Civic Gifts

Civic Gifts

VOLUNTARISM AND THE MAKING
OF THE AMERICAN NATION-STATE

Elisabeth S. Clemens

The University of Chicago Press   CHICAGO AND LONDON

The University of Chicago Press, Chicago 60637
The University of Chicago Press, Ltd., London
© 2020 by The University of Chicago
Published 2020
Printed in the United States of America

29 28 27 26 25 24 23 22 21 20   1 2 3 4 5

ISBN-13: 978-0-226-55936-0 (cloth)
ISBN-13: 978-0-226-67083-6 (paper)
ISBN-13: 978-0-226-67097-3 (e-book)
DOI: https://doi.org/10.7208/chicago/9780226670973.001.0001

Library of Congress Cataloging-in-Publication Data

Names: Clemens, Elisabeth Stephanie, 1958–author.
Title: Civic gifts : voluntarism and the making of the American nation-state / Elisabeth S. Clemens.
Description: Chicago : University of Chicago Press, 2020. |
Includes bibliographical references and index.
Identifiers: LCCN 2019024386 | ISBN 9780226559360 (cloth) |
ISBN 9780226670836 (paperback) | ISBN 9780226670973 (ebook)
Subjects: LCSH: Voluntarism—United States—History. | Charity organization—United States—History. | Social service—United States.
Classification: LCC HN90.V64 C55 2019 | DDC 302/.14—dc23
LC record available at https://lccn.loc.gov/2019024386

♾ This paper meets the requirements of ANSI/NISO Z39.48-1992 (Permanence of Paper).

For Dave, with thanks beyond measure

Contents

Introduction 1

1: Principles of Association and Combination 27

2: Civil War, Civic Expansion:
The "Divine Method" of Patriotism 49

3: Municipal Benevolence 73

4: The Expansible Nation-State 103

5: "Everything but Government Submarines":
Limits of a Semi-governmental System 139

6: In the Shadow of the New Deal 177

7: The People's Partnership 213

8: Good Citizens of a World Power 235

9: Combinatorial Politics and
Constitutive Contradictions 257

Acknowledgments 277
Appendices 281
List of Abbreviations 295
List of Archives 297
Notes 299
References 365
Index 393

Introduction

Finding no sort of principle of coherence with each other in the nature and constitution of the several new republics of France, I considered what cement the legislators had provided for them from any extraneous materials.

EDMUND BURKE, *Reflections on the Revolution in France*, p. 191.

A considerable part of our morality and our lives themselves are still permeated with this same atmosphere of the gift, where obligation and liberty intermingle.

MARCEL MAUSS, *The Gift*, p. 65

During 1933, his first year in office, Franklin Delano Roosevelt faced a host of challenges and crises. Many were met with the establishment of new public programs and federal agencies, the alphabet soup of the FERA, AAA, CCC, and NRA.[1] In contrast to his predecessor, Herbert Hoover, Roosevelt insisted that the federal government could legitimately provide direct aid to suffering citizens rather than deferring to private, voluntary relief efforts. From this vantage point, the New Deal exemplified state-building and government expansion accompanied by the marginalization of private charity and civic benevolence.[2] In the words of Willie Stark, one of the great fictional protagonists of the period, public services would be "Free. Not as charity. But as a right."[3]

But those years of financial crisis also threatened a more personal project in social welfare: Roosevelt's polio facility at Warm Springs, Georgia. Unsure how he would pay the mortgage on the resort that he had purchased in 1926 and made available to other polio patients, Roosevelt welcomed help from a rising star of the public relations industry. With a burst of activity, Carl Byoir organized thousands of parties, dances, and other charitable events in January 1934 to support the "Committee to Celebrate the President's Birthday." Expected to generate $100,000, the celebrations brought in over $1 million and gave the President good reason to reassess the potential of private charity.[4] If, in the desperate winter of 1934, voluntary fund-raising could produce such results, citizen philanthropy might prove powerful in other ways.

Over the next few years, the Committee acquired its lasting name as the "March of Dimes" for the care of polio victims and research toward a vaccine. Its complex choreography of civic and business groups focused on the president—always recovering, never a cripple—as a symbol of a nation still reeling from its own social and economic afflictions. Those who had received government relief could discharge their sense of indebtedness by giving back to the president and, thereby, aiding fellow citizens who had previously extended help to others. But this mobilization in support of the president's personal cause had broader political implications as a cure for the apathy that had taken hold as the Depression continued into its fourth and fifth years. As one Red Cross official commented in 1935, looking at the situation through the lens of the earlier world war, "There was shell shock then. There is depression shock today."[5] At this time of crisis, voluntarism and the organization of civic benevolence proved to be powerful social technologies to mobilize collective action and generate a sense of solidarity. Civic gifts and organized benevolence provided those "extraneous materials" that Edmund Burke had thought necessary to hold together a republic.

What Roosevelt had discovered—or, more accurately, rediscovered— was the power of a model of social relationships that rarely figures in studies of modern state-formation and nation-making although it has repeatedly surfaced in American political history.[6] The giving of gifts, extended through expectations of reciprocity, can generate social ties and solidarity even among strangers. During the Revolutionary War, contributions flowed from one colony to another. Echoing Burke's imagery, defenders of one of the early post-Revolutionary associations hoped that their Society of the Cincinnati—a voluntary association of former officers of the Continental Army—would provide "cement to the union" and "a hoop to the barrel."[7] During the Civil War, Americans on both sides volunteered, raised funds, and knitted to support their militaries. In its debut as a great power, the United States gathered 60 percent of the funding for World War I through voluntary loans and donations. In 1943, during the Second World War, 84 percent of those surveyed by George Gallup reported that they had given to the American Red Cross in the preceding year. As the United States expanded its system of social welfare during the postwar decades, voluntary and nonprofit organizations were prominent ingredients in this new wave of nation-state-building.[8] As Marcel Mauss understood, liberty and obligation intermingle in the gift.

As elected officials and engaged volunteers repeatedly discovered, gifts can help to make nations as well as to build states,[9] generating ties among citizens mobilized as a people. National identities have been understood as "imagined communities" or "stories of peoplehood,"[10] but such collective identities may be enacted as well as imagined. In the materials produced by and about the March of Dimes, the themes of quasi-military but benevolent mobilization and national unity are pervasive. The argument was captured in a cartoon published in the *Arizona Republic* and clipped for Roosevelt's files (figure 1): the parade stepping off to distant battle included rich men's dimes, poor men's dimes, labor's and capital's dimes, Democrats' and Republicans' dimes, and your dime (but note that women's dimes and the dimes of racial and ethnic minorities are absent).[11] In a classic expression of civic nationalism,[12] traditions of voluntarism and charity were incorporated in a project of nation-making. But, through the practices of national fund-raising, nation-making aligned with the activities and projects of state agencies and government officials. (See figure 1.)

This cartoon identifies the tensions generated when co-constructing a state (understood as a centralized means for mobilizing and allocating resources) and a nation (defined as a shared category of membership and, therefore, of political solidarity). A military line-up of private categories of identity and association—wealthy and poor, labor and capital—is juxtaposed to symbols of the major political parties, a private citizen, the president, and a young polio victim. This political configuration involves at least two kinds of sociological transformation.

First, individuals are encompassed by organized groups or identity categories. This accomplishment is easily taken for granted in contemporary social science and social life. But, in the early Republic, the very fact of association offended commitments to personal liberty and freedom of conscience, powerful legacies of the nation's revolutionary founding. "Shall every one of us be subject to the interpretation of every other one who claims authority over conscience?" asked a leading ethicist of the early nineteenth century of the multiplying associations that would come to be known as the Benevolent Empire.[13] Against such strong claims for freedom of conscience and individual liberty, the deeply institutionalized, profoundly taken-for-granted status of civic association in American political culture could not be assumed but had to be accomplished. That accomplishment, however, was so effective that organized voluntarism and civil society are often equated with liberty in a way that would make little sense to those earlier critics who linked association to despotism and the suppression of individual freedoms.[14]

The second transformation articulated civic associations with the organization of state power. Read through his experience with the centralized

FIGURE 1. Cartoon by Reg Manning, first published on the front page of the *Arizona Republic*, January 20, 1939. Image courtesy of the Franklin Delano Roosevelt Presidential Library.

administrative state in France, Alexis de Tocqueville celebrated the voluntary associations of the United States as bulwarks against despotism. But in a political culture marked by strong anti-statist currents, a national government of limited capacity could extend its power through collaboration with private actors, whether individuals or associations, in what Michael Mann has theorized as a mode of "infrastructural power."[15] Rather than consistently resisting "the despotism of the parties or the arbitrariness of the prince,"[16] associations may sometimes extend centralized power. These organizational technologies and cultural practices produced a potent engagement of private action with public projects, what Brian Balogh describes as the "associational state."[17]

The resulting coproduction of public goods cannot be understood simply as the co-optation of private actors by the state or as the capture of the state by private actors.[18] "Infrastructural power is a two-way street," making state actors dependent on the collaboration of others and vice versa.[19] This mutual dependency takes on a particular character within a regime premised on popular sovereignty. Governing arrangements that rest substantially on infrastructural power create opportunities for non-state actors to withdraw their consent from joint projects, including mobilization for war and provision of relief to fellow citizens in times of natural disaster or economic distress. To the extent that mobilization is "expansible,"[20] citizens can abandon the coproduction of government action whenever they judge that the crisis has passed.[21] Consequently, infrastructural power is a source of both instability and dynamism in the construction of nation-states.

In the United States, the resulting trajectories of change have been shaped, at least in part, by the character of organizations that are not directly or consistently under the control of state elites. State-building has often articulated public bureaucracies with voluntary associations, businesses, and the emerging forms of electoral democracy (albeit restricted to adult white men and, in some cases, then further limited by property qualifications).[22] All this did not come together seamlessly. The constitutive contradictions of political liberty and slavery, free and unfree labor, were built into the governing framework, requiring a host of institutional innovations to stabilize this fraught combination, and then only for a few decades. Less explosive, but perhaps more persistent, the elaboration of civic forms of reciprocity created recurring friction in a polity centered on the image of the independent, self-sufficient citizen. Yet, despite the tensions between these different models of political and economic relationships or relational geometries, the gift—in all its variations as reciprocity, mutuality, and charity—proved useful to those engaged in the experiment that was a democratic revolution. With available models of deference and hierarchy rejected, the gift represented one possibility for generating ties among individual rights-bearing citizens. What Marcel Mauss had understood as "one of the human foundations on which our societies are built" might also serve as the "extraneous materials" that Burke thought necessary to cement a new political order.[23]

Such a combination might be taken as a guarantee that the nation would be virtuous and benevolent. And, indeed, the prevalence of voluntary associations in the civic life of the United States has made such moral language pervasive, producing a distinctively "civic" political culture. For those opposed to the growth of state power or committed to popular control, the coproduction of government represented an important limit on bureaucratic expansion.

But the reliance on voluntarism has also reinforced the salience of private inequalities and exclusions in the public domain, although quite differently than the categorical exclusions of the Jacksonian democracy of white adult men. The social logic of the gift transforms the privileged into leading citizens,[24] while enabling the not-necessarily egalitarian inclusion of those marginalized by disenfranchisement. The legacy of this trajectory of nation-state-building is an architecture of governance that is less than fully visible and structurally porous, open to the influence of not only voluntary associations but also of private wealth and business concerns.[25] And as earlier configurations of infrastructural power have eroded, their legacies include openings for new combinations of public and private.

States as Constructions

Theories of the state typically start with a reflection on what "the state" is. This form of theorizing is taxonomic. The classic answer comes from Max Weber, who defined the state by its monopoly of legitimate violence within a territory.[26] This definition then frames the question as "is this a state or not?" The result draws attention to what constitutes legitimacy or which other social actors possess the capacity for violence or how political relations might be organized across extended or discontinuous territories. Having identified some configuration as a "state," scholars can then ask about its attributes: Is it a strong state or a weak one? An absolutist monarchy or constitutional monarchy? A republic or a democracy?

But Weber's own vast writings, as well as the contributions of other political sociologists, provide warrants for restating the question: *how* is a relatively centralized organization of legitimate power constructed? As with all constructions, states are built out of available materials. Existing social networks, material resources, and elements of culture may be combined or transposed from one domain of social life to another.[27] In Mann's formulation, "Societies are constituted of multiple overlapping and intersecting sociospatial networks of power."[28] State-formation represents a special case of such overlapping networks in which network intersections result in concentrations of power and, eventually, taxonomically distinctive kinds of state.[29] Actors or groups that sit at the intersection of diverse networks then have opportunities—though no guarantees of success—to use their positions to exert influence over actors who lack such leverage.[30] States are constructed at, and through, the intersection of networks. In the process, state-building restructures the possibilities and forms of interaction, competition, and collaboration.

If states are built out of "multiple overlapping and intersecting sociospatial networks of power," state-building must be understood as a fundamentally combinatorial project. As Pierre Bourdieu explains, "We have someone who does things by makeshift, combining elements that are borrowed from previous states and constructing jigsaw puzzles."[31] The topography of overlapping networks provides opportunities for entrepreneurship and institution-building through the combination of diverse sources of power and the "transposition of relational ties and practices across domains."[32] That topography may also be marked by durable zones of tension and instability, where incompatibilities between those elements repurposed for state-building remain unresolved or imperfectly stabilized. In some rare instances, "innovative recombinations cascade out to reconfigure entire interlinked ecologies of 'ways of doing things,'" producing far-reaching transformations of institutional arrangements, including political orderings or states.[33]

This theoretical imagery poses a question that has received far less attention. If social networks are meaningfully different, characterized by distinctive patterns of ties and etiquettes for interaction, we should expect combinatorial moments to be followed by contradiction, conflict, and possibly dissolution. For many reasons well established throughout the social sciences, like and unlike should not be easily combined. Classics of anthropology document the importance of distinctions between sacred and profane as well as the power of taboo to delineate categories of persons, activities, or things in the world.[34] Cognitive scientists, cultural sociologists, and organizational scholars concur on the consequential importance of boundaries and classification systems that separate distinct kinds.[35] So how, and under what conditions, do some recombinations of relational logics or models prove to be relatively durable while others do not?

A part of the answer to this question can be found in the claim that state-building involves shifts from indirect to direct rule (empire-building follows a different pattern). In a system of indirect rule, a would-be

monarch defeats a chieftain in battle and demands that the defeated chieftain swear fealty and enforce the monarch's will among that chieftain's
followers. Because indirect rule co-opts "local and regional powerhold-
ers without utterly transforming their bases of power," the geometry of
authority between the central ruler and his or her multiple subordinates
need not be uniform or standardized. Indirect rules allows for the decoupling of diverse models of power and authority.[36]

A second strategy involves establishing direct rule through the development of an officialdom recruited on merit rather than connections. In
early modern Europe, the Catholic Church provided a path to advancement by men of talent but few connections. This model was imitated by
secular rulers.[37] For Max Weber, the separation of office from person was
the key to the development of rational-legal or bureaucratic forms of rule.
These forms of "depersonalized power"[38] depend not solely on selection
by merit, but also on the fusion of an ethic of impartial professionalism
with corporate solidarity in locales such as military schools and recruitment into agencies characterized by an esprit de corps harnessed to
public service.[39] But the implementation and deployment of this power
depended on the cultivation of personnel who are at least partially disembedded from networks premised on other kinds of ties: obligations to
family, fealty to co-ethnics, or action guided by religious commitments
external to the state.

The construction of such capacities for direct rule "gave rulers access
to citizens and the resources they controlled through household taxation,
mass conscription, censuses, police systems, and many other invasions of
small-scale social life."[40] In the process, these techniques of counting, mapping, and penetrating the economic and social lives of subjects aligned the
resources and relationships across different networks. Local economic activity could be encapsulated in a tax, collected by state officials, and then
transformed into a ship or the means for waging a war. A monarch's whim
could produce a law to be observed by all at the risk of some punishment.
In a sharp divergence from premodern societies characterized by distinct
internal and external economic ethics,[41] markets were not "limited by ir-
rational restrictions" but sustained by frameworks of rational bureaucracy
and calculable law that exemplify the move from indirect to direct rule.
Rather than being embedded in local social networks or particularistic
relationships, all subjects are reachable by the central power.

Taken together, the transition from indirect to direct rule and the development of bureaucracy have been central to accounts of the modern
state. Yet not all states and nation-states have followed this path. Some
very successful developmental states are characterized by "embedded

autonomy," described by Peter Evans as the extensive but not complete entanglement of state officials with private industry. Even where a substantially centralized bureaucratic system has been constructed, political power may rest on the mobilization of networks that extend across domains of social activity, the combination and rearticulation of available models of social order.[42] This harnessing of formally nonpolitical relationships and social networks to projects of state-making is central to Michael Mann's concept of "infrastructural power" understood as the "capacity to actually penetrate society and to implement logistically political decisions."[43] But, like those earlier forms of indirect rule, such configurations of infrastructural power represent points of instability and even potential defection within governing arrangements.

Once recognized, the centrality of "infrastructural power" to state-formation has generated important new perspectives on American political development. Described by Samuel Huntington as a marooned bit of Tudor statecraft,[44] the organization of governance in the United States has been marked by the linkage of public projects and private capacities. Whereas the United States appeared as an anomaly in the context of modernization theory's teleology of political development, the concept of infrastructural power has reconfigured Steven Skowronek's "weak" state or "state of courts and parties" of the early nineteenth century into what Brian Balogh (echoing Alexander Hamilton) portrays as a "government out of sight" organized through relational networks that were not recognized as officially governmental.[45] Private persons were commissioned to perform government functions, post offices were located in trading posts and general stores, small but growing streams of public subsidies from different levels of government flowed to private voluntary associations that took responsibility for providing some public service. This broad trajectory of political development was additive in that private capacities for collective action were appended to formal state authority, a state best described as "associational" or captured in the complex machinery of a Rube Goldberg cartoon.[46] But this trajectory also injected tension and dynamism into American configurations of governance.[47]

But the linking of diverse networks becomes vulnerable when social ties are based on different relational models or geometries. The potential for disruption, conflict, and perhaps, innovation, exists whenever extrapolitical networks and relationships are implicated in a project of state-building. As Noah Webster warned shortly after the American Revolution, "whenever such societies attempt to convert the private attachment of their members into an instrument of political warfare, they are, in all cases, hostile to government."[48]

So what happens when such combinations are attempted? One possibility is that these efforts fail, generating outrage, charges of impropriety, insult, and pollution. Such condemnations are a reliable alarm system and are often followed by efforts to reinforce the distinctions around fields of interaction through "boundary work" that clarifies how relational logics or etiquettes should be deployed by particular actors or in the course of appropriate actions.[49] Thus wherever "intersecting sociospatial networks of power" are mustered into projects of state-building, the invention of new techniques and the intensification of formalization appear as methods for stabilizing those combinations and intersections. Grounded in the power to tax and the authority of the state in establishing relationships of trusteeship, legal structures are one means for segregating motives, creating institutional separation between benevolence and the pursuit of self-interest. In many instances, sacred, legal, and social prohibitions are layered upon one another, testifying to the substantial cultural and political work required to delimit fields of social action governed by distinct and even incompatible logics of appropriateness.

But boundaries are not only obstacles, they are also challenges and opportunities.[50] Transgression, recombination, and hybridization may produce innovations and new opportunities or advantages. Efforts to stabilize such combinations may generate organizational innovation and new practices, even as they fail to fully resolve the underlying contradictions between relational geometries or logics. The result is a seeming paradox. Combinatorial state-building creates institutions of depersonalized rule while also injecting sources of change and zones of instability into the structure of political orders. Consequently, the architecture of governance generates distinctive trajectories of institutional reproduction, contestation, and change.

This paradox clarifies the significance of the unexpected prevalence of charity and benevolence in a liberal democratic polity such as the United States. By transposing relationships of gratitude and reciprocity into political life, advocates of organized benevolence generated resources and solidarity in support of both nation-making and state-building. Charity and gifts are potent, if far from perfect, methods for enacting political solidarity among citizens despite pervasive social and economic inequalities. Generalized exchange generates a felt sense of solidarity that is a valuable resource for those attempting to cultivate loyalty in times of crisis, even on the part of those who were excluded from full membership in the polity. But gifts also create relations of dependence and expectations of gratitude, thereby threatening the civic equality and liberty of citizens. The puzzle is to understand how charity and the gift became central elements in a purportedly liberal and individualistic political culture.

From Gifts to Peoples

In anthropological theory, the gift performs a sort of social alchemy. The giving of a gift creates a social tie where none existed and something in the gift itself—the *hau* or spirit of the thing—requires reciprocation, extending that tie in time, producing a potentially durable piece of social structure. Because they are based on the relational logic of the gift, charity and symbolic exchange constitute powerful means for social mobilization. They represent variations on *reciprocity*, one of the three major forms of nonmarket social organization identified by Karl Polanyi.[51] Although anthropologists have associated these social models of reciprocity primarily with premodern societies—the Kula ring of the south Pacific, potlatch rituals of the Pacific Northwest[52]—the organizing capacity of symbolic exchange was not eliminated by the rise of modern markets and rational bureaucracies.[53] Contemporary social psychology has documented the capacity of systems of indirect exchange to promote a sense of solidarity,[54] a process magnified and intensified when harnessed to modern public relations and propaganda departments or linked to existential crises of war and disaster.[55] Within many major religions and civilizational traditions,[56] extended forms of symbolic exchange and charity have constituted collective identities and provided a basic infrastructure for social welfare and even national finance.

Because gifts generate relationships, and sometimes hierarchy, they can contribute to both nation-making and state-building. Whereas "nation" is often presumed to map onto some prior—indeed primitive or primordial—shared ethnos, language, or religion, the study of nationalism has been transformed by Benedict Anderson's understanding of nations as "imagined communities," constituted through newspapers, maps, museums, and mass culture that sustain a vision of belonging as simultaneous presence within the space demarcated by a particular bloc of color or a boundary line on a map.[57] Through flows of goods and people, conversations and printed commentary about happenings, and commemorations of great events and individuals, persons of all sorts may help to constitute—and continually reconstitute—themselves as a "people."[58] The sense of a shared fate when confronted with external threats may generate new political identities. National identities may also be assigned, inscribed, and enforced by state documents and policies, fueling the transformation of a complex and often fluid distribution of identities into distinct national groups and national minorities.[59]

But nations may be enacted or performed as well as imagined or imposed.[60] Even before the nation's birth, not-yet Americans made use of charitable networks to supply the blockaded city of Boston with its port closed in retaliation for the Tea Party of December 1773. Because the people of Boston were understood to be suffering for a nation or polity that had not yet been formally declared, communities throughout the colonies contributed sheep, cattle, barrels of rice, and the occasional pipe of brandy to the Boston Committee on Donations.[61] The attributes of the intended beneficiaries marked the limits of membership in this imagined community and carefully protected the economic independence expected of those qualified for full citizenship. The Boston Committee promised that relief would go to laborers thrown out of work by the port closure and not to the lazy or indigent. A portion of the goods were sold in order to raise funds to support work projects for these worthy unemployed. From the start, civic benevolence was recognized as a threat to the economic self-sufficiency at the heart of liberal understandings of citizenship. Consequently, its uses were carefully monitored and frequently criticized.

In addition to policing the boundaries of civic membership, the Committee on Donations harnessed well-established practices of community self-help to the politics of revolution.[62] In aid of Boston, individuals contributed, communities collected contributions, and all these efforts were reported in the colonial press, linking actions to relationships to imaginings of political membership. Such efforts represented both a "story of peoplehood"[63] and a concrete organization of flows of resources and political commitments. As historian T. H. Breen has argued, with the activities of the Boston Committee on Donations, "we are witnessing the creation of a huge charitable infrastructure that had obvious political possibilities."[64] Even before the establishment of a national government, the colonists made use of social technologies—including but certainly not limited to benevolence and charity—that enabled collective action without resort to state coercion (although often depending on significant social pressure). As a significant experiment in voluntarism, the Committee on Donations demonstrated how networks of benevolence contribute to state-building projects. National membership could be embedded and enacted as well as imagined. Charity and gifts had the power to create ties, and therefore the political solidarities that sustain nation-making.

Multiple Traditions and Constitutive Contradictions

But benevolence was a problematic resource for organizing governance. Insofar as the formal framework of politics was premised on commitments to equality and liberty—however partial and imperfect—these organizational innovations and experiments generated contradictions. Such tensions are central to the "multiple traditions thesis" advanced by Rogers Smith, which "holds that the definitive feature of American political culture has not been its liberal, republican or 'ascriptive Americanist' elements but, rather, this more complex pattern of apparently inconsistent combinations of the traditions, accompanied by recurring conflicts."[65] The very plurality of these efforts underscores the extent to which the politics of nation-state-building have been fundamentally combinatorial in the sense of drawing on a range of intellectual traditions and working with an assemblage of available elements of social organization.

Gratitude, indebtedness, and dependency were at odds with the founding principles of the new nation, at least insofar as they applied to the adult white men (and scattered others) who could make effective claims to liberty and equality. When the better-off give to those who are less well-off, gift-giving may produce relations of dependence that are marked by expressions of gratitude and the acknowledgment of indebtedness. The core problem is evident from the list of those excluded from full citizenship in the new republic: "most African Americans, native Americans, women, men who had not attained their majority, and adult white males who did not own land" along with paupers, felons, migrants, and the insane.[66] In many, if not all of these instances, some form of dependence or lack of self-sufficiency (economic or otherwise) provides the rationale for exclusion from the electorate. Not surprisingly, these same categories were often invoked to identify those who were appropriate objects of charity.

Because the receiving, if not the giving, of gifts carried the risk of dependence and indebtedness, managing the coexistence of civic benevolence and democratic governance has been no simple task.[67] Within the Christian tradition, as well as many others, benevolence expresses care for others as well as one's own state of spiritual well-being. Yet benevolence in the form of charity has troubling implications for equality.[68] Reflecting on the status of "the poor" in modern society, Georg Simmel contended that "if . . . the recipient of alms remains completely excluded from the teleological process of the giver, if the poor fulfill no role other than being an almsbox into which alms for Masses are tossed, the interaction is cut short; the donation is no social fact, but a purely individual fact."[69] In Simmel's analysis, an unreciprocated act of generosity reduces the receiver to something less than fully human and certainly less than fully civic: "an almsbox."

In this way, giving may generate power relationships that are at odds with liberal democratic commitments to equality and individual self-sufficiency. Many founders of the liberal tradition in political theory recognized this threat, expressing concern over the political implications of gifts and charity. Thomas Hobbes, John Locke, Adam Smith, and

Bernard Mandeville all did their best to characterize gifts as voluntary and expressive on the part of the giver rather than as acts that created ties and obligations.[70] In his discussion of charity, Locke pointed directly to the danger of dependence: "a Man can no more justly make use of another's necessity, to force him to become his Vassal, by with-holding that Relief, God Requires him to afford to the wants of his Brother, than he that has more strength can seize upon a weaker, master him to his Obedience, and with a Dagger at his Throat offer him Death or Slavery."[71] These arguments shared Simmel's insight that the gift was incompatible with the political standing of independent participants in market exchange as well as free and equal citizens.

Similar fraught interactions between charity and political freedom were central to Hannah Arendt's comparison of the American and French Revolutions. The latter's descent into the Terror, she argued, was a product of the revolutionaries' attitude of compassion toward the poor.[72] Compassion positioned the poor as less than full citizens, excluded from political membership by the claim of leaders to care for, speak for, and act in the name of the poor: "Pity may be the perversion of compassion, but its alternative is solidarity. It is out of pity that men are 'attracted toward *les hommes faibles*', but it is out of solidarity that they establish deliberately and, as it were, dispassionately a community of interest with the oppressed and exploited."[73] In Arendt's analysis, the path from compassion to totalitarianism led through charity's corrosive effects on the humanity of its beneficiaries.

Then how can the pervasiveness of voluntarism and patriotic giving in the process of nation-state-building be explained? Recall Bourdieu's image of the state-builder as "someone who does things by makeshift, combining elements that are borrowed from previous states and constructing jigsaw puzzles."[74] Although the historiography of American politics is structured around distinct ideological frameworks[75]—liberalism, republicanism, Christianity, among others—the practical answer was often "all of the above" plus models of collaboration drawn from family, fraternalism, and the world of work. In a search for models of social ordering that were uncorrupted by patriarchal monarchy and deference to aristocracy, the colonists-who-would-be-citizens turned to ancient history, religious doctrine, natural science, and everyday life. Despite its taint of monarchical favor, the chartered corporation was also available for repurposing.[76]

Every new combination had the potential to create tensions. Should the Republic be made rigorously Christian or should churches be ordered along republican principles? Political experience drove religious change as people sought to align the ordering of democratic life with religious engagement. Elias Smith, who had left his position as minister of a well-respected Baptist church to proclaim his own religious liberty, called upon others in 1809: "Let us be republicans indeed. . . . Many are *republicans* as to *government*, and yet are but half republicans, being in matters of religion still bound to a catechism, creed, covenant or a superstitious priest. Venture to be as independent in things of religion, as those which respect the government in which you live."[77] Under the pressure of such demands for consistency, the trajectory of American political development was shaped not only by the ascendance and eclipse of different lineages of political thought, but also by the dynamics that were set in play by the complementarities and contradictions among them.

The national motto—*E Pluribus Unum*, or "out of many, one"—summed up the challenge. Adopted by Congress in 1782, the phrase captured a central project of nation-state-building that has been renewed by the incorporation of new territories, most already-claimed by indigenous peoples defined in their own way, as well as by repeated waves of immigration. In American history, themes of cosmopolitanism and benevolence expressed efforts to constitute peoplehood in a manner that did not depend on ethnic, religious, or linguistic homogeneity (even as it could, and did, sustain severe forms of ethnic and racial exclusion). If, by 1787, America was a nation in the sense of a people with a self-understanding of shared membership (a claim doubted by no less that George Washington and undercut by the absence of the term from the new Constitution[78]), that accomplishment was premised on overlooking differences of religion and language as well as profound exclusions of race. Because American national identity developed in conflict with others—whether the English people to whom many American colonists had thought themselves to belong or with native Americans and enslaved Africans—these strong external boundaries could be combined with methods for relaxing or obscuring, rather than eradicating, social differences or heterogeneity. This option reflected not simply virtue, but absolute necessity in a set of colonies where many spoke a different language (German was the most prevalent alternative to English) or practiced a different religion (not long before, Quakers had been persecuted as heretics in Massachusetts while others were exiled to Rhode Island for their Baptist faith).[79] The challenge was how to create a sense of national belongingness in a multiply diverse population, to fashion a public role for the wealthy and advantaged within a democratic polity, and to mobilize those who were not fully entitled citizens. The "nation-ness" of the United States would be repeatedly challenged by each new wave of immigration as well as the succession of generations that eroded the common experience of the Revolution as a basis for shared membership.

At the time of the Revolution and through much of the early Republic, the possible political uses of organized benevolence were debated only episodically. Within the cohorts of the American Revolution, "many now argued that 'gratitude' was 'a kind of counterpart of benevolence,' an enlightened republican substitute for monarchical subjection and deference." The power of benevolence to forge ties within a farflung and socially varied proto-polity was offset by the potential threat to the civic standing of those on the receiving end of such good intentions. "Americans in the years following the Revolution remained uneasy over their attempts to make their republican ideas of equality compatible with gratitude and the inequality it suggested."[80]

Most debates focused on other resources for imagining political order: the martial and republican virtues of the ancient world or the tradition of contract theory inherited from Hobbes and Locke. Yet even in these early discussions, some political actors sought to ground political institutions in natural affections in the same way that the Declaration of Independence and Constitution appealed to natural law and natural rights: "The natural feelings of love and benevolence between people could become republican substitutes for the artificial monarchical connectives of family, patronage and dependency, and the arrogance, mortification and fear that they had bred."[81] The further this civic affection extended from immediate circles of family and friends, the greater its potential for expressing political virtue.

In this vision, benevolence—whether in the form of active philanthropy or everyday altruism—offered a powerful model for building expansive and cosmopolitan ties in a nation not yet fully conceived. As Craig Calhoun has argued, liberalism on its own is unequal to the task of constituting a democratic political order: "Liberalism informs the notion of individual agency but provides weak purchase at best on membership and on the collective cohesion and capacity of the *demos*."[82] This, for many theorists, represents the problem of obligation in a liberal polity: "Collective action and the broad manifestations of mobilization that go beyond private initiative are blind spots in the national story of unencumbered individualism."[83] The political salience of gift-giving and reciprocity has been hidden in that blind spot. Equality and inclusion are optional rather than necesary. As a consequence, civic benevolence has functioned as a particularly powerful but volatile component of the mix of models for political organization, sanctioned by Christian doctrine but often at odds with commitments to other political ideals including individual liberty and democratic equality.[84]

As a distinctive and durable way of "doing" peoplehood, civic benevolence promised to transcend—without actually erasing or resolving—differences of race, ethnicity, gender, religion, class, region, and even partisanship through a celebration of voluntary activity.[85] Generosity among friends or neighbors within one's community could be projected nationally without requiring actual unification or consistency of sentiments. This proved to be a durable recipe for collective mobilization at a national level. Reflecting back on the first years of fund-raising success, a presidential aide closely involved with the March of Dimes declared, in the wake of a contentious electoral season, that "the annual Birthday Party has been a great unifier of people . . . the rallying ground, more than ever before, for the unification of our people and an eradicator of any hang-over of ill feelings from this year's election campaign."[86] From this vantage point, the mobilization of civic benevolence, even in the aspirationally egalitarian form of citizen philanthropy, not only transcended but also healed the rifts of electoral politics.

But nation-making is inevitably contested and such confident assessments were far from universally shared. Civic benevolence often provoked charges of damage done to the dignity of citizens. Only a few years before that presidential aide's praise of the unifying power of the March of Dimes, a newspaper incorrectly reported that the National Association for the Advancement of Colored People had contributed to the national campaign. This "news" was countered forcefully; no such contribution had been made because no facilities supported by the effort were open to African American citizens.[87] In response, a research and treatment center was opened at the Tuskegee Institute in Alabama which received both an autographed, framed photograph of the President (high in the ranking of personal acknowledgments) and, in 1939, a grant for $161,350 from the National Foundation for Infant Paralysis, "the largest made by the foundation."[88]

The contested and imperfect circuits of civic benevolence were disrupted by conflicts around class as well as race. Only a year after the end of the Second World War, the Congress of Industrial Organizations (CIO) withdrew from the joint fund-raising model of wartime, complaining that "our efforts to create a more wholesome understanding between Red Cross chapters and local labor groups were discouraged at every turn." Yet labor leaders continued to express the hope that "the Red Cross will become a truly American Red Cross, democratized for full participation for everyone in the community."[89] Given the fraught relationship between the liberal image of the self-sufficient citizen and normatively valued practices of charity, how was it possible to enact benevolence toward others without undermining the ideal of free and equal citizenship (at least among adult white men potentially capable of self-sufficiency)? If, in Stein Rokkan's phrase, the nation is a solution "to the problem of cultural unification within a sovereign territory,"[90] how were civic benevolence and voluntarism combined with principles of liberal individualism in the making of an American nation-state?

The Argument Ahead

By the time Alexis de Tocqueville visited the new nation in the early 1830s, the cultural construction of civic benevolence and voluntarism was well under way. Foreign observers were reliably impressed by the ways in which Americans voluntarily joined collective efforts to produce public goods. The uneasy combinations and latent contradictions in such formations would later be crisply diagnosed by sociologist Claude Fisher as a combination of the beliefs that "each individual is a sovereign individual" and that "individuals succeed through fellowship."[91] As with the March of Dimes, reciprocity and the relational geometry of gift-giving could serve as "social glue"[92] or "cement to the union." To the extent that diverse and formally incompatible components of social organization are articulated in a system of governance, how did they come to hang together and what dynamics were set in motion?

This analysis begins with the puzzling contrast between the vivid cultural incompatibility of benevolence and liberty in the political discourse of the early republic and their thorough entanglement in the policy discourse and governing arrangements from the Civil War through the middle of the twentieth century. By the early eighteenth century, a politics fueled by threats to personal liberty had emerged, generated by a lack of economic opportunity combined with demographic pressures. Prospects for self-sufficiency dimmed, straining existing webs of interdependence: "For a large number of men coming of age in the 1740's and 1750's the contrasting statuses of free and unfree, dependent and independent, came to represent stark alternatives."[93] These intense concerns about personal independence sparked resistance against authorities that threatened subordination: new laws imposed by the British Empire or decrees issued by clergy. This resistance took form in new revolutionary associations and organizations; these in turn were denounced as dangerous to personal liberty. But although controversial, association mattered centrally for nation-state-building in the United States, not least because there was comparatively little other social material to work with once the framework of British imperial rule was rejected. Only after a long and contentious debate over the propriety and purposes of association, both religious and secular, did benevolence take on a new form that mobilized private persons around public purposes.

To reconstruct the combinatorial politics and organizational innovation that produced this distinctive conjuncture of organized benevolence and liberal democracy, the analytic strategy is "neo-episodic."[94] After mapping the sites and moments where discourse, conflict, and innovation intensify around the political role of benevolence, the analysis then positions these episodes as historically interconnected cases within a sequence of historical development. Changes in behavior, discourse, or law signal episodes in which the relationship of benevolence and liberal citizenship is salient; those episodes are then understood as historically linked moments of "iterated problem solving" in which each partial resolution changes the terms for the next round of wrestling with the possible articulations of these two relational models or geometries.[95] Each episode that produced a new configuration of infrastructural power—an architecture linking voluntary associations and state agencies in a governing arrangement—was likely to be contested. Each version of the "Rube Goldberg state"[96] produced its own politics and provided opportunities for organizational innovation, legislative action, and legal intervention that might stabilize otherwise volatile combinations.

When the crisis had passed, legacies remained. Pieces of law, organizational models, and memories of mobilization were left on the path of institutional development.[97] The result was often a durable zone of opportunity for combinatorial politics, activated by the constitutive contradictions among the multiple traditions and diverse relational models that organize American life: the commitment to individual liberty as a foundation of political ideology and market institutions; the hierarchical structures of both the state and the large firm; and the normative celebration of generosity, reciprocity, and solidarity. Voluntarism developed as a central feature of the connective framework that makes possible the co-constitution of a polity by these diverse relational geometries. It operates as a transformer that connects appliances running on one current to an electrical grid conveying another or a valve that prevents the pressure in the main lines from destroying the interior plumbing of a home.[98] In a society and political culture simultaneously committed to individual liberty and equality, organizational hierarchy, and moral reciprocity, the requirements for effective connecting structures were demanding and dynamic.

The argument cycles across topics and sites: war, economic crises, and natural disasters at the local, national, and international level. By repeatedly surveying the shifting terrain, the analysis tracks not only what happens at any given juncture of nation-making and state-building, but also how participants in an extended debate over governance confronted successive challenges with different assumptions, resources, and organizational models. Although wars, hurricanes, and economic depressions tend to figure in quite separate literatures, those who mobilized in response recognized how they drew on similar repertoires despite the substantive differences between the crises. In a speech kicking off the 1938 campaign for the Greater New York Fund (which supported private social service agencies), John D. Rockefeller Jr. opened his remarks by drawing an explicit parallel to the United War Work Campaign of 1918: "Selfish individualism has gotten us nowhere. Altruistic cooperation points the way out. . . . The meeting in the old Madison Square Garden represented a cooperative, altruistic endeavor irrespective of race or creed; that is what this meeting represents. The purpose of that meeting was the promotion of social welfare and health agencies; that is the purpose of this meeting. The only difference between the two meetings lies in their fields of activity. That meeting was in the interest of work among the soldiers in the camps. This meeting is in the interest of work among the Citizens of Greater New York."[99] Deep dives into archives document particularly dense nodes in the networks of American voluntarism, revealing the recurring dilemmas of aligning benevolence with the dignity of democratic citizens.[100]

Images of construction recur throughout the argument for a key theoretical reason. Arthur Stinchcombe made the central point in a discussion of blueprints. These diagrams are most elaborated at the points where different crafts have to align their products—where pipes have to fit into walls, where ductwork cannot disturb an architect's aesthetic.[101] Similar challenges occur along the junctures of distinctive fields of activity. Sometimes, most of the action concerns imposing and reinforcing boundaries that are marked by a proliferation of taboo, normative evaluations, and law. But where the goal is to articulate one field with another—to claim governing powers for civil society or to harness voluntary associations to state projects—the task is not (or not only) to impose boundaries and categorical distinctions. Instead, contradictions and tensions are relaxed or obscured while organizational innovation may generate new models of articulation and methods of disarticulation and decoupling. Inevitably, specific outcomes are contingent and vary across episodes of mobilization and political competition. But the cumulative result has been an institutional elaboration that obscures the ways in which the legacies of one era are repurposed to meet new challenges, conflicts, and opportunities.

These repeatedly recognized contradictions between charity and democratic dignity as well as between liberty and association underscore the puzzle of how organized civic benevolence came to be established as a durable—and developmentally significant—component of an American nation-state with its celebration of liberal political principles and democratic egalitarianism. This unlikely combination is the product of a sequence of iterated problem-solving, efforts to generate solidarity and capacities for expansive collective action to meet emergencies or to advance political visions. The sequence can be traced to the revolutionary Committee on Donations that provided "proof of concept" but left little in the way of either organizational or ideological legacies. In the first decades of the nineteenth century, the establishment of a legal framework and cultural competence for widespread associationalism changed the terms for possible alignments of benevolence with a democratic polity (chapter 1). The dual imperatives to act with benevolence toward those in need and to respect the dignity of fellow citizens led to the articulation of practices and institutions that carefully segregated enfranchised men from categories of noncitizens or not-quite-citizens—children, women, the ill or insane, immigrants, Native Americans, and former slaves—as appropriate objects of charity. This division of labor between the domains of charity and citizenship was destabilized as Americans first deployed charitable practices in massive support for soldiers during the Civil War (chapter 2) and then as methods for meeting the social challenges generated by industrialization and urbanization (chapter 3).

Under the pressures of crisis and world war, these alignments were reordered once again. The municipal model of civic governance was rearticulated with national institutions and political identities (chapter 4). The possibilities created by this new alignment were tentatively explored in the response to the San Francisco earthquake of 1906 before the potential of a fully national mobilization of voluntary association was realized during the First World War. Economic production, war funding, military support, and refugee relief all called upon the practices of voluntarism in order to generate vast new capacities for national government without a commensurate increase in the powers and resources of formal institutions. In this vision, civic benevolence was a source of sustained coordinated capacity for action and also an inoculation against the appeal of radical statism. The limits of this solution were exposed in the effort to transpose wartime models to domestic crises, above all by the economic crisis of the Great Depression (chapter 5). In the effort to mobilize voluntarism to meet the unprecedented scale of suffering, the architecture of voluntarism collided with the contradictions between benevolence and democratic standing, a collision that was not cushioned by the invocation of military service nor by the obvious crisis of natural disaster. In the end, these efforts were insufficient to the magnitude of the crisis, but their legacy was a framework of nationally coordinated voluntarism that would be a resource for later projects requiring expansive but not statist governance.

In many tellings of American political history, Hoover represents the end of voluntarism; Franklin Delano Roosevelt ushered in the modern welfare state, centralized government, and entitlements. But the story is not so simple (chapter 6). Initially, the Roosevelt administration rejected the social technology of voluntarism, but this stance did not survive for long. On a personal basis, FDR discovered that his own philanthropic efforts for polio victims could be sustained by mass citizen philanthropy; the March of Dimes began as the "Committee to Celebrate the President's Birthday" and this national exercise in gift-giving was a kind of reciprocation that addressed the sting of dependence on government relief. Nor were federal financial resources sufficient to meet all the demands; steadily over the course of the 1930s, changes in tax law and the regulation of government spending opened up the channels through which resources flowed to service-providing civic organizations.

World War II saw a last full flowering of this form of civic benevolence, mobilized in support of the troops but also in aid of Roosevelt's foreign policy hemmed in by an isolationist Congress during the early years of the crisis (chapter 7). In the wake of the war and Roosevelt's death, his allies attempted to institutionalize this civic mobilization in peacetime while Republicans and business elites sought to dismantle the linkage of patriotic philanthropy to presidential politics, particularly of the Democratic variety. The result was a nonprofit sector with far fewer obvious political overtones, one that facilitated both care for those left out of the nation's incomplete welfare state and the self-provisioning of communities in areas such as the arts, higher education, and medical services. In the process, the charities that entered the decade of the 1930s emerged as nonprofit organizations after the Second World War (chapter 8).

Each of these efforts to articulate voluntary organization and state authority shaped subsequent rounds of conflict and innovation. Tax subsidies for individual and business charitable contributions fueled an expanding field of what came to be known as nonprofit organizations. Although federal revenues continued to expand for decades after the Second World War, restrictions on government growth meant that this burgeoning field of privately managed organizations was ever more important for the implementation of policy and ever more dependent on public funding. This consolidation of this new organizational form, the nonprofit organization, enabled the great expansion of a domain of publicly recognized and funded (either through tax-subsidized donations or direct government grants) but privately managed organizations that acted in the name of the public good. The capacity of government action expanded while its identity was blurred, throwing up obstacles to accountability. In time, the nonprofit sector would itself become the basis of yet another burst of state expansion: Lyndon Johnson's Great Society and War on Poverty that directed federal funds and rights to support through private organizations, both nonprofit and for-profit. The result has been a distinctive type of state in which many public activities take place in private venues at a distance from mechanisms of electoral accountability.[102] Even as the era of mass membership voluntary associations waned, this method for mobilizing governance left behind an open architecture of legal possibilities and policy models that would be inhabited—hermit crab-like—by new waves of social movements, philanthropic initiatives, and profit-making enterprises.

As voluntary or nonprofit organizations have become more dependent on government funding rather than community-encompassing fund-raising, they have also lost at least some capacity to sustain an experience of peoplehood constituted through generalized reciprocity. The dances, pranks, and door-to-door drives of the March of Dimes and the coordinated giving-and-allocating of the Community Chests have been displaced by fragmented fund-raising campaigns that are decoupled from the large-scale benevolence of multiplying philanthropic foundations.[103] Exceptions for religious and charitable organizations that were written into the core components of the New Deal order in time provided openings for efforts to dismantle key welfare and social insurance provisions that had come to seem like stable features of the policy landscape.[104] The institutional legacies of one political moment or crisis have shaped the possibilities in the next. As a consequence, midcentury civic benevolence was no more likely to be stable and final than any of the earlier combinatorial forms of governance that have been central to American political development.[105]

To what extent does this account of the coevolution of civic benevolence and nation-state represent simply another variation on narratives of American exceptionalism? With respect to the invention of a system of democratic governance based on (incomplete) manhood suffrage, the United States and France were engaged in parallel experiments although the French Revolution led to very different organizational configurations. Private associations were expelled from the French civic sphere or tightly regulated while *fraternité*—or the relational model of friendship—was evoked as the binding agent in a public sphere purged of inherited relations of deference and dependency.[106] Many elements of the evolving structure of American governance were borrowed from or shared with other political traditions. In discussions of the "Darkest England" scheme, British Victorians imagined a welfare system managed entirely by the Salvation Army. From 1931 through the end of the Second World War, the annual fund-raising drive known as the *Winterhilfswerk* supported relief work in Nazi Germany.[107] Social relations of friendship, charity, and benevolence were ingredients in many projects of nation-state-building.

But even within the United States, there were important variations in how relational geometries were combined and articulated. As Drew Faust has written of Confederate nationalism, "The conflict between the notion of absolute power and the ideology of reciprocity central to paternalism had placed contradictions at the heart of the system long before the Civil War erupted," tensions that were exacerbated by efforts to reconcile the demands of evangelical Christianity, market society, and democratic rights even if these did not extend beyond the limits of white male suffrage.[108] Taken separately, the challenges, ingredients, and recipes for governance that generated a particular model of the nation-state were not unique to the United States.[109]

Nor were the practitioners of civic benevolence in the United States alone in recognizing the political potential of voluntarism. Alexis de Tocqueville's celebration of voluntary associations in American democracy was followed by the utopian hopes of Peter Kropotkin, the "anarchist prince," who found foretellings of a postcapitalist society in voluntary associations including the Zoological Society of London, the English Lifeboat Association, and the Red Cross.[110] American pragmatists and reformers concurred in locating possibilities for governance in community groups and voluntary efforts.[111] Even that strong defender of free markets, Friedrich Hayek, refused to oppose individualism and voluntary association, arguing that "the case of the individualist rests, on the contrary, on the contention that much of what in the opinion of many can be brought about only by conscious direction, can be better achieved by the voluntary and spontaneous collaboration of individuals."[112] For those who wrestled with questions of governance in the modern world, voluntarism was repeatedly identified as a promise and possibility only to be obscured by sharper oppositions of individual rights and state power.

In the absence of a blueprint provided by a dominant ideology or theorist, sequences of crisis and response produced a distinctive and practical model for mobilizing resources and generating national solidarity. This model was elaborated over the same decades that the country emerged as an economic, geopolitical, and military superpower. Elements of this model were borrowed or exported, carried by missionary efforts, by international voluntary associations and, with the onset of the Cold War, by democracy-promoting government programs both covert and overt. Many parts of the world witnessed expanding zones of private activity claiming some public purpose but beyond the full control of elected officials. By the late twentieth century, transnational recipes for governmental reform and alternative forms of governance—the Third Way, the New Public Management, social entrepreneurship, public-private partnerships—embodied efforts to promote public ends in ways that were not limited to official state institutions.[113]

This history of the combinatorial politics that have made the American nation-state speaks to contemporary projects of remaking and recombination: the marketizing forces of neoliberalism, novel public-private partnerships, claims for social entrepreneurship, effective philanthropy, and distributed governance. Within each of these efforts there is a proposal to transpose models of social relationships from one kind of organized activity to another and to combine diverse networks into systems of governance: to treat citizens as if they are customers, to encourage investors to be public-minded, to invite the governed to participate in governing. Champions of such projects invoke the potent language of benevolence, of goodwill toward others that is often joined to voluntary contributions and philanthropic gifts. Critics assert that the open architecture of governance creates opportunities for wealthy donors or organized interests to pursue their goals under the cover of benevolence.[114] Such calls for recombination and rearrangement signal projects of social change, provoking outrage, generating resistance, and producing innovation and new possibilities in the process. The zone of dynamic and unstable interpenetration between liberal ideals of citizenship and practices of benevolence and reciprocity endures, shaping future trajectories of political development.

1

Principles of Association and Combination

Private associations of men for the purposes of promoting arts, sciences, benevolence or charity are very laudable, and have been found beneficial in all countries. But whenever such societies attempt to convert the private attachment of their members into an instrument of political warfare, they are, in all cases, hostile to government. They are useful in pulling down bad governments; but they are dangerous to good government, and necessarily destroy liberty and equality of rights in a free country.

NOAH WEBSTER, "The Revolution in France" (1794)[1]

In declaring their independence from the British Empire in 1776, North American colonists embarked on a spiraling sequence of practical problem-solving. What organization of governance could be squared with commitments to life, liberty, the consent of the governed, and the principle that all men are created equal? Each of these terms was the focus of heated debates and seemingly endless dilemmas could be produced by different combinations of these concepts. If liberty allows individuals to achieve different levels of economic success, in what sense are all men (or, at least, adult white men) still equal? If the governed consent to a system of rule and therefore domination (at least in the interval between elections), in what sense are they still free?

At a philosophical level, such questions continue to fuel reflection and debate. But, in practice, the tensions between these proclaimed ideals and practical problems of governance generated a rich history of organizational innovation and recombination. To the extent that these diverse models of citizenship and social order were durably reproduced yet substantially incompatible, they represented a set of *constitutive contradictions* or intrinsic tensions that have driven American political development.[2] The compromises between the self-government of free citizens and an extensive economy based on slavery were the most fateful of these contradictions.[3] But they were not the only tensions that became embedded—more or less securely—in the new kind of political order ushered in by a revolution in the name of self-government.

In rejecting traditional models of monarchical rule and declaring all men equal, the inheritors of that revolution added degrees of difficulty to the project of constructing a new form of government. Authority should not offend the equality of (male, white, ideally property-owning) citizens. Solidarity should be imagined in ways that do not threaten individual liberty. The French Revolution celebrated one possible solution to these dilemmas in its motto of *liberté, egalité, fraternité.* Leading revolutionaries, argues Pierre Ronsavallon, put *fraternité* or friendship "at the center of social life," judging it to be "the most complete and necessary form of the social bond. Friendship, as a form of social cement, thus ceased to belong exclusively to the realm of private affections and took on a collective dimension that called for a pledge and implied a responsibility to all members of the society."[4] These interpersonal bonds were critically important given the French Revolution's pronounced hostility to forms of intermediate or corporate social organization, including the clubs, associations, and religious congregations.

Although differing from friendship in its specifics as a social form, benevolence had a similar capacity to function as "social cement," linking individuals to collective projects and a sense of the social. The distinctiveness of the American effort to invent democratic governance is evident in the trans-Atlantic commentary of the time. Europeans, observes historian Joyce Appleby, "were astounded by the presence of social order in America in the absence of social solidarity. Federalist leaders shared this sense of the situation and 'saw their principal political problem as one of adhesion: how to keep people in such a large sprawling republic from flying apart in pursuit of their partial local interests.'"[5] Absent some basis for solidarity, governance would be more difficult still. As Alexis de Tocqueville would observe a few decades after the American Revolution, "When the bonds among men cease to be solid and permanent, it is impossible to get large numbers of them to act in common without persuading each person whose cooperation is required that self-interest obliges him to join his efforts voluntarily to those of all the others."[6]

One response would be to work mightily on the mobilization of self-interest. Within the decade or two following the adoption of the Constitution, political entrepreneurs were inventing a new organizational form— the mass political party—to facilitate action and mobilization within the institutional framework. But a second possibility was to create new kinds of bonds. Alongside the invention of the mass political party, a new form of civic or voluntary association flourished and came to be taken as the distinctive feature of this new democratic polity. Associations might generate solidarity among free citizens and serve as vehicles for organizing across community and state lines.[7]

Although the Constitution of 1789 established jurisdictional boundaries for state and federal governments, it provided much less guidance on how to organize across those jurisdictional lines and at the intersection of different domains of social life.[8] This silence, in turn, provoked efforts to remedy the perceived fragility of the new constitutional order and counteract the fissive dynamics within the federal system. During those first decades of the new Republic, this structural challenge repeatedly provoked organizational innovation. Secret or selective associations, such as the Masons and the Society of the Cincinnati, created and sustained networks among neighbors, between occupational interests, and across state lines.[9] The First Bank of the United States emerged as a "great regulating wheel" at the center of a system of relations with the state banks in the management of public and private credit.[10] Operating in the space opened by the ongoing disestablishment of religion across the colonies-turned-states, multiplying reform groups advocated for temperance, founded Sunday schools, and evangelized on the western frontier as part of what came to be known as the "Benevolent Empire" or the "Evangelical United Front."[11] Each of these organizational experiments was a response to the weaknesses that many perceived in the new constitutional order. All represented combinations of private association and official political institutions that might produce a novel system of governance capable of replacing the monarchical and imperial arrangements rejected by the Revolution.

The problem, as Noah Webster insisted, was that such political combinations might be "useful in pulling down bad governments; but . . . dangerous to good government." His diagnosis, written in response to the escalating Terror of the French Revolution of 1794, turned on the role of the Jacobin societies, which "were voluntary associations, unclothed with any legal authority." Yet to enforce the decisions of the Convention across the entire country, these societies were "clothed with the sanction of a constitutional form. . . . A single club, by this curious artifice, gave law to France." One association claimed to represent and direct the whole. Read through this analysis of the extreme phases of the French Revolution, the logic connecting association to political danger is clear: "By this principle of combination, has a party, originally small, been enabled to triumph over all opposition."[12] Webster's analysis resonated with the concerns of Federalists disturbed by the growing political presence of new "Democratic" societies: "The societies seemed to adopt techniques of insurrection appropriate for the imperial crisis but at odds with the new republic's political structures. . . . 'Nobody will deny the usefulness of popular Societies, in cases of revolutions,' noted one observer."[13] But associations, however useful they might have been as vehicles of justified revolutionary mobilization, carried the potential for the emergence of faction, the tyranny of a well-organized minority, and the subversion of the sovereignty of the people as a whole.

The potent threat that Webster and many of his contemporaries attributed to political association may surprise readers whose understanding of American civil society derives from a stylized summary of Alexis de Tocqueville's *Democracy in America*. Based on extensive travels less than four decades after the publication of Webster's essay, that classic analysis celebrated private associations as the key to the robustness of American democracy, a striking contrast to the much different aftermath of revolution in France.[14] Viewed through this trans-Atlantic comparison, Tocqueville portrayed association as a "principle of combination" that moved easily across the spheres of civil, political, and economic life, generating capacities for collective action and shaping new kinds of political selves.[15] Viewed historically, however, the political role of private association poses a different question to an analysis of nation-state-building. How were "self-created societies," condemned in those terms by no less than President Washington, transformed from threats to the republic into legitimate and familiar vehicles for a wide range of civic activities that might even function as a shadow form of governance?[16]

The practical history of making "self-created societies" both safe for American democracy and useful for nation-state-building involved experiments with and refashionings of already familiar organizational models. "Self-created" societies threatened to displace the exercise of popular sovereignty with a cacophony of partial interests, subordinating individual conscience to organizational goals and extracting individual contributions with their dauntingly efficient associational machinery. A resolution of these dilemmas, however partial, required the invention of new organizational forms and etiquettes to engage private association with public projects, the defining feature of "infrastructural power." The corporate form was harnessed to benevolence and then to sweeping reform mobilizations, anchored by a new discourse of "voluntarism." But the efflorescence of organizing also fed on itself, with movements seeking to capture other associations, resulting in multiplying lines of schism and conflict. Although the organizational experiments of those decades after the revolution produced a new political ordering, it was an ordering fraught with constitutive contradictions among the assembled pieces that would shape the trajectory of nation-state-building.[17]

Self-Created Societies as Political Threats

In the aftermath of the Revolution, Americans divided over the question of whether revolutionary means could be deployed for post-revolutionary purposes. Once a new sovereign nation was established, many argued, the right to revolution was extinguished. The "freedom of assembly" enshrined in the Bill of Rights protected the ability of communities to protest unjust policy, but this was something quite different than the modern freedom of association that guarantees the rights of particular groups to organize themselves apart from the majority.[18] The central issue was captured by the contrast between "constitutional" and "self-created" societies. Those organizations of patriots that had been established through "conventions" at the level of towns or colonies could claim to represent the people. By tracing their origins to an established political authority, they rebuffed accusations that they represented only themselves and therefore constituted factions hostile to popular sovereignty.[19]

When societies were "self-created," however, even the unquestioned patriotic service of members was no guarantee against such suspicions. The Society of the Cincinnati, whose membership was restricted to "officers and their first-born sons," was attacked as "an attempt by a nationally connected political and military elite to create an American nobility" while also functioning as a charitable mutual benefit association to provide relief for "the unfortunate members, or their widows or heirs."[20] There was no consensus on the place of such private, restricted, even secretive associations within a new kind of polity. As critics of the Cincinnati charged, "self-creation removed the society from legal constraint and allowed it to usurp a power forbidden to the states or the nation," namely the creation of a hereditary nobility.[21]

Disagreements over the legitimacy of self-created societies and the organized expression of public opinion also fueled conflicts between the emerging configurations of Democratic-Republicans and Federalists. These debates intensified in 1793 and 1794 with the tax resistance that would become the Whiskey Rebellion[22] and the shifting character of the ongoing revolution in France. In that context, President Washington criticized "self-created societies" as a threat to the government.[23] Having accepted the office of "president general" of the Society of Cincinnati, Washington then led the annual meeting through a revision of its own charter, abandoning its hereditary character, excluding foreign membership, and surrendering control of any funds to state legislatures: "the American states and people could not accept the hybridizing of private benevolence and coordinated public leadership."[24] Through these changes, "the promiscuous mixing of mutual benevolence and state- and national-level political didacticism would be ended."[25] Washington's distrust of private association was shared by Jefferson who, as late as 1824, "worried that they 'may rivalise and jeopardize the march of regular government.'" Like Washington, Jefferson "believed that permitting the spread of voluntary associations and corporations would threaten equality by allowing a small minority, a cabal, to exercise disproportionate influence over public life."[26]

If private attachment threatened true popular sovereignty, the seemingly admirable qualities of benevolent action also endangered claims to political equality. Unreciprocated gifts were understood to generate dependence and a sense of personal humiliation. They might also allow the privileged few to accumulate concentrated power. One early experiment in combining patriotic organization and charity, the Washington Benevolent Society, provoked precisely this criticism in the form of accusations that it was "bribing the needy and avaricious under the mask of benevolence."[27] Here, benevolence threatened political virtue to the extent it reduced less-advantaged citizens to dependence on the gifts of others, an acknowledgment of their lack of self-sufficiency and independence.

Beyond the fear that charity-as-bribery might taint electoral processes, many saw benevolent organizations as threatening the fundamental principles of a free republic. Attacking the "Benevolent Empire"—a network of organizations that included the American Tract Society and the American Bible Society as well as promoters of Sabbatarianism and Sunday schools—Ephraim Perkins, a Unitarian farmer from upstate New York, argued that these societies were fueled by "the small but increasing contributions which, by the most skillful management, are squeezed out of the pockets of all ages, sexes and conditions, and mostly from the women and children of our country." They had acquired an "influence exercised openly or covertly . . . over the public sentiment, even in civil matters and touching candidates for public office." Drawing comparisons to wealthy pre-Reformation monasteries in England, Perkins urged his readers to "look at their splendid establishments of various kinds at home, and their gigantic schemes starting into existence abroad in the four quarters of the globe, the execution of which, upon the scale professed and contemplated, would require a sum probably equal to our national revenue." The state-like qualities of private voluntary association were central to the perceived threat: "Consider the sums collected annually, quarterly and monthly in various ways, with the regularity of a legal tax, and which is viewed, from the force of habit, by thousands, of as high and binding obligation as an established system of tythes."[28] Thus efforts to link formal political networks and authority to practices of charity and benevolence attracted disapproval and repeated condemnation.

Experiments in political association provoked multiple critiques. Elites worried that the mobilization of "interests" would undercut deliberation on the public good while other citizens were quick to identify conspiracy as the motive behind any private association.[29] This suspicion of association persisted for decades. Elected to the presidency in 1800, Thomas Jefferson benefited from the efforts of the Democratic-Republican societies even as he questioned the political legitimacy of associations.[30] As Jefferson was followed in that office by a sequence of his allies—James Madison and then James Monroe—the dominance of one political network created the conditions for an "Era of Good Feelings" in which earlier association-driven conflict seemed a temporary aberration.[31]

Yet the resurgence of conflict with the election of 1824 (thrown into the House of Representatives after an election that split support among Henry Clay, Andrew Jackson, and the ultimate victor, John Quincy Adams) highlighted the still-unresolved legitimacy of partisan association. In the elections of 1828, Jackson's supporters advanced a transformative party-building project while the opposing Whigs charged that Democratic leaders inculcated "slavish loyalty among their constituents and were dependents themselves on the spoils of party patronage."[32] The resulting emergence of partyism out of a tradition of anti-partyism rested on a claim that only Jackson's Democracy truly represented the people.[33] This "solution" to the problem of party in the still-new republic, however, left no ideological space for an organized opposition and electoral contestation. Signs of coordinated action in politics were easily perceived as evidence of conspiracy, a trope that would figure in the anti-Masonry, anti-Catholic (or "Know-Nothing"), and anti-Mormon mobilizations of the 1820s through the 1840s.[34] Fears of association that had taken shape in response to the Society of the Cincinnati or the Democratic-Republican societies of the 1790s resurfaced and fueled new controversies from the 1820s up to the Civil War.

In the absence of a legitimated alternative for organizing political action, the reaction was to fight fire with fire. As one Democratic paper proclaimed, "'When *factious* men *combine*, . . . *patriotic* men must *associate*.'"[35] Challenged by the new Democratic party, the Whigs reacted with reluctant imitation, invoking the threat of Jacksonian Caesarism as sufficient justification for acting "as if" they were a party themselves in order "to rescue and preserve the Constitution."[36] But as this model of political organization began to gel, its actually-existing representations faltered. The Whigs collapsed by the 1850s and the Democrats were divided by sectional schism during the election of 1860. Other reinventions of association, however, would prove more consequential as a basis for the wartime mobilization that loomed on the horizon. And, here, benevolence was high on the roster of motives for organizing.

The Case for Voluntary Association

In 1803, Lyman Beecher gave a sermon in East Hampton, Long Island, on the topic of "The Practicability of Suppressing Vice, By Means of Societies Instituted for that Purpose."[37] Beecher would become a major figure in the evangelical reform movements of the 1820s and 1830s as well as the father of a famous brood that included the author of *Uncle Tom's Cabin*, a champion of education for women, and one of the leading evangelical preachers of decades to come. He assumed the ends of reform; the importance of the sermon lay in its argument for the means to those ends.

Beecher's analysis began from political, indeed civilizational, premises. In light of the decline of many of the great republics and empires of the past, was it inevitable that the American republic should follow the same course? No, he asserted, so long as the virtuous would take action. Invoking George Washington's words, he argued that religion and morals were necessary supports for political virtue. Acknowledging that individuals were likely to lament sin but to assume that someone else was better able to combat vice, Beecher contended that "what the individual could not do in that he was weak, many individuals combined can do with ease, because they are strong. The exertion for each is not so great, and the censure, divided among many, is not feared . . . he speaks more readily, and with greater efficacy, because he speaks the sentiments of many, and is conscious that numbers are prepared to uphold him, and back his reproof." By shaping public opinion, "an association of the sober, virtuous part of community, if that union become extensive, will have irresistible influence to stigmatize crimes, and to form correctly that opinion which is known to possess such influence over the minds of men." Beecher went on to envision a distributed, networked associational project of political preservation and uplift:

> What can we do to preserve the nation; a small town, and one only among thousands? We can do our part. The nation is formed by the addition of such small districts; it is preserved by their purity, and destroyed by their vices. Every town is a member of the body politic, and, if a healthful member, is a great national blessing; let every town reform, and the reformation will be national. Who can tell how far the influence of our example may extend? How great a matter a little fire may kindle? Who can tell how much kindness God has for us? Already has he enkindled an extensive zeal to find the blessings of religion abroad;

and may we not hope, that he will add to it, a zeal to secure the fruits of religion at home.

Thus the fate of the nation, even if foreseen by God, was potentially in the hands of men who might "gradually improve ourselves, and improve the society in which we live."[38]

Beecher's 1803 sermon heralded a powerful and consequential project of publicly engaged association operating through public opinion and moral pressure on individual behavior rather than electoral mobilization.[39] The invocation of "reform" as a motive for association, rather than a threat to liberty, stressed the responsibility of citizens-as-Christians for the well-being of their nation and the salvation of their fellow citizens. Within the political and intellectual circles of New England, these arguments were advanced by Yale president Timothy Dwight as well as Beecher. Dwight founded a student society at Yale; its alumni went on to lead moral reform associations across the expanding nation.[40] Beecher helped to establish the American Temperance Society, another site of intense organizational learning that shaped a cohort of leaders of other reform efforts.[41] Combined with the efforts of many others, their activities contributed to a new architecture of public engagement and collective action.

In associations, reformers such as Dwight and Beecher found a substitute for the informal support and surveillance once credited with maintaining social order. Inspired by a handful of societies founded in the United States in the1790s as well as models provided by British missionary efforts, associations to promote Sunday schools, temperance, and orphanages all sought to counter the perceived decline of traditional community and morality.[42] In the decades after Beecher's 1803 sermon, momentum built, fueled by religious revival, heightened concern over the irreligiosity of the westward-moving frontier, and the disestablishment of churches across all the former-colonies-turned-states.[43] In the new nation's cities, bulging with immigrants from both the countryside and overseas, better-off residents were called upon to aid their less fortunate neighbors—or to combat vice, crime, and social decay. Urban missions, friendly visiting, and "free churches" offered alternatives to traditional community self-help and mutuality by allowing some people to organize coordinated benevolence directed at others, often outside their immediate social circles.[44] Such efforts often required cooperation despite difference as well as coordination across regions. Not surprisingly, the results were sometimes powerful, sometimes destabilizing, sometimes both.

The landscape of religious association was marked by cross-cutting pressures of cooperation and separation. To follow only one chain of interactions, in 1801 the Congregationalists and Presbyterians agreed on a Plan of Union through which they would cooperate in missionary activities to create and staff churches across the multiple frontiers. Ministers trained in the Congregationalist seminaries could staff some of the pastor-less churches in areas of new settlement, whether Presbyterian or Congregationalist. Although they disagreed on models of church governance (indeed, at this point the mostly disestablished Congregational churches had not yet formed a national association of their own), both denominations were committed to versions of Calvinist doctrine and collaborated in creating a novel interdenominational mechanism to collect funds in settled areas and redistribute them in support of new churches. The arrangement soon generated conflict. Congregationalists charged that the Presbyterians were favoring their own western churches in the allocation of funds; Presbyterians critiqued the doctrinal innovations within Congregationalism that would lead to Unitarianism.[45]

As tensions built within this alliance, there were further innovations in religious cooperation based on models that were extra-denominational and multi-denominational.[46] These were the pillars of the "Benevolent Empire," all established in the 1810s and 1820s: the American Colonization Society, the American Bible Society, the American Sunday School Union, the American Tract Society, the American Home Missionary Society, and the American Temperance Society. Although each pursued its distinctive mission, most combined characteristic elements: governance was lodged in a chartered corporation, controlled by trustees (typically a mix of clergy and laypeople drawn from multiple denominations); funds were raised through appeals to local congregations, societies, and supporters; and the combination of accumulated funds and ties to economic elites promoted the adoption of business methods for evangelical purposes.[47] Supporters of these endeavors clearly understood the role of these organizations as forms of governance, with one identifying the "late Bank of the United States" as a model for the American Bible Society while the American Tract Society envisioned "its Publishing Committee as 'the Supreme Court of the Society.' "[48]

Drawing on the organizational resources of religion, missionary societies, and reform associations, the organizations that made up the "Evangelical United Front" promoted Sunday schools, temperance, abolition, and other causes linked to their vision of a moral society. This vision was backed by considerable resources. In the mid-1820s, six of the large benevolent societies—the American Sunday School Union, the American Home Missionary Society, the American Tract Society, the American Education Society, the American Bible Society, and the American Board for Missionaries—had total combined revenues of approximately $100,000. By 1830, that total had surpassed $450,000.[49] To put this in context, in 1830 total federal government spending amounted to $15.1 million. Most went to fund the army, navy, interest on the debt, pensions, and veterans' compensation, leaving $5.2 million—just over eleven times the combined budgets of these six large benevolent associations—to cover all other functions.[50] So while organized voluntarism certainly could not match the resources of the federal government, these associations commanded funds that were not insignificant in comparison.

The power of this combination of organizational models, financial resources, and practices was exemplified by the American Temperance Society. Beecher himself was a founding member. Within three years, it claimed one hundred thousand members, organized through one thousand chapters. In less than a decade of existence, the claim rose to five thousand chapters joined by one million individuals. The society combined the traditional powers of congregations (members were urged to deny church membership to those who drank or trafficked in alcohol), the political-economic tactics of consumer boycotts (refusing to do business with those who sold liquor), and influence on public opinion through pamphlets, lectures, and the emotional impact of public meetings.[51] Taken together, these elements of the program represented a substantial force, evidenced by the fierce and hostile responses of some of those who were subjected to this plan of religiously inspired benevolence. As a "weary traveller" wrote to an Ohio newspaper in 1830:

> Not many days ago, I stopped at a public house in this part of the country to rest my weary body, where the landlady entertained me for an hour or more with a set of high-keyed vituperations upon all the Societies which humanity and piety rejoice in . . . and sir, had I . . . lately fallen down from Jupiter, I should have taken them to be a set of cannibals seeking to fatten themselves upon the ruin of mankind. I should have regarded Temperance Societies to be the unholy combinations of most malicious beings, bent on depriving the world of liberty: and in case I should meet one of the members of such a Society, I should have expected nothing better than to be knocked down with a jug of whiskey. I should have thought the American Bible Society, and the American Tract Society, were most industriously engaged in pilfering and purloining money from the pockets of the poor, and using their ill-gotten pelf for the destruction of what little comfort and happiness remained to man after the fall.[52]

As with the original "Presbygational" Plan of Union, the goal of these national benevolent organizations was to spread and sustain the Christian faith—or at least Protestant variants of it[53]—across areas of new settlement as well as in cities where populations were expanding with new immigrants. But these translocal, extra-denominational efforts of the national benevolent organizations threatened the authority of local congregations and clergy, most notably through the "agency system" in which fund-raisers visited congregations to generate enthusiasm for their particular cause—Bible distribution, Sunday schools, or temperance— and then transform that enthusiasm into monetary contributions to be sent back to headquarters in New York City. As a "Village Pastor" complained in the pages of the *Baltimore Literary and Religious Magazine*, the proliferation of fund-raising agents for benevolent associations undercut the position of clergy within their communities.[54] Some were also concerned that the methods of the benevolent agents, appealing to the sympathies of congregants, corroded the proper character of action informed by faith:

> Great meetings are held; the agent comes with his manufactured "public opinion" in the shape of a string of resolutions. . . . No doubt much money is so collected, but are pastors aided? Do we not here see the very cloven foot of "new measures," so much decried? Excitement and not principle? Here too is benevolence as an *extra work*, associated with *meetings* and *cards* and *pledges*—much talk of a *missionary* spirit, as something grown up in the nineteenth century, with a great deal more, all calculated to foster a spasmodic purse-opening.[55]

Another correspondent suggested that congregations should organize themselves around a clear and rational system of benevolence: "To each cause should be designated a season of the year, when it may have free access to the charities of the people, and receive all that they propose to give it during the year; and then it should stand aside and give place to other objects."[56] Anticipating methods that would be celebrated as "discoveries" decades later,[57] these practices of distributed fund-raising articulated local congregations with a field of national and even transnational efforts by the early 1830s.[58] Through such innovations, "the Benevolent Empire and its denominational allies had forged a common organizational culture committed to a pious orderly society. They comprised a virtual proxy nation that counteracted the centrifugal forces of the market revolution and partisan politics." But precisely because of the impressive organizational resources mobilized through this "Federalist-Benevolent nation-building project," the character of that organization itself became a political issue.[59] While champions of the Benevolent Empire argued that association was the means to realize the divinely intended purposes of the nation-as-political-experiment, its critics contended that organization itself was a threat to foundational principles, above all that of individual liberty and freedom of conscience.

Reconciling Association and Liberty

Although not necessarily hostile to reform, critics of the Benevolent Empire looked on these organizational innovations with dismay, seeing in them a profound threat to liberty. In his 1829 essay, "Remarks on Associations," the Reverend William Ellery Channing drew a distinction between natural (or God-created) associations of family, community, or country and artificial associations. The latter, he argued, emulated the "grand manoeuvre" of Napoleon or "the concentration of great numbers on a single point," but in so doing posed a serious threat to the virtue of individuals and their pursuit of understanding of the divine in man and nature.[60] He proposed that "the value of associations is to be measured by the energy, the freedom, the activity, the moral power, which they encourage and diffuse."[61] The danger lay in the tendency of association or organization to concentrate power:

> Associations often injure free action by a very plain and obvious operation. They accumulate power in a few hands, and this takes place just in proportion to the surface over which they spread. In a large institution, a few men rule, a few do every thing; and, if the institution happens to be directed to objects about which conflict and controversy exist, a few are able to excite in the mass strong and bitter passions, and by these to obtain an immense ascendancy. Through such an association, widely spread, yet closely connected by party feeling, a few leaders can send their voices and spirit far and wide, and, where great funds are accumulated, can league a host of instruments, and by menace and appeals to interest can silence opposition.[62]

Rather than seeing in associations a power that could protect minority opinion (foreshadowing Tocqueville) or an instrument for the domination of free institutions by organized factions (following Washington and Jefferson), Channing worried about the capacity of organized associations to suppress individual exercise of conscience: "an influence is growing up, through widely spread societies, altogether at war with the spirit of our institutions, and which, unless jealously watched, will gradually but surely encroach on freedom of thought, of speech, and of the press."[63]

These debates over the threats posed by association to individual liberty, reason, and divine word merged with conflicts over the danger they posed to—and through—national government. Such concerns extended the emerging splits between Jeffersonians, who constructed proto-party systems anchored by multiplying newspapers, and the Federalists. As they gradually retreated from active electoral participation, Federalists organized their own protopartisan associations—the American Republican Society, the Sons of Washington, the Washington Association, and the Washington Benevolent Society (estimated to have over 200 chapters and 2,500 members at the time of the War of 1812) among others[64]— and then shifted to build new kinds of social and cultural institutions. The disagreements over political principle motivated fine distinctions in practice: proponents of association argued that individuals expressed political opinions while associations provided merely sociability; others argued that associations imposed a set of political positions as a requirement for membership.[65]

This fear of the coercion intrinsic to association resonated with other forces in electoral politics. Linked by their shared base of support in New England, the reform associations of the Benevolent Empire were perceived by their critics as "a menacing hydra, much as Jacksonians were obsessed with the power of a 'monster' bank."[66] That sense of threat was reinforced by the efforts of reform organizers to strengthen their project; the controversy came to a head in debates around the charter sought from the Pennsylvania legislature by the American Sunday School Union. Denied in 1828, "amid cheers in Philadelphia's poor wards and Democratic charges that the ASSU wished to become '*dictator to the consciences of thousands*,' "[67] the controversy testified to the durable and deeply felt contradictions between the model of associational activism and the operating logic of democratic politics.

One response was a proposal to bring the evangelical reform movement even more explicitly into politics.[68] By the 1830s, the abolitionists sought to use the U.S. Post Office as a channel to extend their arguments to readers in the Southern states. Although federal law required Post Office officials to be impartial in delivering any publication they received, suppression of a mass mailing by the Anti-Slavery Society by postmasters went unpunished.[69] Instead, opponents of abolition sought to have new federal powers written into the Post Office Act, explicitly permitting postmasters to refuse to transmit material of objectionable content. The threat here was "the federal government had been captured by a malignant 'slave power' intent on destroying the liberties of freemen throughout the United States." In opposition to what was understood as an effort to secure federal enforcement of state laws, those who sought to preserve the independence of the post office "regarded both antiabolitionists and Sabbatarians as powerful lobbies intent on using the government in order to dominate the public agenda."[70]

In the controversies over the charter for the American Sunday School Union and the proposed Sabbatarian legislation governing the Post Office, popular democracy and champions of individualism agreed in rejecting governmental endorsement of associations, benevolent or otherwise. More fundamentally, what came to be known as the "anti-mission movement" denied the core premise of reformers as articulated in Beecher's sermon of 1803. It was not the place of the self-identified "virtuous" to reform others; the sole source of religious inspiration and instruction was the Bible. Hewing more strictly to Calvinist assumptions of predestination, the anti-mission "Hard Shell" and "Primitive" Baptists rejected the goals of the evangelical reformers as well as the presumption that the work of spreading the gospel should be conducted by organizations other than local congregations.[71]

Moral reformers recognized that such understandings of religious faith and democratic liberty were obstacles to the advancement of their own understanding of a moral nation. As one wrote in 1845, it was "delicate indeed to interfere with the private concerns of any individual, however poor he may be—that claims to be *one of the independent citizens of the United States—one of the sovereign people*."[72] On this point, Channing's argument came full circle to join with Jefferson's dismay at "a vast association, which may be easily perverted to political purposes, which, from its very object, will be tempted to meddle with government, and which, by setting up a concerted and joint cry, may overpower and load with reproach the most conscientious men in the community."[73] Whether the organizing links between citizens and the polity took the form of reform associations, political parties, or conspiracies, all might be seen as threats to individual liberty and the foundational values of the republic.[74]

To untangle his concerns over political liberty, individual conscience, and the projects of reform associations, Francis Wayland set forth a particularly developed consideration of how to align individual moral responsibility with organized benevolence: *The Limitations of Human Responsibility* (1838). Wayland himself was an unusual but significant figure in this era, an Independent Baptist and pastor, trained in medicine and theology, who served as the president of Brown University from 1827 to 1855. He was also a noted moral philosopher whose *Elements of Moral Science* was "fabulously successful," used as a central textbook in many colleges and universities as well as abridged in a widely used high school text.[75] Although less widely read than his textbook, Wayland's reflections on human responsibility represent the application of his influential

moral philosophy to the dilemmas of an Independent Baptist, committed to the primacy of individual conscience and scripture, and a proponent of both temperance and antislavery. These causes were advanced
by the unprecedented voluntary associations of the time that, Wayland
acknowledged, had "been denominated the peculiar glory of the present
age, so emphatically the age of valuable inventions. They are frequently
supposed to be the great moral means, by which the regeneration of the
world is to be effected. They are believed to multiply, almost indefinitely,
moral power, and to give to virtue a predominance over vice, which, in
former ages, it never has possessed."[76]

Acknowledging that he had arrived at some unexpected conclusions
in the course of developing his argument, Wayland began with the primacy
of the moral conscience of individuals as informed by scripture. While
individuals were bound by explicit scriptural commandments—"God has
made known to us our duty to preach the gospel to every creature"—
they were not bound by the interpretations and practices of a particular church, much less those championed by benevolent associations and
cemented by pledges from the membership.[77] Extending this claim for
the primacy of individual interpretation of God's will, Wayland argued
that associations threatened both political liberty and religious freedom
of conscience. This moral danger was diagnosed in an extended analysis
of "the pledge" as an organizational practice. The pledge, Wayland argued
"imposes the form of a moral obligation to believe a particular sentiment
and to perform a particular act."[78] The form of the pledge obstructed an
individual in his obligation to follow his conscience if he came to new
positions on an issue, added the social stigma of breaking the pledge as
an obstacle to a changed conscience, and generally closed pledged members to the persuasive power of the arguments and evidence mustered
by those who had come to different interpretive positions on a particular
issue.

Because of these commitments to individual liberty and rational debate, and despite his own support for the causes of temperance and antislavery, Wayland recognized that expanding reform agendas threatened
his understanding of the relationship between associational members
and their leadership in terms of specific and delimited contracts:

> The moment any departure is made from the original agreement, the as-
> sociation is, in fact, dissolved. The individual members agreed to unite
> for one specific purpose; if the purpose be changed, another association
> is formed, with which the previous members have nothing to do, unless
> they form a new and different compact. Thus, suppose I join a temper-
> ance society, by signing a pledge to abstain from spirituous liquors, and

by my example and precept, in such manner as I think proper, to promote temperance among my fellow men. This is a distinct and definite
matter. It binds me to a particular and specified course of conduct. But
this is all. I delegate nothing to any one. I put myself in no one's power.
I surrender neither my understanding, nor my conscience, nor my liberty, to any man, nor to any set of men. I am in all these things as I was
before.[79]

This reading of associational practices through a rigorous framework
of individual liberty and contract theory captures the moral and conceptual challenges to aligning voluntary associations with individual freedom
of conscience. These dilemmas were far from purely philosophical. This
line of reasoning provided a rationale for the decision of the American
Tract Society to exclude publication of antislavery tracts from their mission. Founded in 1825, the American Tract Society was governed by an
executive committee composed "of fifteen or eighteen men divided into
publishing, distributing, and finance committees." Of those on the publishing committee—ministers drawn from different denominations—any one
was able to veto publishing specific material. The Society's constitution,
explained the secretary in 1852, "allowed it to publish only material 'calculated to receive the approbation of all evangelical Christians.'" So without
unanimity—much less an explicit scriptural command as opposed to scriptural interpretation—on antislavery, the society would not publish tracts
condemning slavery in the same way that it campaigned for temperance
and against gambling.[80] Taking a similar stance, the leadership of the American Home Missionary Society contended "that the organization had no
control over the internal affairs of subsidized churches. Admission to full
membership and communion in Presbyterian and Congregational churches
came only after individuals had convinced the pastor and members that
they had experienced a conversion—that the Holy Spirit had infused their
souls. Condemning slavery as a sin and refusing to aid churches admit-
ting masters, said the officers, would be undermining church discipline."[81]

By building hierarchical and corporate elements into their basic
structure, along with principles of deference to local auxiliaries (above
all, those in the South), these voluntary associations were substantially
insulated from the tides of popular mobilization, abolitionism included.
Even with the support of major donors such as the Tappan brothers of
New York City, abolitionists were unable to push the American Bible Society to reconsider its silence on antislavery. If Catholic priests were attacked for withholding the Bible from their parishioners while gamblers
and drunkards were refused church membership, why did not the same
principles apply to slaveholders "who kept their Negroes ignorant of the

Scriptures"? While such arguments failed to sway the American Bible Society, they fueled schism within the American Home Missionary Society. By 1856, the new, antislavery Home Missionary Society no longer extended aid to churches that admitted slaveholders to membership, amplifying its earlier stance toward congregations that admitted drunkards, those who broke the Sabbath, adulterers, and other moral reprobates.

Given this durable tension between organizational practice and individual conscience, it is not surprising that Wayland eventually confronted the specter that had motivated Noah Webster's reflections on the French Revolution almost a half century before:

> What were the *French Jacobin clubs*, but *voluntary associations*? . . . The right of franchise, that palladium of liberty, was valueless; for elect whom you would to be a legislator, he dared not disobey the mandate of the club. Legislative proceedings were regularly decided upon, in the meetings of these voluntary associations, before they were brought forward in the assembly; and the representatives of the people did nothing but record the mandates of a sanguinary mob. Thus was a tyranny enacted, to which the history of the world affords no parallel; and all this was done by men, who, at first, were associated to discuss abstract principles of right, and who were merely pledged to carry into effect some truly salutary measures of reform.[82]

In this debate, however, Webster and Jefferson and Channing as well as Wayland—not to mention the cheering poor of Philadelphia's working class wards—wound up on the losing side of history. Liberty and association were reconciled by highlighting the freedom of conscience exercised in the decision to join. This resolution made possible the peculiar hybridized claims joined in the concept of voluntarism: that "each individual is a sovereign individual" and that "individuals succeed through fellowship."[83]

Creating an Institutional Framework for Voluntarism

Through the 1820s and 1830s, private associations and corporations became increasingly important vehicles for public action, particularly for the economic and national elites threatened by the ascendance of Jacksonian democracy through the 1820s and 1830s. Represented electorally by the many variants of the Whig party that promoted candidates in national and state elections (National Whigs, Silver Whigs, Cotton Whigs, to name only a few), the proponents of active economic development, moral uplift, and cultural advancement had made inventive use of private associations.[84] By the mid-nineteenth century, leading organizers recognized that they had produced something quite new and significant. Writing to present that history of innovation, one of the leading organizers of antebellum religious reform movements explained: "There being no longer a union of Church and State in any part of the country, so that religion must depend, under God, for its temporal support wholly upon the voluntary principle: it seemed of much consequence to show how vigorously, and how extensively, that principle has brought the influence of the Gospel to bear in every direction upon the objects within its legitimate sphere."[85] Yet the realization of this vision would require a new legal framework for associations, one that would provide a compelling platform for collective action in the name of the public but outside the arena controlled by electoral politics. Other developments long in the making contributed to the creation of a firm legal and cultural foundation for the "art of association" celebrated by Tocqueville and recognized as a potentially powerful vehicle for social reform: the institutionalization of "voluntarism."

While moral philosophers debated the virtues of associations, struggles over the practical and legal meaning of a right of association played out around the established churches. As Johann Neem has documented, dominant denominations such as the Presbyterians and Congregationalists were caught up with the turmoil of revival and challenges to orthodoxy from Baptists and Universalists.[86] Bound by law to pay taxes in support of the established church, some congregants joined reform movements that strove to take control of established churches rather than to exit and wind up supporting a new congregation in addition to the established church. Faced with the loss of control over individual churches, established denominations eased their opposition to the formation of new congregations. In a legal development that would have transformative consequences, over the next decades states began, slowly and unevenly, to adopt unprecedentedly permissive statutes of incorporation, first for churches and gradually for other associations including commercial firms.

These incremental moves toward an "open access order"[87] accelerated as the increase in religious toleration then gave way to religious disestablishment in each of the states by the 1830s.[88] What had once been state-supported religious organizations now "began to compete for members, lacing the country with parishes and networks for fund-raising, proselytizing, and reform." Survival required ongoing mobilization of members and their contributions, particularly in an era when many states had abandoned the Elizabethan Statutes of Charity and the legal framework that sustained charitable bequests and, therefore, a central resource for

building endowments. The result was "an enduring institutional framework for social mobilization, drawing women and men of differing races
and stations into the voluntary sphere."[89] Although it has acquired a much
more general meaning, "voluntarism" in American political development
originated with this transfer of responsibility for a preeminent public
good—organized religious life—from government to private associations.[90] As one early historian of the "voluntary principle" announced,
"We are now about to enter upon the consideration of the resources
which the churches have developed since they have been compelled to
look, in dependence upon God's blessing, to their own exertions, instead
of relying on the arm of the State."[91]

As a recognized anti-political—both non-statist and nonpartisan—
but public organizational form,[92] the voluntary association crystallized
across a series of key episodes in American political development as the
provision of organized religion—a supremely public good—was transferred
from colonial or state governments to private associations of believers, a
process completed in all states by the 1830s.[93] Formerly a tax had been imposed to support congregations of the denomination "established" within
a state or colony (an arrangement resembling that of post-Reformation
Europe), but now believers were made responsible for the material support of their own religious organization.[94] The period of religious disestablishment coincided with a major wave of revivalism. Although the
numbers are inexact and uncertain, estimates suggest that more than
three-fourths of Americans were "churched" in some fashion by the 1840s,
compared to perhaps one in ten in the years following the revolution.[95]
As a consequence, a massively greater proportion of Americans became
familiar with the self-organizing forms that would come to be known
as "voluntarism."

This capacity to harness private action to the production of public
goods could be extended to social support, economic development, and
national security as well as religion. Elected officials appreciated this capacity at a time when the capacities of formal government institutions
remained quite limited. The new state legislatures, particularly those in
the North, contributed to the growing number of private associations.[96]
Taking over the power of granting charters from the Crown, legislators
sought to populate their landscapes with the institutions that signaled
civilization and progress, including colleges, hospitals, and benevolent
associations as well as private corporations that would produce public
goods such as roads and bridges.[97] These developments generated new
lines of conflict. The grant of private corporate existence required legislative assent to the public benefits of the association (a requirement that
could be a substantial obstacle prior to the adoption of more permissive

procedures for incorporation), but once granted who retained that right to determine what was in the interests of the public?

On this question turned one of the most important legal decisions of the new nation, the *Dartmouth* decision that established that once a charter was granted, authority rested with the charter-holders, not with the legislature.[98] This decision heightened the stakes in the granting of charters, but also the awareness of the uses to which private associations could be turned. Bridges and roads were built by private corporations with public mandates and funding. The poor and aged were sustained by benevolent associations that, in turn, often relied on subsidies from state and local government as well as gifts from philanthropically inclined citizens.[99] Colleges and universities were enabled by public grants as well as tax exemptions and were governed by boards composed of representatives of religious, civic, and state interests. Given the widespread suspicion of visible, centralized government, there were obvious benefits to governing by way of delegation to private associations and chartered corporations.[100] Through financial subsidies and grants of authority, this harnessing of civic organizations and private corporations to governmental purposes represented a distinctive kind of political infrastructure, one in which the capacity for governmental action exceeded the resources of recognizably public institutions. If a corporation had been "constitutional" at the moment that it was granted a legislative charter, to what extent could it become self-(re)created through the decisions of its trustees?[101] The grant of a charter was effectively a delegation or forfeiture of one piece of sovereignty over the common good, an insight that helps to explain the intensity of popular opposition to something so seemingly innocuous as the American Sunday School Union.

By the first decades of the nineteenth century, the outlines of a specifically *civic* state were evident. Decades of wrestling with these issues produced an institutional framework for voluntary association that was more legally secure and more widely employed, but also drew a sharper boundary between public and private domains of authority. The result was a greatly expanded sphere of organized reform and benevolence that was at the same time more sharply differentiated, in both legal and political terms, from the formal institutions of government. This transformation rested on a series of innovations. First, the organizational infrastructure of private associations oriented to civic purposes was established in law and practice. This had required discovering a method for defusing the tensions between individual liberty and associational membership. Second, at least some of the latent contradictions between relational geometries were overcome, relaxed, or transformed. Finally, agreements were forged concerning the legitimate relationships between the domains of government and voluntary associations, both of which were sustained by claims to serve the public good. A resolution to the first problem was largely complete by the 1850s, at least in the North.[102] By the eve of what would become the Civil War, the organizational landscape was more densely populated as well as more fragmented and factious. In these ways, the repurposing of private association and the mobilization of voluntary giving represented an important piece of both state-building and nation-making, but both projects remained very much "in progress" midway through the nineteenth century.

In American political discourse, "voluntarism" is ever-present but often inarticulate. As Michael Rogin argued,[103] it developed into an organizational ideology that represented itself as everyday pragmatism. The concept's core claim is that the needs of citizens are best met by their own self-organized efforts, whether in the form of congregations and religious movements, labor unions, farmers' cooperatives, social clubs, fraternal orders, or trade associations. Thus "voluntarism" transcends the opposition of individualism and collectivism that has structured so much of modern political debate. Consequently, American voluntarism has managed to link this privileging of associations with an affirmation of individual liberty and freedom of conscience. In this account, with its echoes of Wayland's reflections on the limitations of human responsibility, social institutions emerge from contracts between individuals. But because membership is freely chosen, just as contracts are freely entered and religious faith freely embraced, the collective actions of voluntary organizations could be understood as consistent with both liberal individualism and market society. The paradox at the center of voluntarism is its capacity to provide a pivot between individual choice and enduring—and often hierarchical and privately controlled—social organization.[104]

In this sense, the doctrine of voluntarism was compatible with the striving of the self-interested individual as well as celebration of relationships of community and occupation, with principles of individual freedom of choice in addition to the mobilization of power through networks of these relationships with political equality and deference toward elites. Voluntarism or associationalism could sustain anti-statism as well as the protection of local hierarchies of status and deference, efforts to construct alternatives to markets as well as the large-scale organizations that could effectively collaborate with the state in wartime mobilization or peacetime projects. So long as these multiple meanings were not laid out in a formal doctrine, the practices and symbols of American voluntarism could function as a powerful if inarticulate discourse for organizing action that was public but not explicitly recognized as an element of formal government.

2

Civil War, Civic Expansion

THE "DIVINE METHOD"
OF PATRIOTISM

Firstly. The Armies of a Nation can be rendered incomparably more efficient by the volunteer aid and assistance of the people,—without the slightest infringement of military discipline, or interference with the constituted medical authorities of armies.

Secondly. The American Civil War affords the brightest precedent of spontaneous *and yet organized* benevolence, and furnishes an example which other nations will do well to emulate.

Thirdly. The whole of the American people—men, women, and children alike, in thus rendering their armies efficient, prove conclusively that the war is not carried on—as many in Europe suppose,   by the Government of a minority, but is waged by the great mass of the citizens themselves. In no other way can you explain the colossal achievements of this Volunteer Commission.[1]

Midway through the nineteenth century, the conditions were in place for a nation-state grounded in and often operating through civic or voluntary associations. As the revolutionary Committee on Donations and the Benevolent Empire had demonstrated, charitable and civic practices could be mobilized on a (proto)national scale. In addition, a legal framework now provided associations with the resources and formal standing necessary to survive beyond event-driven upsurges of activity. In many states and localities, partnerships were established between private associations and governments to manage care for the elderly, orphans, widows, and others who fell outside the requirements of self-sufficient citizenship. But underlying tensions between these two methods—state and voluntary—of "organizing for the public good" remained to be reconciled.

At the outbreak of the Civil War, three conflicting visions of the relationship of private or voluntary benevolence to the nation-state stood in stark relief. One position represented a strongly nationalist but anti-statist and anti-institutional claim. By sustaining the war through popular, voluntary mobilization, the people would hold *their* army close to them, preventing a despotic combination of bureaucratic authority and military power: "the Sanitary and Christian Commissions, in their ultimate results, are to make the armies of the world *the armies of the people and not of kings*."[2] For this camp, the specter of Napoleon loomed large. The importance of this connection between voluntarism and political principle is suggested by a letter from Giuseppe Mazzini, the great advocate of republican government in Italy, to the abolitionist newspaper the *Liberator*. Just after the war ended, Mazzini asked whether someone could provide a "good, accurate primary history" of "the doings of the Sanitary Commission and all that tends to prove the immense vitality of your republican principle? What you have done is so heroic that I feel the profound necessity of having it publicly known in all our countries, and especially in my own." After offering to translate and distribute such a history, Mazzini celebrated the achievements of the U.S. Sanitary Commission (USSC) in political terms:

> Your triumph is our triumph: the triumph of all, I hope, who are struggling for the advent of a republican era. Our adversaries were pointing to the worst period of the old French revolution as to the irrefutable proof of republics leading to terror, anarchy and military despotism. You have refuted all that. You have done more for us in four years than fifty years of teaching, preaching and writing, from all your European brothers, have been able to do.[3]

Although a decided minority amidst the eruption of patriotic voluntarism, a second camp rejected the melding of civic benevolence with national service, seeing it as a corruption of the self-sufficiency central to the dignity of liberal citizenship. Samuel Gridley Howe contended that continued charitable support of the Union effort would distort proper political roles and relationships: "it would be a misdirection of public charity to do what the Government can do, and ought to do, and will do." Rejecting the claim that fund-raising and sewing were necessary to maintain "the patriotic fervor of our women," Howe concluded that "it was only necessary that the country and the cause should be worthy of the devotion of our women in order to secure it."[4]

Finally, a third vision saw civic benevolence as a path to state capacity that bypassed both the strict constraints of electoral democracy and the dangerous powers of a centralized bureaucratic state. In New York City, the elite-dominated Union Defense Committee raised volunteer regiments, collected funds to support soldiers' wives and families, and eventually took charge of public funds to support their voluntary effort. "To a degree not seen before, elite New Yorkers directly usurped governmental functions: The Union Defense Committee was at once an organization of New York's bourgeoisie and simultaneously a quasi-governmental agency."[5] This path—a fundamentally Whig project that would long outlive the Whig party—harnessed social status and community organization to national purposes.[6]

The experience of the war mobilization revealed the obstacles to enacting each of these visions, but the "infrastructural power" generated by the third option provided sufficient proof of concept to inspire later efforts to incorporate civic benevolence in projects of nation-state-building. But to appreciate this accomplishment, it is first necessary to remember why these combinations were neither easy nor obvious. In North and South alike, war-driven voluntarism provoked debates over the proper extent of civilian and military authority, over the articulation of distinct lines of command, and over the propriety of incorporating women into military efforts.[7] Consequently, the direct legacies of the Civil War for civic voluntarism would prove to be limited.[8] But durable templates drawn from wartime experience would inform later efforts to harness the civic to the developing American state.

"A Popular War"

The historical memory of the Civil War has come to be dominated by the "state" components, either the high politics of President Lincoln and congressional conflicts over abolition or the military histories focused (and reenacted) on battlefields (the latter reinforced by the retrospective understanding of the conflict as the first "modern war"). But in the immediate aftermath of the war, some foreign commentators argued that its most distinctive features were not to be found in the combat itself. Reporting on that "good, accurate primary history" requested by Mazzini, one reviewer contended that "to understand the war . . . a large share of attention must be given to the social conditions of the country, to the opinions, sentiments, impulses and desires of the American people, and to the forms in which their exertions to maintain the cause which they had at heart took shape." According to this commentator, the war's "most remarkable feature" could be found in "the conduct and bearing of the people by whom and for whom the war was fought and victory won. It was most remarkable for being in every sense a popular war."[9]

This popular character of the Civil War represented a practical exercise in how to embody political theory in action and organization. Writing to the organizers of the 1864 Great Sanitary Fair in Philadelphia, John Stuart Mill characterized their effort as "so great a work of unselfishness extemporized by the spontaneous self-devotion and organizing genius of a people, altogether independently of the Government."[10] As Americans—particularly in the Northern states—debated the proper form of civic participation in the conflict, they laid out the framework for the distinctive kind of modern nation-and-state that would attract the admiration of Mazzini and Mill from afar.

These efforts played out on an organizational landscape shaped by decades of conflict over the appropriate role—if any—of voluntary associations in the public life of the new republic. By the midpoint of the nineteenth century, repeated revivals, the projects of the Benevolent Empire, along with campaign-driven developments in party organization, had greatly expanded the scope and level of familiarity with the arts of association. Yet this landscape had been repeatedly and profoundly fractured by the felt contradictions of association and charity with the dignity of citizenship understood in terms of the liberty and equality of adult white men.[11] A partial solution had been found in the equation of individual liberty with the choice to join (or leave) a particular congregation or voluntary association. But this lynchpin of voluntarism was insufficient to support a nationwide mobilization of associations in support of the Union war effort.

The Demand for a People's Army

The crisis of the Civil War provided a massive opening for the mobilization of benevolence and the participation of civic associations in national affairs.[12] In large part, this reflected the contested place of the military—as opposed to citizen militias—in the American political imagination. For those who would become American revolutionaries, the appearance of British troops in Boston in 1768 had been a sure sign of Britain's hostile designs on the colonists' freedoms. A standing army, they argued, was antagonistic to liberty by definition. Others contended that the effects of a standing army were determined by its political loyalties. "In Britain, 'the armies are *his* [the King's] *armies*, and their direction is solely by him without any control . . . Here the army, when raised, is the army of the people.' "[13] The hoped-for army was one in which the "mixture of a citizen militia and professional army was vital."[14]

This popular distrust of standing armies aligned with the limited capacities of the national government. Although a state can be defined, following Max Weber's classic discussion, by its possession of a monopoly of legitimate violence within a territory, the formal institutions of American governance were not equal to the task of carrying out a major conflict on its own soil.[15] That fact had been brought home by the British sacking of the District of Columbia during the War of 1812 as well as by the recurrent failure of the "general government" to contain private violence as well as some of the more entrepreneurial efforts of its own military officers.[16] Much of the development of the American military occurred on the nation's peripheries, in the Mexican-American War and in the work of the frontier regiments, the Army Corps of Engineers, and the Topographical Corps.[17] Such limited roles for the military were, for many Americans, consistent with their understanding of what it meant to be a free republic.[18] So even if the federal or "General Government" had possessed capacities for war-making comparable to those of European absolutist states, the declaration of war elicited an outpouring of efforts by state and local governments, associations and corporations, and individual citizens. For the first months of the war, state governments and voluntary efforts played important roles in raising and funding the mobilization and outfitting of troops.[19] In both North and South, military officials issued requests for donations of medical supplies, clothing, and foodstuffs.[20] Many citizens, in effect, demanded to participate as an expression of their patriotism and personal commitment to particular soldiers and the cause in general.

This insistent demand for a popular role in the military struggle reflected a broad cross-national tendency for greater civilian involvement in conflict, both as participants (formally drafted or otherwise) and targets.[21] War represented an opportunity for the demonstration of patriotic loyalty, a particular concern for those whose civic membership was not yet securely established. Catholic nuns represented a third of the nurses in the North, while Irish men volunteered in large numbers for the Union Army (a fact often obscured by the later role of the Irish in draft riots).[22] In New York City, the *Jewish Messenger* reported that a synagogue had taken up collections for the Western Sanitary Commission and the newspaper "take[s] a pleasure in recording this as one more evidence of the deep sympathy our co-religionists feel for their fellow citizens engaged in the patriotic work of vindicating the national integrity and suppressing a baseless rebellion."[23] But it also enacted an emergent theory of the state, or perhaps more accurately the nation-state, that was articulated both in conversations among intellectual elites and through the commitments of a wide cross-section of Americans in the northern states. Already in 1859, Henry Bellows (a Unitarian minister who would become president of the United States Sanitary Commission) offered an organic image to define "the state" as "the great common life of a nation, organized in laws, customs, institutions; its total social being incarnate in a political unit, having common organs and functions; a living body, with a head and a heart . . . with a common consciousness."[24] Those who clamored for recognition of their civic contribution to the war were in effect asserting that the state of "social being incarnate in a political unit" was something to be achieved rather than assumed.

Well before South Carolina troops fired on Fort Sumter, the self-organizing capacities of the American people were getting into gear. A wave of revivalism in 1857 and 1858 had infused new energy into religious gatherings, while muting the connection to social reform that had been a hallmark of the revivals of the 1820s and 1830s.[25] These religiously inspired endeavors were joined by anticipatory military organizing. In Chicago, a clerk mobilized a homegrown military company modeled on the French Zouaves (noted for both their exotic costumes and acrobatic drill routines), while Lincoln's campaign in the second half of 1860 fueled the nationwide emergence of "Wide Awakes," companies of young men marching in uniform, regimented under the light provided by their oil torches.[26] In the words of one account written shortly after the end of the conflict, "The people were going to war, and it was for the people to take care of itself." The capacity for "care of itself" could exist "only in a nation habituated to extra-governmental organization and to associate action, and its whole dependence was upon the readiness and ability of the people to concentrate diffused and individual efforts into a single channel of combined activity."[27]

The engagement of popular voluntary organizations with war-making represented a distinctive method for expanding state capacity,[28] quite different from the establishment of new bureaucracies or professionally dominated agencies. Commentators were very clear that the Sanitary Commission was not only a novel social formation, a "mixed work of humanity and patriotism,"[29] but also something unimaginable in the context of European states. A similar case was advanced for the United States Christian Commission (USCC), the second "great commission," which specialized in the distribution of religious literature and direct emotional support of soldiers by volunteer delegates in the field.[30] This moral claim for the military deployment of voluntarism was further sharpened by the contrast with the development of a more centralized state in the South in the form of the Confederate States of America.[31]

Surveying the history of care provided for soldiers, the Rev. Lemuel Moss, Home Secretary of the Christian Commission, concluded that "there had been in no nation any recognition of the army otherwise than as a machine of the government, to be cared for by the government or not cared for at all."[32] But a new kind of political regime required a new relationship between the people and *their* state. As Moss elaborated:

It was the character of the contest and of our armies that made the Christian sympathy of the people so natural, spontaneous, and beneficent. Such popular exhibitions of patriotic and religious feeling are inconceivable where the army is simply an instrument of oligarchic power, and war is for royal ends alone,—removed from the knowledge and interests of the people. Hon. Geo. Bancroft, in a private letter, remarks:—"Nothing like the self-organized commissions for the relief of our armies ever was before. The Christian Commission is the fruit of our institutions,—*could* not grow up, *would not be allowed* to grow up in any nation in Europe, unless it be in England, and could not there in the huge, free, popular way that we have witnessed here. Republicanism proves herself the friend of charity and of religion, and may the union endure forever. Go on, and write your noble work;—every word of it will be the eulogy of free institutions."[33]

Armies, however, are not free institutions but rather exemplars of hierarchical authority and organized discipline. Although the great commissions were often portrayed as a spontaneous, unstoppable outpouring of some fundamentally American spirit, it was no simple task to manage the linkage of voluntarism to military organization. Toward the end of the war, one commentator observed:

It will be difficult to find two principles more seemingly antagonistic than Military Discipline and Volunteer Philanthropy. The Discipline necessary for the cohesion and effectiveness of armies proceeds from set rules framed upon the experience of long years: it is cold, impassive, unimpulsive, non-eclectic, autocratic, tyrannical; it robs man of his individuality, deprives him of free-will—and looking only at the end to be attained, treats the soldier as a simple part of a great machine, to be strained, forced, and overwrought, if needs be, and cast aside when worn out or otherwise incapacitated. Reverse the position in all its several particulars, and we have the most distant and opposite end of a far-stretching diagonal,—Volunteer Philanthropy.[34]

In combination, voluntarism might contain the despotic potential of a professional army or state bureaucracy. This argument, advanced most insistently by conservative intellectuals and northern elites, asserted that organized philanthropy was both a vehicle for national mobilization and a method for inculcating civic discipline that would have political, economic, and social benefits far beyond its immediate military uses: "An unruly society, devoted to individual freedom, might be in the process of learning that discipline and subordination were good in themselves, and the commissioners wanted to play their role in teaching this lesson."[35]

Thus the same activities that expressed social being in state activities might also transform the character of individual citizens.

Mobilizing a Generous People

For a time, however, organized discipline would have to wait. As word spread of the outbreak of war, individual men volunteered for service, militia companies organized, and voluntary contributions flowed from private wallets and pantries to support the troops, though often specifically *my* sons or *our town's* soldiers.[36] The relatively spontaneous and self-organizing mobilization of support in the North had its counterparts in the Confederate states.[37] And, because support for the war was not unanimous on either side, these political differences also took form in associations such as the Loyal Leagues of the Union effort and the (perhaps largely rumored) Knights of the Golden Circle, who were alleged to be southern sympathizers in northern states.[38] Given this eruption of civic energy, the founders of the Sanitary Commission found that their plans to consult professionally and scientifically on the hygiene of military camps were swamped by the great waves of volunteer efforts to collect medical supplies and food to supplement a military diet of hard biscuits and salt pork. In towns and cities across the North, the existing organizational matrix of churches and clubs spawned new soldiers' relief associations that produced supplies and raised funds.[39]

The explosive growth of voluntarism—often in the form of organized charity or benevolence—was understood as a correlate of a new kind of polity rather than a relic of premodern social provision. This new polity, an unprecedented kind of nation-state,[40] was potentially a challenge to the centralized authority of the federal government as well as the military command. But, at least in the beginning, the difficulties of incorporating civic voluntarism in a wartime project of state-making were offset by the power of organized benevolence to generate a strongly felt sense of national solidarity. At the Great Western Sanitary Fair held in Cincinnati, one speaker proclaimed:

> It was seen that the rulers in this land did not constitute the State, but that here the people made the nation, and, therefore, the people had come forth to the war to defend their own.
>
> We were made then to understand what resistless might lay sleeping among the populations of this land, the reserve force of a free people, energies bound together by unseen National sympathies, and which could be instantly roused and changed into an organized form at the appearance of National danger.[41]

Following the pattern established by the Committee on Donations during the blockade of Boston's harbor almost a century before, civic mobilization was structured by the logic of the gift. Representatives of the two great commissions reported both large gifts—ten thousand from an individual here, half a million dollars in gold from the Pacific states and territories—and small contributions of ten cents here or a treasured item there that demonstrated deep and encompassing popular commitment to the cause.

These practices of patriotic donation have become so central to the enactment of good citizenship in the United States that it is difficult to appreciate how peculiar they appeared to some observers at the time. Reviewing the official history of the USSC shortly after the war, a British reader commented on the importance (as well as "varied and grotesque interest") of the large sums of donations raised in California: "the mode of raising these contributions was no less remarkable than their amount. The 'favourite method' of Californian charity, it seems, is that of selling an article by auction to the highest bidder, with the implied understanding that 'after paying for it,' he is 'to give it back again to the auctioneer, to be resold to the same company.'" This claim was illustrated by vignettes of "a bag of strawberries of herculean size" with each berry sold for a gold dollar, a hare shot during an unexpected train delay and then sold and resold through all the carriages for a total of $157, a defeated political candidate who carried a bag of flour from town to town in Nevada and, by selling and reselling it, collected some $40,000.[42] Nor was California the only site of innovative fund-raising. In April 1864, the Great Metropolitan Sanitary Fair in New York City featured a "sword contest, in which by the payment of $1 a vote might be cast for Gen. Grant or Gen. George B. McClellan." At his death, a noted billiards player, Melvin Foster, was remembered for an appearance "in a tournament in aid of the United States Sanitary Commission, wherein he achieved the distinction of making the best average in a 500-point game of carroms."[43] This "charitable buffoonery," the reviewer concluded, demonstrated "the earnestness of the American people in the cause; since none will deliberately and gratuitously make fools of themselves for that which they do not care for."

Voluntary contributions expressed support for soldiers but also provided a method by which citizens could reciprocate for the military service of others. In a speech given after Vicksburg, Charles Demond of the USCC captured the ways in which the logic of gift-giving provided an infrastructure for enacting patriotic feeling:

> Some one said, "Let us show our gratitude by our gifts," and the crowd came to our table, and for some time we could not take the money as fast

as it was offered. The manner of giving was equally remarkable. "This is my thank-offering," was a frequent remark; "We must take care of the boys who fight for us," another; while a large proportion said with a smile, "If you want more, call on me." Contributions soon began to come in by mail, on each occasion, and continued after we had left the Exchange, until the sums received were $100,000, $60,000, and $50,000.

But large as these gifts were, there are others that in the sight of heaven are larger, I think. An old lady, eighty years of age, lived in Amherst, Massachusetts, and supported herself by her needle. She walked several miles to bring to her pastor this five-cent bill [*sic*] (holding it up before the audience), that he might send it to me to aid the suffering soldiers. Twenty years ago a dying mother gave to her daughter this silver dollar (exhibiting it). She carefully kept the last gift of her beloved mother till she heard of the work of the Commission. Then she said, "If my mother were living I know she would give this dollar to help the soldiers, so I will do what I think she would do," and she put the dear memento into our treasury. A widow in New Hampshire sent her only son to war. He fell and was buried in Virginia. When she heard of what was being done and what was needed in the army, she gave this her wedding ring (showing it) to help the noble sufferers. Such benevolence makes even the smoke and carnage of our terrible battles radiant with the reflected brightness of heaven.[44]

Notice something interesting about these small gifts. However moving the stories, these were not gifts from one person to another. Early efforts of the USSC to facilitate person-to-person provision of necessities and luxury had created an insurmountable logistical burden in a war with multiple and often shifting fronts. Instead of a direct exchange of gifts or provisions for the military service of specific soldiers, what the USSC and USCC produced was a generalized system of reciprocity in which gifts of military service would be reciprocated indirectly. One might give because of a particular soldier, still serving or already fallen, but without the expectation that *this* gift would go to *that* man. Instead gifts would sustain strangers while friends and relatives at the front would be supported by gifts from still other strangers.

This insistence on generalized exchange was central to the political purpose of the Sanitary Commission. The great networks of giving had to be national precisely so that they would not be local or, even worse, sectional. But creating national networks that were also deeply felt was no simple matter. The Reverend Thomas Starr King, the USSC's champion fund-raiser in California (which contributed a total of $1.2 million or one-fourth of the national total),[45] laid out the problem in a lecture on

"The Privileges and Duties of Patriotism." Disagreeing with those moralists who condemned patriotism as a "sectionalism of the heart" and as an offense to the universal love of mankind, Starr King argued that "the Divine method in evoking our noblest affections is always from particulars to generals." For Starr King, the thing that aligned love of particular with love of the nation was the land itself: "an imperial river runs through it to embarrass, and to shame, and to balk all plans of rupture. The Mississippi bed was laid by the Almighty as the keel of the American ship, and the channel of every stream that pours into it is one of its ribs."[46] Thus love of the particular and the national was aligned by assuming that the unity of the land itself was already deeply felt. In practice, that love of a national landscape was enacted through gifts in cash and kind to the Union cause.[47]

Only in the strangest of circumstances would the "Divine method" lead straight from the particular to the national and back again. But tellingly, some accounts did celebrate those moments when circuits of individual relationships and generalized gift-giving coincided in a too-perfectly personalized patriotic moment. One such was reported in *Our Daily Fare*, the newsletter published by the organizers of the Philadelphia Sanitary Fair in 1864:

A Surgeon at one of the Beaufort (S.C.) hospitals relates the case of a soldier who was given over to die; disease and despondency combined had robbed him of all energy and hope. In changing his bed, a Sanitary Commission patchwork quilt was put in place of the ordinary bed spread. It arrested his attention, which for days nothing had been able to excite, there was evidently something familiar in it; he became thoroughly aroused, examined it more carefully, and presently discovered his wife's name neatly written in one corner. His interest in life returned, and he rapidly recovered. The chances that this quilt would be put on the right bed were not one in ten thousand, and the housewife who dedicated, perhaps, one of her treasures to the soldiers, could scarcely have dreamed that it would be the means of restoring her own good man to health. The story seems almost too delightful to be true, yet true it certain *is*, on the word of an army surgeon, and anybody who presumes to doubt it shall be fined a dollar (after worthy Jacob Grimm's fashion of punishing unbelievers) and the proceeds added to the Sanitary fund.[48]

This tale, apocryphal or not, captured the social dynamic at the heart of Thomas Starr King's "divine method of patriotism," "evoking our noblest affections . . . always from particulars to generals."[49] By embedding gifts and voluntary support of loved ones in a system of generalized exchange among citizens and the soldiers of their "people's army," civic solidarity could be infused with both personal love and patriotism.

In the telling of this tale, the complex organization of donation and distribution was relegated to the background. In the mobilization of patriotic solidarity, it was easy to love a landscape, as Starr King envisioned, but it proved harder to love an organization. It was particularly hard when those organizations, notably the USSC, injected inequality and expectations for deference into the fabric of civic voluntarism. For the leadership of the Sanitary Commission, properly *national* patriotic sentiments required deference to the organizational leadership of a small cadre of elite, disproportionately Unitarian, men from cities in the Northeast. These leaders were keenly aware that civic benevolence—just like love of the landscape—could crystallize at local or regional rather than national level.[50] The national leadership of the USSC repeatedly sought to squash the autonomy of local fund-raising efforts, portraying regional mobilization of gifts as a manifestation of the sectionalism that had fueled the turn to war.[51]

Proof of the capacity of civic benevolence to fuel division was found in New York City. Following the eruption of the Draft Riots in July 1863, a combination of private donations and municipal borrowing created a fund to pay the $300 commutation fee for any resident of the Democratic-dominated city who was selected in the lottery and unable to raise the funds or fund a substitute for himself.[52] Here municipal benevolence threatened to undercut the Union effort. If this was a war to preserve the Union, the webs of gift-giving and reciprocity needed to be equally encompassing.

Those webs of giving also required expert discipline, at least in the opinion of the leadership of the USSC. Following the armistice, Bellows reflected on "the 'service' the organization 'rendered the country' by 'standing between the army, as cared for by the government, and the country, which expected impossibilities,' and which foolishly 'proposed to take care of the army by countless State, county, and town committees,' was accomplished by 'defending military discipline' while at the same time 'pacifying the fears and representing the solicitudes of home.'" As Bellows' language makes clear, the formal hierarchy of the USSC was reinforced by a discourse that often belittled ordinary citizens as driven by emotion, disorganized, and expecting "impossibilities."[53]

In a historical irony that makes perfect sense in light of these tensions between the people and "their" commissions, the legacy of wartime benevolence was not linked in popular memory to the "great commissions," but rather to a compelling individual. From the very first days of the conflict, before Commissions were established and organizations imagined, private citizens acted on their own to contribute something to the national struggle. Perhaps no individual exemplified the projection of this will to act more than Clara Barton, who was among those who made their way to the battlefields to offer what comfort, nursing, and sustenance they could. These efforts expressed the fundamental logic of the gift, an unmediated circulation of service and gratitude between soldiers and citizens. But that logic would be transformed as it was harnessed to military discipline and projects of nation-state-building.

Aligning Civic Participation with Military Discipline

From the first onset of hostilities, commentators recognized that the outpouring of civic energies and the motives of popular benevolence conflicted with the organizational principles of the professional military: "The principle was seen from the first, and has been resolutely maintained under all circumstances, that the people's care for the soldiers, if permitted a free and spontaneous course, might become a main dependence of the army, and thus weaken the sense of responsibility and the zeal and efficiency of the official sources of supply and protection. . . . How long and how far, it was continually asked from the very first, is it safe and wise for the nation, in its home character, to undertake to do what the Government can do, and ought to do?"[54] But, faced with a surge of voluntary energy, the government had no choice: "The popular affections and sympathies will force themselves into the administration of army and all other affairs in times of deep national awakening. According to Henry Bellows, the practical question was not, is it best to allow the army to depend in any degree upon the care of the people, as distinguished from the Government?" but rather "How shall this rising tide of popular sympathy, expressed in the form of sanitary supplies and offers of personal service and advice, be rendered least hurtful to the army system, and most useful to the soldiers themselves?" Voluntary contributions, at least according to Bellows, endangered "the order, efficiency, and zeal of the regular bureau." Enthusiastic civic mobilization would have to be tempered, guided, and above all organized: "It could not be deemed wise, much less was it possible, to discourage and deaden the active sympathies of the people."[55]

Such top-down guidance was at odds with the claim of the people to care for their own army. In its initial form, the Sanitary Commission represented an effort by elite, professional men, interested—as their chosen title declared—in the promotion of healthful organization and maintenance of military camps in an era when disease often took as great a toll on soldiers as actual combat. "Can the average death-rate from disease be reduced to a fraction of that which was registered in the Mexican war? This result the Commission believed possible. It was to be accomplished by *prevention* and *succor.*" Here, the response to the problems of a volunteer army was identified as *more voluntarism*, in this case from civilians in support of the military.[56] In this first incarnation, the Sanitary Commission seemed a plausible partner for a military system that was closely tied to the development of engineering and surveying expertise. But despite the efforts of the great commissions to conform to military rather than participatory models in order to facilitate collaboration, approval and acceptance from the military were limited.[57]

Professional military officers often resented the interference of civilian experts in the organization of their camps and the military medical corps was hostile to the "trespassing" of civilian physicians in their jurisdiction.[58] President Lincoln, famously, referred to the USSC as his "fifth wheel."[59] At the end of the war, for example, General William Tecumseh Sherman provided somewhat grudging praise. Recognizing that "the people of the United States should have voluntarily contributed six millions of dollars for the moral welfare of the soldiers employed, in addition to other and vast charitable contributions, is one of the wonders of the world,"[60] he acknowledged that "At times I may have displayed an impatience when the agents manifested an excess of zeal, in pushing forward their persons and stores when we had no means to make use of their charities. But . . . I have always given them credit for good and pure motives."[61] Sherman's "congratulatory" note in honor of the final meeting of the Christian Commission underscores the contradictions between two organizational models. Although the Civil War was recognized as an unprecedented triumph for voluntary associations and proof of the capacity of voluntarism to meet national crises, at least one general had recognized that the combination of "military discipline and volunteer philanthropy"[62] was fraught with tension.

In their official histories, both the "great commissions" stressed the self-discipline required for civilians to gain the military's trust. Anticipating arguments that link state-formation to the constitution of modern, disciplined selves, the volunteers stressed how bringing "home-like" and "Christian" interactions to the military camps would support the self-control of volunteer soldiers and prevent military discipline from mutating into despotism. The same message would be carried by every bandage, book, and provision distributed through the commissions. Writing a historical account of the sanitary movement as it was still in its prime, one organizer claimed that the efforts of the Sanitary Commission

will annihilate forever that wide interval that has always existed between the army and the people. It prevents the soldier from drifting away from the influence of home. It binds him to its tender charities by all that made that home dear; and more than all, holds him with the strongest of all earthly bonds, the sweet influence of woman. . . . . . In short, its tendency is to keep the army *one with the people*, thus rendering it impossible for a tyrant to convert it into an instrument for the accomplishment of his own base ends. The love of spoil, and of a life without moral restraint, that makes a great army so dangerous to human freedom, is thus to be overcome by charity.[63]

Here, organized charity was presented as a protection against both the uncivilizing effects of war and the illegitimate extension of centralized military power into political tyranny. The commissions would "make the armies of the world *the armies of the people and not of kings*."[64]

In their insistent linking of military nationalism, patriotic solidarity, and individual discipline, the founders of the Sanitary Commission anticipated one of the key insights of recent theories of the modern state. Building on the work of Michel Foucault, historical sociologists have demonstrated how systems of belief—in religion, in honor—constitute the selfhood of subjects or citizens in ways that reinforce the governing arrangements. A religious faith that emphasizes how sin leads to damnation produces practices of self-control that encourage conformity to law without requiring extreme coercion or constant vigilance by state agents. The elaboration of a code of warrior honor both sustains and channels elite violence as an element of rule.[65] The Civil War required a comparable response. How could democratic citizens be roused to fight—as well as to support conflict on distant battlefields—without destroying the qualities that maintained civic order in a regime with still minimally developed policing power?

The specifically *civic* character of these concerns was evident in the conflicts that almost immediately arose between the Sanitary Commission and the regular army. Writing in the dark days (at least for the Union armies) of 1863, the future official historian of the USSC, Charles J. Stillé, focused on this conflict of organizing principles. Both the leaders of the USSC and the military valued discipline, but they did not understand it in precisely the same way.[66] Among the causes for "the want of immediate success," Stillé pointed to "the character of the early military education of our higher officers." The West Point system "seems to fail in teaching the young soldier, what is just now the most important quality he can possess for command, the character and capacity of volunteer soldiers. The system of discipline that he has been taught is that which governs the regular army, a system modeled upon the English, which is, with the exception of that in use in Russia, the most brutal and demoralizing known in any army in Europe."[67]

To mitigate the effects of military brutality, it would be necessary not only to educate the officers but also to transform the quality of life in the military for soldiers regardless of rank. The effects of such benevolent interventions were expected to persist after wartime. As Major-General and U.S. Representative Benjamin Butler of Massachusetts (also an important ally of Clara Barton) wrote for the commemorative volume for the USCC: "I think it is largely due to the connections of the soldier with his home and citizenship, thus kept up by the years and kindred associations, that the country is indebted for the sublime but before unwitnessed spectacle, of an army of more than a million veteran soldiers, on the approach of peace, changing at once without shock into a like number of quiet, orderly, valuable citizens."[68] Foreshadowing a century in which the demobilization of soldiers would repeatedly endanger democratic politics, Butler pointed to the effect of benevolence in constituting citizen-soldiers and generating stronger bonds among them.

Benevolence as a Threat to Democratic Dignity

For all its patriotic resonance, civic benevolence challenged core principles of political liberalism, the independence and self-sufficiency of male citizens. Consequently, the claims made by the commissions and their volunteers were contested not only by officers resentful of intrusions by well-meaning volunteers, but also by prominent figures within the "voluntary" effort. Samuel Gridley Howe—physician, abolitionist, member of the USSC, and husband of Julia Ward Howe of "The Battle Hymn of the Republic"[69]—was strongly committed to the USSC's original mission of providing expert advice to the Army's medical service. But this original project was overshadowed by the charitable efforts of fund-raisers and gift-giving. Acknowledging that the flood of donations testified to the "patriotism, zeal, and generosity" of the people, Howe recognized that these contributions had been vitally necessary in the first months before military capacity had been expanded. But he contended that the long-term consequences of sustained donations were damaging to soldiers: "Disguise it as we may, if we continue the present practice beyond the period of dire necessity, *we introduce a system of alms-giving and alms-taking;* and no purity of motive can avert the degrading influence of such a system. I hold that the period of dire necessity has passed."[70]

Howe directly grasped the danger in transposing models of benevolence and charity into the heart of a democratic polity. The giving of a gift—no matter how well-intentioned, patriotic, or generous the motives of the giver—puts the recipient in a position of dependence.[71] Although soldiers were understood to reciprocate through their own sacrifices on the field, even a transient moment of dependence could corrode their self-sufficiency and dignity as citizens.[72] In benevolence, advocates of liberal individualism saw a moral threat, rather than a source of "Christian" or "home-like" relations that would maintain the self-discipline and virtue of soldiers in the field. According to one of Howe's correspondents:

> As with the civilian, the more the soldier is made to depend upon the fruit of his own labor and resources, the better soldier, the better man he becomes. By self-dependence, accompanied by the strict discipline of camp life, he is much more likely to learn the habits of economy, prudence, carefulness, temperance, sobriety, and secure cleanliness; in short to acquire those habits that characterize the true soldier. Who can estimate the value of such habits to the volunteer on his return to civil life? . . . [F]ar better that the soldier shall purchase any such needed extra, with his own earnings, than be supplied by charity; on the principle that one values what he earns or procures, and consequently is more likely to make better use of it.[73]

Howe eventually resigned from the Sanitary Commission, standing by his rigorous liberal commitment to self-sufficiency through "free labor" first as a member of the Freedman's Inquiry Board, which was hostile to any program of one-way paternalism toward freed slaves, and, later, as an active supporter of aggressive vagrancy laws in his role as chairman of the Massachusetts Board of State Charities.[74] In both settings, he anticipated the postwar ascendance of market liberalism protected by legislation and judge-made law.[75] Others once committed to patriotic benevolence took a turn in Howe's direction. Following her experience in the Franco-Prussian War of 1870–71, Clara Barton shifted from relief to the economic rehabilitation of war victims and refugees. Straight food assistance, she worried, would "make of them permanent beggars and vagrants, thus doing for their morale all that the bombardment had done for their physical condition."[76]

Rumors of Corruption

As efforts to harness civic benevolence to national projects, the USSC and the USCC exemplified the many ways in which the logic of the gift conflicted with other templates for social organization: liberal models of citizenship, the market, professionalism, military hierarchy, and state authority. The strains can be traced by mapping rumors and complaints,[77] starting with the possible corruption of the gift by self-serving behavior.

Rumors abounded that donated goods were being wasted and spoiled, sold rather than given to soldiers, or diverted for the personal profit of agents of the commissions. In some cases, there was a germ of truth in these stories; the USSC did sell one load of socks knitted by volunteers to the U.S. Army when the army's own procurement arrangements fell short.[78] But the transposition of the gift from intimate relationships to a large, less personal, national organization ensured that these worries over who benefited from these gifts would continue to fuel rumors. Louisa Lee Schuyler, the chief contact between the men of the Executive Committee and local women's organizations, called for documentation of these proliferating charges: "In almost every village there is the story of a returned soldier, who spent his last dollar for a pot of jelly, and there finds his mother's name on the wrapper. But where is the soldier, and what was his mother's name?"[79]

Donors to wartime efforts also interrogated the motives of those who managed and worked for the two commissions. Both employed paid agents, although salaries at the Christian Commission were substantially lower and much of the work of the paid agents was to oversee a larger force of unpaid volunteers. The USSC was vulnerable to criticism for the high "professional" salaries of $1,500 to $4,000 paid to the officers.[80] Frederick Law Olmsted, now best known as the pioneering landscape architect but then the secretary of the USSC, rebuffed these criticisms with a straightforward appeal to the market: "How long could the war be carried on upon the theory that voluntary and unpaid services are the best or that a patriotic spirit is the best security of discipline?" In contrast to appeals to benevolence and voluntarism, Olmsted insisted that the organization's performance depended upon "getting the best available talent and paying the market price for it."[81]

The character of the Sanitary Commission as a professional, hierarchical organization with a well-paid staff also brought into question the qualities and jurisdiction of voluntarism. Whereas Samuel Gridley Howe had contended that organized benevolence interfered with the proper development of the national state, many of the women volunteers in the war effort came to question whether their own benevolent activity had been commandeered by the national government and therefore represented double taxation. As Louisa Lee Schuyler summarized this line of concern and complaint: "What is the govt. doing? Why can't it do *all*? Why is the Sanitary the Best channel for the gifts of the people?"[82] And if some donors and volunteers complained that they were asked to do too much, others charged that citizens and government alike had failed to reciprocate fully for the military service of their soldiers. One correspondent decried the "numbers of discharged and disabled soldiers in this city forced to beg" and urged the *New York Times* to "again apprise the public of this fact, and request them to assist the [USS] Commission in their laudable endeavors to remove that stain upon our patriotism, viz: A man in Uncle Sam's uniform, forced to beg for bread."[83]

Finally, the histories of the two commissions highlight a problem of scale in the linking of civic benevolence to nation-building. If Thomas Starr King's "divine method of patriotism" called for moving from particulars to generals, the history of the Civil War demonstrated that the process could stall at any point along the way. The Sanitary Commission battled its own "sectional" tendencies as organized efforts in the Midwest—notably in Chicago, Cincinnati, and St. Louis—demanded greater autonomy.[84] A fund-raising innovation, the "Sanitary Fair," encouraged municipal organizing and pride as city after city tried to beat the records set by earlier fairs. Along with fears of corruption, hostility to professionalism, and uncertainty about the extent of state responsibility, the persistence of local and regional loyalties enacted through fund-raising networks presented durable obstacles to any national patriotism grounded in the practices of civic benevolence.

Each of these tensions expressed the durable contradictions between benevolence and the democratic dignity of citizens, between voluntarism and bureaucratic state-building. Rumors of corruption or the indulgences of well-paid staff flagged motives unsuited to wartime. Concerns that voluntarism had been commandeered by the government raised the specter that the army did not belong to the people but that the generosity of the people had been commandeered by an ever more powerful state. And to the extent that all these efforts built on local networks and love of the particular (in Thomas Starr King's formulation), the nationalizing patriotism of wartime was, as Melinda Lawson has argued, always at risk of fracture.[85] Because these tensions were not resolved, the Civil War did not represent a stark turning point in the trajectory of American nation-state-building. But the experience left a significantly altered topography of probabilities,[86] with new distributions of cultural resources and organizing skills. Despite the rapid disassembling of the commissions themselves, the widespread experience of civic voluntarism left behind widely shared practices and organizational models that would shape later efforts to address social ills and cultivate national patriotic commitment.

Legacies of Wartime Benevolence

The Civil War represented an unprecedented effort to harness the practices and discourses of voluntarism, charity, and benevolence to a national project. The scope of these efforts underscores the power of reciprocity as a principal of social organization as well as the potential of voluntarism as a medium for mobilization and commitment of a people to a state. As Ulysses S. Grant recognized, the work of the two "great Commissions"—the USSC and the USCC—had made major contributions not only to the war effort but to the quality of national unity: "To them the army feel the same gratitude that the loyal public feel for the services rendered by the army."[87] To the extent that these webs of benevolent action and organization constituted and continually reinforced that commitment while preempting further resort to state coercion, it is obvious why voluntarism is such a compelling vehicle for political endeavors.

Almost immediately after the war, this lesson was applied to new political projects as Irish-Americans sought to support the independence struggles in Ireland. In 1866, the Directress of the Fenian Society in New York City made arrangements to "receive donations of lint, bandages, medicines, preserves, and such matters as the experiences of the late war have taught the women of America to prepare for those who, in the struggle for the achievement of liberty, as well as in that for its preservation, may fall sick or wounded."[88] This model of patriotic benevolence was sustained through occasional reunions of the veterans of the USCC.[89] Decades later, as the United States geared up for the Spanish-American war, calls were made for the organization of a "national relief association" whose "Formation Will Be in Accordance with the Spirit of the Christian Commission of 1861."[90]

Yet, with the rapid disbanding of both the USSC and USCC, the main line of influence on subsequent civic projects was biographical. The Civil War had been exhausting and tragic, traumatic for many, and yet a peak experience for a number of those who had led—or risen through—the great national mobilization in support of the Union cause. (At this point in the analytic narrative, the Southern elements recede from that national development for a time, overwhelmed by the destruction of the social and economic order of the Confederate States and repelled by the identification of national voluntary associations with the Union effort during the war years.[91]) From the Sanitary Commission, Henry Bellows would go on to play a prominent role in shaping the Republican party not as a force for abolition but as a vehicle for national economic development and business interests. Louisa Lee Schuyler, who oversaw much of the Commission's relationship with the women who served and made preserves and raised funds, would become prominent as an advocate for charity organization, an effort in which she was joined by Josephine Shaw Lowell, a war widow and pioneer of modern social welfare. One outstanding field agent for the Christian Commission, Dwight L. Moody, would in time become the leading evangelist of the Gilded Age. For these

and many others, the experience of the Civil War left a legacy of new organizational skills and models of collective action.

These legacies—the organizational models, practical skills and technologies, as well as a commitment to the civic role of voluntarism—were
perpetuated in diverse ways. They were described in newspapers and periodicals, encountered in the postwar projects of veterans of the USSC
and USCC, and carried biographically in the lives of individuals. A sense
of the trajectories of influence and inheritance can be gleaned from the
often brief records of those lives that were recorded in obituaries for decades after the war (see appendix 1). These are in no way representative in
statistical terms. The decision to publish an obituary is far from random
and undoubtedly skews toward those who were organizational leaders
or advantaged by some other source of social privilege. But, recognizing
these limitations, these assembled lives suggest that there were distinctive, if overlapping, paths taken after the war that would shape the development of civic benevolence in American cities and towns for decades
to come.

As would be expected from its name, the United States Christian Commission appears predominantly in the obituaries of men with religious
vocations. Although a number of the key figures were prominent businessmen—George H. Stuart of Philadelphia and John V. Farwell of Chicago were dry goods merchants, Benjamin F. Jacobs "one of the pioneer
real estate dealers in Chicago," and Adam Scott Pratt a banker from Detroit—their other civic activities tended to cluster in outposts of the "Benevolent Empire" such as the American Sunday School Union, the Young
Men's Christian Association, Bible societies, city missions, and temperance activities. Relatively few connections to secular civic organizations
or politics are mentioned, although Farwell was an elector on Lincoln's
presidential ticket and appointed to the Board of Indian Commissioners
by President Grant. Farwell was also a prominent supporter of Dwight L.
Moody first through the YMCA and later through Moody's own evangelical efforts. Pratt was noted as a member of the Union League, and the Rev.
Dr. Joseph Ford Sutton had memberships in both the Loyal League and
the Sons of the Revolution in addition to being a fellow of the American Geographical Society. The majority of those in this group, however,
spent their careers as ministers in a variety of denominations: Methodists, Presbyterians, Episcopalians, and nondenominational congregations. Some also taught at or led seminaries and universities. This network built on the prewar energies of urban evangelism and returned
to this channel with new intensity and a greatly expanded network of
allies after the war. But the collective impression of the lives lived by the
former agents of the USCC was continuous, in important ways, with

antebellum patterns of revival and organized evangelism that pulsed into waves of social reform and insistently escaped the boundaries of specific denominations.

The obituaries of the men with affiliations to the Sanitary Commission describe a quite different path through life. In contrast to the veterans of the USCC, the male Sanitarians display much more varied occupational trajectories, with ties to business, to the legal and medical professions, to higher education, and to politics and government. Alumni of the USSC went on to serve in Congress, in federal government or on federal commissions, and in state and local office ranging from the state legislature of New Hampshire to the mayor's office in San Francisco. In their avocations, the former Sanitarians distributed their efforts across the evangelical efforts favored by the alumni of the Christian Commission (temperance, urban missions, Sunday schools), the charity organization efforts that also engaged many of the women who had served with the USSC, and leading cultural institutions, historical societies, professional associations, and educational institutions that were all pillars of municipal life in the late nineteenth century. Although only a fraction of the obituaries mentioned the elite civic clubs promoted by Henry Bellows, almost all mention an affiliation with the prominent cultural and benevolent institutions that would come to be organized into new networks of municipal governance through emerging networks of businessmen and civic elites. Taken together, the lives lived by the men of the USSC capture the increasing interconnectedness of civic life in the late nineteenth century and the linking of the civic to political parties and institutions as well as to growing enclaves of industry and commerce.

Finally, although their numbers are small, the lives of the female veterans of the Sanitary Commission illuminate the connections between that wartime experience and the domains of social reform and charity organization. This trajectory is exemplified by Louisa Lee Schuyler, who was the woman most centrally involved in the organization and management of the Commission[92] and then went on to found the New York State Charities Aid Association[93] as well as to serve as one of the original trustees of the Russell Sage Foundation, itself a central actor in the rationalization of municipal benevolence. Others, notably Mary Livermore in Chicago, embodied the ongoing connections with efforts of social reform and uplift, including both woman suffrage and temperance. These activities, like those of the veterans of the Christian Commission, might seem largely continuous with antebellum models of feminine charity were it not for their new engagement with city as well as state government and for the increasingly centralized financial resources of philanthropists and civic organizations. Although the gender politics of the Civil War experience were complex and at times conflictual,[94] at least a handful of women took with them the ambition of playing a larger civic and political role in service to social reform.

Taken collectively, these lives only sketch the web of connections between the experience of wartime civic benevolence and the subsequent emergence of municipal benevolence as a mode of quasi-private, quasi-public governance. The cumulative results of their efforts would become evident when, three decades after the war, the nation's cities staggered under the demands of the depression of 1893 and then mobilized to support a new military effort that would become the Spanish-American War. Through these episodes, alliances were also built with a new cohort of truly rich men and their families, who entered into civic affairs either as individual philanthropists or as benefactors of the great modern foundations. The Sanitarians and evangelicals who had led the civic mobilization during the Civil War would have important second acts in the postwar decades marked by local efforts of urban reform.

But, from the start, it was clear that the incompatibilities of organized benevolence and public affairs were not resolved by the return to civil peace. The coupling of organized benevolence and state authority foundered on the contradictions of reciprocity and self-sufficient individualism, of voluntarism and bureaucratic hierarchy, of amateurism and professionalism. Just before the war ended, a new Republican governor of Illinois devoted a part of his inaugural address to pulling apart the wartime fusion of voluntary and governmental efforts. Gov. Richard J. Oglesby acknowledged that the commissions "have added a new feature to modern warfare and go very far towards mitigating its barbarities." But—and here one must infer the proposal he is rejecting[95]—Oglesby contended that it would be

> better to permit this great agency of the people, the work of their own thoughts, to be left entirely to their own management, operation and control, free from all legislative interference. It is greatly to be feared that any attempt to give it the appearance of an institution supported by law will divest it of its real character, and in a very short time discourage those voluntary and unselfish efforts of the public to support and sustain it, without which it would soon languish and its efficiency become impaired.[96]

The direct legacies of the Civil War commissions were fragmented and often stillborn. Some of the leaders of the Sanitary Commission constituted themselves as the American Branch of the International Committee of Relief for Wounded Soldiers in Geneva, Switzerland.[97] Up in Maine, some anticipated that the local affiliates of the USSC could be transformed into "agencies through whom all claims upon the Government and for the pensions of soldiers and sailors and their families may be prosecuted without expense to the claimants."[98] This "good news for our brave boys" was premature since this responsibility would be assumed by a different voluntary association, the Grand Army of the Republic with its close alliance to the Republican Party. Only in the aftermath of World War I, would the American Red Cross fulfill the role envisioned for its predecessor over fifty years earlier. For the time being, the wartime fusion of civic association and nation-state-building rapidly gave way as the veterans of the great commissions and patriotic benevolence pursued different paths in peacetime.

3

Municipal Benevolence

The Sanitary Commission was not from its inception a merely humanitarian or beneficent association. It necessarily took on that appearance, and its life depended upon its effective work as an almoner of the homes of the land to fathers, brothers and sons in the field. But its projectors were men with strong political purpose, induced to take this means of giving expression to their solicitude for the national life, by discovering . . . that a great scheme of practical service, which united men and women, cities and villages, distant States and Territories, in one protracted, systematic, laborious and costly work—a work of an impersonal character—animated by love for the national cause, the national soldier, and not merely by personal affection or solicitude for their own particular flesh and blood, would develop, purify and strengthen the imperiled sentiment of nationality.

HENRY W. BELLOWS
President, United States Sanitary Commission
Founding member, Union League Club of New York[1]

Writing more than a decade after the Confederate surrender at Appomattox, Henry Bellows acknowledged that his great wartime enterprise had never been entirely about benevolence. The farflung civilian networks of fund-raising and production of supplies had used "a work of impersonal character" to leverage the "personal affection or solicitude for their own particular flesh and blood" into something infused by a robust sense of general reciprocity "animated by love for the national cause, the national soldier, and not merely by personal affection or solicitude for their own particular flesh and blood." While northern troops were mobilized to protect the Union, the United States Sanitary Commission was also at work saving the nation and advancing a distinctive model of the national state.

Following the military surrender and rehabilitation of the Southern States, the sense of a common, nationalist cause in the North contracted. The great wartime commissions were disbanded and components of the effort spun off in new directions or withered into obscurity.[2] But many of those who had been most directly committed to benevolent mobilization soon found new causes. For some, former slaves took the place of soldiers in the field as the focus of uplift. In what W. E. B. DuBois celebrated as the "Ninth Crusade," a number of the women who had been the backbone of war relief headed to the defeated south to provide the education and literacy denied under the slave system.[3] Soon, projects of education and self-help began, claiming—although very rarely realizing—for the freed slave that economic self-sufficiency and civic dignity that could not co-exist with any form of charity.

On a parallel track, organized benevolence was deployed closer to home to counter the social ills of growing cities and new waves of migration, from both Europe and rural America. These efforts created new organizational capacities that shaped the possibilities for relief of poverty and suffering for decades to come. Veterans of the Sanitary Commission helped to found State Boards of Charities with oversight over private agencies; in cities, their initiatives transformed voluntary relief through the establishment of charity organization societies (COS).[4] But none of these projects enjoyed the full-throated support from both elites and ordinary citizens that had been the hallmark of wartime fund-raising projects. Efforts to recruit new allies and sources of financial support reoriented the politics of organized benevolence away from nation-state-building projects to municipal improvement. Here, civic benevolence combined with a different political endeavor: the mobilization of businessmen and commercial elites to secure control over local affairs and promote local economic development. Organized charity met ascendant commerce, in a joint effort to contain the growth of municipal government and tax-based spending.

As a result, the logic of the gift was rearranged; familiar practices of civic benevolence were repurposed as an alternative to emerging party machines.[5] At a moment when property owners had surrendered a portion of their power over and responsibility for civic leadership,[6] demands for expanded public spending controlled by party bosses and sustained by increased taxes threatened private wealth.[7] And private property owners pushed back. Some advocated for civil service regulations and the establishment of public agencies staffed by tested and credentialed experts.[8] Others urged that public relief should be handed over to privately funded voluntary associations in the hope that municipal governments would thereby be insulated from popular demands for greater tax-supported expenditures for aid.[9] Businessmen opposed to the expansion of tax-supported public services were often willing to contribute to voluntary relief efforts. In this respect, the development of charity organization was a piece of a broader reconfiguration of governance that cannot be reduced to either the imposition of moral order and social control or the ascendance of a new class of experts and bureaucrats. Organized benevolence came to anchor a distinctive vision of municipal political economy.

Cities and State-Building

In theories of the state, cities figure in at least three different ways: as sites of capital accumulation, as seats of government, and as distinctively civic polities. Where all three coincide, cities have provided a stage for political contests over how and when capital will be coupled to state-making and what liberties will be secured for citizens. Yet these three elements are not necessarily co-located: economic power may be rooted in agriculture or extraction, government may be located in ceremonial cities, and urban residents may lack the standing of citizens. Different configurations contribute to distinctive trajectories of state-building.[10]

According to Charles Tilly, "cities shape the destinies of states chiefly by serving as containers and distribution points for capital."[11] From the perspective of their inhabitants, however, towns and cities are much more than simple containers for capital. They are also locales of social interaction, economic exchange, and political mobilization. But in the United States, cities have been multiply handicapped as sites for the mobilization of political power. The constitutional framework—adopted when cities such as New York, Boston, and Philadelphia barely counted as urban[12]—recognized only the federal government and the states. So whereas the growth of large cities preceded the formation of modern states in much of Europe, the sequence was reversed in the United States.[13] Cities developed as major centers of capital accumulation within an institutional framework that provided few footholds for the political role of economic enterprise and concentrated settlement. While many of the founders were intent on protecting the rights of property, their concern was not the concentrated property of urban commerce and industry.

This lack of political concern for urban capital was not a matter of simple oversight. The translation of concentrations of investment and capital into political leverage had been blocked intentionally.[14] Many state constitutions severely limited the autonomy of cities, fueling long struggles over home rule. Symbolically, the new nation's capitol was removed from the prominent cities of New York and Philadelphia to a newly created (and, to this day, politically disempowered) place, the District of

Columbia. As a consequence, many historical accounts of the national American state have attended to cities primarily as locations for important events. But cities are much more than settings for politics. Fueled by electoral competition, cities gave rise to new organizational forms—the party machines—that contested elite control of municipal government and threatened possible redistribution of wealth through an expansion of tax-supported services.[15] These new forms of political power were met with still further organizational innovation, driving important—if often overlooked—transformations in American politics. In addition, cities faced their own version of the lack of collective identity that had confronted the new nation at its founding. The problem of constructing patriotic solidarity at the national level existed in a parallel form in the nation's cities. What materials were available to create new forms of social order and governance in the face of explosive growth, in-migration, out-migration, and profound economic change?[16] In many of the nation's cities, an innovative model of distributed governance emerged that both offered a new template for citizenship and accommodated substantial economic inequality.

These projects had important precedents in wartime benevolence. Some of the Civil War efforts, notably the Sanitary Fairs, had advanced a civic vision of public spaces open to all (if effectively limited by admission prices and the core activity of shopping at the fairs). As historian Jeanie Attie explains, just as "Frederick Law Olmsted and Calvert Vaux had envisioned Central Park as a staging ground for the better classes and the masses to share in democratic, urban leisure, so the Metropolitan Fair advanced a harmonious rendition of industrial, urban life and a romanticized vision of the Union."[17] A different configuration was championed by those who successfully proposed a municipal fund to pay the $300 commutation fee for New York City working men selected in the federal draft lotteries—an effort denounced by the city's leading Republicans who recognized that "with their multimillion dollar handout to the poor, the Democrats of the Common Council had established themselves as the preeminent donors in the city."[18] Such projects represented a powerful fusion of benevolence and (anti-)nationalism with the social organization of the city, often exacerbating the ever-present tensions between civic dependence and democratic citizenship.

For the urban reformers of the late nineteenth century, poverty and economic inequality stood front and center in both their diagnoses of civic problems and their proposed remedies. This centrality of inequality meant that the difficulty of reciprocating for benevolent gifts would likely corrode any sense of shared civic membership. The working class might sell their votes, contributing to corruption; public funds channeled through benevolent institutions would generate gratitude that would then take the form of political dependence and potentially fuel class conflict. During the 1857 depression, a New York City plan for unemployment relief drew charges that it was "a demogogical attempt to array the poor against the rich."[19] As with the charges leveled at the Washington Benevolent Society a half century before (see chapter 1), any linking of the "gift" of relief to electoral politics threatened to corrupt individual political liberty. With the expansion of the vote, as Simmel observed, "the poor are not only poor, they are also citizens."[20] To harness benevolence as a basis for political solidarity in a democratic and urban polity required a thorough reworking of the logic of the civic gift.

This reworking animated and roiled urban politics—particularly in the North—for decades after the Civil War. Sweeping economic changes eroded the material prospects for independence and self-sufficiency as de-skilled artisans and casual laborers were buffeted by day-to-day volatility in the demands for their goods and labor.[21] If these workers were forced—or allowed—to turn to public relief, they would be exposed to the alleged moral corrosion of pauperism and ensnared by the political uses of public benevolence. Consequently, many business leaders hoped that charity could preempt depression-driven disorder while preventing any expansion of political patronage (at least patronage that they did not control). The first severe economic downturn after the Civil War, coming only two years after the Paris Commune, set off a cascade of efforts to arrive at new organizational solutions to these problems.

The Depression of 1873

As the winter of 1873–74 took hold, the nation felt the full force of a financial panic that would test the capacity of cities to provide relief to the "temporarily destitute."[22] Unlike the traditional categories of the "worthy poor"—the blind, disabled, widowed, and aged who were held blameless for their inability to support themselves—and the "unworthy poor," the unemployed were understood and often understood themselves to be capable of work. They were, in effect, the "should not have been poor but for. . . ." Given that work was not to be had because of the "reckless speculations of so-called bankers who invested the savings of prudent depositors in moonshine enterprises and baseless securities,"[23] their need reflected lack of opportunity rather than intrinsic moral character. As with the soldiers in the recent war, the challenge was how to provide relief—always potentially demeaning—to those who were seen as blameless in their own unemployment and who would presumably return to the status of full citizens and voters as soon as the economy recovered.

Many, particularly Democrats, blamed the recession on the policy of the Republicans in national office[24] who combined a determination to pay down the wartime debt with alleged unwillingness to economize on government spending. As a consequence, the depression provided an occasion for arguing about government's role in relief. As writers for the *Graphic* baited the *New York Tribune*: "A year ago, for weeks before the Presidential election, the Government works of all kinds swarmed with men under pay. Can the Government give two months' work and pay for a ballot, but nothing whatever for bread? Because our Government is not paternal in the European sense, must it mock the people's hunger with a stone, and when they ask even a fish give them a serpent? Then the sooner we have a paternal government the better."[25] The same lines of debate were evident in Maryland, where the *Annapolis Gazette* responded to proposals from the "United Order of Internationals" to petition Congress on the grounds "that 'all penniless, homeless, and involuntary idle persons' are 'properly the wards of the nation,' and therefore should be supported by the nation" and from "some of the working men [who] met in this city on Sunday, and passed a resolution 'that work on a large scale must be promptly furnished by the people to the people.'" [26]

Insofar as American government was "not paternal in the European sense," the question was how to provide relief in a non-paternalistic, appropriately democratic manner. Those—including the writers at the *Tribune*—who offered the most obvious answer of "no such relief," invoked the comparison to France as evidence of the futility of government-funded work relief: "A Government experiment was tried in 1848–9. Workshops were established and work was supplied. The roll of 5,000 the first week was soon extended to 117,000. Manufacturing proceeded, but no one had money to buy, and soon the workmen actually at work numbered only some 2,000, and Government had the rest to care for. No wonder general bankruptcy followed."[27] Purely public solutions to unemployment, including work relief, were criticized as economically flawed, susceptible to political patronage, and aligned with socialist demands. But this left the question of whether a system of relief appropriate to American principles of government could be imagined, however those principles were defined. In rejecting calls for expanded public employment as un-American, European, or socialistic, critics begged the question of how to respond to economic hardship that was unprecedented in scale.

In communities across the country, the legacies of the Civil War were visible as early as the depression of 1873. Although histories of social welfare in the United States often trace a line directly back to the Sanitary Commission, in the wake of the Civil War both of the great commissions largely disappeared from view as explicit models for civic mobilization.[28] Despite the praise of Giuseppe Mazzini and John Stuart Mill, there is little evidence that Americans took these experiences as templates for the reconstruction of national or municipal polities. But if the commissions themselves were not held up as models, individual veterans of these efforts carried both an orientation to civic service and specific practical solutions back into the civic life of the late nineteenth century, particularly in the growing cities that faced unfamiliar challenges. In New York City, "an informal meeting of a number of persons connected with various churches, benevolent associations, &c." was chaired by Jackson S. Schultz, who had been a member of the Union League Club's committee to raise volunteers for the Union army and had worked with the USSC in staging the Metropolitan Fair. Minutes were taken by Lewis Jackson, who had served as secretary of the Union Meeting of City Missions, and the first remarks reported were given by Morris K. Jesup, a member of the Christian Commission who argued that "no new organization should be formed, but that their efforts should be directed toward strengthening the hands and furthering the work of those now in existence." Central collection of information and coordinated investigations to stymie professional beggars would be the key to meeting the demands of the economic crisis.[29]

Their plans were framed by the debate over the propriety of government-supported work relief. At this same meeting, one participant[30] "deprecated the spirit which led people, in every time of depression, to look to the Government, almost with a feeling of a claim, for assistance." His argument was met by the assertion that "the demands were so great that private charities alone were unable to meet them, and the City Government must do something too." Thus the role of private charity and benevolent associations was caught up in a larger debate over the appropriate division of labor between government and voluntarism as well as, by extension, the financial markets and private firms.[31]

The result of the meeting was the creation of a committee to devise a plan "to relieve destitution without increasing pauperism," which would involve "the union of efforts and the direction of the matter by a single central organization." Yet, in New York City, such centralization proved elusive. Three weeks earlier, one report of efforts to meet the problem of unemployment had provided a catalogue of diverse organizations, some public, some private, some decidedly hybrid or ambiguous: the Commissioners of Charities and Corrections, the Children's Aid Society, the

Workingwomen's Protective Union, No. 38, the Girls' Lodging House, the Free Labor Bureau, the Newsboys' Lodging house, the St. John's Guild, the Five Points House of Industry, and the Prison Association. No doubt many others went unmentioned.[32] Six weeks later, a listing of financial reports displayed still more variety in the efforts of organized charity, both public and private.[33]

Centralization mattered in these discussions as both an organizational technique and a necessary precaution given the political dangers inherent in charitable giving to the needy, who were assumed to be heterogeneous in a very specific way. In an economic crisis, "the poor" consisted of both those who were chronically impoverished—due to poor morals, indulgence in vice, lack of discipline, or disability—and those who would be self-supporting given different economic circumstances. Indiscriminate giving could, therefore, create two kinds of political damage. For the "unworthy," undisciplined benevolence might generate expectations of relief that could easily transmute into claims for a right to relief.[34] On the other side, undisciplined giving governed by sentiment would flow toward those with few scruples against begging while others would hold back out of shame: "few think deeply enough to form an adequate idea of the quiet, unobtrusive, silent misery endured by one class of the poor; by those who have occupied a good position in better days, and whose pride and self-respect, combating with absolute starvation, not unfrequently win the day and leave their victims to die in misery, unnoticed and unrelieved."[35]

This concern for those who had fallen into poverty due to general crisis would be a durable feature of debates over the appropriate forms of relief. Such individuals did not fit into the categories of worthy and unworthy poor. Rather, like victims of natural disasters, they were the "should not have been poor" whose fundamental character was to be self-supporting and who merited respect as once-and-future independent citizens. In these efforts to provide relief in ways that did no lasting damage to the qualities desired of a self-supporting citizen, charity reformers produced an argument about the important differences between begging and soup kitchens: "A man whose pride and self-respect may induce him to bear the pangs of hunger rather than to beg of strangers in the streets would scarcely pass a free soup kitchen, probably with a half famished child by his side, without entering and enjoying a meal."[36] Not surprisingly, many of the unemployed dissented from this characterization of the level of relief that would sustain self-respect. But, notwithstanding one's assessment of soup kitchens, these debates over the provision of relief went beyond questions of social control and moral discipline. The challenge was to provide relief for "those who should not be poor" in a polity that premised citizenship on economic self-sufficiency.

The political concerns that structured debates over emergency relief in New York City were evident across the country. In Chicago, however, the Great Fire of 1871 had left an organizational legacy that created different possibilities for meeting the challenge of unemployment in 1873. Although established decades earlier, the Chicago Relief and Aid Society (CRAS)[37] had been greatly strengthened by its role as the vehicle for receiving and distributing contributions of aid from throughout the nation to those displaced by the tremendous blaze. This outpouring of contributions, imagined by one cartoonist as "the National Hand of Fellowship," represented a potent web of city-to-city, industry-to-industry, and group-to-group ties that had been and would continue to be activated in the wake of disasters of all types. The city council and citizens of Chicago carefully monitored such exchanges, determined to reciprocate appropriately for the generosity shown to them in the wake of the Great Fire. In June 1874, the Common Council adopted a proposal to request the CRAS "to forward all the aid and assistance [to victims of floods in the South] their sense of justice and gratitude will permit" in recognition that "very many of those now suffering did, when we were rendered helpless and in want by our great fire, most nobly contribute to our wants, freely giving their means and extending their kindest wishes." A few months later, as drought and grasshoppers plagued the high plains, donors were assured that "no supplies received by the Nebraska Relief and Aid Society from Chicago or other Eastern cities or towns have been distributed on promises to pay for or return them. . . . All distributions made by the Society will be free and unconditional."[38] In this way, gifts in response to suffering in other cities and states perpetuated the sense of nationwide, if not necessarily fully national, solidarity.[39] (See figure 2.)

In time, the city-to-city circuits of reciprocity would generate an expansive infrastructure for national mobilization. But, with winter approaching and unemployment on the rise, the citizens of Chicago recognized that they would need to raise funds for relief from within their own ranks. The institutional legacies of the Great Fire provided a foundation. After two years of channeling aid to victims of the fire and to rebuilding efforts throughout the city, the CRAS remained in place although "the means of the society are but a tithe [*sic*] of what they were then." By early November, therefore, new fund-raising efforts were underway, including a "grand co-operative movement for the relief of the poor" started by Protestant institutions who "then decided to invite the Roman Catholic and Hebrew societies to co-operate," producing "the first occasion in the

THE NATIONAL HAND OF FELLOWSHIP.

FIGURE 2. "National Hand of Fellowship." Image courtesy of the Chicago Historical Society.

history of Chicago when all denominations joined hands for the noble purpose of relieving the afflicted and distressed."[40]

Limited resources also required greater judgment in their distribution and, at the recommendation of the city's *Sunday Times*, an alliance with the "ladies of Chicago." Because "without organization indifferent results are obtained in science, politics, or benevolence, [t]he women of the city should band themselves at once into parish, ward, or district associations, and make themselves familiar, by kindly visitation, with the condition and the prospects of every family likely to require help." Religious organizations were suggested as a vehicle for this effort, not because of their theological commitments, but "because there are many women who work best in pious squads; who prefer to be harnessed in religious traces, and be driven in the name of the Lord."[41] The paper called upon the ladies to "forego the pleasure of other diversions, and devote themselves to this,—the foreign missionary work, the philosophical club, the bible societies, the art lecture, and the musical recitals will live until next summer, and God's poor will not, if they are not attended to." The crisis was an opportunity to ally the established central relief society with a network of secular and religious organizations, thereby combining proto-professional charity workers with businessmen and female volunteers in a manner familiar from the combination of centralized coordination and funding with the efforts of women volunteers that had been central to the success of the Civil War commissions.[42] Contributions were channeled into projects under public but not strictly governmental control; distribution of relief and the initial determination of "worthiness" would be delegated to women, a disenfranchised category of citizen. But despite the virtues of this arrangement as they were described by the *Chicago Tribune*, it was soon challenged by a highly mobilized, intensely partisan, male electorate.

As in New York City, the depression of 1873 revived calls for expanded public employment. By late December, the Chicago City Council adopted a proposal that the CRAS simply turn over its funds—estimated at $500,000 or more, most of which was a balance held over from the contributions received in the wake of the Great Fire—to the city in order to employ destitute men on public improvement projects. Speaking a few days after a large meeting of the unemployed had been held on the city's west side, Alderman Cullerton proposed that the "Relief and Aid Society be, and they are hereby, requested to expend and distribute the funds in their hands liberally to all worthy persons needing aid, and that, for the purpose of supplying immediate wants, they employ an efficient force to examine into the needs of residents and to relieve the needy to the full extent of their ability." Helpfully, perhaps, he added that "a committee of three Aldermen from each division of the city be appointed by the Mayor to assist the said Relief and Aid Society in the proper distribution of said relief fund."[43]

One champion of the workers, a Mr. Hoffman, portrayed dependence on private charity from voluntary societies as degrading, a gift rather than a right or entitlement to a public resource. The defenders of the CRAS responded with imagery in which the people would provide for the people just as they had "kept the Army close to them" during the Civil War. Mr. Hoffman retorted: "How so? Whose money is it? The Society does not own it. If it belongs to anybody in this wide world it belongs to the destitute; and as destitution is neither a crime nor a disgrace, no destitute person is degraded by accepting it." This claim echoed the sentiment that the people would take care of the people.

In the very next sentence, however, the political stakes in this humanitarian vision became clear: "But for this relief fund, and for the prudent management which has surrounded it, the cry of 'bread or blood' might be raised in our streets this winter, and might still be, if the Society were weak enough to pour it all out in the form of two weeks' wages on the

Hoffman plan, and leave the destitute to shift for themselves thereafter."[44] As those references to the National Workshops in France had signaled, these practical debates over the provision of relief—whether by private charity or by government program—were keyed directly into concerns for the maintenance of political order in a time of industrial unemployment and new kinds of urban poverty.

But a new architecture of organized benevolence would not be consolidated in a single crisis. As the numbers of "temporarily destitute" ebbed, concern over the efficient distribution of aid to the purportedly unworthy poor returned to the fore. Facing another season of "dullness of labor and the reductions of manufactures" in late 1874, the CRAS reasserted the principle that "there are occasions when charity is little less than a crime against society, and the bestowal of relief offers a premium for laziness, beggary, and dissolutions."[45] This line held, both in Chicago and many other cities. But over the course of a series of hard winters and business crises that punctuated the late nineteenth century, this organization of urban benevolence was challenged and, in response, produced one of the key components of a new regime of urban governance: the charity organization society or COS.

Reorganizing Charity and Civic Life

The roots of the American system of social welfare can be traced to public almshouses supported by town and county governments, and the creation of public institutions to house particularly vulnerable populations such as orphans and the mentally ill. By the 1860s, a new model was introduced from England, the charity organization society (COS). The first was established in Buffalo in the 1877; the influential New York Charity Organization Society (NYCOS) followed in 1882.[46] Although the charity organization model built on familiar distinctions between worthy and unworthy poor, it introduced a new emphasis on investigation and the segregation of those in need for distinctive reasons so that those labeled as morally deficient would not influence or degrade those who were indigent for reasons of loss of family, abandonment, ill health, or disability.

With respect to political development, the significance of the charity organization lay in the delegation of a set of public responsibilities for public relief to private actors. Volunteers and private charity workers distinguished the worthy poor from those deemed unworthy of help; aid to the worthy was carefully weighed in terms of the principle that relief should never be more attractive than work.[47] These fine distinctions expressed concern for the corrosive effect of charity upon citizens. Those ineligible for full citizenship—women, children, the mentally ill, and Native

Americans—were particularly appropriate objects of charity (although even here, giving was never to be heedlessly generous). Those whose need was clearly caused by events beyond their control might also be helped; victims of natural disaster and military attack petitioned Congress (with some success) for relief.[48] Among adult men in poor houses, those who were simply receiving aid could be disenfranchised, while those who performed some labor in return for their board in the same institution retained their right to vote.[49] To these categories of worth, the charity organization movement then added attention to the rational distribution of help in order to avoid duplication and fraud as individuals might seek aid from multiple institutions or individual benefactors. As they had been for Clara Barton cataloguing the dead and missing after the Civil War, basic technologies of lists and card files were central to these efforts. The management of these organizational technologies was increasingly in the charge of a paid staff, often including proto-professional charity workers.

This focus on disciplining the delivery of private relief altered the geometry of relationships produced by benevolent giving and receiving. If a beggar knocked on a seemingly prosperous door, the proper response of the homeowner to an appeal for alms was to provide a pre-made ticket or voucher that would serve as an introduction to the COS—and perhaps even to pay a hansom cab to deliver the needy person directly to the agency. Neighbors, churches, and local groups were also sources of referral. The COS staff would then evaluate the applicant, but this resulted in more than a decision on the appropriate economic and moral category. The causes of need and distress had to be identified accurately in order to design an intervention that would address the root cause of the problem.[50] Just as physicians now worry about interactions among different prescription drugs, proponents of charity organization were alert to any additional aid that might undermine a plan of remedies and sanctions.

Ideally, this required all aid organizations to refrain from giving help outside the centrally coordinated system. The same discipline was imposed on would-be donors who "to satisfy their own feelings of pity . . . offer their inadequate doles."[51] Comparing the widow who does washing to support her family and the "widow who passes her days in idleness and her nights in debauchery," Josephine Shaw Lowell warned that generosity to the latter might corrupt the former: "The fact that the first widow may in time come to contrast her lot with that of the second widow, and may prefer the latter, seldom occurs to the almsgiver, nor does he know how desperate a temptation he is presenting daily to his fellow men."[52] Through a new array of organizational practices and exchange relationships, the direct, dependence-inducing relationship between a donor and a recipient was replaced by ties between donors and the various agencies that cooperated with the community's COS.[53]

These organizational innovations rationalized the gift relationship. Benevolence shifted out of the register of pity or the donor's own expressive desire to do good works. Sentiment was displaced by a more reasoned, disciplined discourse about the public good (at least from the vantage point of those in a position to donate). Although this new language of motives did little to lessen the blow to the democratic dignity of those in need of aid, it attenuated the felt demand for personal gratitude in response to assistance. The poor were still profoundly stigmatized as dependent, but the answer to "dependent upon whom?" was now something like "the community" rather than the name of a particular benefactor. If rapid adoption of a form is taken as evidence of its "fit" with perceived problems, the multiplication of the COS suggests the extent to which American cities—or at least many of their businessmen and "leading citizens"—were confronting similar challenges. An 1885 report noted that 170 different charities had responded that they were involved in some way in the scientific reform of giving. An 1887 survey documented 34 functioning COS's; the number would grow to 92 by the time of a report to the 1893 meeting of the National Conference of Charities and Corrections.[54] As organizational innovations decoupled contributions from the emotional demands for gratitude and reciprocity, proto-professional charity workers placed themselves between donors and recipients. But control over the resulting reconfiguration of civic benevolence reflected a second legacy of the sanitarians, the mobilization of elite networks in projects of municipal governance.

Civic Clubs

The combination of high social and geographical mobility, new fortunes, and periodic economic catastrophe made the consolidation of a class of leading citizens a persistent problem in cities across the country. A host of social innovations—elite clubs, elite schools, an expanded stock market that facilitated cross-ownership, and the publishing of "social registers"— were deployed to construct a collective identity of "leading citizens" and their capacity for collective action.[55] Charity organization societies also contributed to the social coherence of elites, property owners, and citizens of somewhat more modest means as they were all called upon to give in moments of civic crisis or for public projects. Other efforts had already organized predominantly male civic sentiment in support of nationalist projects. Some of these, such as the Loyal Leagues, would end with the war itself, but Union League clubs were established in major cities, notably Philadelphia, Boston, and Chicago, in addition to the New York club, which traced its foundation most directly to the USSC.[56] That club's male members invoked the "beautiful union of domestic and public virtues" and, in 1864, the club had sponsored a dinner of tens of thousands of turkeys, which was remembered as "a Thanksgiving table, stretched over so many States, and extending into so many corners."[57] The clubs also operated with a sophisticated social psychology, sponsoring social events to make sympathy with secession—or even with Peace Democrats—socially unacceptable within elite circles. The plan for the club adopted in 1863 established that "the primary object of the Association shall be to discountenance and rebuke by moral and social influences all disloyalty to the Federal Government, and to that end the members will use every proper means in public and private."[58]

The Union League clubs were elite associations of Republican-leaning businessmen, particularly important in cities where municipal government was either dominated or seriously contested by the Democratic Party. In New York City, Mayor Fernando Wood (a Democrat) had suggested that the city declare its neutrality in the war. The violent draft riots of 1863 further heightened the stakes in Republican political organization,[59] linking the virile sense of Civil War mobilization to a concern for civil service reform and attacks on political corruption.[60] The club credited its own 1865 report on municipal government with proving that "New York City has under its present charter fallen into the control of one class of voters—the least intelligent, the least moralized, the least interested in good government,—and that, by their banded power, an inferior class of men is foisted into executive, legislative and judicial offices. It shows that the power of the city is no longer in the hands of those who pay its revenues, and that the brains, and worth, and patriotism of the city are always feebly represented in its councils."[61]

How was the political influence of "those who pay its revenues" and "the brains, and worth, and patriotism of the city" to be secured within electoral institutions founded upon universal white manhood suffrage? The Union League clubs and their allies answered with a call to reform and purify political institutions. In these efforts, the organization of private benevolence was understood as a critical preventive measure that would prevent the flow of tax revenues into relief funds administered by party politicians. Civic-minded elites would donate generously to charities while simultaneously opposing tax-funded government support and applauding the YMCA when it rejected a grant of $5000 offered by the state.[62] Public subsidies for the care of the needy threatened to make voluntary associations dependent upon the state.

Patronage politics often operated by allocating public contracts and government jobs in exchange for bribes or campaign contributions. Charities were not exempted from these arrangements. In New York City, critics portrayed Catholic charitable institutions as auxiliaries of the Democratic machine of Tammany Hall.[63] No less than the boss, William Tweed, "had strategically placed himself on the Senate Committee on Charitable and Religious Societies in Albany, the committee that had regularly rubber-stamped requests from Protestant or nonsectarian charities for state funding." Under Tweed, Catholic charities received almost $900,000 while a total of just over $300,000 went to Protestant, Jewish, and nonsectarian organizations combined. "In 1871, Charles Loring Brace claimed that $30,000 of the $110,000 annual state appropriation on which the Children's Aid Society had come to depend had been lost 'by frauds.'"[64]

Nor were the politics of benevolence unique to New York; the synergies between political patronage systems and organized charity could be observed in many cities and states. Consequently, business elites had good reasons to seek control over the financing of urban charitable organizations. Whether motivated by opposition to popular patronage politics or a desire for greater efficiency in provision for the needy, businessmen's clubs frequently allied with advocates of charity organization to contest partisan control of benevolent institutions. But these alliances stabilized only after new organizational arrangements resolved some of the tensions between the relations of benevolence and the requisites of municipal governance.

The Depression of 1893

In the twenty years since the winter of 1873–74, new forms of benevolent and civic association had appeared in many American cities without cohering into an encompassing division of labor or a culture of common membership. Some city governments had retreated from their earlier role as direct sources of relief, adopting laws to shield property owners from popular demands for increased public spending in response to downturns. In New York City, the Board of Estimate eliminated outdoor relief (aid that did not require residence in an almshouse) and "decided that only funds for excise taxes could be used for public assistance and that that money would only be used to subsidize private charities."[65] But, such restrictions on the role of municipal government in providing relief meant that future crises would challenge voluntary arrangements even more starkly.

The next great wave of mass unemployment in 1893—contemporary estimates ranged from 800,000 to three million[66]—provoked calls for greater coordination among private agencies and reactivated a familiar set of debates, organizational critiques, and proposed solutions across the nation's cities. Reports of the response to the crisis in New York City once again featured recitations of a long list of organizations: "the Charity Organization Society, the Children's Aid Society, the New-York Association for Improving the Condition of the Poor, the Superior Council of the St. Vincent de Paul Society, the United Hebrew Charities, the German Society, the St. Andrew Society, and the New York City Mission and Work Society."[67] In New York City, a major construction project had already helped to organize a collective response as the new United Charities Building provided office space for many organizations nearby the recently opened headquarters of the Federation of Protestant Welfare Agencies.[68] In Chicago, a new coordinating entity, the Central Relief Association, was created to replace the CRAS, which appeared trapped in an ungenerous "charity organization" model just when the financial crisis called for a more expansive and flexible approach to relief.

William T. Stead, a prominent British reformer and innovative journalist, spent the winter of 1893–94 in the city, a visit that would result in his widely read *If Christ Came to Chicago*. In the Central Relief Association, he saw the outlines of a more comprehensive organization of urban governance: "But although the work was well begun, it is only beginning. The whole of the summer might be spent in elaborating a system of co-ordination and co-operation, which is indispensable to any nation and co-operation, which is indispensable to any effort to put the community in a state of siege against exceptional distress." Suggesting that the city be divided into relief districts that coincided with political wards, Stead explained that these ward-based charitable units could then recruit local churches for "the work of visitation. If this were done, and an efficient visiting committee established in each ward, then . . . the citizens would feel that they were adequately equipped to cope with any misfortune which may overtake the community."[69]

As in 1873, discussions of what would constitute adequate relief were organized around a set of categorical distinctions. Some of these centered on membership in the community. "Vagrants" and "tramps" were singled out as the least deserving of respectful relief. Community membership and residence featured as central qualifications for relief. The president of the New York Commission of Charities and Correction made this clear with his promise "that pains would be taken to give proper consideration and care to deserving poor people, but the regular tramps who infest the city should be sent to the Island and prevented from begging in the streets."[70] A second line of exclusion emerged more strongly in a retrospective assessment of relief efforts in various cities published in the *Journal of Social Science* in the autumn of 1894.[71] The collected data spoke to "the great preponderance of foreign-born persons among the applicants for work or aid," estimated at "two-thirds to three-fourths of all the unemployed last winter, who came to be registered, were foreign-born" and a still higher proportion in the mining counties of Michigan.[72] The report from New Haven, Connecticut, however, estimated that although "strangers" to the city constituted a sizeable majority of those applying for aid, "possibly 1 per cent were recent immigrants or their children."[73] Yet the proponents of charity reform were most concerned about a third distinction, between the worthy and unworthy poor. But, in the context of a national economic downturn, the definition of "worthy" became newly problematic.

Although the distinction between the worthy poor (the elderly, disabled, widowed, and orphaned) and their unworthy counterparts (anyone capable of paid employment but unwilling or derailed by drink and other vices) had long governed thinking about relief, the national depression of 1893 again created patterns of hardship that did not fit into this category system. Just as natural disasters and emergencies had long been sources of a temporary category of the relief-worthy[74]—upstanding citizens impoverished by events beyond their control—so the extended economic downturn created a visible population of those who always had supported themselves, wanted to support themselves, but could not find employment. Their change in circumstance was obviously a personal tragedy, as families were evicted and in desperate need of both food and clothing, but it was also a public or political problem for those who were spared the worst of the depression.

In the understanding of many of those who owned property and managed firms, the newly needy of 1893 were not the sort of people who knew their way to the established charities. The reported pattern of withdrawals from savings banks and increasingly busy pawnbrokers suggested that this subset of the unemployed had survived on their own resources for some time. The conclusion drawn was that these unemployed found it difficult to ask for relief but, importantly, that this concern for civic dignity meant that their discontent might translate into political action that could not be ignored. Consequently, this moment of economic distress prompted expressions of concern that echoed those of 1873, but the depth of the crisis produced more lasting experiments with respect to the form of relief, its relation to the provision of public goods, and the organization of both fund-raising and allocation of resources.

The central feature of those newly in need of relief was that these were men—and single working women—who were known to be willing and able to support themselves. So it was important that relief involve work. While this was not an entirely novel element in relief practice—men had long been sent to cut wood, shovel coal, and dig trenches to "earn" a meal and a place to sleep—the new twist was to link relief work to the provision of recognizably public goods in the form of roads and canals. Here, an important initiative was led by a veteran of the Sanitary Commission, Josephine Shaw Lowell, and the Eastside Relief Committee in New York City.[75] Lowell and her colleagues raised funds—from both the public and local property owners—to have streets cleaned, refuse removed, and basements cleared and painted with lime, thereby framing relief as an improvement of public hygiene.[76] In this way, "work relief" lost some of its purely punitive aspect, as a disciplinary measure to assess the worth of the person to be helped. Instead, this revised vision of work relief claimed to connect the recipient of aid to benefits for other residents of the neighborhood. Or, at least, this was the theory of the charity reformers. The head of the city's Society of St. Vincent de Paul observed that for all the advantages of these work programs, "still those who had any self-respect left were continually mortified at hearing the remarks made by passers-by, and it was only the thought of their starving families at home that gave them the moral courage to remain the allotted time."[77]

Charity reformers were also concerned that these formerly self-sufficient citizens would be morally degraded by contact with unscrupulous professional beggars who crowded free employment services and rushed to the front of the line when food, coal, or clothing was distributed. The danger of such moral damage was heightened by a new form of organized charity, the newspaper fund: "the publicity forced on those who received these newspaper gifts, the standing in line, the struggling in the street and at the doors, the publishing of names and descriptions,—all this was a further degradation, a moral stripping naked of the suffering and the poor." Reflecting on the mistakes made in the relief effort the previous winter, Josephine Shaw Lowell singled out these newspaper initiatives as particularly corrosive: "Free lodgings and free meals brought more and more people, for whom again more free lodgings and free meals must be supplied." Perhaps even more dangerous, the newspapers' rationale for relief threatened to undermine the anchoring of relief in benevolence and voluntarism "when, day after day, for weeks and months, the offers of food and clothing were reiterated, and it was made to appear that public opinion was in favor of 'getting something for nothing.'" Anticipating the Depression-era demand that relief be "Free. Not as Charity. But as a Right," Lowell worried that "the socialistic teaching that such gifts were not a favor received, but only a small part of what was due from the rich to the poor, was fostered by the tone of the newspapers."[78]

In New York City, the four newspaper funds accounted for half of the $300,000 raised by donations[79] to supplement the $1 million public appropriation to the Board of Charities and Corrections, an amount barely changed from the previous years. A majority of the remainder of the donated funds came from two politically linked "assessment" systems: a fund raised by contributions from City Officials and Employees and another from Tammany Hall, the Democratic political machine. The sixth and smallest of these "much advertised funds" represented an innovative use of the wage assessment model of fund-raising familiar from relief campaigns organized by leaders of business and commerce. But, displaced from this leadership network, reliance on weekly assessments opened participation in municipal benevolence to the type of mass fund-raising that had characterized the voluntary effort in support of Union forces decades before. The combination of mass fund-raising and economic relief pointed toward a novel architecture of governance.

Leading businessmen, either individually or through their membership in exchanges and chambers of commerce, had long been a major source of contributions in times of disaster. Some employees also contributed, but in ways that highlighted their identification with a firm and lodged control of fund-raising with their employer rather than solidarity with other employees. But early in 1894, the *New York Times* announced the establishment of "a great and far-reaching organization, to be known as the '6–15–99' Club." The person credited with this invention, a surveyor and hydraulic engineer named William D'Hertburn Washington, was described as having "in his veins more historic blood than any other American," being related to the first president on both his maternal and paternal side. He also had a record of leadership in a variety of Democratic organizations (typically of the pro-business or "Bourbon" variety): Chairman of the Executive Committee of the quadrennial convention of the National Association of Democratic Clubs, Secretary of the Iron and Metal Cleveland and Stevenson Club, Chairman of the Twelfth Assembly District Democratic Club, and member of the Executive Committee of the Southern Democratic Association. The "cabalistic title" of his organization referred to the expectation that those who "work for small wages" would contribute six cents a week while clerks would donate 15 cents, and employers 99 cents. If successful, this plan, "favored by many men prominent in business circles" might raise "$13,000 per day . . . in addition to the great sums already contributed to the various charity organizations."[80] That total was never reached; a retrospective report of the relief effort credited the club with raising $7,507.[81] But, in a short time, an organization appears to have been built. In the first week, twelve auxiliary clubs based in firms were organized; that number rose to 234 by early March (supporting a distribution of $1,500 that week to a range of established charitable and relief organizations, including the free labor bureau directly created by the club); a few days later, the claim was 256 clubs with 10,000 members; by the time the fund-raising effort came to its planned conclusion in April, it claimed 270 auxiliary clubs and 10,000 members.[82]

The political vision was embodied in routine practices: "Enrollment blanks are given to persons in each trade, and collections are made each week from those who subscribe. Thus a large fund results from a very small tax on individuals."[83] Reports from Chicago suggest that somewhat similar arrangements for mass fund-raising were emerging to support the relief effort there, although the control of the city's philanthropists and charity experts was not so deeply challenged by newspapers and other new entrants to the field. Early in January, the Central Relief Association called on the "people of this city to contribute one day's wages or income for the relief of the unemployed," promising that "those who contribute can rest assured their money will be in good hands and will be applied where it will do the most good."[84]

The centralized organization of the relief effort stood behind this guarantee, with its record of surveying and investigating the distribution of need. The association "is in a position to discriminate between the worthy and the unworthy. There is no danger that tramps, vagrants, or professional paupers will get any of this money."[85] A clear sense of a non-governmental public emerges from this argument:

> The charitable organizations of the city are working in harmony with it, and the city government itself has recognized it as the official almoner of the bounty contributed. . . . The whole people must devote themselves to the work as they have done on some previous seasons. They now have an agency for the application of relief which represents that whole people, and all that is necessary is for them to make one hearty, unanimous effort and the situation will be under control for weeks to come, by which time it may be anticipated the worst of the trouble will be over. . . . Let Chicago set the good example. Let its people . . . bear each other's burdens."[86]

In an echo of Civil War understandings, the people would take care of themselves, rather than depending purely on alms from the wealthy or on a pauperizing government dole. In February 1894, the Central Relief Association Chairman requested "that every committee among all the trades and businesses throughout the city which has assumed the responsibility of soliciting and collecting funds at once to push its labors to a speedy completion."[87] A few days later, the paper reported progress or completion of "subscriptions" from the Booksellers' committee, the employees of the Edison Electric Light company, the Jewelers' Auxiliary Association, the Building Trades committee, and a number of other firms as well as individuals. In addition, the article noted "the first of a series of five 'hard times' progressive euchre parties to be given by twenty-five members of the Philanthropic committee of the West End Woman's club" had been "well attended, and added to the fund for charity work."[88] Based on specific occupational, religious, and social identities, the relief effort called upon the city's residents to contribute to this centralized effort of voluntary social provision.

In these efforts to respond to the economic distress of the winter of 1893–94, a new system of organized relief began to appear. The arrangement involved shifts in the categories of worth, in the division of labor between public and private, and in relations among existing associations, both commercial and benevolent. Experiments in the organization of fund-raising were equally significant. Although the majority of relief funds and charitable organizations were still raised through subscriptions from and appeals to a circle of relatively wealthy members and donors, at least two large cities saw a revival of the relational models so central to the success of the great commissions of the Civil War. Large-scale, small-contribution systems of fund-raising were harnessed to the centralized, "scientific" distribution of relief to those deemed worthy. Just as the champions of Civil War voluntarism had promised to "keep the army close to the people" rather than dependent upon the Government in time of economic crisis, the call in January 1894 was to let the "people . . . bear each other's burdens."[89]

As in the aftermaths of the Civil War and the depression of 1873, this model of voluntary public provision barely outlasted the crisis. In New York City, the 6–15–99 Club's free labor bureau continued to operate for perhaps another year or two based on a model in which workers had always already reciprocated for relief through their prior donations, shifting from an imagery of charity to one of voluntary and mutual social insurance. In clear contrast to "socialist" claims for a right to relief,[90] this system incorporated those "working for small wages" as donors so long as they had employment and then as worthy recipients of aid as well as a clientele for free labor bureaus in times of widespread economic distress. Echoing the Civil War claim that "the people were going to war and it was for the people to take care of itself," the 6–15–99 clubs in New York City and the "One-Day Wage Relief" in Chicago represented broadly participatory models of collective social provision. But these experiments had the potential to energize demands for tax-supported, government-administered aid and work relief comparable to the National Workshops of 1848 in France. Either way, these claims challenged the control of community elites over an increasingly centralized model of governance through voluntarism.

Infrastructure for a New Urban Citizenship

As the depression ebbed in 1894, decades of reform efforts and a few years of intense organizing of economic relief had begun to reconfigure the political and social landscapes of many American cities. With respect to the allocation and delivery of aid, religious and social agencies were becoming increasingly coordinated. In many cities, the establishment of a formal charity organization society represented the transition of a networked set of associations into a more hierarchical system with proto-professional charity workers now in charge of many key decisions and activities. Such developments could disarticulate charity-induced dependence from democratic political participation and electoral control, often in the name of battling corruption and partisan patronage.

A distinct mode of coordination was also emerging on the fund-raising side of voluntary and public-private systems of economic relief. In contrast to the wartime "divine method of patriotism," which linked personal affections to a nationally encompassing love of country and Union, these urban experiments took a more corporatist form. Donations and volunteer activities were mobilized through membership in religious, community, ethnic, and workplace associations. In a pattern that would be captured by the motto of the General Federation of Women's Clubs, this was "unity in diversity." Interdenominational relief efforts were heralded as innovations in 1873; by 1893, such configurations were commonplace, operating in parallel with fund-raising through firms, organized through industries, sending aid to coworkers or—in the case of natural disasters—to employees and owners in similar lines of industry in different cities and towns. This template for organizing voluntarism embedded individuals in associations or firms or congregations that, in turn, were linked into place-based federations. The result was a durable architecture of governance that had distinct advantages for municipal and corporate elites.

Charity organization provided an important part of this new regime, a link between the fund-raising and relief-delivery sides of a voluntarist system. Such arrangements held down demand for aid while acknowledging the distinctive expertise and suitability of different organizations to help different kinds of clients. Unlike the Civil War efforts, in which the evangelicals of the Christian Commission and the Unitarian leadership of the Sanitary Commission had seen themselves as competitors, this kind of urban division of labor served as a framework within which different denominational institutions could function alongside other benevolent as well as public institutions. In parallel with local charity organization societies, a national movement—with its circuit of conferences and exchanges of periodicals—reinforced the sense of common orientation to the problems of the city, even as territorial feuds and disagreements over method persisted and multiplied.

Inevitably, any such centralized system also created relationships of power and, therefore, patterns of conflict. In Chicago, the winter of 1899 saw a tussle between the "anti-tramp crusade" of the Bureau of Associated Charities and Mayor Carter Harrison over whether or not to keep police stations open overnight as "free lodging-houses for the poor," who would also be provided with coffee and a roll in the morning (a policy intended to preempt the men's raids on "all the bakery and milk wagons they could find in the district"). The mayor won that round, supported by the superintendent of the debtor's prison who explained that "until we have model lodging-houses where men may 'work out' the cost of a night's shelter, I don't see how we can do without free lodging at police stations."

The issue was a microcosm of enduring debates over the appropriate division of labor between government and private voluntary agencies, even when some of the funding for relief came from private donations. As Mayor Harrison argued, "The Bureau of Associated Charities objected last year because we received money and supplies and distributed aid through the Police department. The officials argued that all donations should be turned over to their organization, and relief centered wholly in their hands. Well, we went right ahead just the same, and with splendid results, too. We will do the same thing this year. Unfortunate men may make Chicago a sort of headquarters, but, if they are here, we won't let them starve nor freeze to death on the street. Humanity should be first and the Bureau of Associated Charities second."[91]

The tensions that surfaced in this struggle persisted. A few years later, one Father Basil (who claimed "to be attached to the old Catholic church, and is at the head of the St. John's home for boys") stopped in at a courtroom to inquire, "What does it cost to assault a man?" Having been told that the fine could range from three dollars to one hundred dollars, he proceeded to the offices of the city's charity bureau and attacked Ernest Bicknell, the secretary of the bureau (as well as former head of the Indiana State Bureau of Charities and future director of the Red Cross). Bicknell's battering by the irate Father Basil was alleged to have been motivated by "the refusal of the charity bureau to assist the home financially or to indorse it, in spite of persistent solicitations."[92] Although reports of personal violence were not regular topics in the coverage of organized charity, Father Basil's attack on Bicknell in Chicago certainly resonated with lines of conflict in other cities. But the arrangements championed by Bicknell and his allies constituted a new kind of municipal regime, a public if not electoral order sustained by volunteers (and, later, proto-professional charity workers) and private donations.

This civic order anchored in voluntarism depended on fund-raising, which was in the process of being transformed by the invention of the "campaign model." First perfected by a cadre of fund-raisers for the YMCA in the 1890s, the "campaign method" combined personal solicitation of donors by friends, colleagues, or acquaintances with the urgency of competition against the clock, other communities, or both.[93] Enjoying unprecedented success—first tens of thousands of dollars in a few weeks, then hundreds of thousands—the model was soon adopted by other organizations. Importantly, this model combined the breadth of popular participation with solicitation of large gifts from the well-off and an emerging class of self-acknowledged philanthropists. Large donors might be asked to give an initial gift, perhaps to cover the cost of the drive itself so that small donors could be promised that every penny of their contribution would go to the designated cause with the increasing total tracked using the image of a thermometer or a race. Philanthropists might be called on again to give a capstone gift, taking the drive across the finish line. But those large donors also participated as regular citizens; the records of the Rockefeller family, for example, meticulously note both six-figure gifts to the American Red Cross and contributions of $1 to $25 for the annual Roll Call for members.[94]

The enthusiastic adoption of these new organizational techniques raised sufficient funds to support major civic projects but could also make benevolence unpleasant for donors. Every refusal of a request to donate carried at least a frisson of selfishness and, in some cases, a cost to a friendship or valued relationship.[95] Friendship provided a context within which one person could ask another for a donation to a cause; in the next fund drive, a return favor might be requested. By channeling intensified fund-raising through personal relationships, however, those very relationships could fray as requests for contributions exceeded the etiquette of friendship. Precisely because this fund-raising model was easily replicated, any individual inclined to benevolence could expect to be asked to give repeatedly. As this model became "modular," it was widely copied, confronting individual donors with ever more demands, sometimes from multiple friends, sometimes multiple requests from the same friend or colleague.[96] In addition to erecting buildings and augmenting endowments, these drives produced a predictable wave of backlash as donors resisted the intensification of solicitation.

Coupled with the efflorescence of voluntary associations in the late nineteenth and early twentieth centuries, the development of the campaign method had three important consequences for the relational geometries that infused voluntary projects. First, the tensions between democratic dignity and the dependence that followed from receipt of charity were deflected by new circuits of reciprocity *among* donors rather than *between* donors and beneficiaries. Friends asked friends to contribute to a cause knowing that they might be asked to donate in turn. As a direct consequence, ties of family, friendship, and collegiality were strained as requests for contributions multiplied. In addition, since this model raised funds *for* organizations, the relationship between donors and the ultimate beneficiaries of their gifts was mediated—indeed decoupled—by the role of the organizational staff in actually delivering services and relief. From the turn of the century forward, these charity workers would increasingly model themselves on the professions, establishing training programs, publications, and the other elements of a self-governing occupation.

While the wealthiest donors could erect offices to buffer themselves from the incessant wave of requests (the Office of the Messrs. Rockefeller exemplified this strategy), individual citizens turned instead to the model of federation in the form of community chests. This second innovation met the demands for both insulation from repeated requests and accountability for handling of donations. Because businessmen were well represented among those who were asked to give, they had already faced the question of which causes were legitimate and which would generate "good will" for their enterprises. The intensity of these solicitations had led some organizations, notably the local chambers of commerce, to establish "charities endorsement committees" that vetted potential recipients. Perhaps more importantly, their control of the certification of charities as legitimate gave them leverage to impose a significant reorganization of fund-raising. Rather than each separate organization cultivating its own network of donors, those charities approved by the endorsement committee would be integrated into a single annual effort in the name of the community as a whole.

Not surprisingly, these committees were obvious candidates to perform the same role for the new consolidated fund-raising campaigns that would become known as "Community Chests." The federated campaign or Community Chest first appeared at the turn-of-the-century but would diffuse nationally only during and after the First World War. Just as would-be beneficiaries were now organized through a single point of registration at the COS, so too donors might be "immunized" from all but a single annual request. This model of "financial federation" promised to concentrate all those individual charitable campaigns into one single drive. Just as the campaign method articulated contributions large and small in a single drive, this federated fund-raising generated greater organizational conformity, reinforced by endorsement committees and investigation bureaus. The allocation of funds required those in charge to evaluate the honesty and competence of charitable groups, but also to define a "community interest" that would be legitimately financed by a single annual drive.[97] Typically, only a portion of a city's charities were included in the federated drive, notably in areas such as health, family welfare, recreation, and character building that "reflected both the conservative interests of the business community and that appealed to the general population."[98] At the same time, the category of organizations receiving funds through the Community Chest steadily expanded, as the goal of giving came to encompass "social welfare" as well as charity. By centralizing and standardizing charitable activities within communities, local elites made "modern business methods" the lingua franca of the charitable field and cemented their dual identities as major businessmen *and* leading citizens. Through these governing arrangements, supported by new models of urban citizenship, business leaders extended control over the organized networks of charitable giving and positioned themselves as pillars of the community.

As charitable giving morphed from relationships between specific donors and specific beneficiaries to more durable, organized enterprises, the relational logic of voluntary relief was transformed. In the place of the vocabulary of charity and benevolence, business organizations increasingly adopted a language—and practice—of service that counterbalanced the resentments fueled by social exclusivity. Rotary, which began with a self-conscious strategy of self-interested social closure, soon embraced an ideology of "service" to the broader community.[99] This shift was paralleled in more elite civic circles. As one of Harvey Warren Zorbaugh's informants on Chicago's Gold Coast would explain decades later, "Since the [first world] war, playing the social game is not so *terribly* important as it was before. Everyone still wants to be 'in,' of course, but many are getting off into something else, too. It's not the thing to do just to be a social butterfly any more. Any many social leaders are *really* busy women; nor is it just a matter of teas. Social recognition is increasingly secured through political, civic, and philanthropic work."[100]

This call for service represented an important shift from the initial use of social exclusivity to sustain a new identity as a business class. A doubling or nesting was required to embed exclusive social organization within a broader identity premised on membership in a community defined by common location.[101] Social closure of status groups (whether elite members of the city club or the solid business class of Rotary, Kiwanis, and Lions) had to be articulated with organization of the entire community, such that businessmen could be seen as representing or acting in the interests of all. This mattered not only for the interests of business, narrowly construed, but also for the economic fate of the city given that the well-being of Cleveland would be determined by its ability to compete with Chicago or St. Louis.

Materials for constructing this bridge between class-based membership in networks of donors and civic leadership had been provided by the charity organization society, the campaign model, and federated fundraising. By the last decade of the century, these organizational innovations were knitting together circuits of civic giving with circles of elite control. Taken separately, neither the charity organization society nor the elite civic club nor the campaign method of fund-raising was sufficient for the sort of nation-state-building project once envisioned by the leaders of the USSC. When combined, however, these three innovations provided a powerful if partial solution to the basic contradictions between the logics of benevolence and democracy. Reciprocity was reoriented, with an emphasis on horizontal ties among donors rather than the dependency-generating relationship of donor to beneficiary. Within many American cities, the techniques of organized benevolence continued to develop as they were challenged by—and sometimes helped to resolve—the contradictions between charitable relationships and democratic citizenship.

By the beginning of the new century, therefore, two different but overlapping constellations of public and private effort were consolidating in American cities.[102] In some cities, the central place in the network was occupied by municipal or state agencies, descended from an older regime of public almshouses but now linked to the reform-oriented oversight of new Bureaus of Charities—or of Charities and Corrections. In others, civic organizations such as the chambers of commerce served as hubs both for federated fund-raising and the allocation of resources to private charitable organizations. In both variants, the result was the promotion of a centralized system for managing the flow of publicly oriented but not necessarily governmentally supported activities to manage community-wide challenges of disaster, unemployment, and poverty. These configurations proved most powerful at the local scale and, therefore, reinforced the kind of civic boosterism and regional loyalties that had been the despair of the Sanitary Commission.[103]

These horizontal ties could operate on multiple scales. Mobilized locally, such networks reinforced the particularism of this city or that one. The reasoning from particular to general—Thomas Starr King's "Divine method" of generating patriotism—was short-circuited at the edge of town. To construct a new path from "particular to general loyalties" would require the injection of novel elements and renewed interest by nationalizing elites and elected officials as well as a new breed of foundations capable of distributing gifts on an unprecedented scale. In the first decade of the new century, this remained a nascent alliance, uncertain in its own etiquette and very unevenly developed across the nation's cities. In other configurations, exchanges were envisioned as either among communities or between communities and nation. With this, an entire nation could be bound together by highlighting every citizen's capacity to give something and obscuring the question of who received the goods generated by this practice of citizen philanthropy. The different models of exchange represented different political projects, advanced by different political elites.[104] This chapter has traced the history of the municipal configuration; the next will return to the harnessing of civic groups and organized benevolence to the consolidation of the nation-state.

4

The Expansible Nation-State

Mayor Schmitz to-day took a firm stand against "Citizens' Protective Committees," organized in many sections of the city by men to undertake to regulate the affairs of their neighborhood. Many complaints have been made against these "committees". . . .

The State militia has not been withdrawn, notwithstanding the requests from the mayor and from the Citizens' Executive Committee. Gov. Pardee has not met with the Executive Committee or with the heads of the military and civil authorities at Fort Mason. . . .

It appears that as a rule members of the militia have had a misapprehension of the conditions in San Francisco. They have acted as though martial law were in force, and it was their duty to regulate the affairs of the city according to their individual conception of that law. Since they have been confined to a limited area, however, and the conditions have been explained to them, there has been less complaint from citizens.

There is nothing but praise for the work of the United States Army, the navy and the police. They have acted with reason at all times.

New York Times, April 26, 1906[1]

Nations rarely build states under conditions of their own choosing. Natural disasters, epidemics, famine, and war threaten the well-being of even those citizens who most ardently defend individual liberty and warn against the concentration of power in the hands of government authorities. It is not the disaster itself that produces stronger states with greater capacity. These developments are driven by the rush of demands for effective government action and the improvisations of those who respond to the emergency.

The aftermath of the 1906 San Francisco earthquake displayed all the complexity and indeterminacy of such a moment in American political development. Drawing on an established repertoire of popular associationalism and voluntarism, self-organizing citizens created "protective committees" to police the streets. Even as the city was devastated by the earthquake and overrun by fire, a familiar capacity for local self-organization asserted itself. As one relief administrator observed, "As soon as the population found itself in safety, it lost its mob aspect and became an army of intelligent, competent individuals . . . Thus the relief leaders found their program instantly understood and actively carried out, frequently indeed forestalled by the refugees themselves."[2] Across the country, fund-raising for victims and refugees from the destroyed city began with impressive speed. But these voluntary projects often failed to mesh smoothly with official actions to police the crisis. The whole assem-blage of spontaneous civic action and formally organized authority was far less than the sum of the parts. Uncertain as to their legal mandate, the state militia overreached; the governor struggled to coordinate different sources of public order; the city police and federal military forces were praised for their disciplined and appropriate management of a city first shaken by the earthquake and then swept by fire.[3] In this complex mix of organizational models and capacities, what was lacking was an effective architecture for governance.

This confusion of civic, municipal, state, and national efforts created an opening for new alignments of federal authority with voluntary or-ganizations and resources. After more than a century of contested, frag-mented, multiplying efforts to develop the governing potential of vol-untary associations, a still-limited national government now began to experiment with infrastructural nation-state-building in a much more directly instrumental project of generating "collective power, 'power through' society, coordinating social life *through state infrastructures.*"[4] But the effort to extend the capacity of the national state through civic as-sociations set in motion new struggles over the balance of power. Would control shift to the leadership of those voluntary associations? Would such arrangements constitute new "veto points"[5] where private citizens could withdraw their contributions to the coproduction of public goods? And how would the reordered capacity of this infrastructure of power articulate with the nation-making side of the equation, the challenge of constructing an inclusive patriotic identity to sustain state projects in times of crisis and war?

The alignment of party politics and state capacities gave these ques-tions particular urgency. At the beginning of the twentieth century, civic association had proliferated in regions that leaned Protestant, were eco-nomically advantaged, and tended to favor the Republican Party. This sit-uation set the terms for successive encounters between national projects and civic capacities. Theodore Roosevelt's expansive nationalism was supported by voluntary mobilizations, but also threatened the concentrations of wealth that sustained organized benevolence and voluntarism. A decade later, Woodrow Wilson faced a still more complex situation in which he sought to mobilize the nation-state for foreign war. Recognizing that his Southern Democrats were hostile to federal power, but reluctant to cede militarized patriotism to the Republican-leaning circuits of civic voluntarism, Wilson's war effort constructed an encompassing national identity that attempted to transcend—without resolving— the durable sectional animosities of the Civil War while criss-crossing divisions of race, class, gender, language, and religion. The result was not a tightly centralized Weberian state supported by a uniform culture of national membership, but rather an "expansible"[6] state in which federal projects drew upon and amplified local capacities, solidarities, and prejudices.

The architecture of an expansible state was entwined with new, but still partial and contested, models of national citizenship.[7] An approach to nation-state-building that incorporated civic associations could not avoid importing the identities and exclusions that structured the world of voluntary participation.[8] In this way, any "associative state" created obstacles to an inclusive, solidary sense of political membership at a moment when the scars of the Civil War were still deeply felt, when waves of new immigration had complicated the cultural landscape, and when women, African Americans, and others excluded from full citizenship were demanding equal rights. Under these conditions, nation-state-building required both the alignment of civic organization with government institutions and the development of a framework that encompassed, but did not necessarily erase, durable differences and inequalities. Realized across a decade of crisis and war, the result was an architecture of governance that sustained high levels of mobilization but often damaged the dignity of those who sought to participate as democratic citizens.

This governing arrangement began with an organizational mutation. By ratifying the Geneva Treaty and later granting a federal charter to the Red Cross, Congress created a new kind of entity: a civic association directly linked to the federal executive.[9] Across a series of crises, national leaders explored the potential of this new instrumentality and, more generally, turned to private actors and associations to manage difficult international situations. Like an earlier generation of volunteers in the "great commissions" of the Civil War, the experience of disaster relief, organized humanitarianism, and mobilization of war imprinted a model of effective collective action reliant on voluntarism and decentralized management. The lesson taken by many, if far from all, was that it was possible to mobilize a powerful nation without creating a bureaucratic and potentially despotic state.

Nationalizing the American Red Cross

Nation-state-building in the early twentieth century was shaped by legacies of the Civil War. Although the Sanitary and Christian Commissions had towered over other civic efforts at organized benevolence during the Civil War, a single woman—rather than a voluntary organization—was revered as the embodiment of selfless care for soldiers. Clara Barton was unusual for her time, holding a position as a paid clerk in the U.S. Patent Office and nurturing alliances with a number of members of Congress. Her efforts, while appreciated and indeed legendary among many soldiers, were rebuffed by the authorized nursing operation of the USSC. Consequently, Barton sought out battlefronts where she would have relative freedom of movement to arrange hospital services in support of the Union troops.[10] With the defeat of the Confederacy, Barton joined forces with a survivor of the infamous military prison at Andersonville to publicize the names of those who had died in captivity and to organize a registration service to collate information on dead and missing servicemen. These efforts kept her highly visible in the years after the war, as the veterans of the two great commissions scattered and turned to other tasks. Consequently, when Barton took a much-delayed trip to Europe to recuperate, she was recognized by the founders of the International Committee of the Red Cross (established in 1864) as the most obvious candidate for organizing an American affiliate, a goal that would be met in 1881. In the decades that followed, Barton again proved to be a most unusual woman, lobbying Congress relentlessly until in 1882 the Senate approved the Geneva Treaty.[11]

Unlike the European national societies, Barton committed the American Red Cross to more than the care of troops and noncombatants in war.[12] When floods and hurricanes struck throughout the late nineteenth century, the Red Cross was there, managing a flow of funds and services by which national contributions would restore disaster victims to some semblance of self-sufficiency. Across repeated but unpredictable disasters, the Red Cross operated in a manner captured by that image of "the Great National Hand of Fellowship" that had reached out to help Chicago after the 1871 fire. Along with countless city-to-city offers of aid after tornados and hurricanes—as well as industry-to-industry gifts in which one set of artisans or merchants gathered funds to help their counterparts elsewhere—these networks built from point-to-point benevolence and anchored a moral guarantee of assistance. But just as the inventions of federated fund-raising and community chests had injected a central node into local networks of benevolent gift-giving, so the Red Cross began to reorient relations of city-to-city assistance into a nationalized system.

In this way, Barton and the Red Cross contributed to the process of nation-state-building, constructing a web of relationships that cross-cut region, if not necessarily the other dimensions of social division. Having gone to the aid of African Americans devastated by a hurricane that hit the Sea Islands, Barton would later use their donation to victims of the Galveston hurricane specifically to aid the black community within that stricken city. A collection made by six children was given to a family that now consisted of six orphans.[13] Thus benevolence created a sense of sympathetic connection from American to American within categories of social difference, but not necessarily a patriotic and inclusive solidarity.

But whatever the geometry of a nationalized web of benevolence, its proponents still faced the contradiction between the dependency induced by unreciprocated gifts and ideals of individual self-sufficiency. Over decades of providing care and relief—first for soldiers, then for disaster victims—Barton wrestled with the tensions between the practice of charity and the self-sufficiency expected of liberal citizens. In an address to the 1886 Social Science Conference, she acknowledged that "against all precepts of Christian charity" "handouts of food or money did little real good. Instead they caused expectation and dependence." In order "to aid but not pauperize" in the wake of an emergency, the Red Cross sought to move quickly from the provision of direct relief to a "secondary stage, in which the community is again functioning and the help needed is more educational than material."[14] This distinction finessed the tensions between providing assistance and damaging democratic dignity in that the goal of education is the (re)attainment of the civic competence required of political equals.[15]

The prospects for a nationally organized benevolent machinery shifted decisively when Congress finally ratified the 1864 Geneva Convention in 1882. The American Red Cross became embedded in international treaty obligations.[16] More marked changes followed when the Red Cross received a federal charter in 1900 (revised in 1905) that specified a hierarchical, corporate form tied directly to the executive branch of the federal government. Other voluntary organizations objected, charging that Congressional restrictions on the use of the Red Cross emblem had effectively established a "charitable trust."[17] Whereas Tocqueville had envisioned civic associations as bulwarks against the central administrative state, here was something new: a civic association directly subordinated to the holders of executive office in the federal government. As the official historian characterized the change, "Through these latter provisions the American Red Cross became a quasi-governmental organization more comparable to foreign Red Cross societies which had long since been directly linked with their governments."[18]

In forging this direct link between voluntarism and state authority, the 1900 and 1905 charters set in motion a process that took the Red Cross from grassroots civic voluntarism toward centrally directed organized benevolence. Conflicts over finances tracked this movement. Barton had managed the American Red Cross in much the same way that she had organized her Civil War efforts. Personal expenses and disaster fundraising mingled in ways that were not necessarily corrupt but which certainly fell far short of the "business methods" required of any respectable civic organization by the late nineteenth century. Tensions flared during the Spanish-American War of 1898, as local Red Cross organizations mobilized major operations, raising the question of the proper relationship between the national organizations and various auxiliaries and chapters, some of which had their own complicated status as legacies of earlier Civil War and disaster relief efforts.[19]

Barton's personalized management practices allowed her critics to mobilize under the banner of professionalism. An increasingly contentious debate developed over financial record-keeping, with pro-Barton factions trying to oust anti-Barton factions from the Board and vice versa. In the end, Miss Mabel Boardman, a good friend of one of Theodore Roosevelt's sisters, and her allies were able to reach directly to the president with protests over "irregular methods" and "loose and improper arrangements" in the management of Red Cross funds.[20] The president's secretary sent a letter to Barton informing her that "while it appeared that the President and his Cabinet were constituted a Board of Consultation for the American Red Cross in the new by-laws, 'it is not possible for the President or any of his Cabinet to serve on such a committee, and the President directs me to have it publicly announced that the President and the Cabinet cannot so serve.'"[21] The conflict then escalated with the Boardman faction demanding a Congressional investigation of the finances of the Red Cross. Faced with the prospect of testifying to a Congressional panel, the elderly Clara Barton resigned from the organization with which she was so thoroughly identified.

The federal charters produced an importantly unusual organization. Because the Red Cross was obliged to support the military as well as civilians under the Geneva conventions, the board was composed both of private citizens and specified representatives of relevant Cabinet departments. When, a few years later, the President of the Red Cross was elected President of the United States, William Howard Taft inaugurated a practice that tied the executive branch still more closely to the Red Cross. At the end of his U.S. presidency, Taft stepped down from his Red Cross presidency, creating an opportunity for the office to be offered to his successor. Woodrow Wilson accepted. For decades, this pattern would hold.[22] The President of the United States, as President of the Red Cross, would appoint a chairman and approve the appointment of other members of the board to limited but renewable terms. Those nominations were made by the existing board.[23]

Finally, because the federal charter was held by the national organization, every local chapter held its charter by grace of the national board.[24] One can see here the provisional outline of a powerful if not purely voluntary association, one that linked the President to organizations of local leaders across the nation. By the 1920s, the Red Cross would have chapters in some 2000 out of 3000 counties nationwide. This possibility was never fully realized, not least because a succession of presidents understood the power of the organization as a vehicle for patriotism rather than partisanship in times of crisis. But this organization displayed the lineaments of what Michael Mann terms "infrastructural power" or the realization of that "huge charitable infrastructure" with "obvious political possibilities" that had been foreshadowed by the revolutionary-era Committee on Donations.

With these developments, the era of self-organizing voluntarism ended within the Red Cross. A new leadership took control, identified with the politics of the northeastern and Midwestern elites and committed to increased professionalism, hierarchy, and explicit nationalism. But although key figures in the Red Cross and leading supporters of municipal benevolence often traveled in similar social circles, they were embedded in distinct and sometimes competing civic networks. Whereas charity organization societies and federated campaigns strengthened networks of local ties—particularly within larger towns and cities—the Red Cross had national ambitions. Competing geographies of solidarity developed: a loosely organized mutual aid orientation among the large cities and a national relief system with particular responsibilities for the droughts, floods, and other disasters that episodically incapacitated rural areas and small towns.[25]

The Aggregate of "Trifling Contributions"

In advancing its national ambitions, the Red Cross lacked many of the necessary resources. In the wake of the fights over leadership and the new charter, it remained small. An organization whose machinery had fit comfortably within Barton's home now occupied a room or two in the Department of War. It lacked staff and, in the absence of war, it was unclear what a permanent staff would do. The answer came with a literal jolt when President Theodore Roosevelt turned to the newly rechartered American Red Cross to respond to the 1906 San Francisco earthquake.

Improvising in a moment of crisis, the president asked the General Secretary of the influential NYCOS, Edward T. Devine, to represent the Red Cross in San Francisco. Devine had already set out to travel west. The superintendent of the Chicago Bureau of Charities, Ernest Bicknell (the target of that beating by Father Basil), was also en route with relief contributions mobilized through established circuits of municipal benevolence in towns and cities in Illinois.[26] But President Roosevelt went further, asserting a significant realignment of national and municipal civic authority: "The American National Red Cross, Roosevelt declared on April 16, was the best fitted organization to undertake relief work, and so far as possible the outpouring of the nation's aid should be entrusted to its administration."[27]

In San Francisco, however, civic organization had been quickly reestablished and local leaders saw a threat in the presidential proclamation. Drawing on familiar relationships of municipal self-government and benevolence, a "Committee of Fifty" had been organized to manage the relief effort and "the proposal that public contributions for relief were to be sent to the still little known Red Cross rather than to this local agency was deeply resented. The *San Francisco Chronicle* declared it to be a reflection on the integrity of the city to have an outside agency handle relief funds, and outspokenly attacked the Red Cross for meddling." In the words of the official historian of the Red Cross, "When Dr. Devine reached San Francisco with Ernest Bicknell, not yet formally associated with the Red Cross and at this time representing a number of Illinois organizations which had raised relief funds, they met a decidedly chilly reception." By operating with tact and diplomacy, Devine and Bicknell helped to construct a "co-operative program" in which "all contributions for relief, except the congressional appropriation, were to be pooled and jointly administered." The result of that tact was a new administrative corporation, "The San Francisco Relief and Red Cross Funds, Inc.," to be chaired by a prominent San Franciscan, James Phelan, with Edward Devine serving as Secretary.[28] A new organization was created to articulate a problematic linkage of municipal autonomy and national political authority.

Of the almost $9.7 million in relief funds, $2.5 million was appropriated by Congress and allocated to the Army. The remainder was managed by this new Relief Corporation.[29] While the spontaneous generosity and co-operation of the residents themselves were critical, those leading the relief effort also called on professional social workers, both from San Francisco and on loan from other cities. This attempt to engage proto-professional social workers from the world of municipal benevolence with disaster relief for citizens who were unused to the practices of organized charity produced predictable conflicts.[30] Applications for aid "came in an avalanche and every applicant wanted help at once," but social workers stuck to their standards of systematic investigation. Each case took an average of 43 days to arrive at a final action. In time, Bicknell helped to establish a "Bureau of Special Relief" that "was flexible, . . . could cut corners, had wide powers of discretion, could act upon partial investigation and without reference to a case committee when enough was known to afford a reasonable assumption of facts and needs."[31] With Devine's return to New York City, Bicknell took over his roles both as Secretary of the Relief Corporation and as the designated representative of the American Red Cross.

If the Relief Corporation represented a new organizational model that could align networks of municipal benevolence and self-help with national contributions, it also encountered important limits to the uses of charitable funds for a project of economic rehabilitation. In his memoirs, Bicknell reported that some of those who received unsecured business rehabilitation loans eventually refused to repay those loans and took the cases to court: "Shrewd lawyers were engaged by the borrowers and jury trials were demanded in all cases. The lawyers pointed out that the relief funds had been given by the generous people of the United States, not to be loaned out, but given with promptness and with warm sympathy."[32] Similar claims surfaced during a riot over donated flour and in demands from the "United Refugees" to control the distribution of donated funds. As one woman asserted, "The papers say the money belongs to the people, and I want mine."[33] The legitimacy of the Red Cross as an intermediary in "the care of the people for itself" was contested and far from secure.

Note all the shortcomings of the Red Cross as a partner in this project of national relief to the stricken city: it lacked leadership and staff, had few resources of its own, and could be bitterly resented by local organizations. Although the earthquake relief effort was only a minor piece of Theodore Roosevelt's project of assertive nationalism, the possibilities of this new model of civic association would be there for other presidents to explore. Roosevelt's successor, Taft, had formed a strong preexisting tie to the Red Cross when he served as Secretary of War. As president, he actively promoted the organization, calling for contributions toward a $5 million endowment and endorsing a reorganization in which each state would establish a permanent state committee, ready to serve as financial guardian of relief funds should disaster strike.[34] While the Red Cross mobilized funds for international relief in the case of earthquakes in Italy and famine in China, Taft sent a letter to all governors explaining the purposes of the Red Cross: "Should any calamity occur within the bounds of your State which requires large and unusual relief measures, you are invited to make the freest use of the services of the Red Cross or of its national director [the now familiar Ernest Bicknell] in either an executive or an advisory capacity."[35]

In the aftermath of its relief efforts, the Red Cross was repeatedly strengthened by the gratitude of those who had benefited. In 1908, when the Red Cross first experimented with selling Christmas stamps to support efforts to contain and cure tuberculosis, San Franciscans were crestfallen when demand greatly exceeded supply given their "desire to show their appreciation of the generous activity displayed by the Red Cross Society when San Francisco sorely needed help by making a big record as purchasers of the stamps."[36] Just as Chicago had been quick to raise funds for San Francisco, San Francisco made repeated shows of its generosity, both in donating unused relief funds to the earthquake relief effort for Messina in Sicily and coming in second, after New York City, in the speed with which it met its quota for the national endowment for the Red Cross.[37] Each such step contributed to a slow and halting process of building a broad, mass membership base for an organization that was chartered to represent the entire people yet dependent on donations from wealthy individuals, a greatly enhanced endowment, and sales of Christmas stamps (later renamed "seals" to quell protests from the U.S. Post Office). As one editorial explained in connection with the fight against tuberculosis:

> For funds for this purpose the Red Cross Society is appealing not merely to the rich or the well-to-do, but to the entire population of America rich and poor. The poorer the man the more likely he is to need the ministrations of the society should he be attacked by this fell disease; and there are none so poor, if still able to work and employed, that they cannot in some small degree contribute to their own protection by buying and using the Red Cross stamps, which are a suggestion as well as a contribution. And if the habit can be made general the income will be enormous. The aggregate of the trifling contributions of the whole community will far exceed any possible income from the larger contributions of the rich.[38]

This sustained effort to build an architecture for collaboration—across national, state, and local governments, with networks of municipal benevolence and chambers of commerce—went forward in anticipation of possible war. A former mayor of San Francisco, who was also the former chairman of the San Francisco Relief and Red Cross funds, called for more individual enrollments in the Red Cross.[39] In less than a decade, the American Red Cross would be joined at the hip with the federal government in mobilizing volunteers, activity, and funds for the war effort in Europe.

By December 1917, 22 percent of the American population had made at least the basic contribution that signified membership in the organization.[40] Another decade passed, and the Red Cross would first collaborate with President Herbert Hoover to meet the onset of the Depression, then be at odds with the Franklin Delano Roosevelt administration, but quickly return as a supplement to government efforts and (at least in the case of foreign relief opposed by an isolationist Congress) a direct tool of Presidential politics. But before a system of voluntary support for an activist national government—an expansible nation-state—could take form, one more ingredient would be added: the philanthropic mobilization of new and unprecedented fortunes.

Danger in Big Gifts

During the same years that the federal charter for the Red Cross created stronger ties between national government and organized voluntarism, civic benevolence was transformed by the unprecedented wealth that gave its name to the "Gilded Age" of the late nineteenth century. Each wave of territorial expansion and technological innovation generated new wealth, often overshadowing that of earlier elites. By the early twentieth century, the fortunes of figures such as John D. Rockefeller Sr. and other titans of the new industrial economy profoundly challenged established understandings of the relationship between private giving and public purposes.

This conjuncture of large fortunes and civic benevolence was shaped by earlier conflicts over the legitimacy of association and the potentially antidemocratic power of organized benevolence. Some of the earliest experiments followed the end of the Civil War. Baltimore philanthropist George Peabody (whose junior partner in banking was J. P. Morgan) set the pattern by practicing "the method of partial succor" in support of education for blacks in the southern states.[41] Emphasis was placed on the "partial" inasmuch as Peabody's grants required both political action and financial support from southern state governments. Decades later, Andrew Carnegie would repeat this model of the matching grant in support of public libraries, requiring that municipalities both raise operating funds and adopt any necessary changes to their charters to ensure that his gift of the building and books would receive ongoing public support. As he began to distribute the fortune acquired through his leadership of Sears, Roebuck, Julius Rosenwald followed a similar plan, making his gifts to support schools for blacks in the south contingent on both a measure of public funding from state governments and fund-raising along with sweat equity from the communities that were to receive schools.

Rosenwald adopted the same formula to govern his gifts in support of the construction of YMCA buildings in black communities throughout the nation: the gift was contingent on fund-raising from both black and white communities, typically in a ratio of one-third to two-thirds.[42] By the 1920s, the Rockefeller philanthropies would pursue a similar line in support of the creation of departments of public health within state governments.[43] In each of these projects, the local capacity to raise private as well as public funds to meet a match was central to the expansion of public services and governing capacities.

These philanthropic efforts raised the specter of private wealth determining political outcomes. Although the opposition to associations—and, by extension, to chartered benevolent corporations supported by gifts and endowments—may have been most fierce at the level of popular politics, the sentiment that politics and charity should be kept separate also penetrated into American law. As Olivier Zunz has documented, "Judges always asked first whether a contested gift could be used for challenging existing laws. They declared time and again that citizens could not attempt to alter the law through a bequest of their private wealth."[44] This decision, *Jackson v. Phillips*, privileged democratic politics over private philanthropy, although the exception for bequests for "educational purposes" provided a generous back channel for political influence.

Yet no buffer could be stable in the face of the dramatic growth of private fortunes in the last decades of the nineteenth century and the first three of the twentieth. The question was how this wealth would—or would not—be accommodated by democratic politics. As W. T. Stead had warned in his classic hybrid of social gospel and muckraking, *If Christ Came to Chicago*:

> if millionaires will not distribute their own wealth and use their great position with great souls and hearts, they will find that they will come to be regarded by the hungry and thirsty Demos much as compensation reservoirs are regarded by the inhabitants of the cities who have constructed them to replenish the stream which their thirst would otherwise drink dry. These great fortunes of $70,000,000 and $100,000,000 and $300,000,000 will come to be regarded as the storage service upon which mankind draw in seasons of scarcity and drought. That is the use which society will make of its millionaires, if millionaires do not anticipate the inevitable by utilizing their millions.[45]

Taxes were the means for transforming private wealth into democratically controlled "compensation reservoirs" for public emergencies. Although states had primary responsibility for chartering charitable institutions, regulating bequests, and levying taxes on estates, recent events had drawn Congressional attention to charitable gifts and private civic associations. The Spanish-American War had prompted the country's latest experiment with a federal income tax.[46] Over those same years, Populists had agitated for the introduction of an income tax rather than supporting the federal government through consumption taxes and tariffs that weighed heavily on workers and farmers. In time, this cause gained new allies. During his presidency, progressive Republican Theodore Roosevelt would continue to argue for both a federal tax on bequests, possibly "heavy in proportion as the individual benefited is remote of kin," and a graduated income tax.[47]

This interest on the part of lawmakers reflected concerns over the influence of unprecedentedly large fortunes in American society.[48] When those fortunes were linked to ongoing business enterprises, they were attacked in the language of monopoly and antitrust. But the pivot by the wealthy to charitable giving did not still the controversy, even as contributions reached record levels. Total giving topped $121 million in 1907. Gifts by John D. Rockefeller Sr. totaled over $63 million. Andrew Carnegie placed a distant second, just shy of $9 million.[49] But millions in charitable contributions did not secure immunity from criticism. Members of the Disciples of Christ in Cincinnati protested the acceptance of a Rockefeller gift by their Board of Foreign Missions, arguing that "Cain was no more a marked and discredited man in his day than the president of Standard Oil is at the present time."[50] In his 1907 Commencement Address at Johns Hopkins, Hannis Taylor, former U.S. Minister to Spain, contended that he knew of "no monster so dangerous to the life of a republic as one who can in a moment throw bewildering millions in one direction or the other, especially when those millions grow out of abnormal legal and economic conditions that should not exist."[51]

Private philanthropy was clearly not a straight path to public approval. The trade-offs among liberty, national power, and great wealth surfaced in debates surrounding the propriety of the endowed foundation in a democratic polity. The first President Roosevelt experimented with establishing a foundation when he received the 1907 Nobel Peace Prize for "his services in ending the Russo-Japanese war." Roosevelt used his prize to establish a "permanent industrial peace committee" that would "strive for better and more equitable relations among my countrymen who are engaged, whether as capitalists or wage workers, in industrial and agricultural pursuits. . . . [I]n modern life it is just as important to work for the cause of just and righteous peace in the industrial world as in the world of nations."[52] But even Roosevelt, more determined and energetic than most,[53] discovered that foundations could be recalcitrant tools. His foundation failed to expend any of its resources in the years that followed and, eventually, Theodore Roosevelt requested that Congress pass legislation returning the funds to him so that he might donate the entire amount to World War charities. Congress granted his request.

Commentators saw many dangers in large-scale philanthropy managed by foundations and self-perpetuating boards of trustees. Men might abandon their admiration for "poets, orators, theologians, philosophers, novelists, historians" for "the teachings of the new gospel, which proclaims that nothing is really worth while [*sic*] except the brute force wielded by masses of money."[54] The depth of these concerns became evident in March 1910, when the Senate Committee on the District of Columbia recommended a bill to incorporate the Rockefeller Foundation under a federal charter. At an earlier hearing, Starr J. Murphy (a leading figure in the Rockefeller philanthropies) testified, offering arguments in favor of the expansive language concerning the foundation's purposes: "That the object of the said corporation shall be to promote the well-being and to advance the civilization of the peoples of the United States and its Territories and possessions and of foreign lands in the acquisition and dissemination of knowledge; in the prevention and relief of suffering; and in the promotion of any and all of the elements of human progress." To justify this encompassing statement of mission, Murphy pointed to the comparable language in the federal charter of the General Education Board, which had been established in 1903: "That the object of the said corporation shall be the promotion of education within the United States of America, without distinction of race, sex, or creed." This language avoided the weight of the "dead hand" of the original donor as "the wisdom of living men will always exceed the wisdom of any man."[55]

In response to fears that such a foundation would become a power beyond government control, Murphy insisted that "as a matter of general law . . . the Government always has control of charitable corporations" and pointed to the federal revocation of the Mormon Church's charter because of its commitment to the illegal practice of polygamy; church assets had been redistributed to the public schools of Utah.[56] Murphy deflected suggestions from Edward Devine of the NYCOS (and former Secretary of the San Francisco Relief and Red Cross Funds) that the government select the foundation's trustees, contending that a self-perpetuating board such as Harvard's "secures the best results" precisely because the current members "know the qualities of character and of heart and mind that are required for filling that position better than any outside agency can." Furthermore, if political officials did exert control over the foundation, they would be bombarded by begging letters and in danger of damaging the honor of their position. The Chairman

of the Committee concurred with this last point, noting that he had received more than 100 such requests since introducing the bill for the
incorporation of the Rockefeller Foundation.[57]

This reassurance, however, was for naught. Even at the highest level of
government, officials shared the populist concern over the power of great
wealth. In 1911, word came from a correspondent for the *Chicago Tribune*
that if the bill came to the desk of President Taft (a staunch business-
friendly Republican), he would likely veto it on the advice of the Attorney
General of the United States. Those legal concerns stemmed from the
fact that "In the first place, the foundation avowedly would be perpetual.
In the second place, its Directors would determine what would best advance civilization and apply themselves to its realization, even if the purpose might be the control of the Government of the United States." This
argument was elaborated by other commentators: "It is not a far cry for
the imagination to depict a situation where, in all sincerity, the Trustees
might determine to devote the fund at their disposal to the frustration
of some politico-economic movement favored by large masses of the
people, under which circumstances it is not difficult to imagine a growing state of indignation which would ultimately disregard law and order
and, perhaps, even attain the proportions of a revolution." While the *New
York Times* was skeptical that either the President or the Attorney General could have "been foolish enough to attach his signature to a document setting forth reasons such as we have quoted," their columnist went
on to describe all the safeguards in the proposed legislation that would
prevent such an imagined, antidemocratic outcome, including Congress'
power to terminate the endowment after a set period, the requirement that
the foundation not accumulate revenue and add to its principal, and the
need for "the consent of the President and of three other high Government officials and of the Presidents of five great universities" for appointment of trustees nominated by the existing board of the foundation.[58]

Many of these safeguards had been included as amendments to the
original bill, in an effort to secure Congressional approval of a federal
charter for the proposed foundation.[59] These efforts failed. The public remained skeptical as the Federal Commission on Industrial Relations augmented its inquiry into the "Ludlow massacre" at the Rockefeller-owned
Colorado Fuel and Iron with an investigation of foundations including
"the Russell Sage Foundation, the Baron de Hirsch Fund, all the Carnegie
benevolences, the Cleveland Foundation" and the Rockefeller philanthropies in order "to ascertain if they were a menace to the Republic's
future."[60] Eventually, the Rockefeller Foundation secured its charter from
the legislature of the state of New York, a body that did not demand the
roster of safeguards that had been incorporated in the amended versions

of the unpassed federal bills. Calling for federal regulation of all foundations, one critic observed that "if New York had not given them what
they wanted they would have gone from State to State till they found a
corporate habitation on their own terms. This should not be possible."[61]
But it was.

The New York charter for the Rockefeller Foundation capped a period
in which private fortunes were repeatedly transformed into foundations
in perpetuity: recognized in law, subsidized through tax provisions, and
committed to some public purpose. Because the benefactors of these
foundations—or their survivors—were also likely to be at the center of
webs of municipal benevolence, a new node in the intersecting networks
of civic, political, and economic power was now in place. On the eve of
the U.S. entry into the First World War, a framework had been established
for linking small individual contributions and major donations as well as
circuits of municipal and national solidarity to the federal agencies.

Architecture for an Expansible State

The multiple association-building projects of the early Republic were
echoed by early twentieth-century efforts to link private concentrations
of wealth and organized voluntarism to federal authority. The antebellum vision of "hydras"—invoked with respect to both the Bank of the
United States and the Benevolent Empire—was recast in language of the
large trusts that provided a framework for the extension of private or
corporate power into political arenas and benevolent projects.[62] In 1913,
the "great regulating wheel" that was the first Bank of the United States
was reimagined as the Federal Reserve system in which regional financial
networks were articulated with the federal treasury and monetary policy
to manage a rapidly growing economy. Similar architectures—nationally
focused, but constructed out of private organizational capacity—were
being formed in the worlds of organized benevolence and industrial
manufacturing.

Once again, Ernest Bicknell was in the thick of things. Informed by
his experiences with both the Chicago Bureau of Charities and the San
Francisco Relief Corporation, he promoted a plan for "closely knit cooperation between the Red Cross and the organized charities of the country, under which the trained workers composing the staffs of the local societies could be drawn instantly into the temporary service of the Red Cross
in the event of disaster." This arrangement, he argued, would increase the
capacity of the Red Cross to respond to crises, promote the training of
social workers as well as building professional friendships, while also en-

suring that the disaster effort "could be immediately demobilized when the emergency disappeared."[63] In 1908, Bicknell was named as the first national director of the Red Cross and he proceeded to recruit "carefully chosen" charity organization societies as "institutional members" that would represent the Red Cross in the case of a local emergency and send "trained workers to help in disaster relief elsewhere when called upon to do so by the national director of the Red Cross."[64] This arrangement allowed the Red Cross to respond to more disasters, but quickly exhausted the capacity of charity organizations to release their staffs for emergency service. As a consequence, there "gradually developed an exclusively Red Cross staff capable of meeting relief emergencies without calling on the institutional members at all." In this way, an expansible architecture of governance generated the development of a more powerful and centralized organization, directly allied with the federal government, a process that would be accelerated by the world war that now loomed on the horizon.

Preparedness for war inspired similar governance arrangements in the for-profit economy. Emerging first from professional societies and trade organizations, the Council for National Defense was envisioned as a system of broad participation by American industry, coordinated through the "national mechanism" of the engineering profession and "educational contracts" by which the military encouraged private companies to learn to produce munitions in accordance with army or navy specifications. A competing version was promoted by an executive on loan from American Telephone and Telegraph, Walter S. Gifford (a man whose activities will weave through the chapters that follow). Rather than engaging with engineers located in large and small companies alike, Gifford advocated a more central role for trade associations, arguing that the interests of an entire industry could be represented by a handful of informed experts, most likely from the larger firms.[65]

Both disaster relief and industrial preparedness were choreographed through networks that linked private organizations—whether municipal charities or professional societies—to federal agencies. In both cases, approaches that began as both expansible and broadly participatory gave way to greater concentration of resources in large organizations positioned along the fluid boundary between public agencies and private concerns. With the entrance of the United States into the war in Europe, pressure mounted for a still closer incorporation of privately managed organizations into the national state. But businessmen would be joined by many political officials in resisting that pressure, a stance defined by a deeply held commitment to minimize the centralized power of the federal government.

World War I: Indirect State-Building

At the paradigmatic state-building moment of world war, a Democratic administration controlled the national government. Consequently, officials who had deep reservations about the consolidation of power by the federal government determined the shape of national mobilization. For southern Democrats, the long legacy of the Civil War and the defense of states' rights fed a reflexive resistance to national centralization. For others, distaste for a strengthened national state was rooted in classic nineteenth-century liberalism and the anti-federalism that could be traced back to the party's Jacksonian origins.[66] Even the western populist wing had its own alternative vision of national government, based on an anti-bureaucratic regulatory model that matched national legislation to highly decentralized, and often semi-private, administrative decision-making by local associations.[67]

An aversion to federal intervention was evident in the administration of the draft. Within the administration, debates over the advantages of the draft over a volunteer force were marked by a deep-rooted preference for the latter. Even as the judgment of the regular Army tipped the scales toward the selective service (an evaluation bolstered by the uncomfortable fact that former President Theodore Roosevelt was vocally determined to be the most prominent of the volunteers), those in charge of implementing the policy sought to embed registration in the landscape of civic life. Rejecting a proposal that regular Army officers would conduct registration in U.S. Post Offices, Secretary of War Newton Baker opted to authorize governors to appoint local draft boards and to locate registration activities in established polling places. The call to register opened with "Greetings from Your Neighbors."[68] Baker and "Enoch Crowder, the army's provost marshal general, strove to overcome the lingering and bad memories of the Civil War draft. Crowder kept military officers out of the actual process of selecting draftees and set up a network of more than 4,000 boards composed of local civilians."[69]

This arrangement minimized the transformative effects of military mobilization, allowing local priorities and racial prejudices to shape decisions about who would serve; the national administration intervened to ensure that agricultural labor would not be enlisted disproportionately, but did not contest local assumptions about race or social status. Through the work of those thousands of civilian draft boards, local elites and professionals were drawn into a national military bureaucracy. This reliance on private but intensely civic effort carried over from Baker's decade of service in municipal government in Cleveland and his ideal of "civitism," which combined "Home Rule and the Golden Rule." National government, he thought, could draw on the same wells of local civic commitment: "Addressing representatives of state and local Councils of National Defense in early May 1917, he called on them for help to make registration for the draft an act of civic virtue rather than one of compulsion."[70]

In the War Department itself, discomfort with a strong federal bureaucracy generated an indirect approach to mobilization. Supervising both the military and the nationwide industrial mobilization required to support the American Expeditionary Force, Baker resisted efforts to create a single office with executive authority over economic activities.[71] Advocates of more centralized control, including Bernard Baruch, despaired in the first year of the war: "The more committees, the more lack of coordination. . . . No one wants to give the power to one man."[72] In time, Baruch would take charge of the War Industries Board, using the threat of federal compulsion when needed to secure "cooperation." Yet, significantly, even with a centralizer at its helm, war mobilization remained fundamentally "infrastructural," dependent on the collaboration of private firms and voluntary associations.

This preference for—or acquiescence to—private, voluntary efforts was also evident in the programs to improve the quality of life for troops in training camps and after deployment to Europe. As Raymond Fosdick, director of the Commission on Training Camp Activities, explained, he and Newton Baker "had come firmly to the conclusion that we wanted to work through existing agencies, and that we would create additional machinery only when necessary."[73] "Necessity" was defined by the capacity of existing organizations and the extent to which they adequately represented the nation as a whole. Hoping initially to work solely through the YMCA, Fosdick and the Wilson administration were dismayed to learn "that the Y.M.C.A. had no real Catholic representation on its newly-formed War Work Council" and, unless the Y changed its position, "it would be necessary to admit to the training camps a Catholic organization, probably a Jewish organization, and perhaps indeed, other branches of the Protestant faith, like the Unitarians, which were not affiliated with the Y.M.C.A." The resulting sectarianism, Fosdick feared, would be "out of keeping with the work to be done or with the spirit of unity and cohesion which the government desired above all else to inculcate in the new army." In the months that followed, when Fosdick "saw the three emblems—'K of C' [Knights of Columbus], JWB [Jewish Welfare Board], and YMCA so conspicuously displayed on huts, stationery, and even boxes of candy, I felt that this stratification struck a discordant note in any army whose soldiers were fighting as Americans, not as Catholics, Jews, or Protestants."[74] In this way, the construction of an expansible wartime state out of associations organized around diverse social identities could undercut rather than reinforce national solidarity. State-building and nation-making were set at odds.

But a preference for relying on existing organizations outside government was shared by both businessmen protective of the private economy and Democrats suspicious of enhanced federal power.[75] In the absence of an expanded federal bureaucracy to manage war production, Washington, D.C., was flooded with men on loan from industry. While the out and out donation of one's time and effort ran afoul of federal regulations,[76] many executives were effectively transferred to the government for the duration of the war, arrangements often but not always legitimized by that fig leaf of a "dollar-a-year." The result was a newfound capacity to rework the American economy, centered initially in the Council of National Defense, whose director was Walter S. Gifford. Employed by American Telephone and Telegraph, Gifford would go on to serve a long term as the company's president (1925 to 1948) while also making regular appearances in key roles at the intersection of government, business, and civic life: as chair of President Hoover's committee on unemployment relief, as chairman of the board of NYCOS for much of the 1930s, as chair of the 1943 Red Cross War Fund Drive, and as ambassador to the Court of St. James in the 1950s.[77]

For Gifford, as for the nation, the First World War was an immersion in decentralized but coordinated governance, a project outlined in one of his early reports for the council: "Only eighty persons . . . are drawing salaries for work for the organization, and most of these are clerks and stenographers. More than one hundred highly trained men are giving their entire time to the council without remuneration. Several hundred more are giving a large part of their time." With this combination of paid clerical staff and managerial volunteers, the Council had mobilized over a quarter-million miles of railroad as well as the telephone and telegraph companies in support of the war effort, including settlement of threatened railroad strikes. The procurement of coal, steel, zinc, copper, and aluminum had been handled along with "completion of an inventory, for military purposes, of 27,000 American manufacturing plants." A "great program of airplane manufacture and training of aviators" had been inaugurated by the Aircraft Production Board. Millions of government dollars had been saved "by the co-ordination of purchases through the agency of the General Munitions Board" and members of the medical profession had been mobilized to develop a standardized system of supplies and instruments. Finally, there was a "successful initiation of a movement to co-ordinate activities on the part of the States of the Union for the national defense, brought to a clear and workable focus by the conference of States held recently in Washington at the call of and under the auspices of the council."[78]

Although these arrangements took full form only late in the war, the network of civilian "volunteers" and industry committees profoundly reorganized parts of the American economy: harnessing professional accreditation, standardizing the specification of products, identifying bottlenecks in production and transport, eradicating duplication and conflict in government requisitions and purchases. The financier Bernard Baruch was central to this process as head of the War Industry Board. His appointment had been delayed, not least because of Congressional suspicion of his reputation as a financial speculator. In making his case for himself, Baruch embraced this identity as a speculator, arguing that successful speculation turned on precisely the ability to identify pricing inconsistencies, shortages of key material, and opportunities for arbitrage and brokerage among firms. This network among business leaders was one of the most important legacies for both the American economy and the American state for the rest of the twentieth century. As with the draft board, the economic mobilization forged stronger relationships among both local and national elites. But when it came to war production, these relationships went to the core of business activity.[79]

Although the War Industries Board mobilized these men as leaders of American business, many of those same individuals were simultaneously central to networks of civic activity and charitable networks. Consequently, the "expansible" architecture of the war mobilization operated on parallel civic and economic tracks, generating both dollars and military production through this infrastructure of voluntarism.[80] Despite the recent establishment of a federal income tax by the sixteenth amendment to the Constitution, the Wilson administration opted to finance approximately 60 percent of the costs of the war through voluntary subscriptions to government bonds: the Liberty Loans.[81] Precedents for this effort could be found in financier Jay Cooke's success in raising more than $1 billion through government bond sales during the Civil War,[82] but the four Liberty Loan campaigns—accompanied by a War Savings Program and followed by a Victory Loan campaign—enlisted almost one-third of American citizens as holders of war-related debt. As historian Julia Ott has argued, these expanded financial ties between citizens and the national government anchored an understanding of citizenship in which investing was linked to voting and service.[83]

The mobilization of men, material, and financing all worked through collaborative, cooperative networks of local notables and businessmen, the same sort of men (and very occasionally women) who would be found at meetings of a local chamber of commerce and in the leadership of community fund-raising drives. While the federal-state-local structure (or sometimes simply federal-local, as in the reorganized Red Cross) prevalent among these associations had constituted a nationalizing matrix,[84] the method of war mobilization strengthened ties across levels within any given association. Nowhere was this clearer than in the American Red Cross, due in large part to its uniquely ambiguous identity as a simultaneously civic and governmental entity. The national leadership was quickly shuffled; while some stayed on from the Republican-dominated board in place since the rechartering, new members were recruited from the top tier of municipal civic networks. Along with President Wilson and former President Taft as chairman, the war council included Henry P. Davison of the Bankers Trust Company and J. P. Morgan and Co.; Robert W. de Forest, a leader of the NYCOS and advisor to M. Olivia Sage, the widowed founder of the Russell Sage Foundation; Eliot Wadsworth, a Boston lawyer; Colonel Grayson M.-P. Murphy, a private banker and director of Anaconda Mining Company, among others. This new group of leaders "took over control of the American Red Cross—lock, stock and barrel" and viewed "the American Red Cross as a virtual arm of the Government, [which] they envisaged [as] making an incalculable contribution to the winning of the war."[85]

Change was not limited to new leadership at the top. The new recruits to the Red Cross brought with them business models of organization, explicitly reconfiguring the voluntary organization on the lines of an industry that required decentralized but standardized operations. As Harvey D. Gibson,[86] the first appointee to the new position of general manager, explained: "The future structure of the Red Cross is to be similar in general plan to that of any large national corporation—such as a railroad company, an express company, a telephone company, or any other big industry having branches in many scattered centers."[87] These were not simply talking points. The personnel recruited to the voluntary piece of war mobilization were often deeply experienced in leading practices of business organization. The head of the new "Department of Standards," Frederick P. Small, came from the American Express company; he quickly introduced "a uniform system of Chapter accounting" that involved "a simplified form of double-entry book-keeping especially adapted to Red Cross activities, all financial reports will hereafter be made on standardized forms which will be furnished to the Chapters."[88]

The contributions of businessmen to the war effort extended well beyond the Red Cross and into the terrain of war-making thought to be the monopoly of sovereign states. As hostilities broke out in Europe, the task of coordinating support for American citizens seeking to return was in the hands of a highly successful international mining engineer: Herbert Hoover. Having managed this first task, Hoover then took the lead of the Commission for Relief in Belgium, an entirely voluntary effort to raise funds and deliver food, the latter task involving working out agreements with Germany to transport grain to those in need. The Commission "evoked powers and immunities, was neutral—but . . . waged frequent controversy with both belligerents," leading a member of the British Foreign Office to characterize it as "a piratical state organized for benevolence."[89] Supported by major donors such as the Rockefellers, as well as a swell of small contributions,[90] the Belgian relief effort provided powerful "proof of concept" for a collaborative, voluntarist model of governance applicable even to the challenges of world war.

Controlled by businessmen and professionals, these arrangements created obstacles to engaging citizens and volunteers in the response to a national crisis. Whereas the champions of voluntarism at the start of the Civil War had assumed that citizen philanthropy would "keep the Army close to the people," the dilemmas facing organized benevolence at the start of the First World War rearranged the terms of the challenge. In the process of developing stronger relationships with American business, the Red Cross and other voluntary associations had become closer to the military and to the state. If these organizations were to remain "close to the people," they would need to function as vehicles for national solidarity and patriotism. The solution would be found in revivals of the Civil War's "divine method of patriotism" that articulated small gifts and everyday volunteering with mobilization for modern war.

Patriotic Giving and Nation-State-Building

Given the strong sentiments against intervention in the European conflict, a vital step in national mobilization was to increase civic participation in the patriotic efforts to support the war. As late as the summer of 1917, the Red Cross remained a middling size organization, boasting a national membership of "nearly three and a half million."[91] Recruiting efforts were focused on a Christmas drive that would harness all the moral force of the religious holiday to the national military effort. As one of the drive's corporate partners, the *Saturday Evening Post*, advised its readers: "Your Christmas does not need the usual litter of acknowledgments and Christmas cards this year. It can well take all that for granted. What it decidedly does need is knowledge that from your comfort and security something has gone out to alleviate a little the boundless woe in Europe."[92] Generosity should be rechanneled from networks of family and friends into the national war effort. Every household with a member was to display a transparency of the Red Cross emblem in its windows, with a smaller cross added for each additional member from the family. With candles lighted behind at an appointed hour on Christmas Eve, joined by the pre-arranged ringing of bells at nearby churches, the intent was to create a sense that everyone should join and had joined in the national patriotic effort. Even recognizing that "membership" required only the contribution of one dollar or more, the results were astounding. By the middle of January 1918, the official report was that "Latest Returns from Christmas Drive Indicate Membership of 23,475,000 or 22 Percent of Population."[93] This drive would be followed by another effort in the spring of 1918 to enroll 22 million schoolchildren in the newly established Junior Red Cross; the effort fell well short of the target, but with a membership of 8 million the effort was impressive nonetheless.[94]

Those in charge of the Christmas membership drive understood their accomplishment in political—as well as patriotic and spiritual—terms. The recruitment of so many members was said to embody the character of the United States as a nation: "The recruiting was on a tremendous scale because each one wanted to give—and to give without waste; to give in such a way that the giving would do the most good. Powerless as an individual, each felt his strength grow as the number of his comrades grew. Since Christmas he has felt a giant indeed." With a fifth of the population on its membership rolls, "The American Red Cross is . . . the total of the sympathy and affection of its members. It is the expression of the patriotism and solidity of the nation—as well as it is the fighter behind the line." Membership was portrayed as "spiritual communion in a nation's patriotism," a civic army that supported "our soldiers and sailors on land and sea; and acts as the link between the fighting line and the folks at home. Our allies look upon us as a source of strength and an earnest of faithful endeavor. If we shall do our part we shall not only shorten the war itself, but contribute much to a future lasting peace."[95]

Editorial after editorial expressed the conviction that this massive work of voluntarism would send a message to tyrants and autocrats throughout the world. Although not sufficiently articulate to count as a political theory, one of the clearest statements of this intensely felt civic creed came in response to a violation of its basic premises. The chamber of commerce of Allentown, Pennsylvania, had called for the government to take over many Red Cross tasks and to support these efforts with tax revenues. This resolution for Congressional support of the Red Cross was circulated nationally, drawing a rebuke from the chairman of the Red Cross: "it would be a mistake, at this time, to support Red Cross, even in part, by congressional appropriation." Acknowledging the contributions of volunteers, H. P. Davison argued that the Red Cross "is a great auxiliary to the Government in war, made the more helpful because it claims no time from a rapidly expanded Administration pressed by many problems, recruits no operating personnel from those liable for military duty, and imposes no financial burden or responsibility upon the national treasury." Warning that government support might convert the Red Cross "from a great voluntary humane movement to a department of Government supported wholly by taxation," he urged that "as long as our people have the spirit and the means to go on independently they should be encouraged so to go."[96] As a source of "spiritual communion in a nation's patriotism," the Red Cross promoted solidarity among citizens "anxious to pay more than taxes to help win the war." These arguments assert that the practice of voluntarism literally *makes* a distinctive kind of nation: "Our purpose is to associate the whole nation in an effort not only to manufacture knitted sweaters, surgical dressings, and comfort kits, but to act as a great social force, creating in the people a spirit of self-sacrifice, and mobilizing the enthusiasm, the generosity of the American people."[97]

But the construction of this compelling enactment of peoplehood faced multiple obstacles. Despite the impressive proportion of the population that had joined the Red Cross and made contributions or loans to the War Funds, the world war began as a less-than-fully-national effort. A half century after the end of the Civil War, distrust still marked relations between the children and grandchildren of Confederate and Union loyalists. Furthermore, the support of those excluded from full citizenship— women, African Americans, Native Americans—was uncertain as were the loyalties of the large immigrant populations who had direct stakes in the European conflict. The national totals reveal stark regional differences, reflecting great differences in wealth, racial inequality, as well as exclusion, and the persistent identification of the Red Cross with the northern effort during the Civil War. Membership rates were dramatically highest in the northeast and Midwest; markedly lower in the southern states.[98] (See table 1.)

Although its success was partial and uneven, patriotic mobilization for war aspired to the national motto of "e pluribus unum," out of many, one. In its membership and fund-raising drives, the Red Cross exemplified this distinctive mode of nation-state-building. Anyone could invest in the Liberty Loans—women, blacks, children, recent immigrants—and thereby enact their own citizenship in financial terms. Because the Red Cross understood itself to be the pinnacle of American voluntarism, its publications dwelt on the details of civic integration, repeatedly describing how donations linked marginal men and women to the national cause. One story featured Indians, "nearly all full-bloods," who were not citizens but had agreed to donate a sack of wheat each from their harvest and to serve in the military if needed. Another item concerned a mountain man, coming down into town with a pet bear cub: "the advertisement

TABLE 1. Statistics of Membership Drive (All Figures in Thousands)

Division	Population	Membership November 1	Quota	Christmas Members	Total Membership	Percentage of Membership to Population
Atlantic	14,740	1,011	2,015	2,800	3,811	.26
Central	15,365	2,000	1,189	3,600	5,600	.36
Gulf	6,198	86	304	384	470	.08
Lake	10,466	834	1,063	2,300	3,134	.29
Mountain	2,041	70	181	276	346	.17
New England	5,988	480	964	670	1,150	.19
Northern	4,268	212	388	658	781	.18
Northwestern	2,905	155	361	693	948	.29
Pacific	3,404	273	467	327	600	.18
Pennsylvania	8,875	502	1,192	1,600	2,102	.24
Potomac	5,370	156	356	250	406	.08
Southern	10,219	171	438	370	542	.05
Southwestern	13,854	435	1,162	3,250	3,785	.27
Totals	106,693	6,385	10,000	17,188	23,475	.22

Source: "Latest Returns from Christmas Drive Indicate Membership of 23,475,000 or 22 Percent of Population," *RCB* 2 (5) (January 28, 1918), 4. Note that the values do not add up properly; the article begins with the claim that "the work of compiling returns from the recent Christmas Membership Drive has progressed to the point of substantial accuracy" but then qualifies that "in the accompanying table, however, the figures will be found closely to approximate the final count." Division descriptions are from *RCB* 1 (20) (September 25, 1917), 3.[a]
[a] Atlantic (Connecticut, Delaware, New Jersey, New York); Central (Illinois, Iowa, Michigan, Nebraska, Wisconsin); Gulf (Alabama, Louisiana, Mississippi); Lake (Indiana, Kentucky, Ohio); Mountain (Colorado, New Mexico, Utah, Wyoming); New England (Maine, Massachusetts, New Hampshire, Rhode Island, Vermont); Northwestern (Idaho, Oregon, Washington); Northern (Minnesota, Montana, North Dakota, South Dakota); Pacific (Arizona, California, Nevada); Pennsylvania; Potomac (Maryland, Virginia, West Virginia); Southern (Florida, Georgia, North Carolina, South Carolina, Tennessee); Southwestern (Arkansas, Kansas, Missouri, Oklahoma, Texas).

for his sale to 'some one desirous of aiding the Red Cross and at the same time gaining a bear'" that was described as "playful, as gentle as bears ever get, interesting and smart."[99] From the Eastern Penitentiary in Philadelphia, "Inmate B1381," a "life prisoner," offered his services—along with those of other inmates—in making knitting needles for the war effort.[100] In each vignette, adult men marginalized by reason of race, distaste for civilization, or incarceration were incorporated into the polity through the mechanism of their gifts. For adult men, however, voluntarism was never to preempt a more fundamental relationship of citizen to state: military service. Repeatedly, articles explained that any men of draft age working for the Red Cross had been exempted due to disability by their draft board.[101] For men at the margins, by comparison, voluntarism was a path back to civic membership.

Voluntarism also enlisted those whose usefulness as citizens was uncertain, none more so than women past the age when they could make a meaningful contribution by way of "republican motherhood."[102] Without strong bodies or useful skills, these women still made small contributions to a grand vision of the war effort. A woman from Arkansas wrote to say:

> I work some every day for the Red Cross and put in one day every week a' gathering up eggs. I sell them and turn the money into the bank for the Red Cross. Some will say what is it to you and I tell them that of course I haven't got any boys gone yet but I don't know how soon I will have. I know that the boys in France are risking their lives to save our country and I want to help all that I can. Some tell me that it helps the bankers. I don't know and I want to get some information; maybe it will help me in the work. I am fifty-eight years old but I can help in this war.[103]

Yet another account linked the late nineteenth-century hope that voluntarism would heal the wounds of the Civil War through a new vision of encompassing citizen solidarity. A Home Service worker traveling in the south wrote to a friend this account of one experience:

> We saw a colored woman in North Carolina who was born in slavery, and had never in all her life gone further than ten miles from home, where she still lives with her old mistress. Neither woman ever married, and they have shared the same bed-room as mistress and servant for years. She is bent and white-haired and feeble, but with her gnarled hands she has just learned to knit.
>
> Between the intervals of hobbling painfully back and forth between kitchen and dining-room she has managed to knit washcloths for the Red

Cross. They went to France, with her name and address attached, and the soldier who got one of them wrote her a letter of thanks. She can not read, but the letter has been read to her so many times that she knows it by heart; and it is the proudest moment in her day when she can produce it from the bosom of her dress, where she always carried it, and tell you just what it says.[104]

Born in slavery, female, elderly, childless, and illiterate—all these disqualifications from full civic membership were recited by the Home Service worker only to be overcome by a small gift sent to France, reciprocated by a thank you note from a soldier.

Nothing captured the strained quality of these arguments for the worth of contributions from unskilled women than the never-ending controversies over knitting. Knitting marked the liminal zone of civic usefulness. It was, in an important sense, the most useful task that could be accomplished by people otherwise useless for war (and, consequently, was once an important feature of war mobilization around the globe). The home production of jellies and pickles so important in the Civil War was a thing of the past; the manufacture of surgical bandages remained an important voluntary contribution to the war effort (although with warnings that the collection of sphagnum moss should be left to those with special training). But knitting represented a useful activity that could be done by individual volunteers even though, arguably, sweaters could be produced more efficiently and effectively by machine manufacture. In response to concerns, both the Secretaries of War and the Navy made official statements confirming the value of this contribution and urging all, particularly the women, to keep knitting.[105] The War Industries Board sent out queries to both textile manufacturers and small merchants concerning the availability of knitting yarn for purchase by the government. And, as in the Civil War, rumors circulated that the knitted goods produced by volunteers were being sold, to soldiers or others. The Red Cross moved quickly to rebut the rumor as "emphatically not true."[106]

The dangers in linking voluntarism and citizenship were highlighted by the mobilization of children in the war effort. Despite the immediacy of the crisis, both President Wilson and the leadership of the Red Cross insisted that the activities of the newly established Junior Red Cross *were not* to be judged by the scale of their contribution to the war effort but by the long-term effects in fashioning a particular type of citizen: disciplined and self-sufficient, motivated to civic generosity by deeply held spiritual commitments rather than by the—potentially authoritarian—exhortations of teachers or exploitation by parents.[107] But, properly managed, the voluntarism of children could overcome both the corrosive lack of economic discipline among the poor and the divisive potential of a society of immigrants. The underlying theory of civic socialization was captured in a story about George, an "incorrigible" boy in a classroom for immigrant children somewhere in the Mountain Division. As his teacher explained, the Junior Red Cross "happened" to George in a powerfully positive manner:

> He wanted to learn to knit because his partner had learned, and it was fun to roll the ball [of yarn] up and down the aisle, when the teacher wasn't looking.
>
> I did my best to get the boys enthused and when the woman who canvassed our district in the interest of the conservation of food made her report, I was gratified. Calling at the home of George, she started in to explain the object of her visit. "I know all about it," said the mother. "My Cheorge watch like a cat on the table. 'Clean your plate or Hoover get you,' he say. I think he go crazy. Last night I go in the room and what you think, he sit up in the bed and knit so fast he can. I say, 'What you do, Cheorge?' He tell me 'I knit for the soldiers. Mrs. Kelley say we knit night and day. No time to be lost.' What you think?"
>
> George, and others [*sic*] boys of his type, their minds concentrated on the knitting, forgot to be mischievous and had good lessons. Several months ago George was promoted. He still minds his knitting, and, en passant, his teachers.[108]

Although the discourse of voluntary mobilization promised a direct connection between any citizen—regardless of age, gender, race, religion, or social status—and the nation, the organized structure of voluntarism amply allowed for the persistence of segregation in everyday activities. The melting pot was still on low heat, but even a lumpy and uneven inclusiveness was celebrated. Reciting the work of various local groups in the Junior Red Cross, one official speech described how

> American Children of many nationalities are in the ranks of the Red Cross workers. Tim Ford, the prize draftsman of the Tonopah, Nevada, auxiliary, made furniture for Red Cross houses. In spite of his name, Tim was a full blooded Chinese. The Blue Bird club was a group of Chinese girls, somewhere in the Pacific Division, each of whom made at least one garment for a soldier. Little Italians, busy in their American schoolrooms making clothes for other Italians who fled across the Piave before the oncoming Austrians, felt a great pride in the big-hearted, long-armed country of their adoption. Race prejudices gave way before sympathy of ideals.

There were twenty-six small Japanese in the Rick Spring School in New Castle, California. A year ago they organized their School Auxiliary to sew for French refugees. East and West met in the great American schoolrooms. Out of the war must come a brother-hood that will reach the national frontiers, and the children, still free from prejudice and bitterness, the inevitable concomitants of war, learned this wide sympathy from the Red Cross.[109]

The rhetoric of these arrangements represented both persistence and change in the relation of racial identities to civic identities. In the late nineteenth century, it had been important for Clara Barton to match the contributions of black residents of the hurricane-ravaged Sea Islands to black victims of the Galveston hurricane, just as members of a trade in one city would collect funds for their counterparts in another who had been stricken by disaster. These practices created a complex web of benevolence and gratitude while maintaining lines of ethnic, racial, and occupational distinction.

By comparison, the World War I configuration allowed—but did not require—the preservation of separateness in terms of the production and gathering of contributions, but these civic gifts then flowed across divisions of race, religion, age, gender, and station in life.[110] The washcloth made by an elderly black woman born into slavery in the South travels to an unspecified (but presumably white) soldier in France and a note of gratitude returns. As a solution to the problem of constructing a nation-state in a society riven by differences, exclusions, and inequalities, the organized voluntarism of the First World War displayed a double-edged quality. It constructed an encompassing "story of peoplehood"[111] that was compatible with either the strengthening or the transcendence of exclusionary categories of racial and ethnic identity.[112]

In a moment of national mobilization that required the combined efforts of those excluded from full citizenship, resurgent Southern Democrats, the heirs of racially progressive northern abolitionism, and adherents to a strong strain of anti-imperialism and Christian uplift, this malleable combination of civic inclusion and group exclusiveness was politically powerful. It provided a framework in which some African Americans seeking to realize their equal citizenship could choose to "close ranks" through service and voluntarism. But such alignments with the national war effort produced schisms as others pointed to the persistent—and at times intensified—practices of discrimination and ideologies of inequality that were woven through wartime voluntarism.[113] But working against these centrifugal forces was an increasingly complex articulation of governance and civic practice.

Institutionalizing Civic Philanthropy

These invocations of a people united with government in a voluntary effort were not simply talk. This expansive discourse of voluntarism was harnessed to an unprecedented effort to recruit new members and solicit donations to support the war effort, to expand the capacity of government without actually increasing the extent of government administration. But to succeed in these war-related missions, the volunteers needed money, lots of money. The response to that straightforward need produced some of the most lasting shifts in the place of benevolence in national life. Among these was a tendency for expansive civic benevolence to obscure growing economic inequality. A system in which everyone was equal in giving what they could was also a system that provided a secure place for the large fortunes that had driven the formation of modern foundations and fueled new practices of large-scale philanthropy.

But foundations were not the only large donors to be incorporated in the wartime circuits of patriotic giving. The success of the war fund drives, particularly the second, depended not only on the generosity of individual businessmen and the inheritors of industrial fortunes, but also on direct contributions from corporations, many newly prosperous with wartime contracts. For many firms, the new requests—or perhaps demands—for contributions posed no problems; the owner of a private firm was the firm and required no authorization to divert some of the company's earnings to a civic or charitable purpose. But with the growth of stock ownership, publicly owned corporations represented a growing share of the national economy and these firms were bound by different fiduciary constraints. National banks, for example, were explicitly restricted from diverting earnings for any purpose other than dividends, investment, losses, and the regular costs of business.[114] A great many of the businessmen who had been recruited as volunteers to play leading roles in the war effort came precisely from those companies that were least able to signal their support for the effort through corporate contributions.

This dilemma helped to fuel one of the less-noticed aspects of the war mobilization, but one which would set important precedents for the support of voluntary organizations for decades to come: the revision of the regulation and tax treatment of charitable contributions. The first major change came as part of the debate over the financing of the war effort. Congress spent much of 1917 debating the War Revenue Act, considering the character of the taxes to be imposed—on personal incomes, war profits, or consumption—as well as the progressivity of each of those taxes. The substantive political question was, who would bear the financial costs of the war? Would these fall on the wealthy, on corporations enjoying wartime prosperity, or on a wider range of citizens through taxes on personal income and on consumer purchases?

Relatively early in the debate, the question of charitable contributions was addressed, prompted by telegrams from two pillars of the New York City financial community who had communicated their concerns to a Columbia economist, Samuel McCune Lindsay, who in turn passed the issue on to Senator Henry French Hollis, a progressive Democrat from New Hampshire.[115] Two financiers from New York City, Jacob Schiff and Felix Warburg,[116] explained that they gave significant donations to Jewish philanthropies, that these important philanthropies depended on charitable donations, and that Congress might consider deducting such contributions from their gross incomes before the income tax was calculated. Such a deduction would be consistent with precedents set in state-level estate taxes and resonated with the exemption of various categories of educational, scientific, and benevolent organizations from federal corporate excise taxes.[117] The so-called Hollis Amendment was passed, a rare success for its sponsor, and established the precedent for the charitable tax deduction that would become a permanent feature of the American income tax code,[118] one that privileged charitable giving over other forms of private consumption.[119]

This addition to the tax code was augmented by regulatory changes that permitted national banking associations to contribute to the Red Cross War Fund Drive for the duration of the war. Because a number of states tied their regulation of banks to the national statutes, this shift in federal policy also covered a number of state-chartered banks. Passed just in time for the second war drive, which topped its goal of $100 million by $68 million, this temporary shift in regulation was not extended to all firms or beyond the end of the war. The status of business charitable contributions would remain uncertain, hedged about with efforts to preempt charges that managers were diverting profits from dividend payments to shareholders, until another round of tax revision in 1935. But just as major philanthropists had found a method for combining their one large gift with the contributions of many citizens through matching grant programs, the unprecedented national fund drives allowed for corporations, millionaires, new immigrants, working folks, children, and leading citizens to join in one patriotic fund drive.

These diverse flows of contributions had to be combined with an experience of solidarity if patriotism were to trump class just as it had incorporated (without eradicating) ethnic and racial difference. Reminiscent of the Civil War Sanitary Fairs that were imagined as embodiments of a well-mannered but inclusive civic sphere, those engaged in mobilization for the First World War presumed that voluntary activity could over-come deep social and economic divisions. But because the war effort asked for participation as well as impersonal contributions, the incom-patibility of charitable donations and democracy was once again an is-sue. The fact that soldiers were serving, however, gave them immunity from the stigma associated with receiving help (after the war, generous contributors and devoted volunteers would be taken aback by overtones of resentment of their efforts by the troops, a resentment that reliably appeared and reliably surprised after almost every war).

More symbolic work also had to be done on the giving side if privileged donors were to avoid the impression that their contributions required gratitude from soldiers and sailors. Consequently, elite participation was cloaked in performances of humility as well as a military model of service. In his accounts of the moral quality of voluntarism, John D. Rocke-feller Jr. repeatedly turned to accounts of status abdication. Recounting his visit to a military camp, he described "one man, the leading citizen of a large city in New York State, well-to-do, successful, highly regarded at home, I found cleaning the washroom at the Y.M.C.A. headquarters one morning, as though that had always been a part of his daily duty."[120] Any expectation of gratitude could be minimized by the humility of the giver. So just as federated fund-raising disembedded charitable giving from networks of friendship, the etiquette of volunteering called for efforts to purge the substance of social status from acts of benevolence.

A barely-yet-born public relations industry helped greatly. At the opening event of the first Red Cross fund drive, the picnic "was served on the lawn surrounding the home of General Hugh L. Scott, Chief of Staff, by the Refreshment Corps of the District Chapter. Differences in wealth and station were forgotten in the great common cause and the luncheon party was a picturesque mingling of the great and the near great in a democratic way." This portrait of patriotic solidarity was cap-tured for a national audience: "The moving picture operators were pres-ent at every turn, taking pictures of New York Millionaires eating fac-tory made pies, ham sandwiches and drinking out of tin coffee cups, made in the field kitchen of the local chapter. The members of the War Council, Mr. Taft and Miss Mabel T. Boardman were popular favorites with the camera men."[121]

This well-choreographed scene could not erase all the difficulties in-volved in a national mobilization that linked everyman's dime to the con-tributions of multimillionaires. For those on the most privileged end of the economic spectrum, the war fund drives drew on a familiar repertoire of fund-raising methods and entertainments. For the Second Red Cross War Fund in 1918, the Greater New York Organization ran a competition

of 31 10-person teams; team #4, composed of women with marital ties to
wealth and political prominence, beat out team #24 captained by John D.
Rockefeller Jr. for top honors.[122] Gala balls and fund-raising competition
were central to the social life of organized benevolence as it had developed in American cities during the late nineteenth century. But when
these events were held in the name of the "truly needy"—the widows
and orphans and ill and aged—the recipients were expected to reciprocate with gratitude. When fund-raising supported soldiers, however, the
social geometry was reordered; gifts to support soldiers were to be accompanied by gratitude for *their* service.[123]

As in the Civil War, great care was taken to ensure that the mass mobilization of benevolence did not turn soldiers and sailors themselves into
dependents. In Europe, General Pershing ordered that the YMCA sell
cigarettes to the troops, insisting—despite the organization's objections—
that "his soldiers should not be objects of charity. They were not to be
pauperized."[124] Official policy was clear that civic groups would bear
no financial responsibility for the support of the families—and perhaps
widows and orphans—of those serving in the armed forces. Benevolence would not be allowed to undermine men's status as economic
providers for their families. Servicemen were required to set aside a
fixed portion of their pay to be sent home to their dependents and to
purchase life insurance; their contributions were then augmented by
the government. In order to avoid penalizing family breadwinners as
well as to "install thrift, and better to preserve equality and democracy
among the members of our own forces," service men without dependents
were required "to deposit with the government so much of the half-pay
as is not allotted, these deposits to bear interest at 4 per cent per an-
num, compounded semi-annually."[125] The civilian volunteers of the Red
Cross were expected to fill the moral and advisory, but not financial,
vacuum left by the absence of a husband or father.[126] These roles, however, required new kinds of volunteers, trained to mediate between an
increasingly rationalized, bureaucratic, professionalized system of state
agencies and the particular, personal, emotional concerns of individual
citizens.

Just as the experience of mobilizing for world war transformed the
capacity of the federal government to harness civic organization, so too
the years of effort reshaped the internal relations and organizational culture of the voluntary associations themselves. Because the American Red
Cross had a uniquely close partnership with government and military
authorities, the changes in its character were particularly pronounced.
Controversy flared over the apparent "militarization" of the organization; its officers were authorized to wear a designated uniform while

operating in theaters of war. The civilian leadership sought to dispel concern, explaining this as simply a practical solution that allowed Red Cross workers to operate in areas out of bounds to civilians and to locate themselves within the hierarchies of military etiquette.[127] Faced with individuals primed for volunteer activity, voluntary organizations were not necessarily welcoming. Rather than directly translating levels of interest and energy into organizational projects, staff and leadership continually monitored how grassroots initiatives might affect the character and reputation of existing organizations.

These internal conflicts flowed directly from the organizational mutation that defined the American Red Cross: a civic organization, charged with representing all of the nation's people, but linked closely to the office of the President of the United States and a number of executive departments. Compared to the "great commissions" of the Civil War, the Red Cross was much more thoroughly entwined with civilian and military authorities at the national level than in the earlier conflict. Yet for all its privileged and fiercely defended status, the Red Cross was only one of many examples of how the "expansible" American state mobilized for war by drawing on the individual leaders and organizational capacities of civic voluntarism. In part, this was the result of necessity, as a relatively underdeveloped administrative machinery confronted the challenges of mobilization. But it was also a matter of values and choice. As Herbert Hoover moved from his role as leading volunteer to government appointee in 1917, he persuaded President Wilson that the entity overseeing grain shipments to Europe—the United States Food Administration—should be set up as an independent agency precisely because it would be easier then to dismantle it when the need had passed.[128] Across the federal government, the expansible state was constructed so that it could be dismantled, at least in part.

Make It Unanimous!

The Armistice demonstrated the limits of nation-state-building that took preexisting associations as its building blocks. "Make it unanimous!" had been the call for the 1918 Christmas Roll Call; none of the detailed quotas that had focused membership recruitment during the winter of 1917 would be assigned, declared the organizers. But the November armistice undercut the urgency of the drive and the beginnings of the great influenza outbreak further hobbled a plan for civic mobilization that depended on community gatherings and church services to generate enthusiasm and peer pressure. Not surprisingly, the results disappointed, even as the leadership attempted to put the best face possible on the outcome:

Seventeen million persons in a single organization is a mighty big thing, just of itself. Numerically the persons thus registered almost equal the voters of the United States who cast their ballots for presidential electors at the election of 1916. The national spirit which the army of mercy reflects in concentrated form is something to thrill the world in the dawn of a new peace the same as it did in the depressing days of war. The power for service of such an organization is incalculable.

When the idea of universal Red Cross membership was developed the war still was raging. Had it continued there is no doubt that the enrollment would have shown really stupendous figures. But happily the hostilities were brought to an end, the natural effect being to curtail much of the enthusiasm which war stirs in the hearts of men and women. Any feeling, however, that there would be a reaction inimical to the permanency of the American Red Cross on the broader lines planned, has been dissipated by the Roll-Call. Under the circumstances its result is wonderful. It further is to be borne in mind that physical circumstances, notably the prevalence of the influenza epidemic, greatly embarrassed the Roll-Call in many parts of the country.[129]

In retrospect, the unfortunate motto for the 1918 Christmas Roll Call captures the limitations of wartime voluntarism as a framework for national solidarity. But substantial interest, energy, and loyalty remained. Despite all the distractions of the 1920s, the infrastructure for an expansible state remained in place, awaiting the next crisis. Some efforts were made to repurpose the local community defense boards into a civic system of self-government.[130] A decade later, the Mississippi Flood of 1927 would exemplify the full-flowering of civic voluntarism linked to executive leadership. Although the great commissions of the Civil War had quite quickly been disassembled, this mode of mobilizing voluntarism in response to national crisis survived the armistice this time, carried forward by the meteoric career of the "master of emergencies," Herbert Hoover.

5

"Everything but Government Submarines"

LIMITS OF A SEMI-GOVERNMENTAL SYSTEM

> This does not exhaust the list of governmental channels of cooperation, it merely serves to illustrate it. We have used everything but government submarines. We have seen this interplay between the government and the Red Cross in time of war and now in time of disaster. It is not at all a phantasy of imagination to speculate upon the possibilities of similar interplay in other peace-time and normal business of the Red Cross.
>
> JAMES FIESER, Vice-Chairman, American Red Cross, April 1929[1]

The Civil War was mobilized on a still sparse social and political landscape. Beyond the Post Office, much of government operated indirectly through the tariff system or by delegating government activities to private individuals.[2] National firms and continent-spanning railroads lay in the future. Consequently, when private organizations and state authorities demobilized at the end of the war, many of their accomplishments were abandoned. Only in time, and largely through the metamorphic forces of municipal politics, did they develop into new forms of collaborative governance and social provision.

The situation in the wake of the First World War was vastly different. Mobilization amplified the capacities of the professional military, national government, organized business, large-scale philanthropy, and federated civic associations. The legacy of these efforts has informed an influential account of American state-building as proceeding "from warfare to welfare."[3] But with respect to the role of voluntarism, the development was not so linear. Although wartime fundraising had created a parallel "voluntary" system of taxation (or, in the words of John Seeley, a system of "gift extraction"),[4] the moral legitimacy of this system rested on the fact that the recipients themselves contributed military service to the nation. Consequently, the end of conflict required a recalibration of benevolence to situations where the beneficiaries might be citizens who had not always-already reciprocated through military service.

At both national and municipal levels, the 1920s revealed the complex-
ities and challenges of this task. The baseline was set by the success of the
closely choreographed coordination of government agencies, business
firms, and voluntary organizations that was a hallmark of the First World
War. But after the war, some of the key actors—notably the American
Red Cross—struggled to establish a new sense of mission.[5] Absent the
goal of victory over a morally condemned foe, intensified social pressure
was required to keep the machinery of giving in motion. Other components of the wartime infrastructure of civic benevolence more easily
found a central role in peacetime, above all the municipally oriented Community Chests. Only a dozen or so had been established before the conflict, but the form spread widely as War Chests were organized and later
converted to local purposes after the armistice and just in time for an
economic downturn in 1920–21.[6] Just as wartime voluntarism had been
championed in order to limit the expansion of federal government, municipal benevolence was revived with a mission of containing the expansion of tax-supported public services. In cities across the country, these
efforts to perpetuate wartime civic giving produced their own critics as
community fund-raising came to be experienced as an undemocratic tax.
Consequently, postwar efforts to refashion civic benevolence again raised
the issue of the democratic dignity of those who benefited as well as those
who were exhorted to give.

Revivals of civic nationalism represented a second potential challenge
to local elites in the form of a singular champion. No one had greater authority in making claims on civic benevolence than Herbert Hoover,
the "Great Humanitarian" whose mastery of large-scale organized voluntarism had been demonstrated throughout the war, from the initial
evaluation of American citizens from Europe through postwar food relief. Hoover's last major pre-presidential triumph as Secretary of Commerce, the response to the Mississippi Flood of 1927, provided compelling proof of the power of voluntarism in collaboration with government
and industry. Armed with this lesson, Hoover would confront the growing industrial unemployment and widespread drought that fueled a deep
national depression in the late 1920s. But when voluntary efforts faltered,
particularly by the winter of 1931–32, a population already accustomed
to "voluntary taxation" was primed for a greatly expanded governmental
role in social provision.[7]

Bracketed by war and economic crisis, the 1920s illuminate both the
possibilities and profound limitations of harnessing an infrastructure of
civic benevolence to national political projects. Absent wartime's motivations for giving, organized benevolence was experienced as coercive,

damaging the democratic dignity of those citizens who might need relief and adding insult to those now pressured to give. Voluntarism and charity came to be coded as strongly partisan in the Congressional struggles to come up with an adequate response to the devastation of the Great Depression. As demands overwhelmed the capacities of these arrangements by the late 1920s and into the 1930s, the conditions for a moment of field transformation would emerge. But those possibilities were shaped by the decade between world war and economic crisis.

Legacies of War

For years after the armistice of November 11, 1918, civilian suffering in Europe prompted familiar charitable efforts—drives for donations, calls for used clothing that could be refashioned into garments for the children of France, Austria, Poland, and beyond. Red Cross nurses divided their efforts between care for troops as they awaited their return to the United States and combating the epidemics that accompanied civilian hunger and displacement. Perhaps most tellingly, the knitting proceeded in a halting fashion, calibrated to shifting rationalizations for continued American engagement with Europe. A call went out to cease producing items in khaki and navy yarn for the soldiers and sailors. This was followed by appeals to the knitters for more colorful layettes that would celebrate new life and demographic revival in France.[8] Suffering abroad and hopes for European renewal inspired ongoing generosity.

This was not purely a project for civilian volunteers. Organized benevolence was directly authorized and financially supported—if not actually delivered—by the U.S. government. Food was at the center of these efforts, reflecting both the very real possibility of famine in Europe and the politically dangerous problem of agricultural surpluses that depressed prices in domestic grain markets.[9] These surpluses were in part the result of the efforts of the U.S. Food Administration, headed by Herbert Hoover, to promote wartime production increases and conservation by consumers.[10] Voluntary contributions were blended with government appropriations and purchasing credits made available through quasi-government enterprises. No single instrumentality was sufficient to the challenge that seemed to require "inter-governmental action on an enormous scale. As previously stated, the pending relief task is so enormous that governmental action alone can [not] deal with it. But it is becoming more and more apparent that the call which government will make for aid will involve in time the utilization of every resource of volunteer relief agencies."[11] Even after the armistice, many American citizens remained both emotionally engaged and financially supportive of the relief and rehabilitation of Europe. At the head of many of these efforts was Hoover himself.[12]

As foreign relief efforts extended wartime voluntarism, organizations also struggled to redirect their efforts homeward. The Wilson administration had given the Red Cross primary responsibility for the reintegration of veterans into civilian life.[13] Given the possibility of political discontent among veterans, this work was politically significant: "A recent survey of demobilization indicates . . . the need for a helpful and efficient Red Cross service among the men who are coming home if they are to re-enter civil life with a rational attitude toward their duty as citizens and the government in general." This required encouraging veterans to make use of the benefits linked to their military service, including "vocational training with pay, this for the wounded and disabled; retaining government insurance; the readiness of the United States Public Health Service to care for them absolutely without cost . . . should any illness or incapacity develop as a result of war service; allotment problems, correctness of pay, and so on." These benefits "have to be presented in a human way, in a heart-to-heart fashion—have to be 'sold' to the men, as social workers use the term."[14] At the most basic level, veterans often needed help in establishing eligibility and filling out the requisite forms.[15] In a society not yet accustomed to regular interaction with large-scale bureaucracies, the efforts of relatively educated citizens (sometimes serving as volunteers, sometimes as paid staff) prepared the ground for more intensive public social provision.

The Red Cross highlighted the importance of individualized case work as justification for its work with demobilized veterans:

> One of the questions frequently asked is why the Government does not do what the Red Cross is doing? The Government is compelled to confine itself to a standardized service, treating all men more or less alike. The Red Cross can go into all the ramifications of the individual case and help the man overcome his peculiar handicaps and obstacles. The Government must stick to the essentials of the job. It has a gigantic and difficult task to accomplish the obvious work, common to the handling of every case of a disabled man. It cannot take infinite pains with every case. What it does for one, it must be prepared to do for all who are eligible, whether they need it or not.

By comparison, the Red Cross and other voluntary organizations were "under no such obligation" to treat veterans with uniformity and could tailor services to individual needs: "Through its system of Chapters and its representatives located at all the strategic points along the way, the

Red Cross is a combination claim agent, friend, adviser, teacher and general *fides Achates* of the disabled man. Such a role would be very difficult, if not impossible, for the Government."[16] Here the tension between equal rights and individual situations was clear, opening a door to the injection of local preferences and prejudices at the same time promoting the legitimacy of accepting government benefits.

As late as 1921, the Red Cross commented that "rather curiously, it is occasionally necessary for the Red Cross representative to persuade a man to take advantage of what the Government has to offer. Sometimes his family fails to understand what the Government provides and counsels him against applying for training. A great deal of explaining may be necessary before fears are dispelled."[17] This reticence, even aversion, to accepting help revealed the problematic boundary between government entitlements based on service and intrusive charity work. This was a potential source of conflict in every encounter between a Red Cross volunteer (or paid staffer) and a veteran. Even in wartime, Home Service had operated on morally dangerous ground "reaching as it does, into those delicate and confidential relationships in everyday life. Its battle is not among bursting shrapnel and screaming shell, but rather where lonely parents, distressed wives and children, and confused returned service men are waiting for the advice and care of the 'Greatest Mother in the World.'"[18] Any extension of these services into peacetime, once the fathers and husbands had returned from the war, threatened to reduce these families to an inappropriate dependency.

Finally, voluntarism could be a vehicle for the reintegration of veterans as valued members of civic communities. As of late 1920, 2554 of 3171 chapters reported that they were still engaged in war work (out of a national total of 3649 chapters). Other major activities included Junior Red Cross, home hygiene, public health nursing, home service extension, and production.[19] The Red Cross also helped to form thousands of new Boy Scout troops, both to socialize the young and to "give to men, especially returning soldiers and sailors qualified to act as Scout leaders, an opportunity to further serve their country by enlisting as Scoutmasters, Assistant Scoutmasters, Members of Troop Committees and Members of Local Councils."[20] Yet, with the war over, the diminishing sense of civic responsibility made it difficult to mobilize funds and volunteers to help restore veterans to their position as breadwinners and valued members of their communities.

In its efforts to claim a place in postwar society, the American Red Cross deployed all the methods of propaganda and public relations developed during the war. Movies made the case for peacetime voluntarism.[21] By late 1919, "American Junior" was in production with its story of the resistance of a wealthy man to the organization of a Junior Red Cross chapter at the school attended by his daughter and the daughter of his gardener. His opposition, based on the conviction that such voluntarism was appropriate only in wartime, melts when the gardener's daughter uses her first aid lessons to save the life of his young son who has toddled into a pond. The willingness to serve others, supported by appropriate training, trumped class divisions and prejudices against peacetime voluntarism. In a second film, a "successful wife and mother" is drawn into an active role in the community through her sympathy for the mother of a soldier still in Europe. The effort to find employment for the soldier's sister, to gain assistance from a public health nurse, and to protect the sister from the predations of an unscrupulous supervisor all generate an appreciation of the Red Cross on the part of everyone involved. Every issue is resolved and "Joe Harrigan, the soldier, returns with gratitude in his heart for the help of the Red Cross while 'over there,' and deeply appreciative of the assistance Home Service has rendered his family."

For all these public relations efforts, the virtuous cycle leading from wartime to community-building proved feeble. Absent war or crisis, the impetus to give was not sufficient to fuel the grand system envisioned by Red Cross leaders. Nor were Americans eager to ask for help, particularly when delivered in a manner reminiscent of social work and charity care. By mid-decade, the Red Cross had faltered in its attempt to transpose its organizational capacity for military support and refugee relief to domestic programs. Instead, the organization redefined itself around rural public health nursing, first aid, and lifesaving classes.[22] A project of community surveys brought greater coordination with "the extension departments of the state universities and the agricultural colleges, the Farm Bureau movement, the Grange, the rural Y.M.C.A and Y.W.C.A., the Society of Equity and a number of child-welfare societies,"[23] thereby steadily building an infrastructure for governance and provision in small towns and farming districts. Given a flood, tornado, hurricane, or fire, voluntary fund-raising and relief work could be mobilized. But, for the time being, the most visible legacy of the great national voluntary effort of the war was to be found in the nation's cities.

Businessmen Ascendant, Civic Benevolence Transformed

Although Red Cross officers, nurses, and volunteers had been prominent actors in the war, much of the heavy lifting of wartime fund-raising and Liberty Loan campaigns was done by the clubs and associations that were a fixture of American cities and towns. These experiences accelerated the coordination of voluntary efforts that had begun decades earlier with the establishment of charity organization societies, chambers of commerce, and the first Community Chests. In the years before the war, proponents of a unified and rationalized regime of fund-raising and social service faced uphill battles in many cities. In Chicago, the papers of Julius Rosenwald, the president of Sears, Roebuck, speak to the sustained effort and repeated frustration that confronted even a prominent and generous philanthropist. Although the city had a long tradition of organized benevolence and active civic organizations,[24] conflicts over control repeatedly blocked the creation of a federated campaign or community chest. Pieces of such a regime were in place, including the "Bureau of Charities" once managed by Ernest Bicknell (the victim of that battering by Father Basil and later national director of the Red Cross), but fund-raising was scattershot and driven by crises. In 1908, for example, a "Business Men's Relief Committee" had raised $58,000 for relief in the face of higher unemployment, funds that were to be distributed independently of the Chicago Bureau of Charities. The division of effort between businessmen and charity workers was further complicated by the separate federations or proto-federations of Catholic and Jewish charities (secular agencies and mainline Protestant charities often cooperated in a third camp).[25]

One of the legacies of war was greater support, at least in theory, for collaboration among voluntary associations. A decade after the 1908 effort, a new Chicago Council of Social Agencies replaced the Bureau of Charities, but as one of Rosenwald's correspondents bemoaned, "The great trouble in Chicago is that we have had dozens and dozens of organizations, each doing its own work in its own way, without the slightest correlation or coming together on the matter of plans, policies and intersections."[26] In 1922, hoping to leverage contributions from local benefactors and philanthropists into broad public support for the voluntary efforts of private social agencies, the Commercial Club sponsored a study of "raising of finances for the social purposes of Chicago." The study represented an "opportunity to sell to a wider public the idea of co-ordination, co-operation and fore-planning."[27]

Published in 1924, the resulting study was prefaced by a plea to Chicagoans to consider the cumulative power of their individual contributions: "What became of the bill you gave that pretty girl who tagged you on State Street in the name of children's charity, or of the small check you mailed a month ago in answer to a heart-reaching letter of appeal?" Business methods were then invoked: "If it had been a thousand dollars, or even a hundred, you would have looked on it as an investment and taken pains to be rather sure what returns you—or somebody else—would receive. . . . Yet . . . this steady patter of carelessly given money, this almost mechanical reaction of a monster city to the cry of its poor and unlucky, swells the tide of yearly giving in Chicago to almost fifty million dollars." The advantages of federated fund-raising, the study claimed, were evident in the 150 cities that had adopted this practice, including "forty-nine of the seventy-four largest cities." Often inspired by an appeal from the public for "relief from constant taxation, and of the agencies for relief from the struggle for existence," federated funds tended to increase the total number of donors and the size of large gifts, while reducing fund-raising costs and stabilizing finances for social agencies.[28] But these gains came at the cost of "centralized control; the danger that the spirit of progress may crystalize into an inflexible institution." Charitable agencies feared the loss of direct ties to their supporters and, for some, "of freedom to develop the religious aspects of their work, and character building organizations feel that a general grouping of all social effort detracts from their ideal of self-support."[29]

In Chicago, the desire for organizational autonomy won out. At a conference called by the Council of Social Agencies, only seven of the 57 delegates preferred a community chest model. The major result was a new committee on the financing of social work, carefully balanced among competing interests.[30] New York represented similarly difficult terrain for centralized coordination and would only manage a merger of the two venerable charitable societies—the NYCOS and the Association for Improving the Condition of the Poor—in the 1930s. The failure of the Community Chest movement in Chicago and New York makes clear why federation was such a significant development when it succeeded. By uniting diverse business groups and social elites in the financing, and therefore supervision, of private social welfare agencies, the community chest represented an alternative to control through an elected city council and a method for limiting the expansion of tax-funded city services.[31]

Federation rearranged the networks of obligation that linked donors and beneficiaries, displacing relatively direct ties between wealthy donors and the needy poor. Instead, the "Chest movement has tended to lessen the gap between these two extremes by deepening the top layer of subscribers, and also by thickening the lower level of beneficiaries so that now only the thinnest partition divides the two."[32] As the pool of contributors widened, control centralized in the Chests themselves, eroding the autonomy of individual agencies while mapping more closely onto municipal culture and identity. As the *Survey* observed, "the way people speak the name of a thing often betrays their conception of the thing itself. For instance, some say community *chest*, and we catch their thought in terms of dollars; others say *community* chest and thus reveal their sense of fellowship. . . . In Cincinnati the accent is ever on *community*— community of responsibility, community of effort, community of life."[33]

The fund-raising totals in Cincinnati document the lasting legacy of wartime fund-raising on municipal political economies. From 1920 to 1930, the totals ranged between $1.6 and $1.9 million and then surged above $2 million in the depression years of 1931 and 1932. For every year after 1920, more than 70 social agencies participated in the Chest's federated fund-raising drive, which was reoriented to include organizations that supported the self-provisioning of the working and middle class as well as relief for the neediest. As one commentator noted, "Many large gifts in practically every chest are predicated pretty directly upon the inclusion of the Y.M.C.A., the Y.W.C.A., and the Boy Scouts in the campaign, to say nothing of health agencies and hospitals."[34] Just as the federated campaign had reoriented the circuits of gifts and gratitude from the vertical ties of donor and beneficiary to the horizontal ties among those who gave, this shift from charity to "social welfare" positioned individual citizens as *simultaneously* donors and beneficiaries within a system of municipal membership. (See figure 3.)

But in this voluntarist system, all citizens were not equal. As separate fund-raising campaigns were consolidated into annual drives for the Community Chest, leading businessmen (along with their wives) became ever more central in networks of giving and receiving as a growing proportion of gifts were made directly by corporations.[35] Because the chambers of commerce—directly or indirectly—determined which agencies and services were "in the community interest," businessmen also gained influence over veteran philanthropists and charity workers. Charities were expected to conform to business understandings of what constituted a well-run organization: an unpaid board of at least five persons, efficiency and avoidance of overlap with other organizations, strictures on questionable fund-raising methods, limits on entertainment and fundraising expenses, and "complete audited accounts, both American and foreign, prepared by a Certified Public Accountant or the foreign equivalent."[36]

These requirements of the National Investigation Bureau, which had been established to evaluate charities during the First World War, could be used to coerce.[37] Solicitors were said to have lists of the amounts expected from each local business or individual. Chain stores were advised to follow the practice of "setting aside and maintaining a definite budget for civic and charitable work of recognized merit" in order to demonstrate that they were good citizens of a local community rather than outposts of a faraway corporation. Corporate policy suggested that "local employees be given the widest opportunities and encouragement for active personal participation in all recognized community activities, to the end that they will merit recognition as good citizens as well as good merchants."[38] The Community Chest "made giving less an act of personal

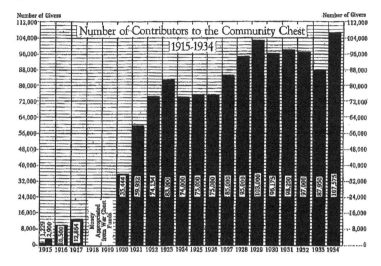

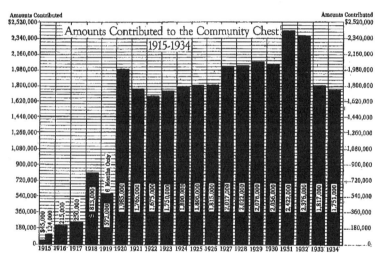

FIGURE 3. Cincinnati Community Chest. Source: The Community Chest of Cincinnati and Hamilton County, *The First Twenty Years, 1915–1935* (Cincinnati, Ohio: The Community Chest of Cincinnati and Hamilton County, 1935), pp. 35, 43.

charity than a form of community citizenship, almost as essential as the payment of taxes."[39] But unlike taxes, these funds were controlled by private committees, often dominated by members of the business elite rather than social workers and reformers. This configuration of obligation diffused broadly into community networks and practices, consolidating a model of "localized" citizenship that combined the performance of civic virtue with increasing centralization of fiscal control.[40]

These consolidating networks of municipal control were challenged on multiple fronts, by rivals both old and new. Responding to disappointing enrollments in the late 1920s, the national leadership of the American Red Cross instructed chapter membership committees that "in places of business one of the office force [is] to be appointed by the employer at the request of the Roll Call Committee direct or preferably through a Chairman of a business group of which that firm is a unit, to canvass his fellow employees. People should be asked to join by those they believe have a right to ask them."[41] Annual drives would appoint chairmen to serve as liaisons to particular target groups: unions, women's clubs, and above all workplaces. In this way, calls to participate in a community or national drive could be embedded within immediate networks (and, indeed, relations of authority) at the same time that they were linked into national fund drives, thereby bypassing the federated control of municipal elites.

Where such group-based relationships existed, the returns could be impressive, as evidenced by a report from A. C. Sprague, the employment manager of the B. F. Goodrich Company in Akron, Ohio, a few years later.[42] Published shortly after Franklin Delano Roosevelt's inauguration, Sprague's account summarizes the effort to articulate individual choices to give with the bureaucratic hierarchy of increasingly large firms through a system of pledge cards distributed at the workplace that authorized deductions from contributor's paychecks. The plan was simultaneously egalitarian—including everyone "from President to Office Boy and from Superintendents to Sweepers"—and implemented through "department heads and distributed to the individual employees." Above all, the plan was formally voluntary: "The employee followed his own judgment—no pressure—no sales talk—no coercion—no follow-up. If he turned the card in he was thanked. If not, no questions were asked." More than 40 percent of the 10,000 "members of the B. F. Goodrich organization" participated, representing almost half of the total enrollments for the entire Ohio county.

The fund-raising campaign at the Goodrich plant embodied both the strengths and the stakes in this method of mobilizing social networks. As Mr. Sprague made clear, one of the virtues of this arrangement was that it both built on and contributed to the "group-mindedness" of his employees, reinforcing their relationship to the company. "Our people participate in a contributory Group Life Insurance plan, and in contributory Group Sickness and Accident Insurance. We are uniformly successful in group support of our local Community Chest year after year. We use our group purchasing power in making it possible for our people to purchase coal from any qualified coal dealer on credit at a cash price. Wherever the group buying power can be exercised without disturbing regular channels of trade, we use it."[43] But the heightened importance of membership in the corporate community potentially undercut the community-wide webs of benevolence and reciprocity represented by the federated campaigns of the nation's community chests. As historian Christopher Capozzola has argued of the First World War, American civic culture at this time was a "culture of obligation," generating heated contests over the question of "obligation to whom or to what?"[44]

The linkage of networks of charitable giving and organized business generated new grievances. Business leaders, it turned out, had a strong preference for spending on direct relief rather than the family-based case-work that defined social work as a profession. As economic conditions deteriorated in the late 1920s, the staff of agencies established long before the founding of Community Chests might be handed a budget that required cutting their own salaries as well as the proportion of resources directed to case work. In some quarters, social workers began to argue that relief should be recognized as a responsibility of public agencies—fully funded by taxes—while voluntary fund-raising should be reserved for support of the kinds of intervention that were distinctly the domain of private social work agencies.[45]

Businessmen's claim to represent the community was also contested. Critics argued that "plutocracy" was an apt description for privately supported social work: "The community chest resembles democracy in that under it the people pay a tax. But there is taxation under all forms of government. Democracy consists in the people's control of the expenditure, directly or through their representatives. Control by businessmen and representatives of existing social agencies is" best described as "taxation without representation."[46] The greater efficiency that was *the* defining advantage of federated fund-raising undercut the voluntary quality of voluntarism. The intensified fund-raising within institutional settings and workplaces transplanted the "voluntary gift" into a domain of authority, increasing "the number of the comparatively poor from whom money is obtained." This intensified social pressure to contribute—sometimes described as a "hold up"—undermined the social logic of using charity to generate moral obligation to community: "the element of free choice which is the essence of giving is excluded."[47] But these conflicts would not break out into the open until the strains of the depression overwhelmed municipally organized charitable relief, eventually reorganizing relations between voluntary and governmental action in the United States. Before that happened, there would be one final triumph for the strong form of decentralized but networked voluntarism emblematic of the First World War. It would be led by one of the celebrated heroes of that effort: Herbert Hoover.

Return of the Great Humanitarian

In 1921, Herbert Hoover left the American Relief Administration and its efforts to relieve hunger in postwar Europe in order to serve as Secretary of the Department of Commerce, where he organized a President's Conference on Unemployment that brought together experts and key stakeholders from government, business, and the world of organized charity. But convening did not lead to taking charge; Hoover argued that responsibility for meeting the problem lay at the municipal level. Arthur Woods— a former schoolmaster at Groton and New York City Police Commissioner as well as future president of the board of Rockefeller Center and grandson-in-law to J. P. Morgan—was assigned to provide mayors with information and to encourage them to appoint voluntary committees rather than calling for government contracts for public works.[48] Here, the masters of nationally mobilized voluntarism insisted that municipal benevolence take the lead.

In resisting calls for public spending, Woods and Hoover acted on their firm belief that any form of dole threatened the moral foundations of society. Hoover had invoked this argument to oppose the provision of food relief to Belgians who had the option to work for the German occupiers during the war. The same argument held for domestic unemployment. Woods recited the accomplishments of voluntary associations and government officials acting as volunteers: in Chicago, fire chiefs had required householders to clear their premises of flammable materials, creating "many short time jobs"; in Schenectady, New York, the same results were achieved by "enforcing rigidly the local ordinances concerning snow removal and the like." Churches in Dallas and the Women's City Club in Chicago canvassed members and citizens for odd jobs that could be assigned to the unemployed. Cities and towns across the country raised voluntary funds to support work relief while some municipalities were able to make emergency appropriations for public works: "The sales of municipal bonds for public works in 1921 were about double those of any previous year, and nearly three times the amount of those for any year before the war." Corporations experimented with programs of work-sharing to minimize further unemployment.[49] Yet despite all these efforts, there were continuing calls for greater government spending, whether local, state, or federal.[50] But with a return of industrial prosperity in 1922, Hoover and his allies concluded that voluntary efforts choreographed by government had been more than sufficient to the challenge.

This validation of collaborative voluntarism was repeated by the response to the catastrophic flooding of the Mississippi River in 1927, an effort led by then-Secretary of Commerce Hoover. As the flood engulfed parts of more than twenty states, Hoover appointed a special committee. The Red Cross made an appeal for $5 million to support the relief effort "but ever more serious flood conditions caused it to be doubled within a little more than a week. As it then became evident that this was still not enough, further appeals were issued that led to the final total collection of $17,000,000."[51] This mass giving was coordinated with material contributions from federal departments and agencies (including Navy, War, Treasury, Agriculture, and Commerce), state-level departments of public health, the mobilization of "federalized National Guard units (normally under the command of individual state governors), the major foundations, the American Legion, the Red Cross, and local civic mobilizations."[52] The variety of participants resembled the initial response to the San Francisco Earthquake of 1906, but it was now harnessed to a centrally choreographed system of federal leadership.

Nationalized fund-raising was critical for this response and "Hoover put the Red Cross at the very center of the no-cost-to-the-federal-government relief effort."[53] Echoing themes familiar from the Civil War, offers of small gifts were celebrated: "an 11-year-old girl arose and said: 'I have five cents; may I give that?'" Just as San Francisco, recovering from earthquake and fire, had sought to reciprocate by its support of other Americans in need, the post-flood "Roll Call" in the Mississippi Valley showed gains in membership, doubling and even tripling in some states. The official interpretation stressed that this was more than straightforward reciprocation for aid received in the past, but rather "a new interpretation of the fundamental responsiveness of the American people, which, even though it be in gratitude, is also in recognition of the fact that the people who are in distress experienced the helping hand of their Red Cross, representing their own countrymen, learned to know that it is good."[54] Joining the Roll Call was not simply discharging a debt, but signaled the embrace of a different model for citizenship.

Yet, echoing the experience of the First World War, that model embodied the contradictions of a system of national solidarity composed of associations grounded in diverse localities, entrenched prejudice, and competing identities. Again, the implications were particularly clear when it came to matters of race. Early in the relief effort, charges of severe discrimination were made. Evidence supporting those charges accumulated: African Americans provided with less help, subjected to "work or starve" policies, and held in refugee camps until "reclaimed" by the planters for whom they share-cropped. Covering the controversy in the *Chicago Defender*, Ida B. Wells-Barnett quoted a correspondent from Mississippi who asked, "why can't the Race, who are 90 percent of the actual flood sufferers, share in that $14,000,000 relief fund which the country sent freely to the flooded district?"[55] Echoing complaints that donated jam and socks were sold by the USSC, charges were made that sharecroppers were being forced to purchase food relief that had been provided as a donation from the Red Cross to plantation owners.[56] For years, critics would accuse the Red Cross of having promoted a modern form of slavery in response to the crisis.[57]

In response to these accusations, the Red Cross appointed a "Colored Advisory Commission" headed by Dr. Robert R. Moton of the Tuskegee Institute. The final report highlighted how a national framework for voluntarism accommodated local practices, however discriminatory. Officially, the Red Cross "made no differentiation in its policies between individuals or racial groups. The organization, however, is largely built upon Chapter units operating on a county-wide basis which, in the final analysis, have immediate control of local administration." This combination of relatively uniform national policy with local implementation reflecting local race relations also characterized the selective service during World War I (see chapter 4) and the implementation of emergency relief early in the New Deal (see chapter 6). The Commission recommended that "one colored worker should be appointed for every white representative of the National organization," citing initial reports that conditions had been better in camps where local African Americans had some administrative role. Such practices, the Commission argued, quoting from a magazine article by Dr. Moton, demonstrate "the wisdom and helpfulness of inter-racial cooperation, in all matters affecting the colored people—an example which would well be followed by all branches of our Government including federal, state and municipal."[58]

While Moton's complimentary comments about the Red Cross were far from universally shared, his recognition that voluntary organizations could be models for government captured a possibility of the moment. As civic organizations took on responsibility for larger and more complex crises, they developed new social technologies, new practices for penetrating and managing aspects of social life that had been relatively insulated from formal government intervention.[59] Far from constituting a bulwark against expansion of the centralized bureaucratic state, civic associations could be capable adjuncts of national efforts and make possible a distinctive division of labor between public and private, government and voluntarism. At a 1928 Citizens' Conference on "Community Responsibility for Human Welfare," Hoover observed that education had begun as an overwhelmingly private project and yet the United States had become the "first in the world to develop the responsibility of the community to free and universal education."[60] He predicted that responsibility for public health was similarly well on the path to moving from private to public responsibility.

Former Secretary of War Newton Baker laid out a similar prognosis for family welfare work, stating that "in his opinion, private agencies should not carry on services that could be conducted as well by the city government."[61]

But expectations could also move in the opposite direction, with voluntary organizations tasked with properly governmental responsibilities. In its work with returning veterans, the Red Cross recognized the danger of such blurred lines and encouraged veterans to have their checks sent to general delivery at the Post Office rather than the local Red Cross Chapter. This would avoid any impression that the chapter would "deduct for loans made to the veteran. Such a practice would be just cause to criticism. Loans should, of course, be considered an obligation by the veteran, but they should be collected on a case work basis, and not by anything savoring of a 'dunning process.'"[62]

As expectations for assistance increased, so did the vigilance with which the Red Cross distinguished itself from the government. "The Red Cross does not make loans to disaster sufferers," declared Chairman John Barton Payne in 1928. "Help is freely extended and creates no obligation of the recipients." The relief policy ruled out assistance to public utilities, roads, railroads, and public charities, and instead "deals with people and aims to put them on their feet and to enable them to be self-supporting."[63] These policies did not prevent resentment from citizens who may have once been donors but were now in need of aid.[64] And, as in 1873 and 1893, the most difficult cases were "those who should not have been poor." This category, which would swell to unprecedented levels in coming years as victims of flood and tornados were joined by those impoverished by widespread drought and deep industrial decline, required the most care and elicited the most innovation.

From Community Chest to Block-Aid

The onset of what would become the Great Depression posed an unprecedented challenge to the nation's capacity for relief and to Hoover's reputation as "master of emergencies." Predictably, the now-President returned to the methods that had served him so well in the face of famine abroad and inundation at home. Organizations such as the Red Cross and the Community Chests were generic motors that could be harnessed to new projects. Hoover also established new organizations to serve as clearinghouses for information and plans, as "trouble-shooters" and "booster engines" that would operate with and through "the Association of Community Chests and Councils (ACCC), the Family Welfare Association of America (FWAA), the Red Cross, the Russell Sage Foundation, and the religious-based charities," among others.[65] Yet his efforts to create a private

TABLE 2. Community Chests and Amounts Raised, 1914–1931

Year	Number of Chests	Amount Raised ($)
1914	1	22,437
1919	12	14,224,740
1924	180	48,850,000
1929	329	72,743,916
1930	363	75,108,792
1931	377	83,213,428

Source: Walker (1933: 1205). From data compiled by the Association of Community Chests and Councils.

"national relief fund" foundered on the competing claims of the municipally focused Community Chests and the nationally oriented (and redistributive from urban to rural and town to town) Red Cross. In the end, "all that Hoover could get was a special Red Cross drive for drought relief funds and some unpublicized Red Cross assistance in Appalachia's coal-mining towns, a program that was later taken over by the American Friends Service Committee with money from the Hoover-controlled American Relief Administration" that was left over from Belgian food relief efforts.[66] Miners and other workers in rural industries were among the first to fall between the pillars of voluntary provision, rebuffed by the Red Cross that held tight to its mandate of responding to natural disasters (which, when seriously pushed, was extended to include agricultural drought) and overlooked by the municipal networks that focused on urban workers.

But for all these shortcomings, the first wave of citizen philanthropy in response to what was becoming the Great Depression was more than impressive. The economic downturn coincided with ongoing efforts to expand the social basis for giving. In New York, the COS had gone from 8,000 donors in the early 1920s to 17,000 by 1927.[67] From this baseline, the dramatic increase in charitable receipts in 1929 represented the mobilization of private voluntary effort as an alternative to public programs, a commitment central to Hoover's vision of associationalism. The $72 million raised by Community Chests in that year represented only a fraction of the charitable contributions elicited by the distress of the Depression—albeit one that began to approach the leading source of federal "stimulus" through the $200 million appropriation for federal aid to road construction—even without counting the relief donations in still Chest-less Chicago and New York City.[68] (See table 2.)

The fall-off in Community Chest contributions after 1929 reflected not only the direct effects of economic hardship that transformed donors into would-be beneficiaries of relief, but also a growing recognition that even the most ambitious voluntary relief plans were unequal to the magnitude of the need. In New York City, by the fall of 1931, municipal relief had already been augmented by new state government bonds championed by then-governor Franklin Roosevelt as well as private fund-raising. The Prosser Committee used familiar methods of soliciting through networks of businessmen and elites to collect $18 million to provide work to the unemployed over the winter. The pressures of managing this massive relief effort began to transform key practices of private social work agencies, including even their insistence on investigation as a precondition for aid. In some agencies, "interviewers were . . . instructed to use their judgment, send such men to work at once and turn in their cards for investigation afterwards." These deviations from established norms of social work were justified on the grounds that "in any comparison of assistance through work as against that of outright relief, it is well to remember that a landlord more readily waits for his rent and that credit at the corner grocery store is continued when a man has a steady job." As in earlier economic downturns and emergencies, relief changed in ways that would minimize damage to the civic standing of the previously self-sufficient: "What happens to peoples' [*sic*] souls in a time of depression is as important as what happens to their bodies."[69] Government agencies, private social work organizations, leading businessmen, elite civic networks, neighbors, landlords, and merchants collaborated—at least in such idealized portrayals—in the effort to extend aid in ways that would preserve an appearance of self-sufficiency for the duration of the crisis.

Even before 1931 had ended, it was clear to many that the initial $18 million in private relief was not enough. Despite its novel "mass canvass" based on the newly available technology of a commercial telephone directory,[70] the Prosser Committee effort had remained a comparatively elite endeavor with 80 percent of the proceeds coming from only 3 percent of the 80,000 who made donations.[71] A confidential report to Harry Hopkins (then at the head of New York State's Temporary Emergency Relief Administration or TERA)[72] noted that some Protestant churches opposed another coordinated city-wide drive and "evidently desire to push relief in their own parishes without suffering outside 'organization.'"[73] The funds provided by the sale of TERA bonds were running low and the economy showed few signs of revival. As a stopgap, a complex arrangement was worked out in which a private voluntary relief effort, the Emergency Unemployment Relief Committee (EURC), made a loan to the city government to allow payment of wages to those on public work relief, guaranteed by funds from the city's portion of a state appropriation.

The demands of the situation had made it clear that no single, institutionally pure solution to the unemployment crisis was sufficient. Harvey Gibson, chairman of the EURC (and, in succession, president of the Liberty National Bank, New York Trust Company, and the Manufacturers Trust Company as well as Red Cross Commissioner in France and then all of Europe during World War I), underscored this point early in January 1932: "I wish to emphatically point out that the money available from the EURC for Home Relief and Work Relief is inadequate by a great amount to meet the distress existent this winter because of unemployment without the help of the City. This fact becomes more and more obvious to our Committee daily."[74] In a city weary of fund-raising, most of those who were willing to give had given repeatedly as they were solicited for pledges at work, in their clubs, by their friends. Yet the level of need in the winter of 1931–32 was greater than expected and additional relief campaigns in the following year were anticipated.

The situation called for innovation. The design of what became known as the "continuation" campaign of the EURC sought to tap donors who had not been reached by earlier campaigns. The new plan, Block-Aid, sought to collect contributions from all of the city's boroughs and to create

> a distinct permanent value in that it provides an organized group which can be called upon in any emergency for a community endeavor within any given block. And it furnishes a complete record of each of 10,000 blocks, with a description of the buildings on those blocks, the types of people living or working therein, names and addresses, telephone numbers of block chairmen, block treasurers and innumerable Block-Aiders, with their addresses, telephone numbers, and a record of the capacity and willingness to work of each during the present campaign.[75]

The intention was to look beyond the immediate need for relief in order to create a durable, centralized institutional framework for voluntarism that penetrated communities far beyond the reaches of established donor networks.

To design this plan, leading New Yorkers turned to the John Price Jones Company. The firm's founder was a veteran of the WWI Office of War Information and would be a leading figure in the modern business of institutional fund-raising.[76] The company's roots in the fund-raising for the wartime Liberty Loan campaigns were of a piece with much of the leadership of the effort in New York City. The chair of the EURC was Harvey D. Gibson. He would go on to be Red Cross Commissioner to Great Britain (1942–45) and then for all of Western Europe (1944–45), capping his Red Cross Service as National Chairman in 1946–47.[77] This nexus of business leadership and government service was amplified within the Block-Aid campaign, whose board included, to name only a few, Cornelius Bliss (son of a one-time Secretary of the Interior, long-time president of the Association for Improving the Condition of the Poor, and fixture on the boards of New York City's leading cultural institutions[78]), Henry P. Davison (son of the World War I chair of the Red Cross War Council, partner at J. P. Morgan, trustee of Groton School, and vice-chairman of the New York chapter of the American Red Cross[79]), as well as Marshall Field (of the Chicago department store fortune), banker E. Roland Harriman, Dr. Harry E. Fosdick of the city's powerful Riverside Church (and brother of Raymond who had been a leading figure in the recreational and morale efforts for the troops in the First World War), and Col. Arthur Woods, the former New York City Police Commissioner, close ally of the Rockefellers, and soon-to-be chair of Hoover's President's Emergency Committee on Employment (PECE).

But if the guiding networks of Block-Aid were elite—linking the worlds of business, philanthropy, and government—the organizational plans required more widespread enrollment of volunteers in the hope of raising funds from a wide swathe of New Yorkers in regular small donations that echoed earlier War Fund and Liberty Loan programs. Both the name "Block-Aid" and the campaign's iconography evoked wartime patriotic solidarity to support organized benevolence in response to economic crisis. (See figure 4.)

In a manner reminiscent of the Civil War's "divine method of patriotism," which had linked personal affections to Union patriotism, the plan was to harness neighborliness to meet a national economic crisis in a manner that would encompass if not erase lines of social difference and division. The hope, expressed in an endorsement from Will Rogers (comedian, screen star, and a moral voice for the public through much of the Depression), was that this would be a model that could be adopted widely:

> This isn't just one of those plans. This is the most human thing I've heard of. . . . Now if you organize into communities like you say, you have done something that no big city has ever really done before. It looks to me like other cities ought to do the same thing. . . . You can quote me as saying that it looks like the best scheme I know. You can't put it too strong. No, sir, this thing's fine.[80]

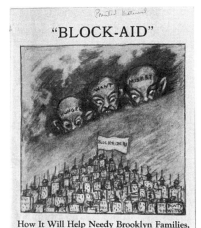

FIGURE 4. "Block-Aid" posters from the John Price Jones collection in the Baker Library, Harvard Business School.

   With an explicit commitment to find new sources of support, campaign organizers promised that volunteers would not be called on to ask
their friends for money. Instead, the campaign itself was to be a form of
work relief, particularly for unemployed white collar workers who were
exemplars of "those who should not be poor." The idea was to "staff" an
organization—rather than relying on volunteers—but to do so at a moment when the crisis itself provided a supply of men of unusually "high
caliber." "It is safe to say that there has never been a time in charity or
relief organizational work when so many men of such high standing and
unusual ability were available for organization work at almost no cost."[81]
In yet another variation on work relief, unemployed newspapermen
would craft portraits of those in need by translating case reports from
social welfare agencies into touching vignettes.[82] Publicity skills honed in
wartime fund-raising were combined with the social scientific technique
of community fund-raising to inform a demographically targeted strategy
for maximizing the results of the campaign.
   Organizers believed theirs to be the first ever "direct appeal" on radio,
complete with exhortations to "call this number now." But they combined
new technologies with familiar reliance on distinguished citizens to ask
for support. Of the four-minute radio speeches (a format that itself was
a throw-back to the Liberty Loan campaigns), the greatest response—in
terms of both donations and recruitment of volunteers to the leadership
ranks—was to J. Pierpont Morgan, who delivered his first ever radio speech
from the library of his mansion. Morgan also underscored how Block-Aid
represented citizen philanthropy, rather than the usual civic philanthropy,
in that it involved "going to everybody—to those who have little, and to
those who have much—and asking for help for relief work in such small
amounts that no one who has seen with his own eyes, or heard from others
of the greatness of the need will hesitate to give the sum asked for." Block-
Aid, he explained, "is the only plan that I have seen or heard of by which a
great sum may be raised over a period of months and without undue hardship on any giver; and a sum coming from a far greater number of people
than has ever before been brought into one common effort for the good of
the Community. We have reached a point where the aid of Governments,
or the gifts of individuals, no matter how generous, are insufficient to meet
the conditions which have come upon us. So we must all do our bit."[83]
   Morgan's appeal to his listeners as "my friends" recapitulated a theme
of the campaign, simultaneously inclusive and hierarchical. Possible Block
Captains were alerted that "within the next 48 hours an invitation will
come to you from one of the most respected men in your neighborhood
to join him as a Leader in a Great Social Enterprise."[84] These potential
recruits had been identified in an earlier stage of the project, when white

collar men of "high caliber" had surveyed neighborhoods and consulted
with branch bank managers, police captains, clergymen, school principals,
and "anyone with a wide knowledge of the residents of the district" (proposed chairmen, however "must <u>not</u> be a politician or a man too closely
identified with any political party"). The second element of the survey
was to assess the quality of the residences in order to link them to suggested contributions ranging from 10 cents per week for cold water tene-
ments to one dollar a week for the "best type homes, apartments, stores,
offices, etc."[85] Thus the plan simultaneously recognized status differences
and promised status rewards to those who participated and took leadership roles. "Block-Aiders therefore become a group of selected leaders
to whom New York will turn in any crisis. The backbone of New York."[86]

In what must be one of the most unusual "joint billings" in any speaker
series, Morgan's radio address was followed two days later by a speech by
Norman Thomas, many time presidential candidate of the Socialist Party.
Making clear that his condition for speaking was that he "speak from the
heart the truth as I see it," Thomas made a politically perceptive case
for pragmatic cooperation in voluntary fund-raising. After invoking the
spirit of the Easter season, he made clear that "I do not think Block-Aid
is intended to be, or indeed can be, a successful conspiracy of the rich to
make the poor pay for unemployment relief. Still less do I believe that it
can be that great spy system the Communists profess to fear. It is an attempt by volunteers to enlist systematic support for the Work Bureau and
other relief, which on the whole is being as well and humanely administered as funds permit and may cease operation without this aid." Having
given this highly qualified support, Thomas concluded with the hope that
Block-Aid would "convincingly demonstrate the need of far more drastic
action by public authorities. It is the plain truth that the best collector of
relief is the income and inheritance tax collector. So far the great mass of
unemployed workers have been amazingly docile."[87] As Robert Moton
had hoped for policies to promote racial equality and Herbert Hoover
feared for organized private relief, Norman Thomas recognized the possibility that the principles structuring projects of private voluntary relief
might be translated to government programs, indeed entitlements.

This highly qualified endorsement of Block-Aid was informed by a
keen awareness of the relational politics of mass fund-raising for relief.
Thomas urged Block-Aiders to "be sensitive and reverent in discovering and reporting the need that pride has hid. Let them remember that
they are part supposedly, of a democratic, neighborly civic organization;
that their neighbors' political opinions in this instance are none of their
business; and that they frequently have not the power and should not
have the gall to try to imitate some of our employers who arbitrarily tax

their workers without representation and without giving their workers a chance to explain their own burdens in order to fill a company quota to go over the top." Thomas' refrain of "democracy and brotherhood" signaled his awareness of the resentment that could be triggered by the solicitation of funds and the provision of relief. The power of employer over employee or of investigator over potential recipient could threaten the autonomy and dignity of democratic citizens. Responding to calls that this mass fund-raising effort provide 80 percent of the total "continuation campaign" in order to match the contributions of the well-to-do in the previous autumn's Prosser Committee, Thomas retorted that "they owe far more than 80% of the free surplus of the cost of existence and they did not give anything like 80% of the total relief when one reckons in the relief of friend to friend." He reminded his listeners that "we cannot be herded like sheep if we think and act like men."[88]

Recipients of this emergency relief also established a tone of equality rather than dependency and democratic diminution. The final report for the program described an employment bureau waiting room that embodied a distinctive kind of egalitarian solidarity:

> Each morning after the men were seated in the big room a member of the staff spoke to them of the Bureau's intention to treat "every man alike," no matter what his race, his religion or political creed—that every man would be interviewed in his right turn, that the man who had not a friend in New York to write a letter for him, would have just the same chance to state his case as the men who came bringing all sorts of letters from district leaders, ministers, social workers, police captains, judges or other people of prominence. It was a straight talk. The quick, sincere applause with which it was always answered confirmed one's belief that men can be counted on to respond to any appeal which smacks of what they call "a square deal."
>
> Of the general good feeling that seemed to lay hold of the waiting group one might cite this incident:—One morning, a man from somewhere in the crowd broke out in song. He sang well. The men listened. As applause ceased, someone shouted, "Let's give him first place in the front row for that." He was shoved up. And then, "who else wants to try"? Four followed—negro, Slav, Irish, Scotch. By shouted vote of "yeas," each was moved up to be part of the next group to move downstairs to the interviewing room. The practice was kept up for several days. It stopped when some men tried substituting speeches for songs.[89]

Nowhere was the complex etiquette of democratic dignity more clear than in the question of the relationship of those who benefited to those who donated. The initial idea, floated in December 1931, followed the model of the innovative East Side Relief project organized in response to the depression of 1893, in which unemployed residents were employed to shovel snow, pick up garbage, and otherwise maintain the public space on their assigned block, which might or might not be in their own neighborhood.[90] Yet organizers had learned the pitfalls of this arrangement and shifted to an arrangement that echoed the practice of decoupling giving from receiving in order to maintain anonymity. Neighbor would help neighbor, but a policy of anonymity would prevent relief from producing degrading personal dependency:

> We will make it a neighborly plan. But we do not want to embarrass families who will be supported by our plan. Therefore, we will keep their names secret. They may live around the corner from you or in the next block but you will not know it. But if you live in Greenpoint, then it will be a Greenpoint family you will help support. If you live in Williamsburg, you will help a Williamsburg family. It will be [a] plan of neighbor-help-neighbor."[91]

This arrangement located authority for identifying worthy recipients in the collaborations between Block-Aid and the relief agencies, generating conflict when "the block insisted on caring for one of its own residents and some exceptions were permitted for reasons of local policy. In general, however, each block was discouraged from selecting as its beneficiary a family living in that block."[92]

These concerns notwithstanding, the organizers of Block-Aid celebrated their project as a provisional model for campaigns anticipated for the autumn and winter to come. As a "basis for future campaigns . . . it was felt that the Block Community Organization, if successful, might prove a more satisfactory means of combing the city for small gifts from large numbers of people than was the Mass Canvass last fall. It was believed too, that many of these block units would function as local relief agencies within the blocks, caring for individual cases of need without the necessity of referring them to outside agencies."[93] In addition to this capacity for mass fund-raising, Block-Aid represented a model of voluntarism that could be widely applied precisely because it diverged dramatically from the norm of American charity practice in identifying its intended beneficiaries as "those who should not be poor":

> The majority of the people coming to us were straight, honest people. They came for one reason—a job that would mean a bit of a wage to keep them going until the turn of the tide. They were as capable of managing

their own affairs as any average group of people. They wanted relief neither from public or private purse. The pathways to the regular relief organizations were unknown to them. Time after time, when interviewers in
their attempt to determine need, dragged out brave and tragic stories of
struggle and distress, the remark was made—"Never mind that. Give me
a job and we'll pull out of this ourselves." One could make every effort
to meet them on their own high ground, (*noblesse oblige*). The Bureau
endeavored to make its rule for this group rather than for the smaller
group, who, already familiar with the many sources of relief in the city,
were among the first to crowd the doors of the newly created agency.[94]

The importance of Block-Aid in the spring and summer of 1932 did
not lie in the funds collected for unemployment relief in the last months
before FDR's election to the presidency would open the possibility for
the radically different approach to unemployment envisioned by Norman Thomas. Rather, Block-Aid contributed to a cognitive shift.[95] Those
who were most deeply committed to the power of mass voluntary fund-
raising embarked on an innovative plan and, in the end, came to understand its limits in an economic crisis of this magnitude. Even in New York
City, where the private charitable economy was more developed than
anywhere else in the nation, private funds failed to meet the needs of a
population devastated by unemployment. It had been difficult to recruit
all the necessary Block Captains. The "men of high caliber," expected to
run the bureaucratic and accounting machinery, turned out to lack the
necessary skills. Canvassers were caught between fund-raising models
built around workplaces and residential communities; commuters would
claim to have given already elsewhere. Anticipating future developments,
the final report observed that "the campaign was not made visual" (although it did have two official theme songs).[96]

Most strikingly, organizers confronted the challenges of extending a
peacetime philanthropic campaign well beyond the social and cultural
home territory of these forms of social action:

> The decision to make the campaign truly city-wide, brought the work
> into large sections such as Williamsburg, Brownsville, East New York,
> etc., whose residents have never before participated in any large phil-
> anthropic undertaking. It was necessary to build from the ground up,
> overcoming racial, political and denominational prejudices; and to give
> much time to finding salaried and volunteer workers who could deal
> with the foreign-born and often-times illiterate prospects.[97]

The extended crisis changed the terms of its own resolution.[98] Because fund-raising totals were both unprecedented and clearly inadequate, many citizens gained new information about the actual extent of unemployment and the insufficient capacity of organized benevolence to meet the challenge. None recognized these limits as thoroughly as some of the most committed and important donors: "People who had once deplored the growing proportion of relief funds coming from city and state coffers were now urging larger appropriations and more public bureaucracy, especially for areas without community chests or Red Cross assistance."[99]

Recognition of the limits of voluntary relief surfaced even among Hoover's allies and appointees to his new coordinating entities: the President's Emergency Committee for Employment (PECE), which was replaced by the President's Organization on Unemployment Relief (POUR) in 1931 and placed under the direction of Walter S. Gifford, a veteran of the economic mobilization of the First World War (chapter 4) and at the time president of both the NYCOS and American Telephone and Telegraph. Members of PECE had already broken with Hoover to support a proposal from Senator Wagner of New York that federal funds be appropriated to support state employment agencies. Arthur Woods, who had led Hoover's response to the much smaller employment crisis of 1921, resigned from PECE and "became an open advocate of federal relief grants to the states on the same basis as the grants for road building."[100] In time, even Gifford himself testified to his support for federally funded relief in principle, although in practice he thought relying on private relief was inevitable because "we have . . . built up the system the other way."[101]

The pressure that persistent unemployment placed on the barrier between federal funds and unemployment relief was felt beyond the leadership circles of government and voluntarism. Although most correspondence in Hoover's presidential files supported his opposition to linking federal funds to charitable relief efforts, at least one correspondent, a banker no less, articulated the position that would come to be dominant in the Roosevelt administration:

> I believe in the Red Cross for ordinary times and events. In the cities we have the community chest, to which I contribute regularly for the dependents of our city, but the drought is very unusual and covers the country people. I think they should be helped and that adequately; but it all should be done by law and the money raised through the income tax. No other way is democratic and fair and by it the burden falls on those who can pay it and in just proportion.
>
> Now if you attempt to raise it by soliciting methods; you will penalize the good people and put an unjust burden on them and the stingy will

not contribute. This city is typical; I know some rich citizens who will not give; no orator can touch their hearts; and the generous ones who are already doing much will be compelled to do more.

I beg of you to try and have money raised by law and taxes; no other way is fair to all.[102]

In other conversations about how to meet the crisis, arguments were made for a "both/and" approach that would appreciate the distinctive civic and psychological effects of philanthropy while not limiting relief to private funds. As one New York City businessman, Gilbert B. Bogart, wrote to Harry Hopkins, then an aide to Governor Roosevelt, "The raising of emergency funds either by contribution or by state legislation as was done by Gov. Roosevelt is absolutely necessary, but the relief must not stop there, we must . . . create a new National spirit so that those who are in a position to do so will render direct assistance to one or more of their less fortunate personal acquaintances. So organized that the people of every community will feel that it is their individual job and pleasure to help themselves by helping others." Bogart backed his recommendation with an appeal to his wartime experience "as Assistant Director of Sales of the Government Loan Organization. The problems of the masses to day I understand because they are my own."[103] One of Hoover's correspondents focused on the sheer social unpleasantness of nonstop charitable fund-raising and suggested that "a nation like this could provide food and clothes for the destitute of this year by employment mostly and if not by that means by government management supported by taxes."[104] Criticism alone would not be sufficient to generate institutional transformation, but a shift toward tax-supported relief was beginning.

Among elites and small donors alike, the extended depression unraveled commitments to organized benevolence as a method of governance. Personal unpleasantness, insufficient funds, and the uneven generosity of those deemed capable of giving by their neighbors all combined to turn one opinion, then another, against the well-established circuits of municipal benevolence. Ironically, no organization was more central to the breakdown of relationships between government and charity than the voluntary association that had long been closest to government: the American Red Cross.

Benevolence Politicized

Hoover's signature initiatives in response to the growing economic crisis embodied his commitment to generating relief from the very system of private employment and production that was shuddering under the strains of the depression. In the autumn of 1930, he had turned to familiar models of collaborative voluntarism and established PECE, and later POUR, to address the problem of industrial unemployment and to forestall the growing demands for some sort of government intervention to relieve suffering and need, both in the nation's cities and in the drought regions. Hoover also pressured the Red Cross to move beyond its traditional mandates defined by war and natural disaster to address the destitution produced by severe drought. In this effort, he met with strong resistance, securing only a special Red Cross drive for drought relief rather than a broad organizational commitment.[105] But these efforts did not prevent the eruption of controversy in Washington. By December 1930, open political conflict over relief broke out. President Hoover accused Congress of introducing $4.5 billion in relief measures (a figure arrived at by counting every reintroduction of measures) and of "playing politics at the expense of human misery." Congressional Democrats fired back, even as many of their Republican colleagues rose to the defense of a President who had consistently failed to consult them on policy and legislation.[106] Thus as Hoover promoted an unprecedentedly expansive vision of voluntarism, the response was a more insistent articulation of the legitimate role of the federal government in relief.[107]

With the confluence of massive drought and increasing industrial unemployment at the end of the decade, the implications of this script for charitable citizenship became explosive. In the context of a widespread economic downturn *and* a federal income tax that fell more heavily on the rich, President Hoover and his allies fiercely opposed any program that would create a pipeline between the U.S. Treasury and direct relief.[108] This connection between relief policy and the tax code would surface again late in the year when the U.S. Treasury announced that it expected that over $1 billion in deductions for charitable contributions would be taken on income tax returns.[109] Senator Thomas Heflin (D-Alabama), a recently defeated lame duck, chimed in, arguing that "no one calls the huge donations to the railroad companies a dole. No one calls the millions donated to the shipping interests a dole. They have been granted by the hundreds of millions of dollars. But the very moment we ask for help for those who are weak and those who are destitute and those who are hungry, it becomes a dole." Senator Hattie Wyatt Caraway (D-Arkansas) underscored this attack on the categories that had organized debates over public and private charity for a century or more: "everywhere we hear highbrows declaring their opposition to the dole, just as if a charity from the government is any more a dole than a charity through the Red Cross. Of course, Red Cross dole is not Government dole; but any form of charity is a dole."[110] And if all government spending was a dole, the options were either to cut all spending or to morally reconfigure "the dole" into the entitlements of the modern welfare state.

As forces in Congress condemned the ineffective response to the drought and famine (not to mention industrial unemployment), both options were considered. Senator Caraway (D-Arkansas) proposed that $15 million be appropriated for the Department of Agriculture to make loans for the purchase of food, while the House considered a joint resolution to appropriate $30 million to the American Red Cross "for the purchase of food and clothing for the purpose of relieving distress among the unemployed and in drought-stricken areas, and for other purposes."[111] As these debates intensified, they focused on a set of distinct issues. First, what were the resources available to the Red Cross and how were they being used? Members of Congress recited details of Red Cross finances: its assets, various endowments, the division of resources between the national organization and the local chapters.[112] The question of whether relief should be restricted to the victims of the drought or should also include the urban unemployed sparked sharp sectional differences. Finally, and most furiously, debate flared over the possibility of appropriating public funds to be spent by the Red Cross.

In many respects, this proposal should not have been controversial. In both the World War and the 1927 flood, Red Cross efforts were sustained by large quantities of supplies from the U.S. Army and other public agencies. The Depression-era Congress would often look back to these precedents, quoting the House debate of 1919, albeit with some confusion as to whether $100 million to Europe or $20 million to Russia for food relief was at issue. But it was generally agreed that there should be no direct cash transfer between the federal government and individual citizens; voluntary associations were to intervene lest a true dole do damage to its intended beneficiaries. "The one thought that inspired their intense activities at that time was that the distribution ought not to be made by the President, but that it ought to be made by the American National Red Cross. At that time the Red Cross never raised its voice against distributing Federal funds. It was willing, apparently, to take $25,000,000 of the money of the people of the United States and go across the sea and enter the soviet republics and administer to sufferers there the funds of the people of the United States."[113]

But not all recipients and currencies were morally equivalent.[114] Throughout Congressional debates and press coverage, the distribution of goods owned by the government—whether military tents for the homeless or surplus grain and cotton—appeared far less threatening to citizen virtue and to the organizational character of the Red Cross than did any distribution of government money to those in need. Consequently, controversy focused on an amendment offered by Senator Joseph Taylor Robinson (D-Arkansas) to appropriate $25 million from the U.S. Treasury to be given to the Red Cross to provide food relief.[115] To preempt the Robinson proposal, Senator Reed (R-Pennsylvania) offered an amendment (eventually defeated) to delay the decision on an appropriation until the outcome of the Red Cross $10 million drive was known. Playing defense for the administration, he argued that "the very integrity of the Red Cross is at stake, and I think we ought to postpone a Government contribution to give the Red Cross a chance to put through the drive which they themselves have started to fill up their funds by voluntary offerings."[116] But in the wake of much heated debate and parliamentary maneuvering, on January 19 the amendment was passed by the Senate (56 to 27) with the support of Democrats as well as of a group of insurgent Republicans.[117]

The House, which was more closely allied with the President than the Senate, then took up the issue with what many perceived as delaying tactics. Although highly unusual, the House held hearings on the amendment that some of Robinson's allies suspected were intended to ensure that a vote would not take place before the scheduled adjournment of Congress on March 4. Hugo Black, then a Democratic Senator from Alabama and later an Associate Justice of the Supreme Court, contrasted administration support for a loan program that covered animal feed and seed with its opposition to federal support for food relief. Black's caustic commentary clarified how methods for delivering relief had become aligned with distinct partisan positions: "we find the administration forces holding hearings to prove the soundness of philanthropy for the mule and parsimoniousness for the citizen. . . . The governmental feeding of a mule is the quintessence of patriotism, while the governmental feeding of a hungry child will destroy the pillars of the Republic."[118]

Hoover confirmed this analysis: "My own conviction is strongly that if we break down this sense of responsibility of individual generosity to individual and mutual self-help in the country in times of national difficulty and if we start appropriations of this character we have not only impaired something infinitely valuable in the life of the American people but have struck at the roots of self-government."[119] Within the Red Cross, the national leadership allied with Hoover to rebuff calls from local leaders for government relief. Under the banner of "Save the Red Cross!" the *Washington Daily News* challenged "the judgment of those 11 board members who presumed to reverse the very purpose of the Red Cross and refused the duty laid upon the Red Cross by the congressional charter under which it operates."[120]

With consideration of the Robinson Amendment slowed in the House, some Senators began to warn of the need for a special session. In the meantime, the Red Cross intensified its efforts to raise $10 million for drought relief, aided by public statements from Hoover and a committee formed of leading political and business figures. The high stakes—both humanitarian and political—in this fund drive led to new procedures, including a decision in New York City to "depart radically from its policy of past campaigns for relief funds by dropping its traditional method of merely receiving contributions from those motivated by the spirit of generosity. Instead, it will begin the first personal canvass in its history in solicitation for funds."[121]

By this point, of course, the city's Prosser Committee and the "extension campaign" of the Emergency Unemployment Relief effort had demonstrated the possibilities. For large donors, the political implications were also clear; John D. Rockefeller Jr. specified that his $250,000 contribution was contingent on Congress *not* approving a federal appropriation.[122] Early in February, a new compromise ended the deadlock between House, Senate, and White House with the approval of an agreement to add $20 million to loan programs for "agricultural rehabilitation." Although there was no specific mention of using the loans for food, supporters of the Robinson amendment reassured themselves that one could not have agricultural rehabilitation with dead farmers. The Red Cross fund drive continued on through February, passing the $10 million target only after the middle of March. Contributions arrived slowly.[123]

These congressional debates over drought relief highlight conflicts over the appropriate relationship of voluntary relief to public funds. Hoover argued that the first line of response to crisis should be voluntary and that only after voluntary, local, and state efforts had failed could federal aid even be considered. Yet he contended that the power of voluntarism was so great that this last resort would never be required:

"I will accredit to those who advocate Federal charity a natural anxiety for the people of their States," the President said. "I am willing to pledge myself that if the time should even come that the voluntary agencies of the country, together with the local and State governments, are unable to find resources with which to prevent hunger and suffering in my country, I will ask the aid of every resource of the Federal Government, because I could no more see starvation among our countrymen than would any Senator or Congressman. I have faith in the American people that such a day will not come."[124]

Even such discussion of the possibility of public relief, some argued, might endanger the efficacy of voluntarism. Alternatively, such debates could incite a flurry of private charity to forestall government provision of relief. As Congress deadlocked, a contributor of $100 to the Red

Cross explained the delay of this gift: "I should have sent this check earlier had there been no talk of a large appropriation of the public moneys by Congress. It now looks as if the public moneys will not be used for this purpose unless private subscriptions prove inadequate. The American Red Cross has never yet failed to raise from private sources the money needed in an emergency like this. I hope it will not fail now. At any rate I want to do my part."[125]

For President Hoover and his allies, voluntarism was both central to what it meant to be American and antithetical to government intervention. In opposing the Robinson Amendment, they invoked the distinctive character of the Red Cross and, by extension, all voluntary associations.[126] Representative Tilson, the Republican Majority Leader in the House, amplified this argument, asking, "Shall we stab [the Red Cross] to death and make it a cold, lifeless thing by substituting for it a governmental bureau, bound with red tape, administering a Federal dole?"[127]

The supporters of the Robinson amendment did not dismiss the distinctive virtues of voluntary organizations. Instead they argued that the suffering of drought victims outweighed any damage that could come to the Red Cross from handling government funds. They minimized the capacity of federal dollars to corrode charitable motives by pointing to the many precedents for collaboration that ranged from floods to foreign relief. With loans for food off the table in Congress, at least for a time, Congressional advocates of federal drought relief attacked the categories that underlay the opposition of voluntarism and direct government aid: "The objectors to the appropriation of $25,000,000 characterize this appropriation as a 'dole' and that it is socialistic meaning 'state socialism.'" Rejecting this argument, Mr. Granfield (D-Mass.) asserted that "to render assistance when an emergency exists is not a 'dole,' neither is it 'state socialism.' It is the response of humanity to the justifiable call for help, and the effort of the Government to assist its distressed people, performing a natural and proper duty."[128] The struggle over the respective responsibilities of the Red Cross and the government had become deeply embedded in class politics.

If the champions of voluntarism had one discourse about the morality of money, those in need of relief had others. Without diminishing the generosity of others, the sting of charity-induced dependency was fierce. Speaking for his constituents in the state hit hardest by the drought, Senator Thaddeus Caraway (D-Arkansas) insisted that "no one down in my State . . . wants charity. We have lots of poor people, but they wanted to preserve their lives and their self respect if they might be allowed to do so. . . . They would rather have been allowed to borrow and to pay even exorbitant interest rather than to have to apply for charity. Lots of them will suffer before they will accept it. But this proposal is the only thing now before the Congress. We have to have it or get nothing."[129] The words of one Arkansas farmer undercut every celebratory account of the Red Cross: "Asked why he had not applied for aid, he replied that he had known the Red Cross during the war overseas and 'God help me if I ever thought I'd have to ask them to feed me if I got home alive.' His wife suggested that maybe 'we have held our heads a little too high, but it's hard to get down in the class of the shiftless.' "[130] In the pages of the *New York Times*,[131] an Arkansas state legislator drove home the point: "Our distressed people have been humiliated by men of national prominence, and it is up to us to take care of them." These "reckless, desperate citizens"[132] were not only humiliated, but they might prove dangerous to those very privileged interests that opposed federal direct relief and its demands on income tax revenues: "When they see their loved ones starving, sick, and dying, it is enough to make Bolshevists out of them; it might make communists out of them."[133] Senator Copeland (D-New York) warned that "we sit here so complacently, imagining that the social structure is safe; that the political structure is beyond danger!"[134]

Ironically, one of the sites of destabilization lay within the Red Cross itself. While the national leadership, drawn from privileged circles and closely allied to President Hoover, defended a bright line between government funds and charity, many members and local volunteers had a different understanding of the responsibilities of their organization. As a federally chartered voluntary association whose mandate derived from an international treaty, the legal form of the Red Cross was deeply at odds with the dominant model of voluntary association as fundamentally participatory. Informed by that cultural model, many of those attending the National Meeting of the Red Cross in Washington, D.C., in April 1931, thought that they should have a say in Red Cross policy toward relief. The conflict over the Robinson Amendment was still fresh. In order to suppress an incipient rebellion among the volunteers, the national leadership devoted a keynote session to a lecture by their legal adviser on the corporate nature of the American Red Cross. This lawyer emphasized that the Red Cross was not a democratic, grass-roots organization but a *corporation*. The organizational charter was held by the national entity and chapters operated only by charter from that entity.[135] Consequently, Red Cross activities aligned more easily with hierarchies of charity and benevolence than with the egalitarian reciprocal relationships of mutualism that had such strong bona fides in American political culture.

Like so many episodes in Congressional history, the controversy produced relatively little in policy and perhaps less in results. Ultimately, many farmers were unable or unwilling to take up the terms of the agricultural loan program. Yet the arguments made during these two or three months early in 1931 capture an important turning point in the politics of public and private relief. By defending the voluntary character of the Red Cross as moral and fundamental to American identity, Congressional opponents of the Robinson amendment provoked a rethinking of the meaning of charity in a democratic society. By staunchly opposing any federal programs of drought or unemployment relief, Hoover firmly embedded voluntarism generally—and the Red Cross quite specifically—in a highly partisan coalition.[136] Hoover's opponents responded with fierce arguments about the class-based nature of the opposition to federal relief, creating an opening to rethink relief as compatible with democratic citizenship. In seeking some way out of the deadlock between charity and "the government dole," politicians began to elaborate different understandings of the role of voluntarism and of the relationship of citizens and the federal government.

Although Congress adjourned as scheduled in March 1931, the Depression continued and with it efforts to provide relief through public or private means. In June, Governor Pinchot of Pennsylvania, a progressive Republican, called on the Red Cross to aid the hungry children of miners, arguing that the state had exhausted its funds. The chairman of the Red Cross, Judge John Barton Payne, denied the request, explaining that the "organization deals only with emergencies,"[137] which by definition could not be prevented by the responsible behavior of moral individuals. Anticipating a new wave of demands for relief in the winter of 1931–32, Walter S. Gifford of POUR continued coordinating relief efforts. Localities mobilized fund-raising drives in anticipation of the winter's needs. In New York City, both old-line charities such as the Association for Improving the Condition of the Poor and depression-creations such as the Emergency Unemployment Relief Committee joined in helping thousands of individuals and families.[138] The Red Cross continued to address rural famine and drought-driven devastation, penetrating into local economies and family decision-making to an unprecedented degree.

But this intensification of voluntarism was a last gasp, even for the Hoover administration. During the next Congressional session, the Red Cross figured only marginally, as a vehicle for the distribution of large quantities of government-owned crops and cotton to the needy.[139] Looming larger was the creation of the Reconstruction Finance Corporation, which would make loans to the state for public works that would generate employment. But although private charity had proven inadequate to the need and inappropriate for citizens, the question of whether public money could be a legitimate—and sufficient—source of relief remained. Although robust intervention would wait until Roosevelt's inauguration in 1933, the arguments over drought relief challenged the cultural

categories that made moral distinctions between public and private relief. In the words of Senator Walsh (D-Massachusetts), "two things about
this [Robinson] amendment are objectionable: First, to take money from
the public funds and give it to a private agency; and, secondly, to let the
private agency administer the fund when we have Government officials
in every section of the country and whose activities will not cost us a dollar."[140] By rejecting claims for the superior moral virtue of private relief,
those opposing strong claims for voluntarism prepared the ground for
direct forms of federal relief for those in need.

There was also a positive moral case for federal relief grounded in a
model of reciprocity between citizens and states. As articulated by Congressman Edward Eslick (D-Tennessee):

> These very families in distress contributed their sons to the American
> Army as offerings on the western front to save the civilization of the
> world. The folks back home, of their means and through their taxes,
> contributed to the $100,000,000 appropriated February 25, 1919, as
> a revolving fund for furnishing foodstuffs to the hungry people of Eu-
> rope. . . . We who have seen the generosity of the Nation shown to the
> hungry people of the Old World wonder why it is that our women and
> children, without fault on their part, come with outstretched hands to
> the Congress of the United States and say, "We are hungry and need your
> help," get the answer that we can not feed you because it means to adopt
> the dole system in the United States.[141]

Here, paying taxes, making voluntary contributions, and sending sons
to war are all evidence of the generosity of citizens and proof that they
had "always already reciprocated" for relief. Given this prior generosity,
they could receive aid in times of distress without endangering their status as full citizens. But for this emergent understanding to take institutional form, the political conditions would have to change. And that did
not happen during 1931 or 1932.

Despite the glaring inadequacy of voluntarism in confronting the economic crisis, the early years of the Great Depression left a lasting mark
on the articulation of private associations and public agencies. Much of
that legacy lay on the "private" side of the boundary constructed between
state and society. Fund-raisers moved toward a more encompassing
definition of community responsibility, developing new techniques for
enrolling participants across lines of class, ethnicity, race, and religion.
However imperfectly executed, these efforts represented a significant re-
orientation of the geometry of civic gift-giving. Campaigns such as Block-
Aid sought to repurpose the circuits of wartime nationalist philanthropy

at the scale of cities and towns in economic distress. Reliance on the exclusive networks of elites and business leaders gave way to an imperfect version of generalized exchange in which all were supposed to give so that all in need could receive.

This emerging configuration suggested a resolution of one of the most durable and potent contradictions between the relational geometries of charity and liberal citizenship: the damaging dependency generated by the unreciprocated gift. Whereas the nineteenth-century charity organization societies had decoupled horizontal circuits of reciprocity among donors from the vertical authority of social workers over clients, at least a few of the municipal relief programs of the early Depression—notably Block-Aid—went further to reconstruct the experience of asking for and receiving relief. Anonymity shielded beneficiaries from donors; in some cases, the presumption of moral failing and chiseling was displaced by the working assumption that applicants (or at least some of them) were "straight, honest people," in the sense of "those who should not have been poor" (see chapter 3). These developments were far from universal; private relief continued to reinscribe hierarchies and exclusions based on gender, race, and ethnicity and these same categorical inequalities would be built into the core Social Security programs of the New Deal through the exclusions of agricultural and domestic workers.[142] But in the last flourishing of private voluntary relief before Hoover's electoral defeat, some proponents of voluntary relief began to find a path beyond the incompatibility of dependency-inducing relief and self-sufficient citizenship. Although the momentum would soon shift to the expansion of federal and state relief, the challenge would remain to make public provision "Free. Not as Charity. But as a Right."[143]

6

In the Shadow
of the New Deal

In our American scheme of things it has been proved again and again
that progress in matters concerning the welfare of the people of our
nation is best obtained not by leaving everything to the Government,
but by having strongly organized groups of informed citizens working
through volunteer agencies to aid, amend and stimulate government
agencies.

"The Citizen & Social Welfare"
Charity Organization Society of New York, c. 1935[1]

Four years into the Depression, Herbert Hoover's commitment to voluntary relief was profoundly discredited. Across the nation, private
charities, religious organizations, and mutual associations had failed to
meet the unprecedented calls for assistance. Thus when Franklin Delano
Roosevelt took office in March 1933, policy turned sharply toward federal
funding, state matching grants, and public administration of relief. The
Federal Emergency Relief Administration (FERA), under the leadership
of Harry Hopkins, embodied this new approach. In his first regular order
to state governments, Hopkins established that "grants of Federal emergency relief funds are to be administered by public agencies. . . . This ruling prohibits the turning over of Federal Emergency Relief funds to a private agency. The unemployed must apply to a public agency for relief, and
this relief must be furnished direct to the applicant by a public agent."[2]

In retrospect, this turn from private charity to public relief has seemed
unremarkable. Overwhelmed by the crisis, voluntary organizations were
clearly not up to the task—a conclusion reached by many donors and
private social workers as well as those in need of relief.[3] In such tellings,
the Depression is a catalyst for the "laggard" United States to catch up on
the path toward a modern welfare state taken by other industrial democracies. Yet, at the time, not all voluntary associations shared this assessment. Instead, they argued, private charities constituted an impressive

infrastructure for the delivery of publicly funded relief.[4] Stung by Hopkins' policy, Red Cross leaders advised one another to lie low until government programs inevitably failed and they were again called upon to take the lead in meeting the crisis.[5] Why should the government create or adapt an alternative to the national network of private charities that was already in place and only in need of new funds to sustain their relief efforts?

This hoped-for return to delegated governance through voluntary associations was far from unfounded. The Depression might well have taken the form of an extension—and intensification—of long-standing practices of public subsidy to private charities. Hopkins, after all, was a product of the world of private charities. He began his professional career in a New York settlement house, moved to the Association for Improving the Condition of the Poor, and, after a spell with New York's Bureau of Public Welfare, served for two years as the Gulf Coast Regional Director for the American Red Cross.[6] In Congress, there were ample precedents for appropriating public funds for disaster relief.[7] In addition to providing supplies and funds for crises such as the San Francisco Earthquake of 1906 and the Mississippi Flood of 1927, Congress had made major appropriations for foreign relief, notably in the aftermath of the First World War and in response to the Soviet famine of 1921–22. So even if President Hoover had been adamantly committed to a voluntary approach to emergency relief, why was the well-established model of appropriating public funds to support the work of voluntary associations not adopted by the incoming Roosevelt administration?

The bright line that Hopkins drew between public funding and private organizations reflected the long history of struggle over the role of voluntary organizations in responding to disasters, particularly the intense conflicts over the appropriate response to the massive drought and surging unemployment of 1931 and 1932. Charity had been politicized as the nexus of relationships between the well-off and the needy, between citizens and the state. As the Works Progress Administrator for Pennsylvania declared late in 1934, "wherever organized exploitation is conducted on a grand scale, organized charity, too, must operate on a similar basis."[8] If exploitation were eradicated, organized charity would be marginalized. Yet just as the New Deal failed to align with the existing division of labor between government and voluntarism, that infrastructure was not abandoned.

Given that the Roosevelt administration began with a stark expulsion of private charity from public programs, we might expect this "turning point" to produce a purely public regime for securing the social and economic rights of citizenship.[9] In many respects, the New Deal exemplifies the classic conditions for institutional change: a once-dominant institutional logic overwhelmed and discredited; a significant change in control of political power linked to advocacy of an alternative model. Yet even this combination of delegitimated institutions, powerful economic shock, and entrepreneurial advocacy of an alternative did not expunge private charity from American governance. While the depression would erode the categorical logic in which receipt of charity was antithetical to citizenship and the domain of rights, it would also open possibilities for novel combinations. The result was a deeper incorporation of voluntarism into the national project and the organization of governance. In a dialectical fashion, the encounter of the New Deal with the world of private charity both intensified long-standing contradictions and generated a novel synthesis that would come to be embodied in the postwar "nonprofit sector." Nurtured by expanded tax exemptions and multiplying "partnerships" with government, this newly named nonprofit sector would figure centrally in subsequent expansions of governance at all levels, local, state, and federal, as well as in resistance to those expansions.

Over the course of the 1930s, the division of labor between public and private shifted from Hopkins' bright line to a more complex collaboration between government agencies and voluntary associations.[10] Whereas Hoover had championed voluntarism, Roosevelt's speeches articulated a model of generalized reciprocity—enacted through taxes as well as charitable contributions—as the moral basis of democratic citizenship.[11] Like Hoover, the future members of the Roosevelt administration were familiar with the choreography of voluntarism and government, but after years of crisis they had become deeply disappointed in these methods.[12] Following the sweeping electoral victories by Democrats in 1932, they turned toward a more purely public system in which federal funds flowed to state agencies staffed by government employees. In the process, a clearer boundary was drawn between the jurisdictions of public and private fund-raising and relief efforts. For a moment, a cleanly articulated division of labor between private voluntary agencies and government programs seemed possible.

But members of the administration, including Roosevelt himself, soon discovered the limited capacities of the federal government. In response, private agencies continued to transform some of their hallmark methods and mandates. Business allies successfully advocated for privileged treatment of their contributions to support such private voluntarism and began to rehabilitate arguments for voluntarism as an alternative to and bulwark against big government. As the Depression extended through the end of the decade and the warnings of another global war intensified, a still more far-reaching recombination of public agencies and voluntary organization took shape.

Prelude to the New Deal

In 1931, then-Governor Roosevelt sparked a public conversation about how to best respond to the Depression. At his urging, the State Legislature of New York had approved a $20 million dollar bond issue to relieve unemployment during the winter of 1931–32.[13] The act began by firmly establishing a division of labor: "While the duty of providing aid for those in need or unemployed because of lack of employment is primarily an obligation of the municipalities, nevertheless, it is the finding of the State that in the existing emergency the relief and assistance provided for by this act are vitally necessary to supplement the relief work accomplished locally and to encourage and stimulate local effort in the same direction."[14] Those municipal efforts—as in 1873, 1893, and 1920 (see chapters 3 and 5)—involved varied combinations of public funds and private fundraising.[15] The key shift in New York was the addition of state-level bond financing for the Temporary Emergency Relief Administration (TERA) to this well-developed infrastructure for providing an admittedly minimal level of relief in an economic downturn.

Suggestions came from across the country as to how best to use the funds to meet an increasingly unprecedented crisis. Some correspondents proposed public programs that would also solve their personal economic dilemmas, whether through the purchase of potatoes from Idaho or beans from farmers' cooperatives to feed the people of New York. Larger policy goals—retirement pensions, taxes that would limit chain and department stores, or suspensions of the union wage scale—were offered as remedies for the employment crisis. Others advocated funding road work as a source of manual labor or proposed familiar utopias of agricultural settlements for the urban unemployed. As one man explained, "I am and I believe every good citizen is opposed to charity, because charity breeds idleness and idleness breeds crime and surely we have too much of both, at this time. I think the men in charge of the distribution of that money should purchase a large tract of land, one on which you could work from five hundred to a thousand men for as many months as the depression lasts; in addition to furnishing that many men work you could build up the property and make it worth many times the original cost, and make it a foundation for future emergency." He did, of course, have his own piece of property already in mind for sale to the state government.[16]

A very few endorsed an expanded charitable effort, augmented by public funds. One of the rare advocates of this approach criticized the way in which the role of churches in relief had been dismissed by one TERA official and urged that "the churches from Coast to Coast" make a survey of the poor. With these new government funds, the churches would "now be as well equipped as the Salvation Army. We all know the Salvation Army Relief is 100%—every dollar counts—not so when rendered by political organizations." Such an arrangement would have the added advantages of bringing "those who are in distress under the good influence of the churches" and of reaching "a class who are too proud to go to the public or political places for relief."[17] Still others drew explicit parallels to the civic mobilization during the Great War, calling for the creation of a network of advisory committees and activities that would "create a new National spirit so that those who are in a position to do so will render direct assistance to one or more of their less fortunate personal acquaintances." With the appropriate effort, "the people of every community will feel that it is their individual job and pleasure to help themselves by helping others."[18]

For the most part, those who mentioned charity did so to underscore the point that the unemployed wanted jobs "not charity." This sentiment also militated against an expansive system of government relief. Discussing the possibility of supporting FDR for president, one correspondent observed that if the Governor were to consider a large-scale loan to help the unemployed, "we know . . . it would be used for the benifit [*sic*] of the people by putting them to work at building certain things which would help the people in general to get something for their money instead of having a DOLE which would only tend to make the people lazy like they are over in England."[19] As another correspondent observed, "Charity is a wonderful thing if properly placed. But in a good many cases it is a breeder of bums. The country spends millions for Charity and not one half reaches the proper channels it is either made a football for the Politicians or made a subject of petty graft."[20]

But notwithstanding this seemingly blanket rejection of charitable methods, the same letters often endorsed practices familiar from the voluntary fund-raising. The insight that large sums could be raised if many people gave just a little informed a number of the proposals sent to Governor Roosevelt and his State Relief Administration.[21] Ever hopeful that one such scheme would also provide employment for himself, one repeat correspondent sketched plans to raise funds by asking those with savings accounts to spend a portion, by banning cars more than five years old from the public streets, and even by leveraging one of the most vital of everyday purchases:

It might interest you to know that there are about three million cups of coffee sold in Greater New York during a period of twenty-four hours. Now if you set aside a Coffee Day and have a committe [*sic*] get the nickel for the one cup that the public would drink extra on that day which I believe everyone would do for the great cause, you will benefit $100,000 or better without anyone being put out.[22]

A few writers went beyond the standard declaration of "jobs not charity" to detail the difficulties of extending relief to a newly recognized group among the unemployed: white collar workers. For them, it was argued, the methods of social workers were so offensive that they would rather starve than to accept relief. As in earlier economic crises and natural disasters, here was another group of "those who should not be poor." J. W. Boies, writing "on behalf of a Pacific Coast Group of non-partisan welfare workers" to President Hoover but copying Governor Roosevelt among others, invoked the " millions of capable citizens who, while seeking honest work, will starve rather than apply to Charitable Organizations."

Civic dignity was at the heart of their concerns. "Agents of Welfare Societies—with the best motives—are entering such homes to pry into the private affairs of many of these self-respecting citizens of this American Commonwealth" who desired only work of a sort that they could perform, being "unsuited for the heavier construction kind on Roads, Tunnels, Buildings etc." One proposed remedy was an emergency food credit plan to allow white collar workers to keep shopping through the winter, preserving both their physical existence and their dignity. The receipt of aid would be hidden while their exercise of consumer choice would be publicly visible: "some such plan for Food-credits will accomplish more in responsive citizenship of higher-standards than a cruel recourse to the present Bread-lines or enforced appeals to Charity by those millions of Uncle Sam's Voters, who will soon be looking to the new Administration for immediate relief from their long enforced state of un-employment."[23] As with earlier programs to support soldiers and sailors, public programs needed to provide adequate relief in ways that would not corrode the civic virtue of beneficiaries.

What the TERA actually did was refund 40 percent of the funds spent by municipalities on qualified forms of relief. State policy drew a bright line between work relief paid in cash and "work for relief" (in the form of food baskets or clothing or coal) which was ineligible for the state refund.[24] The goal was to use public funds to sustain a labor market in a time of low demand, not to create a generalized entitlement to relief. This decidedly limited endorsement of government responsibility was consistent with the philosophy that Roosevelt had expressed to the graduating class of Syracuse University in June 1930, requesting "the intelligent interest of the younger generation in answering how much further this extension of governmental functions shall go." Rather than "adding new functions year by year" in response to "a sometimes ill-considered popular demand," he urged the graduates to contribute to "such a careful and intelligent study . . . that we shall be able as a sovereign people to outline a structure of government limited definitely in its functions."[25] Events pushed the governor and soon-to-be President to add more programs and revenue to state government than he could have foreseen at the time of this graduation speech. Although he understood the state as an "organized society of human beings, created by them for their mutual protection and well-being,"[26] Roosevelt's ideal of a "government limited definitely in its function" raised persistent questions about the appropriate division of labor between public programs and voluntary efforts.

Government Limited Definitely in Its Function

Roosevelt and his administration came to Washington, D.C., in March 1933 with experience in using substantial public funding for relief and a recognition that the political meanings of private charity had been transformed. In the aftermath of the 1930–31 fight over the Red Cross and drought relief, voluntarism was now firmly linked to the Republican party and long-standing moral arguments for private charity were starkly opposed to an emerging discourse of relief as a democratic entitlement. This discourse might idealize reciprocity between citizens and state as had been done by Representative Eslick, who invoked those citizens who had "contributed their sons . . . as offerings on the western front."[27] Others, including Roosevelt as Governor, had already asserted the fundamental responsibility of the government to care for its citizens because the opportunity to work was shaped by social conditions and economic policy: "home relief is in no sense charity. Home relief is being given to individuals to whom *society will have failed in its obligations* if it allows them to suffer through *no fault of their own*."[28] Government responsibility for providing employment had to be assumed in order to legitimate federal relief for unemployment.

To transform the category of relief, the right personnel had to be recruited to staff a program based on shared responsibilities across local, state, and now federal jurisdictions.[29] His successor as governor of New York, Herbert Lehman, implored FDR to refrain from appointing Harry Hopkins to head the new federal relief administration.[30] But, when it came to the services of Harry Hopkins, nation trumped state. With the creation of the Federal Emergency Relief Administration (FERA) in May 1933, Hopkins moved rapidly to consolidate the dominance of public agencies and their independence from private charity. This effort required a great deal of political arm-twisting to get state governments to appropriate the required matching grants.[31] In the process, the core relationships of relief—among the needy, the case workers, politicians, and local elites— were haltingly realigned with federal policies and programs.[32] Although volunteers and private charities continued to promote their own role in the national project of relief, Hopkins persisted in pulling relief into the public domain. Following up on his first order that federal funds could be expended only by public agencies, by early summer he signaled that personnel would have to shift from private agencies and be sworn in as public officials before August 1, 1933.[33]

For all his official efforts to draw a bright line between government and charity, Hopkins did not fully abandon the world of private charity and philanthropy. Correspondence to the FERA came in on the same forms used by social work agencies for confidential referrals; Hopkins also used the methods of case work investigation, with multiple confidential interviews, to map the political landscape of states and cities as he developed strategies for implementing federal aid provisions. Like those who had been in charge of Hoover's unemployment programs, Hopkins made his way to the Rockefeller Foundation to request support for the new emergency relief effort. Even if government was to be the primary funder of relief, private philanthropy was needed for support that would be less easily secured from Congress. In particular, Hopkins wanted data, a request that aligned more closely with the mission of the Rockefeller Foundation than had Hoover's earlier request for support of demonstration projects in family food provision.[34] The Special Trustee Committee allocated $50,000 to support five statisticians to work on a census of relief cases being carried out by FERA. In order to maximize the economic and policy benefits of this award, "work relief clients can be used to carry on the details of the work."[35] Private philanthropic support of government research on the implementation of public policies simultaneously generated public employment as work relief. The allegedly bright line between public and private relief was blurred from the start.

As a Right, Not as Charity

Looking only at flows of public funds, the exclusion of voluntary agencies was all but complete by the winter of 1933–34. In New York City, these private organizations were distributing more than twice as much in 1934 as they had in 1929.[36] But as a proportion of the total, private relief spending had dropped from over 25 percent of the total relief spending in 1929 to less than 4 percent by 1934 (see table 3). Public funds (not including the "semi-official" sources) had increased from over $7 million to more

TABLE 3. Relief Spending in New York City, 1929–1934 ($)

	1929	1930	1931	1932	1933	1934
Private Agencies[a]	2,549,881	5,289,771	15,354,435	18,821,275	13,211,332	6,016,099
Semi-Official Agencies[b]	n/a	361,451	2,135,606	3,689,018	2,643,250	1,850,406
Public Agencies[c]	7,493,412	9,021,041	28,768,074	57,673,506	93,427,242	157,161,233
Total	10,043,293	14,672,263	46,258,115	80,183,799	109,281,824	165,027,738
Private as percent of Total	25.4	36.1	33.2	23.5	12.1	3.6
Public as percent of Total	74.6	61.5	62.2	71.9	85.5	95.2

Source: "Private and Public Agencies' Relief Outlays for 5-Year Period," *New York Times* (July 28, 1935), N2.[d]
[a] Includes the American Red Cross (NYC and Brooklyn), the Salvation Army, various professional, charitable, and family service agencies.
[b] Includes the Mayor's relief committee and the School Relief Fund of the Board of Education.
[c] Includes state work projects, city work relief, Home Relief Division, Department of Public Welfare, and the Board of Child Welfare.
[d] As the source note explains, the table presents "the figures on unemployment relief expenditures by private and public agencies for the years 1929 to 1934 inclusive. They do not include the cost of administration of relief or institutional relief expenditures by the city and private agencies, such as those involved in the operation of the municipal lodging houses and shelters by the Salvation Army."

than $157 million and now constituted over 95 percent of the total expenditures for relief in New York City. Both funding and personnel rapidly shifted to the public sector. The passage of the Social Security Act in that year—with its programs of old age and unemployment insurance along with aid to dependent children—promised to further diminish any role for private relief. But in a society where accepting aid was deeply tied to assumptions of dependency, "it would be necessary first to remake many of the fixed attitudes" and to overcome "this state of the public mind . . . a moral coma with an effusion of evil."[37]

With strong endorsements from the President on down, Harry Hopkins set out to implement economic relief understood as a right, not as charity. As recently as 1932, the *Chicago Tribune* had called for the "disfranchisement of the unemployed."[38] Rejection of the equation of relief with dependency and, therefore, disqualification for full citizenship involved more than changing political etiquette.[39] The legitimation of public relief was a complex practical project of implementing a new right of citizenship that would displace models of charity that both informed the practice of social workers and were a source of shame for those in need. To accomplish this, Hopkins turned to a cadre of experienced professional social workers. The roster of those recruited to FERA included Aubrey Williams, who had been a social worker in Ohio and Wisconsin (and would go on to lead the National Youth Administration).[40] The Civilian Conservation Corps (CCC), the first of the New Deal programs to create jobs for the unemployed, was headed by W. Frank Persons, who had worked both with the NYCOS and, during the war, for the Red Cross.[41] Frank Bane came out of the regulatory world of state boards of charity and would soon become the first head of the Social Security system.[42] Many had internalized the lessons that the first years of the Depression had taught about the limits of voluntarism and private relief in the face of a global economic crisis.

These formerly private social workers maneuvered between well-established relief practices and the new priorities of Roosevelt's administration: "There was not time to cut a new pattern."[43] Not surprisingly, the Red Cross was a particular source of conflict. Touring the Dakotas, where people were wearing rags and subsisting on soup made from Russian thistles, journalist Lorena Hickok did her job as the eyes and ears for Hopkins: "They say the Red Cross is holding back a lot of clothing throughout this area, and they are very bitter about it. The Red Cross people say they have to hang on to it, 'to meet emergencies.' Good God. I'd like to know what constitutes an emergency in the eyes of the old ladies who seem to be running the Red Cross!" Further conversations with the head of one local Red Cross Committee confirmed that flannel, quilts, and clothing were stockpiled in a padlocked storeroom in readiness for some more deserving crisis.[44]

But even those social workers and government officials who supported the new policy—including Hickok and many federal appointees—brought beliefs and practices from the pre-Depression world of social work and social relations.[45] Many of these involved strong assumptions of social inequality and morality that were at odds with Roosevelt's pronouncement that the needy would not endanger their standing as citizens by applying for relief. The Federal Emergency Relief program of 1933–34 was exceptionally unrestrictive in specifying the qualifications for relief. The only qualification was need, whether the needy were male or female, married or single, black or white, or even on strike.[46] But the long tradition of making fine categorical distinctions about worthiness for relief was not easily displaced. As Hickok toured the country in those years, she repeatedly noted how relief administrators made special efforts to preserve the dignity of their white relief applicants and, above all, their white white-collar relief cases. When possible, these formerly white-collar citizens would be given cash relief, rather than grocery orders, and social workers took what care they could to protect these people from the indignities of "intake" offices and home visits.

These efforts reflected a challenge that would have been familiar to charity workers of the 1890s or to the Red Cross staff assembled in San Francisco in 1906. "Charity methods" were understood as stigmatizing because they had been meant to stigmatize, to make both public and private relief unattractive to those in need. Consequently, when these methods were deployed as "standard operating procedure" in an economic crisis of unprecedented scale, the meanings long associated with social work practice were not easily erased. From Salt Lake City, Hickok reported the assessment of one veteran social worker that relief clients "seem to mind most being 'regimented.' They hate like poison having certain days set when they may visit their case worker in her office. They loathe being investigated all the time. They want to be 'on their own' with wages. However little, to spend as they see fit."[47] The shift from private to public management did not resolve the underlying relational tensions.

Many newly governmental social workers also remained committed to the case work method, which required investigation before relief and interventions tailored to the needs of particular individuals and families. Unlike the "mass" relief of soup kitchens and breadlines, this individualized treatment was championed as a method of preserving the moral character of citizens as they survived on relief through a difficult but presumably abnormal time. But even with these good intentions, the transposition of social work methods and personnel to the public domain created new threats to the civic standing of relief recipients. Businessmen sought to verify credit applications against the public relief rolls. Absolute confidentiality, they argued, was not warranted because "this is no longer a matter of the social worker supplied with private charity funds who can deal more effectively with a relatively few problem cases if working in secrecy." To have the disbursement of "hundreds of millions" of public monies "clouded in secrecy certainly gives a wonderful opportunity for abuse and corruption."[48]

Under the earlier system of relief administered through private voluntary agencies, these invidious distinctions had been drawn outside the domain of formal rights and obligations. Even as fund-raising had become increasingly rationalized and efficient in large communities and corporations, smaller towns managed the tricky etiquette of raising money within communities to help members of those same communities. Organizations such as the Junior Red Cross sought to avoid the stigmatizing equation of aid with inequality by coupling broad-based giving—including from the needy themselves—and unmarked receiving:

> Here is Jimmy Jones. It is winter and his feet are almost on the ground. His father has been out of work for weeks and another pair of shoes is too much of a strain on the family budget. Jimmy hates to go to school in those old "dogs" of his. Then one day he is furnished with a good new pair, and he doesn't mind sitting next to the well-shod John Smith. Now, John Smith, like Jimmy, is a Junior and he has contributed money to the Junior fund which bought those shoes for Jimmy, but he has not the slightest notion how Jimmy got them. The fund is wisely administered by the Junior chairman of the local Red Cross Chapter in consultation with the school authorities, that no child may acquire a smug and patronizing attitude towards those his money has aided.[49]

For the Junior Red Cross, adult supervision of the expenditure of funds insulated the equality of membership from the inequality of benefits. By decoupling giving from receiving, anonymity could be maintained as it had been in the Block-Aid effort in New York City a few years earlier. But once relief was funded by the government, the cloak of anonymity that had been deployed to protect the dignity of those on relief was condemned as an obstacle to accountability for public funds.

The transfer of responsibility for relief to government also made it less easy to evade or obscure the contradictions between formal political equality and deeply entrenched social inequality. In a society characterized by deep racial and gendered inequalities, there simply was no mathematical solution to a relief allotment that would be both uniform in terms of government policy and culturally appropriate given assumptions of racial hierarchy held by much of the electorate. In 1930s America, where some citizens were widely assumed to be more equal than others, local officials were ever aware of (and often sympathetic to) the dangers involved in a program that was to serve both whites (and particularly those who had lost white-collar jobs) and "thousands of Mexican and Negro families" along with American Indians. As one Texas official told Lorena Hickok, "If it's a choice between a white man and a Negro, we're taking the white man. . . . We've got to, because of the mental attitude of the whites. We've been threatened with riots here." In her letters to Hopkins, Hickok herself repeatedly returned to the central dilemma of how to implement an equal right to relief in a society marked by stark inequalities of race and class. She pondered with evident moral discomfort whether government should keep nonwhites, particularly domestic and agricultural workers, "out of peonage and on relief, thereby, unless we spend a whole lot more money, actually forcing the white man's standard of living down to that of Negro and Mexican labor?"

To finesse these contradictions between categorical inequalities and the concept of equal rights, a system of differentiated relief was used in some locales. Hickok provided a particularly detailed description of the arrangements in Tucson, Arizona, where relief applicants were put into one of four classes on the basis of a combination of occupational skills, social status, and race. Each group had a separate intake system and office: "no mixing." The most privileged group ("engineers, teachers, lawyers, contractors, a few former businessmen, architects, and some chemists who used to be connected with the mines") received not only the largest amount of relief ($50 per month) but also the largest proportion in cash (50 percent). In Class D, the almost 1500 "low class Mexican, Spanish-American, and Indian families" received $10 a month, all in kind. While setting different standards for different types of recipients (a familiar practice in the earlier world of private charity) might circumvent the problem of aligning equal rights with social hierarchies, Hickok didn't "see how the Federal Government could go in for that sort of discrimination."[50]

The establishment of a right to relief also required acknowledging the political standing of recipients with respect to the other rights of citizens.[51] According to FERA policy, if "clients" "wish to join labor unions, or the leagues or councils of the unemployed, we have assumed they have a right, as American citizens, to do so."[52] Just as the administration of relief was not to marginalize citizens in hierarchical relations of dependence, it could not demand partisan political loyalty of government staff or undercut their standing as democratic citizens. As Aubrey Williams, assistant administrator of FERA, explained to the director of the Philadelphia County Relief Board: "no one gives up his right as a citizen when he becomes an employee of the Federal Emergency Relief Administration. Employees have all the rights which go with citizenship in this country, such as the right to organize, right of assemblage, right of free speech, etc. They have the right to criticize and express opinions."[53]

This policy entailed a complex choreography of the roles of citizen, social worker, and professional above politics that disembedded federally funded relief from the civic and political networks that had structured the organization of municipal benevolence.[54] Public funding for the care of voters and their dependents, delivered as a subsidy to a private charity organization, was the functional equivalent of a Thanksgiving turkey, a Christmas basket, or a job on the city payroll. These patronage relationships were threatened by the Hopkins rule that federal relief funds be handled by public officials employed by public agencies, many of whom were professional social workers with a record of hostility to patronage politics.[55] The pushback was particularly fierce in Chicago, where a consolidating Democratic machine had mobilized against the nomination of FDR in favor of a second presidential run for Al Smith.[56] Once elected, Roosevelt needed allies in state governments to authorize the "matching funds" required by many federal programs and to manage the implementation of relief programs without doing damage to the reputation of the administration. Faced with an unreliable partner in the Democratic governor, Hopkins and Roosevelt made accommodations with the Chicago Democratic machine and one of its most important constituencies: the powerful organized Catholic Charities of the city. In a move that undercut the authority of professional social workers in one of their great municipal strongholds, Hopkins made one striking exception to his insistence that public funds be handled by public officials employed by public agencies. For the purpose of delivering relief in Cook County, the Archdiocese of Chicago was recognized as a public agency.[57]

Even where religious and private charities were unable to secure such major concessions, the space for private charitable efforts was not eliminated. Assuming that the government could restore a functioning economy, problems would still remain: "Unemployment has become an agglomeration of population problems, and relief has been asked to take care of them all. Adhering to the magnetized core of pure unemployment are all the steel shavings of our disorganized and shifting age. If we demagnetize the core the accretions fall away. We can put them back where they came from or we can find a new place to put them." For private agencies, the goal was to reinvent themselves as the "new places" for these problems, "the steel shavings of our disorganized and shifting age." The result was not the displacement of private and voluntary social provision but its transformation.

The Transformation of Private Relief

Following Hopkins' rule that federal relief would be administered solely by public agencies, private organizations regrouped yet again. Whereas Roosevelt and Hopkins suggested a functional division of labor aligned with different kinds of "adjustment," private charities claimed a role as innovators and experimenters, as "the pathfinder in method and technique."[58] A NYCOS pamphlet from the mid-1930s argued that the COS has "complete freedom of action and thus can deal with distressed men and women, not in mass fashion but as individual persons, each with difficulties peculiarly his own. Such an experienced organization is able, in the course of its daily work, to throw light on many of the larger social questions now confronting us—unemployment, housing, delinquency and crime, mental suffering, broken homes, child guidance. It becomes, in a very real sense, a human welfare lighthouse, constantly revealing to the public the underlying causes of our social ills." In this way, private innovations might identify paths forward for public policy. Significantly, the final page of the pamphlet is devoted to a list of "milestones" that "the C.O.S. has created or had an important part in creating." These included city and state agencies, two new kinds of courts, laws, and new private voluntary organizations, associations, and exchanges.[59]

This contrast of the mass quality of public relief with the individuated services provided by private organizations was a central feature of the emerging division of labor, echoing earlier arguments made by the Red Cross for its distinctive role in working with veterans of the World War and their families.[60] In a follow-up report on their Christmas appeal of 1935, the NYCOS explained that "the Society's contribution is the personal service of our caseworkers—assistance in meeting new and baffling situations, guidance in health, housing and vocational matters, protection for children, help with household budgets, and continuous friendly efforts of many kinds looking to the preservation of family morale and the restoration of self-confidence and self-dependence."[61] Among the leaders of private charity, this argument came to be known as the "rehabilitation thesis." The role of private agencies in providing advice and mediating between individuals and a complex world rife with "new and baffling situations" justified continued support of private charity despite greatly expanded government funding of relief.

But tax support for relief also required that charities take great care in the demands that they made of supporters to give voluntarily as members of the community. Since the onset of the depression, corporations and individuals had been asked to give twice, as taxpayers to support public relief as well as private donors who would make a routine annual contribution and go "over and above" to meet the excess caseload produced by the employment crisis. But, Arthur Packard of the Rockefeller philanthropies argued, "the 'over and above' basis cannot be justified any longer with the large sums of money from public sources." Private agencies would need to develop a new mission, to cut "their coat according to their cloth in one of two ways; either by relinquishing their independent campaigns and join in a functional group campaign or abandoning their practice of receiving contributions from the same source twice through this method."[62]

In New York City, the Citizens Family Welfare Committee adopted the "rehabilitation" rationale by acknowledging that the city was helping

320,000 families at a monthly cost of $18 million while private charity supported only 20,000 at $500,000 per month. But despite this apparent financial insignificance, the Welfare Committee argued that "the people helped by the private agencies have involved problems. They require too much study, understanding and intensive work to fit into mass relief."[63] Echoing the rationale for giving responsibility over veterans to the Red Cross (chapter 4), prevention and rehabilitation tailored to individual cases constituted the core mandate for private charity. It was critical, the Welfare Committee argued, to pay attention to "what taxes don't do."

> Taxes go into the great fund the Government is using to keep people alive.
> They provide these people with mere subsistence.
> They do not get down beneath the surface.
> Tax funds cannot be used to support the private agencies. Government funds cannot by law be applied to support of private institutions.
> The alternative would be to scrap the private agencies, demolish the whole fabric of human relationships they have built, and start from scratch.
> **Otherwise private relief and private support must go on.**[64]

The "rehabilitation thesis" did not presume a stark division of labor between private and public efforts, but rather a much more complex and dynamic relationship between voluntarism and government. A vibrant voluntary sector, it was argued, would improve the quality of government programs while preserving qualities of individual and social life that would be damaged by direct contact with the mass, uniform character of public relief. Government relief might sustain those in need, but only private welfare agencies—so they claimed—could restore citizens to self-sufficiency.[65] As some leaders within voluntary associations and private agencies recognized, "We should not bury ourselves in the rut of our own Red Cross experience; for a rut, after all, is nothing more than an elongated grave."[66] This would require experimentation and innovation on the part of private agencies.

During the first years of the Roosevelt administration, this case for going beyond the "mass relief" of government programs often had a decidedly partisan edge. Community Chest campaigns "repeatedly conjured up an image of federal domination to rouse Americans to new heights of private effort" and appealed to conservative businessman "by laying particular stress upon private philanthropy, individual responsibility, and local control."[67] Yet such arguments did little—at least initially—to dampen federal pressure on states, counties, and municipalities for the creation of new public relief agencies and to appropriate the matching funds required by federal relief authorizations.[68] This shift to public spending reinforced a more clearly democratic understanding of the criteria for distributing relief and a more restricted sense of the clientele for private agencies: those with particularly complex and compound needs, requiring special help to be rehabilitated toward self-sufficiency.

As private agencies redefined their mission, they also sought to reestablish their financial stability by recruiting a new set of donors. Although the plummeting decline in overall individual charitable contributions finally reversed in 1934 (as measured by deductions from the federal income tax, which was still overwhelmingly a tax on elites), these gifts were redirected from traditional charity and relief toward fine arts, religion, and, above all, education.[69] With this shift in the philanthropic attention of the truly wealthy, local charitable organizations renewed their efforts to build the broad-based popular support and participation that had been introduced to municipal fund-raising by the Community Chests and campaigns such as Block-Aid in New York City. For example, the NYCOS appealed "at this time for *members rather than money*—for a strengthened interest among the citizens of this community in a program of social work endeavor which has stood the test of more than half a century and which, judged by experience, was never more important than today."[70]

This emphasis on members reflected an ongoing shift in strategy for major voluntary relief agencies. Hewing to the principle that "for the people, by the people" applied to charity as well as government, a philanthropic yet democratic solidarity could be fostered by expanding the number of contributors and extending practices pioneered by private employers in earlier fund-raising drives. Rather than a union or employer responding *seriatum* to each request for support, firms and government agencies adopted policies of automatically deducting a set amount or percentage from each paycheck and then pooling these contributions (however truly voluntary) so that they could be allocated either by managers or by a designated employee committee. In New York City, city employees were expected to make a 1 percent payroll contribution. Post office workers, firemen, and policemen responded to the intensification of fund-raising by creating general funds, financed by monthly payroll contributions (up to 25 cents for firemen, 10 to 50 cents for policemen).[71] In many appeals, one of the first actions was to appoint chairs for business, labor, professionals, and other organized groups.[72] Disaster preparation also reinforced occupational identities, with dentists and others laying out plans for rapid mobilization in times of need.[73] As Andrew Morris has argued, these were important, if often unrecognized, precedents for war bonds and payroll tax deductions during WWII.[74] Systems of workplace-based giving, increasingly linked to the routinized technologies of regular payrolls, reoriented key pieces of fund-raising machinery away from both networks of elites and the web of churches, community associations, and fraternal orders long central to American conceptions of civil society.

Thus the first years of the New Deal were marked by parallel lines of development in the financing of relief. The first—far larger in scale, political salience, and public visibility—was the dramatic expansion of tax-funded, government administered relief and the passage of Social Security programs that were portrayed as if they were individually funded savings accounts rather than dependency-inducing gifts from other taxpayers.[75] Moving along a second track, private agencies reconfigured their fund-raising and their organizational missions.[76] The move away from strong categorical distinctions between the worthy and unworthy poor that had been evident in Block-Aid's characterization of applicants for relief as "straight, honest people"[77] now took the form of a call for individualized treatment of complex cases.[78] Given that the federal government had taken on unprecedented responsibility for supporting the unemployed, those who were in a position to make large donations were in no hurry to transfer that mandate back to private agencies, although many very much hoped to limit the duration and scale of the federal experiment. But as private voluntary associations turned toward business for support, their relationship to both labor markets and business strategies was also being transformed.

"In Just the Same Careful Way as Investing"

If Harry Hopkins had sought to draw a bright line between government relief programs and the world of private charity, the response to his efforts had the effect of blurring the lines between business and voluntary associations. While private relief organizations had long counted on business leaders as major contributors, many such businessmen failed to subject charities to the same expectations that they would apply to a contract or acquisition (see chapter 5). Strong ties between individual agencies and their supporters often thwarted efforts to impose financial discipline, particularly in cities—including both Chicago and New York—that had not yet established a Community Chest system.[79] But, because private charity now made jurisdictional claims in terms of "what taxes cannot do," these organizations opened themselves to increasingly strict expectations with respect to efficiency and efficacy. As John D. Rockefeller Jr. asserted in 1932, "giving ought to be entered into in just the same careful way as investing. . . . Whether we expect dividends in dollars or in human betterment, we need to be sure that the gift or the investment is a wise one and, therefore, should know all about it."[80]

John D. Rockefeller Sr., his father, had constructed a family office that provided him with research and advice in responding to requests for donations. But, if private giving as a whole were to be as careful as that of the largest philanthropists, it would be necessary to create a shared method for evaluating the work of private agencies. These efforts often took the form of "information bureaus" that, like rating agencies such as Dun and Bradstreet,[81] reported on the legitimacy and financial status of potential recipients of charitable contributions. But the establishment of such an agency could allow a single charitable organization to gain influence over a broader field of activity as the charities endorsement committees of local chambers of commerce had done in many cities a decade or more before. In New York, the COS acknowledged that its own donor-serving Bureau of Information and Advice was perceived as such a threat. But as private charities added auxiliary functions, they also blurred their identity as charities in the eyes of the public and, perhaps more importantly, of their donors.[82]

The logic of accounting in the gift economy of private charity was not easily aligned with the business methods of the day nor could it be purged of implications for the distribution of power. As corporate donors and major philanthropists sought to make the world of private voluntary agencies accountable in business terms, they generated a surge of "going to scale" similar to that produced by the mobilization for the First World War. Organizations did not simply persist or fail, they transformed themselves. Two of the strongest and most established bastions of private charity—the NYCOS and the Association for Improving the Condition of the Poor—merged in 1939 to form the Community Service Society, an organization that would be at home in the nonprofit sector of the postwar years.[83]

As private agencies conformed more closely to "business methods" and became accountable to major donors, many charitable organizations also became less "voluntarist" in the core sense of relying on volunteers. As the organizers of Block-Aid had recognized, fund-raising could become a source of paid work relief that was particularly suited to white-collar workers. Voluntary agencies and not-for-profit institutions became sites for—rather than providers or adjudicators of—unemployment relief. Early in the Depression, emergency relief had added work relief in nonprofit agencies to the more familiar forms of temporary public works and city projects. In 1931, New York City's emergency relief payroll "for January was $1,519,570. Of this amount $863,299 was paid for labor on city properties, the balance, $656,271 for labor in non-profit institutions."

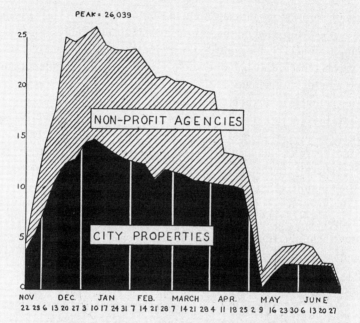

EMERGENCY WORK BUREAU
RECORD OF PLACEMENTS MADE
NOVEMBER 17, 1930 TO JULY 1, 1931

PERSONS
EMPLOYED
(THOUSANDS)

PEAK = 26,039

NON-PROFIT AGENCIES

CITY PROPERTIES

NOV   DEC   JAN   FEB.   MARCH   APR.   MAY   JUNE
22 29 6 13 20 27 3 10 17 24 31 7 14 21 28 7 14 21 28 4 11 18 25 2 9 16 23 30 6 13 20 27

The top line shows the total number of persons employed
by the Bureau. At the time of the peak of 26,039 there were
15,000 employed on city properties, and 11,039 in nonprofit agencies.

45

FIGURE 5. "Emergency Work Bureau Record of Placements Made." Image courtesy of the Rockefeller Archive Center (OMR II 2 F, Economic Interests, Box 21,
Folder 177).

Many nonprofit agencies were initially reluctant, questioning "how such
people could be fitted into their somewhat specialized work."[84] But—
particularly in the winter months and particularly as a response to the
problem of responding to white collar unemployment—nonprofits accounted for a substantial portion of the sites for work relief.[85] (See figure 5.)

By 1937, a study of 85 settlement houses found that various "workers whose services were, in a sense, volunteered by the government," represented a third of the total staff, including those paid by the Works Progress Administration (WPA) or the National Youth Administration with relatively little regard for the specific programs and needs of the settlement houses. Not quite one-quarter were "regular paid staff" with the remainder comprising "volunteers giving regular service," students, and residents who were not counted among the paid staff. The class character of the volunteers also shifted in some settlements as it became "increasingly difficult" to get middle and upper class volunteers. "The unemployed were a hitherto largely untapped source. Settlements found that many of these people would 'offer their services for the sake of having something to do' and to keep their skills, such as typing, from getting rusty."[86]

Just as voluntary agencies came to resemble workplaces, the magnitude of the crisis also scrambled clean divisions between business investment and charitable giving. Private individuals could contribute to relief in ways that resembled business investment rather than charitable giving. As John D. Rockefeller Jr. summed up the family's contributions to meet the unemployment crisis late in 1931:

> I am giving immediate work to men at Rockefeller City in the amount of millions of dollars. Mr. Debevoise could get from Fr. Todd an estimate of no. of men to be employed there bet. now and next June also probable total wages that will be paid them. At Tryon Park I am spending about $2,000,000. Mr. Fosdick can put similar data there. In view of these facts which it may be well to publish, certainly to tell Unemployment Com, my present feeling is that $1,000,000 from Father and me will be our full share and probably more.[87]

As the scale of tax-supported relief programs expanded during the early New Deal, business leaders made stronger demands for accountability and efficacy, while voluntary associations came to understand themselves as sites of employment as well as vehicles for good deeds and moral uplift. The result was a deeper interdependence of business wealth and the budgets of voluntary agencies. The question of "how to pay" infused a broad range of policy issues, including the ratification of the 21st Amendment that ended Prohibition and renewed the excise taxes on alcohol, thereby lessening demands to expand taxes on the wealthy. But post-Prohibition alcohol taxes were insufficient to compensate for expanded government spending and the still meager tax revenues generated by a depressed economy. Eventually, the Roosevelt administration proposed legislation that would be adopted as the 1935 Wealth Act, better known as the "soak the rich" tax,[88] which raised both individual and corporate income taxes as well as estate taxes for the wealthiest. But, at the urging of representatives of the Community Chest movement, the administration accepted one amendment as the bill made its way through Congress: an allowance of a charitable deduction for businesses capped at 5 percent of income.[89]

This amendment resolved an area of legal ambiguity. Since at least the 1920s, some firms had deducted charitable contributions as normal business expenses based on the claim that they served to cultivate community goodwill.[90] But the legal status of this practice was uncertain. During the First World War, banks that were regulated by the federal governments (or by state governments whose regulation piggy-backed directly on federal regulations) had received special authorization from Congress to contribute to the War Funds; the War Revenue Act had also allowed for the deductibility of charitable contributions from individual income taxes (see chapter 4). Early in the Depression, similar legislative authorization for charitable contributions had been given to a number of public utilities by the New York State legislature.[91] Other corporations made their relief contributions indirectly, by issuing special dividend checks accompanied by a suggestion that the check be signed over to the American Red Cross or some other relief effort.[92]

Even as federated fund-raising campaigns had come to depend significantly on corporate contributions, the status of these contributions was unsettled: did managers have the right to divert profits from stockholders? These principal-agent questions, which would infuse classic discussions such as Berle and Means' *The Modern Corporation and Private Property* (1932), were circumvented by decisions to distribute special dividends to shareholders.[93] Yet many corporations continued to give directly, despite the uncertain status of these expenditures. They also often deducted those contributions as business expenses—for the cultivation of "goodwill"—until the practice was decisively overruled in a 1934 decision.[94] Incited by increased rates of taxation on the wealthy, philanthropists joined corporations to reverse this decision. By simultaneously endorsing corporate charitable contributions and high tax rates on wealthy individuals, this combination of court decisions and public policy constituted a pivot point in the financing of private charity.

The creation of the corporate charitable deduction introduced new categorical exclusions related to political activity. Corporations could deduct up to 5 percent of their income as charitable contributions, but "to qualify for this exemption, a corporation could not give to an agency whose major function was legislation." This chilling effect added to the disapproval of political activity by agencies that was already felt in many Community Chest cities. "As early as 1937, Lea Taylor, head of Chicago Commons, stated that tax exemption provisions 'had been used by the Council of Social Agencies (CSA) as a means of preventing action on social legislation.' Hence, the granting of tax exemptions for charitable contributions restricted the social action programs of private organizations. These restrictions were not present during the Progressive Era and may partially explain why settlements were more involved in reform in the early 1900s."[95]

If the tax code created a new legal framework for nonprofit organizations, another key exception was introduced by the Social Security Act. In order to protect religious organizations from federal legislation, employees of all nonprofit organizations were excluded from the provisions of federal social insurance programs. Private social workers quickly recognized that they were disadvantaged by this arrangement and advocated loudly and long for passage of an amendment that would bring them under federal jurisdiction in this respect.[96] But, once adopted, the exclusion of benevolent organizations from federal mandates was fiercely protected by others. This seemingly minor element of the Social Security legislation would, in time, allow for the development of a substantial beachhead of organizations outside the mandates of federal labor law. A loose thread was incorporated into the path-dependent developments set in motion by the Social Security programs, one that would be pulled much later as religiously affiliated schools and hospitals claimed exemptions from multiple federal regulations.

Finally, for those who had championed the public provision of social support, other policy developments steadily erased the bright line between public funds and private agencies. By 1935, federal funds were permitted to flow to private homes for the elderly and other exceptions followed.[97] As one veteran policy activist lamented, "virtually unchallenged and undebated, the principle established with the first large-scale federal welfare program, the Federal Emergency Welfare Administration [*sic*], that public funds should only be expended by public agencies, was quietly repudiated."[98] But whereas this reversal is often associated with the expansion of federal social programs during the 1960s War on Poverty programs,[99] the turn to new forms of collaboration between the federal government and nonprofit organizations had begun in the very shadow of the New Deal. Thus before the beginning of the Second World War, the financial footing for a recognizably modern nonprofit sector was in place.

Business contributions to private agencies not involved in politics could function as part of a political strategy. By the late 1930s, champions of voluntary efforts were explicit in their challenge to preempt expansion of the New Deal—particularly to health care and higher education—by demonstrating the financial and managerial potential of private fundraising.[100] Opponents of the New Deal continued to invoke the Red Cross as an alternative to expansion of public programs, arguing "that the Federal Government in its distribution of relief should have more widely availed of the voluntary services of this agency of its own, which was, during and following the World War, the most extensive and efficient instrument of mercy that humanity has ever known." Conservative critics of Social Security also held up the Red Cross as a model of "appropriate financial responsibility." In 1938, the John Price Jones Company—the fund-raising firm that had designed the 1931 Block-Aid program to support private unemployment relief—was working with the Sentinels of the Republic to raise funds for "a moving picture show, making a popular demonstration of the wasteful and dangerous policies of the Government, employing humor and satire."[101]

As John D. Rockefeller Jr. put it to the honorary chairmen of the 1939 Greater New York Fund campaign, the reasons for participation included concern for the welfare of the city's citizens as well as commitment to cooperation "among Catholics, Protestants and Jews irrespective of race or creed," but also out of concern that "failure to support adequately these privately operated health and welfare agencies may mean ultimately the taking over by government of their functions—an eventuality to be avoided at all costs."[102] Here, JDR Jr. echoed Tocqueville's classic account of voluntary associations as a bulwark against the expansion of the administrative state or, in his language, despotism. For proponents of the New Deal, therefore, an independent and oppositional population of private charities posed a potential political threat, which was described with unusual bluntness by one state administrator of the Works Progress Administration (WPA): "when I say that these economic parasites had regimented all their forces to 'gang up' on President Roosevelt, I mean all their forces, including the forces of servile organized charity—that brand of organized charity which is twin brother of organized greed."[103]

Rather than "crowding out" or displacing private agencies from their traditional activities, the mid-1930s saw a more complex renegotiation of relationships between public programs and private charities. In many cities, private voluntary agencies and federated fund-raising networks now framed their jurisdiction in terms of the "rehabilitation thesis," leaving large-scale public relief and public works employment to the government, whether local or state or federal. In endorsing the 1938 Mobilization for Human Needs (the national fund drive of the community chests),[104] Roosevelt reinforced this new understanding: "Community leaders . . . have welcomed the acts of their government as a liberation of their efforts, as an opportunity to move forward on the front of social progress."[105] The president again used the social workers' language of "adjustment" to define jurisdictional boundaries: "Direct relief is aimed at many problems of human misfortune—adjusting maladjusted families, taking care of the sick, tiding over a great number of kinds of crises in family life. Work relief is aimed at the problem of getting jobs for normal people who can give useful work to the country, and seeking adjustment of a maladjusted society rather than an adjustment of maladjusted individuals."[106]

The head-to-head combat between public and private relief was de-escalated as private charities distanced themselves from the core policy concerns of the New Deal. The Red Cross focused on disaster relief and reinvigorated the concern for public health evident in its initiatives from the 1920s, reframing these efforts under the rubric of "safety." Workplace safety, water safety, highway safety, first aid—all these gained prominence in the organization's roster of activities. But as private voluntary agencies created a new role for themselves, President Roosevelt also discovered new uses for organized benevolence. After the first flush of emergency relief, the Roosevelt administration was candid in acknowledging that government could not do everything by itself. The heat and hostility toward private charity, which had been fueled by controversies such as the proposed Congressional appropriation for the Red Cross, faded as many acknowledged that neither government nor private efforts on their own were equal to the need. Together, they just might be.

Presidential Philanthropy and National Solidarity

The Rooseveltian revival of citizen philanthropy began with a very personal cause. The initial signs of a rapprochement appeared in the first year of his presidency, with the organization of the Committee to Celebrate the President's Birthday in the winter of 1934 (see Introduction). This effort, which would soon take the name of the March of Dimes, provided striking evidence of the power of civic benevolence to mobilize loyalty around the person of the president and the cause of finding a cure for polio. The March of Dimes also provided an opportunity to rebalance the debt of gratitude that many citizens felt toward Roosevelt because of their reliance on federal relief.

The case for the March of Dimes was made with multiple, familiar metaphors for national solidarity and mobilization. The call to the birthday balls—"We Dance So that Others Might Walk"—promised a synthesis of enjoyment and benevolence in the service of fellow citizens. Yet despite the upbeat message and the employment of an experienced public relations staff, the initial organizing in late 1933 and early 1934 resulted in only 3000 local committees—half the number hoped for by those in charge of the fund-raising. So, using an approach that was "90 percent political," the organizers turned to "local Democratic Party officials and patronage appointees." As one local volunteer explained, "It had to be. We had to work with our friends."[107] This rooting of a national project of citizen philanthropy in partisan ties was vulnerable to any turn of the political tide. As Roosevelt came under fierce criticism for the court-packing scheme of 1937 and recession returned in 1938, refusal to participate in the March of Dimes became one way of signaling political opposition to the president. The wife of one Republican leader captured the sentiment, declaring that "I am willing to contribute to the [polio campaign] on any day but Roosevelt's birthday."[108]

Just as Hoover's fight against federal relief funds had marked the Red Cross in strongly partisan terms, so the March of Dimes was repeatedly at risk of being coded as a Democratic rather than philanthropic endeavor. Those seeking funding from the March of Dimes recognized the implicit logic of gift-giving and reciprocity as it translated into both benevolence and politics. In 1938, a Congressman from Iowa wrote to Marvin McIntyre, Secretary to the President, forwarding a letter from an orthopedic hospital in his district "complaining that we have been unsuccessful so far in obtaining the appropriation from the Foundation for the local Children's Hospital."[109] By the late 1930s, correspondence among the leaders of the annual drive repeatedly raised concerns that "precisely the same considerations that started it now threaten to kill it—or at least make it difficult or impossible for it to succeed. . . . Over-emphasis on the President's birthday has persuaded many that it is all political ballyhoo. People—not all Roosevelt haters—won't serve or help. Some establishments won't let us solicit or put up posters."[110]

To counter claims that the voluntary effort was a partisan project in disguise,[111] FDR's close advisors emphasized that the March of Dimes produced benefits for all communities. After an experiment with a 70–30 split between the national foundation and local committees, the 1937 campaign switched to an arrangement in which all funds went to the National Foundation and then were distributed according to local need, an arrangement in which "Your Community May Receive More Than It Raises!" The text of this pamphlet explicitly invoked both the imagery of donations as "life insurance" for communities and the nationally redistributive practices of Red Cross disaster relief as opposed to the locally centered practices of the Community Chest.

But this usurpation of local control met with strenuous objections. In response, the 1938 campaign was based on "the fifty-fifty method" just like many of the core Social Security programs (although the flow of funds was reversed).[112] Half the funds raised would stay in the community to support treatment and aid to families with a member stricken by polio; half would go to the national foundation to support research toward a cure. The national foundation, these aides hoped, would take care that research grants were widely distributed throughout the country. With a close eye to the implications of ritual, the leaders of the campaign would no longer present an oversized display check directly to the President, implying that the campaign funds were a personal gift. Instead, the President would be presented with a report from the lead fund-raisers (although he would continue to be photographed with an impressive birthday cake—made and donated by union bakers—to celebrate the occasion).[113] With these changes, the March of Dimes was on track once again. By 1939, one Roosevelt aide reported that "during the period from January 20, to February 20, 1939, approximately 861,000 pieces of mail matter containing currency were received at the White House in connection with the drive to raise funds for the National Foundation for Infantile Paralysis."[114]

Even for the Roosevelt loyalists with the greatest animosity toward Hoover's program of voluntarism, the March of Dimes exemplified the broader potential of civic benevolence. In the place of the monolithic power of the federal government, campaigns celebrated the decentralized but aggregated power of fellow citizens—united in a cause that just happened to be personally important for the President. This imagery was not restricted to presidential philanthropy. A pamphlet from 1937 illustrated the "power of concentrated money" with references to how contributions to the Red Cross provided relief to tornado-struck communities, how individual efforts combine to fight a war on multiple fronts, and how individual payments were pooled in life insurance plans. "An insurance company doing a national and international business obviously serves your community better than if each city, village and hamlet were to organize its own local company. The United States, as a nation, is stronger than if each state pursued its separate plans without regard for national unity."[115] In these ways, Roosevelt demonstrated his appreciation of the capacity of civic giving to generate solidarity and inclusion, thereby contributing to the project of nation-making at a moment of economic strain and ever-imminent conflict.

Roosevelt recognized that organized benevolence was both a patriotic practice and a tactical instrumentality for a president with substantial but limited formal powers. Consequently, he worked to regain some of the capacity for action that Hoover had possessed by virtue of his close ties to the major national voluntary associations. In the winter of 1934–35, FDR encouraged giving to private charity, which would lighten

"as far as possible the relief drain on the Federal, State, and local governments."[116] Quickly, however, this image of charity taking up a portion of
the same load carried by government gave way to calls for a distinctive
new division of labor. Harry Hopkins, now the WPA administrator, addressed a national symposium on the administration of relief: "the immediate future holds out tremendous opportunities and responsibilities for
private organizations in connection with rehabilitating individuals and
families long denied the privilege of employment and normal existence.
The bulk of public assistance probably will be financed from tax funds, but
numerous opportunities will be open to private organizations to provide
intensive family service of the type which citizens are not yet ready to
accept as a public responsibility."[117] With this speech, Hopkins signaled a
new functional division of labor between charity and government. Em-
bracing a version of the "rehabilitation thesis," he foreshadowed how private foundations and the nonprofit sector would come to understand
their relationship to government in the post-WWII period as innovators
and experimenters whose successful programs would then be models for
public policy.

     Roosevelt also recognized that the Red Cross constituted a mecha-
nism for transforming the moral understanding of citizenship. Battered
with charges of partisanship toward Hoover, entangled with the large
banks and big business, and compromised by accusations that it was "essentially a war machine preparing for the next war,"[118] the Red Cross had
hit new lows. In numerous messages and speeches, FDR began to rehabilitate the organization's reputation, endorsing the linkage of voluntarism
and citizenship that had been Hoover's signature theme.[119] In a telegram
to the 1934 national Red Cross conference, the President explained that
"IT HAS OCCURRED TO ME THAT THE ACTIVITIES OF THE RED
CROSS MAY HAVE A MORE FAR-REACHING EFFECT THAN IS GEN-
ERALLY APPARENT. YOU HAVE WORKED TO DEVELOP AMONG OUR
PEOPLE A FEELING OF RESPONSIBILITY IN THE MISFORTUNE OF
OTHERS. YOU ARE THE INSTRUMENT OF EXPRESSION OF A GREAT
GROUP OF AMERICANS WHO HAVE GIVEN GENEROUSLY FOR HU-
MAN WELFARE IN TIMES OF DISTRESS OR EMERGENCY."[120] Later
in the same convention, Eleanor Roosevelt underscored the linkage of
citizenship to the organization: "The Red Cross . . . is a part of the life of
the country and all of our citizens should be members."[121] Although these
affirmations from Franklin and Eleanor Roosevelt might be dismissed as
empty political talk, their statements signaled a far-reaching revision of
the relationship between public programs and private charities.

     Before long, charities themselves adopted the same linkage of voluntarism and citizenship: "It is one of the true romances of a democracy that a whole people can unite in such a common expression of human brotherhood. . . . The small sum asked from each citizen is as a self-imposed poll tax which every man, woman and every child . . . should be happy to pay, because it gives every one, whatever the amount, a share in showing human kindness which is, after all, the best thing in the world with all its hardships and bitternesses and despairs." This linkage of giving as a social good (rather than as an expression of individual religious or moral commitments) was taken still further by Edward Stettinius Jr., chairman of the 1938 Red Cross roll call in New York, recently named chairman of U.S. Steel, future director of the wartime lendlease program, Secretary of State, and U.S. Ambassador to the United Nations: "Viewing the purposes of the organization in a larger sense, contributions to the Red Cross are not charity, but 'part of the social overhead required for maintaining the morale of the nation and its people.'"[122]

Echoing the discourse of earlier national campaigns from the Civil War's "divine method of patriotism" to the circuits traveled by knitted goods during the First World War, FDR emphasized the capacity of citizen philanthropy to transcend social divisions: "The American Red Cross is an institution [in] which our people in every walk of life and in every section of the nation can unite in a common tie of brotherhood. It knows no distinction of race, creed or color. There are no boundary lines, either State or national, in its never-ending mission of mercy for those who are in distress."[123] This celebration of variety became more pronounced toward the end of the decade as the threat of war increased. Reports of fund-raising created imagery of a diverse nation unified in charitable giving:

> Funds continued to pour in from the most varied sources. Ninety North Carolina road gang prisoners sent $10.60 from their small funds ordinarily used for smoking supplies and other necessities. From the Eskimo village of Gambell in Alaska came $60.50 obtained through the sale of ivory carvings by the village's arts and crafts association.
>
> A check for $26 came from a foreman and twenty-two men working on a WPA project in Kentucky. In Rochester a Polish woman who had no funds to contribute raised $2.52 for the relief agency by selling lilies of the valley picked from her garden.

Even without going beyond the boundaries of New York City to find convicts and Eskimos, reporters listed donations of 77 pennies from one man, a "small contribution" from a blind woman, "$20 of my hard-earned money working as a waitress" from a Scandinavian woman, and then contributions in the hundreds and thousands of dollars from wealthier individuals and corporations. Lacking funds to give, patients in hospitals did their bit by sewing.[124] Thus, in covering fund-raising efforts, reporters anticipated the "melting pot in a foxhole" convention of World War II films and echoed the "unity in diversity" of those vignettes of marginalized men contributing to the mobilization for what would soon come to be known as the First World War.[125] Yet there was a key difference in the imagery of incorporation-through-voluntarism in play during the New Deal as contrasted with the First World War or the Mississippi Flood relief effort. Rather than multiplying vignettes that first emphasized difference or marginality and then gift-giving and reciprocity, the language of the New Deal stressed voluntary contributions as the enactment of a "people's partnership." This was not a benign slogan, but rather signaled a commitment to disrupting the control of local elites over the private voluntary agencies— and the expansive networks of civic fund-raising that supported them.

This combination of voluntarism-as-nationalism and tactical political maneuver surfaced in Roosevelt's deliberations over naming a new chairman of the Red Cross following the death of Admiral Cary Grayson (who, earlier in his career, had been the personal physician of Woodrow Wilson—clearly a loyal Democrat). Using his powers as ex officio president of this federally chartered voluntary organization, Roosevelt could reshape the role of the Red Cross in relation to governmental activities. James L. Fieser, the long-time director of domestic operations and vice president of the organization, wrote to Marvin McIntyre, secretary to the President:

> You and he may not know it, but I represent the popular or "left" aspect of things in the Red Cross. Other forces in it stand for "silk stocking" dominance. I take credit for making it a people's organization and stressing partisanship all around. It has not been an easy role at any time. We are two kinds of an organization, one the dinner coat, dowager type, the other, which alone has interested me since my first venture in the 1913 Ohio Valley Floods, 25 years ago this March, has to do with saving lives and making for better living, through disaster relief, first aid, life saving, highway emergency stations, home and farm accident protection and similar work. There is mud and blood and sweat in this end—the real Red Cross. I hope we may again have a Chairman who stands for these.

The note drew a prompt response: "I want to see Fieser of Red Cross Monday or Tuesday. F.D.R."[126]

In addition to the President's patronage of the March of Dimes and his rapprochement with the Red Cross, Roosevelt gave his support to private fund-raising efforts linked to business and the traditional (and often conservative) supporters of private charity. Relations with the Community Chests remained strained, although the president dutifully recorded a message each year to kick off the federated fund-raising effort that now went under the name of the Mobilization for Human Needs. But even if the specific relationship was not warm, Roosevelt had recognized the potential for large-scale citizen philanthropy as a vehicle for national mobilization and, perhaps just as importantly, community elites and businessmen were compelled to recognize that the President was a virtuoso when it came to methods of leadership that they had presumed were their own.[127] Roosevelt had, in effect, stolen their methods and mastered an approach to civic mobilization long felt to be the distinctive property of business and community elites. At the level of tactics, civic benevolence was too potent to be banished from national politics, no matter how strong its association with the discredited administration of Herbert Hoover.

The Roosevelt administration also recognized the ways in which private voluntary agencies and civic benevolence could contribute to nation-state-building, particularly in an era of unprecedented but still profoundly contested federal expansion. Alongside the discursive linkage of the Red Cross and voluntarism to good citizenship, new working relationships were established between public and private agencies. Some were quite mundane, with the Red Cross offering safety classes to workers in the WPA, the Civilian Conservation Corps (CCC), and the National Youth Authority. Others were more inventive, including a suggestion that a national voluntary association whose president was the U.S. President might be an instrument for monitoring state governments within a federal program, effectively circumventing the 10th Amendment in an effort to ensure accountability:

> Will you think over the possibility of asking the Red Cross to assume responsibility for checking and reporting on the unemployables on the relief rolls whose care will become a state and local responsibility after we (the Federal Government) assume total charge of the employables?
>
> The suggestion was made that in this way the Red Cross could be given a useful task and if in a given State, the State and its localities were failing to take care of the unemployables, the finding of that fact by the Red Cross would have possibly more public effect than if the fact were found by the Federal Relief organizations.
>
> At least this is something worth thinking about.[128]

Although this suggestion for deploying the Red Cross to monitor the federal-state division of labor in unemployment relief does not appear to have resulted in anything, a more robust collaboration in the provision of services was forged in a series of devastating floods in the late 1930s. Only a few years after the Red Cross and the federal government had been posed as mutually exclusive sources of drought and unemployment relief, reporters described:

> a system of improvised and complicated, yet surprisingly close-fitting, gear meshes. All the services that have to do with the labor and mechanical processes of lessening and curbing the flood mesh in with the regular army engineers' expert direction of flood control activities. All the services capable of lending a hand to relieve human suffering mesh in with the Red Cross. Both the major cogs of the army engineers and the Red Cross mesh in with the master cog at the White House.[129]

Tens of thousands of WPA and CCC workers were reassigned to levee and flood protection projects. The Red Cross called in boats from the Navy, the Coast Guard, and other public services and used WPA workers to drive CCC trucks to CCC camps to house those made homeless by the floods. Voluntarism also provided a loophole for engaging parts of the military in a domestic crisis: "As Naval Reservists, they can not, under the present law, be ordered to perform active duty in peace-time without their own consent, but they have voluntarily responded to the many appeals of the civil authorities and have rendered an extensive amount of outstanding service in the rescue and safeguarding of life and property, and on a non-pay basis." As with the plan to use the Red Cross to monitor state relief to "unemployables," voluntarism was invoked as means of maneuvering through a thicket of constitutional and jurisdictional restrictions.[130]

If floods demonstrated the closely meshed relief machinery of government and charity working together, such cooperation was also evident as the economy once again entered into a downturn, the so-called Roosevelt Recession of 1938. By this point polling provided a metric of public opinion. When asked "'Do you think relief should be given as work relief or as direct cash relief?' 90 percent of the voters interviewed answered 'Work relief.' Voters on relief voted four to one for work relief; voters in the middle and upper economic brackets, nine to one." But to provide such relief, representatives of business and the community chests now lobbied for yet another program of federal-state matching grants. Charles P. Taft of Cincinnati, representative of both a storied family of conservatives and the National Citizens Committee of the Mobilization for Human Needs, appeared in Congress to argue for "federal relief grants to the states on a fixed percentage matching basis (not necessarily 50–50; more probably 75–25). To what extent funds would be used for work or direct relief would be for the states to determine, as would standards of eligibility for relief."[131]

This proposed plan represented something close to a complete reversal of Hopkins' bright line of 1933, an arrangement in which federal funds would flow to state and local governments working closely with private social agencies. Indeed, this was part of the rationale of the proponents who argued that "it would rehabilitate state and local responsibility for their own people, remove the possibility of a 'relief bureaucracy,' permit of more flexible programs and stimulate greater local participation in determining ways of meeting needs."[132] The "flexibility" advocated by those allied with the Community Chests would have at least two important political consequences. First, power would be returned to those local networks and agencies long associated with municipal benevolence; second, local discretion would undermine the entitlements associated with new categories of relief for the aged, dependent children, the blind, and the disabled that were just completing the period of initial accumulation of funding under the Social Security Act of 1934. But, echoing themes from his 1930 speech to Syracuse graduates as governor of New York, Roosevelt was clear that federal spending should not be extended indefinitely. States, localities, and private agencies would have to take responsibility for the unemployables and other needy members of their communities and to fund those efforts themselves.

Although Roosevelt showed no interest in subsidizing local control of relief with federal matching grants, he continued to see the Red Cross as a vehicle for conducting politics by other means. This was particularly evident in the domain of foreign policy, where the nationalization of charitable sensibilities, reinforced in each annual Red Cross roll call, underscored an identification of private voluntary gifts with national purpose. Constrained by an isolationist Congress, Roosevelt repeatedly used charitable relief to project U.S. support for foreign countries. The president endorsed a $1 million drive for civilian relief in China—a drive that admittedly fell short and closed after raising only $250,000 (which was augmented by $200,000 from the Red Cross general fund).[133]

This fusing of voluntary relief and government effort culminated in 1940. Eight years earlier, the Red Cross (urged on by President Hoover) had declared that it would not accept a $25 million appropriation from Congress to aid in drought relief. But, with the onset of war in Europe and the mobilization of Red Cross activities to raise funds for refugees, Roosevelt resurrected the possibility of Congressional appropriations as gifts to charitable organizations:

Many millions of dollars have been given to the Red Cross for relief purposes in Europe, but I feel that the government itself should greatly add to the assistance that is now being given.

In the pending Relief Bill before the Congress we are making possible expenditure of over $1,000,000,000 for the relief of the needy unemployed in the United States. And in addition to this, large further sums are being spent from day to day by States and municipalities for the care of the needy who cannot be given employment on work-relief projects.

In view of these large sums spent at home, I feel that the Congress would receive nationwide support if it were to add an appropriation to the Relief Bill in the sum of at least $50,000,000 as a token of our deep-seated desire to help not only Americans but people who are destitute in other lands.[134]

And Congress agreed. In contrast to the fierce fight over the Robinson amendment to appropriate $25 million to give to the Red Cross for drought relief in the hard winter of 1930–31, Roosevelt's proposal for a congressional "gift" of $50 million was rapidly approved. Rather than portraying the congressional appropriation as antithetical to voluntarism, newspaper coverage made clear that the situation required *both* government and charitable funds. The $50 million would not "obviate the continued Red Cross need of private contributions" nor "lighten the burdens which the Red Cross already has assumed in furnishing clothing, medicines and ambulances to the war wounded and needy." The most immediate of those burdens were met in the summer of 1940 as the Red Cross announced that it had pulled within $176,000 of its fund-raising goal of $20 million, almost double the $10 million collected when the President called for the congressional appropriation six weeks earlier.[135] The preparation for war thus cemented a new working partnership between the federal government and private charities or, to use the term that would gain prominence in the following decades, the nonprofit sector.

Institutional Legacies

In demanding that aid be "Free. Not as charity. But as a right," Robert Penn Warren's fictional protagonist posed a binary choice. That binary also implies a teleology—from charity to rights—that has informed some of the most influential theories and histories of the modern welfare state.[136] But to draw an arrow from there to here, to accept a stylized picture in which private charity enters the Depression and the framework of a modern welfare state comes out at the other end, misses the complex politics over the division of labor itself. If, as Timothy Mitchell suggested, the relation of state and society should be understood "not as the boundary between two discrete entities, but as a line drawn internally within the network of institutional mechanisms through which a social and political order is maintained,"[137] then it is important to explain where it gets drawn and why. In addition to establishing the foundational components of a welfare state—a set of entitlements or rights—these policy battles transposed practices and templates from the world of charity into public programs. The shift to public funding did not eradicate the ways in which the provision of relief enacted categorical differences between employable men, typically white, and women as well as disadvantaged minorities.[138] From the exclusion of agricultural and domestic workers from core social insurance programs to the moral policing of women receiving Aid to Dependent Children, elements of what had been voluntary practice became embedded in public policy.

Private voluntary agencies also continued to function as part of the system of social provision, where they often contributed to the reproduction of racial and ethnic inequality,[139] maintained boundaries between public and private,[140] and provided a beachhead for the political mobilization of opponents of further expansions of the New Deal order. Although, at the time, the adoption of the business charitable deduction and the exclusion of nonprofit organizations from Social Security requirements might have seemed like minor concessions, these policies represented loose threads that would eventually provide openings to those seeking to unravel public systems of social provision. For all that the New Deal set American political development on the path toward a modern welfare state, "even settled paths," as Marc Schneiberg has argued, "are typically littered with flotsam and jetsam—with elements of alternative economic orders and abandoned or partly realized institutional projects."[141] These remnants of the pre–New Deal order would become resources for later political struggles to redefine the articulation of public and private in American governance.

Looking at the Depression from the vantage point of the 1920s, the question was why the Roosevelt administration did not build upon the existing infrastructure of public and private collaboration to construct an expansive system of relief on well-established foundations. Viewed from the middle of the 1930s, however, the puzzle is how this ascendance of public provision failed to inaugurate a fully public system. Instead, by the end of the decade, and certainly by the close of the Second World War, the United States had returned to a system built on complex collaboration between public and private agencies sustained by both public and private resources. President Roosevelt had recognized citizen philanthropy as a powerful instrument both for raising resources outside of Congressional control and for mobilizing networks of gift-giving and reciprocation that flowed symbolically through the presidency. The first would prove important in both limiting the expansion of federal obligations to social provision and circumventing an isolationist Congress in the years before the official outbreak of the Second World War. The second would help to sustain patriotic solidarity during wartime.

7

The People's Partnership

And the Finns have not forgotten. Sixteen months ago I was in Finland, the invited guest of the Finnish nation. . . . An elderly farmer came to the hotel, stopping me on the steps, to explain that he had come some 200 miles; that he had brought for me a present; that he had had a family of nine children; that they had all grown to manhood and womanhood, strong in mind and in body; that they owed it to the American people; that during that dreadful time the children had embroidered an American flour sack with woolen yarns of their own making. He wishes for me to have it. That flour sack was embroidered with the American Flag.

Herbert Hoover's address at Madison Square Garden
on behalf of the people of Finland, December 20, 1939[1]

Although the nation was not yet out of depression, civic mobilization surged in the late 1930s with the anticipation of war. Some of the first events expressed the importance of reciprocity within American political morality. Of all those displaced by the initial campaigns of German expansion and annexation, few elicited more spirited support and sympathy than the Finns. While it might seem odd that so much enthusiastic support was rallied for a small nation with so few co-ethnics within the United States, the outpouring of donations made perfect sense within the moral calculus of American political culture. Alone among the debtor nations of the First World War, Finland had repaid its war debt in full. Reciprocity merited repeated generosity.

The Finns were respected for honoring their debts and extending aid in turn to other nations. Although "Finland [had] scarcely finished burying her dead," when Norway was invaded by Nazi Germany in April 1940, "Helsinki hospitals stripped themselves of all equipment not absolutely essential in order to repay Norway for aid sent when Finland was fighting Russia."[2] Other national attributes also inspired relief efforts. Athletic organizations raised funds because Helsinki had already been chosen to host the Olympics in 1940 (these games would eventually be canceled), and the Finns, it was said, were "a sporting people" both in their history of athletic accomplishments and their current role as underdogs against the vastly larger Soviet forces.[3] The Service Club Farmers of Huron, South Dakota, collected a rail car full of wheat, which they offered to either ship to Finland or convert to a cash donation. (Hoover requested cash).[4] Women's organizations raised funds and, in February, the Rockefeller family contributed $100,000, the largest donation to date.[5] Whimsical social events were also planned, including an affair for several hundred guests at the Coq Rouge club in New York, complete with "wall designs of polar bears, penguins, puffins and other creatures, skis and flags."[6]

   This civic benevolence extended beyond conventional understandings of charity to include preparation for war. Finnish War Relief Inc. processed remittances to Finland "for any purpose specified by the donors, including armament and ammunition."[7] The original mission of the international Red Cross movement, to offer neutral support to wounded soldiers and beleaguered noncombatants, had been breached during the First World War. But the immediate linkage of benevolence to ammunition suggested that few illusions of neutrality survived. Well before the attack on Pearl Harbor in December 1941, the machinery of voluntary fund-raising was put into gear. By mid-December 1939, almost 200 groups were already registered with the State Department to collect funds for war relief as was required by the Neutrality Act.[8] More parties for Finland followed, along with "Paris Chantant" to send kits to French soldiers on the Western Front, "A Night in an English Music Hall" to support "Bundles for Britain," and "A Night in Scandinavia" for support of the American-Scandinavian Field Hospital.[9] In a reprise of the "charitable buffoonery" that had drawn comment from foreign observers during the Civil War, fund-raising efforts included "tin cans on street corners and cocktail parties for dogs."[10]

   In its overall character, this wave of voluntary fund-raising repeated patterns familiar from the Civil War and the First World War as well as many conflicts, crises, and natural disasters in between. Once again, the United States was facing the threat of military conflict with comparatively few armed forces and little dedicated capacity for war production. Once again, mobilization for war depended on harnessing the capacity of voluntary and civic groups to raise funds, produce supplies, and sustain the morale and political support of American citizens.[11] Yet this extended coproduction of state capacity to wage war was constructed on institutional foundations that had been fundamentally transformed by the legacies of the First World War as well as the experience of the Depression and the New Deal.

The familiar recipes for an "expansible state" were invoked, but in contrast to earlier wartime mobilizations, the capacity of federal government was now far larger in proportion to the resources that could be mobilized through voluntary associations.[12] With respect to the Red Cross, social workers wondered whether "in such matters as home service will it pick up where it left off in the other war when there was no nationwide public welfare organization."[13] Planning memos proliferated, spelling out complex divisions of labor among public and private agencies.[14] Voluntary efforts were more tightly integrated with both the presidential administration and a rapidly proliferating array of government agencies and programs. But if knitting had represented the outer limit of useful voluntary contributions to the war effort two decades before, what could civilians offer to a government whose capacities had increased massively in response to the depression? The possibility of meaningful volunteer contributions to the coproduction of war were minimized by technological advances and the professionalization of social work.[15] Consequently, it became ever more challenging to convince civilians that their donations would contribute to the safety and support of their soldiers. To bridge this gap, the public relations and advertising industries that had been nurtured by the First World War came back with full force. Yet some of those fiercely committed to the familiar model of voluntary mobilization in support of a nation at war pushed back against intensified federal intervention. Humorously, although with an edge, the vice-chairman of a local defense council in Pennsylvania threated "to blackout this community at the approach of an enemy armed with an organization chart."[16]

The result was a reconfigured articulation of voluntarism and state capacities during the war, one simultaneously pervasive and fragile, linked to the fortunes of the president who was the emotional focus for so much of the nation. Mobilization for war energized contests over the leadership of fund-raising efforts and activities in familiar circuits of community chests, once again transformed into war chests. But this resurgence of voluntarism encountered practices of national governing that had been profoundly changed by a decade of federal policy expansion during the New Deal. The model of the expansible state was reconfigured and control over key decisions migrated further into government agencies, out of the hands of community networks and the councils of private citizens that had been so prominent during the First World War. As a consequence, the possibilities for citizens to withdraw from the coproduction of war were limited, although far from eliminated.[17] The result was a greatly strengthened national state, deeply marked by, but no longer so dependent upon, civic mobilization.

The Politics of War Relief

Wartime fund-raising began in solidarity with the Finns, built on efforts to aid China under Japanese occupation, and rapidly expanded with support for those under attack or already refugees in the proliferating conflicts that would become the Second World War. Even before a formal declaration of war, this wave of support for war relief became entangled with politics. It could hardly have been otherwise when Finnish War Relief was led by former president Herbert Hoover, who recruited many of his colleagues from the food relief effort for Belgium during the First World War. Particularly during the 1936 election, Hoover had been active as a speaker against the New Deal[18] and there was talk that he would run for the presidency in 1940. Other rumors suggested that President Roosevelt had already approached Hoover to ask him to lead American war relief in an indirect effort to remove Hoover from the political scene in advance of the elections. As with most such rumors, both were forcefully denied by the appropriate spokesmen.[19]

As the nation was drawn into the war, first through the support of allies and then through military conflict, debates over the place of voluntary effort spoke to a barely sublimated conflict over the appropriate role of the federal government. As Hoover warned when he took up the job of Finnish war relief, "The four old horsemen of the Apocalypse . . . now have outriders dashing over the entire world. The coming of Famine, Pestilence, War and Death is preceded by five advance horsemen who leave misery and grief in their tracks. Imperialism, the destroyer of nations; Intolerance, the destroyer of minorities; Statism, the destroyer of personal liberty; Agnosticism, the destroyer of Christianity, and Hate, the destroyer of human accord—these lead the way for the four horsemen of Revelation."[20] The threat of "statism" to liberty was the charge that struck closest to domestic politics. Although both Roosevelt and his critics made the case for a mixed system of private enterprise, voluntary effort, and government programs, they envisioned the balance among these in quite different ways. Over the course of the war, Roosevelt's model was ascendant. With respect to voluntarism, he supported efforts at coordinating fund-raising, but stopped short of full centralization—particularly under the control of the Community Chests linked to municipal networks of business and civic leaders who were often hostile to the New Deal. The social networks that had long organized community-level voluntarism were profoundly challenged by the administration's insistence that organized labor be incorporated into the management of wartime fund-raising, a key piece of reimagining the Red Cross as the "people's partnership."

Hoover and Roosevelt were not the only participants in the political skirmishes around the question of war relief.[21] Roosevelt was not yet officially running for an unprecedented third term, but his vice-president, John Nance Garner, was already on the presidential primary ballot in Wisconsin and New York.[22] Garner, who had been speaker of the House before the 1932 election, retained powerful connections within Congress and opposed government appropriations to relieve refugees of wars in which the United States was not a participant. The fear that the United States *might* become a participant only strengthened the resolve of many in Congress—as well as both the National Association of Manufacturers and the United Mine Workers—to resist appeals for humanitarian aid.[23] For Roosevelt, therefore, privately organized war relief efforts represented an important opportunity to circumvent Congressional isolationism.

In addition to the disagreements over whether charitable efforts would involve the United States in the growing wars in Europe and East Asia, Americans were also unsure about who would qualify to receive aid. By the summer of 1940, questions swirled over the military implications of humanitarian war relief: "If Britain can hold out on land will she permit charitably minded America to feed Europe for Adolf Hitler?" The commitment to neutrality that informed the founding of the International Committee of the Red Cross came up against the politics of military alliance: "Pending an answer to this question, the American Red Cross is delaying the dispatch of further 'mercy ships' to France. . . . Before others depart, Britain and Germany must agree to allow them safe passage."[24]

During the First World War, the effort to feed starving Belgium had required a complex choreography that delivered aid to a country under occupation while ensuring that this aid would not help the war effort of the occupier. No comparable effort was mobilized during the Second World War; such debates would reemerge only after V-E Day in 1945 over whether and how to aid the citizens of former enemy powers. But even if the focus was to be on mobilizing voluntarism to aid one's own nation at war, there was significant room for disagreement over the appropriate division of labor among a greatly expanded state apparatus and multiple voluntary networks based on different understandings of civic membership and tied to diffcrent interests or constituencies. Settlements carefully worked out between public and private agencies, across levels of government, were destabilized as the federal government took a much larger role in leading the wartime mobilization. In the process, private voluntary agencies and practices of voluntarism were integrated still more tightly into the making of the American nation-state.

A Contested "American Collectivism"

The surge of contributions to war relief also threatened to upset the balance between federal and local contributions to relief work at home. For years, the Roosevelt Administration had held fast to the WPA as a limit against further expansion of federal commitments to fund relief efforts. "The American Way," Roosevelt insisted, was for the federal government to organize and fund work relief projects for the "employables" (or at least as many of those who could be accommodated in the limited number of projects) and for state, county, local, and private funding to take care of the rest. That remainder had been whittled down as "the categories" or "the insurances" came into operation and removed many of the aged, the blind, the dependent children, and the widows from local relief rolls as they qualified for new kinds of federal assistance (pointedly described with the language of insurance not "relief").[25] But many fell between the categories and were still in need of relief and other supports. Consequently, private fund-raising, particularly through the Community Chests, remained an important component of social provision. Private funds—combined with contributions from local and state governments—were to take care of those who did not qualify for either employment on public works or "the categories" as well as the complex cases that were understood to be the particular sphere of private welfare agencies.[26] If citizens diverted their contributions to war relief abroad, the voluntary component of local relief might be undermined.[27]

In the aftermath of the attack on Pearl Harbor, almost half of the existing community chests converted to "war chests." A national drive, under the familiar banner of the "Mobilization for Human Needs," was kicked off by a radio speech from the President. This promised to create greater unity and coordination in the funding of voluntary contributions to the war effort and care for those at home. In the assessment of one observer, "the war, which has had a streamlining effect on many forms of organized effort," had reduced the "competitive friction between established private agencies and the emergency groups raising funds for foreign war relief (it still hasn't disappeared entirely)." The result was that "in war chest towns, the established social agencies get together with the war relief groups—United Service Organization (USO), British, Russian, Chinese relief, etc.—in a single fund-raising drive" with the goal of raising over $175 million, some $75 million of which would be divided among the leading war relief organizations.[28]

Although calls for unified, universal mobilization dominated public debate, behind the scenes there was serious disagreement. Would there would be one overarching organization of civic associations and, if so, who would lead that civic alliance? Past politics mattered here, as did the potential for bringing voluntary organizations more fully under presidential control. In May 1941, the Community Chests and Councils, Inc. proposed that were war to come, "there shall be organized in each community ONE WAR-TIME CAMPAIGN, which will include not only appeals for war services (such as the American Red Cross, the United Service Organizations, and the Foreign Relief agencies) but also appeals for all-time services of the local Chest and other agencies."[29]

The analysis behind this proposal was that the Community Chests had come to embody local solidarity that could be harnessed to the war effort and the more encompassing project of nation-state-building. A few months before the attack on Pearl Harbor, an old social worker friend, David Liggett, wrote to Harry Hopkins about the prospects for "the unification of our feeling toward national defense."

> It seems to a great many community leaders . . . that the Administration, and the President in particular, has not realized this sizeable potentiality. You know better than anybody in the land, Harry, how people will rally in united fashion to humanitarian appeal. There's a common denominator here which has re-vitalized our concept of government and its social responsibilities. You are largely responsible for, and can be justly proud of that new concept and practice of government. There is a common denominator here which has, in practice, during the last twenty-five years, made for the kind of community unity which has come out of the Community Fund movement in approximately 600 American cities. This unity is a great moral force, and you could make a worthy use of it right now, but, unfortunately, the trend is all in the opposite direction.[30]

Liggett wrote in response to FDR's decision to authorize separate fund-raising campaigns for the Community Chests (soon to become war chests), the USO, and the Red Cross. This decision was an attempt to resolve the contentious relationship of the Red Cross as the expression of a national people to the Community Chests as vehicles for the care of specific communities by the members of those communities. Hoping to head off divergent and competing fund-raising efforts, the Community Chests had approached the Red Cross with a proposal for a single, unified drive. The Red Cross, not surprisingly, rejected this proposal, replaying a conflict that had repeatedly erupted over the past decades.[31] Instead, Chairman Norman H. Davis invoked the distinctive charter of the American Red Cross and its responsibility "to furnish volunteer aid to the sick and wounded of armies" as well as serving as the "medium of communication between the people of the United States of America and their

Army and Navy." The Community Chests were, the Red Cross claimed, poorly suited as vehicles for a truly national effort: "The Red Cross is a national organization with 3,728 Chapters and 6,585 Branches covering every country and community in the country, whereas Chests exist in only about 550 cities and towns. When the Red Cross is dealing with the national emergencies of war or disaster its fund raising plans must be applicable in all the communities of the country." Perhaps most importantly, the Red Cross recognized that the activity of fund-raising was itself central to the organization's vitality: "The practical effect of this proposal is that the Red Cross would surrender its direct contact with the people in about 550 cities and towns where there are Community Chests."[32] For all those who carped that the one dollar contribution required of the Roll Call rendered Red Cross membership hollow, the leadership affirmed that "Membership is recognized as real by those who join."[33]

FDR's decision was endorsed, a few weeks later, by the *New York Times.* Their editorial argued that while recognizing the value of centralization, "it would be a grave error to lump too many together in the interest of efficiency or the belief that patriotism and war-stimulated generosity will give the same answer in every case. People give by a free choice and from particular motives."[34] This decision seemed to validate the decades-long effort by the Red Cross to resist absorption by the Chests and affirm their distinctive relationship to the people and their military.

But for David Liggett, who wrote personally to Hopkins rather than in any official capacity, the decision to endorse multiple fund-raising efforts was unwise. It "seems both unnecessary and contrary to sound procedure to split up a unity which should not only be preserved, but which is vitally needed as a contribution towards a united national front with regard to backing up the President's splendid leadership in foreign affairs." Although FDR had recently invoked Abraham Lincoln as a model of a wartime president, "his Red Cross letter is a gesture in the direction not only of secession, but also in the direction of disruption of an indispensable country-wide unity, which goes a lot deeper than just a joint war-defense campaign.... The President's dictum sets a whole psychological pattern which in turn sets up a veritable row of toppling dominoes which goes through the whole private welfare field." Although Liggett himself had been a recipient of Red Cross services in the earlier war and had been employed on their staff in Cleveland, he "particularly deplore[d] the Presidentially-sharpened spearhead of isolationist procedure that is now shoved into the vitals of the very unity which we need so much more than we needed it during the two decades following the World War. We need it now, and we can't very well do without it now."

The circuits of patriotic giving would create competing civic solidarities. If those allied with the Community Chest saw a missed opportunity to harness wartime fund-raising to the municipal solidarity cultivated "between the Rockies and the Appalachians" where isolationist sentiments ran particularly high, the leadership of the Red Cross welcomed the assurance that they would continue to raise funds on their own to support a distinctive mission with respect to the conflict.[35]

The Red Cross also recognized the links between organized fund-raising and patriotic solidarity. James Fieser, long-time officer of the Red Cross, forwarded to Hopkins a confidential memo he had written to defend the substantive meaning of membership in the organization. Reacting to charges that Roll Call contributions represented only the thinnest sense of belonging,[36] he attributed this critique to "New York where the membership . . . has always been discounted by the few who dominate there and who consistently, over the years, have failed to bring the people—the democracy of that great Chapter—into a sense of participation and proprietorship in its affairs." In this sense, the 1918 call to "Make It Unanimous!" was still the appropriate goal, even if the achievement of such goal (barely imaginable) would bring in funds far exceeding the budgeted needs of the organization.[37] Elsewhere across the nation, he argued, membership produces "a group of interested stock-holders, an example of democracy which we fight to preserve." Furthermore, if the Red Cross were to shift from this emphasis on the total count of members to a focus solely on the amount of funds raised this would breach one of the important bright lines defining the place of voluntarism in governance: "A dollar approach would tend to simplify the hope of many that major Red Cross functions would be absorbed by the government where much larger sums of money may become available for each through taxation."[38]

In the absence of a single unified voluntary effort in support of the war, policy choices by the Roosevelt administration and military leaders translated into conflicts and slights at the organizational level. To take only one example, commanders in Europe decided that the task of operating clubs and hotels for soldiers on leave should be delegated to a single organization: the Red Cross. With recreational programs located on military bases now under military control, this policy about clubs and hotels squeezed out the possibilities for the proliferation of Salvation Army doughnut huts and USO clubs that had been a defining feature of the First World War. Worse still, the Red Cross was seen by some to be conducting its operations in a way that offended the core motives for the tradition of American voluntarism.

In a series of "postcards" from Europe, popular journalist Ernie Pyle brought this festering issue to the surface with his praise for the Red Cross. Focusing on those hotels operated for soldiers on leave in places such as London, Pyle reassured his reader that "the Red Cross in this war is doing something brand new and wonderfully interesting." Scale was part of what was impressive: "one immense organization is doing one big thing in a colossal way." But how it was doing this was equally striking: "because the Red Cross is a relief organization and not a spiritual one, it completely absolves the soldier from having to pray for his chocolate bar." Creating further distance from a tradition of voluntarism as a mechanism of moral uplift, Pyle pointed out that both the Red Cross and the Army Special Services knew that "a fighting man on leave isn't going to sit around with folded hands and a lily-white look on his face." Instead "if a soldier comes in tipsy at night, the Red Cross is more likely to help take off his shoes for him, than it is to kick him out." Some hotels even saved beds "for soldiers who will show up late at night in a condition of needing to lie down real quickly. All these Peck's bad boys may get a tongue-in-the-cheek 'scolding' next morning, but nothing worse. Soldiers are appreciative of this."[39]

Other donors and voluntary associations were not amused. Now best remembered as the author of a classic of management theory, *The Functions of the Executive*, Chester Barnard was serving as chairman of the USO. He made his displeasure clear in a memo to the group's General Policy Committee that was sent with a copy of the offending postcards: "The marked and excerpted paragraphs I think are fairly to be taken as attacking our member agencies, the principles of their work, and the ideals and religious convictions which they represent." Barnard found the "attitude that countenanced the publication" was "one of sneering at the philosophy of our work and therefore at that of the religious institutions of the country; and of glorifying a purely secular approach . . . to the point of publicized condonement of bad habits and bad morals." Pyle's commentary was made all the worse by the fact that the Red Cross had reproduced the articles in a "postcard" form to be sent to family and friends at home, offering "a deep affront not only to our member agencies and to all religious groups in the United States, but also to the British private war work agencies doing work for our soldiers, nine of which are of religious character." Furthermore, Barnard was confident that "the decent people of this country cannot support a Red Cross indulging in this kind of defamation, and perhaps will not support one whose conception of recreation and morale as presented in these articles is so nearly brutish."[40]

This episode endangered financial support for the Red Cross from no less than the Rockefellers, who had long been the nation's leading donors in times of war, crisis, and natural disaster. Early in 1943, John D. Rockefeller Jr. wrote to Chairman Norman Davis. Reiterating his commitment to their personal friendship, Rockefeller nevertheless raised the possibility that it might be necessary to "withhold further support" in response to "any requests for personal service, endorsement or contribution which may come to me from Red Cross representatives."[41] While Rockefellers would continue to give to the Red Cross, the tensions between religious motives for giving and voluntarism-in-service-of-the-state were unmistakable. As the Red Cross came to understand itself as a "people's partnership" and allied more closely with the Roosevelt administration, ties to the long-standing networks of religiously imbued benevolence were strained. A decade after the organization had been aligned with Hoover's side in the partisan fights over federal funding for relief, it now risked being seen as an appendage of the Democratic administration.

In addition to the perceived affront to their vocabulary of motives, those accustomed to leading roles in civic benevolence were challenged on other fronts. Most striking was the rapid mobilization of organized labor as a full partner in the exercises long associated with leading businessmen and elite associations. The subscription list for a fund-raising rally at Madison Square Garden was topped by one Jack Pollard, "secretary-treasurer of the Garage Washers and Polishers Union, Local 272." By the day before the event, he submitted receipts for 1,000 individual tickets at fifty cents to two dollars each and seven boxes at $100 each.[42] Labor unions linked their participation in fund drives by the Red Cross and the Community Chests to "a universal check off plan for union dues."[43] The process of mobilizing the nation through civic benevolence injected class conflict into the realm of philanthropy, once securely dominated by social and economic elites.

The resulting competitions over the control of wartime fund-raising posed particular challenges for the Red Cross as it sought to realize its newly embraced identity as the "People's Partnership." As James Fieser recounted in a reflection on Red Cross relations with organized labor:

> Recognizing the designation of the Red Cross as a "Peoples' Partnership," I conceived it to be our job to enlist these millions in our national effort. As a money raiser, I also became increasingly conscious of the fact that more than four-fifths of our national income is in the hands of individuals receiving $5,000 a year or less. I proceeded on the idea that the American Red Cross, as such, was not committed to or against any social or economic ideology, or any race or religion. I resisted the few attempts to use the Red Cross to promote the prestige of labor, except in so far as support of the Red Cross naturally reflects credit on all who support it. And I equally resisted the few attempts to handicap our labor policy on the part of those who took the position that labor dollars were welcome but cordial labor relations, as such, were not.[44]

Fund-raising drives had long worked through existing associations and affinities, linking members of different religious groups or employees of different firms into a broad web of giving directed by elites, often business leaders. But the incorporation of labor unions into this framework raised new questions about these intersecting relational geometries. As working people, union members lacked the spare time and financial freedom to take on fund-raising responsibilities as unpaid volunteers. But if they were to be paid, who should pay? Larger and stronger unions answered "the union should pay." This meant that the fund-raiser would be both a member of the union and financially dependent on the union to cover a part of his or her working day devoted to the Red Cross campaign. For workers in industries with financially weaker unions, however, the options were less clear. If they were paid by their employer but given release time, then their appeals to fellow workers were marked by dependency on business owners.

Recognizing the dilemma, the Red Cross offered to pay workers directly for fund-raising, but this provoked protest for those who equated the Red Cross with an ethic of pure volunteering. From Cincinnati, the county chairman wrote that the Executive Committee was "unanimously and unalterably opposed to the arrangement which the National Red Cross has made with the CIO and AF of L Unions for the collection of funds." This criticism, they insisted, was "by no means an anti-labor attitude, rather it is absolute opposition to paying anyone for the collection of Red Cross funds! We feel that if this arrangement is fair and proper for the CIO and AF of L Unions, then it is equally so for fraternal, church and other groups or unions. And with the precedent already established, it would be difficult to refuse them! In our opinion it is contrary to Red Cross spirit and principles, and therefore it should be terminated immediately."[45]

Voluntarism on the Home Front

In the run-up to war, the demands of mobilization destabilized the barely settled division of labor between private voluntary and governmental agencies at all levels. For private agencies, the war brought new energy to citizen philanthropy with community chests reporting their highest totals since the early years of the Depression. Giving was accompanied by increasing interest in volunteering, although it was uncertain what those volunteers could actually do given that the military planned to provide many services for itself, thereby minimizing the opportunities for the adventures in voluntarism that had drawn so many to service in the Red Cross during the First World War. While war mobilization strengthened

the position of nationalizing organizations such as the Red Cross over local efforts, it also raised questions concerning the relation of government
provision for the military to the tradition of the people taking care of its
own army. Even before Pearl Harbor "all welfare, recreational, and health
activities under the defense program" were transferred to the Federal Security Administration. The decision by the War Department to "run its
own show" was attributed to the need for " 'impartiality toward all civilian welfare agencies, coupled with the fact that it is deemed impracti-
cable to permit every such agency to maintain establishments to military
reservations.' The only exception to this rule, and one specifically authorized by act of Congress is the establishment of Red Cross field directors in camps and cantonments."[46] A year later, an opening would be
provided to the USO to participate in providing recreational facilities in
the camps,[47] supported by the request of a $150 million appropriation by
Congress.

The geography of war also mandated a stronger redistributive system
of financing within the Red Cross. Cities along the Pacific Coast that
"have a war on their door steps" and served as embarkation points for
tens of thousands were "unanimous in asking that we take all the local
budgets, add them to the national and equalize them nationally . . . it is
unfair to slap the entire cost upon them when they hold the fort and represent all of the United States."[48] Similar arguments applied to the communities adjacent to large military bases whose size "completely overwhelmed local capacity, however willing, to set up adequate community
services for them," even with support from federal funding. In the effort
to set up a "coordinated public-private program," the exact specifications
of responsibility and recognition were critical. One of the thorniest issues
was what signage to put on the buildings. The federal government suggested "USO" but "the agencies say that in each instance the name of the
operating agency also should appear, though possibly in smaller letters."
Their rationale was that while their efforts were "not an extension of the
program offered by the army within the camps. Rather it is an extension
of home community life."[49]

Finally, the war undercut the administration's insistence that states,
localities, and private agencies were responsible for relief cases not covered by federal works programs or the "categories" of social insurance.
On both state and local levels, "public agencies have been concerned
that the principle should be maintained which has prevailed since 1933
that public funds should be expended through public agencies." These
agencies worried that they would be unable to meet basic personnel
needs as trained social workers and potential recruits to the profession were drawn to better-paid employment elsewhere in the defense

mobilization. Industrial preparation for war eased the pressure on federal and local work relief programs as some workers, particularly the
relatively young and relatively skilled, found employment in defense production.[50] But because the geographies of the defense industry and need
for relief were not aligned, the war-driven economic recovery did not
automatically benefit the less-employable or unemployable who were
left behind. Following the patterns set in the First World War and the
1920s, federated fund-raising—largely under the umbrella of the Community Chests and Councils, Inc.—was deployed to manage the flows
of funds at the intersection of taxes and contributions and demands
for social support. In the process, networks of community leaders and,
above all, businessmen, were restored to a position of local influence that
had been substantially undermined during the 1930s. But in contrast to
World War I, the locus of control over these civic and business networks
migrated toward the centers of formal government power and party
strategy.

   In May 1941, Mayor La Guardia of New York City was appointed head
of the new Office of Civilian Defense (OCD) and charged with organizing "communities over the country for the maximum industrial defense,"
stimulating civilian morale, and "setting up . . . skeleton civilian defense
organizations for actual physical defense in the event that should become
necessary." Eleanor Roosevelt headed the Community and Volunteer
Participation Division. Just as FDR had placed a series of lifelong Democrats and personal allies at the head of the Red Cross and the March of
Dimes, those in charge of the articulation of community organization
to the national war effort were exceedingly close to the administration,
drawing charges that "the OCD was being converted into a 'social reform
organization.' "[51]

   The scale of the war effort led to changes in the symbolically freighted
and carefully negotiated division of labor among government agencies
and the military, private firms, and voluntary groups. Within the Federal
Security Agency, the OCD and the Office of Community War Services
created unprecedented coordination between the national war effort and
local agencies as well as voluntary associations.[52] Initiatives such as the
face-to-face information efforts of the Organizations Service Division
within the OCD sought to promote "real understanding [that] comes
from participation of the citizen's mind through group discussion of issues and policies" by providing materials (including pamphlets, speak-
ers, and films) to "women's clubs, civic groups, trade and industrial organizations, churches, fraternal societies, youth groups, labor unions,
patriotic groups, service clubs, and professional organizations, [which]

have extensive programs of public information to help their members understand better the broad problems which war is bringing to the community."[53] Even the Red Cross abandoned its long-standing policy of accepting only in-kind aid from the government and agreed "to accept governmental reimbursement for major expendable items."[54]

The allocation of specific responsibilities to public and private agencies was guided by deeply entrenched assumptions about the dignity of soldiers as citizens. As had been the case during the First World War, careful attention was paid to avoiding any policy that resembled the provision of relief. An initial plan proposed that "supplementary assistance" to dependents of those in service "was to be administered by the Federal Security Agency through the existing state and local public welfare system, with grants based on a means test and the budgetary need of the individual family." This arrangement, of course, smacked of unemployment relief and social welfare casework. Instead, Congress raised the amount of the automatic grants given to servicemen, "thus increasing the cost to the government but not providing any flexibility to meet emergencies." Allowances for those dependents were then jointly financed by a deduction from service pay and a government contribution.[55] While soldiers and sailors might serve as symbols to elicit wartime benevolence, they were never to be placed in the position of receiving charity.

With these programs, the federal government extended its "infrastructural power" in the most instrumental sense, aligning private voluntary agencies and associations to wartime goals. "In the majority of the largest cities, the planning committees of these private community organization agencies, the CSAs, have become the nuclei of the Civilian War Services Committees in the fields of Health, Welfare and Recreation." In cities, some CSAs used the "block organization" (familiar from the private relief efforts in New York City in the winter of 1930–31; see chapter 5) which was described as "the most successful method yet developed in urban neighborhood organization. Rural districts are covered by the Neighborhood Leader system organized by the Extension Service of the Department of Agriculture."[56] Even the individual act of volunteering could now come under the umbrella of a federal program, the U.S. Citizens Service Corps.[57] In some sense, these arrangements still constituted an "expansible state" in which much of the capacity for governance was constituted by and mobilized through private firms, voluntary associations, and individual volunteers. But all were now more firmly anchored to formal agencies. Reflecting on his wartime experience, one commentator recalled the "1942 octopus, the Office of Civilian Defense, and its restless welfare tentacles."[58] Within cities and regions, these initiatives—however successful or contentious—laid the foundations for new architectures of governance in the postwar era.[59]

The vast array of government relief and social programs was also incorporated into the war effort. When some in Congress attempted to trim the WPA budget to prioritize military spending, the agency's supporters successfully reframed its programs as defense measures.[60] The CCC was reimagined as a training program for militarily useful manpower in the form of tens of thousands of drivers, mechanics, cooks, mapmakers, and radio operators.[61] Of course, the CCC itself could not impose mandatory enlistment, but some state and local relief programs introduced "work or fight" requirements for single men on relief. (In many cases, these policies were rescinded in the face of outraged reaction to these new rules as infringing on basic liberties.)[62] Even as the war was ending, planning committees were imagining a "United States Department of Welfare" in the form of a cabinet-level federal agency that would encompass "Education, Health, Recreation, Welfare, and Social Insurance."[63]

Mobilizing Support for the War

As the wartime regime expanded, the administration still recognized that voluntarism and charitable giving had a place within an unprecedentedly powerful American nation-state. In a joint appeal with Wendell Wilkie, the 1940 Republican candidate for the president, Roosevelt "reiterated that the Federal Government 'cannot and ought not' attempt to cover the entire field of social service and that the failure of private charity to grow would be a national calamity."[64] The question was which organization—or configuration of organizations—could best generate support for the war and national solidarity. The architecture of voluntarism familiar from the First World War represented one possibility, carefully documented and sustained by alumni of that effort. But critics argued that "the use of emergency organizations staffed by business leaders proved too favorable to business interests in the last war" and would be unnecessary given the institutional achievements of the New Deal that had the capacity needed to manage a war economy.

Well before the formal entry of the United States into the war, the roles of government officials, business leaders, and organized labor were already fiercely contested. The 1939 Mobilization Plan had provided that "the control of the war economy should not be entrusted to government officials already in service, but to 'patriotic business leaders of the Nation.'" For guidance in mobilizing for war, plans formulated and filed away after World War I were taken off the shelf and efforts were underway to reproduce the earlier system of wartime collaboration with industry. One immediate consequence of this policy was a War Resources Board that lacked any representative from organized labor.[65] Consulting boards were formed with representatives of industry, foreshadowing the return of the dollar-a-year men to an administration that had, by the late 1930s, established its reputation as being unfriendly to business. As FDR morphed from "Professor New Deal" to "Dr. Win the War," those formerly castigated as "economic royalists" would be welcomed in to do their part in mobilizing the nation for war.

There were also political considerations: "Opponents of emergency organizations also stress their 'undemocratic' character. Appointed by the President without senatorial confirmation they wield, without direct authorization by Congress, unusual and extensive powers."[66] The scale of charitable fund-raising established the stakes in control of voluntary efforts to support the war. Barely one year after German tanks had crossed into Poland, American citizens had contributed $20,924,120 to the American Red Cross War Relief Fund alone (the original goal had been set at $10 million, then doubled to $20 million).[67] This sum represented both a financial resource and a testament to the capacity of this voluntary association to focus and energize national mobilization in a nation that was not yet at war.

Perhaps more importantly, Roosevelt found that his ex officio position as president of the Red Cross (and, in time, the appointment of his close colleague Basil O'Connor as head of that organization as well as the Foundation for Infantile Paralysis or the March of Dimes) allowed him to harness citizen philanthropy to his own goals, particularly in foreign policy where they were blocked by an increasingly isolationist Congress. This push had started early in his first administration, with the President's seemingly benign suggestion to shift the cabinet departments that would be represented on the board to align more closely with the demands of national unemployment and drought relief. The chairman, then John Barton Payne, demurred, citing the organization's federal charter. An opportunity to align the Red Cross more closely with the nation's priorities arose in 1935 with Payne's death; as president ex officio of the Red Cross, FDR appointed Admiral Cary Grayson, a military medical man who had served as Woodrow Wilson's personal physician (see chapter 6). Grayson's death in 1938 prompted a stream of suggestions for the next appointment. Some suggested former President Herbert Hoover,[68] while other letters named distinguished businessmen and long-time volunteers and chapter officers with the Red Cross itself. But FDR returned yet again to the veterans of the Wilson administration, appointing Norman Davis, who had served as Assistant Secretary of the Treasury and

Undersecretary of State. Chairman Davis' death in 1944 provided yet another opportunity and this time FDR appointed one of his closest personal allies, Basil O'Connor, who was his law partner in the 1920s, served as chairman of the Infantile Paralysis Foundation, and was a close confidant throughout Roosevelt's entire time in the White House.

From within the Red Cross, Vice President James Fieser advocated for a populist understanding of the organization's identity:

> This Red Cross, in this great Republic of ours, has emancipated itself from the controls and fixations which have kept the Red Cross little and ineffective in many countries where only "the right people", socially or financially, counted, where the Red Cross is a patronized movement, conducted on a tea or garden party basis. The American Red Cross is the People's Red Cross, the people's partnership. It is no lip service to say "millions belong to it, millions work for it, millions benefit by it". There is no tongue in our cheeks when we sit down with representatives of Protestant, Catholic and Jewish organizations, the great labor and agricultural unions and federations, the women's clubs, the veterans' organizations, and the service clubs of America and discuss, with complete frankness and friendliness, the ways to increase this people's partnership and its improvement in the world's key democratic nation, in this fight for democracy. These diverse elements, many with economic and other differences, meet with the Red Cross with a confidence otherwise reserved alone for our flag and government. We still hear the fear occasionally expressed that there is too much exclusiveness in this or that spot in Red Cross but in great measure this feeling has gone overboard during recent years.[69]

But the transformations generated by closer work with the military threatened to erode the power of voluntarism as a kind of performative propaganda. Within the Red Cross, there were calls from James Fieser (long-time supervisor of disaster relief and now vice president in charge of Domestic Operations) to restore the annual National Convention and its responsibility for "recommending nomination of people for Central Committee vacancies." As he argued, "We were nearly alone in not having our Convention this year. We are a part of the nation's machinery for patriotic participation and should be the last to relinquich [sic]." Later in the same lengthy memo to the Chairman, Norman Davies, he again suggested appointments to the Central Committee that would not only strengthen its connections to the Roosevelt administration, but make it more representative of the national population. In addition to Harry Hopkins and Eleanor Roosevelt, he suggested "someone from a Midwestern city," the Ohio valley, or "a labor man of the younger group, perhaps from a railroad brotherhood would be a good thing psychologically in breaking up a tradition of big business and society domination." Concluding this list, Fieser explained that "ultimately I favor a Negro also to keep in step with other organizations."[70]

The "people's partnership" rested on a deep sense of generalized reciprocity among citizens, on the home front or in the armed services. Whereas charitable fund-raising throughout the Depression had been dogged by the problem of "receiving" by citizens who would be demeaned by their dependence on relief, this constraint on the elaboration of nationwide citizen philanthropy fell away during wartime. As in the First World War, a full circuit of exchange among citizens and citizen-soldiers could be established, this time amplified by the greater extent of military service and less obstructed by the still-aristocratic character of the earlier war's officer corps. Fund-raising efforts deliberately forged links between personal relationships and a massive project of citizen philanthropy, embedding that imagined community in enacted relationships. This cultural accomplishment was carefully documented by Robert Merton in *Mass Persuasion* (1946), his study of a one-day war bond drive centered on a radio marathon by Kate Smith. Carefully coding the content of her appeals, Merton's study captured the symmetry of appeals to sacrifice. Notably, these appeals were particularly effective in producing subscriptions when they were heard by individuals whose sons and brothers were in service, but whose location was then unknown. Merton himself offered an explanation grounded in social psychology:

> Within this context of emotional stress, Smith's appeals were taken by mothers as presenting a means of coping with the apprehensions that crowded in upon them. They felt themselves at the mercy of incalculable circumstances. . . . For, tormented by terrible forebodings, these mothers acted as though the *particular* bond they bought would directly safeguard their own sons in battles, as though *their* bonds would set in motion circumstances which would bring their boys safe through war.[71]

Direct ties to those in overseas service led to contributions and subscriptions, which led to still more subscriptions from citizens "who had a less immediate, a psychologically less compelling stake in the war."[72] The relational underpinnings of such voluntary war drives were equally evident on the receiving end, where soldiers were keenly sensitive to any perceived slight in the circuit of exchange. As documented by one component of the *American Soldier* surveys, the attitudes of troops toward the Red Cross were not governed by individual attributes or biography (e.g., education, rank, rural/urban, time in service) but rather by their assessment of the relational quality of their military experience (appendix 2). The strongest associations with a positive attitude toward the Red Cross and a likelihood of recommending that friends and family contribute were their assessments of officers (shows real interest, willing to do anything asked of his troops) and Red Cross girls (willing to date both officers and men). To the extent that the lived experience of service confirmed an egalitarian circuit of sacrifice and interaction, citizen philanthropy was a legitimate means of national participation.

Back in the United States, voluntary fund-raising amplified the claim that donations reinforced the bonds between soldiers and citizens, bonds that constituted the solidarity of the nation and, in the language of the Civil War, kept the army close to the people. A flyer for the 1943 War fund drive urged readers:

> Tell everyone you meet about the vast scope of Red Cross services to our Armed Forces. To those few who ask: "Why doesn't the Government do it?" there is a straightforward answer. These men who are giving up their jobs and homes and life itself, for us, are *our* men. The Red Cross is *our* Red Cross, personally ministering to their needs in our behalf, and the spirit of its great work rests on the voluntary nature of the support which we, by our own free will, give it. To the men in the Service, the Red Cross is a living symbol—of our love and compassion and the gratitude we have in our hearts for those who are sacrificing so much for us.[73]

The key point is that the process of fund-raising was not to be understood primarily as a means of raising money or providing services. By mobilizing large numbers of volunteers who would engage their personal and professional networks, fund drives constituted the nation as a moral and emotional collectivity. The Red Cross presented itself not as "a mere machine set up for humanitarian purposes," but as "a great organization filled with life and representing the active sympathy and aid which millions of our citizens are eager to render to the men of our armed forces—which they are rendering, in all the local camps in America and at our far-flung naval posts scattered over the Seven Seas."[74] Civic benevolence generated patriotic solidarity.

Civic Disengagement

The Chairman of the Red Cross, Thomas Lamont, did not exaggerate in his claim that the American Red Cross, along with the other wartime voluntary efforts, was not "a mere machine." A series of confidential polls commissioned from George Gallup confirmed this claim, finding that 71 percent of respondents reported that they had contributed to the Red Cross in 1946 compared to 84 percent in 1943 and 79 percent in 1945 (for "have you ever given money to the Red Cross?" the responses ranged from 92 percent in 1943 to 96 percent in 1946). But across the same years, the numbers replying that they had heard something unfavorable from a member of the World War II armed forces rose from 10 percent in 1943 to 55 percent in 1946. Leading sources of complaint were charging for services "when they shouldn't and when other organizations do not, an absence of any help from the Red Cross, and favoritism toward officers."[75] This mode of civic mobilization carried the potential for its own unraveling.

As if foretold by the conclusions of the Gallup poll of 1946, this national mobilization of reciprocal service and philanthropy proved fragile. As veterans returned with stories of the shortcomings of Red Cross service, disillusionment with the organization followed the same relational lines that had so effectively fueled wartime fundraising. Donors could also be easily offended. Asked for an additional donation to defray the costs of seats to be given to disabled soldiers at a Madison Square Garden benefit concert, a key Rockefeller adviser expressed disapproval "that the contributions thus received may swell the total of Red Cross income. It strikes me as a money-raising device purely and simply, and I think it is a shame to exploit the presence of these disabled soldiers in this way."[76]

With the enormous flood of war-fund-raising, the Rockefeller family office worked to figure out the relationship between Red Cross revenues and expenditure. Their analysis concluded that "in each of the past 2 years at least actual receipts have approximately doubled the sums actually reported as spent. The differences have accumulated in surpluses to keep the organization in a position whereby it practically has, at the beginning of any one year, sufficient reserves to finance the entire program for that year and that program each year proves to be about double what it was in the preceding year." This was judged an appropriate reserve for the duration of the war, but the analysis already signaled that a lasting reserve on this scale was not to be desired: "Presumably these reserves would be effectively used in financing the program of the Red Cross as it rapidly diminishes at the cessation of hostilities and without such heavy reliance upon the public."[77] The Rockefellers remained committed to the idea of applying the brakes to Red Cross fund-raising once the war was over.[78] The outcome was that the Red Cross gradually spent down its $68 million post–World War II reserves on disaster relief, creating the conditions for a financial crisis in 1955–56 when confronted with a hurricane in Puerto Rico, floods in Kentucky, and cyclones in Texas and the Southeast.[79]

The cumulative effects of competition among organizations and social networks were intensified by the erosion of a sense of mission, the fading

away of a civic compulsion to give. Among donors, both individual philanthropists and corporate leadership resisted the indefinite extension
of the wartime regime of fund-raising. This concern surfaced in a 1947
conversation between Arthur W. Packard from Rockefeller and Walter S. Gifford of the USO.[80] In private conversation, Gifford was critical
of the continued pace of fund-raising by the Red Cross:

> I think they are raising too much money. I don't think they are cutting
> down as much as they could. They still have a lot of money. What is
> their philosophy? That is a question that I have been trying to get at. . . .
> So far as their service to men in uniform is concerned, they probably
> have got enough to meet their needs for a year without asking for any
> more. . . . I should be sorry to see them go overwhelmingly over the top
> on their drive because of the popularity of the cause. It will tend to make
> them over confident and may kick back at them later and entrench their
> spending practices.[81]

In the years following the end of World War II, the unified fund-drives
of wartime gave way to increased competition, dissent, and mutual recrimination. Understood as a "civic nation," the wartime state had mobilized the enactment of citizenship within a nationally imagined community, deploying languages of obligation and gratitude. Fund-raising efforts
deliberately forged links between personal relationships and a massive
project of citizen philanthropy, embedding that imagined community in
enacted relationships as Americans were called "to join the war effort in
order to protect the state that protected them."[82] During wartime, this
political commitment to inclusiveness reorganized relationships across
regions, among powerful associations, and between business and labor.
Perhaps most significantly, patriotic fund-raising and volunteering connected a vast web of associations directly to the projects of the federal
government and the President himself. The principles of the "expansible
state," that had been evident in episodes of mobilization since the early
nineteenth century, were invoked as the nation-state met the challenge
of world war for a second time. But this was a temporary fusion of voluntarism and state-building, one that would soon be challenged by champions of anti-statism and riven by lines of conflict suppressed for the duration of the war.

8

Good Citizens
of a World Power

If unity has as its main purpose mutual defense against a common
threat, it provides no basis for a permanent peace except to help buy
time to engage in genuine peace-making. The latter calls for an understanding of the underlying nature of the threat and a positive answer—
a democratic faith—around which men everywhere can rally; an answer which provides the means of mobilizing free people to cope with
and overcome communism, fascism, and other "mass irrationalities".
Since these "irrationalities" grow out of the perversions of human nature, the "answer" must lie in generating moral and social forces which
strengthen the personal and collective integrity, the sense of responsibility, and the concern for people essential to free society.[1]

In 1943, more than 80 percent of Americans surveyed by George Gallup
reported that they had donated to the American Red Cross during the
past year.[2] Other war charities benefited from elevated levels of giving
and, at the same time, citizens purchased war bonds in large numbers.
Although all these contributions were understood as "voluntary," the
scale of citizen support for the war exemplified the consolidation of a
civic culture in which giving and loaning were powerful enactments
of citizenship. Linked to the nationalization of economic activity and
a revered wartime president, this pattern of citizen engagement was a
formidable political resource. Although the expanding power of national
government was evident in the wartime draft, rationing and price controls, as well as the introduction of a mass income tax, the practices of
voluntarism continued to suffuse the experience of citizens. This reflected a particular design for state-building; the highly intrusive Office
of Price Administration, for example, "organized its field staffs to include
large numbers of unpaid volunteers, partly because of limited funds and
partly as a democratic technique to foster public understanding and acceptance of the necessary price and rationing control."[3] Through the

purchase of war bonds, contributions to the Red Cross, and time contributed to government agencies as volunteers, Americans affirmed their
connections to the nation-state.

But by 1946, the regime of wartime solidarity expressed through civic
benevolence was already at risk. The American Red Cross commissioned
another confidential poll from George Gallup. This time, they found that
support had fallen dramatically, particularly among those who had direct
ties to someone serving overseas. Troubling as this discontent among
veterans and their families was to the Red Cross, it represented only one
dimension of the destabilization of the wartime model of national mobilization. In an extension of patterns evident for decades, and especially
in the mobilization for what had been the Great—not yet First—World
War, military mobilization had driven the United States Government
to expand in ways that depended massively on extended collaborations
with private organizations to rally support, to produce war material,
to provide aid to the troops, and to discipline the civilian population.
Reliant as it was on local business leaders, corporate executives, and a
nascent category of public relations experts, this model of governing
through public-private collaboration simultaneously increased government power and delegated a portion of control to private individuals
and organizations.

Under FDR, however, this method of mobilization had been firmly
tied to the person of the president. This configuration blurred the boundaries between patriotism and partisanship in ways that generated lasting
suspicion that depression and war would pave the way to some combination of socialism and durable Democratic hegemony.[4] Although calls
for a single coordinated war fund drive were never fully realized (in this,
as in almost every administrative matter, FDR preferred to have multiple
players in a single field), many groups had chafed at the partial centralization of control whether in the Red Cross or the war chests. These tensions festered, breaking into the open after FDR's death in 1945. Reaction against Democratic domination of the presidency was exacerbated
by the federal requirement that organized labor be given a seat at the
civic "roundtables" that played such an important role in the mobilization
of resources and public support for national efforts during war, natural
disaster, economic crisis, and renewed war. This demand represented
a "nationalization" of associational governance in at least two senses:
an intensification of Presidential direction of civic mobilization and
an opening of the architecture of civic associations, long controlled by
business and community elites, to new participants including organized
labor.

FDR's death and the end of the war triggered renewed debate and conflict over the relationship of voluntary effort, charitable fund-raising, and the national state. Roosevelt's allies would try to repurpose wartime configurations for peacetime, revisiting the challenges confronted by the Red Cross in the 1920s. Others advocated a stronger rejection of government's central role and a return to more local networks of civic responsibility. For some, this meant the "local" of bowling leagues and Parent-Teacher Associations that were populated by returning veterans, their spouses, and burgeoning families.[5] But, perhaps more significantly, this was also the local of chambers of commerce and community hospital boards that occupied the center of networks boosting economic development.[6] All three of these configurations—nationalized citizen philanthropy, local-civic alliances, and local-business networks—can be characterized as "infrastructural" or "associational," but they supported very different distributions of power and understandings of national membership and obligations.[7]

These contending templates for control over civic efforts set the terms for a postwar political struggle. The city-centered mapping of Community Chests was at odds with the national–small city–rural configuration of the Red Cross. Many business leaders disengaged from community federations, where community elites and social workers were influential leaders, reconstructing civic benevolence along the lines of the firm. The tensions between organized labor and civic elites multiplied as cause-based organizations and ethnic associations asserted control over the donations and voluntary effort of their members. Yet, at a moment when American voluntarism was central to the ideological opposition to Communism,[8] voluntary activity flourished even as its connections to the nation-state eroded. Henry Ford II made the case for federated fund-raising in the form of an Industrial Fund in explicitly political terms:

> Because I believe that we in this country are turning to Government more and more to get things done for us in what sometimes appears to be the soft and easy way. Many people are very much afraid that we are in danger of going too far, that we are in danger of forgetting that we <u>are</u> the Government. And that the more we give up relying on ourselves, the more we lose the capacity for being self-reliant.
>
> We all know—because we have seen it happen elsewhere—that freedom never is lost suddenly, overnight. It is lost over a long period of time, by a long chain of small neglects of duty and responsibility. In other words, very plain words, our rights and privileges are seldom actually <u>taken</u> away from us—we <u>give them up</u>, they are <u>abandoned</u>.[9]

The result of this conflict and competition would be a strange hybrid political regime that linked a celebration of voluntary participation in local politics and an expansive internationalism in support of the Cold War national security state. This moment of national dominance, the high water mark of "the American century," was marked by a puzzling combination of voluntarism and statism that would shape the trajectory of postwar political development in lasting ways.

Experiments at War's End

As the United States elaborated its postwar role in international affairs, philanthropy—both elite and "citizen"—once again proved an attractive tool for American influence. These efforts were not initiated by government alone. As had been the case since the early nineteenth-century missionary societies, civic and voluntary associations were not shy when it came to launching their own endeavors overseas.[10] In the wake of their extensive involvement in the recent war efforts, this was not a moment when private voluntary associations retreated from foreign projects or decoupled their activities from the national interest. As he attempted to solicit a gift from John D. Rockefeller Jr. for activities in Russia, Rufus Jones of the AFSC explained that "we have long felt that we ought to have a Quaker Unit of Relief working in Russia for the effect it would have on the Russian people, and, eventually, on our American relations with Russia." Such a project might have "a very far reaching effect on the whole attitude of the Russian people toward America."[11] Although this proposal to establish feeding stations for children in Stalingrad was eventually put on the back burner, the AFSC remained a central, if often little noticed, player in the extension of American influence. As an article in *Nation's Business* explained, "as the A.F.S.C.'s fame has spread, foundations, institutions, religious groups, even governments, have given them huge sums, especially in certain emergencies when no other organization is so well fitted for the relief role."[12]

Whereas many elite private charities balked at close cooperative relationships with government, remembering the bruising fights of the early 1930s, the AFSC had a different understanding of the relation between their voluntary efforts and government funds. They freely acknowledged that "the demands are so vast that only governments have adequate resources to meet the current crisis." Yet it was important that those funds be delivered through personal relationships to meet a need for "small determined, reconciling services of sympathy and understanding and for the new patterns of cooperation which resourceful and dedicated workers can try out in small but fresh and direct ways."[13] Gifts were linked to purposes rather than to membership, making the organization an attractive vehicle for donors wary of still more entanglement with politics.[14]

As was true of the Great Depression, the Occupation raised questions about the division of labor between private philanthropy and government effort. Reflecting on a request from the AFSC to the Rockefellers for support of neighborhood centers in Germany, Robert C. Bates confessed "there is a question in my mind as to whether needs of this kind, which seem to me pretty basic in the rehabilitation of an occupied country ought to be left to private philanthropy to deal with."[15] Private charity was also unclear whether it ought to be the broker between elite philanthropists and government action, a question that gained urgency as John D. Rockefeller III responded to a request from John J. McCloy, U.S. High Commissioner for Germany, for a gift of $100,000 in securities to the AFSC (that would come from John D. Rockefeller Jr.) to be used in ways McCloy "would consider strategic in hastening the rehabilitation of the German people."[16] McCloy's intention was to use these funds for scholarships, school fees, and other small grants that would cultivate goodwill. Even for high government officials, private philanthropy could be a source of critically important discretionary funds (as both Hoover and Hopkins had shown in their own requests to the Rockefellers during the first years of the depression). But provision of such discretionary funds stretched the bounds of what was understood as charitable. The AFSC, for example, had been advised that "the Committee could not properly turn over the funds to Mr. McCloy for his disbursement." While sympathizing with the purpose of the project, the AFSC was unwilling to "be a conduit only."[17]

In time, these and other similar efforts would inform a distinctive conjuncture of philanthropy, foreign policy, and social sciences. Echoing the AFSC's concern for the effects of personal contact on attitudes toward the United States, conferences and commissioned studies discussed how intervention could create new social capacities in addition to more narrowly conceived technical improvements or economic growth. The central claim involved the moral qualities of nations, which were understood as necessary components of national strength. Still profoundly shaped by wartime encounters with totalitarianism and the ongoing politics of the Cold War, postwar elites sought to articulate a vision of what is now called "soft power," which reserved a central role for voluntary action. As the final report of a conference on the international impact of the United States convened by the AFSC explained: "The suggestions made here stem from the basic premise that there must be, underlying the free world's collective actions today, a conviction and a sense of responsibility based on something more dynamic than fear of a common enemy."[18]

In this analysis, private efforts were not understood as simple substitutes for government action, but rather as a necessary means to attain national ends. Only by working through private individuals and voluntary organizations could national interests be realized abroad.

A Legacy Envisioned

As a new articulation of voluntarism and state power emerged within foreign policy, the parallel articulation in domestic politics was increasingly contested. Just as Herbert Hoover had been the embodiment of the ties between charity and citizenship during the 1920s, the person of Franklin Delano Roosevelt had come to anchor this combination after more than a decade of fund-raising for polio and fund-raising for war. His death in 1945 removed a central pillar of the regime of nationalized reciprocity. Although the 1946 drive for the March of Dimes set records as a kind of national memorial for the late president, thereafter the efforts became more problematic and revived only as the prospect of a successful vaccine came into view during the 1950s.[19] As wartime expectations of national unity faded, the postwar years brought efforts to redefine the linking of charity and citizenship in ways that were simultaneously patriotic and partisan.

From the late 1940s through the 1950s, Roosevelt's long-time allies worked to perpetuate the connection of voluntary giving to a strong national identity, notably through the mechanism of national blood-banking and the continuing war against polio. Those who had been closest to President Roosevelt had witnessed how extended networks of civic benevolence sustained the capacity and legitimacy of state action. The implications of this model of governance and solidarity were clear to Basil O'Connor, FDR's former law partner, founding president of the National Foundation for Infantile Paralysis (which received 50 percent of funds raised by the March of Dimes), and as of 1944, president of the American Red Cross. Situated at the intersection of structures of civic organization and formal political institutions, O'Connor understood what might be accomplished by a peacetime alignment of nation and citizen through the logic of the gift.

O'Connor proposed a domestic substitute for wartime mobilization as a method of generating national solidarity. He argued that a national system of blood banking would provide a moral framework for national unity, "a program of, for, and by the people of this nation":

> The goal of the National Blood Program is to provide blood and blood derivatives, without charge for the products, wherever needed throughout the nation. . . .

The program is a cooperative project in which hospital and medical authorities, public health officials, and the American Red Cross will participate to ensure the soundest policies and the highest possible standards of operation.

The most important participant, however, must be the citizenry. The *need* of the people *for* blood has been our motivating force in establishing this new program. And only the *generosity* of the *people* in *donating* their blood to the sick and injured will provide the power to drive this program forward with sustained momentum. . . .

What if the donor cannot actually trace, with his own eyes, the use of his blood to the beneficiary? Each gift of blood will have tangible value to someone in need. The picture is clear. It needs only to be made vivid in the minds of the American people.

A pint of blood given by John Doe rests in the storage vault of a blood center. Not far away on a main highway, two cars come speeding toward each other and collide. Their occupants are torn by broken glass and twisted metal and suffer great loss of blood. John Doe's blood is rushed to the bedside of one of the victims, who has well-nigh bled to death, and is poured into his veins. John Doe's blood has helped to save a life.

Another donor's blood has been processed into plasma and held for emergency use. Weeks later a fire breaks out in one of the city's large buildings. Dozens of residents suffer shock and terrible burns. This plasma is poured into the veins of one of the victims, even before there is time to transport her to the hospital. The donor's gift of blood has lessened shock and suffering. . . .

The blood of generous citizens, donated to the general welfare, will be the raw material out of which may come great discoveries in the amelioration or prevention of some of mankind's worst enemies. Men and women—the volunteers of America—could not give of themselves to a finer cause. Yes, this is truly a milepost for all the participating chapters. Likewise it is a milepost for the medical world.[20]

This passage, quoted at length, links themes of civic solidarity, preparedness, and progress in a textbook plan for an extended system of indirect exchange.[21] Through the practice of donating blood, citizens give gifts that then forge ties of gratitude among strangers (and, by extension, contribute to a vast system of mutual insurance against unexpected accidents and threats to health). These acts of generosity contribute to the repair of the damaged bodies of fellow citizens, but they also sustain the progress of science and medicine that will contribute to the well-being of all, present and future generations alike.

For the five years that he led the organization, Basil O'Connor worked to realize this vision of a national infrastructure of benevolence consistent with democratic commitments and expansive participation. He pushed the first major amendments of the Red Cross charter since Mabel Boardman and her allies had ousted Clara Barton in 1902. (Boardman herself died in 1946, only a year after stepping down from the position of Red Cross secretary that she had held for decades.) The revised charter shifted power to the local chapters that would now elect a clear majority of the board, the remaining seats to be filled either ex officio by representatives of the federal cabinet departments or by nominations from the current board.[22] At the tail end of a long Democratic administration, having provided relief to citizens and support to soldiers, the Red Cross stood on the verge of a stronger alignment with basic democratic principles. But, in many respects the shift came too late to forestall criticism, defection, competition, and a slide from national influence.

In the face of opposition fueled by a suspicion of any extension of the Roosevelt-Truman political hegemony as well as fear of government expansion into a national health service, O'Connor's attempt to transpose a model of nationalized civic benevolence from wartime to peacetime foundered. But the defeat of O'Connor's national blood-banking plan was only a first move in a broader effort to realign voluntary efforts with different structures of power and circuits of exchange. The business leaders and community elites who had long watched as Roosevelt gained leverage over local networks of voluntary associations were now poised to retake control.

A Legacy Undone

The possibility of constructing a national infrastructure of benevolence was undermined by political developments set in motion by the Roosevelt administration itself. With its roots in the tradition of deference that stretched back to the antebellum Whigs, organized benevolence did not necessarily mesh smoothly with the expansion of democratic rights and participation pushed by the New Deal and wartime mobilization. The friction surfaced early in relationships between the Red Cross and the Congress of Industrial Organizations.[23] While the CIO had participated in multiple wartime drives led by the Red Cross, frustrations had mounted at the failure of the Red Cross to provide meaningful opportunities to participate in the volunteer services and decision-making of the organization. Early in 1946, the CIO withdrew from joint fund-raising, asserting that "the Red Cross had not indicated any interest in the CIO's efforts to promote volunteer participation in home nursing, first aid, and other essential Red Cross volunteer work, and that 'our efforts to create a more wholesome understanding between Red Cross chapters and local labor groups were discouraged at every turn.'" Holding out the possibility of a rapprochement, the CIO expressed its hope "that under your [Basil O'Connor's] leadership the Red Cross will become a truly American Red Cross, democratized for full participation for everyone in the community."[24]

If the union members of the CIO felt that they had been excluded because of their politics from full membership in the "community" as represented by the American Red Cross, other organizations put themselves forward as more appropriate representatives of *local* rather than *national* community. The alternative was represented by the resurgence of federated fund-raising, once practiced by the hundreds of "community chests" but increasingly under the banner of "United Funds." Pioneered in Detroit in 1949, the United Fund model expressed a growing recognition by business leaders of the potential importance of corporate philanthropy and employment-based giving. Echoing advice given to chain stores in the 1920s that they should participate in community chest drives to secure local support, the new configuration gave greater financial control to business leaders by virtue of their corporate role rather than on the basis of membership in some more encompassing civic elite.

Through community relations programs, business groups strengthened their network ties to other civic and patriotic organizations. The simultaneously class-based and ideological motivations were captured by the title of a chamber of commerce pamphlet from 1948: *Program for Community anti-Communist Action.*[25] At the same time, business leaders made a case for seizing an opportunity produced by the conjuncture of increasingly steep taxes on corporate profits with the 1935 adoption of a corporate charitable contribution. A leading embodiment of the intersection of business, academia, and philanthropy, Beardsley Ruml instructed corporations in how to set up nonprofit corporate entities to take advantage of the deduction for 1951; Alfred P. Sloan Jr. made a special case for corporate donations to higher education, arguing that "any system of colleges limited to governmentally supported schools would be a standing temptation to politicians to exercise political control over what is taught in the class rooms."[26]

This co-optation of citizen philanthropy by business provoked criticisms of "taxation without representation" that echoed those that had been directed at the community chests in the 1920s.[27] A second threat to encompassing civic benevolence came from the emergence of a new kind of fund-raising effort: the "medical voluntaries," such as the American Heart Association and the American Cancer Society, that adopted well-honed methods of fund-raising but disembedded them from networks of reciprocity at either the community or national level. From the perspective of the Red Cross, these health-related organizations, the United Funds, and the new philanthropic assertiveness of large business all threatened its core understanding of national patriotism articulated through voluntarism. The Red Cross charged that the idea of united fund-raising was "being 'actively sold' to business leaders, large corporations and membership organizations, in Michigan by the United Health and Welfare Fund of Michigan, Inc., and on a nation-wide scale by the Michigan unit as well as by Community Chests and Councils, Inc., of New York."

As wartime solidarity receded, the conflicts over the relationship of the Red Cross to the Community Chests that had flared in the 1920s resurfaced, driven in large part by the "corporations and employee groups" that accounted for a large portion of contributions to community chests.[28] In response, Red Cross leadership issued a statement as to "Why The American National Red Cross Does Not Permit Participation in Any Joint Fund Raising Campaign."[29] This argument was couched in an extended analogy to world politics:

> One argument against communism is the fact that under this system those who deserve to be better off are not and those who do not deserve to be better off are. To a considerable extent this has been the experience of Community Chest agencies. The weak and less needed organizations must ride in on the wake of the stronger ones. Without much question it can be said that the Red Cross, because of its very nature and purpose as a national and international force, deserves to be better off financially than possibly can be provided through any communized fund-raising device.[30]

These conflicts turned on money and power. Familiar complaints were recited, that local Red Cross chapters had joined Community Chests with the assurance of certain distributions from the united drives yet those assurances were not honored. Revenues were slashed, memberships declined, and "most chapters identified with chests tended to become more and more localized in their point of view and to lose sight of the fact that they were the agents of a national organization governed by a Congressional Charter. Furthermore, in some instances, the chapter's identity in the local community faded almost to the vanishing point. . . . Chests tended to become dictatorial and to assume vested authority over chapters along with other member agencies." Apart from the implications for the amount of funds raised or needy persons served, each separate fund-raising effort sustained a particular network of influence and particular understanding of the relational quality of civic life. Thus the conflicts surrounding national charities and the civic role of philanthropy were not necessarily expressions of populist resentments, but the mutual suspicion of distinctive subsets of the many, many elite networks that organized life within and across the nation's communities.

At the national meeting in 1949, the Red Cross "struck out . . . against 'coercive' attempts to federate all welfare fund drives in one annual appeal." Red Cross officials argued that " 'compulsory federated fund raising' would be controlled first on a state-wide and eventually on a national basis. The system would produce one mammoth annual financial campaign carried on simultaneously throughout the country 'under the direction of this national authority.' "[31] In the alternation of "community" and "national," two different configurations of voluntarism are visible. The first, represented by the Red Cross, linked local chapters to the national organization with its presidential imprimatur. But this configuration linking local and national was weakened by the postwar revisions of the Red Cross charter. The second, exemplified by the Community Chests and Councils, Inc., built on municipally centered organizations, very loosely linked through regional and national ties.[32] In this arrangement, gifts were directed within the community under the control of local elites, but increasingly contested by groups that demanded that their contributions support causes of particular personal concern or causes that were closely linked to group identity at the same time that individual private agencies wrested back a measure of control over their finances from central budget committees.[33]

Eventually, the Red Cross succumbed to the pressure from a handful of powerful local chapters to participate in joint fund-raising in industrial plants that allowed only one fund-raising drive per year. This agreement was hedged about with conditions—that the Red Cross would determine its own budgetary means added into the total amount of the drive, that the Red Cross would retain the right to organize independent drives in the broader community—but the change of principle was clear. By-then-former Red Cross president Basil O'Connor blasted the policy change, arguing that payroll deductions "no matter how dressed up, are compulsory assessments on employes [*sic*] for health and welfare activities." This compulsion, O'Connor argued, undermined the pretense of voluntarism as a legitimate alternative to public social services:

> If funds for health and welfare are to be obtained by assessment, then the proper mechanism to use is obviously the power of taxation where the burden falls on all and not just on labor.
>
> If the public will not voluntarily support voluntary associations for health and welfare, the indication is that the public believes such

associations should no longer exist and that health and welfare should be totally a matter of governmental operation. That seventy million people annually support the March of Dimes shows clearly that the public has reached no such decision.[34]

Echoing the late 1920s, the theme of voluntary fund-raising as a prophylactic against expanded taxation regularly appeared in arguments for the Red Cross. Defending the size of the organization's projected budget in 1949, President E. Roland Harriman questioned the demand that the Red Cross return to its prewar scale: "Why should Red Cross be the only organization, Government, welfare or business to return to any predetermined level? . . . America still is growing and all of us are doing everything in our power to keep it growing. Red Cross is part and parcel of that growth, particularly with respect to national defense." The failure to support those activities would have undesirable political consequences, he warned: "If the Red Cross and other agencies do not give the people what they need and what they have learned they want and can get, the only road left open may be for the Government to take over. That means taxation instead of voluntary contributions."[35]

In the space of a few years, networks of corporate leaders had substantially regained control over the circuits of civic benevolence, leading critics to see "voluntary" fund-raising as a new form of economic dictatorship capable of coercing employees to donate funds to support services that could be funded more democratically through taxation. Proponents of these new models, including Henry Ford II, argued that workers were also plagued by multiplying fund-raising drives and organized labor continued its cooperation with employers in organizing community fund-raising.[36] On this dimension, the postwar politics of civic benevolence shifted the balance between a charisma-driven nationalizing mode centered on the presidency and a much more municipally centered, business-dominated form of mobilization—and even then, the focus tended to shift from the community to the firm and its employees. As a consequence, the philanthropically sustained sense of common membership in a national community eroded. Focusing his comments on the "ingrate crisis area" of Flint, Michigan, which had been struck by a tornado in 1954, Red Cross President E. Roland Harriman complained that "the pattern had been to wait until 'the Red Cross finished the job of meeting basic needs.' . . . In the future, he said, 'communities that don't help themselves in the total responsibility of a disaster can hardly expect to be recipients of nation-wide generosity.'"[37]

In parallel with these shamings and scoldings, others attempted to revive the sense of national obligation and solidarity. As fund-raising efforts fell short in 1953, Mamie Eisenhower made a "personal appeal to the mothers of America," calling for them to donate both funds and blood. Attempting to explain the troubling shortfall, the First Lady speculated, " 'What they perhaps do not realize is that the same pint of blood they contribute can be processed into gamma globulin and also into serum albumin, the blood derivative which our Korean combat wounded need so desperately.' Through the Red Cross, therefore, Mrs. Eisenhower stressed blood today did double duty. 'We can help children walk and wounded to live.' "[38] In these appeals, the faded spirit of wartime civic benevolence reappeared but the results fell short of the national solidarity that was to have been generated by circuits of blood donation and receipt within a unified citizenry.

The shift from national networks of benevolence to more restricted circuits of mutual aid was evident across policy domains, including disaster relief and medical care. The same tension between the inclusive "indirect exchange" envisioned in O'Connor's plan and the organizational features of the postwar health care system produced a schism within blood-banking over issues that went to the heart of a Maussian model of gift exchange.[39] Whereas the Red Cross under O'Connor had envisioned a system in which blood would be donated without compensation and available to all those who needed it, the medical societies—at least in the vicinity of New York City—were interested in linking the provision of blood to the financial practices of private hospitals. Consequently, they promoted a system in which donors would receive "credits" for donations that would entitle them to a certain amount of blood for themselves if needed (at a ratio of up to four pints for every one pint donated) and, at a slightly less generous rate, to other family members. The Red Cross protested that if a system of credits was to function it needed to recognize that blood donation often happened in the context of group membership—in fraternal lodges, unions, churches, workplaces—rather than narrowly within the bounds of family.[40] Credits, they argued, needed to be transferable to co-members in these organizations. But these arguments did not persuade the leadership of professional medical societies and their breach with the Red Cross widened further. Here, civic benevolence was not only de-nationalized, it was increasingly individualized and disembedded from the networks of giving and receiving that had been a feature of the American landscape for more than a century.

In the years following the end of World War II, these cumulating conflicts over specific forms of associational voluntarism fractured the landscape of civic benevolence along multiple dimensions. The unified fund-drives of wartime gave way to increased competition, dissent, and mutual recrimination as various groups and constituencies contested the right of any one group to represent and choreograph the generosity of the American people.[41] Among donors, both individual philanthropists and corporate leadership resisted the indefinite extension of the wartime regime of intensified fund-raising.[42] As wartime mobilization ebbed, new civic models were promoted but the institutional frameworks that had supported fully fledged configuration of nationalized voluntarism and benevolence remained. Thus new civic projects came to inhabit a well-developed framework of privileges, exemptions, and regulations.

A Transformed Organizational Landscape

This splintering among civic organizations was accompanied by a re-treat into professionalism. The charity organization societies and relief boards that had provided a venue for recognition and coordination of be-nevolence prior to the New Deal emerged from the Second World War as entities dedicated to professional therapeutic work with a mix of paying and subsidized clients.[43] In the years immediately after the war, social service organizations oscillated between two quite different understand-ings of their role, alternately acting as private charities or as professional nonprofit agencies. Thus the winter of 1947 brought appeals that would have seemed quite familiar a half century earlier: "For $15 one of these children will find a wealth of warmth in a bright new coat. $10 will fit his little sister into a sturdy snowsuit, and $5 will keep a youngster snug with a set of galoshes, mittens and stockings."[44] Yet by later that spring, one study committee of the same organization, the Community Service Society of New York (the product of a merger between the Association for Improving the Condition of the Poor, established in the 1840s, and the NYCOS, est. 1882) reported: "In the light of our study it would ap-pear that in the process of growth and expansion the Family Service Department has been undergoing a gradual change in function, as evi-denced by the greater emphasis on research and staff development and by a deepening of the content of case work, to the point where it has become more nearly a family-counseling and child-guidance service."[45] Relationships between organization and donor as well as organization and client were transformed, minimizing the traditional ties of benevo-lence between donors (or the organization as their representative) and clients.

These organizational changes extended the division of labor between government and private efforts articulated early in the New Deal. Whereas FDR had spoken about government's responsibility for "economic maladjustment" and charity's jurisdiction over "individual maladjust-ment," the language now referenced the relationship of those providing and receiving services. The key distinction conflated references to commerce and totalitarianism, drawing a line between "mass" services and "individuated" or "retail" services.[46] Urging support for the Community Service Society of New York, Frederick Sheffield wrote to Laurance Rockefeller:

> This new society is equipped to do all of the jobs that the prior organizations did and do them more effectively and more efficiently. . . . My personal belief is that unless the right kinds of private charitable organizations are supported in these days, the future of each individual's relationship to his community will become more and more dependent upon government and less and less individualistic. The particular charity, moreover, reaches down into the very roots of the troubles which so many charities have to help and for which so much government expenditure is necessary.[47]

Whereas the nation-centered civic benevolence of wartime had emphasized how each small gift incorporated individuals into a national struggle, here the emphasis was on private charity as a limit on the intrusion of government service that were understood to threaten democratic values. Thus the linking of mass citizen benevolence to national projects and patriotism eroded. And, as a consequence, circuits of reciprocity were reoriented.

With the struggle over government financial support for relief and social services largely settled in the affirmative, nonprofit organizations confronted the question of how to motivate supporters to make contributions above and beyond their mandated taxes. Absent the rallying force of a national crisis or presidential charisma, how could people be persuaded to give freely in order to forestall the need to expand mandatory taxation to support those same community services? In the fund-raising drives of the 1950s, charitable motives were displaced by references to business calculation infused with political commitments: "This is a straightforward business appeal. The century-old Community Service Society is in the business of helping to keep sound the New York community in which you do business, to help protect the community's family life—the bedrock of democracy."[48]

Yet for all these changes, the mobilization of resources in the nonprofit sector continued to rely on networks of personal reciprocity.[49] These were recalibrated to accommodate the expansion of widespread, almost mass-market solicitation, and to convey respect for the individual choices made by donors rather than inherited family ties to a particular organization.[50] Fund-raisers understood the extra influence that came with an appeal embedded in a personal or business relationship. As the Community Service Society reported in December 1955: "Every effort has been made in this campaign to increase the extent of personal solicitation of our more generous contributors." Leaders drawn from civic groups and businesses had "taken responsibility for approaching certain individuals with whom they have influence." Even if person-to-person meetings were not possible, "the campaign organization has been built up with an aim to providing the most effective signatures on the mail solicitations, e.g. executives in Wall Street have been written to by fellow executives; lawyers have been approached through letters signed by one of several prominent lawyers serving on the campaign committee, etc."[51]

In this respect, the pattern following the Second World War paralleled that after the First. While the Red Cross, the organization most closely identified with the national military effort, fizzled and fractured in peacetime, the municipal pieces of the fund-raising machinery were quickly repurposed and even strengthened. In response to fires and floods, circuits of giving built on and even strengthened relationships in the world of work, either through quasi-mandatory assessments of employees within a firm or the interpersonal persuasion (and pressure) of organized businessman-to-businessman solicitation. The resulting funds supported a wide range of activities ranging from the self-provisioning of an expansive middle class through scouting groups and the YMCAs and YWCAs (which, in turn, were increasingly orienting themselves to recreation rather than spiritual uplift[52]) to the support of the professionalized social service agencies that now dealt with "clients," some of whom paid for services, others of whom were subsidized by funds raised through federated campaigns.

As Basil O'Connor had argued with respect to joint fund-raising within industrial plants, this represented something very close to a system of taxation, but a system that was most "mandatory" for workers and over which business leaders exercised considerable control. The limits of this system would be revealed in the 1960s, as multiplying strains on the fabric of urban life would invite new federal interventions. Ironically, these interventions would be "contracted out" to the very system of nonprofit organizations that had been sustained as a bulwark against the expansion of tax-supported community services. The successful transformation of private charity agencies into nonprofit organizations had been promoted by opponents of government expansion, but became the matrix for new patterns of government expansion. Rather than settling on one side or the other of the ideological opposition of free markets and statism, American governance continued to straddle both, prompting efforts to characterize and legitimate this hybridized state of affairs.

Retheorizing Public and Private:
The Rockefeller Special Studies Project

In cities across the nation, networks dominated by businessmen had edged out many competitors for control over civic benevolence by the 1950s. But, given the context of world politics, this resolution was ideologically unsatisfactory; it failed the test of demonstrating the vibrancy of participatory democracy in the United States. Precisely because the greatly expanded national government that emerged from the Second World War had posed profound challenges to long-standing beliefs about the value of democratic participation and voluntarism, many of those most committed to voluntarism now felt the need to articulate those commitments in the context of an anti-totalitarian moment. Those same philanthropists who had been intimately involved in the prosecution of the war and postwar refugee relief sought a rationale for preserving their valued ties to government officials while reaffirming the role of the voluntary associations and local involvement.

A sense of that genuine interest in supporting local political involvement is provided by the extended conversations among the Rockefeller philanthropic advisers over a request that came to Nelson Rockefeller to support a community organizer in Chicago by the name of Saul Alinsky. Just as Nelson's father and grandfather had given considerable attention to building new forms of community government in the 1920s, the request was taken quite seriously. The staff commissioned a relatively lengthy evaluation of the organization, which focused on the question of whether there was something distinctive to the community (Back of the Yards) or the organizer (Alinsky himself) that would prevent this effort from serving as a replicable model. The conclusion was that Alinsky was probably one of a kind, but the real bar to making a contribution came from the organizational template that Alinsky had adopted for the Industrial Areas Foundation. In a participatory mode, any contribution to the organization made you a member of the corporation. The Rockefeller enterprises were not about to accept that sort of entanglement of their corporate identity with that of a community organization. In the end, Alinsky's request was declined.[53]

The thickness of the file on this particular request, however, testifies to the fact that at least one very important philanthropic enterprise was not satisfied with an understanding of voluntarism that centered on business-controlled community fund-raising. The small 'd' character of voluntarism mattered as much as the equation of voluntarism with anti-statism in the context of the Cold War. This commitment to reviving forms of local political participation and community control was not restricted to the Rockefellers and was, very conveniently, compatible with the continued strength of the national state, at least in certain policy domains. One model of political order turned on a division of labor between a centralized national government that would manage big challenges such as defense, foreign policy, and the business cycle, while local arrangements would provide citizens with a "voice in the control of the immediate forces that affect his home, the character of his neighborhood, or the conditions under which he works."[54]

The result was an understanding of the relation of public and private that differed markedly from the stark contrasts of federal government and voluntarism exemplified by Herbert Hoover's conception of "the American System." Instead, voluntarism offered what would later be labeled a "third way" that could preserve individual liberty while acknowledging the need for some form of governance and regulation.[55] Thirty years after the publication of Hoover's manifesto, the Rockefeller Brothers Fund sponsored the "Special Study Project," intended in part as preparation for Nelson Rockefeller's planned run for the presidency. The project, directed by a young Henry Kissinger, brought together a marquee set of the Cold War liberal elite—drawn from politics, business, academia, religion, and beyond—to reflect on the big questions of the postwar world. In this sustained effort to develop both a philosophical stance on American democracy and a programmatic basis for public policy, the members of one panel described a regime defined by the significant—but far from total— interpenetration of public and private activities. The analysis began with reflections on the still-vivid encounters with totalitarianism:

> Particularly in times of emergency, but even at other times, there is a besetting temptation in political life. It is the temptation to push reason of state into the private areas of society and to turn nonpolitical voluntary associations into instrumentalities of an encircling political power. The extralegal persecution of conscientious objectors, the refusal of private enterprises to give employment to individuals only because these individuals subscribe to radical doctrines—these are examples of practices that erase the line between the state and the rest of society.[56]

But rather than using this warning to endorse a bright line between the civic sphere and the state,[57] the Rockefeller panel recognized—with clear approval—that a growing comingling of public and private efforts or "widespread private government, nourished and supported, indeed, by the deliberate action of the state, is an intrinsic feature of a free society."[58]

> It is a mark of a free society, we have said, that it draws a line between the areas that are subject to state control or legal coercion and those in

which the private judgment of individuals or voluntary groups will prevail. At any given moment, however, there is usually an entire zone where the public and private sectors fade into one another. The recognition that certain private associations serve crucial social interests that must receive public support is reflected, for example, in provisions of the income tax laws which make contributions to private educational and charitable institutions in part tax deductible. Again, associations within the professions—for example, bar associations—have long enjoyed a delegated authority from the state and are recognized as the quasi-official representatives and protectors of particularly important sectors of the public interest. To take still another example, in recent years a new form of partnership between government and private enterprise has been worked out in the field of atomic energy. On all sides during the last generation new hybrids have emerged—independent public corporations, private corporations that are created to do only government work, research centers staffed by private groups and financed by public funds. Few of these activities fit into simple and conventional categories separating the 'private' and the 'public.'[59]

This interpenetration of private organizations and public purposes was recognized not as a problem to minimize but as an opportunity to exploit. As the secretary to Panel VII on "The Moral Framework of National Purpose," a young Robert Heilbroner argued that private organizations, including churches but also public institutions such as schools, were important sites for closing "the gap between moral lip service and moral practice." Voluntary associations might also contribute, although here the panelists were very aware that the large "corporate" voluntary organizations that were increasingly prominent did not represent the kind of participatory association celebrated by Tocqueville.[60]

In important respects, this vision of civic participation reversed many of the important precepts of the model of citizenship that had been deployed by nation-builders since the nation's founding. In the prime of this effort, the period extending from the Civil War through World War II, civic benevolence did constitute a "divine method of patriotism," to quote Unitarian preacher and Civil War fund-raiser Thomas Starr King. Local ties enacted in participation were embedded in the social imaginary of an extended system of national solidarity. Gifts circulated among strangers, linking diverse places and types of people without requiring direct social ties. Envisioned on this national scale, organized civic benevolence would constitute a reinforcing armature for a political order ever-threatened with secession and group conflict.

What had changed by the time of the Rockefeller Special Studies Project was a systematic blurring of the distinction between public and private with a corresponding shift in focus to the contrast between large hier-archical organizations (whether federal agencies or voluntary associa-tions) and meaningful participation at the individual and interpersonal level. The social landscape of *public* schools and *private* churches as roughly equivalent arenas for meaningful participation by individual citizens co-existed with a recognition of the role of a powerful national government, particularly one that would project its (putatively benevolent) power in a contested and dangerous world. This dual vision was already evident in the late 1940s, when projects such as the "Letters to Italy" campaign sought "to enlist civil society in general—and immigrants and their chil-dren, in particular—in a defense of the American Way overseas."[61] Similar strategies were deployed during the Kennedy administration, in which military strength was coupled with the "authentic" personal engagement of the Peace Corps or later Vista in American cities. It would emerge in yet another configuration during Lyndon Baines Johnson's Great Society, in which massively expanded federal funding for poverty relief and eco-nomic development would flow through community nonprofits, many of which traced their lineage back through the professionalized social ser-vice organizations of the 1950s to the reform-minded groups of the turn of the century. In the Toquevillian imagery, voluntary associations rep-resented important bulwarks against the expansion of the administrative state. By the 1960s, however, they constituted vehicles for the extension of federal efforts. Government raised revenues and then funds—attached to rules made by either Congress or federal agencies—flowed to state and local governments as well as nonprofit organizations.[62]

Perversely, at least from the vantage point of those who had champi-oned voluntary social service as a bulwark against state expansion, this configuration allowed for the continued escalation of federal spending and the ongoing attenuation of governmental control and accountability. Public funds were channeled to private organizations in an enormously complex web of contracts, grants, and subsidies that continues to defy efforts at regulation or even documentation. Thus the effort to dismantle the national configuration of civic benevolence out of concern that it would unduly enhance the power of the presidency has had the result of enhancing the scale of government while disguising and degrading the capacity of any political actor or institution to oversee the operations of this vast new system of associational governance.

This greatly expanded web of federal, state, and local grants to non-profit organizations has had the additional effect of undercutting the power of community-level federated fund-raising to enact a strong sense of municipal membership. While the leaders of the community chest movement had presumed a set of common concerns to motivate contributions and direct the resulting funds, by the late 1950s and 1960s, newly mobilized groups increasingly charged that such centralized fund-raising-and-distributing models overlooked or misunderstood the needs of their particular community or cause.[63] Patterns of giving, like those of distributing funds, became increasingly fragmented and difficult to map clearly into civic identities. Although levels of giving and donating have continued to fluctuate, subjects of celebration and anxiety, these exchanges no longer effectively enact the model of civic benevolence that had been such a powerful force in mobilizing the nation across a series of crises culminating in the Second World War.

The result was a period of flux in which some groups defected from centralized fund-raising, others made plays to wrest control from the groups that had dominated the wartime organization of civic benevolence, still others turned from nationalizing benevolence to fund-raising that would strengthen those institutions—particularly in health care and higher education—that would serve as bulwarks against state expansion and pillars of domains of private enterprise. The terms of conflict involved the level of voluntary giving as well as the locus of control. Economic elites came to understand giving by citizens as an obstacle to the expansion of a consumer economy at the same time that they recognized the potential of a newly conceptualized nonprofit sector as a site for setting boundaries on the expansion of public social provision. This potential for limiting explicitly public programs was underwritten by expanding streams of tax-subsidized contributions, enabled by the linking of a long-standing individual deduction for charitable contributions with the introduction of a mass income tax as well as the regularization of corporate charitable contributions. As federal spending programs increasingly recognized nonprofit organizations—whether social welfare agencies, community hospitals, or research universities—as legitimate recipients of public funds, the ingredients were in place for the distinctive brew of public and private efforts that has come to characterize American governance in the second half of the twentieth century.[64]

9

Combinatorial Politics and Constitutive Contradictions

Words signifying ends and means, or values in general, have a double relation to the times in which they emerge. Their meanings are determined by problems recognized and purposes pursued; their use is a sign of the values of the times. They, in turn, define and relate values and processes; their analysis is an instrumentality of understanding of action.

RICHARD MCKEON, "Responsibility as Sign and Instrumentality"[1]

On the level of pure theory the most disparate views and tendencies are able to co-exist peacefully, antagonisms are only expressed in the form of discussions which can be contained within the framework of one and the same organization without disrupting it. But no sooner are these same questions given organizational form than they turn out to be sharply opposed and even incompatible.

GEORG LUKÁCS, "Towards a Methodology
of the Problem of Organisation"[2]

Trying to make sense of the French Revolution as it unfolded, Edmund Burke wondered "what cement the legislators had provided" for this new political order "from any extraneous materials." What could stabilize the instantiation of novel revolutionary ideologies in the complex layerings of inherited political practices and social forms?[3] Had Burke pivoted to look west across the Atlantic, rather than east across the English Channel, his question would have been equally on point. For decades, indeed centuries, after the American Revolution, nation-state-building was a work in progress. Crises, chronic challenges, and political visions fueled an ongoing organizing process in which diverse materials were combined and recombined to generate both new capacities for governing and revised "stories of peoplehood."[4] Through such iterated problem-solving, the American nation-state has been invented and reinvented.

Diverse "extraneous materials" have been employed in these efforts: private individuals and firms, racial and ethnic solidarities, religious faiths, and ideological commitments. Repeatedly, however, relations of reciprocity, practices of voluntarism, and discourses of benevolence have been harnessed to political projects, often advanced through the efforts of voluntary associations. This was the feature of American democracy that captured the imagination of Alexis de Tocqueville during his visit to the new nation in 1831. During the Civil War, John Stuart Mill and Giuseppe Mazzini similarly singled out the capacity of "the people" to mobilize in their own interest as the distinctive and admirable feature of American politics. During the first and second world wars, voluntary efforts were understood not simply as instrumental additions to the war effort but as object lessons in political virtue that countered the threats of tyranny and totalitarianism. In the 1950s, Nelson Rockefeller's Special Studies Project recognized "an entire zone where the public and private sectors fade into one another" as various associations exercise "a delegated authority from the state and are recognized as the quasi-official representatives and protectors of particularly important sectors of the public interest."[5]

The names given to these activities have shifted over the decades and centuries. The use of "charity" and "benevolence" declined markedly by the middle of the nineteenth century, with the former resurging during occasional recessions and crises.[6] "Alms" also receded from American vocabulary, steadily and gradually. "Philanthropy" crested during the era of the Benevolent Empire, while the use of "nonprofit" began to surge in the 1930s. While all represented forms of "voluntarism" (itself gaining in popularity over the twentieth century), these nouns embodied subtly varied models of the relationship between donor and beneficiary and engendered distinctive tensions with understandings of democratic citizenship. Faced with crises or committed to projects, political actors have repeatedly drawn upon the social networks, familiar practices, and moral resources of voluntarism to construct the sort of "charitable infrastructure" with "obvious political possibilities" that had been represented by the Boston Committee on Donations during the early years of the Revolution.[7]

This pattern of building and rebuilding the nation-state with materials from outside of formal political institutions is intrinsically unstable. The delegation of authority to private entities of any kind creates challenges to political accountability that multiply in a "government out of sight."[8] In addition, these private entities may establish relationships to citizens that are at odds with the models of citizenship recognized within formal political processes. Prisoners contracted out to private employers have been subjected to conditions akin to peonage, firms awarded government contracts are not held to the same requirements for open meetings and freedom of information requests that apply to government agencies, and citizens may be charged additional fees in order to submit their tax returns or meet the terms of their parole. Thus the "zone where the public and private sectors fade into one another" is laced with tensions and contradictions.

Although benevolence and charity have decidedly different normative valences than peonage, lack of transparency, and extortionate fees, they generate an analogous set of incompatibilities. Gift-giving—of kindness, or alms, or symbolic exchange—has the capacity to create ties beyond immediate kinship or community. It is, therefore, a potent form of social cement. But the relationships generated in this way may also entail dependency, the expectation of gratitude and reciprocation, and consequent resentment at the absence of opportunities to contribute. During World War II, the CIO complained that the Red Cross "had not indicated any interest in the CIO's efforts to promote volunteer participation."[9] Uncoupled from acts of reciprocation, such obligations offend the equality and independence of the liberal ideal of citizenship, intensified as the discrepancies between formal political equality and economic inequality grow. An architecture of governance that developed to harness civic voluntarism and mass patriotic giving to the production of public goods has created opportunities for the deployment of unprecedented private wealth in the name of *privately determined* public goods.[10] Thus, the relationship between benevolence and democratic dignity functions as a constitutive contradiction. It both enables the construction of a powerful national state in an anti-statist political culture and establishes a durable zone of instability in those configurations of governance.

Across multiple crises and political projects, this powerful yet volatile relationship has generated a distinctive trajectory of political change. This specific—perhaps even exceptional—historical account of American political development can be understood in terms of a set of more general theoretical claims. First, that states and nations and nation-states are products of political ordering that employ diverse materials. The forms of voluntarism—of private action oriented toward public, or at least shared, projects—are culturally available social technologies that have been repeatedly repurposed for nation-state-building. Such political use of voluntarism is far from unique to the political development of the United States, but it has been particularly important there due to the deep-rooted anti-statism that infuses much of American politics.

All these "elements that are borrowed from previous states" and put together as "jigsaw puzzles"[11] may be perfectly compatible with one another, but this is certainly not inevitable. Such combinatorial politics resembles bricolage rather than consistent system-building and, therefore, embeds tensions and contradictions within political life, particularly in the topography of infrastructural power.[12] Efforts to contain these tensions and to harness connections across diverse networks may generate organizational innovations and institutional legacies such as laws that define or segregate kinds of action. The result is a type of path-dependency that is anchored not in one specific solution, but rather in a durable zone of instability and reconfiguration.[13]

Constitutive Contradictions and Institutional Change

For much of its history, American politics has been marked by partial and contentious combinations of charity or benevolence and liberal citizenship. Restated in the language of institutional theory, two models or geometries of social relationships have been repeatedly linked in the course of political projects, both domestic and international.[14] For government, streams of voluntary contributions might represent a solution to the provision of public goods without requiring increased taxation. For charities and voluntary associations, government's authority to tax (and exempt from taxation) incentivized giving far beyond the unaided capacity of their own fund-raising drives. But for all the benefits of such partnerships, the two models of social relationship remain fundamentally at odds.

Recall Willie Stark's demand that government provide support to citizens "Free. Not as charity. But as a right." However well-intentioned, gifts entail dependency. Consequently, the meshing of voluntarism and charity with a substantially liberal polity represents a particular kind of institutional accomplishment in which these conflicting relational models were reconciled in new organizational arrangements and through cultural transformations. Some individuals inevitably loom large at particular moments—Clara Barton, Herbert Hoover, FDR, and numerous Rockefellers among others—but the emphasis on excavating the models of action that guided their efforts to meet public challenges requires an historical account of the organizing principles of public life.[15]

Here, a brief detour through the languages of cultural and organizational sociology is helpful. Recall the central empirical puzzle: How did the American nation-state come to incorporate cultural models of both liberty and benevolence that were once held to be deeply incompatible, at least when applied to citizens with full standing? Translated into theoretical terms, this puzzle can be restated as: How do conflicting relational logics or cultural models come to be linked in a stable institutional arrangement? Although the availability of multiple logics or schemas is now widely recognized in social theory (often accompanied with the image of a "tool-kit" or "repertoire"),[16] there has been relatively little theorizing about when and how these models may or may not be combined and transposed. What work is required to harness formally incompatible models to one another?

The answer to this question turns on the character of different historical moments. As Ann Swidler has argued, over long stretches of "settled" time, tensions between social domains and models of order may be diffuse. Cultural practices are taken-for-granted rather than requiring explicit ideological justification.[17] But in moments of conflict and mobilization, claims are often made that an entire domain of activity should be organized in one way or another. Recall the charge leveled by Elias Smith in 1809: "Many are republicans as to government, and yet are but half republicans, being in matters of religion still bound to a catechism, creed, covenant or a superstitious priest. Venture to be as independent in things of religion, as those which respect the government in which you live."[18] In order to advance such claims, periods of rapid social change or contestation also prompt the heightening of differences: "Bursts of ideological activism occur in periods when competing ways of organizing action are developing or contending for dominance. People formulate, flesh out, and put into practice new habits of action."[19]

In general, moments of crisis or "unsettled times" will be marked by two opposing tendencies: both the increased effort by proponents of one logic or organizational form to capture all resources and the intensified defense of clear categorical distinctions. In the case of American charity, such claims sometimes turned on efforts by national government to harness the entire field of benevolent organizations and voluntary donations to national projects. During both World Wars, for example, fund-raising was centralized through war chests and community chests. By the autumn of 1918, civic leaders and representatives of large donors had come together to form the National Investigation Bureau of War Charities and a bill had been introduced into Congress to centralize control of all war charities in the Department of Justice. Although these efforts to harness private charity to war mobilization were cut short by the November armistice, similar efforts were made during the Second World War. Responding to concerns over competing fund drives, President Roosevelt created

"The President's War Relief Control Board" to register all agencies solic-iting funds for foreign relief and private organizations.[20] As an expanded income tax and "voluntary" payroll deductions for war bonds and stamps were layered[21] onto a system already in place for charitable contributions, there was an opening where all the organizational and cultural resources of citizen philanthropy might have been captured by the gravitational pull of the federal government.[22]

Not all crises, however, drove the consolidation of charity and citi-zenship. Fearing the extension of federal powers, President Hoover re-acted to the drought and unemployment that would become the Great Depression by calling for greater coordination and efficiency of charity, but insisting that such voluntary efforts must remain private and entirely distinct from government programs.[23] A pamphlet published by the Emergency Employment Committee of New York asked "Is this Man on Your Christmas List?" and pointed out that assistance for the "man without a job" could be given in the same spirit as a Boy Scout outfit for Buddy, a doll house for Judy, or a briar pipe for Uncle John (see Fig-ure 6).[24] But the tensions between the normative models of benevolence and citizenship created a receptive audience for the claim of a citizen en-titlement to relief without any taint of charity. Willie Stark again provides the refrain: "Free. Not as Charity. But as a Right."

The durable contradiction between charity and liberal citizenship pro-vided opportunities for countermobilization. The expansion of govern-ment programs was often met by resistance from civic elites who sought to ground a culture of charitable citizenship in local community. Calls to meet public necessity with private charity were decried as inappropriate in a polity of free and equal citizens. As long as adherents to one norma-tive model or set of rules are able to repeatedly reanchor their model in distinctive resources and networks, there is no reason to expect that such episodes of heightened conflict will result in the triumph of one way of organizing political and civic relationships over another.

The expansion of the jurisdiction of one model of social relationships may also have the effect of undermining its own central premises. Thus as communities place greater demands on voluntary associations to ad-dress public problems such as poverty or public health, the linking of charitable fund-raising to community pressure could profoundly erode the voluntary character of those civic gifts. Consequently, rather than a progressive teleology that moves from one dominant form to another, it is possible that great swathes of institutional change will involve oscillations between and repeated hybridizations of the rules of the game or models of appropriate organizational form.[25]

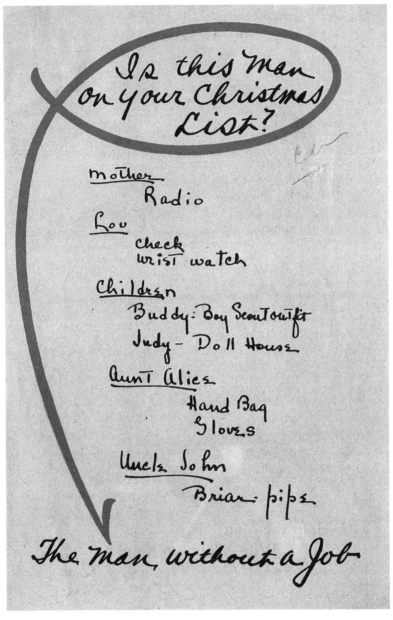

FIGURE 6. "Is this Man on Your Christmas List?" Image courtesy of the Rockefeller Archive Center (OMR II 2 F, Box 21, Folder 187).

Combinatorial Politics in American
Political Development

Viewed through the lens of comparative politics, the history of the American state has seemed anomalous, a deviation from the trajectories followed by governing arrangements in Europe and elsewhere. Instead of conforming to the model of centralized, bureaucratic, autonomous public authority often equated with the modern state, American governance has been organized through *both* public institutions and private organizations or individuals. This type of regime relies on what sociologist Michael Mann has called "infrastructural power," allowing for the development of "power to coordinate civil society" without a commensurate increase in the scale or visibility of formal public institutions.[26] The apparently "weak state" observed by scholars of nineteenth-century American politics has been recharacterized as a system of governance that relied significantly on these "sinews of power" that extended far beyond the visible boundaries of official institutions.[27]

Attention to infrastructural power has been central to dispelling what historian William Novak has termed "the myth of the 'weak' American state." The existence of a rich network of collaboration with private individuals or organizations helps to explain how such a small national government—measured in terms of its budget or personnel—could expand across a continent and mobilize for modern wars, both civil and overseas. But if infrastructural power helps to explain the capacity of the American state, this concept has been less effective at addressing two related questions: if governance is constituted through infrastructural networks, then who governs?[28] And what happens in the encounter of a system of delegated and distributed governance with liberal democratic understandings of citizenship?

To answer these questions, it is necessary to go beyond the modifier of "infrastructural" to investigate the specific configurations of associational involvement in governance and, by extension, conflicts over control of critical networks in these expansive state-linked collaborations. Over the course of the nineteenth and twentieth centuries, the "associational state" repeatedly morphed into new forms, at times more closely linked to the building of new federal agencies and capacities and at others more aligned with those opposed to the expansion of federal powers. Different arrangements of infrastructural strength advantaged different political actors and were consistent with different policy visions. Antebellum Whigs and Gilded Age elites both turned to infrastructural configurations to advance public projects, often pushing back against increasingly democratic urban polities. The Whig party may have collapsed before the Civil War, but this form of Whig practice endured. A different variant, celebrated as the "associative state," was championed by Herbert Hoover as Secretary of Commerce and then as President in the 1920s.[29] This vision of self-organizing action among private firms and organizations has often been understood as an alternative to the expanded government of the New Deal, with its array of new regulatory agencies, citizen entitlements, and social insurance programs. Viewed across these two successive presidencies, party politics plays out as a contest over the extent of associational or collaborative government, with more conservative administrations favoring limits on the role and size of public agencies and programs. Expanded reliance on voluntary associations could double the influence of those opposed to expanded public provision of services: directly through the control of the executive or legislatures and indirectly through the influence of local elites on the networks of private charity and civic mobilization.

Despite the hostility of many conservatives to the expansion of state intervention (at least with respect to social provision and economic regulation; military mobilization and national security are different issues), this standard account misses the important ways in which associational politics and governance have proved attractive regardless of an administration's ideological commitments. Roosevelt himself did not shy from harnessing civic and voluntary groups to public projects. Examples can be found in the policy responses to the depression years of the 1930s, in his own signature project of civic benevolence, the March of Dimes (originally known as the "Committee to Celebrate the President's Birthday"), as well as the national mobilization in support of World War II.[30] Rather than rejecting the associational methods linked to the conservative opposition to the New Deal, Roosevelt managed a transformation of purpose and control. If this moment of crisis can be understood as a political competition for loyalty and obligation,[31] Roosevelt appeared a clear winner and, in the process, the president engineered a decisive shift in the control of civic benevolence and the ramified system of associational governance.

A part of his achievement consisted in re-centering the emotional focus of civic benevolence on the presidency itself, while at the same time establishing the foundations for a welfare state in which appeals made in the register of benevolence would be displaced by claims on the basis of recognized rights for relief and social provision. But precisely because a transfer from government to an individual citizen may be named in many ways—as charity or entitlement—the institutionalization of rights-based social policies was vulnerable from the start to the politics of renaming: as patronage, as relief, as a gift. In the days after the 2012 presidential election, for example, defeated Republican candidate Mitt Romney offered explanations for his electoral loss: "What the president, the president's campaign did was focus on certain members of his base coalition. Give them extraordinary financial gifts from the government. And then work very aggressively to turn them out to vote. I mean it's a proven political strategy, which is, give a bunch of money from the government to a, to a group and guess what? They'll vote for you." In a conference call with large donors, he spelled out a rationale that turned on the incompatibility of gift-giving and liberal democracy: "What the President did is he gave them two, two things. One, he gave them a big gift on immigration with the Dream Act Amnesty Program. Number two, put in place Obamacare which is, which basically is $10,000 a family. . . . The giving away free stuff is a, is a hard thing to compete with."[32]

The equation of government benefits to citizens with "gifts" provoked a predictable reaction. In a conversation with his most generous supporters, Romney himself did not express any sense of personal diminishment as the recipient of their contributions, yet those who were characterized as beneficiaries of Obama's "gifts" immediately recognized the implied denigration of their motives as voters and citizens.[33] Despite decades, arguably centuries, of effort to harness benevolence to national mobilization, the underlying conflict between the relational geometries of the gift and of liberal citizenship persisted, erupting in a small flurry of press conference remarks and reactive commentary.

As a political event, this episode did not have lasting consequences beyond reinforcing the focus on economic inequality and political power that had already become a hallmark of this period in American politics. But the controversy embodies the persistently incomplete and unstable linkage of two different and demonstrably contradictory relational geometries[34]: the form of the gift and the model of liberal citizenship. Gift-giving, particularly as generalized exchange, has the capacity to generate solidarity that may augment both national identity and state capacity to mobilize resources. But in a democratic polity, these advantages are offset by the threat that receipt of a gift, and therefore dependence, poses to civic standing. Consequently the durable zone of unstable linkages and repeated ruptures at the intersection of voluntary organizing and democratic politics poses a more general theoretical question for institutional theory in the social sciences. If the combination and transposition of organizational models are an important mechanism of institutional change, how can we account for the persistence of such zones of unstable settlement? It is precisely such zones or fault lines—*constitutive contradictions*[35] in the language used here—that facilitate efforts at combination and recombination.

Categories and Legacies

It requires work to keep incompatible organizing elements in a viable relation with one another.[36] Voluntarism and democratic electoral politics represent alternative methods for determining and producing public goods. But they embody very different understandings of the relationships between the rights and values of those making decisions and the rights and values of those affected by them. As a model of collective action, voluntarism privileges the moral commitments of those who act to promote some value or achieve some goal. Unlike arrangements that center on representation or accountability, there is no necessary requirement for the consent of those directly influenced by their actions nor of the broader polity whose members might hold strong preferences about the issue.

The tensions between democratic principles and organized voluntarism infused antebellum American politics (specifically in the form of the Benevolent Empire). Nascent party organizations and new institutional rules—notably the "gag rule" that required petitions in favor of abolition—worked to obstruct voluntary efforts to advance controversial goals (temperance and woman suffrage in addition to antislavery) from disrupting compromises carefully constructed within the framework of democratic electoral politics. The voluntarism of abolitionists threatened change without the consent of slave-holding citizens and their representatives in Congress. For those whose behavior and property were threatened, the efforts of these voluntary associations appeared as illegitimate acts of coercion and even domination. Thus one of the challenges of political order in the early republic was to establish rules delimiting the appropriate domains for these two ways of doing collective action with respect to matters of public concern. In the case of abolition, the moral and instrumental forces aligned behind slavery were eventually overcome. But the underlying question of how to articulate a relationship between voluntarism and democratic government remained.[37]

In time, the courts developed a clear rule for limiting the scope of at least one form of voluntary action in support of a public cause: the charitable bequest. In a late nineteenth-century case, *Jackson v. Phillips*, the Massachusetts court was asked to determine the legitimacy of a will that included two bequests related to politicized causes: one to an organization that promoted the advancement of now-free African Americans and the other to an association pledged to support the not-yet-successful cause of woman suffrage. The decision allowed the former, but not the latter, asserting that charitable bequests could not be allowed to preempt political processes: "a gift must be 'applied consistently within existing laws.' "³⁸ Note that nothing stood in the way of living individuals making non-deductible contributions to organizations promoting changes in the law. This distinction highlights the carefully constructed but vulnerable boundaries between the spheres of tax-subsidized benevolence and democratic politics. This case established a hierarchical relationship between democratic politics and civic benevolence, mandating the right of the former to determine the boundaries of the latter.³⁹

Once articulated by the courts, this linkage of the legitimately charitable to the avoidance of politics worked its way through organizational populations. For a student of late nineteenth-century voluntary associations, it is often difficult to find a bright—or even a blurred—line between groups dedicated to benevolence and those committed to bringing about change and social uplift through the legislatures or the courts. But over the first decades of the twentieth century, the boundary sharpened, particularly as a distinction once centered in matters of inheritance was extended to the new national income tax established in 1916.

With this new framework for public revenue, a distinction between the charitable and the political that once was relevant primarily to the dead was now injected into every decision to make a donation by someone wealthy enough to be covered by the federal tax (and doubly so for those who also sat on boards of organizations that might endanger their status to receive charitable donations). By the 1930s, the force of this categorical distinction in the tax code pushed—or at least provided cover for—further changes in the organizational field as trustees of settlement houses increasingly banned meetings that might be construed as political from the premises of their organizations and thereby furthered the depoliticization (and concomitant professionalization) of these associations.⁴⁰ The consequences of this distinction between the charitable and the political persist to the present, with the leaders of nonprofit organizations regularly *underestimating* the kinds and extent of political activity in which they may engage without endangering their tax status.⁴¹

By following the tax code, one uncovers a political process that drove a clearer distinction between the political and the charitable—at least on the giving side of the relationship—over the course of the late nineteenth and much of the twentieth centuries. This sharpening of the boundary, in turn, made the project of linking the benevolent patriotism of the nation to the administrative structure of the state ever more challenging. This process traces a persistent zone of contention over which activities and ends should fall within which moral and regulatory domain. We know that there are two meaningfully different fields in play precisely because of this extended pattern of conflict.

Much of the change evident along this fault line has not taken the form of the displacement of one logic by another, but rather of the transformation or substitution of individual elements within an institutional grammar.[42] By distinguishing between causes that operated within and outside of the bounds of "existing law," *Jackson v. Phillips* changed what had been understood to be a "may" statement regarding bequests to politically engaged benevolent associations into a "must not." Originally located in the sphere of probate courts, this "must not" was generalized when the charitable deduction was incorporated in the federal income tax as a part of the War Revenues Act of 1917. The contradictions between benevolence as a method for producing public goods and the claims of democratic politics as a source of law were stabilized through the imposition of a rule that hooked into multiple regulatory domains (probate, income tax, and by the mid-1930s eligibility for federal funding for social services). The result was a boundary dividing not charity and government, but charity or nonprofit organizations and democratic politics.

This multiply reinforced boundary between the logics of benevolence and democracy has been repeatedly challenged by the core moral claims of voluntarism, namely that private action legitimately could and should be directed to public ends. By the 1970s, an opposing process took hold as 501(c)(3) organizations pushed the boundaries of allowed behavior, eventually leading to a partial splitting as 501(c)(3)'s established twinned 501(c)(4)'s that were allowed a greater political role at the cost of losing tax-exempt status for contributions. The classic case concerned the Sierra Club and the eventual formation of the Sierra Club Legal Defense Fund.[43] Here, organizational elaboration and disarticulation were employed to manage the tension between voluntarism and electoral democracy. For decades, the institutional rules governing 501(c)(4)'s appeared to define a legitimate place for political-but-not-electoral activity by supporters of a tax-exempt 501(c)(3).[44] But in time, another court decision—this time *Citizens United* of 2010—redefined publicly oriented contributions as *political speech* (rather than tax-deductible charitable contributions), opening a wide breach in the boundary that allowed massive private funds to flow into 501(c)(4)'s where they gained cover of anonymity and then flowed on to political action committees.

This extended example illustrates how the management of tensions between competing relational geometries or logics involves boundary work: the construction, breaching, and reinforcement of distinctions among domains of activities and sets of legitimate participants in those activities.[45] But it also reveals how those efforts have fueled organizational innovations that routinize the linking of distinct relational models, even when those geometries are formally incompatible, generating controversy whenever the conjuncture of democratic dignity and "receiving gifts" becomes too fraught. Each episode of innovation may be reinforced through policy and law; the legacies of each episode, in turn, shape the possibilities for subsequent projects of nation-state-building. In addition to the elaboration and reinforcement of boundaries, organizational hybridization and disarticulation are mechanisms for the management of tensions between relational geometries. The combination of brighter boundaries and more complex elaboration results in a paradoxical outcome: distinctions are both more explicit in law and more difficult to recognize—or more easily evaded—on the ground. The result may be a durable zone of conflict, innovation, and combinatorial politics.

The resulting organizational forms often operate to disarticulate the obligations and dependencies generated by benevolence from the conception of liberal citizens as independent and self-sufficient. But this has not always been the case. Particularly in the nineteenth century, the price of receiving relief or charity was loss of—or at least serious symbolic damage to—one's standing as a citizen. The histories of organized benevolence offer innumerable accounts of the resentment generated by the exercise of social control and the shame at felt dependence on the part of those who received aid.[46] Commentators and critics repeatedly linked the receipt of aid to a sense of disqualification for full citizenship. From laws that disenfranchised paupers to the comments about "gifts" made in the wake of the 2012 presidential election, the underlying contradiction endures.

So long as benevolence reinforced political inequality and exclusion, it provided a robust relational foundation mobilizing those who understood themselves as members of a specific community: elites within a given city, members of a particular religious or ethnic group.[47] When circuits of giving are located within restricted communities, they may fuel political fragmentation. But the persistent tension between benevolence and civic standing has been repeatedly counterbalanced by a deeply felt need, evident since at least the traumatic sectionalism of the Civil War, to incorporate all those whose support for the nation might waver in a sense of encompassing patriotic membership. The key to this innovation, the organized mobilization of patriotism, was to return to the gift as a social form, recognizing that everyone, however poor, still has something to contribute.

This recipe was most powerful when harnessed to the well-being and suffering of soldiers who had given themselves (whether fully voluntarily or by the force of the draft) to some national cause, but it could also be invoked in response to natural disasters and economic crises. Through the 6–15–99 club formed in the Depression of 1893, Red Cross relief in countless disasters, Community Chests, and the March of Dimes, the linkage of mass giving to targeted distribution created capacities for governance without necessarily expanding the capacity of state agencies. In contrast to Hannah Arendt's analysis (see Introduction), the key to the political power of civic benevolence was that compassion and pity were harnessed to the production of solidarity, rather than in opposition to it. But this required the organizational disarticulation of giving and receiving, of democratic dignity and dependence on others.

The configuration of civic benevolence illuminates how an organizational form can stabilize the linkage of relations built on incompatible relational geometries. The patriotic literature of the Civil War, as well as the First and Second World Wars, is filled with a distinctive genre of tales of civic generosity from those with the least to give. Difference and inequality are foregrounded, but are overcome by the circulation of civic gifts, as in that tale of an elderly, unmarried, childless, illiterate woman who had been born a slave but learned to knit so that she could make a contribution to the mobilization for the First World War. Unnamed penitentiary prisoners contributed as did an elderly Cherokee who had fought for the Confederacy during the Civil War but, a half century later, made a gift to support the reunified nation in its first venture into armed conflict in Europe.[48]

As idealized in these tellings, the organized effort to produce voluntary contributions from *all* Americans brought multiply-marginalized persons into a relationship of benevolence, gratitude, and recognition with citizen-soldiers at the front or fellow citizens in need. But these relationships were typically indirect or imagined rather than directly experienced. Although the discourse of voluntary mobilization promised a direct connection between any citizen—regardless of age, gender, race, religion, or social status—and the nation, the organized structure of voluntarism amply allowed for the persistence of particularism, localism, and segregation in everyday activities. As contributions flowed one way to soldiers and thank-you notes returned to the home front, solidarity was created without any necessary disruption to the categories of difference and inequality that ordered American society at any given time.

At the center of these networks of contribution and gratitude were organizations such as the "great commissions," the American Red Cross, and the USO that facilitated projects of generalized exchange as expressions of national solidarity. These formal organizations mediated the tensions between the form of the gift and liberal citizenship by transcending the need for direct ties between donors and beneficiaries, those exchanges that could do so much damage to the civic standing of the beneficiary. In the hubbub of fund-raising or the "production rooms," everyone gave; fund-raisers asked for donations, but not for their own benefit. Instead it became possible for everyone to understand themselves as a donor. Those at home gave to soldiers and seamen, soldiers and seamen gave to preserve the liberties of all citizens.

The same model was apparent in fund-raising to support benevolent activities in times of peace. The perfection of the "campaign model" in the 1890s provided a recipe for large-scale solicitation of small contributions linked to large gifts from the wealthy. Here again, the recipe required that everyone give (at least that was the theory). Through the efforts of organizations such as the Community Chests and the March of Dimes, those funds were then allocated to a network of social service organizations, staffed by professional (or proto-professional) social workers and volunteers. Here again, there was no need for a direct relationship between donor and beneficiary, with all its potential threat to the civic standing of the recipient. And, through that choreography of small gifts, those at risk of needing aid from such agencies might well have been contributors in the past or would be capable of imagining themselves as contributors in the future.

Even when donors and beneficiaries were known to one another socially, any sense that gratitude was obligatory or even coerced could be obscured by clever organizational arrangements. In particular, promises of anonymity to recipients made it possible to accommodate charitable giving to democratic principles; the self-same child could be both donor to the Junior Red Cross and beneficiary of organized giving in the form of a new pair of shoes.[49] By aggregating and obscuring gift relationships, "citizen philanthropy" became a means of collective self-provisioning that obscured the relations created by charity in preference to the performance of solidarity among civic equals.

Contemporary ethnographic work has explored such complex choreographies of interaction at the core of nonprofit organizations. In *Making Volunteers*, Nina Eliasoph illuminates the world of "empowerment projects" intended to aid disadvantaged youth through their engagement in civic projects. As she documents in compelling detail, the joint invocation of "disadvantage" and "citizenship" among the teenagers produces a reliable stream of awkward situations, sometimes but not always met by inspired performances that transcend the inherent contradictions of such situations. Failed performances sharply illuminate the tensions. One youth group "was *told* that it won the award [of funds for a minivan] for having done 'service to the community.'" But the program for the celebratory luncheon listed "Community House: Van to transport needy youth."[50] Economically disadvantaged teens had earned distinction by helping the needy through food drives and the community through litter pick-ups, only to find that they themselves were now cast in the role of "the needy."[51] As with the outrage that greeted Mitt Romney's postelection comments about gift, the rawness of their resentment signals the uneasy coexistence of benevolence and democratic dignity, making the accomplishment of institutionalized civic benevolence all the more theoretically interesting.

Voluntarism Reconsidered

In their specifics, the entwined histories of civic benevolence and liberal democracy represent a distinctively American narrative of the innovative management—and, at times, exploitation—of contradictory principles of social organization. The same organized social welfare projects "empower" their participants and position them as "needy," setting up predictable clashes at gala luncheons where young citizens are expected to show gratitude to generous donors. To avoid such clashes, the elaboration of organizations along the boundary of democratic politics and civic benevolence articulates relationships between broader fields of social activity ordered by conflicting expectations. In a culturally heterogeneous society, powerfully shaped by anti-statist political commitments, civic practices of voluntarism and patriotic gifts contributed to the development of a highly consequential configuration of infrastructural power: the not-so-weak American nation-state.

But if the examples are particular to the United States, this understanding of the relation of organizational forms to their broader sociocultural context has a distinguished genealogy within organization theory that merits renewed attention. The challenge, as the late French sociologist Michel Crozier argued, is to explain "the pattern of change, and not the amount of change itself." In an effort to disentangle the study of bureaucracy from the Weberian ideal-type, Crozier framed his study of a factory and a public agency in France by a specific concern for rule-driven dysfunction as a characteristic of bureaucratic organization. But although *The Bureaucratic Phenomenon* begins with a comparative case study of these two organizations, it concludes with an effort to ground that comparison in an understanding of the tensions within French culture and to extrapolate to an explanation of the trajectories of change characteristic of different societies.

To this end, Crozier began with a characterization of French culture as encompassing specific, historically constituted, expectations about interaction and relational order. Speaking of the mid-twentieth century, he observes that "the privileges and particularisms of the *ancien régime* have gone. But the same patterns—individual isolation and lack of constructive co-operative activities on one side, strata isolation and lack of communication between people of different rank on the other—have persisted."[52] He then argues that characteristic forms of organizing collective activity serve as relatively, if far from perfectly, effective methods for resolving such contradictions:

> Face-to-face dependence relationships are, indeed, perceived as difficult to bear in the French cultural setting. Yet the prevailing view of authority is still that of universalism and absolutism; it continues to retain something of the seventeenth century's political theory, with its mixture of rationality and *bon plaisir*.[53] The two attitudes are contradictory. However, they can be reconciled within a bureaucratic system, since impersonal rules and centralization make it possible to reconcile an absolutist conception of authority and the elimination of most direct dependence relationships.[54]

But if Crozier is correct, differently constituted contradictions may generate distinctive trajectories of institutional change. In American political development, diverse models of social relationships have been repeatedly combined: liberal models of citizenship premised on self-sufficiency and liberty, a democratic culture that sustains expectations of equal rights and dignity, concentrated power and hierarchy in private firms and public agencies (above all the military), and the elaboration of practices and circuits of giving. Across the history of American nation-state-building, this last component has been central to managing these otherwise conflicting relational geometries. Voluntarism facilitates political inclusion despite the persistence of deep and damaging categorical inequalities. Voluntarism enables the coproduction of a powerful nation-state within an often deeply anti-statist political culture. Voluntarism, animated by the distinctive logic of the gift, has contained the development of centralized, bureaucratic national state while also contributing to a process of nation-state-building that has produced a major world power.

As a consequence of these built-in tensions and contradictions, rupture and destabilization are built into this trajectory of political development. But these possibilities are also opportunities. While we often think of political change as shifting the balance between the market models championed by neoliberals and strengthened systems of public social provision, one lesson of American political development is that a third possibility can be found in the coproduction of governance by a variety of public and private organizations. While civic engagement and social capital are often celebrated on the input side of democratic politics,[57] the history of voluntarism as a component of nation-state-building represents one form of open architecture that engages both public and private effort at multiple scales as a form of aspirationally democratic governance.[58]

Nothing is certain about the realization of those aspirations. By relying on voluntary associations and private firms to implement public projects, the American architecture of governance allowed for the pursuit of national projects that generated solidarity while long delaying the construction of a centralized, bureaucratic national state.

In the past, this mode of mobilization has enabled powerful responses to crises of war, depression, disease, and natural disaster. Such efforts often reinforced the influence of privilege and the operation of inequalities, but also represented potent moments in which democratic citizens insisted that government depended not only on popular consent but popular contribution. Through the expansive mobilization of voluntary efforts, ordinary citizens could "make the armies of the world *the armies of the people and not of kings.*"[59] To recover such a possibility in the present, will involve not restoration, but innovative combination and recombination.

Acknowledgments

Although reciprocity is central to *Civic Gifts*, gratitude overwhelms as I come to the end of this project. Early support for a study of the forms of social provision came from both the National Science Foundation (SES-9911428) and the University of Arizona Foundation/Office of the Vice President for Research. As research assistants, Martin Hughes, Jennifer Murdock, Steve Nelson, and Wade Roberts all helped to break ground. A semester of leave at the Udall Center for Studies in Public Policy allowed me to wrestle with the first formulations of the central research question, which repeatedly devolved into something like "why is American government so complicated?" My efforts to reframe that puzzle were sustained by the extraordinary community of political and organizational sociologists at the University of Arizona, including Neil Fligstein, Woody Powell, Marc Schneiberg, and Sarah Soule as well as a number of wonderful graduate students who have become outstanding researchers in their own right. Only after going down a number of blind alleys did I realize that this intractable question could be translated into a puzzle about institutional change. If institutions are transformed through the combination of already-existing cultural models, when and how are the contradictions between those models stabilized, contained, or transcended?

But while sorting out that puzzle, I had the opportunity to join a trio of collaborations that both delayed and enriched this project. With support from the American Sociological Association's Fund for the Advancement of the Discipline, Julia Adams, Ann Shola Orloff, and I convened a gathering of colleagues to produce a wide-ranging assessment of historical sociology that became *Remaking Modernity: Politics, History, Sociology* (Duke, 2005). In my writing of the volume's conclusion, all the contributors invited and pushed me to clarify an approach to the analysis of historical change. With support from the Committee on Philanthropy and the Third Sector at the Social Science Research Council, and contributions from its members and many fellowship recipients, Doug Guthrie and I organized the conference that produced *Politics and Partnerships: Voluntary Associations in America's Past and Present* (University of Chicago, 2010). Finally, the Neubauer Collegium for Culture and Society at the University of Chicago provided two rounds of support for "The History and Theory of the Democratic State," a multifaceted collaboration that began with Bernard Harcourt, Jim Sparrow, and Steve Sawyer before it expanded into a series of interlinked conferences co-convened with Ann Orloff, Kimberly Morgan, William Novak, and the France Chicago Center as well as a manuscript workshop. Tony Chen, Jane Dailey, John Mark Hansen, Brayden King, Kimberly Morgan, Kelly Moore, Steve Sawyer, and Jim Sparrow all gave generous and incisive readings that have made this a much better book.

As would be expected of a project long in the making, versions have been presented at many conferences and department colloquia. These discussions generated more insights than I can fully acknowledge, leaving me deeply grateful to the faculty and students at Arizona, Berkeley, Copenhagen Business School, Iowa, Northwestern, Notre Dame, Stanford, Stockholm University, Toronto, Yale, the University of Chicago Center in Beijing, Zhejiang University, the Institute of Humanities and Social Sciences at Beijing University, and the Lilly Center on Philanthropy in Indianapolis. An invitation from Benjamin Z. Kedar, Ilana Friedrich Silber, and Adam Klin-Oron to join a seminar in the memory of Shmuel Eisenstadt at the Van Leer Jerusalem Institute pushed me to think carefully about mechanisms of institutional change. Special thanks are owed to Deb Meyerson, Woody Powell, and Rob Reich, whose invitation to talk at the Stanford Center on Philanthropy and Civil Society led me to discover the overall trajectory of the argument as well as to Erica James, who included me in a weeklong seminar on faith-based organizations and the security state at Santa Fe's School for Advanced Research. I am also indebted to all the archivists and research librarians who provided assistance at the National Archives, the Herbert Hoover Presidential Library, the Franklin Delano Roosevelt Presidential Library, Special Collections at the University of Chicago, and the Rockefeller Archive Center, which also provided a grant for archival research and the invaluable advice of Tom Rosenbaum. My thanks to all my colleagues at the Department of Sociology at Chicago for so many rich conversations and to the Albion Small Fund for a subvention for publication. Bijan Warner wrangled public opinion data and Josh Pacewicz contributed close readings of classic community studies. I am particularly indebted to the late Don Levine for reminding me, with a combination of insistence and enthusiasm, to reread Simmel's essay on "The Poor."

I'm grateful in innumerable ways to friends, colleagues, and institutions that made it possible to bring this project to a close. Ann Orloff and

I formed a writing pact that pushed both of our manuscripts forward. A year at the Center for Advanced Study in the Social and Behavioral Sciences was a true gift, combining great collegiality with fellow fellows who provided models of compassion and grace when life took difficult turns. Particular thanks, both personal and intellectual, to Carol Heimer, Louis Hyman, Margaret Levi, Barbara Risman, and Dan Rodgers. Both Heather Haveman and Sidney Tarrow provided keenly critical and enormously generative readings of the manuscript as it took final form, as did the two reviewers for the University of Chicago Press, one anonymous and the other, Brian Balogh, who is among the very most generous of the many scholars thanked here.

But all the insightful comments, constructive suggestions, and forceful criticism weren't actually enough to get across the finish line. For this, I thank a few university lawyers who, in one long policy meeting during my year-long return to administration, unintentionally persuaded me that my life as a scholar was sure to be sacrificed to the bureaucracy so I might as well send in the revised manuscript as it was. Forty-eight hours later it was in the hands of Doug Mitchell and Kyle Wagner at the University of Chicago Press, who secured a final pair of reviews and cheered on the last few revisions before handing off the manuscript to Elizabeth Branch Dyson, Dylan Montanari, and then Mary Corrado for her meticulous editing. Those revisions were finished only hours before a grand party to celebrate Doug's retirement after an extraordinary career at the Press. Along with lawyers, my desire to enjoy a toast in good conscience was a powerful motivation.

My deepest thanks are personal: to my late mother, Dorothy Thelen Clemens; to my father, Bill Clemens; and, above all, to Dave Larson. This book has been part of our lives together for a long time. It would have been impossible to finish without him, although I know he is profoundly grateful that the last words are now written.

Appendix 1

TABLE A1.1. Selected Members of the United States Christian Commission (from obituaries and other biographical sketches available from ProQuest Historical Newspapers, 1865–1920)

Name	Occupation	Affiliations	Source
Rev. Gilbert Ray Bent	Methodist Minister		*Boston Daily Globe* (September 6, 1915), 10
Rev. S. L. Bowler	Clergyman, Maine Financial agent, Bangor Theological Seminary	Supervisor of hundreds of delegates in USCC	*Boston Daily Globe* (November 2, 1914), 6
Rev. G. H. Bringhurst	Clergy, Protestant Episcopal Church, New York City	Missionary worker in New York slums Organizer of Midnight Missions	*New York Times* (March 27, 1903), 9 *Washington Post* (March 27, 1903), 3
John V. Farwell	Head of dry goods firm VP Chicago Board of Trade	YMCA Board of Indian Affairs Presidential Elector for Lincoln Temperance activities and religious services for prisoners	*Chicago Daily Tribune* (August 21, 1908), 4
Rev. Mr. Godfrey	Itinerant evangelist for the faith of "Cosmic Reformation"		*SF Chronicle* (September 29, 1895), 9 (not an obituary)
Rev. George A. Hall	State Secretary, New York YMCA Wesleyan Methodist minister	Traveled with evangelist Dwight L. Moody	*New York Observer and Chronicle* 82 (9) (March 3, 1904), 278

Name	Occupation	Affiliations	Source
Dr. Henry Clarke Houghton	Professor of Physiology Dean and Professor at the New York Opthalmic Hospital	Medical Societies New England Society	*New York Times* (December 2, 1901), 1
Sandford Hunt, D.D.	Minister		*The Methodist Review* (January 1897), 3
Benjamin F. Jacobs	Real estate dealer, Chicago	Sunday school and church work YMCA	*Chicago Daily Tribune* (January 20, 1902), 3
Rev. Dr. Thomas Kerr	Nondenominational minister, Rockford, Ill.		*Chicago Daily Tribune* (December 14, 1894) (not an obituary)
Dwight L. Moody	Shoe salesman Leading national and international evangelist	YMCA, Chicago North Market Mission Sunday School	*SF Chronicle* (December 23, 1899), 3
Rev. Lemuel Moss, D.D. LL.D.	Minister Professor of Systematic Theology, Bucknell President, University of Chicago, 1874–75, then Indiana University, 1875–84[a]	Baptist	*The Watchman* (July 21, 1904), 23
Adam Scott Pratt	Dept. of Treasury Attorney for various national banks General insurance business, charter member of National Life Insurance Co. of America Financial agent for YMCA	Central Union Mission Washington Humane Society Trustee, Howard University Director, American Bible Society VP, Washington Bible Society Organizer, Associated Charities Trustee, National Homeopathic Hospital Member, Union League	*Washington Post* (July 3, 1900), 7

Name	Occupation	Affiliations	Source
David Preston	Detroit banker	Director of Michigan branch of the USCC	*Christian Advocate* (May 5, 1887), 285
George H. Stuart	Head of dry goods commission house Director of Philadelphia banks and insurance companies	American Sunday School Union YMCA Board of Indian Commissioners Presbyterian	*Chicago Daily Tribune* (April 12, 1890), 7 *Christian Advocate* (April 17, 1890), 241
Rev. Dr. Joseph Ford Sutton	Minister	New York Presbytery Loyal Legion Sons of the Revolution Fellow, American Geographical Society	*New York Times* (June 1, 1912), 11
Rev. Edward Warren Virgin	Methodist Clergyman	Delegate to world's first school convention in Paris	*New York Observer and Chronicle* 89 (September 29, 1910), 414

[a] For an account of Moss's termination at the University of Chicago after one year, see John W. Boyer, *"Not as a Thing for the Moment, But for All Time: The University of Chicago and Its Histories,"* Occasional Papers on Higher Education 20 (Chicago: The College of the University of Chicago, 2010), pp. 64–65.

TABLE A1.2. Selected Male Members of the United States Sanitary Commission (from ProQuest Historical Newspapers, 1865–1920)

Name	Occupation	Affiliations	Source
Henry Abbott	Cashier of the Winchester National Bank	1869–70, member lower house of New Hampshire Legislature 1873–74, member New Hampshire State Senate	*New York Times* (February 13, 1898), 7
Dr. Cornelius Rea Agnew	One of the founding group of USSC A.M. M.D. Surgeon General of State of New York Professor, College of Physicians and Surgeons Manager, New York State Hospital for the Insane	Trustee, Columbia College Trustee, College of Physicians and Surgeons President, Medical Society of the State of New York Member, various opthalmological societies VP, Union League Club Elder, Fifth Avenue Presbyterian Church	*New York Genealogical and Biographical Record* 19 (4) (October 1888); American Periodicals, p. 179
John A. Anderson	Ordained minister 12 years as U.S. Representative from Kansas Appointed consul at Cairo, Egypt, by Pres. Harrison	Trustee, California State Insane Asylum President, Kansas State Agricultural College Judge, U.S. Centennial Commission Republican	*Chicago Daily Tribune* (May 20, 1892), 5 *SF Chronicle* (May 20, 1892), 4
Dr. Henry W. Bellows	Ordained pastor (Congregational, Unitarian)	Sanitary Convention for Improvement of Urban Health, 1859 Founder, Union League Club Original member, Century Club Phi Beta Kappa Harvard Alumni Association	*Chicago Daily Tribune* (January 31, 1882), 5
Henry L. Boltwood	Principal, Evanston Township High School, Illinois	"Widely known as the author of a new system of orthography"	*New York Times* (January 25, 1906), 9

Name	Occupation	Affiliations	Source
Rev. Peter H. Burghordt	Pastor Employed by government as of 1875	Chairman, standing committee on Temperance of Washington City Presbytery	*New York Evangelist* 57 (31) (August 5, 1886); American Periodicals, p. 8
Col. H. P. Bush	Appointed to command Second Brigade, National Guard of California		*San Francisco Chronicle* (June 1, 1905), 15 Not an obituary: "Gains Command Through Merit"
Bishop T. M. Clark	Episcopalian prelate Author		*New York Times* (September 8, 1903), 8
Francis Stephen Dyer	Grocer	Massachusetts Society for the Prevention of Cruelty to Animals	*New York Times* (November 21, 1892), 4
Ezekiel Brown Elliot	Actuary and Electrician Telegraph Actuarial work for New England Mutual Life Insurance	Hamilton College American Statistical Association Secretary, U.S. Revenue Commission (until 1869) Representative of the Treasury Department to the Civil Service Commission	*American Academy of Arts and Science, Boston, Proceedings* 24 (May 1888–1889): 447.
Dr. George Jackson Fisher	M.D.	President, State Medical Society of New York President, Village of Sing Sing	*New York Times* (February 4, 1893), 5
Rev. Edward Griffin	Pastor of Hancock Church, Lexington MA	Williams, Harvard, Heidelberg, Berlin Foreign missions American College at Aintab Massachusetts Historical Society American Antiquarian Society American Historical Association	*Congregationalist* 85 (7) (Feb. 15, 1900); American Periodicals, p. 229

Name	Occupation	Affiliations	Source
		Colonial Society of Massachusetts Bostonian Society Prince Society New England Historic Genealogical Society Winthrop Club Overseer, Harvard Trustee of Wellesley, Abbot, Radford, and Lawrence Academies	
Ralph N. Isham	Surgeon	Founder, Chicago Medical College (now Medical School of Northwestern University) Chicago Historical Society University Club Presbyterian	*Chicago Daily Tribune* (December 16, 1900), 59 "Gallery of Local Celebrities"
Orange Judd	Agricultural journalist and philanthropist	International Sunday School System Inventor of Crop Reporting System Member, Board of Indian Commissioners	*Chicago Daily Tribune* (December 28, 1892), 6
Isaac Kerlin, M.D.	Physician Pennsylvania Training School for Feeble-minded Children	Director, colonization plan on the Island of Vache	*Medical and Surgical Reporter* 69 (22) (November 25, 1893); American Periodicals, p. 829
Ezra Butler McCagg	Lawyer, Chicago	Chicago Historical Society Chicago Astronomical Society Trustee, "old" University of Chicago Chicago Academy of Science	*Chicago Daily Tribune* (August 3, 1908), 8

Name	Occupation	Affiliations	Source
		Trustee, Eastern Hospital for the Insane at Kankakee President, Bar Association President, Chicago Club Member, Loyal Legion	
John Strong Newberry	State Geologist of Ohio Professor of Geology and Paleontology at Columbia College School of Mines	Explorations along the Colorado and Columbia Rivers Judge, 1875 World's Fair in Philadelphia National Academy of Sciences Torrey Botanical Club	*New York Times* (December 9, 1892), 5
Frederick Law Olmsted	Landscape Engineer	American Museum of Natural History NYC Metropolitan Museum of Art First Commission of the National Park of the Yosemite and Mariposa Work with municipal governments in Boston, Philadelphia, Baltimore, Wilmington, Del., San Francisco Joint Committee on Buildings and Grounds of Congress Niagara Falls Reservation Committee Trustee, Harvard, Yale, Amherst, and other public institutions	*Chicago Daily Tribune* (September 8, 1890), 1 Letter from Geo. L. Andrews, *Chicago Daily Tribune* (September 2, 1903), 16
James Otis	Politician Mayor, San Francisco	Member, Republican State Central Committee, California President, Mercantile Library Association	*San Francisco Chronicle* (October 31, 1875), 5

Name	Occupation	Affiliations	Source
James Park Jr.	Steel Manufacturer, Pittsburgh	President, Dime Savings Institution Incorporator of the Western Pennsylvania Hospital University trustee Ward rep. on Allegheny council	*Magazine of Western History* 4 (4) (August 1886); American Periodicals, p. 524
Edward Parker	Flour Merchant Member, New York Produce Exchange	Veterans' Association of the 23rd Regiment	*New York Times* (January 25, 1916), 9
George Spencer Russell	Newsdealer, apothecary Employed at *Boston Globe* for 25 years	Superintendant of Boston YMCU [*sic*] Grand Army of the Republic	*Boston Daily Globe* (October 28, 1913), 10
Professor Arthur Searle	Harvard professor of astronomy Worked in statistical department of USSC		*Boston Daily Globe* (October 25, 1920), 3
Edwin M. Snow, M.D.	City Register of Births, Marriages and Deaths Health Physician and Health Officer at Quarantine Superintendent of Health (elected) Superintendent of State Census/ National Census for Rhode Island Inspector of Hospitals for USSC Chairman of Rhode Island Cattle Commission	Member, Common Council of Providence National Prison Congress Secretary, State Board of Charities and Corrections Fellow, Rhode Island Medical Society Member, various medical societies American Public Health Association "In politics Dr. Snow was a Republican, in religion a Baptist"	*Medical News* 54 (1) (January 5, 1889); American Periodicals, p. 27
Charles J. Stillé	Lawyer, Historian Provost, University of Pennsylvania 1868–1880	President of the Board of Directors of the Eighth School Section of Philadelphia Protestant Episcopal Communion	*Pennsylvania Magazine of History and Biography* 24 (1) (1900): 1. "In Memory of Charles Janeway Stillé, LL.D"

Name	Occupation	Affiliations	Source
Rev. Treadwell Walden	Episcopal clergyman Writer USSC Commission to investigate prisoners of war		*Boston Daily Globe* (May 22, 1918), 8
John C. Wetmore	Construction engineer (supervised cutting of the Yazoo canal) Ohio State military agent	"On intimate terms with Presidents Lincoln, Grant, and Garfield"	*Washington Post* (August 14, 1895), 1
Rev. John S. Whitman	Pastor	Williams, Union Theological Society American Board of Foreign Missions American Bible Society American Tract Society New York Presbytery	*New York Times* (March 1, 1909), 9
Sir Edward Wigglesworth	"Noted dermatologist," Boston	Harvard, Class of 1861	*Chicago Daily Tribune* (January 24, 1896), 8

TABLE A1.3. Selected Female Members of the United States Sanitary Commission (from ProQuest Historical Newspapers, 1865–1920)

Name	Occupation	Affiliations	Source
Antoinette Akin	"Prominent worker" in USSC Author of volumes of verse and prose		*Los Angeles Times* (November 24, 1903), 3
Elizabeth Dodge	Pioneer in California, 1852 Served in Philadelphia hospital during the war		*Los Angeles Times* (December 10, 1896), 6 Not an obituary: "Woman Warrior: A Nurse of the Civil War Who is not Unkown [*sic*] to Fame"
Mrs. Ellen Terry Johnson	Treasurer, Western Reserve Branch of USSC Secretary, New York State Charities Aid Association		*New York Times* (December 26, 1896), 5
Mary Livermore	Teacher Associate member of USSC	Raised Baptist, but later embraced "liberal" views "held many offices in societies for the promotion of temperance" Woman suffragist	*New York Observer and Chronicle* 83 (33) (August 17, 1905), 201
Clara Jessup Moore	"Literary and philanthropic labors" Pennsylvania branch of USSC	Union Temporary Home for Children	"Mrs. Bloomfield Moore Dead" *New York Times* (January 6, 1898), 6
Laura Wolcott Parker	Nurse USSC	Massachusetts Indian Association Trinity Church Daughters of the American Revolution "Interested in missionary and philanthropic work"	*New York Observer and Chronicle* 79 (4) (January 1, 1901), 112

Name	Occupation	Affiliations	Source
Louisa Lee Schuyler	Founder, New York State Charities Aid Association	Trustee, Russell Sage Foundation Works to remove insane from poorhouses. Organizer, first training school for nurses	"College Honors for Women," *Outlook* (January 16, 1915); American Periodicals, p. 355. Not an obituary.
Mrs. Helene De Kay Townsend	Member, Oyster Bay USSC (New York)		*New York Times* (February 5, 1895), 6

Appendix 2

American Soldier S-170, 1944
(survey conducted in China-Burma-India theater)

TABLE A2.1. Regression of Q29 ("Does Red Cross do a good job of handling personal/family problems?" 1 = yes)

	Model 1	Model 2
Age (in months)	1.007	—
Tenure (in months)	1.017	—
Q17 (% of officers willing to go through anything)	1.001	—
DUMMY VARIABLES		
Q18rc (officers have interest in your welfare)	2.261***	2.236***
Q35rc (Red Cross girls treat you as really important or equals)	9.210***	9.075***
Q36rc (RC girls date officers only)	.634*	.640*
Drafted	1.563*	1.478
Constant	.203**	.404***
N	730	749
-2LL	732.286	751.639
Nagelkerke R²	.365	.364
% predicted correctly	76.2	76.4

Source: The American Soldier in World War II: Trend Study on Attitudes (United States) [USAMS1944-S170] Directed by Dr. Samuel A. Stouffer for the Research Branch, Information and Education Division, War Department, field dates: October–November, 1944, sample: White and Negro enlisted men, stationed in China-India-Burma

Note: *p < .05, **p < .01, ***p <. 001

Reported coefficients have been exponentiated.

• Q29: "FROM WHAT YOU KNOW, HOW WELL DO YOU THINK THE RED CROSS IS HANDLING EMERGENCY PERSONAL AND FAMILY PROBLEMS?" (recoded into 1 = well, 2 = not well)

• Q17 "HOW MANY OF YOUR COMPANY OFFICERS ARE THE KIND WHO ARE WILLING TO GO THROUGH ANYTHING THEY ASK THEIR MEN TO GO THROUGH?" (recoded: "all" = 100%, "most" = 75%, "about half" = 50%, "some" = 25%, "none" = 0%)

• q18 "DO YOU FEEL THAT YOUR OFFICERS HAVE AN INTEREST IN YOUR PERSONAL PROBLEMS AND WELFARE?" (recoded: 1 = yes, 2 = no)

• Q35 "HOW DO MOST OF THE RED CROSS GIRLS YOU KNOW ACT TOWARD ENLISTED MEN?" (recoded: 1 = really important people OR as equals, 0 = look down)

• Q36 "WHAT HAVE THE RED CROSS GIRLS WHOM YOU HAVE KNOWN HERE IN C-B-I DONE ABOUT DATES?" (recoded: 1 = date only officers, 0 = dates with both OR dates with enlisted men only)

• Drafted: "recruit" recoded to drafted/not drafted

Abbreviations

AAPSS	*Annals of the American Academy of Political and Social Science*
AFSC	American Friends Service Committee
ANRC	American National Red Cross
ARC	American Red Cross
CCC	Civilian Conservation Corps
CIO	Congress of Industrial Organizations
COS	Charity Organization Society
CR	*Congressional Record*
CRAS	Chicago Relief and Aid Society
CSA	Community Service Agency
EURC	Emergency Unemployment Relief Committee
FERA	Federal Emergency Relief Administration
NYCOS	New York Charity Organization Society
NYT	*New York Times*
OCD	Office of Civilian Defense
PECE	President's Emergency Committee on Employment
POUR	President's Organization on Unemployment Relief
RCB	*Red Cross Bulletin*
RCC	*Red Cross Courier*
SMM	*Survey Mid-Monthly*
TERA	Temporary Emergency Relief Administration (State of New York)
USCC	United States Christian Commission
USO	United Service Organization
USSC	United States Sanitary Commission
WP	*Washington Post*
WPA	Works Progress (later Projects) Administration
YMCA	Young Men's Christian Association
YWCA	Young Women's Christian Association

Archives

ARC	Records of the American National Red Cross, National Archives and Records Administration, College Park, Md.
EURC	Emergency Unemployment Relief Committee (2nd). John Price Jones Papers, Baker Library, Harvard Business School
EURC-BCO	Emergency Unemployment Relief Committee (2nd). Block Community Organization
FDR-POF	President's Official File, Franklin Delano Roosevelt Presidential Library
FDR-PPF	President's Personal File, Franklin Delano Roosevelt Presidential Library
HHPL-PP	Herbert Hoover Presidential Library—Presidential Papers
HHPL-SF	Herbert Hoover Presidential Library—Subject File
HLH-FDR	Harry L. Hopkins Papers, Franklin Delano Roosevelt Presidential Library
JPJ	John Price Jones Papers, Baker Library, Harvard Business School
JRP	Julius Rosenwald Papers, Special Collections, University of Chicago
OMR	Office of the Messers. Rockefeller
RAC	Rockefeller Archive Center
RBF	Rockefeller Brothers Fund
RFA	Rockefeller Foundation Archives
WPA-FERA-CF	Records of the Works Projects Administration, Federal Emergency Relief Administration Central Files, National Archives and Records Administration, College Park, Md.

Notes

Introduction

1. Federal Emergency Relief Administration, Agricultural Adjustment Administration, Civilian Conservation Corps, National Recovery Administration.

2. Charity, philanthropy, and benevolence constitute an overlapping cluster of terms for acts that benefit others. The first, charity, delimits this meaning by highlighting the identity of beneficiaries as poor or needy; the second, philanthropy, is linked to the aim of advancing human welfare. Benevolence encompasses both of these meanings and has the added advantage of being a term in general use within American political discourse. For a discussion of the influence of this vocabulary within American history, see Friedman (2003).

3. Warren (1946: 277). Willie Stark, the populist lawyer-turned-governor at the heart of Robert Penn Warren's *All the King's Men* (winner of the 1947 Pulitzer Prize and the Best Picture Oscar in 1950), has been frequently linked to the historical figure of Governor Huey Long of Louisiana. Warren, however, downplayed the connection.

4. Roosevelt had purchased Warm Springs by committing a large portion of his personal fortune to the project. Public donations provided substantial support in the years before the depression, but fell dramatically from $369,000 to $30,000 per year between 1929 and 1932. At this time, Byoir represented an oilman accused of questionable business practices. Oshinsky (2005: 39, 47–50).

5. James T. Nicholson, "Home Service and Its Social Value" (April 9, 1935), 7. ARC, RGIII, Box 8, 929.1801 News Releases, #44765–7752, 1935–1936. Dulles (1950: 296).

6. But see Reich et al. (2016). Foundational works in this area include Warner (1908) and Watson (1922). For historical accounts of charity and philanthropy in American political development, see Bremner ([1960] 1982); Katz (1986); McCarthy (2003); Patterson (2000); Zunz (2012). For a cross-national survey of the relationships between charity and the surveillance state, see James (2019).

7. Harris (1995: 124); on Hamilton's use of "cement to the union," see Balogh (2009: 97–105). For a second use of the image of union-as-barrel, see Pelatiah Webster as quoted in Haselby (2015: 55). A few decades later, John C. Calhoun would

argue for a "perfect system of roads and canals" as a method that would "counteract every tendency to disunion" (quoted in Howe 2007: 87). On the problem of unity in American history, see Higham (1974).

8. Harris (1995); Ott (2011: 55); "A Study of the Public's Attitude toward the American Red Cross with a Supplement Dealing with World War II Veterans" (June 28, 1946), ARC, 1935–1946, RG200, Box 764, 494.2; Smith and Lipsky (1993). On the postwar Community Chests and United Ways, see Barman (2006).

9. Lainer-Vos (2013).

10. Anderson ([1983] 1991); R. Smith (2003).

11. This absence is surprising given that much of the work of incorporating women's groups—and, at least on a symbolic level, racial minorities—through civic philanthropy had been accomplished during the campaigns in support of the Civil War and the First World War. Reg Manning, *Arizona Republic*, January 20, 1939. FDR-PPF 4885: Committee for the Celebration of the President's Birthday, 1939.

12. Gerstle (2001). As will become evident, however, this form of civic nationalism could incorporate ethno-nationalist mobilization in a web of patriotic reciprocity. See, in particular, chapter 4 on civic philanthropy during the First World War.

13. Francis Wayland (1838: 22) went on to draw explicitly political parallels with religion: "The difference between the Romanism of St. Peter's and the Romanism of fanaticism is, that the former is the despotism of *one*, the latter the despotism of the *many*. In principle they are the same, one and indivisible."

14. Tocqueville recognized this threat but attributed it to European associations whose members "respond to orders as soldiers in the field. They profess the dogma of passive obedience, or perhaps it would be better to say that upon enlisting they offer up all they possess of judgment and free will in a moment of sacrifice. Within such organizations a tyranny often prevails that is more unbearable still than the tyranny exerted over society by the government they attack" (2004: 222). For a critical discussion of arguments that portray the United States as fundamentally liberal in its political culture, see R. Smith (1993).

15. Mann (1986); Tarrow (2015).

16. Tocqueville ([1839] 2004: 219).

17. Balogh (2015). This analysis builds on the work of Ellis Hawley (1974; 1998). For an extension to the present, see Tarrow (2015).

18. For examples of state capture arguments, see Domhoff (1996), Kolko (1967). An alternative assessment of the balance of power between public agencies and private organizations is captured by the concept of the "embedded autonomy" of the state (P. Evans 1995).

19. Mann (1993: 59).

20. Katznelson (2002 and personal communication) appropriated the term "expansible" from John C. Calhoun, champion of the slave-holding states, who used it to describe a novel military structure. See M. S. Fitzgerald (1996).

21. Mann (1993: 59).

22. On the varieties of restrictions on white male suffrage, see Brown (1952); Keyssar (2000); Pflugrad-Jackisch (2010).

23. Mauss (2000: 4). The terminology of relational models, geometries, and logics captures increases in the clarity or rigor of schemas that organize social interaction and, therefore, the increasing possibility of recognized contradiction. On "institutional grammar," see Crawford and Ostrom (1995).

24. Clemens (2010).

25. Balogh (2009; 2015); Clemens (2006); Morgan and Campbell (2011).

26. Weber (1978: 908–909). Weber also characterizes states as "compulsory associations claiming control over territories and the people within them." P. Evans (1995: 5).

27. As Sewell (2005: 320) explains: "I begin by considering the notion that the social may be thought of as a 'language game' and end by suggesting that it must also—simultaneously and dialectically—be thought of as a 'built environment.'" For important discussions of combinatorial analysis, see Padgett and Powell (2013); Sewell (1993); Swidler (1986).

28. Mann (1986: 1).

29. Mann begins with a variation on Weber: "The state is a differentiated set of institutions and personnel embodying centrality, in the sense that political relations radiate outward to cover a territorially demarcated area, over which it claims a monopoly of binding and permanent rule-making, backed up by physical violence" (1986: 37). Although Mann's approach provides an opening for a processual analysis of iterative state-building, in the second volume of his *Sources of Social Power* the analysis is once again taxonomic, focused on variations across "four higher-level crystallizations: capitalist, militarist, representative, and national." Mann (1993: 81).

30. Padgett and Ansell (1993).

31. Bourdieu (2014: 95). In a related metaphor, Slauter (2009) describes state-building as "a work of art."

32. This emphasis on social constructions as recombinations of existing material derives from a classic essay by Claude Lévi-Strauss on *bricolage* and has informed the theoretical orientation often described as "cultural institutionalism." See, for example, Armstrong (2002); Clemens (1997); Clemens and Cook (1999); Sewell (1993); (Swidler 1986).

33. Padgett and Powell (2013: 5, 7). A similar combinatorial imagery appears in Charles Tilly's (1992) contention that the relationship between the military and capital (the organizations of violence and of economic production) was central to the emergence of the early modern state in Europe. Puzzling over the unexpected prominence of the Dutch Republic as an early modern global power, Julia Adams (2005) highlighted how elite family structure and political power were entwined while Philip Gorski (2003) excavated the harnessing of religious discipline to the expansion of state control over subjects. Bruce Carruthers (1996) located the emergence of a particularly potent British state in the linkage of networks of finance to the military requirements of Crown and Parliament. While studies of early modern Europe have focused on the emergence of a particular kind of monarchical state, the argument that durable configurations of power are built out of and through

diverse social networks is shared by scholars of empire, of fascism, and of post-communism; S. Berman (1997); Riley (2010); Stark (1996).

34. Douglas (1966; 1986); Eliade (1959).

35. Kroneberg and Wimmer (2012); Lamont and Molnár (2002); Negro et al. (2010).

36. As Karen Barkey (2008) has concluded of empires, such arrangements are conducive to greater tolerance of diversity precisely because they minimize the institutional work required to construct lines of direct rule. See also Eisenstadt (1963); Joyce and Mukerji (2017); Kiser and Tong (1992); Mukerji (1997).

37. H. Berman (1983); Lancaster (2005).

38. Joyce and Mukerji (2017: 2).

39. P. Evans and Rauch (1999); McDonnell (2017).

40. Tilly (1992: 25); for a contrasting formulation, Foucault (2010). On the development of capacities for taxation, see also Brewer (1988); on the "primitive accumulation" of symbolic power, see Loveman (2005).

41. Internal economic ethics required fairness, reciprocity, and "an ethic of charity and the avoidance of calculation of gain from loans within the community" but impose no such ethical restrictions when dealing with outsiders. Collins (1980: 931).

42. Foucault (2010); Mitchell (1991).

43. Mann (1993: 59). Over the course of Mann's historical analysis (1986, 1993), the quality of being "infrastructural" shifts from media of coordination that may be promoted by those with political power (e.g., coinage, literacy), through linkages of social networks in ways that produce interdependence and therefore a distribution of control, onto the Weberian ideal type of a bureaucratic state that controls the means for penetrating and controlling civil society. For the latter interpretation, see Soifer (2008).

44. Huntington (1968).

45. Balogh (2009); Skowronek (1982).

46. On the image of a "Rube Goldberg state," see Pressman and Wildavsky (1984); Clemens (2006); Morgan and Campbell (2011: 9–10); Nackenoff and Novkov (2014).

47. See Orren and Skowronek (2004) on "intercurrence."

48. Webster (1794), "The Revolution in France" (consource.org, downloaded October 7, 2015); see Wood (2009: 203). On Webster's political evolution, see Rollins (1976: 416–419).

49. Gieryn (1983).

50. R. Evans and Kay (2008); Fligstein (2001).

51. Polanyi ([1944] 2001: 49–50). For the purposes of this argument, reciprocity is understood as a cultural form or relational geometry following Simmel's analysis in "Faithfulness and Gratitude": "One might say that here gratitude actually consists, not in the return of a gift, but in the consciousness that it cannot be returned, that there is something which places the receiver into a certain position with respect to the giver, and makes him dimly envisage the inner infinity of a relation that can neither be exhausted nor realized by any finite return gift or other activity" (1950: 392). An alternative approach considers reciprocity as a property or attribute of social structure. See, for example, Gouldner (1960); Martin (2009).

52. In addition to Polanyi, see Malinowski (1922), Mauss ([1950] 2000). For more recent theoretical treatments, see Godbout (1998), Godelier (1999); Silber (2009).

53. Zelizer (1997).

54. Molm et al. (2007); Simpson et al. (2018).

55. As Barry Schwartz (1967: 2) observed, "The charity potlatch is an important mode of the public presentation of self." See also Eckstein (2001); Healey (2000).

56. Robbins (2006).

57. Lainer-Vos (2013); Anderson ([1983] 1991).

58. Bodnar (1992); Breen (2004); Brubaker (2005); Calhoun (2007); Barry Schwartz (1991). External threats may be particularly important: repeated conflicts with France were central in constructing the political identity of "Britons" out of an assemblage of Englishmen, Scots, and Welshmen. In contrast to presumptions that nationalism derives from primordial identities, Colley (1992: 6) contends that "Britishness was superimposed over an array of internal differences in response to contact with the Other, and above all in response to conflict with the Other." See also Calhoun (1993); Eley and Suny (1996); Greenfeld (1992); Hobsbawm and Ranger (1983); Sahlins (1989); A. Smith (2003).

59. Brubaker (1996).

60. Lyn Spillman and Russell Faeges (2005: 434–35) contrast conceptions of nation as grounded in prior collective—often understood as ethnic—identities with a more recent literature that focuses on the political idioms and symbolic repertoires through which a strong sense of "political community" is constructed.

61. While discussions characterized these contributions as freely given, the line between compulsion and voluntarism was easily blurred. Breen (2010: 119–120).

62. Contributions and "popular financial support" had also enabled the Anglo-Dutch invasion of Britain by William of Orange a century before. Pincus (2009: 232–233).

63. R. Smith (2003).

64. As Breen (2010: 117, 121) documents, this effort was accompanied by novel metrics: "many newspapers published a weekly report—a kind of box score of political responsibility—listing either the town or, in some cases, the individual offering support."

65. R. Smith (1993: 558). On the interplay of Protestant, republican, and liberal understandings of virtue in the late eighteenth century, see Kloppenberg (1987).

66. Keyssar (2000: 2, 61–65).

67. As Breen (2004: 9) explains: "The colonists . . . had first to assure themselves that in an emergency distant strangers would come to their support. Abstract principles—the stuff of popular political ideology—made sense within a framework of trust, a vast web of assumed reciprocities that required time and patience to negotiate."

68. Clemens (2017a).

69. Simmel and Jacobson (1965: 125). See also Lee and Silver (2012: 138); Fiske (1992). I am grateful to the late Donald Levine for reminding me to return to readings done years before in his graduate seminars that had informed my own approach to social organization.

70. "Contract in Hobbes's definition was *mutual*, the gift was not; the general distinction left no room for a reciprocity of gifts. Hobbes instead characterized the asymmetrical gift, the free gift without right to expect a return, as the gift in his contract-based society." Liebersohn (2011: 29–30).

71. Locke ([1689] 2004: 30).

72. "Poverty is . . . a state of constant want and acute misery whose ignominy consists in its dehumanizing force; poverty is abject because it puts men under the absolute dictate of their bodies, that is, under the absolute dictate of necessity. . . . It was under the rule of this necessity that the multitude rushed to the assistance of the French Revolution, inspired it, drove it onward, and eventually sent it to its doom." Arendt ([1963] 2006: 50).

73. Arendt ([1963] 2006: 79).

74. Bourdieu (2014: 95); on Bourdieu and the gift, see Silber (2009).

75. See, for example, Rodgers (1992); R. Smith (1993).

76. Maier (1993); Kaufman (2008).

77. In the decades immediately after the Revolution, many denominations had been shaken by attacks upon the legitimacy of clerical authority while surges of revivalism produced new denominations (often labeled as "sects") whose internal governance conformed more closely to democratic principles. Hatch (1989: 69–70).

78. Wood (2009: 38–39). Historian Max Edling has also observed that "it may be an exaggeration to claim that America in 1787 was a stateless nation, but it is not a great one" (2008: 220).

79. Fischer (1989: 194–95), Phillips (1999).

80. Wood (1991: 224–225). See also Van Burkels (1984: 60).

81. Wood (1991: 220); see also L. W. Banner (1973: 24–26). Decades later, Thomas Jefferson and his allies would underscore the affective basis of patriotism. Rather than relying on law and regulation to constitute the nation, argued Senator Nathaniel Bacon of North Carolina, the people "must be bound together by love." Quoted in Balogh (2009: 115–116).

82. Calhoun (2007: 151). On the role of friendship or *fraternité*, as a solution to the post-revolutionary problem of order, see Ronsavallon (2007).

83. Block (2007). On the problem of obligation in a liberal polity, see Pateman (1979); Walzer (1970). For explorations of this question within American history, see Westbrook (2004); Capozzola (2008).

84. A variety of different political theories converged in the presumption that the right to vote should be linked to economic standing interpreted either as "having a stake in society," being subject to the taxing power of government or a member of a community by virtue of paying taxes, or being free of dependence on others represented by the status of a pauper, tenant, or unpropertied laborer. Keyssar (2000: 5, 9–14, 29, 61–62).

85. Gerstle (2001).

86. Keith Morgan to Missy LeHand, November 6, 1940, FDR-PPF 4885: Committee for the Celebration of the President's Birthday, 1939.

87. Rogers (2007). "Warm Springs Bars Negro Boy," *New York Sun* (October 14, 1936); "The National Foundation for Infantile Paralysis, Speech of Basil O'Connor, President, at Tuskegee Institute, May 22, 1939," FDR-PPF 4885: Committee for the Celebration of the President's Birthday, 1939; Missy LeHand to Basil O'Connor, January 27, 1941, FDR-PPF 4885: Committee for Celebration of President's Birthday, 1941.

88. "Paralysis Center Set Up for Negroes," *NYT* (May 22, 1939), 15; "The National Foundation for Infantile Paralysis, Speech of Basil O'Connor, President at Tuskegee Institute, May 22, 1939," FDR-PPF 4885: Committee for the Celebration of the President's Birthday, 1939; Missy LeHand to Basil O'Connor, January 27, 1941, FDR-PPF 4885: Committee for Celebration of President's Birthday, 1941. On the embedding of racial inequality in civic benevolence, see Guglielmo (2010).

89. "CIO Agency Ends Red Cross Tie-Up," *NYT* (April 15, 1946), 29.

90. Rokkan (1973: 13).

91. C. S. Fisher (2010: 10).

92. Haveman (2015: 22).

93. Appleby (1976: 7, 19–20).

94. The term is borrowed from Michael Mann (1986: 3), who in turn invokes Ernest Gellner. In justifying the case selection and comparative strategy in his classic *Social Origins of Dictatorship and Democracy*, Barrington Moore made a similar case for focusing on political innovation rather than diffusion (1966: xiii).

95. Haydu (1998).

96. Clemens (2006).

97. Schneiberg (2007).

98. On voluntarism as articulating demands for uniformity of provision and respect for individuality, see Clemens (2017b).

99. "Address introducing the Mayor at the opening rally of The Greater New York Fund," (February 24, 1938) OMR III 2 A, Box 4, Folder 166, JDR Jr. PERSONAL, Cooperation and Stewardship.

100. Thus archives do not represent cases for analytic comparison, but are analogous to key informants in an ethnographic study. The Rockefellers, for example, considered themselves responsible for 5 percent of the giving in a national crisis such as World War I or the Mississippi Flood of 1927. Consequently, they were very concerned with monitoring what others gave and, more generally, many of those involved in private relief and welfare work made a point of keeping the Rockefeller philanthropies up to date on their efforts. The Hoover archives also function in this way; as a record of Hoover as a key actor but also as a repository of traces in dense and ongoing conversations about the relation of government programs and private voluntarism. The Red Cross was both a key organization operating at this boundary and a profoundly territorial organization intent on protecting its distinctive jurisdiction; as a consequence, the organizational archives also record the activities of many potential competitors.

101. Stinchcombe (2001: 55–75); Fligstein (2001).

102. For exemplary recent studies of the characteristically public-private regime of social provision in the United States, see Hacker (2002); Morgan and Campbell (2011).

103. Barman (2006).

104. Harwood (2002).

105. For complementary analyses of American federalism as a source of political dynamism, see Callen (2016) and Tani (2016).

106. Ronsavallon (2007).

107. Manson (1906); see also Eifert (1997); G. S. Jones (1971: ch. 13); Tennstedt (1987).

108. Faust (1988: 79).

109. On the comparison of polities by mapping relations in the distribution of practices, see Fourcade et al. (2016).

110. Kropotkin ([1896] 2015: 103–109, 127–134).

111. Follett ([1918] 1998). On voluntarism as a means of confronting the Great Depression, see Dewey (1984: 57–58).

112. Hayek (1948: 16).

113. To name only a few examples from a vast literature, see Suleiman (2003); Wolch (1990).

114. Callahan (2017); Giridharadas (2018); Reich (2016); Reich, Bernholz and Cordelli (2016).

Chapter One

1. "The Revolution in France" (consource.org, downloaded October 7, 2015); see Wood (2009: 203).

2. This theoretical claim builds on literatures in institutional analysis and historical sociology. For analytic reviews, see Clemens and Cook (1999); Clemens (2005, 2007).

3. For only one example from a vast literature on the consequences of this founding contradiction, see Einhorn (2006). The form of a "two possibilities in one polity" argument has also been deployed in accounts of citizenship (e.g., Gerstle 2001) and political ideologies (e.g., Dionne 2012).

4. Ronsavallon (2007: 26). On the deployment of friendship as a relational model in the politics of the early Republic, see Koschnik (2000: 237–239).

5. Appleby (2000: 25); Wood (1996: 6).

6. Tocqueville ([1839] 2004: 600). As Gordon Wood argues, "this latently republican society . . . was still largely agricultural and rural, and it possessed as yet few modern alternatives to traditional personal and kinship relations to tie itself together . . . Americans had fewer opportunities than Englishmen to substitute impersonal market exchanges and a cash nexus for older personal and patriarchal connections." For a critique of Woods' characterization of the Revolution as essentially an erosion of dependency and deference, see Appleby (1994).

7. The "association" had an earlier history as a cross between a petition and an individual oath. In 1584, "associations" were circulated in response to a threat to

Elizabeth I. The Assassination Plot against William III provoked much larger—and eventually mandatory—associations to pledge loyalty to the monarch, with signatories grouped by locality, occupation, as well as religion, both domestic and in the colonies (Pincus 2009: 464–465). For significant discussions of the role of associations in American political thought and practices, see Gutmann (1998); Rosenblum (1998). On U.S. laws of association, see Novak (2001); on the "mixed" corporation and nonprofit corporation, see Howe (1979: 99); Levy (2016).

8. On the arrangement of governance in the early Republic as a "neo-composite" state, see Brooke (2009: 4–5).

9. Brooke (1996); Harris (1995).

10. Lomazoff (2012). A particularly controversial organizational innovation, the mass political party, began to take form over those early elections despite repeated and widespread condemnation. McCormick (1966); B. W. Brown (1971).

11. D. W. Howe (2007: 192). "These institutions [Sabbath schools] may terminate in an *organized system of mutual co-operation* between ministers and private Christians, so that every church shall be a disciplined army . . . in the grand onset against sin." A Reverend Ely quoted in Blau (1946: 26, italics in original). The "travelling" plan of Methodist circuit riders represents another example of innovation in religious forms of expansive coordination. Hatch (1989: 87). See Dorsey (1998) on the consequences of religious democratization on Quaker benevolence.

12. (consource.org, downloaded October 7, 2015).

13. Quoted in Koschnik (2007: 34); see also Schoenbachler (1998).

14. Tocqueville ([1839] 2004: 607) recognized the ambivalence so evident in Webster's essay: "In democratic countries, political associations are in a sense the only private entities that aspire to rule the state. Accordingly, governments nowadays look upon associations of this kind as medieval kings looked upon great vassals of the crown: they feel a sort of instinctive aversion to them and engage them in combat wherever they meet. By contrast, they feel a natural benevolence toward civil associations, because they can see readily that these, far from encouraging citizens to take an interest in public affairs, serve to distract them, and encourage them instead to become involved in projects that cannot be carried out without public peace, thereby averting revolution. But they fail to see to it that political associations multiply and greatly facilitate the growth of civil associations, and thus by avoiding a dangerous ill they deprive themselves of an effective remedy."

15. "It is through political associations that Americans . . . acquire a general taste for association and familiarize themselves with its use. . . . they take the lessons they learn this way and carry them over into civil life, where they put them to a thousand uses." Tocqueville ([1839] 2004: 608).

16. The shifting character and role of association have figured prominently in recent contributions to the history of the early republic. See Brooke (1996); Elkins and McKitrick (1993: 451–488); Koschnik (2007); Neem (2008); Wood (2009: 485–495).

17. Writing on the corporation, Pauline Maier (1993: 83) explains that "Americans salvaged from a rejected past those English legal traditions and practices that suited their republic, modified them to fit . . . 'an enlightened age,' and began a

trajectory of development that, in time, produced results dramatically different from the precedents with which it began." Matthew Schoenbachler (1998: 241) offers a kindred account of combination embodying durable tensions: "The Democratic-Republican Societies thus demonstrate not only the compatibility of democratic hopes and republican fears, but also the ways in which Americans of the early republic created a radically new, yet oddly familiar, language of politics."

18. Neem (2008: 40–42).

19. Koschnik (2007: 31); Brooke (1996: 292).

20. Koschnik (2007: 101); Harris (1995: 122). In 1784, the Society recommended that its state chapters acquire legislative charters to insulate them from such criticism. Maier (1993: 82).

21. Harris (1995: 116, 135).

22. Schoenbachler (1998: 254); Gould (1996).

23. McCarthy (2003: 27); Wilentz (2005: 60–65).

24. Harris (1995: 140).

25. Harris (1995: 138). A number of state societies, including that of New York, refused to ratify these changes.

26. Quoted in Neem (2008: 22). See also Wood (1991: 296).

27. Quoted in Koschnik (2007: 78).

28. Ephraim Perkins, A "Bunker Hill" Contest, A.D. 1826, reprinted in James D. Bratt (2006: 58–59). On opposition to the Benevolent Empire, see Bratt (2004); Wyatt-Brown (1970). On the conservative politics of the establishment of the Benevolent Empire, see Rollins (1976: 418–419). The anti-religious turn within the French Revolution provoked a stronger identification of American republicanism with religious piety. Banner (1988).

29. Wood (1991: 207, 244–245). For related debates in English popular politics, see Rudbeck (2012); on the sustained hostility to independent associations and charities in France, see Ronsavallon (2007) and C. Adams (2007).

30. Wood (2009: 140–73).

31. By the 1820s, as Leonard (1994: 23) has argued, "an antiparty, partyless democracy was the normal political practice of the states." Ratcliffe (1995: 220) makes a similar point about a different set of political contests: "Rejection of their National Republican associations ensured that political Antimasons would both denounce organized parties and yet become one." On the emergence of parties, see Altshuler and Blumin (1997); Formisano (1974, 1999).

32. de Leon, The Origins of the Right to Work (2015: 34). For an extended discussion, see Holt (1999).

33. Leonard (1994: 27). The question of the appropriateness of party organization differs from that of whether party formation is a product of top-down mobilization or an expression of substantive interests and conflict in the electorate. On this question, see Ratcliffe (1973).

34. D. B. Davis (1960). On whether Anti-Masonry should be understood as a mobilizing issue or as a vehicle for voters seeking an alternative to other party factions, see Formisano and Kutolowski (1977); Ratcliffe (1995).

35. *Richmond Enquirer* (March 7, 1835), quoted in Major Wilson (1988: 429).

36. Quoted from the *National Intelligencer* (various dates, 1835) in Major Wilson (1988: 426). On the anti-partyism of the 1840 campaign by William Henry Harrison, see Carwardine (1983: 62–63).

37. Beecher (1804: 8); see also Abzug (1994: 30–56); Wilentz (2005: 269–272).

38. Beecher (1804: 8–9, 17, 18, 20–21).

39. Locally based reform organizations and charities had been established in a number of American cities in the 1790s; these in turn often drew on recent British innovations in civic organization. See, for example, Abzug (1994: 39–40); B. L. Bellows (1993: ch. 1); Haviland (1994); Wright (1992).

40. Harris (1993: 458–459) on the political importance of "disinterested benevolence." Thus voluntary organizations could provide a partial substitute for organizing a political party: "One reason why the Whigs were able to keep insisting on the evil of political parties is that the benevolent societies (mainly led by Whigs and promoting the kind of reform Whigs wanted) provided them with an alternative mode of organizing in pursuit of their social objectives. The rise of political parties, along with the danger that they would become patronage-oriented, could only tend to undercut the influence of the cause-oriented voluntary associations." Howe (1979: 157).

41. Boyer (1978: 12–14); Hall (1982: 172–177); Hall (2010).

42. Abzug (1994: esp. ch. 2); Boyer (1978: 12–21); Young (2006: 62–74).

43. Abzug (1994); Haselby (2015).

44. Boyer (1978); Carwardine (1972: 327–340); Smith Rosenberg (1971).

45. Abzug (1994: 110, 160–161); Griffin (1960); Young (2006).

46. The earlier American Board of Foreign Missions (est. 1810) had been created within the loosely organized framework of the Congregational Church. Edwards (1919: 437).

47. Nord (2002: 147–71).

48. Elias Boudinot quoted in Haselby (2015: 245). One student of Timothy Dwight, Calvin Colton, developed into a fierce critic of revivalism and "the many works of the benevolence 'hydra.' He objected most of all to its political activism, denouncing temperance crusading as 'Protestant Jesuitism,' abolitionism as 'sedition,' women's rights as a reversal of nature." For Colton, "the Benevolent Empire represented a 'usurpation' of public authority that threatened American liberties." Bratt (2004: 88). See also Bratt (2001).

49. Young (2006: 73).

50. *Historical Statistics of the United States*, Table Ea636–643. George McKenna (2007: 3) provides a higher estimate of the scale of this endeavor: "In the generations following the Revolution, Congregationalists and Presbyterians from New England carried their campaigns of evangelical Calvinism into the upper Midwest and other areas of the Puritan diaspora, and by the 1830s their voluntary organizations of evangelization and moral reform had combined budgets larger than that of the federal government." See also McCarthy (2003: 81).

51. Abzug (1994: 89–90).

52. A Weary Traveller, *Observer and Telegraph* [Hudson, Ohio] (June 10, 1830), n.p. *19th Century U.S. Newspapers* (accessed November 22, 2015), Gale Document Number: GT3012089490.

53. Edwards (1919: 439).

54. A Village Pastor, "Hints on the Agency System," *Baltimore Literary and Religious Magazine* 6 (1840): 117. This essay was also printed in the first volume (1839–40) of *The Western Peace-Maker, and Monthly Religious Journal*, where it was followed by an essay from "Home Missionary" on the subject of "How Shall Funds Be Raised for Benevolent Purposes?" *Western Peace-Maker, and Monthly Religious Journal* 1 (7) (May 1840): 290–295. See also Bratt (2004: 74–75).

55. "Hints on the Agency System," p. 119.

56. It was particularly important to broaden the base of those who gave. The Panic of 1837 revealed the danger of overdependence on a few philanthropists such as the Tappan brothers who had been pushed into bankruptcy: "when worldly speculation has adsorbed [*sic*], or adversity destroyed, the resources of the more wealthy, the enterprises of benevolence have been greatly retarded. We must guard against similar disaster, in future, by expecting more from the common people, and leaning less upon the rich." "How Shall Funds Be Raised for Benevolent Purposes?," p. 293.

57. See discussions of federated fund-raising in chapter 3 and of efforts to broaden the base of donors during the Great Depression in chapters 5 and 6.

58. "How Shall Funds Be Raised for Benevolent Purposes?," pp. 292–293.

59. Brooke (2009: 20–25); Griffin (1959: 199–203, 209–210).

60. On this line of argument, see Gross (2003: 45–47); Brooke (2009: 20–25). A related threat, important for Thomas Jefferson's critique, was that endowed charities effectively held on to resources that might otherwise be deployed in the advancement of citizens and enterprise (Neem 2013: 40). The same argument might be directed at corporations more generally; see Maier (1993: 71).

61. Channing ([1829] 1858: 283, 295, 302); Meyer (1973).

62. Channing ([1829] 1858: 305). Later in the essay, Channing continued: "few things are more to be dreaded, than organizations or institutions by which public opinion may be brought to bear tyrannically against individuals or sects. From the nature of things, public opinion is often unjust; but, when it is not embodied and fixed by pledged societies, it easily relents, it may receive new impulses, it is open to influences from the injured. On the contrary, when shackled and stimulated by vast associations, it is in danger of becoming a steady, unrelenting tyrant, brow-beating the timid, proscribing the resolute, silencing free speech, and virtually denying the dearest religious and civil rights." (1858: 307).

63. Channing ([1829] 1858: 305).

64. Koschnik (2007: 69–71, 77). According to Koschnik, "Whereas the Sons of Washington and the Benevolent Society concentrated on partisan sociability and the organization of national celebrations, the American Republican Society and the Washington Association directly involved their members in Federalist election-

eering efforts. Acting as partisan organizations that challenged James Madison's administration and turned out to support Federalist candidates, the societies simultaneously rejected partisanship and assumed the mantle of disinterested patriotism as they condemned Republican measures and men." (2007: 69).

65. Koschnik (2007: 52–61).

66. Hatch (1989: 170).

67. Boyer (1978: 8).

68. The pastor of the Third Presbyterian Church in Philadelphia made the case "that the 'Christians' of the United States form themselves into a pressure group, transcending sectarian lines, to prevent the election of 'opponents of Christianity,' such as 'Pagans, Socinians, Mussulmen, Deists.'" Blau (1946: 22). The desire to preempt such mobilization has been cited as one reason for the early adoption of general, routinized procedure for the incorporation of religious organizations. Seavoy (1978: 38). See the discussion of "open access orders."

69. R. R. John (1997: 97).

70. R. R. John (1997: 108).

71. Hatch (1989: 177–179).

72. Quoted in Boyer (1978: 77, emphasis in original).

73. Channing ([1829] 1858: 326). Note how this echoes T. H. Breen's characterization of the revolutionary Committee on Donations as a "charitable infrastructure that had obvious political possibilities" (see Introduction).

74. Neem (2008: 25).

75. Madden (1962: 348).

76. Wayland (1838: 90–91).

77. A core commitment to the combination of scriptural literalism and individual responsibility informed Wayland's argument: "shall we take God himself as the interpreter of his own will, or shall every one of us be subject to the interpretation of every other one who claims authority over conscience. The former is the doctrine of Protestantism, the latter of Romanism." Wayland (1838: 22; for an extended critique of "Romanism," see p. 85).

78. Wayland (1838: 98).

79. Wayland (1838: 113).

80. Griffin (1959: 210–216). A second feature of the constitution of the American Tract Society was that it allowed current members of the executive committee great control over the election of that committee, a power exercised at the 1858 annual meeting that attracted some 1200 attendees and, after heated speeches and maneuvers on the part of the abolitionists, reelected the existing executive committee.

81. Griffin (1959: 203).

82. Wayland (1838: 105).

83. C. S. Fisher (2010: 10).

84. D. W. Howe (1979: 20). See also Hall (1982: ch. 8). On American "Whiggery" as shaping political behavior and discourse, see Howe (1979). For an extended

example of such a combination of economic innovation and concern for social stability, see Dalzell (1987).

85. Baird (1856: 365). See also "In What Sense, and To What Extent, Is the Church a Voluntary Association?" [Volutnray in original], *Western Peace-Maker and Monthly Religious Journal* 1 (4) (1839): 156–159.

86. Neem (2008: 21–23, 51–54). On the pre-revolutionary antipathy between political liberty and religious establishment, see Bailyn ([1967] 1992: 246–272).

87. North, Wallis, and Weingast (2009: 21–25). On this point, there is a striking contrast with France, that other great experiment in organizing democracy. See Ronsavallon (2007).

88. Neem (2008: 22, 154–155).

89. McCarthy (2003: 25); Zollman (1924: 33–35).

90. As one early study explained, "In the eyes of the law each religious organization possessed a two-fold character. As a voluntary religious organization it was practically free from state interference. As an economic unit, however, it was a legally constituted body possessing the right to acquire property and to conduct its own financial affairs. In this latter capacity religious organizations acquired a semilegal character and like all other incorporated bodies might claim protection of the state." Edwards (1919: 439).

91. Baird (1856: 261).

92. Rogin (1962).

93. In this tendency, American society of the period was at one with its counterparts in Europe where proliferating clubs and associations were features of urban, commercial life. As governments—monarchical and revolutionary alike—retained strong controls over association (which might easily turn to conspiracy), benevolence provided an attractive premise for social organizing. As Linda Colley (1992) has documented for late eighteenth-century Britain, benevolent projects prompted the establishment of associations in which merchants and manufacturers mingled with the occasional aristocrat for purposes of both philanthropic goals and political discussion.

94. Neem (2008: 111–117). See also Baird (1856: 262–263). Book IV is devoted to "The Voluntary Principle in America; Its Action and Influence."

95. Wilentz (2005: 267). See also John (1990); Wyatt-Brown (1971).

96. The trajectories of institutional development diverged between North and South: "while the free states saw a complex interplay of regulatory power and the elaboration of civil associations and corporations, the relative thinness of civil society in the slave states made the internal police powers of courts and communities all the more potent." Brooke (2009: 9). On the South, see Lockely (2007). On the use of the corporate model in New England, see Kaufman (2008).

97. Neem (2008: ch. 3); McGarvie (2003).

98. McGarvie (2003).

99. For a particularly rich case of the entanglement of local politics and benevolence, see B. L. Bellows (1993).

100. Balogh (2009: 13–15); Wood (1991: 318–319).

101. For example, in 1784 the state of New York adopted a law that excluded members of the clergy from membership on boards that controlled the property of local congregations. "From the American point of view the right of the laity to direct the management of finances was incontestable, and in 1815 all church property in the United States whether protestant or Catholic in which the laity formed a controlling majority. In so far as Catholic churches followed this procedure, however, a fundamental principle of Catholic administration had been set aside." Edwards (1919: 439).

102. Neem (2008). On sectional differences in institution-building and organizational foundings, see Brooke (2009).

103. Rogin (1962).

104. This same melding of individualism and associationalism would still infuse Herbert Hoover's celebration of *American Individualism* written almost a century after the final disestablishment of religion in the states. Noting the "extraordinary growth of organizations for the advancement of ideas in the community for mutual cooperation and economic objectives," Hoover asserted that "in these groups the individual finds an opportunity for self-expression and participation in the moulding [sic] of ideas, a field for training and the stepping stones for leadership" (1923: 41–42).

Chapter Two

1. E. C. Fisher (1864: 16–17). For the historical context of this development, see Kestnbaum (2005).

2. "The Far-Reaching Influence of the Sanitary Commission," *Our Daily Fare* 5 (June 13, 1864): 36.

3. "Letter from Mazzini," *Liberator* (July 7, 1865): 106. For another example of "lessons learned" abroad from the USSC, see Frances Power Cobbe, "The American Sanitary Commission and its Lesson," *Fraser's magazine for town and country* (March 1867): 75, 447; British Periodicals, p. 401. On the centrality of "Union" to the motives and meanings of the Civil War in the North, see Gallagher (2011).

4. S. G. Howe (1862: 22).

5. Beckert (2001: 117).

6. A similar configuration of charity-as-patriotism was evident in the development of British nationalism. "Charity . . . was meant to regenerate the donors as well as their beneficiaries. Giving money to a patriotic cause would root out the apathy and division that had sometimes been evident in 1745. Men and women would be redeemed and reunited in philanthropy and victory over the French would naturally follow" Colley (1992: 92).

7. See, for example, Brockett and Vaughan (1888: 47); Norris (1998: 326). On the multiple and conflicting relational models evoked in the South, see Faust (1988: 78–79, 82–84).

8. On the indirect but significant influences of the Civil War on economic organization, see M. R. Wilson (2006: ch. 6).

9. Review of Charles J. Stillé, *History of the United States Sanitary Commission*, *North American Review* 104 (214) (January 1867): 142.

10. "Letter from John Stuart Mill [Written to the Editorial Committee of Our Daily Fare]" *Our Daily Fare* 11 (June 20, 1864): 95–96. This newsletter was "published during the continuance of the Great Sanitary Fair held in Philadelphia in 1864."

11. Universal white male citizenship had been a work in progress. Not until 1851 did white men without property gain the right to vote in Virginia (Pflugrad-Jackisch 2010: 22–23).

12. Brockett (1863). A much later account claims that an American merchant in London had composed this work in response to "the bias of the people on the question of the war" and recognition that "England, jealous of the prosperity and growing power of the United States was willing that the Union should be dissolved and the states relegated back to their original condition." "Civil War Charities," *NYT* (February 2, 1902), SM 5.

13. Bailyn ([1967] 1992: 112–115, 355). The quotation is from Noah Webster, *An Examination into the Leading Principles of the Federal Constitution . . . by a Citizen of America* (Philadelphia, 1797).

14. Bailyn ([1967] 1992: 356). An echo of these concerns would be heard in debates over the relationship of state militias to the U.S. Army in the mobilization for World War I. Palmer (1931: ch. 4).

15. For the classic characterization of the nineteenth-century American state as a "state of courts and parties" (in contrast to the modern bureaucratic administrative state), see Skowronek (1982). For more recent, critical discussions of this conceptualization, see Novak (2008); R. R. John (2008). Yet even the critics would not claim that the federal government circa 1860 had the organizational capacity and resources to sustain a multiyear, multifront war.

16. Opal (2013).

17. Balogh (2009: 171); see also Adler (2012).

18. As Tocqueville ([1839] 2004: 766) asserted, "War does not always deliver democratic peoples into the hands of military government, but it cannot fail to bring about a vast increase in the prerogatives of civilian government. It almost inevitably leads to centralization in the latter of control over men and things. If it does not lead immediately to despotism by way of violence, it gently pulls in that direction by way of habit."

19. Beckert (2001: 117); M. R. Wilson (2006: 6–10).

20. Norris (1998: 313, 317).

21. Kestnbaum (2005: 273–277).

22. Maureen Fitzgerald (2006: 102).

23. "Local News," *Jewish Messenger* (April 25, 1862), 120.

24. Quoted in Frederickson (1965: 70).

25. Long (1998: 94).

26. Goodheart (2011: chs. 1 and 5); Grinspan (2009).

27. Review of Stillé, *History of the United States Sanitary Commission*, *North American Review* 104 (214) (January 1867): 142.

28. In the words of Katherine Prescott Wormeley, one of the nurses who served under the Sanitary Commission, the Commission "is the great artery which bears the people's love to the people's army." Quoted by Allan Nevins in his preface to Maxwell (1956: v). See also Garrison (1999).

29. *The Sanitary Commission* (1864: iii).

30. Attie (1998: 159–166) provides an important account of the tensions and competition between the two commissions.

31. Bensel (1990: 6–17).

32. Moss (1868: 42). The USCC differed from the USSC in its warmer embrace of traditional understandings of benevolence and humanitarian sentiment as well as its rejection of the use of "paid agents" rather than motivated volunteers. The poet Walt Whitman, who served as a wartime nurse and "believed intensely in the power of love and pity, expressed a fairly common opinion when he railed at the Sanitary agents as 'hirelings.' . . . Whitman, as a thoroughgoing anti-institutionalist, believed that the spontaneous spirit of benevolence could not survive formal organization and the professionalization of service" (Frederickson 1965: 106–107).

33. Moss (1868: 60). Emphasis in original.

34. E. C. Fisher (1864: 3–4). See chapter 1.

35. Frederickson (1965: 105). On discipline and state-building, see Gorski (2003).

36. Attie (1998: 104–106).

37. See Wills (2001); Norris (1998).

38. Grant (1955: 13).

39. *The Sanitary Commission* (1864: 52–54); Jeffrey (1998: 210–217). The administration of these contributions injected concerns over unwise charity and the "unworthy poor" into the war effort (Geisberg 2009: 50).

40. The USSC's leading fund-raiser in California, Thomas Starr King, preached on "The New Nation to Emerge from the War" (June 17, 1862). Posner (1964: 298).

41. Boynton (1864: x).

42. Review of "Stillé's *History of the United States Sanitary Commission*" in the *Spectator.* Reprinted in *Littell's Living Age* (August 24, 1867), 509.

43. "The War Day by Day: Fifty Years Ago," *Boston Daily Globe* (April 4, 1914), 107; *NYT* (July 8, 1888), 16.

44. Moss (1868: 253–254).

45. Peterson (1993/1994); Posner (1964); Simonds (1917).

46. Wendte (1921: 169, 176); Wagner (1952).

47. This call to patriotism can be understood as the sentimental correlate of earlier efforts to promote an interest-based nationalism through internal improvements and the expansion of trade relations across regions. Minicucci (2001).

48. "True and Good," *Our Daily Fare* 1 (June 8, 1864), 3.

49. Wendte (1921: 169).

50. Maxwell (1956: 97–104).

51. Moss (1868: 165).

52. Bernstein (1990: 44–54, 64–65, 201–202).

53. Attie (1998: 77).

54. *The Sanitary Commission* (1864: iv–v).

55. *The Sanitary Commission* (1864: v).

56. *The Sanitary Commission* (1864: v).

57. Maxwell (1956: 193–195).

58. Accounting provided an opening for criticism. An investigation of purported discrepancies in the financial report of the USSC concluded that "The more we see of the operations of this Commission, the more we are convinced that . . . its affairs have been loosely managed, and that though it has unquestionably done much good, it has, by its expensive management, imposed unnecessary labor and financial burdens on the community. There was work it might have done at one-fourth the expense, without supplementing the duties, not to say the prerogatives of the Government." *Medical and Surgical Reporter* (January 21, 1865), 12, 15; American Periodicals, p. 243.

59. Maxwell (1956).

60. By comparison, the bond drive led by financier Jay Cooke raised $1 billion and the U.S. Army Quartermasters' Department reported a total of $47 million in small arms purchases (1861–66). Lawson (2002: 40–41); M. R. Wilson (2006: 231, 235).

61. William Tecumseh Sherman to George H. Stuart, U.S. Christian Commission. January 19, 1866. Quoted in Moss (1868: 238–239).

62. E. C. Fisher (1864).

63. "The Far-Reaching Influence of the Sanitary Commission," *Our Daily Fare* 5 (June 13, 1864): 36.

64. Ibid.

65. On the uses of Foucault's concept of governmentality in the historical analysis of state development, see Gorski (2003); Ikegami (1995).

66. The ambiguous place of civilian volunteers operating at the front was reflected in the comprehensive statement of the laws of war that the Union adopted for the Civil War. The property of churches, hospitals, and "other establishments of an exclusively charitable character" was not to be appropriated as was government property but "may be taxed or used when the public service may require it." "The enemy's chaplains, officers of the medical staff, apothecaries, hospital nurses and servants, if they fall into the hands of the American army, are not prisoners of war," although commanders might choose "to retain them" or the captured staff and volunteers might choose to remain with captured soldiers. Volunteers and charitable organizations were surrounded by a zone of discretion, both their own and on the part of military commanders. General Orders No. 100, reprinted in Witt (2012: 380, 382).

67. Stillé (1863: 15).

68. Moss (1868: 243–244). Butler is remembered in Civil War history for his declaration that slaves were contraband of war and, therefore, effectively free once captured by or surrendered to the Union troops.

69. Dr. Howe was also alleged to be a member of the "Secret Six" who provided financial support to the radical abolitionist John Brown, whose 1859 raid on Harp-

er's Ferry was intended to spark slave rebellions throughout the southern states. Wilentz (2005: 747–748); Showalter (2016: 144–145).

70. S. G. Howe (1862: 11, 12–13).

71. The mobilization of benevolence in support of the war, argued Howe, also undermined the proper development of the national state. "'You are unsound in your ideology,' he wrote to Bellows: 'I think you stand in the way of the action of those natural principles,' which would allow government 'to do its duty.' Tendering his resignation, Howe announced: 'I cannot bring myself to believe that it is wise to urge the people to do the government work any longer.'" Quoted in Attie (1998: 107).

72. Goldberg (2007) contends that entitlement programs directed at fully recognized citizens (soldiers, white working men, etc.) have been repeatedly paired with programs for marginal or disadvantaged groups (e.g., freed slaves, agricultural and domestic workers, women and minorities) which often draw on tropes of charity and dependence. Howe's argument, however, speaks to the consequences of extending those tropes of charity to those whose full standing as citizens is not in question.

73. S. G. Howe (1862: 13–14).

74. Stanley (1992: 1287).

75. de Leon (2015: ch. 5).

76. Quoted in Pryor (1987: 163–164). A model of economic rehabilitation that used charitable donations to subsidize wage labor was used by the revolutionary Committee on Donations and would be a persistent feature of voluntary responses to disaster through the early years of the Great Depression.

77. For a powerful example of such analysis in the context of the Second World War, see J. T. Sparrow (2011: ch. 3).

78. Attie (1998: 174–175).

79. Quoted in Attie (1998: 153).

80. Attie (1998: 162).

81. Quoted in Maxwell (1956: 11).

82. Quoted in Attie (1998: 138).

83. M. W., "Relief of Discharged and Disabled Soldiers," NYT (March 9, 1865), 5.

84. Attie (1998: 108); Maxwell (1956: 101–104, 186–188).

85. Lawson (2002: 183).

86. Padgett and Powell (2013).

87. Ulysses S. Grant, Lieutenant-General, to Geo. H. Stuart, Chairman USCC, January 12, 1866. Quoted in Moss (1868: 238).

88. "An Irish 'Sanitary Commission,'" Irish American Weekly (April 28, 1866), 2.

89. "The Late Christian Commission," Chicago Daily Tribune (July 25, 1880), 9; "Tenth Reunion of the United States Christian Commission," Christian Advocate (August 8, 1889), 64, 32; American Periodicals, p. 512; "The Christian Commission: Close of a Four Days' Meeting at Mountain Lake Park, Md.," WP (August 4, 1896), 7. By the 1890s, the "Christian Commission of the United States" is identified as the successor of the USCC. "For Soldiers and Sailors," WP (January 20, 1893), 7.

90. "Civil Aid for Soldiers," NYT (April 24, 1898), 14; "As They Did in '61: Philanthropists Plan National Sanitary Commission," Chicago Daily Tribune (May 1, 1898), 10.

91. On the effects of sectional rifts on voluntary associations, see Neem (2010).

92. See Attie (1998: 133–135). Also Brockett and Vaughan (1888).

93. Schuyler recruited a number of her colleagues from the USSC to the work of charities visiting, which then transformed into the Charities Association (Cross 1961: 295–296).

94. See Attie (1998).

95. Oglesby's comment may have been directed toward a proposal to incorporate a home for disabled soldiers and sailors. Enabling legislation passed Congress in March 1865 and established a list of 100 incorporators. But in October 1865, General Meade complained that he had three times gone to Washington, D.C., and each time the meeting failed to meet the required quorum of 50 incorporators. "A Home for Disabled Soldiers and Sailors," *NYT* (March 5, 1865), 6; "Gen. Meade On Our Sick And Wounded Soldiers," *NYT* (October 26, 1865), 5. During the same months, the leaders of the USSC secured a legal opinion as to the propriety of using funds collected for the relief of soldiers in the field to support the creation of a Sanitarium "for the succor of discharged soldiers—that is, of men who no longer belong to the army, but who are turned adrift on the world . . . or after reaching home either from poverty or ignorance, or friendlessness, or from delay in procuring their pensions." "The Sanitary Commission," *NYT* (February 26, 1865), 5.

96. "Inaugural Address of Richard J. Oglesby, Governor of Illinois," *Chicago Tribune* (January 17, 1865), 3. The implications of mingling public funds and voluntary effort reverberated through Illinois politics. In 1883, the private benevolent Illinois Eye and Ear Infirmary (itself supervised by a number of USSC veterans and supported by private donations, grants from other benevolent associations including the CRAS, and the State Board of Charities) provoked charges that the government financial contribution set a precedent for public relief to those suffering from all medical maladies rather than those of the eye and ear alone. The State Board of Charities rejected this reasoning: "The answer which has always overcome this objection is that the eye and ear require surgical treatment which general practitioners, especially in the country, cannot ordinarily give, and that the salvation of the eye of a poor person through skillful treatment by saving him from blindness saves him at the same time from pauperism, thus relieving the community of a prospective and permanent burden." "The Illinois Eye and Ear Infirmary," *Chicago Daily Tribune* (May 15, 1883), 11.

97. "News and Miscellany," *Medical and Surgical Reporter* (February 17, 1866), 137.

98. "Good News for Our Brave Boys," *Maine Farmer* (July 27, 1865), 2.

Chapter Three

1. H. W. Bellows (1879: 5–6).

2. Within the USSC, tensions between the elite, male national leadership and the predominantly female volunteers suppressed enthusiasm for turning the organization to new peacetime purposes (Attie 1998: ch. 8).

3. DuBois ([1903] 1994: 16). On the Freedman's Bureau, see Goldberg (2007: 31–75).

4. Ruswick (2013: 20–22).

5. In the history of social welfare, the legacy of wartime benevolence is often presented as part of the development of scientific charity and professional welfare. Those found to be tramps, chronic paupers, and "defectives" would be dispatched out of town or institutionalized. When investigation established a need for aid, the destitute would be incorporated in a system of oversight and intervention that was the kernel of modern social work. A. F. Davis (1967); Greeley (1995); Katz (1986); Peel (2012).

6. Bridges (1984); Einhorn (1991); Hartog (1983); Heale (1976).

7. Kaplan (1978).

8. Finegold (1995); M. R. Wilson (2006: 209–210).

9. As systematic knowledge of the relation between relief and poverty expanded in the late nineteenth century, a number of prominent charity workers acknowledged the need for larger and more sustained government commitments to funding relief (Ruswick 2013: 176).

10. Sassen (2006).

11. Tilly (1992: 51).

12. Using the threshold of 2,500 residents, the United States could boast 24 "urban places" as of 1790. Only five topped 10,000, led by New York City at 33,000. At this time, the population of Paris had exceeded half a million while that of London was approaching one million. https://www.census.gov/population/www/docu mentation/twps0027/tab02.txt.

13. Tilly (1992: 61) invokes sequencing to explain how it was possible for a powerful English state to emerge despite the existence of London, specifically that London became a trading power after the consolidation of the monarchy and parliament.

14. Frug (1980: 1074–1080, 1096–1109).

15. Bridges (1984); Einhorn (1991); Erie (1988); Katznelson (1982).

16. For a later statement of this challenge, see Zorbaugh ([1929] 1976: xix).

17. Attie (1998: 205).

18. Those municipal Democrats "hoped that their indiscriminate style of giving—without detailed investigation of the recipient or personal tie between recipient and donor—would become the city's dominant form of charity" (Bernstein 1990: 53).

19. Quoted in Bridges (1982: 68).

20. Simmel and Jacobson (1965: 124).

21. Bernstein (1990: 78–85).

22. Kaplan (1978: 205).

23. "Labor and Its Prospects," *New York Herald* (November 10, 1873), 5.

24. An opinion piece from the *Buffalo Commercial* (reprinted by the *New York Tribune*) asserted that "the fearful drain has been going on for two or three years, and unless it is stopped a crash will come. We have taken from the pockets of the

people during the past year about $100,000,000, and applied it to the extinguishment of the debt. By so doing, we have depleted the recuperative energies of the country to precisely that extent." A writer for the *Tribune* responded that: "Paying off debt destroys no wealth. It simply transfers it. . . . We owe as a people a sum which is nearly equal to a tenth of our wealth. We owe it mainly to each other. We propose to reduce steadily the Debt, so as to diminish the burden of interest. We believe this is true economy." "This Country On Its Way To The Poorhouse," *New York Tribune* (February 22, 1870), 4. See also Sinisi (2003).

25. The essay continued: "We maintain . . . that it is the part of wise, sound, governmental policy to take advantage of a crisis like this to finish the work it has on hand and carry out new plans of public utility, for the double reason that the work can be done more cheaply than at other times, and that in this way it identifies itself with the interests and welfare of the people. The government can thrust its hand into Wall-st. [*sic*] to relieve brokers and save bankers from failure. Let it show the same interest in the workingmen it has shown in merchants and stock jobbers and millionaires. And the same principle applies with added force to our City Government." "What to Do For the Poor," [reprinted from the *Graphic*], *New-York Tribune* (November 13, 1873), 2.

26. "Wisdom in Charity." The question followed: "Well, but who are the people? Are not the men who passed this resolution a portion of the people, and what other portion do they expect to provide them with employment?" The editorial concluded by urging state legislatures to make appropriations for public works and for the public to support "the best of the existing organized charities" while all should avoid "insane imitations of the miserable class warfares [*sic*] and jealousies of Europe." "Winter and the Working Class: What Can be Done to Find Employment for the Destitute," *Annapolis Gazette* (December 12, 1873), 3.

27. "Self-Help in the Panic," *Commercial Advertiser* (November 15, 1873), 2. For similar debates over the benefits of private contracting versus government production for war, see M. R. Wilson (2006: ch. 3).

28. Digital searches of American newspapers from 1866 to 1900 provide little support for the claim that the Commissions were direct models for subsequent efforts. The commissions are mentioned most frequently in obituaries, in notices of reunions (particularly of the Christian Commission), and in conjunction with mobilization in response to the Spanish-American War of 1898. Only in the last of these are the Civil War Commissions taken as explicit models for new efforts. But the individuals involved in the wartime efforts were active participants in the efforts to address problems of unemployment in an increasingly industrial and commercial society.

29. "Wisdom In Charity. Efforts to Devise Measure for Relieving the Prevailing Destitution without Fostering Public Pauperism," *New York Tribune* (November 21, 1873), 2.

30. Dorman B. Eaton was a prominent attorney who had allied with Henry Bellows, founder of the USSC, in promoting a Sanitary Commission bill in the New York legislature (Duffy 1968: 568–569).

31. "Wisdom in Charity."

32. "The Darkest Side of the Panic," *New York Tribune* (October 31, 1873), 2.

33. "Charity's Balance Sheet," *New York Tribune* (January 1, 1874), 4.

34. "But now, after several weeks of depression, another suppliant for the favor of HERCULES appears, and sundry organizations, such as the Internationals and the Workingmen's Central Executive Committee, combine to solicit from State and Federal authorities the furnishing of work on a large scale to those who are out of employment. These organizations do not ordinarily favor Government interposition in labor matters, unless, indeed, it puts money in their pocket or adds to their hours of idleness but now they look to Government as a guardian, and would have it take up the industries which individuals and corporations have laid down." "Self-Help in the Panic."

35. "The Duty of Public And Private Charity," *New York Herald* (February 8, 1874), 8.

36. Ibid. At least some Chicagoans located the boundary between two kinds of poor in the same place: "A soup-house in each division, it is claimed, would be hailed with joy by those who are really destitute and are too proud to beg." "The Relief and Aid Society," *Chicago Daily Tribune* (January 7, 1874), 8.

37. For a different naming system, see McCarthy (1982: 64–67).

38. "The Council: Aid for the Southern Sufferers," *Chicago Daily Tribune* (June 2, 1874), 2; "The Grasshopper Region," *Chicago Daily Tribune* (November 7, 1874), 2.

39. http://www.greatchicagofire.org/item/ichi-63817. The National Hand of Fellowship; Engraving, 1871 (ichi-63817).

40. "Charity," *Chicago Daily Tribune* (November 9, 1873), 3.

41. "Their members will know, as the officers of the chief society cannot, just where the funds ought to be applied; they will learn where the sick are lying, and the timid poor are hidden; they will trace out shrinking misery, and feed and clothe, with grateful delicacy, those whose sudden indigence has been thrust upon them by Christian speculators, yet who dare not go out in public and ask for meat. The winter's poor will be largely of this class." The paper promised to announce the formation of "new associations of charity in every portion of the city." As importantly, congregation-based efforts would not be hampered by the rivalries that existed among "the directresses of the Orphan asylum [who] do not send into parts unknown somebody who will have to take help from 'that other church.'" "Organized Charity," *Sunday Times* (Chicago, Illinois) (November 16, 1873), 6.

42. "Grand Co-Operative Movement for the Relief of the Poor," *Chicago Daily Tribune*, 3.

43. "The Council: The Demand of the Unemployed," *Chicago Daily Tribune* (December 23, 1873), 3. The *Tribune*'s editorial staff responded that aldermen "of all others, should be excluded from participation in the distribution of the public charity. As a class, they are unfitted by habit, association, and official position for an honest, faithful, and equitable administration of any such responsible duty." "Mr. Hoffman's Remedy," *Chicago Daily Tribune* (December 25, 1873), 4.

44. "Last Night's Meeting," *Chicago Daily Tribune* (December 27, 1873), 4. The Tribune's editorial staff welcomed the "demolishing of all delusions, shams, and misrepresentations" to the effect that the City of Chicago had neither funds nor authority to expand public works in response to unemployment and that the "Relief and Aid Society have the means and machinery to relieve every case of actual want in the city." "The Essence of the Whole Matter," *Chicago Daily Tribune* (December 28, 1873), 8. But given that only one in four applications for aid from the CRAS was found worthy, the conflict lay in the determination of "actual want."

45. "The Duty of the Relief and Aid Society," *Chicago Daily Tribune* (November 12, 1874), 4.

46. Boyer (1978: 145–147).

47. Katz (1986: chs. 1–3).

48. Landis (1997).

49. Steinfeld (1989).

50. Lowell ([1884] 1971: 93–94).

51. Lowell ([1884] 1971: 95).

52. Lowell ([1884] 1971: 93).

53. Cross (1961: 291).

54. Ruswick (2013: 19).

55. Haydu (2008); Roy (1997); Sklar (1988); Beisel (1997); Domhoff (1974).

56. Lawson (2002: chs. 3 and 4).

57. H. W. Bellows (1879: 70).

58. H. W. Bellows (1879: 37).

59. See Bernstein (1990); Beckert (2001: ch. 7). In an extended analogy between the riot and the crucifixion of Christ, Reverend Octavius Brooks Frothingham observed of the rioters that no "passages in the history of human projects" are more dreadful "than those which tell how men have resisted, pushed away, reviled, cursed, beaten, mobbed, crucified their benefactors." Asserting a parallel between God who had given his son and the inventors and investors responsible for the wonders of industrialization, he argued that "if ignorance makes men mad with inventors, how much more will it make them mad with reformers, philanthropists, redeemers, who bring an uncomprehended and altogether fathomless benefit to their social and moral estate!" The sermon also dwelled at length on the abolitionist credentials and charitable acts of a couple whose home was targeted by the rioters (1863: 6, 9, 11–12).

60. M. R. Wilson (2006: 209–213). Exploring the motives of the rioters, Frothingham observed that while conscription may have been unknown in the United States, to more recent immigrants from Europe it was "a horror only too well known" that "suggests tyranny in its most arbitrary form, the tearing of people from their homes to fight battles in whose issue they were not interested" (1863: 15).

61. H. W. Bellows (1879: 92–93). For similar efforts in Chicago, see Grant (1955: 75).

62. H. W. Bellows (1879: 106–107, 129).

63. Maureen Fitzgerald (2006: 110, 112–113). On the political-religious conflicts over the public funding of charitable institutions, see also Crenson (1998).

64. Maureen Fitzgerald (2006: 113).

65. Kaplan (1978: 207).

66. Rezneck (1953: 325).

67. "To Relieve Distress: Charitable Societies in this City Working Together," *New York Tribune* (December 23, 1893), 4.

68. Ruswick (2013: 20–21).

69. Stead ([1894] 1964: 141–142, 153).

70. "To Relieve Distress," 4.

71. "Relief of the Unemployed in the United States During the Winter of 1893–94," *Journal of Social Science* 32 (November 1894): 1–51.

72. Chicago and Boston collected this information, but the experience of those two cities was generalized on the grounds that "there is no reason to doubt that New York, Philadelphia, Pittsburg, and others would show the same preponderance." "Relief of the Unemployed," 11.

73. "Relief of the Unemployed," 13.

74. Dauber (2013).

75. Waugh (2001).

76. Harry Hopkins would later describe his involvement with relief work on public parks in 1915 as a key inspiration for certain New Deal programs (see ch. 5). Roll (2013: 21); J. Hopkins (1999: 151).

77. "Relief of the Unemployed," 24.

78. "Relief of the Unemployed," 20.

79. "Relief of the Unemployed," 31, in the subsection "The Situation in New York City: The Winter of 1893-94" (from a report by Charles D. Kellogg).

80. "New Scheme to Raise Money," *NYT* (January 10, 1894), 9. "Of Good Old Virginia Blood," *NYT* (February 11, 1894), 20.

81. "Relief of the Unemployed," 31.

82. "6–15–99 Club Begins Work," *NYT* (January 14, 1894), 5; "Help the Unemployed Poor," *NYT* (March 4, 1894), 8; "Work of the 6–15–99 Club," *New York Tribune* (March 5, 1894), 7; "Work of the 6–15–99 Club," *New York Tribune* (March 26, 1894), 5; "To Make More Money for the Poor," *NYT* (April 8, 1894), 9.

83. "That The Poor May Not Want," *NYT* (January 21, 1894), 7. The *New York Times,* which was not listed among the four newspaper-based funds, accounted for most of the coverage of the 6–15–99 plan.

84. "The One-Day Wage Relief," *Chicago Daily Tribune* (January 7, 1894), 28.

85. "The One-Day Wage Relief."

86. "The One-Day Wage Relief."

87. "Money Is Needed For Relief," *Chicago Daily Tribune* (February 21, 1894), 8.

88. "Subscriptions to the Relief Fund," *Chicago Daily Tribune* (February 25, 1894), 15.

89. "The One-Day Wage Relief."

90. "There is no doubt that certain utterances by the socialists, who have recently assumed to speak for labor, have had considerable effect in checking the tide of subscriptions for the relief work. It seems evident that some of our citizens have

an idea that 'the unemployed' are nearly all socialists, and that a good many of the wage earners of this city look with favor upon the notions peculiar to the socialistic labor party." "Boom the Relief Fund," *Boston Globe* (March 1, 1894), 4.

91. "Mayor to Aid Tramps," *Chicago Daily Tribune* (December 13, 1899), 9.

92. "Basil Beats Bicknell: Head of St. John's Home Assaults Charities Secretary," *Chicago Daily Tribune* (March 14, 1903), 4; see also, "Row Disrupts a Society: Home Finding Association Officers Resign," *Chicago Daily Tribune* (May 28, 1904), 3. On Bicknell, "Tells of Red Cross Work," *Chicago Daily Tribune* (June 10, 1909), 2.

93. Cutlip (1965: 26, 38–50).

94. Welfare Interests—General, American Red Cross, Membership Dues, 1936–1942, RAC OMR, III 20 Box 1, Folder 5.

95. Polletta (2002: 16–20); on participatory etiquette, see Eliasoph (1998).

96. This situation was aggravated by efforts of the nascent fund-raising profession to activate still more relationships. Starting with Harvard in 1905, college ties were harnessed to fund-raising and by the 1920s many private colleges linked ongoing solicitation of alumni to original endowments and large philanthropic gifts. Cutlip (1965: 242–271); see also Geiger (1985). This systematic trolling for gifts intensified as some of the earliest practitioners of this model of charitable fund-raising transformed their experience into a new profession. In the aftermath of World War I with its unprecedented mobilization of national fund-raising, individuals such as John Price Jones would develop systematic registers of donors that would be used and augmented across multiple drives. Individuals could—and did—complain, but the business of fund-raising became a juggernaut in the twentieth century.

97. See Clemens (2010a).

98. Barman (2006: 23).

99. Charles (1993).

100. Zorbaugh ([1929] 1976: 61). Participation in service-oriented civic organizations could also serve as a vehicle for the displacement of older elites by an ascendant upper middle class. Davis, Gardner, and Gardner (1941).

101. As many of the classic community studies noted, the old elites—W. Lloyd Warner's "upper uppers"—did not usually engage in this sort of activity. Using events listed in the *New York Tribune*, political scientist Gabriel A. Almond ([1938] 1998: 113, 114, 192) calculated that only 4 percent were charitable during the "Social Season of 1882–83," a proportion that grew to 8 percent by 1900 and to 28 percent in 1935. See also F. T. Martin (1911).

102. For a rich comparative account of these processes, see Haydu (2008).

103. Attie (1998: 108, 172). As historian Melinda Lawson (2002: 17) explains, "But where commission leaders encouraged national identity by challenging persistent state and local identities, organizers of the Sanitary Fairs converted localism into a *vehicle* for the construction of a preeminent national identity."

104. Peter Dobkin Hall (2010: 170) has documented a similar pattern of differences in the models of civic activity cultivated by alumni of Harvard and Yale in the late nineteenth century. The former exemplified "an ideal of leadership . . . ex-

ercised through powerful centralized institutions located in metropolitan centers," the latter working "through broadly disseminated networks of community luminaries guiding organizations in villages and towns across the country."

Chapter Four

1. "New Earthquake in San Francisco," *NYT* (April 26, 1906), 1.

2. Bicknell (1935: 36).

3. On the relief effort, see Davies (2011).

4. Mann (1993: 59).

5. Immergut (1990).

6. The term "expansible" derives from John C. Calhoun's plan for an antebellum national army. See M. S. Fitzgerald (1996); Katznelson (2002).

7. Gerstle (2001).

8. Kaufman (2003).

9. The charter of the American National Red Cross "may be found in Title 36 of the U.S. Code" but that section "classifies the ANRC, and the ANRC alone, as a 'treaty obligation organization.'" Kosar (2006: 3).

10. Oates (1994); Pryor (1987). By the time of the First World War, the Red Cross itself would fudge this issue, representing Barton as part of the US Sanitary Commission from which the reconstituted Red Cross traced its lineage.

11. Pryor (1987: 156, 204–207, 325).

12. Pryor (1987: 195); Dulles (1950: 14).

13. Pryor (1987: 232–233).

14. Pryor (1987: 249).

15. On the relational dynamics of mentorship, see Polletta (2002: 74–75).

16. In an effort to clarify a later organizational dispute, one official explained: "Our organization, as the result of its peculiar prerogatives and obligations, has been held by the government to be a quasi-governmental agency and to it alone the government looks for the accomplishment of the tasks prescribed by the Geneva convention." Jason S. Joy, Acting Vice Chairman, ARC to Howard J. Rogers, Manager, Atlantic Division, ARC (August 18, 1921). ARC, 1917–1934, Box No. 68, Folder 041.

17. "The issue was settled only through a compromise that modified the disputed section to prohibit the fraudulent use of the Red Cross insignia" (Dulles 1950: 18). See also Kosar (2006: 21).

18. Dulles (1950: 11, 18–20, 77–78); Kosar (2006).

19. Pryor (1987: 307–16); Dulles (1950: 19–20).

20. Boardman, like the Roosevelts, was a product of the social milieu of the Union League Club and the legacy of its nationalist projects (Pryor 1987: 330–339).

21. Dulles (1950: 71).

22. "Designation by Our Presidents of the American Red Cross as the National Relief Agency: The Historic Proclamations of Five Chief Executives," *RCC* 8 (5) (March 1, 1929): 12–16.

23. Dulles (1950: 77–78).

24. In her study of the very large membership associations, Theda Skocpol (2003: 26–28) notes that many had a federal-state-local organization that mapped onto the framework of electoral federalism. The Red Cross is a decided and important exception. After a brief experiment with creating state organizations, the Red Cross settled on a national-local structure.

25. The tension between these geometries repeatedly surfaced in the form of conflicts with the Community Chests. See, for example, "Eighth National Red Cross Convention: A Well-Spring of Work, of Inspiration, of the Spirit of Service," *RCC* 8 (10) (May 15, 1929): 5–9.

26. Bicknell (1935: 12–14). The rapid mobilization of relief contributions in Illinois expressed expectations for reciprocity. Chicago had received an outpouring of donated relief funds in the aftermath of the great fire of 1871 and quickly collected funds for San Francisco. The consequences of this city-to-city aid endured for decades by entrenching major civic organizations as central gatekeepers.

27. Dulles (1950: 104).

28. Dulles (1950: 103–104); Bicknell (1935: 23–28). The local sensitivity to federal efforts to take control was heightened by the fact that San Francisco was in the midst of a major scandal and trial over mayoral corruption. Davies (2011: ch. 2).

29. Bicknell (1935: 35n).

30. Bicknell (1935: 45).

31. Bicknell (1935: 42–43). As Bicknell explained, "we were aiming to conserve our heavy field artillery by substituting the machine gun for lighter field operations in which speed and mobility were possible."

32. Bicknell (1935: 47–48). The lawyers, Bicknell alleged, "scathingly criticized the committee for using this sacred trust fund for commercial purposes. These lawyers also demanded to know what the corporation proposed to do with any money it might collect from these borrowers. The San Francisco relief was finished and what right would the committee have to the repaid funds? In every case the juries decided against the corporation and those loans, amounting in the aggregate to several hundred thousand dollars, were never repaid" (Bicknell 1935: 52–53).

33. Quoted in Davies (2011: 76–77).

34. "Millions Needed for Red Cross," *San Francisco Chronicle* (December 8, 1909), 2; "Red Cross Has Twenty-Eight State Boards," *San Francisco Chronicle* (October 23, 1910), 26. The system of state branches was soon scrapped due to the recognition that "the tie between State and Nation was too loose to assure united country-wide policy and action, while financial responsibilities were too widely diffused" (Bicknell 1935: 95).

35. "Taft Explains Red Cross Uses," *San Francisco Chronicle* (July 11, 1909), 37.

36. "Red Cross Stamps: A Commodity for Which There Has Been a Brisk Demand," *San Francisco Chronicle* (December 27, 1908), 24.

37. "Red Cross Sends First Funds to Victims: Fifty Thousand Surplus from San Francisco Relief Purse Goes to Italy," *San Francisco Chronicle* (December 31, 1908), 3; "San Francisco Raises $75,000 for Red Cross," *San Francisco Chronicle* (January 20, 1911), 5.

38. "The Society of the Red Cross," *San Francisco Chronicle* (December 16, 1908), 6.

39. "Red Cross Is Urged to Act," *San Francisco Chronicle* (November 12, 1907), 5.

40. Dulles (1950: 87); *RCB* 2 (5) (January 28, 1918): 4.

41. Walters and Bowman (2010); Malczewski (2009: 963–1000).

42. Julius Rosenwald also supported multiple Hebrew charities as well as settlement projects for Russian Jews. Consequently his great support of the YMCA movement exemplifies the expansive ecumenism that characterized many projects of municipal benevolence (Elfenbein 2001: 64–65; see also Ascoli 2006).

43. Fosdick (1958: 38–40).

44. Zunz (2012: 78). For the later judicial and regulatory history of these distinctions, see Thorndike (2016: 13).

45. Stead ([1894] 1964: 97).

46. "Tax on Legacies: General Instructions Issued by Commissioner of Internal Revenue," *WP* (July 17, 1902), 7; "Grants Vanderbilt Claim," *WP* (May 5, 1905), 11; Prasad (2012: 125–128).

47. "President's Message to Congress Deals with Nearly Every National Problem," *WP* (December 5, 1906), 8. The principle of taxing gifts to more direct kin at lower rates than to distant members of the family had been included in the inheritance tax element of the war revenue act of 1898. The actual rate would also increase with the total size of the estate. "The War Revenue Bill," *WP* (June 10, 1898), 4.

48. Phillips (2002: 47–54).

49. "Giving Away $121,356,973, Charity's Gain for 1907," *WP* (December 22, 1907), E14.

50. "Oppose Rockefeller Gifts," *WP* (February 1, 1907), 3. This $10,000 was only one installment of a larger contribution that critics (including former Congressman Thomas W. Phillips) charged should "be returned to the giver, on the ground that it is tainted and not honestly earned." " In time the gift was accepted, but the report acknowledged that "objection had been raised to the acceptance of the Rockefeller gift, and that no more money would be 'solicited' from the same source." "Accepts Rockefeller Gift. Christian Church Missionary Society Finds $25,000 Not Tainted," *WP* (October 13, 1907), 11.

51. "Danger in Big Gifts: Hannis Taylor Talks of Modern Multimillionaire," *WP* (February 23, 1907), 11; Reich (2016).

52. "President Peace Hero," *WP* (December 11, 1906), 3.

53. Theodore Roosevelt recognized that voluntary associations—and above all the federally chartered Red Cross—could be useful vehicles for circumventing the obstacles to action posed by Congress, particularly in the case of foreign policy. "Roosevelt's Latest Message Shows a Keen Desire for Greater Power," *WP* (December 16, 1906), B2; "President Not Heeded: Congress Has Proved Obdurate to Many Appeals," *WP* (March 3, 1907), 10.

54. "Danger in Big Gifts," 11. This article also spoke to the dangerous effects of large donations on universities: "If this thing goes on, we can soon close all departments of our universities except those that apply the principles of physical science to the production of material wealth or its equivalent."

55. *CR, 61ˢᵗ Congress, Second Session,* Report No. 405, Incorporation of Rocke-feller Foundation (March 16, 1910): 2, 4, 6.

56. For a summary and discussion of this case, see B. A. Campbell (1990: 166–169).

57. *CR, 61ˢᵗ Congress, Second Session,* Report No. 405 (March 16, 1910): 10, 11, 13, 14.

58. "The Rockefeller Foundation," *NYT* (May 13, 1911), 12.

59. "The Rockefeller Foundation," *NYT* (January 17, 1913), 12.

60. In addition to issues of industrial unrest, the scope of the investigation in-cluded the question of "whether perpetuating organizations such as the Rockefeller Foundation are a menace to the future political and economic welfare of the na-tion." This statement of mission reflected the concern, expressed to the Commis-sion, "that the creation of the Rockefeller and other foundations was the beginning of an effort to 'perpetuate the present position of predatory wealth through the corruption of the sources of public information.'" "To Investigate All Foundations," *NYT* (December 17, 1914), 6.

61. "Urges Federal Rein on Big Foundations," *NYT* (January 19, 1915), 7.

62. Erik Loomis, "Eight Ways We're Headed Back to the Robber Baron Era," July 5, 2012, http://www.salon.com/2012/07/04/eight_ways_were_headed_back_to _the_robber_baron_era/.

63. Bicknell (1935: 68).

64. Bicknell (1935: 80–81, 97–98).

65. Cuff (1973: 26, 47–48). For a review of the competitive publishing efforts that sought to shape the historical interpretation of these efforts, see Cuff (1970: 11–13).

66. Herring (1964).

67. E. Sanders (1999: 387–389).

68. Cramer (1961: 97, 137). Deep commitments to voluntarism were eroded by the practical demands of military mobilization on a large scale. Baker's friend, Brand Whitlock, wrote, 'There was a time in my life when I should have been op-posed to conscription but knowing what I know now, and seeing what I have seen I am confident that it is the only practicable way for democracy to protect itself'" (Beaver 1966: 31). See also Geva (2015).

69. Cooper (2009: 396–397); Geva (2011).

70. Cramer (1961: 49); Beaver (1966: 34).

71. Beaver (1966: 6); Palmer (1931: 49, 94–109).

72. Coit (1957: 166).

73. Fosdick (1958: 148). See also Bristow (1996).

74. Fosdick (1958: 149–150).

75. Eisner (2000); Berk (2009: 162–163); see also Cuff (1973). One legacy of the war, however, was an increasing openness to a greater government role: "It took another generation and the outbreak of another war to obtain public support for the idea that club houses and books and many of the other factors that make for a rounded life within the limits of our military establishments are an essential part of the nation's direct responsibility toward its troops" (Fosdick 1958: 151–152).

76. In a plea for contributions of telescopes, spyglasses, and sextants, Assistant Secretary of the Navy Franklin Delano Roosevelt reminded donors that all items should be "securely tagged" with their name. He explained that "as the Government cannot, under the law, accept service or material without making some payment therefore, one dollar will be paid for each article accepted, which sum will constitute the rental price, or, in the event of loss, the purchase price, of such article." "Thousands of 'Eyes' Still Needed for Our Navy," *RCC* 2 (6) (February 4, 1918), 3. Codified in the Anti-Deficiency Act of 1905, this prohibition on the unauthorized acceptance of volunteers or voluntary donations was intended to preserve congressional control over the power of the purse, since today's donations might provide a basis for tomorrow's claims on the treasury. Raymond Natter, "Outlawing Volunteers: Congress vs. the President," http://ultimatehistoryproject.com/anti -deficiency-act-history-behind-the-governement-shutdown.html (accessed January 27, 2018).

77. Gifford was central to the networks linking business, benevolence, and government, serving also as a trustee of the Rockefeller Foundation and the General Education Board, President of the Harvard Alumni Association, member of the advisory council for the Tuskegee Institute, and director of the First National Bank of New York, U.S. Steel Corporation, and the Greater New York Fund. "Hoover Appoints Gifford to Set Up Federal Board and Mobilize Idle Relief," *NYT* (August 20, 1931), 1; "Walter S. Gifford Dies; Ex-Head of A.T. & T.," *NYT* (May 8, 1966), 1, 82.

78. "Council of Defense Reshapes Industry," *NYT* (June 25, 1917), 2.

79. Coit (1957: 147–158). Hoover used an argument for voluntarism to secure the autonomy of his Food Administration from other federal bureaucracies. "Voluntarism may also be understood as a tool in the administrative process itself, an ideology that sophisticated administrators like Hoover wielded in their general struggle for power and legitimacy" (Cuff 1977: 364).

80. See Capozzola (2008).

81. Ott (2011: 55).

82. Lawson (2002: 40).

83. Ott (2011: 55–74). Investing in government was portrayed not only as patriotic but also as a means of reinforcing individual self-sufficiency and staving off the threat of poverty in old age.

84. Skocpol et al. (2002).

85. Dulles (1950: 140, 146). As Dulles comments a few pages later, "The roll of Red Cross administrators began to look like a Directory of Directors."

86. Gibson had begun his career with the American Express Company, working his way from office boy in Boston to assistant manager of the financial department in New York. From there he went on to major roles at the Liberty National Bank and, following the war, as President of the New York Trust Company and the Manufacturers Trust Company of New York. The Gibson/Woodbury Charitable Foundation, http://www.gibsonwoodburyfoundation.org/harvey-gibson.html (accessed April 8, 2016).

87. "Address of Harvey D. Gibson," *RCB* 1 (6) (July 28, 1917): 2.

88. "Chapters Now Report to Headquarters on Standardized Forms," *RCB* 1 (22) (October 1, 1917): 1. The Departments of War and Treasury exerted strong pressure to steer local fund-raising into single federated campaigns. "Talk delivered by Mr. John D. Rockefeller, Jr. At the residence of Mrs. Arthur C. Jones, September 10, 1918." OMR III 2 Z, JDR Jr. Personal Speeches, Box 2, Folder 73.

89. Burner (1979: 89). In this relief effort, the lines of future conflicts were evident as Hoover staunchly resisted proposals to provide relief to the unemployed. Although such a "dole" was given to many Belgians so that they would not need to work for German enterprises, "Hoover himself expanded on a Dutch plan for a Neutral Industrial Commission for Belgium that would put the unemployed to work in their own prewar industries and exchange contraband manufactures for food" (Burner 1979: 88). See also Gaddis (2005: 5).

90. Little (2009).

91. *RCB* 1 (11) (August 25, 1917): 2.

92. Business firms contributed in diverse ways: newspapers and magazines donated advertising space, utility companies sent out reminders to join with their December bills. "Red Cross Should Lead Xmas List, Says Saturday Evening Post," *RCB* 1 (33) (December 17, 1917): 7.

93. *RCB* 2 (5) (January 28, 1918): 4. Skocpol's (2003: 24–25) threshold for inclusion as a "large membership association" is 1 percent of the entire U.S. adult population (or of the male or female adult population for gender-segregated organizations).

94. "How Junior Red Cross 'Happened' to a Western Boy," *RCB* 2 (31) (July 29, 1918): 7.

95. "Our New Opportunity," *RCB* 2 (3) (January 14, 1918): 3.

96. "H. P. Davison Says Congressional Appropriation for Red Cross Would Be Mistake," *RCB* 2 (6) (February 4, 1918): 4.

97. "Our New Opportunity," 3; Henry P. Davison, "Red Cross Now Ministering to Wounded Nations," *RCB* 1 (19) (Sept. 21, 1917): 1.

98. "Latest Returns from Christmas Drive Indicate Membership of 23,475,000 or 22 Percent of Population," *RCB* 2 (5) (January 28, 1918): 4. In the wake of the relief response to the Mississippi Flood of 1927, membership in some of the southern states doubled and even tripled. "Early Roll Call Returns of Flood Areas Indicate Great Increases," *RCC* 7 (1) (January 2, 1928): 17.

99. "Pet Bear Sold to Aid Cause," *RCB* 2 (42) (October 14, 1918): 11; "War Teaches Valuable Lessons to American Indians," *RCB* 2 (37) (September 9, 1918): 2.

100. "Convict Offers to Make Knitting Needles for Red Cross," *RCB* 1 (30) (November 26, 1917): 4.

101. "Statement Defining Red Cross Policy Regarding Men of Draft Age," *RCB* 2 (28) (July 8, 1918): 2. See also "No Slackers Admitted to Paris Staff of Red Cross," *RCB* 2 (4) (January 21, 1918): 3.

102. Kerber (1980); Zagarri (1992).

103. "Aged Helpers in the Great Work," *RCB* 2 (32) (August 15, 1918): 7.

104. "Old Mammy's Letter from France," *RCB* 2 (39) (September 25, 1918): 7. The term "mammy" signaled a project by some elite white women to honor the

contribution of black slave women to southern families by erecting a memorial in the nation's capitol. The effort simultaneously reinforced prejudices of gender and race while trying to heal the memories of those divisions. Robertson (1998).

105. "Secretary of War States Department's Attitude Regarding Sweaters," *RCB* 1 (30) (November 26, 1917): 3; "Secretaries of War and Navy Encourage Women's Red Cross Work," *RCB* 1 (31) (December 3, 1917): 2; "Knitting Situation Set Forth by General Manager Gibson," *RCB* 1 (31) (December 3, 1917): 3; Dulles (1950: 170–171). The Red Cross promoted both the use of knitting machines in the "production rooms" and hand knitting.

106. "Seeking Stocks of Knitting Yarn," *RCB* 2 (36) (September 2, 1918): 1; "Articles Made for the Red Cross Are Not Sold," *RCB* 1 (22) (October 1, 1917): 4.

107. Here the concerns presaged worries about authoritarian or demagogic uses of voluntarism at the same time that they looked back to nineteenth-century concerns about parents who would exploit their children by sending them out begging. "Red Cross Junior Membership Joins with War Savings Bureau to End Child Exploitation," *RCB* 2 (32) (August 5, 1918): 1.

108. "How Junior Red Cross 'Happened' to a Western Boy," 7.

109. "Mobilizing the Children," pp. 9–10 (1919? date in pencil) Folder 102.1 "JUNIOR RED CROSS, organization, functions, plans, program, 1917–1921," ARC, 1917–1934, Box 80.

110. The limits of this solution would be tested by the question of blood donation during and after the Second World War. See Guglielmo (2010).

111. R. Smith (2003).

112. I am grateful to Ann Shola Orloff for this insight.

113. On the cross-cutting currents of race and wartime mobilization, see Ellis (1992); Keith (2001).

114. "Law Passed Permits National Banks to Contribute to A.R.C. during This War," *RCB* 2 (22) (May 27, 1918): 6.

115. "Progressive Democrat from New Hampshire" has been an empty set through much of American political history. But by virtue of a deadlock in the New Hampshire legislature, which still selected U.S. Senators in 1913, Hollis came to serve a single term. During the debates over the War Revenues Act, he appears as a regular ally of notable Republican progressives: Hiram Johnson of California, Robert La Follette of Wisconsin, and William Borah of Idaho. At various moments in the extended debates, these senators formed the core of a consistently defeated alliance advocating more steeply progressive taxes and an overall revenue package that would fall most heavily on individual incomes and excess profits. "Hollis Amendment Exempts Charity Donations from Tax," *RCB* 1 (24) (October 15, 1917): 4; "Two Internal Revenue Rulings Favorable to the Red Cross," *RCB* 2 (7) (February 11, 1918): 3.

116. Schiff and Warburg were both leading figures at the investment firm of Kuhn, Loeb, and Company, major philanthropists, and a members of multiple major corporate, philanthropic, and university boards.

117. Zunz (2012: 86–87).

118. At the time of passage, the charitable deduction to the income tax was expected to be a temporary wartime measure (Zunz 2012: 88).

119. "Hollis Amendment Exempts Charity Donations from Tax," *RCB* 1 (25) (October 15, 1917): 4.

120. "Service to our Soldiers and Sailors," by John D. Rockefeller Jr., Reprinted from Review of Reviews. Date in pencil as 1915. RAC OMR III 2 Z B1 F43, p. 392. *American Review of Reviews* 58 (4) (October 1918): 391–393.

121. As in the Civil War, rumors repeatedly circulated charging that items donated to the Red Cross were for sale or even that soldiers were *required* to pay for goods given as civic gifts. "Red Cross Launches $100,000,000 Campaign. National Conference Outlines Plans for Raising of World's Greatest War Relief Fund," *RCB* 1 (3) (May 31, 1917): 1–2.

122. Welfare Interests—General, American Red Cross, War Fund Campaigns, 1917–1918. RAC OMR, RG III 2 P, Box 1, Folder 9.

123. "Rumors against Red Cross to Be Vigorously Hunted Down," *RCB* 1 (24) (October 15, 1917): 4; Almond ([1938] 1998: 190–191).

124. Palmer (1931: 4).

125. *RCB* 1 (12) (August 27, 1917): 2.

126. "The Red Cross as Elder Brother," *RCB* 1 (16) (September 13, 1917): 2; "Home Service Presents Delicate and Difficult Task," *RCB* 1 (25) (October 22, 1917): 3.

127. "The Use of Military Titles by Red Cross Officers," *RCB* 1 (10) (August 20, 1917): 2.

128. Cuff (1970).

129. "The Roll-Call," *RCB* 3 (1) (December 30, 1918): 4.

130. On the postwar Community Councils of National Defense, see John Willis Slaughter to Starr Murphy (January 31, 1919), RAC OMR II 2 F, "Economic Interests," Box 19, Folder 168.

Chapter Five

1. Address of James L. Fieser, Vice Chairman, ARC, April 22, 1929 (#29153). ARC, 1917–1934, Box 87, 104.502. On the Red Cross as "semi-governmental," see Fieser quoted in "Unique Status of the Red Cross among National Social Agencies," *RCC* 8 (6) (March 15, 1929): 12.

2. See Introduction and Balogh (2009).

3. Eisner (2000).

4. Seeley et al. ([1957] 1989: 5).

5. In organization theory, this is the problem of goal succession, theorized in Paul Sills' (1957) important study of the March of Dimes after the successful development of a polio vaccine and thus the negation of its central mission.

6. Cutlip (1965: 149).

7. Hawley (1998).

8. "Suspension of Knitting," *RCB* 3 (2) (January 6, 1919): 3; "Knitting Plan Perfected," *RCB* 3 (7) (February 10, 1919): 1–2. Following in this spirit, knitting was

also proposed as a vehicle for economic rehabilitation, "to give employment to thousands of refugee women in France, Belgium, Italy, Rumania, Servia [*sic*], Montenegro, Palestine, Albania, and other war-swept countries, and thereby help them to help themselves." "Yarn and Needles to Europe," *RCB* 3 (13) (March 24, 1919): 1.

9. Prasad (2012: 68).

10. Recall "Cheorge" who watched food use like a cat. Ch. 4.

11. "The Greater Relief Work," *RCB* 3 (3) (January 13, 1919): 4.

12. Burner (1979: 84–92).

13. "Hark Ye, Military Relief Men," *RCB* 3 (32) (August 4, 1919): 1.

14. "Get the Story to the Men," *RCB* 3 (32) (August 4, 1919): 4; "What Is the Red Cross Doing for Disabled Service Men?" *RCB* 5 (14) (April 4, 1921): 1–3, 6; "Old Jobs or Better for All Wounded Men," *RCB* 3 (11) (March 10, 1919): 8.

15. Clemens (2017b).

16. "What Is the Red Cross Doing for Disabled Service Men?," 2.

17. "What Is the Red Cross Doing for Disabled Service Men?," 1–2.

18. "Planning Red Cross Home Service Future," *RCB* 3 (25) (June 16, 1919): 4.

19. "American Red Cross Chapter Activities," *RCB* 4 (46) (November 8, 1920): 8.

20. "Boy Scout Week—June 8–14," *RCB* 3 (22) (March 26, 1919): 3.

21. "Red Cross Work on the Film," *RCB* 4 (1) (December 29, 1919): 1.

22. "Planning Red Cross Home Service Future," 1, 4; "Home Service in Peace Will Benefit All," *RCB* 3 (33) (August 11, 1919): 5; "National Bureau Reorganizes," *RCB* 3 (41) (October 6, 1919): 5; Dulles (1950: 243–255); Gilbo (1981: 95–97).

23. "Tackling Rural Problems," *RCB* 3 (25 [*sic*, should be no. 46]) (November 10, 1919): 6.

24. McCarthy (1982); Schneiderhan (2015).

25. Executive Committee of the Business Men's Relief Committee to Julius Rosenwald, May 12, 1908, JRP, Box 4, Folder 12.

26. Minnie F. Low, Bureau Director, Central Bureau of the Jewish Charities of Chicago to Julius Rosenwald, January 17, 1917. JRP, Box VI, Folder 8.

27. Willoughby G. Walling to Julius Rosenwald, May 25, 1922. Box VI, Folder 8, JRP. One model was found in the St. Louis "Community Council," whose 40 institutional members were required to incorporate, form a "responsible board," and conduct annual audits by a certified public accountant. "The Saint Louis Plan," October 28, 1924, JRP, Box VI, Folder 9.

28. "Fifty Million Dollars," 16. Undated typescript, JRP, Box VI, Folder 9. The folder includes a press release announcing the publication of this pamphlet dated April 24, 1924. In this notice, the total of charitable funds raised is given as $86 million.

29. "Fifty Million Dollars," 17.

30. Three business groups were guaranteed representation, as were the Associated Catholic Charities and the Jewish Charities of Chicago. The remaining members would come from the Council of Social Agencies, divided between board members and representatives of the executive staffs of member agencies (typically professional social workers). The Committee had authority "to approve dates for the periodical city-wide campaigns by all agencies using the campaign method

to raise current operating expenses, and campaigns for all special purposes other than to meet current operating needs, such as buildings, building sites, deficits, expansions, etc." Report of the "General Study Committee on Financing Social Agencies," October 14, 1925; Chicago Council of Social Agencies, The Financing of Social Agencies, Proposal 1. Submitted by the General Study Committee, February 1926. JRP, Box VI, Folder 10.

31. These consequences played out in the 1930s, as social workers and settlement workers displayed more vigorous support for the New Deal in Chicago, New York, and the minority of large cities *without* Community Chest structures. Trolander (1975).

32. "Community Chest Corollaries," *Survey* (June 15, 1925), 344.

33. "Ten Years of Federation in Cincinnati," *Survey* (February 15, 1925), 591. The emphasis on community level federation was understood as a threat to the missions of some settlement houses. Speaking of the "deficit fund system" (in which a centralized fund covered deficits in the budget of member agencies that took primary responsibility for their own fund-raising), Jane Addams argued that "were Hull-House to join even in a deficit fund system, she believed that it 'would lose its individuality and the right to guide its own destiny.'" After the death of its champion fund-raiser, however, Hull House soon moved to join the deficit fund system in Chicago (Trolander 1975: 57).

34. Homer W. Borst, "Community Chests and Relief: A Reply," *Survey* (October 15, 1930), 74.

35. Trolander (1975: 31). The tax status of corporate contributions was still uncertain at this time; those that were made were frequently deducted under the heading of "business expenses" for the cultivation of customer and community goodwill.

36. Cutlip (1965: 143).

37. Bookman (1932). On normative and coercive isomorphism, see DiMaggio and Powell (1983).

38. Todd (1932); Russell et al. (1931: 32).

39. Bremner ([1960] 1982: 141).

40. Barman (2006: 19).

41. J. Franklin McFadden, "Permanent Membership Committees for Red Cross Chapters" (April 25, 1929), ARC, 1917-1934, Box 87, Folder 104.502.

42. A. C. Sprague, "The Roll Call in Industry," 12th Annual Convention, April 24-27, 1933, pp. 1-2. ARC RG II, Box 90, 104.502.

43. On the (often contested) articulation of firms as sites of moral community, see Haydu (2008); Jacoby (1997).

44. Capozzola (2008: 6).

45. Morris (2009).

46. Not surprisingly, the backlash involved a call for—and in some places a turn to—new public agencies to control relief. "What Happened in Columbus," *Survey* (May 15, 1926), 261-263. In Cincinnati, "the community chests had 'refused to organize the factories and workshops of our city for solicitation,' preferring to solicit house-to-house until the development of a system of industrial solicitation that eliminated undue pressure." Bookman (1932), quoted in Clemens (2010: 189).

47. Joseph Lee, "The Chest and Social Work," *Survey* (March 1928), 749–750; see also Robert W. Kelso, "Banker Control of Community Chests," *Survey* (May 1, 1932), 117. In Boston, these concerns translated into a ban on fund-raising in schools, with a single exception made for the Red Cross.

48. Because "Hoover viewed the 1921 Conference on Unemployment as a gigantic educational device . . . he thought it almost completely successful in arousing local and state cooperative actions for ending unemployment." But "the conference produced little cooperative spirit among the nation's large cities like New York, Chicago, and Detroit. The programs begun with so much fanfare in the smaller cities soon waned" (J. H. Wilson 1975: 92); see also Gaddis (2005: 17–19, 61–66).

49. Arthur Woods, "The Unemployment Emergency," *North American Review* 215 (797) (April 1922): 454–455, 457. On the turn to collaborative governance in the 1920s, see Alchon (1985); Hendrickson (2013).

50. Gaddis (2005: 71–72).

51. Dulles (1950: 270).

52. Zunz (2012: 111–112).

53. Zunz (2012: 112).

54. "Junior Spirit Quickens Life of the Whole School," *RCC* 7 (1) (January 2, 1928): 11; "Early Roll Call Returns of Flood Areas Indicate Great Increases," *RCC* 7 (1) (January 2, 1928): 17.

55. Barry (1997: 192–194); Spencer (1994:172–174); Mizelle (2014: 75–99); Ida B. Wells-Barnett, "Flood Refugees Are Held as Slaves in Mississippi Camp," *Chicago Defender* (July 30, 1927), A11; J. Winston Harrington, "Deny Food to Flood Sufferers in Mississippi," *Chicago Defender* (June 4, 1927), 1.

56. Spencer (1994: 178).

57. John L. Spivak, "Shady Business in the Red Cross," *American Mercury* 33 (131) (November 1934): 272–274.

58. "The Final Report of the Colored Advisory Commission. Mississippi Valley Flood Disaster, 1927." The American National Red Cross, Washington, D.C. October 1929, ARC 271, 11, 19, 27. In HHPL-PP, Box 61, American National Red Cross Correspondence Nov. 1929 to Feb. 1931.

59. Hawley (1974); Clemens (2017b).

60. On infrastructural state-building with respect to education within the American federal system, see Steffes (2012).

61. "The Community Responsibility for Human Welfare," *RCC* 7 (6) (March 15, 1928): 5–6.

62. "Checks in Care of Chapters," *RCC* 7 (1) (January 2, 1928): 30. Notice the parallels with the refusal to repay donation-funded loans following the San Francisco earthquake (Bicknell 1935: 47–53).

63. John Barton Payne, "Disaster Relief Policies of the American Red Cross," *RCC* 7 (4) (February 15, 1928): 16.

64. P. H. Byrns, "Upholding Community Morale in Rehabilitation Time," *RCC* 7 (18) (September 15, 1928): 14–15.

65. Hawley (1998: 166).

66. Hawley (1998: 167). An aide to Hoover, Fred Croxton, was quoted as explaining that "the President is contemplating a major move to raise central funds for relief. This may damage the local drives of Community Chests and other organizations. In any event, I think it should be kept separate and distinct from the work here." E. E. Hunt to Col. Arthur Woods, October 27, 1930, "Hoover, Herbert (Relief) = Apr.-Nov. 1930 = President's Emergency Comm. For Employment," HLH-FDR Box 41. For a Democrat's account of this period of the relief effort, see Hopkins (1936: 17–23).

67. A (declined) request from the Charity Organization Society to the Rockefellers suggests the resources required to shift from elite networks to a broader fund-raising base. The COS explained that an increased number of contributors "did not mean a corresponding increase in the income. The smaller donors reached by mail in the first year do not give substantially more than it costs to get them to join. Nearly 90 percent of them, however, continue contributing the following year without any cost beyond one letter. This method has the financial disadvantage of having the expense come all at the beginning, an especially serious problem at present as the Society is facing a heavy deficit for immediate relief of the unemployed." Proposal submitted by the Charity Organization Society (March 29, 1928; signed by Thomas B. Appleget, Secretary). RAC OMR III 2 P, Box 7, Folder 7.

68. By the 1950s, 1,900 cities and towns had community chests. Sills (1957).

69. *The Report of the Emergency Employment Committee New York City. October 1, 1930. July 1, 1931.* RAC OMR Unemployment and Economic Planning—Unemployment Relief, 170.4, RG 2 F, Box 21, Folder 187, 21, 33–34.

70. EURC-BCO. ORGANIZATION. Vol. 13, C-160 TO: MR. TUCKER. FROM MR. BRAKELY. CC TO MR. STAPLES. November 21, 1931. The mass canvass was based on a business telephone list—of 149,000 names—for the borough of Manhattan. In other boroughs, it took the form of a house-to-house canvass similar to those of the Red Cross.

71. *Plan of the Block Community Organization ("The Block-Aiders") in New York City, June, 1932.* vol. 163–3, p. 4. This total did not include each donor who contributed to firm-based large contributions.

72. Roll (2013: 30).

73. Banta to Mr. Hopkins, "Churches" (February 8, 1932). EURC-BCO, C-163.

74. EURC (2nd). Publicity. News Releases. No. 406. Vol. VIII EURC, Immediate Release. JPJ.

75. *Plan of the Block Community Organization* (1932: 5).

76. J. P. Jones (1954); Cutlip (1965: 170–187). Jones guided campaigns for war funds, hospitals, cathedrals, and many colleges and universities, playing a major role in the building of Harvard's endowment.

77. The Gibson/Woodbury Charitable Foundation, https://gibsonwoodbury foundation.org/harvey-gibson.html (accessed July 24, 2016).

78. "Cornelius N. Bliss," *NYT* (April 17, 1949), 28.

79. "Henry P. Davison, Banker, 63, Dead," *NYT* (July 3, 1961), 15.

80. EURC. Printed Material. No. 406. Vol. IX. *The Block Community Organiza-*

tion. A Preliminary Statement of Plan." An activity of the Emergency Unemployment Relief Committee, 29 Broadway, New York, N.Y. [February 5, 1932], JPJ.

81. EURC. *Printed Material. No. 406. Vol. IX The Block Community Organization. A Preliminary Statement of Plan."* [February 5, 1932], 5, JPJ.

82. EURC-BCO. ORGANIZATION. Vol. 13, C-160. TENTATIVE PLAN FOR THE TEST DISPOSAL OF TWENTY-FIVE SPECIAL CASES UNDER THE ADOPT-A-FAMILY PLAN. December 22, 1931, 2–3.

83. "Radio Address by Mr. J. P. Morgan from Stations of the National Broadcasting Co. on March 23, 1932," pp. 1–2. EURC. Publicity-Radio. No. 406, Vol. VII, JPJ.

84. EURC. *Printed Material. No. 406. Vol. IX The Block Community Organization. A Preliminary Statement of Plan."* [February 5, 1932], 10, JPJ.

85. EURC-BCO. ORGANIZATION. Vol. 13, C-160 Block Community Organizations: HER; Feb. 3, 1932. "Instructions for District Organizers," JPJ.

86. *EURC. Printed Material. No. 406. Vol. IX The Block Community Organization. A Preliminary Statement of Plan.* [February 5, 1932], 10, JPJ. This last phrase highlighted in red.

87. Release. March 26th. "Norman Thomas, 'socialist leader.'" March 25 on WABC of CBS EURC (2nd). Publicity. News Releases. No. 406. Vol. VIII, JPJ.

88. Release. March 26th. "Norman Thomas, 'socialist leader,'" 3–4.

89. *Report of the Emergency Employment Committee New York City, October 1, 1930– July 1, 1931,* p. 17, JPJ. "Unemployment and Economic Planning—Unemployment Relief." 170.4. RAC OMR RG2 F, Box 21, Folder 187.

90. EURC-BCO. ORGANIZATION. Vol. 13, C-160 TO: MR. TUCKER. FROM MR. BRAKELY. CC TO MR. STAPLES. November 21, 1931, JPJ. "The request will be for a contribution to support one or more unemployed persons which will pay for work done by such persons for contributors in that block during the Winter. These persons will be assigned to the block by the Unemployment Committee and will, where possible, be residents of the block."

91. EURC. Printed Material. No. 406. Vol. IX. *The Block Community Organization. A Preliminary Statement of Plan.* [February 5, 1932], JPJ.

92. EURC-BCO. ORGANIZATION. Vol. 13, C-160 FINAL REPORT. BLOCK COMMUNITY ORGANIZATION (BLOCK-AID). EURC/GB/7/14/32, 41, JPJ.

93. EURC-BCO. ORGANIZATION. Vol. 13, C-160, FINAL REPORT, 6. Beyond funds and organization, "the educational goal of the Block-Aid campaign was the education, by word of mouth, from neighbor to neighbor, of large numbers of people . . . as to the relief needs among the residents of New York City. Actually, a large percentage of the 57,000 workers estimated to have been enrolled in the campaign gained a considerable personal insight into the situation in the city as a whole, and particularly among the residents of their own neighborhoods. Furthermore, probably 250,000 contributors became aware of the fact that the relief problem was becoming increasingly serious and was no mere fiction on the part of the newspapers or other publicity" (63–64).

94. Report of the Emergency Work and Relief Bureau of the Emergency Unemployment Relief Committee, October 1, 1931–August 1, 1932. Prepared by W. H.

Matthews, Director of Bureau, Raymond W. Houston, Assistant Director, Miss Ol-
lie A. Randall, Assistant Director. EURC (2nd), Work Bureau, No. 406, Vol. V, JPJ.

95. McAdam (1982: 34–35).

96. EURC-BCO. ORGANIZATION. Vol. 13, C-160. FINAL REPORT, 46–47, 70, 69.

97. Ibid., p. 47. But if intentions were inclusive, the results were uneven. On
African American participation, see "Fully Supports Block-Aid Drive," *New York
Amsterdam News* (April 27, 1932), 15; "Harlem Falls Back in Relief Campaign," *New
York Amsterdam News* (May 4, 1932), 2. JPJ.

98. For an extended version of this argument, see Clemens (2015).

99. Hawley (1998:168)

100. Hawley (1998: 168).

101. Burner (1979: 267).

102. W. B. Farris to Herbert Hoover (January 21, 1931), American National Red
Cross, Correspondence 1931 January 21–25, Box 61, HHPL-SF.

103. Gilbert B. Bogart to Harry Hopkins, October 7, 1931 (letterhead of Kallen &
Company, Members New York Curb Exchange, 49 Broadway, New York City),
HLH-FDR , Box 7, "Plans and Suggestions for Relief, 1931."

104. Mrs. Watshall to Hoover. HHPP-SF, ANRC, Correspondence, 1931 February 2. [n.d., received February 2, 1931].

105. Hawley (1998: 165–169); Hamilton (1982).

106. "Men, Misery, and Mules," *Time* (December 22, 1930), 12. PECE was followed by POUR. On the limited capacity of POUR, see A. Cohen (2009).

107. For a version of this argument, see Clemens (2010b). See also Paul Kellogg,
"Drought and the Red Cross," *Survey* 65 (February 15, 1931), 525; "Country Crying
for Relief from the Relief Fight," *Literary Digest* 108 (9) (February 14, 1931), 9.

108. Senator Thomas Heflin (D-Alabama) spelled out the connection: "The
administration is for exempting the large income-tax payers and the corporations
of this country from paying increased taxes toward this relief . . . To exempt the
Federal Government means that you are going to place on the backs of the small
property owners in every municipality and in every State the increased taxes for
relief, not for this year, not for next year, but for several years. With their property
depreciated, with themselves out of work, these people are to bear the entire burden! In a word, the poor must take care of the poor so far as the Federal Government is concerned." *CR* (January 14, 1931), 2157. For an account of this period of
political conflict, see Hopkins (1936: 33–41).

109. This compares to $518 million in charitable deductions taken in 1929. "Fore-
cast a Record in Tax Deductions," *NYT*, November 22, 1931, 54. A similar argument
was made at length by future Supreme Court Justice Hugo Black (D-Alabama), *CR*
January 19, 1931, pp. 2545–2547. Democratic Senators Heflin of Alabama and Smith
of South Carolina contrasted the proposed $25 million appropriation for relief with
the $160 million in income tax returns funded in the past year. *CR* (January 28,
1931), 3374.

110. *CR* (January 19, 1931), 2547, 2561.

111. *CR* (January 9, 1931), 1754, 1899.

112. *CR* (January 14, 1931), 2152, 2154–57; *CR* (January 15, 1931), 2249.

113. *CR* (February 3, 1931), 3854.

114. Zelizer (1997).

115. *CR* (January 15, 1931), 2219.

116. *CR* (January 19, 1931), 2534.

117. *CR* (January 19, 1931), 2563–2564; "$25,000,000 Relief Passed in Senate," *NYT*, January 22, 1931, 48.

118. *CR* (January 27, 1931), 3253–3254.

119. *CR* (February 3, 1931), 3857. See also "Hoover Acclaims Red Cross's Record as Vindicating Him," *NYT* (April 14, 1931), 1. *CR* (January 19, 1931), 2547.

120. *CR* (January 30, 1931), 3578.

121. "Red Cross to Start Personal Canvass," *NYT* (February 13, 1931), 2.

122. "Amer. Red Cross, Disaster Relief Contributions" (handwritten list July 1951) and Arthur W. Packard to Mr. James G. Blaine (Jan. 26, 1931). RAC OMR, Welfare Interests General, RG III, 2P, Box 2, Folders 19 and 19A. Although much of the correspondence around this contingent gift could not be located in the Rockefeller archives, the terms are noted in a handwritten list (apparently taken from the files of the National Investigation Bureau) that summarized John D. Rockefeller Jr.'s contributions for disaster relief since 1923. An entry for February–March 1931 noted "$250,000 Amer Red Cross Drought Relief Fund (Goal $10,000,000). Understanding was if Congress should make appropriation for same purpose, JDR Jr's contribution would be returned on request." Attached to Yorke Allen Jr. to Dana S. Creel (September 11, 1953). RAC OMR Welfare Interests—General, American Red Cross, Contributions, 1930–1957, III 2 P, Box 2, Folder 19A.

123. "Red Cross Asks Aid for Lagging Drive," *NYT*, March 2, 1931, 15; "Drought Fund Past $10,000,000 Mark," *NYT* (March 19, 1931), 4.

124. "Hoover Opens Way to End Drought Fund Deadlock as Congress Rift Widens," *NYT*, February 4, 1931, 1. In the Senate, Vandenberg (R-Michigan) was a proponent of this argument. *CR* (January 19, 1931), 2540.

125. "$51,319 Needed Here in Red Cross Drive," *NYT* (February 6, 1931), 2. A *New York Times* editorial making the same argument had been inserted in the *Congressional Record* two weeks earlier (January 17, 1931), 2429.

126. Rep. Treadway of Massachusetts. *CR* (January 30, 1931), 3661.

127. Tilson's remarks were read into the Senate record. *CR* (February 2, 1931), 3747.

128. *CR* (January 30, 1931), 3667.

129. *CR* (January 19, 1931), 2537. Various proposals for loans for food purchases had foundered on requirements that the Government would have first claim on the borrowers' collateral—the land and future crops that were already burdened with the liens central to the tenant farming system of the South.

130. Woodruff (1985: 106–107).

131. Read into the *CR* (January 30, 1931), 3577.

132. Heflin, *CR* (February 3, 1931), 3844.

133. Heflin, *CR* (January 28, 1931), 3375.

134. *CR* (January 19, 1931), 2548.

135. ARC, RG 2, Box 89, Folder 104.502. Address by H. J. Hughes, Legal Adviser, 4/15/ 1931, "Some Legal Aspects of the Red Cross."

136. This politicization ran contrary to long-term Red Cross policy that encouraged a rigorous separation of its own members, and particularly leadership, from electoral politics. In separate memos from the 1910s, 1920s, and 1940s, the national headquarters reiterated the recommendation that any local leader who ran for office should first resign their Red Cross position and Red Cross leaders should be careful that any endorsement of candidates was understood to be strictly personal. In a response to a younger Harry Hopkins, then working as director of the Gulf District, the national headquarters also ruled out most forms of legislative lobbying, allowing only for the legitimate possibility that Red Cross officials might appear in order to give expert testimony on matters central to the organization's own experience. H. J. Hughes to Harry L. Hopkins (January 19, 1920) ARC, RG 200, Box 68, 051.001 LEGISLATION.

137. "Holds Red Cross Cannot Aid Miners," *NYT* (July 9, 1931), 48.

138. "Gibson Committee to Disband September 30," *NYT* (June 5, 1933), 1; "Vast Food Supply Aided Needy Here," *NYT* (August 8, 1933), 6.

139. The degree of penetration into the on-the-ground activity of governance was impressive. According to Robert E. Bondy, National Director of Disaster Relief for the Red Cross: "Today, April 12, 1932, out of a total of 3,600 Red Cross chapters, exactly 2,000 are participating in some form of unemployment relief. Over half of the counties of the country are benefiting from this Red Cross service, varying as it does from full responsibility for Family Welfare service to these supplemental services of clothing production, care of transients, employment service, gardening projects, school lunch projects and so on. Those 2,000 chapters in their service to civilians and veterans have dealt in recent months with fully 1,177,000 persons.

"Parallel with that development is the nation-wide distribution through 1,826 chapters in the five weeks yesterday since the enactment of the Law, of flour benefiting over 6,840,000 persons. Geared to function on immediate call in any emergency, the Red Cross machine in this short time has mastered the details of flour milling, transportation, wheat grading and distribution of a tremendous commodity surplus." ARC, RG II, Box 89, 104.502.

140. *CR* (January 19, 1931), 2554–2555.

141. *CR* (January 30, 1931), 3664–3665.

142. C. Fox (2012); Goldberg (2007); Mettler (1998); Quadagno (1994).

143. Warren (1946: 277).

Chapter Six

1. "The Citizen & Social Welfare: An Opportunity for Participation," C.O.S.N.Y., c. 1935. RAC OMR, RG III 2 P, "Welfare—General Interests," Box 7, Folder 74.

2. Quoted in J. Hopkins (1999: 83).

3. L. Cohen (1990: ch. 5); B. R. Fox (1969). With respect to fraternalism, David Beito (2000: 222–228) argues that there was as much retrenchment as collapse.

4. Hammack (2003: 269–270); J. Hopkins (1999: 83). Mr. Cavin to Mr. Fieser, "Subject: 'The Future of the American Red Cross.'" May 6, 1933. ARC, RG 200, Box 78, Folder 102.

5. Don C. Smith to Mr. Fieser. "Subject: 'The Future of the American Red Cross.'" May 5, 1933. ARC, RG 200, Box 78, Folder 102.

6. On Hopkins' early career in social work and public welfare, see J. Hopkins (1999: chs. 4–7); Roll (2013: 21–33).

7. Landis (1997).

8. Text of an address delivered by Edward N. Jones, Works Progress Administrator for Pennsylvania, at a testimonial dinner to James J. Law, retiring postmaster of Wilkes-Barre, held Saturday night, December 14, 1935, in the Hotel Sterling, Wilkes-Barre, PA. RG 69: WPA-FERA-CF, 1933–36, "State" Series, March 1933–1936, Pennsylvania 400, Box 249, PC 37, Entry 10.

9. On the concept of turning points, Abbott (2001: 240–260); with respect to path dependence, Pierson (2000).

10. For example, the NYCOS devoted 10 percent of its efforts to unemployment relief in 1929 but 89 percent by 1933. "Charity Organization Society," memo dated April 17, 1934. RAC OMR, III 2P, Welfare Interests—General, Box 6, Folder 73.

11. For an illuminating discussion of the relationship between welfare state retrenchment and the erosion of social solidarity in Europe, see Berezin (2009).

12. These included Frances Perkins, Roosevelt's future Secretary of Labor, who clashed with Hoover over claims for statistical evidence of an improving employment situation. A. Cohen (2009: 181–184).

13. "New York Unemployment Relief. A Summary of the Activities of the Temporary Emergency Relief Administration of New York State From November 1, 1931 to June 1, 1932. For Release September 6, 1932. Members Harry L. Hopkins, NY, Chairman; Charles D. Osborne of Auburn; John Sullivan of New York." HLH-FDR Box 7, "Plans and Suggestions for Unemployment Relief, 1932."

14. Quoted in Lundberg (1932: 547).

15. Previously, the New York State Legislature had authorized the city "to increase its amount of revenue bonds from $2,000,000 to $12,000,000 for the year 1931, $10,000 of which was to be available for materials and labor for work to be done in the city of New York in order to relieve the condition of unemployment." *Report of the Emergency Employment Committee New York City, October 1, 1930–July 1, 1931*, p. 8. "Unemployment and Economic Planning—Unemployment Relief. 170.4 RG2 F, Box 21, Folder 187. OMR. To support the relief effort in Chicago, Cook County attempted to sell "$6,250,000 in tax-anticipation warrants" in 1932, but "few people would buy them." Only sustained pressure exerted on the mayor, bankers, and industrialists by organized unemployed and representatives of social agencies eventually produced sales sufficient to keep the relief stations open. Trolander (1975: 96).

16. F. T. Tierney to Governor Franklin D. Roosevelt (September 23, 1931), HLH-FDR, Box 7, "Plans and Suggestions for Relief, 1931."

17. F. W. Greenwood to Walter W. Pettit (August 4, 1932), HLH-FDR, Box 7, "Plans and Suggestions for Relief, 1932." This plan shared features with a proposal

to delegate social provision in Britain entirely to the Salvation Army under the "darkest England" scheme of the late nineteenth century. See Manson (1906: 121–123, 191).

18. Gilbert B. Bogart to Harry L. Hopkins (October 7, 1931), HLH-FDR, Box 7, "Plans and Suggestions for Relief, 1931."

19. Chas. J. Jackson to Franklin Delano Roosevelt (September 21, 1931), HLH-FDR Box 7, "Plans and Suggestions for Relief, 1931."

20. From M. H. Knapp, no specific addressee, n.d., HLH-FDR, Box 7, "Plans and Suggestions for Relief, 1931."

21. "3 Idle for Each Job, Work Listing to End," *NYT* (December 4, 1931), 21.

22. Louis Herman to Jesse Isidor Strauss (October 24, 1931; also October 5, 1931; November 2, 1931), HLH-FDR, Box 7, "Plans and Suggestions for Relief, 1931."

23. J. W. Boies to President Herbert Hoover (November 18, 1932), HLH-FDR, Box 7, "Plans and Suggestions for Relief, 1932." The same principles had been at play a few years earlier in "A 'Charge It to Santa' Toy Shop: Greenville, S.C. Chapter Gift Enterprise," *RCC* 7 (4) (February 15, 1928), 26. Because "acceptance of charity only adds to the burden of grief," unemployed parents were enabled to "shop" for presents "and the Red Cross would guarantee the charge account with Old Santa."

24. Lundberg (1932: 547).

25. "Roosevelt Urges Government Study," *NYT* (June 10, 1930), 16. On Governor Roosevelt's policy response to the Depression, see A. Cohen (2009: 184–185).

26. Quoted in A. Cohen (2009: 187).

27. See chapter 5.

28. Emphasis added. Quoted in J. Hopkins (1999: 72).

29. For background on "grant-in-aid" arrangements, see P. H. Douglas (1920a, 1920b).

30. Telegram from Herbert Lehman, governor of New York, May 19, 1933, TERA Correspondence, 1931–1933, HLH-FDR. On the role of Frances Perkins in advancing Hopkins' appointment, see A. Cohen (2009: 206–207).

31. *Memorandum on Governor Pinchot's Letter of June 10th* (June 27, 1934), WPA-FERA-CF, 1933–36, "State" Series, March 1933–1936 Pennsylvania 400, RG 69, Box 249, PC 37, Entry 10.

32. From Pennsylvania, the executive director of the State Emergency Relief Board wrote Hopkins requesting after-the-fact approval of a violation, the allocation of $3000 "to enable undernourished children of relief families [sometimes accompanied by their mothers] to be placed in camps operated by local agencies, such as the Salvation Army, the Lutheran Inner Mission, the Pittsburgh Association for the Improvement of the Poor, etc." Eric H. Biddle to Harry Hopkins, November 21, 1934. WPA-FERA-CF 1933–1936, RG 69, Box 249, PC 37, Entry 10.

33. "Bars Private Groups Handling Federal Aid," *NYT* (June 27, 1933), 6; "Broad Policy Set on Federal Relief," *NYT* (July 14, 1933), 8. For an example of implementation, Eric H. Biddle, executive director, Pennsylvania State Emergency Relief Board, July 27, 1933. WPA FERA Central Files, 1933–36, RG 69 Box 250, PC 37, Entry 10.

34. Arthur W. Packard to Fred C. Croxton, The President's Committee on Unemployment Relief (June 17, 1932), "Unemployment and Economic Planning, Miscellaneous Plans," 170.3 RG RAC OMR, RG II 2 F, Box 21—Economic Interests, Folder 182.

35. Harry Hopkins to E. E. Day, October 14, 1933. RFA, 1.1; Project Series 200 United States, Box 332, Folder 3946, FERA 1933. A year later, Hopkins once again approached the Foundation to support a study of the Civilian Works Administration and Public Works Administration, but this was postponed given the political uncertainty over the future of federal relief programs.

36. New York City was also an exception more locally: "In most cities in the rest of the state private relief has never been very extensive. It has been the practice in a number of cities for private family welfare agencies to obtain public funds for relief disbursements" (Lundberg 1932: 553). See also Swift (1934).

37. Aubrey Williams, "The New Relief Program: Three Great Aims," *NYT* (April 1, 1934), xxi.

38. Quoted in Trolander (1975: 102).

39. In the words of President Roosevelt, "The Federal Government has no intention or desire to force either upon the country or the unemployed themselves a system of relief which is repugnant to American ideals of individual self-reliance." Williams, "The New Relief Program."

40. A. Cohen (2009: 268–269).

41. "W. Frank Persons, 1876–1955," *Social Service Review* 29 (4) (1955): 405; A. Cohen (2009: 218).

42. "Frank B. Bane, 89, First Social Security Chief," *NYT* (January 29, 1983), 9.

43. Williams, "The New Relief Program."

44. Lowitt and Beasley (1981: 67–68).

45. For a comparative analysis of the casework method as an interpretive lens, see Peel (2012).

46. During a strike wave, Eric H. Biddle, relief administrator in Pennsylvania, telegrammed to Hopkins that "I HAVE ISSUED INSTRUCTIONS TO LOCAL BOARD IN THAT COUNTY BASED ON RULING STATE BOARD TO EFFECT THAT IT TAKE NO PART IN INDUSTRIAL CONTROVERSY AND RELIEF BE GRANTED ON SOLE BASIS OF NEED." (July 21, 1933). WPA-FERA-CF. 1933–36. RG 69, "State" Series, March 1933–1936, Pennsylvania 400, Box 250, PC 37, Entry 10.

47. Lowitt and Beasley (1981: 322).

48. G. I. Chadwick, Manager, Carlisle [Pennsylvania] Credit Exchange to Harry Hopkins. August 7, 1935. NARA RG 69 FERA Central Files 1933–36, Box 249, PC 37, Entry 10.

49. Junior Red Cross, "Lesson XX" [N.H. 208, Rev. March 1934]. ARC, 1917–1934, Box 80, Folder 102.1.

50. Lowitt and Beasley (1981: 228, 231, 240–242); see also Clemens (2017b). On racial and ethnic inequalities in relief practice, see C. Fox (2012); Mizelle (2014: 123–150).

51. The linkage of relief status to voting was thinkable, but not widely so. A 1938 Gallup survey asked if respondents agreed with the suggestion "that persons on relief should not be allowed to vote." Only 19 percent agreed and 76 percent rejected the suggestion that party affiliation made a difference in getting relief in their community (USAIPO 1938–0132; survey fielded September 15–20, 1938).

52. "This hold [*sic*] also for workers employed on the staff in the states and localities." Williams to Dorothy Kahn. October 12, 1935. NARA RG 69 FERA Central Files 1933–36, Box 249, PC 37, Entry 10.

53. Ibid.

54. This concern reignited with a vengeance in late 1930s as federal work relief programs were strained by the "Roosevelt Recession" of 1938 and the first implementation of old age assistance was suspected of "being made a tool for local politicians." "Trouble," *SMM* 74 (9) (September 1938): 289.

55. B. F. Schwartz (1973); Tani (2016).

56. G. D. Jones (1974: 253).

57. L. Cohen (1990: 268–270); G. D. Jones (1990: 18).

58. Address delivered by James L. Fieser, Vice Chairman, ARC, Seattle, Washington, September 17, 1933. ARC RG 200, Box 68, 041, Washington State Conference of Social Work.

59. "The Citizen and Social Welfare: An Opportunity for Participation," Charity Organization Society of New York, n.d. RAC OMR, III 2 P, Welfare—General Interests, Box 7, Folder 74.

60. See chapter 4 and Clemens (2017b).

61. Stanley P. Davies to Mr. and Mrs. Rockefeller, 3rd, March 18, 1935. RAC OMR, III 2 P, Box 7, Welfare Interests—General, Folder 74.

62. Arthur W. Packard, memorandum on "Conversation with Miss Hoey— Unemployment Relief Campaigns, Fall of 1934," April 25, 1934. RAC OMR, II 2 F, Economic Interests, Box 22, Folder 204. On the "over and above" rationale, see Arthur W. Packard to John D. Rockefeller, Jr., October 26, 1933. RAC OMR, II 2 F, Economic Interests, Box 22, Folder 204.

63. This claim foreshadows contemporary analyses of the outsized contribution of a small number of complex cases to the total cost of health and social welfare programs. "A Job Taxes Won't Do," Citizens Family Welfare Committee, n.d. RAC OMR, II 2F, Economic Interests, Box 22, Folder 204.

64. "A Job Taxes Won't Do." Emphasis in original. See also James G. Blaine to John D. Rockefeller, Jr. (October 23, 1933) RG II 2 F, "Economic Interests," Box 22, Folder 204, OMR.

65. Williams, "The New Relief Plan." See Clemens (2017b) and note the parallels with the Red Cross arguments for its role in supporting returning veterans after World War I.

66. Mr. Baker to Mr. Bondy (July 27, 1934), Folder 102—"Organizational Trends," ARC, National American Red Cross, RG 200, Box 78.

67. Trolander (1975: 59).

68. Trolander (1975: 65); Tani (2016).

69. The figures reported came from a compilation of tax returns from New York, Chicago, Philadelphia, Baltimore, Washington, and Boston conducted by the John Price Jones company. "Gifts to Charity Increased in Year," *NYT* (January 14, 1935), 17.

70. Charity Organization Society, "An Opportunity for Participation," [n.d.] RAC OMR, Welfare Interests—General, III 2 P, Box 7, Folder 74. Efforts to generate more popular support did not preclude appeals to traditional philanthropic supporters.

71. Police Department, City of New York, Office of the Police Commissioner, January 24, 1933, General Order No. 1, RELIEF FOR THE UNEMPLOYED, "Plans and Suggestions for Relief, 1933," HLH-FDR, Box 7; "Firemen Will Vote on Levy for Charity," *NYT* (March 7, 1938), 19; "Levy on Police Pay to Assist Charity," *NYT* (March 4, 1938), 25; "Post Office to Open Chest Drive Sunday," *NYT* (April 29, 1938), 23.

72. The integration of voluntarism and business was strengthened by rules allowing corporations to deduct charitable contributions up to 5 percent of their net income. "Charity Drivers," *Time*, September 28, 1936, 15.

73. "Dentists in Disaster Plan," *NYT* (July 20, 1938), 11.

74. Morris (2015).

75. Cates (1983).

76. Large donors remained attentive to the scale of participation—as well as to the amounts given—in community-based drives. At times, however, they sought to raise funds for emergency relief quietly, fearing that a large-scale campaign would create the impression among the needy that ample funds were available for their support. Packard to JDR Jr. October 26, 1933. RAC OMR RG II 2 F, "Economic Interests", Box 22, Folder 204.

77. EURC-BCO ORGANIZATION. Vol. 13, C-160 FINAL REPORT. BLOCK COMMUNITY ORGANIZATION (BLOCK-AID). EURC/GB/7/14/32, p. 41. JPJ.

78. On cross-national differences in social work practices during the Depression, see Peel (2012).

79. Major donors in New York City acknowledged that the overarching emergency relief fund drives in the early 1930s were functional equivalents of Community Chests, at least as far as family welfare agencies were concerned. "Family Welfare Committee of New York City," RAC OMR II 2 FR, "Economic Interests," Box 22, Folder 204.

80. Quoted in Clare M. Tousley, Assistant General Director of the Charity Organization Society to John D. Rockefeller, III. November 27, 1933. RAC OMR, III 2 P, Box 7, Welfare Interests—General, Folder 74.

81. Carruthers and Ariovich (2010: 9–10).

82. Arthur Packard, memo of a conversation with Mrs. Bevier. October 24, 1933. RAC OMR, III 2 P, Box 7, Welfare Interests—General, Folder 74.

83. John D. Rockefeller, Jr. to Walter S. Gifford, February 24, 1939. RAC OMR, III 2 P, Box 7, Welfare Interests—General, Folder 74.

84. *Report of the Emergency Employment Committee New York City, October 1, 1930-July 1, 1931*, p. 14. "Unemployment and Economic Planning—Unemployment

Relief. 170.4 RG2 F, Box 21, Folder 187; Worth M. Tippy to JDR Jr. (April 5, 1932) RAC OMR 2F, "Economic Interests," Box 21, Folder 187.

85. *Report of the Emergency Employment Committee New York City, October 1, 1930-July 1, 1931*, p. 46. "Unemployment and Economic Planning—Unemployment Relief. 170.4 RG2 F, Box 21, Folder 187. A parallel development emerged in the field of public relief with the introduction of "work-study" programs for college students under the National Youth Administration. Loss (2012: 68–79).

86. Trolander (1975: 46–47). Later in the 1930s, as unemployment fell and war mobilization began to ramp up, many of these "government workers" were withdrawn, creating new pressures for agencies to either reenergize a corps of volunteers or to shift to new models of funding.

87. JDR Jr. to Mr. Packard [n.d.]. Handwritten in pencil. UNEMPLOYMENT AND ECONOMIC PLANNING—UNEMPLOYMENT RELIEF. 170.4. RAC OMR RG 2 F, Box 21, Folder 187. This theme also appears in JDR Jr.'s *The Technique of Soliciting*.

88. Thorndike (2009). For a broader historical account of efforts to reduce income taxation during the New Deal, see I. W. Martin (2013: ch. 3).

89. In the final legislation, rates were raised on all incomes over $50,000 and the top rate increased from "59 percent on incomes of more than $1 million to 75 percent on incomes of more than $500,000." The corporate income tax ranged from 12.5 percent (for incomes over $2,000) and designated four brackets with the highest at 14 percent on corporate incomes over $40,000. Thorndike (2009: 45–56).

90. Williams and Croxton (1930: 29–31); Marchand (1998: 166).

91. These arrangements generated durable controversies over whether the corporate contributions would be charged to operating expenses and therefore passed on to consumers. "Sifts Charity Gift by Phone Company," *NYT* (February 4, 1932), 11; "Utilities Receive Charity Permits," *NYT* (August 7, 1934), 25; "Governor Vetoes Corporation Gifts," *NYT* (March 17, 1935), 24.

92. For discussion of this practice during the First World War, see "Welfare Interests—General American Red Cross—War Fund Campaigns, Contributions," RAC OMR III 2 P, Box 1, Folders 10–12.

93. On World War I background of these concerns, see Cutlip (1965: 151–152).

94. On goodwill and depreciation, see David W. Brazell, Lowell Dworin, and Michael Walsh, "A History of Federal Tax Depreciation Policy," Office of Tax Analysis (May 1989); see also Courtis (1983).

95. Trolander (1975: 59–60); John A. Fitch, "The Nature of Social Action," *SMM* 76 (7) (July 1940): 220.

96. "Here in Washington," *SMM* 74 (11) (November 1938): 349; Glen Leet, "Amendment Season for Social Security," *SMM* 74 (12) (December 1938): 375; "And So On . . . ," *SMM* 76 (2) (February 1940): 69. For a historical review, see Harwood (2002). The introduction of a minimum wage law in New York State drew protests from "a representative of Catholic charities, speaking also for the YMCA, the Boy Scouts, and the Salvation Army." By 1942, legislation (Condon Bill) had been introduced proposing "a blanket exemption from the minimum wage law for any employment by an agency 'organized and operated exclusively for religious, chari-

table, moral, and mental improvement or educational purposes. . . .' This measure is being opposed by many individuals and groups that have been active in securing the enactment of social legislation in New York and in helping safeguard its administration." "Agencies as Employers," *SMM* 78 (4) (April 1942): 115.

97. Hammack (2003: 269–270).

98. Elizabeth Wickenden, quoted in Morris (2004: 275).

99. Smith and Lipsky (1993).

100. "The Ever-Ready Red Cross," *NYT* (October 22, 1934), 14; "Social Act Perils Security of All, Says W. W. Aldrich," *NYT* (July 11, 1936), 1.

101. Seymour Wheeler to Mr. W. P. Murphy (January 29, 1938), "Sentinels of the Republic," no. 518, vol. 1, JPJ.

102. "Remarks of John D. Rockefeller, Jr. at the dinner he gave on behalf of the other honorary chairmen of the Greater New York Fund to the Select Gifts Committee at the Union Club on Thursday, March 23, 1939." RAC OMR III 2Z, Box 4, Folder 173, JDR Jr. PERSONAL, Personal Cooperation—Fundraising.

103. Address delivered by Edward N. Jones, WPA Administrator for Pennsylvania, December 14, 1935. NARA, RG 69, WPA FERA Central Files 1933–36, Box 249, PC 37, Entry 10.

104. The Mobilization for Human Needs had been organized by former Secretary of War, Newton D. Baker, and succeeded in reversing the decline in contributions to the Community Chests during the early 1930s. Allen T. Burns, "Twenty-Five Years of Growing," *SMM* 74 (4) (April 1938): 101–102.

105. "President Hails Private Agencies as Essential to Effective Relief," *NYT* (October 15, 1938), 19.

106. Franklin Delano Roosevelt, "Radio Address for the Mobilization for Human Needs, Washington D.C.," March 11, 1938 (www.presidency.ucsb.edu).

107. Quoted in Oshinsky (2005: 49).

108. Quoted in Oshinsky (2005: 52). Others charged that Roosevelt himself was benefiting financially or that the promised access to the facility at Warms Spring or other polio services had not been forthcoming.

109. Edward C. Eicher, Member of Congress, to Marvin H. McIntyre, Secretary to the President (February 4, 1938). FDR-PPF 4885: Committee for the Celebration of the President's Birthday, 1938.

110. Hugh Johnson to Steve Early (January 16, 1939). FDR-PPF 4885: Committee for the Celebration of the President's Birthday, 1939. Keith Morgan to Steve Early (August 2, 1939); Stephen Early to Keith Morgan (August 4, 1939). FDR-PPF 4885: Committee for the Celebration of the President's Birthday, 1939.

111. Stephen Early, Secretary to the President, to Keith Morgan (January 19, 1939), FDR-PPF 4885: Committee for the Celebration of the President's Birthday, 1939.

112. "To Unify the Fight" A NEW NATIONAL FOUNDATION FOR INFANTILE PARALYSIS (pamphlet, n.d.), FDR-PPF 4885: Committee for the Celebration of President's Birthday, 1937.

113. Keith Morgan to Steve Early (August 2, 1939), FDR-PPF 4885: Committee for the Celebration of the President's Birthday, 1939.

114. Stephen Early responds to a query (February 3,1939) from Stanley Russ, Southland Hotel, San Antonio Texas. Response dated February 21, 1939. FDR-PPF 4885: Committee for the Celebration of the President's Birthday, 1939.

115. "To Unify the Fight" A NEW NATIONAL FOUNDATION FOR INFANTILE PARALYSIS. FDR-PPF 4885: Committee for the Celebration of the President's Birthday, 1937.

116. "President Urges Aid for Charities," *NYT* (October 23, 1934), 1.

117. "Private Charity Is Held Essential," *NYT* (October 21, 1935), 5.

118. John L. Spivak, "Shady Business in the Red Cross, *American Mercury* 33 (131) (November 1934): 258.

119. Karl (1998: 248).

120. "President Praises Aid of Red Cross," *NYT* (April 10, 1934), 6.

121. "Red Cross Renews Pledge to Nation," *NYT* (April 12, 1934), 25. Chief Justice Charles Evans Hughes echoed this argument a few years later. See "Hughes Acclaims Red Cross Spirit," *NYT* (December 8, 1938), 24.

122. "The Ever-Ready Red Cross," *NYT* (November 13, 1937), 18; "Stettinius Urges Aid to Red Cross," *NYT* (November 10, 1938), 29.

123. "Roosevelt Issues Red Cross Appeal," *NYT* (November 12, 1935), 17.

124. "Red Cross Fund Reaches $6,591,000; Convicts and Eskimos among Contributors to War Relief," *NYT* (June 5, 1940), 17; "War Relief Funds Stress Need of Aid," *NYT* (May 27, 1940), 7; "Patients in Hospital Sew for Red Cross," *NYT* (July 15, 1940), 19.

125. Although, as Paul Fussell (1989: 128) notes, this military multiculturalism was limited to film and fiction. In the realm of advertising, World War II was fought by and for Anglo-Saxon Americans.

126. James L. Fieser to Marvin McIntyre (February 27, 1938); "Memo for Mac," (March 7, 1938). FDR-POF 124, Box 1: American Red Cross 1938. The appointment went to Norman Davis, another veteran of the Wilson administration who had held positions in both the Treasury and State Departments.

127. One public relations wizard, Bruce Barton, confronted a gathering of businessmen with the claim that "the present occupant of the White House is preeminent among all men in public life in his ability to think in selling terms and speak in advertising language" (Marchand 1998: 206).

128. MEMORANDUM FOR HON. HARRY HOPKINS AND ADMIRAL GRAYSON, from FDR (March 20, 1935) FDR-POF 124, Box 1: American Red Cross 1935.

129. "Relief Machinery Runs Smoothly," *NYT* (January 31, 1937), 65. See also "President Hails Private Agencies as Essential to Effective Relief," *NYT* (October 15, 1938), 19; "California Floods Spreading Wide," *NYT* (February 12, 1938), 19.

130. Franklin Delano Roosevelt to Admiral Grayson (May 7, 1936) FDR-POF 124, Box 2, American Red Cross 1936.

131. Gertude Springer, "This Business of Relief," *SMM* 74 (2) (February 1938): 37.

132. Springer, "This Business of Relief," 37. For an extended discussion of this period in relief politics, see Clemens (2017b).

133. "Roosevelt Praises Appeal for Chinese," *NYT* (May 15, 1938), 9; "China Relief Drive Ended," *NYT* (June 16, 1938), 9.

134. "Asks $50,000,000 to Aid Refugees," *NYT* (June 12, 1940), 25; "Roosevelt Moves to Help Red Cross Aid the Refugees," *NYT* (July 28, 1940), 1.

135. "Red Cross Warns on Need of Gifts," *NYT* (June 15, 1940), 8; "Red Cross Aid Seen in Roosevelt Plea," *NYT* (June 13, 1940), 19; "Roosevelt Sets Up Machinery to Aid Europe's War Victims," *WP* (July 28, 1940), 1.

136. To provide only a few examples, T. H. Marshall (1950) provided a template with his succession of civil rights, political rights, and social rights. The influence of this teleology is captured in the titles of a number of the most influential historical accounts such as Katz (1986) or A. F. Davis (1967).

137. Mitchell (1991: 78).

138. Mettler (1998); Quadagno (1994).

139. C. Fox (2012).

140. Morris (2009).

141. Schneiberg (2007: 47).

Chapter Seven

1. "Text of Hoover's Address at Garden Mass Meeting for Finnish Relief," *NYT* (December 21, 1939), 12. The section heading immediately above this passage is "Present Made in Gratitude." See also "A Vast Problem," *SMM* 76 (1) (January 1940): 14.

2. "Finns Send $500 To Repay Norwegians," *NYT* (May 6, 1940), 3. On Finland's reputation for honoring her debts, see also "Text of Hoover's Address at Garden Mass Meeting for Finnish Relief"; "Using Finns' Debt Payment," in "Letters to the Times," *NYT* (January 8, 1940), 10.

3. "Help for Finland Pledged in Sports," *NYT* (January 5, 1940), 28; "Sportsmen Help Finns; Jockeys and Automobile Races Subscribe for 2 Ambulances," *NYT* (February 3, 1940), 2.

4. "Offer Car of Wheat for Finnish Relief," *NYT* (January 1, 1940), 4.

5. "Help of 3 Groups Sought for Finns," *NYT* (December 24, 1939), 22; "Rockefeller Gives $100,000 For Finns," *NYT* (February 22, 1940), 4.

6. Good intentions do not guarantee a mastery of natural history. "Finn Relief Party in Arctic Setting," *NYT* (March 1, 1940), 24.

7. "Hoover Broadens Aid to the Finns," *NYT* (February 20, 1940), 3.

8. Until late 1939 the organizations involved were not required to register under the terms of the Neutrality Act because there was no proclamation of war. "Americans' Funds Aiding Victims of War in Belligerent Countries," *NYT* (December 14, 1939), 10. By March 1941, some three hundred relief organizations were registered with the State Department. "President Orders War-Relief Study," *NYT* (March 14, 1941), 13.

9. "Cabaret Parties Will Benefit Local and War Relief Groups," *NYT* (March 3, 1940), 49.

10. "Chaotic Appeals," *SMM* 77 (4) (April 1941): 119.

11. These civic ties can be understood as harnessing "private obligations" to address a relative weakness in liberal political theory. Westbrook (1990).

12. On World War II and American state-building see B. H. Sparrow (1996); J. T. Sparrow (2011); M. R. Wilson (2016).

13. Gertrude Springer and Kathryn Close, "War and Welfare," *SMM* 78 (1) (January 1943): 3.

14. Harry L. Hopkins to DeWitt Smith (April 3, 1942), FDR-HLH. Hopkins advised Smith that "I frankly do not think it is too important and think you can waste an awful lot of time working on precise language the Government may not agree to."

15. Springer and Close, "War and Welfare," 3, 6.

16. James B. Bamford, "Listen Washington! The Local Community Talks Back," *SMM* 78 (3) (March 1942): 72.

17. After victory had been declared in Europe, threats of mutiny from troops facing possible transfers to the Pacific Theater shaped war strategy.

18. Hoover (1936).

19. Arthur Krock, "Hopes That Mr. Hoover and Red Cross Can Work Together," *NYT* (December 15, 1939), 34; "War Relief Story Denied by Hoover," *NYT* (December 15, 1939), 13.

20. "Mr. Hoover Tackles Another Relief Job," *NYT* (January 21, 1940), 97.

21. Testifying to Congress for the first time since he had served as Secretary of Commerce under President Coolidge, Hoover stated that $40 to $50 million dollars would be required to aid the Polish people (with one-fourth coming from the United States) and that "such humanitarian assistance embraces no threat of involvement in European wars." "Hoover Backs Bill for Polish Relief," *NYT* (March 1, 1940), 1.

22. "The Nation: Candidates' Progress," *NYT* (April 7, 1940), 69.

23. "Congress Is Cool to Loan for Finns; Garner against It," *NYT* (January 18, 1940), 1. The National Association of Manufacturers asserted that "the inevitable result of any act of our government extending loans, credits or other official aid is to transform private and personal sympathy into public action. That is the first governmental step of national assistance to one belligerent against another. Such action is likely to excite reprisals and thus lead to ultimate involvement in war." "Miners Hit NLRB, Hail Wagner Act," *NYT* (January 31, 1940), 13.

24. "Agencies Here Give $20,000,000 Abroad," *NYT* (July 7, 1940), E5.

25. See Clemens (2017b).

26. On the "New Alignments," see Morris (2009: 76).

27. "In the 'Chests,'" *SMM* 76 (1) (January 1940): 19.

28. Albert Deutsch, "War Chest: FDR Opens Annual Drive for Nation's Social Agencies," *PM* (October 5, 1942); clipping in "Unemployment and Economic Planning, Miscellaneous Plans. Mobilization of Human Needs, 170.3, RAC OMR RG 2F, Box 21, Folder 186, Economic Interests.

29. Quoted in The Chairman (Norman H. Davis) to Chapter Chairmen, "Joint Campaigns" (May 20, 1941), HLH-FDR (Groups 124), Container 130, Aircraft Production (Requirements)—American Red Cross, 1945, "American Red Cross—1941."

30. David Liggett to Harry Hopkins (August 30, 1941), HLH-FDR (Group 124), Container 130, Aircraft Production (Requirements)—American Red Cross, 1945, "American Red Cross—1941."

31. This relationship proved to be a durable source of conflict, particularly as it became entangled with questions of the relationship of the Red Cross local chapters to union-led fundraising among organized labor. Guy Emerson to Norman H. Davis (March 24, 1944), HLH-FDR (Group 124), Container 130, Aircraft Production (Requirements)—American Red Cross, 1945, "American Red Cross—1941."

32. The Chairman to Chapter Chairmen, "Joint Campaigns" (May 20, 1941). "American Red Cross—1941," HLH-FDR (Group 124), Container 130.

33. James L. Fieser to The Chairman, "Membership" (September 13, 1941).

34. "President Halts Welfare Merger," *NYT* (June 8, 1941), 34; for a typescript of the press release, HLH-FDR (Group 124, Container 130). "The Red Cross Stands Alone," *NYT* (July 4, 1942), 6. Reprint, RAC OMR III 2 P, "Welfare Interests—General, American Red Cross," Box 2, Folder 21.

35. To minimize conflicts, the Red Cross postponed its annual roll call until spring so that it would not coincide with other drives. Thomas W. Lamont to John D. Rockefeller Jr. (July 17, 1942), RAC OMR III 2 P, "Welfare Interests-General, American Red Cross," Box 2, Folder 21.

36. Fieser, who also forwarded the memo to the Chairman to Harry Hopkins, was a strong advocate for greater internal democracy within the Red Cross and this infused his analysis of membership, describing "the ignorance of those who discount membership and the democratic participating principle which it represents. They have not looked eye to eye with chapters at regional conferences and annual meetings in big and little places across the country. They have forgotten the impact of chapter leadership which is really membership leadership, at our annual convention." "American Red Cross—1941," HLH-FDR (Group 124), Container 130. This debate resonates with more contemporary discussions of check-writing versus active participation in voluntary associations. See Putnam (1995: 67); Skocpol (2003: 210–211).

37. The tension between maximizing members and carefully allocating money was an important element in the conflict between the Red Cross and the Community Chests. Kathryn Close, "Directions for Giving," *SMM* 78 (3) (March 1942): 68 [67–70].

38. James L. Fieser to Harry L. Hopkins (September 15, 1941); James L. Fieser to The Chairman, "Membership" (September 13, 1941), HLH-FDR (Group 124), Container 130, Aircraft Production (Requirements)—American Red Cross, 1945, "American Red Cross—1941."

39. "American Red Cross in Great Britain" by Ernie Pyle. RAC OMR, Welfare Interests—General, American Red Cross III 2 P, Box 2, Folder 21.

40. Norman Davis to JDR Jr. (January 14, 1943). RAC OMR, Welfare Interests—General, American Red Cross, Annual Campaigns, 1940–1943, III 2 P, Box 2, Folder 21; Chester I. Barnard to Members of the General Policy Committee (December 22, 1942), RAC OMR III 2 P, "Welfare Interests—General, American Red Cross," Box 2, Folder 21.

41. John D. Rockefeller, Jr. to Norman H. Davis (January 8, 1943). RAC OMR III 2 P, "Welfare Interests—General, American Red Cross," Box 2, Folder 21.

42. "Hoover Extending Fund Organization," *NYT* (December 19, 1939), 13; "U.S. Labor Generous in Help for Finland," *NYT* (February 18, 1940), 29. The relief effort even overcame the deep divisions between the AFL and the CIO. "Labor Calls Truce to Help the Finns," *NYT* (December 29, 1939), 2.

43. James L. Fieser to "Mr. Davis" (October 3, 1942), HLH-FDR (Group 124), Container 130, Aircraft Production (Requirements)—American Red Cross, 1945, "American Red Cross—1941." Fieser acknowledged these negotiations as part of "this job of explaining our labor agreements, down into the U.S.A. where the money comes from."

44. Guy Emerson to Norman H. Davis (March 24, 1944), HLH-FDR (Group 124), Container 130, Aircraft Production (Requirements)—American Red Cross, 1945, "American Red Cross—1941." At the end of this long memo, Emerson asserted that "disagreement over details must not be permitted to stand in the way of a four-square effort to achieve a true peoples' Red Cross. No American has the right to bring into this sacred forum his private emotions or prejudices. We are in a world crisis where feelings run high, and where many of the old anchorages are gone. In this complex era the Red Cross stands perhaps alone as a universal humanitarian organization, as a symbol of unselfish cooperation which is of immeasurable human importance. . . . . Our labor effort is only one of many fields in which the ideals of the Red Cross have been tested in action."

45. John G. Holters (County Chairman, Cincinnati and Hamilton, ARC) to Basil O'Connor (November 29, 1945), HLH-FDR (Group 124), Container 130, Aircraft Production (Requirements)—American Red Cross, 1945, "American Red Cross—1941."

46. "Waiting for the Green Light," *SMM* 77 (1) (January 1941): 16. Later that year, Charles P. Taft, "a Cincinnati lawyer long identified with the YMCA and with Community Chests and Councils, Inc.," was appointed as the assistant to the federal coordinator of these programs. *SMM* 77 (3) (March 1941): 74.

47. "The USO—and note those initials well; they'll be much in evidence from now on—includes: the YMCA, YWCA [Young Women's Christian Association], National Catholic Community Service, Salvation Army, Jewish Welfare Board, and the National Travelers Aid Association. With Travelers Aid added, this is the same group which organized in November as the National United Welfare Committee for Defense." Gertrude Springer, "For Soldiers Off Duty," *SMM* 77 (3) (March 1941): 75.

48. James L. Fieser to "Mr. Davis" (October 3, 1942), HLH-FDR (Group 124), Container 130, Aircraft Production (Requirements)—American Red Cross, 1945, "American Red Cross—1941."

49. Gertrude Springer, "For Soldiers Off Duty," *SMM* 77 (3) (March 1941): 75, 77. "Mr. McNutt [head of the FSA] and his advisers, including Mr. Taft, have held to the idea of a coordinated public-private program which would invoke a maximum of local activity and participation, serve the home folks as well as the newcomers, and carry on as a part of community life when the high powered defense effort is

behind us. . . . . The USO presented itself as a going concern in terms of organization, with a unified front for money raising, and with influential citizen backing willing to accept responsibility. Its proposed program, while not exactly coordinated, was tangible, following lines familiar to many people."

50. Hoey (1942: 12); Gertrude Springer and Kathryn Close, "Relief in These Times," *SMM* 77 (11) (November 1941): 315, 321.

51. "LaGuardia to Head Home Defense," *NYT* (May 20, 1941), 1; "Landis Regroups Civilian Defense," *NYT* (February 4, 1942), 1.

52. Hillman (1946).

53. Laves (1943: 1027, 1033).

54. DeWitt Smith to Geoffrey May (March 20, 1942), HLH-FDR (Group 124), Container 130, Aircraft Production (Requirements)—American Red Cross, 1945, "American Red Cross—1941."

55. Stevenson (1942: 597–598).

56. Frost (1944: 86–87); "War Welds Folk in San Francisco," *NYT* (June 25, 1942), 22. On the model of "block organization," see I. T. Sanders (1949).

57. This program had a lasting influence: "the Division of Volunteer Participation of the Office of Civilian Defense did, however, establish the pattern for VISTA and similar community-action agencies." Duncan R. Jamieson, "Review of *The Challenge to Urban Liberalism: Federal-City Relations during World War II* by Philip J. Funigiello," *Journal of Southern History* 45 (2) (May 1979): 297–298.

58. Geoffrey May, review of *Social Service in Wartime*, ed. Helen R. Wright, *AAPSS* 327 (January 1945): 227; "The Welfare Agencies, the O.C.D., and the Red Cross," *Social Service Review* 16 (2) (June 1942): 323.

59. May and Ward (1942).

60. "Here in Washington," *SMM* 76 (6) (June 1940): 200.

61. "Youth," *SMM* 76 (12) (December 1940): 362. Collaborative arrangements were also put in place to manage conscientious objectors. The American Friends Service Committee established a camp for C.O.s that offered "constructive service to a rural community" in the form of "painting, carpentering, landscaping about the sawmill, making time studies of efficiency in the mill, doing demonstration clearing of young timber. The cooperative is under the advisory direction of the New England Experiment Station of the U.S. Forest Service."

62. "Certainly Not," *SMM* 76 (7) (July 1940): 225.

63. Hillman (1946: 183); Stevenson (1942: 601).

64. "Roosevelt Joins Willkie in Plea for Welfare Aid," *NYT* (October 4, 1941), 1.

65. Tobin and Bidwell (1940: 51–52).

66. Tobin and Bidwell (1940: 53).

67. "Red Cross Aid Fund $1,000,000 over Top," *NYT* (September 12, 1940), 7.

68. This suggestion was not a new one. Louis A. Johnson to Marvin H. McIntyre (January 28, 1935) FDR-POF 124, Box 1 (American Red Cross 1935), FDR-POF 124 (American Red Cross 1938).

69. Mr. Fieser to Mr. Thorne, "Advisory Committee" (June 18, 1942), "American Red Cross—1942," HLH-FDR (Group 124), Container 130. See also Dulles (1950:

363–364). By 1944, even Mabel T. Boardman—a leader in the ouster of Clara Barton who had for decades served as Secretary—retired and served only as an honorary member of the board.

70. James L. Fieser to the Chairman, "Closer Tie-in with Administration through Central Committee Appointments" (April 2, 1942), "American Red Cross—1942," HLH-FDR (Group 124), Container 130; James L. Fieser to "The Chairman" (September 22, 1942), HLH-FDR (Group 124), Container 130, Aircraft Production (Requirements)—American Red Cross, 1945, "American Red Cross—1941." In December 1942, Fieser forwarded a collection of these memos written as he toured the country in the fall of 1942 to Hopkins.

71. Merton (1946: 116). Sacrifice was linked to servicemen (26 percent of time used for appeals), civilians (20 percent), and Kate Smith herself (5 percent). Merton (1946: 50).

72. Merton (1946: 129).

73. Flyer: "Announcing the 1943 Red Cross War Fund of New York City." RAC OMR III 2 P, Box 2, Folder 23.

74. Thomas W. Lamont, Chairman, ARC National Advisory Committee to JDR Jr. (July 17, 1942). 7/17/1942. RAC OMR III 2 P, Box 2, Folder 20.

75. "A Study of the Public's Attitude toward the American Red Cross, with a Supplement Dealing with World War II Veterans," pp. 17, 20. George Gallup, June 28, 1946. ARC, 1935–1946, RG200, Box 764, 494.2 Also, in the 1942 report, Gallup insisted that "it should be possible to dramatize the fact that in the case of any given contributor the life of his own son or of his neighbor's son might be saved by the Red Cross."

76. To: Mr. John D. Rockefeller, Jr., From: Arthur W. Packard, May 19, 1944 Subject: Special Red Cross Gift. Within Rockefeller circles, the concerns about public attitudes toward the Red Cross were linked to questions about the financial transparency in its reporting. It was in this context that the Red Cross commissioned the first of a series of confidential surveys from George Gallup. Arthur W. Packard to Mrs. John D. Rockefeller Jr. (October 2, 1942). RAC OMR III 2 P, "Welfare Interests-General, American Red Cross," Box 2, Folder 19A.

77. "All the figures relating to the projection of needs are based upon fundraising years, which do not coincide with fiscal accounting periods—a circumstance which makes difficult the rationalization of actual experience with projected plans." Arthur W. Packard to John D. Rockefeller, Jr., "American Red Cross Campaign" (February 10, 1944), RAC OMR III 2 P, Box 2, Folder 24.

78. Arthur W. Packard to Files (July 3, 1945), "American Red Cross—Conversation with Mr. James McClintock—June 9, 1945."

79. "Red Cross Trims Budget in Crisis," *NYT* (May 3, 1957), 56.

80. "Walter S. Gifford Dies," *NYT* (May 8, 1966), 1, 82.

81. MEMORANDUM. To: The Files, From: Arthur W. Packard, Subject: Conversation with Mr. Walter Gifford, American Red Cross, March 13, 1947. RAC OMR RG III 2 P. Box 1, Folder 1. General Marshall served for one year as president of the American Red Cross in 1949–50 between terms as Secretary of State and Secretary

of Defense. Some local chapters also protested that the fund-raising targets were too high. "Discount 'Revolt' on Red Cross Goal: National Aides Cite Only Three Protesting Units—O'Connor Urges 'Democratic' Way," *NYT* (January 7, 1948), 2.

82. Westbrook (1990: 588). On nationalism as "imagined community," see Anderson ([1983] 1991).

Chapter Eight

1. Donald C. Stone, "Projects for Increasing U.S. Effectiveness in Working with Peoples of Other Countries." December 1952. RAC OMR III 2 E, Cultural Interests, Box 51, Folder 508.

2. The American Red Cross commissioned a series of "confidential" polls from George Gallup. "A Study of the Public's Attitude toward the American Red Cross" (October 8, 1943); "A Study of the Public's Attitude toward the American Red Cross with A Supplement Dealing with World War II Veterans" (June 28, 1946; this report includes comparisons to the 1943 and 1944 surveys). ARC, 1935–1946, RG 200, Box 764, 494.2.

3. P. Campbell (1944: 108).

4. Alfred P. Sloan Jr., "Industry's Post-War Responsibilities," *Vital Speeches of the Day* 8 (January 1, 1943): 174–177. Delivered to the Annual Congress of American Industry, December 4, 1941.

5. Mettler (2005); Putnam (2000).

6. Barman (2006); Clemens (2010a).

7. The stakes in these different arrangements can be traced through the durable conflicts over whether Red Cross chapters should join their local Community Chest. This was already an issue during the First World War, and, as of October 1, 1932, the Red Cross adopted a formal policy prohibiting chapter or branch membership in Community Chests. "Red Cross Chapters and Community Chests," N.H. 572, August 1934. ARC, RG 200, Box 345, folder 221.012. As of 1946, the Red Cross reiterated its opposition to joint fund-raising. RG 200, Box 548, folder 221.012.

8. Herzog (2011); Zunz (2012: ch. 5).

9. "Remarks of Mr. Henry Ford II at Greater New York Fund Meeting" (April 12, 1950), 9. RAC OMR, III 2, "Welfare Interests—General," Box 13, Folder 122.

10. Baker (1991).

11. Rufus M. Jones to John D. Rockefeller Jr., February 5, 1947, and February 18, 1947. RAC OMR, III 2 E, Cultural Interests, Box 51, Folder 507.

12. G. Don Fairbairn and John La Cerda, "Silence! Brothers at Work," *Nation's Business* 35 (May 1947): 44, 62. RAC OMR, III 2 E, Cultural Interests, Box 51, Folder 507.

13. Fairbairn and La Cerda, "Silence! Brothers at Work."

14. The connections between voluntary effort and governmental presence overseas varied by country and concern. Not surprisingly, the two were particularly close in the U.S. occupation zones in Europe and Japan. RAC OMR, III 2 E, Cultural Interests, Box 51, Folder 507.

15. Robert C. Bates to Dana S. Creel, October 23, 1952. "American Friends Service Committee—Neighborhood Centers Project." RAC OMR, III 2 E, Cultural Interests, Box 51, Folder 507.

16. John D. Rockefeller 3rd to John J. McCloy, February 24, 1950. RAC OMR III 2 E, Box 51, Folder 510.

17. Dana S. Creel, Memorandum on "Conversation with Hugh W. Moore, American Friends Service Committee, regarding Mr. R. Jr.'s gift to McCloy, June 6, 1950. Julia E. Branson, Secretary, Foreign Service Section, to John Hobart, Lou Schneider, Barbara Graves, AFSC, NYC, July 14, 1950. RAC OMR III 2 E, Box 51, Folder 510.

18. Donald C. Stone, "Projects for Increasing U.S. Effectiveness in Working with Peoples of Other Countries." December 1952. RAC OMR III 2 E, Cultural Interests, Box 51, Folder 508.

19. Sills (1957); Oshinsky (2005).

20. RAC OMR, Welfare Interests General, RG III 2 P. Box 1, Folder 1. American Red Cross. "Dedication Address by Basil O'Connor, President, The American National Red Cross. At the inauguration of THE NATIONAL BLOOD PROGRAM. Rochester, New York, January 12, 1948." After accepting O'Connor's resignation in 1949 (he was succeeded by General George Marshall), President Truman praised O'Connor for having "given your country a relief agency capable of efficient work through strictly democratic processes." "Truman Appoints Marshall President of the Red Cross," *NYT* (September 23, 1949), 1. For a description of those "democratizing" changes, see "Red Cross Revision Favored by Group," *NYT* (September 21, 1946), 9.

21. Molm et al. (2007); Simpson et al. (2018). President Truman echoed this theory of extended benevolent exchange: "In the continuance of our diligent work toward a just and enduring peace, it is very heartening to observe that however peoples may differ on political and economic issues, under the banner of the Red Cross they can unite for the betterment of mankind." "Truman Says Unity Is Red Cross Role," *NYT* (June 19, 1946), 20.

22. "Red Cross Revision Favored by Group." On the history of the charter, see Kosar (2006).

23. Fones-Wolf (1994: 137–143).

24. "CIO Agency Ends Red Cross Tie-Up," *NYT* (April 15, 1946), 29. Expressing the hope that the Red Cross would become "a truly people's organization," the letter "recalled that on Nov. 15, 1945, Mrs. Eugene Meyer, wife of the Publisher of The Washington Post, and co-chairman of the women's foundation committee on reorganization of community services, charged that a group of conservatives within the American Red Cross had determined to force Mr. O'Connor out of his position on the ground that he was too friendly to labor." Mrs. Meyer had claimed that "your very respectable, supposedly honorable but very bitter and very obtuse old fuddy-duddy leaders resent the fact that labor is gaining a foothold in the management of the Red Cross." See "Red Cross Warned against Reaction," *NYT* (November 16, 1945), 10.

25. Fones-Wolf (1994: 160).

26. Beardsley Ruml and Theodore Geiger, *The Five Percent* (National Planning Association, Planning Pamphlet, No. 73, August 1951); Alfred P. Sloan Jr., "Business Has an Interest and Duty to Help Them," *Challenge* 1 (1) (October 1952): 18 [17–19]. See also Gerhard D. Bleicken, "Corporate Contributions to Charities: The Modern Rule," *American Bar Association Journal* 38 (12) (December 1952): 999–1002, 1059–1061.

27. Bookman (1932).

28. Mimeographed report from National Information Bureau, Inc. March 1, 1956. "The American National Red Cross," p. 4. RAC OMR, RG III 2 P, Box 1, Folder 1.

29. Issued April 30, 1946. ARC, RG200, Box 548, 221.012, Community Chests. In 1929, the Red Cross Central Committee had adopted a policy that required locals to "solicit memberships and funds independent of any other joint fund raising agencies." In 1941, the Red Cross severed connections with the Community Chest movement over the proposal for a united drive, predicting "that other agencies would follow suit with the result that the very existence of the Chest would be jeopardized. However, no stampede ever took place and interestingly enough most Chest officials, where separations were affected, soon came to the conclusion that they were in a better position by not having the responsibility for raising the large sums required by the Red Cross from year to year. This conviction was strengthened by the interesting discovery that a contributor does not tend to reduce the amount he gives to other agencies because of his Red Cross contribution any more than is the case in his financial support of the church. . . . . On the other hand, by independent campaigns, chapters uniformly [sic] experienced no difficulty in securing greatly enlarged sums of money, for both local and national Red Cross purposes, and as a by-product were able to reinstate a consciousness of individual membership in the Red Cross." Quoted in The Chairman (Norman H. Davis) to Chapter Chairmen, "Joint Campaigns" (May 20, 1941), HLH-FDR (Groups 124), Container 130, Aircraft Production (Requirements)—American Red Cross, 1945, "American Red Cross—1941."

30. "Why the American Red Cross is opposed to participation in any joint fund raising campaigns," October 1, 1945. ARC, RG3, Box 548, 221.012 Community Chests.

31. "Red Cross Decries United Campaigns: Independent Fund Raising Is Fostered in Pamphlet at National Convention," *NYT* (June 29, 1949), 25. Local chapters faced suspension of their charters for joining such federated drives. "Red Cross Warns Pittsburgh Unit," *NYT* (June 28, 1949), 31.

32. Tellingly, the champions of the Red Cross portrayed their rivals as nationally centralized despite the considerable evidence that both the Community Chest and United Fund models centered control in municipal or corporate communities.

33. Barman (2006); M. Brown (2018).

34. "Joint Fund Drives by Red Cross Hit," *NYT* (August 15, 1951), 39.

35. "Harriman Fights Cut in Red Cross," *NYT* (January 7, 1949), 26.

36. "Remarks of Mr. Henry Ford II at Greater New York Fund Meeting," (April 12, 1950), RAC OMR III 2 P, "Welfare Interests—General" Box 13, Folder 122.

37. Gladwin Hill, "Red Cross Declares Itself Tired of Aiding Ingrate Crisis Areas," *NYT* (March 15, 1954), 1.

38. "First Lady Spurs Red Cross Drives," *NYT* (March 22, 1953), 2.

39. Mauss ([1950] 2000).

40. "Red Cross Leaves Blood Bank Group," *NYT* (May 21, 1945), 29; Titmuss (1971).

41. Barman (2006).

42. "MEMORANDUM. To: The Files, From: Arthur W. Packard, Subject: Conversation with Mr. Walter Gifford, American Red Cross, March 13, 1947." RAC OMR, Welfare Interests General, RG III 2 P. Box 1, Folder 1. American Red Cross. See also "Discount 'Revolt' on Red Cross Goal: National Aides Cite Only Three Protesting Units—O'Connor Urges 'Democratic' Way," *NYT* (January 7, 1948), 2.

43. Morris (2009).

44. Mrs. Oswald B. Lord, Board of Trustees, CSS to Mrs. David Rockefeller, midwinter 1947, in Folder 75 "Community Service Society," Box 7, RAC OMR III 2 P.

45. RAC OMR III 2 P, Box 7, Community Service Society, Folder 75. Draft of Report from Yorkville District Committee (April 24, 1947).

46. RAC OMR III 2 P, Box 7, Community Service Society, Folder 75. Community Service Society, Symposium I—Human Relations in Science and Practice, January 29 and 30, 1948.

47. Frederick Sheffield to Laurance S. Rockefeller (November 15, 1939). RAC OMR III 2 P, Box 7, Community Service Society, Folder 75.

48. RAC OMR III 2 P, Box 7, Community Service Society, Folder 75. A Memorandum to Private Businesses and Executives of Corporations from the Community Service Society, 1948.

49. Advising in response to a request from the Community Service Society, Arthur W. Packard of the Rockefeller Family Office suggested to Mrs. Laurance Rockefeller that "unless a gift were to be made because of friendship with a solicitor, we would not recommend that any other gifts be made by members of the family." Arthur W. Packard to Mrs. Laurance S. Rockefeller (January 21, 1949). RAC OMR III 2 P, Box 7, Community Service Society, Folder 75.

50. Mrs. JDR 3rd to Keith McHugh, March 26, 1957. RAC OMR III 2 P, Box 7, Community Service Society, Folder 75.

51. "STATUS REPORT OF THE CSS FAMILY FUND," RAC OMR III 2 P, Box 7, Community Service Society, Folder 75.

52. Zald and Denton (1963).

53. RAC OMR, III 2 P, Box 13, Folder 120, Welfare Interests-General, Chicago Area Projects, Industrial Areas Foundation, 1941–46.

54. "The Rockefeller Panel Report on American Democracy; The Power of the Democratic Idea; Special Studies Project Report VI," 41. RAC RBF, RG V4G, Box 48, RBF, Special Studies Project, Folder 531.

55. Hayek (1948: 16).

56. Rockefeller "Special Studies Project Report VI," 54.

57. This principle informed the 1949 Hoover Commission Report on government organization; acknowledging the role of independent federal agencies, the report insisted on "a clear line of control from the President" (Kosar 2011: 4).

58. Rockefeller "Special Studies Project Report VI," 58. On the use of the term and form of the "quasi governmental" entity, see Kosar (2011: 4–5).

59. Rockefeller "Special Studies Project Report VI," 55–56. One debate prompted by this blurring concerned the relevance of due process and civil rights within private organizations, particularly business corporations. Many, including notable figures such as Adolf Berle, argued that if liberal democracy were to be preserved in conjunction with a modern economy, it would be necessary for large organizations to develop or conserve a moral character (Clemens 2009).

60. Robert Heilbroner to Henry A. Kissinger, March 21, 1957. RAC RBF, RG V4G, Box 48, RBF, Special Studies Project, Folder 540. On the distinction between corporate and federated (e.g., composed of membership-based chapters) associations, see Sills (1957).

61. Wall (2008: 242). The "Friendship Train" of 1947 embodied the same approach as "a private scaled-down version of the Marshall Plan . . . designed to stave off Communism abroad and strengthen a cold war consensus at home by mobilizing American citizens into an international humanitarian effort." Inspired by a nationally syndicated columnist, Drew Pearson, "a Friendship Train" would "circle the nation, collecting private donations of food and medicine for the famished millions of Europe." This vision was realized with the support of movie producer Harry Warner, in a manner reminiscent of the coupling of celebrity and local civic benevolence familiar from the Civil War through the March of Dimes.

62. Clemens (2017b).

63. Barman (2006).

64. For examples of this large literature, see Hacker (2002); Smith and Lipsky (1993); Wolch (1990).

Chapter Nine

1. Special Studies Project, Subpanel VII—Papers, McKeon, Richard. Papers VII-1, "Responsibility as Sign and Instrumentality," 1947. RAC RBF, V4G 48, Folder 547.

2. Lukács (1971: 299). Quoted in Cuff (1977: 365).

3. One answer in the French case was the third term of "liberté, egalité, fraternité." Ronsavallon (2007).

4. R. Smith (2003).

5. "The Rockefeller Panel Report on American Democracy; The Power of the Democratic Idea; Special Studies Project Report VI," pp. 55–56. RAC RBF, RG V4G, Box 48, RBF, Special Studies Project, Folder 531.

6. See Google Ngram Viewer for Books (American English).

7. Breen (2010: 117–120).

8. Balogh (2009).

9. "CIO Agency Ends Red Cross Tie-Up," *NYT* (April 15, 1946), 29.

10. Callahan (2017); Giridharadas (2018); Reich (2016).

11. Bourdieu (2014: 95).

12. On "intercurrence," see Orren and Skowronek (2004).

13. In the social sciences, path dependence has typically been understood in terms of "lock-in" or the ways in which initial conditions and early events restrict the possibilities of subsequent change (Pierson 2000). By contrast, the combination of diverse elements of social structure may produce zones of durable instability, more akin to a fault line.

14. In sociological institutionalism, it is often assumed that relational models—of exchange, family, etc.—are nested within differentiated "fields" of social activity (Friedland and Alford 1992; Fligstein and McAdam 2012). The argument here treats this mapping of forms directly or uniquely into fields as possible but not definitional.

15. This focus on organizing principles, models, or templates is central to the cultural and relational turns in political sociology. Rather than focusing on abstract rights or attributes associated with individual political actors, the central insight is that there is a "prefigurative" quality to the ways in which political actors organize themselves to act politically (Polletta 2002). What follows, if one accepts the argument that state-society relations are central to state development, is that the models that organize collective action are also infused into formal governmental orders. As Charles Tilly summed up this point, "This relational approach to state and culture generates social structures and processes from culturally embedded interactions" (1999: 410). While the "quick thinking" at the center of practice theory may be involved, particularly in those moments when conflict flares at the violation of some expectation, the process of coordinating collection action is centered on the more explicit "slow thinking" that can be traced in archival documents (Lizardo and Strand 2010).

16. DiMaggio (1991), Swidler (1986), and Sewell (1993) provide the theoretical framework. For applications to social movements and political contention, see Armstrong (2002); Clemens (1997); Polletta (2002); Tilly (1995).

17. Note how this claim resonates with the passage from Georg Lukács at the start of this chapter. Luckács, however, focused on the coexistence of conflicting ideological commitments in discourse but the capacity of practical organization to bring those contradictions into focus.

18. Quoted in Hatch (1989: 69–70). In the decades immediately after the Revolution, many denominations had been shaken by attacks upon the legitimacy of clerical authority while surges of revivalism produced new denominations (often labeled as "sects") whose internal governance conformed more closely to democratic principles.

19. Swidler (1986: 279).

20. Cutlip (1965: 141-43, 404, 407); Walker (1933: 1204).

21. Thelen (2002).

22. For a discussion of this possible trajectory, see Riley (2010).

23. Clemens (2010).

24. "Is This Man on Your Christmas List?" RAC OMR II 2 F, Economic Interests, Box 21, Folder 177.

25. Cutlip (1965: 507–509); Oshinsky (2005: 189). On models of institutional change, see Clemens (2005); Leblebici et al. (1991); Lounsbury et al. (2003).

26. Mann (1986: 477).

27. This characterization of the United States as governed by a "weak state" has a long history, but is often linked to Stephen Skowronek's (1982) characterization of nineteenth-century government as a "state of courts and parties." On "infrastructural power," see Mann (1984). In the context of American political development, see Balogh (2009, 2015); Clemens (2006); Novak (2008); Tarrow (2015, 2018). The phrase "sinews of power" is taken from Brewer (1988).

28. The classic statement of this question comes from Dahl (1961). Dahl's commitment to a pluralist analysis of American politics put him at odds with those who underscored the pervasive power of elite networks. For a review of this debate, see Khan (2012).

29. Hawley (1974). See also Alchon (1985); Hendrickson (2013).

30. See Clemens (2010b); Morris (2009).

31. For the development of this concept in the context of the First World War, see Capozzola (2008: 6): "Looking at the history of a liberal society like the United States, it might seem that Americans have never really had to think much about their political obligations, let alone act on them. In the later wars of the twentieth and twenty-first centuries, liberal individualism, an economy of consumption, a nationalized culture, legally protected civil liberties, and an expanded federal state all played more prominent roles in public life. But even so, throughout American history, a citizenship of obligation has always coexisted with one of rights, as a patchwork of political cultures supported a hybrid state as jumbled as Uncle Sam's ill-fitting suit."

32. The audio recordings of some of these conversations as broadcast by ABC News can be found at: http://www.youtube.com/watch?v=Ly2wHIge4Ug. *The Rachel Maddow Show* combined these audio clips obtained from ABC with videotape of multiple critical reactions from Republican and Democratic politicians to the equation of these government benefits with "gifts": http://www.youtube.com/watch?v=_zQ7SjpSBBU. For additional reporting of the incident, see: "Romney: Obama's Gift Giving Led to Loss," *WP* (November 14, 2012), http://articles.washingtonpost .com/2012–11–14/politics/35507210_1_mitt-romney-obama-campaign-louisiana -and-scott-walker; "Mitt Romney Blames Election Loss on 'Gift' Obama Gave to Minority Groups," *Guardian* (November 14, 2012), http://www.guardian.co.uk /world/2012/nov/14/romney-blames-election-loss-gifts.

33. As Elon James White asked: "Do Romney and the Republican Party understand how insulting this line of commentary is? These groups didn't vote for Obama because they disagreed with Republican policies or anything. . . . Everyone just wanted free stuff! I'm wearing my brand-new platinum chain that says, "Government handouts, bitchez" in diamonds that Obama sent me right this very moment." "Romney: Obama Gave Voters 'Gifts'" (November 15, 2012), http://www.theroot

.com/blogs/elongated-thoughts/romney-obama-gave-voters-gifts. This sense of personal and civic insult echoed across progressive blogs. "Romney Says Obama Gave Out Gifts to Get Votes. Where's My Golden Box?" (November 14, 2012), http://www.dailykos.com/story/2012/11/14/1161734/-Romney-says-Obama-gave-out -gifts-to-get-votes-Where-s-my-golden-box.

34. For a related concept, see Kellogg (2009).

35. See chapter 1 for a more complete discussion. In historical accounts, the canonical constitutive contradiction in American political development is that between liberty and slavery. But, as I suggest in that earlier discussion, we can find a number of other lines of generative cleavage that run through the political history of the United States and, no doubt, that of most other societies.

36. It is here that cultural construction and maintenance of categorical boundaries collides with both the classic institutionalist vision of the diffusion of legitimate forms through a population of individuals, organizations, or nations and the more agentic neo-institutionalism of transposition and combination of forms. The possibilities for—and obstacles to—organizational innovation and institutional change may be illuminated by an extended mapping of at least one boundary between fields. That plural is crucial, given that the conceptual power of "institutional logics" presumes the capacity for contradiction and incompatibility. Empirically, such incompatibility should be evidenced by persistent fault lines of conflict and efforts to insulate and decouple domains of action from one another. Clemens and Cook (1999); Schneiberg and Clemens (2006).

37. On voluntary associations and the emergence of mass interest group politics, see Clemens (1997).

38. Zunz (2012: 78). See also Clark (1960); Morris (2009: 114); Thorndike (2016).

39. This hierarchy of authority was also evident in the right of governors and later legislatures to authorize—or withhold—charters for corporations or to set limits on activities or mandate minimum and maximum resources. Zollman (1924).

40. Trolander (1975).

41. Berry (2003).

42. Crawford and Ostrom (1995).

43. Zunz (2012: 206–207).

44. Tellingly, the IRS locates the prehistory of the 501(c)(4) in requests by the U.S. Chamber of Commerce and employers' associations to recognize an exemption for "civic and commercial" organizations. http://www.irs.gov/pub/irs-tege /eotopici03.pdf.

45. Gieryn (1983).

46. Goldberg (2007).

47. On elites, see Almond ([1938] 1998) and Zorbaugh ([1929] 1976). On ethnic solidarity, see Kaufman (2003).

48. See chapter 4.

49. ARC, 1917–1934, RG 2, Box 80, 102.1 Junior Red Cross (Organizations, Functions, Plans, Program, 1922–1934), JUNIOR RED CROSS Lesson XX [N.H. 208, Rev. March 1934].

50. Eliasoph (2011: ix).

51. "Empowerment Projects are supposed to blend different kinds of people and different kinds of organizations—civic association, state agency, nonprofit organization, family, and cultural tradition. Since funding is usually short-term, all of this blending has to happen flexibly, rapidly, and transparently, with documentation for multiple sources, each with a separate form. Organizers celebrate all this melting of stiff boundaries, finding it exciting and empowering. But the blending also produces tensions, as it is often hard to juggle this many different types of relationships all in one place, all at once—as the anger in the awards luncheon shows." Eliasoph (2011: 2).

52. Crozier (1964: 218, 226).

53. Per Crozier, "the arbitrary will of the ruler."

54. Crozier (1964: 222).

55. This dynamic resonates with the systems-and-crises imagery that has informed so much historical sociology, focused on the formation of regimes and the rupture of those regimes by revolution. Clemens (2005).

56. Shmuel Eisenstadt (1964: 235) described a similar path out of structural functionalism to the explanation of historical change: "the general 'predilections' to change inherent in any social system become 'concretized' or 'specified' through the process of institutionalization."

57. Following Putnam's (2000) influential analysis, connections between social capital and democratic politics are often made at the "input" side, in the relation between community networks and electoral participation. Civic benevolence draws attention to the "output" side, to the relationship between voluntarism and government agencies in the coproduction of public goods.

58. Both as scholars and practitioners, Ganz (2009) and Han (2014) offer new models for engaging social networks with political and advocacy campaigns. For a discussion of how municipal politics might provide opportunities for a new model of progressive politics, see Tani (2016).

59. "The Far-Reaching Influence of the Sanitary Commission," *Our Daily Fare* 5 (June 13, 1864): 36.

References

Abbott, Andrew. 2001. *Time Matters: On Theory and Method*. Chicago: University of Chicago Press.

Abzug, Robert H. 1994. *Cosmos Crumbling: American Reform and the Religious Imagination*. New York: Oxford University Press.

Adams, Christine. 2007. "In the Public Interest: Charitable Association, the State, and the Status of *utilité publique* in Nineteenth-Century France." *Law and History Review* 25 (2): 283–321.

Adams, Julia. 1996. "Principals and Agents, Colonialists and Company Men: The Decay of Colonial Control in the Dutch East Indies." *American Sociological Review* 61 (1): 12–28.

———. 2005. *The Familial State: Ruling Families and Merchant Capitalism in Early Modern Europe*. Ithaca, N.Y.: Cornell University Press.

Adler, William D. 2012. "State Capacity and Bureaucratic Autonomy in the Early U.S.: The Case of the Army Corps of Topographical Engineers." *Studies in American Political Development* 26 (2): 107–124.

Alchon, Guy. 1985. *The Invisible Hand of Planning: Capitalism, Social Science, and the State in the 1920s*. Princeton, N.J.: Princeton University Press.

Almond, Gabriel. (1938) 1998. *Plutocracy and Politics in New York City*. Boulder, Colo.: Westview Press.

Altshuler, Glenn C., and Stuart M. Blumin. 1997. "Limits of Political Engagement in Antebellum America: A New Look at the Golden Age of Participatory Democracy." *Journal of American History* 84 (3): 855–885.

Anderson, Benedict. (1983) 1991. *Imagined Communities: Reflections on the Origin and Spread of Nationalism*. London: Verso.

Appleby, Joyce. 1976. "Liberalism and the American Revolution." *New England Quarterly* 49 (1): 3–26.

———. 1994. "The Radical Recreation of the American Republic." *William and Mary Quarterly* 51 (4): 679–683.

———. 2000. *Inheriting the Revolution: The First Generation of Americans*. Cambridge, Mass.: Belknap/Harvard University Press.

Arendt, Hannah. (1963) 2006. *On Revolution*. New York: Penguin Books.

Armstrong, Elizabeth A. 2002. *Forging Gay Identities: Organizing Sexuality in San Francisco, 1950–1994*. Chicago: University of Chicago Press.

Ascoli, Peter Max. 2006. *Julius Rosenwald: The Man Who Built Sears, Roebuck and Advanced the Cause of Black Education in the American South*. Bloomington: Indiana University Press.

Attie, Jeanie. 1998. *Patriotic Toil: Northern Women and the American Civil War*. Ithaca, N.Y.: Cornell University Press.

Bailyn, Bernard. (1967) 1992. *Ideological Origins of the American Revolution*, enlarged ed. Cambridge, Mass.: Harvard University Press.

Baird, Robert. 1856. *Religion in America: Or, an Account of the Origin, Relation to the State, and Present Condition of the Evangelical Churches in the United States, with Notices of the Unevangelical Denominations*. New York: Harper & Brothers, Publishers.

Baker, Paula. 1991. *The Moral Frameworks of Public Life: Gender, Politics, and the State in Rural New York, 1870–1930*. New York: Oxford University Press.

Balogh, Brian. 2009. *"A Government Out of Sight": The Mystery of National Authority in Nineteenth-Century America*. New York: Cambridge University Press.

———. 2015. *The Associational State: American Governance in the Twentieth Century*. Philadelphia: University of Pennsylvania Press.

Banner, James M. 1988. "France and the Origins of American Political Culture." *Virginia Quarterly Review* 64 (4): 651–670. http://www.vqronline.org/essay/france-and-origins-american-political-culture (accessed January 22, 2016).

Banner, Lois W. 1973. "Religious Benevolence as Social Control: A Critique of an Interpretation." *Journal of American History* 60 (1): 23–41.

Barkey, Karen. 2008. *Empire of Difference: The Ottomans in Comparative Perspective*. New York: Cambridge University Press.

Barman, Emily. 2006. *Contesting Communities: The Transformation of Workplace Charity*. Stanford, Calif.: Stanford University Press.

Barry, John M. 1997. *Rising Tide: The Great Mississippi Flood of 1927 and How It Changed America*. New York: Simon and Schuster.

Beaver, Daniel R. 1966. *Newton D. Baker and the American War Effort, 1917–1919*. Lincoln: University of Nebraska Press.

Beckert, Sven. 2001. *The Monied Metropolis: New York City and the Consolidation of the American Bourgeoisie, 1850–1896*. New York: Cambridge University Press.

Beecher, Lyman. 1804. *The Practicability of Suppressing Vice, By Means of Societies Instituted for that Purpose: A Sermon Delivered before the Moral Society, in East-Hampton, (Long-Island), September 21, 1803*. New London, Conn: Green.

Beisel, Nicola Kay. 1997. *Imperiled Innocents: Anthony Comstock and Family Reproduction in Victorian America*. Princeton, N.J.: Princeton University Press.

Beito, David. 2000. *From Mutual Aid to the Welfare State: Fraternal Societies and Social Services, 1890–1967*. Chapel Hill: University of North Carolina Press.

Bellows, Barbara L. 1993. *Benevolence among Slaveholders: Assisting the Poor in Charleston, 1670–1860*. Baton Rouge: Louisiana State University Press.

Bellows, Henry W. 1879. *Historical Sketch of the Union League Club of New York, Its Origins, Organization, and Work, 1863–1879*. Union League Club House, printed by G. P. Putnam's Sons, New York.

Bensel, Richard. 1990. *Yankee Leviathan: The Origins of Central State Authority in America, 1859–1877*. New York: Cambridge University Press.

Berezin, Mabel. 2009. *Illiberal Politics in Neoliberal Times: Culture, Security and Populism in the New Europe*. New York: Cambridge University Press.

Berk, Gerald. 2009. *Louis D. Brandeis and the Making of Regulated Competition, 1900–1932*. New York: Cambridge University Press.

Berle, Adolf A., and Gardiner C. Means. 1932. *The Modern Corporation and Private Property*. New York: Macmillan.

Berman, Harold J. 1983. *Law and Revolution: The Formation of the Western Legal Tradition*. Cambridge, Mass.: Harvard University Press.

Berman, Sheri. 1997. "Civil Society and the Collapse of the Weimar Republic." *World Politics* 49 (3): 401–429.

Bernstein, Iver. 1990. *The New York City Draft Riots: Their Significance for American Society and Politics in the Age of the Civil War*. New York: Oxford University Press.

Berry, Jeffrey M., with David F. Arons. 2003. *A Voice for Nonprofits*. Washington, D.C.: Brookings Institution Press.

Bicknell, Ernest. 1935. *Pioneering with the Red Cross: Recollections of an Old Red Crosser*. New York: The Macmillan Company.

Blau, Joseph. 1946. "The Christian Party in Politics." *Review of Religion* 11 (November): 18–35.

Block, James E. 2007. "Agency and Popular Activism in American Political Culture." In *Formative Acts: American Politics in the Making*, edited by Stephen Skowronek and Matthew Glassman, 52–74. Philadelphia: University of Pennsylvania Press.

Bodnar, John. 1992. *Remaking America: Public Memory, Commemoration, and Patriotism in the Twentieth Century*. Princeton, N.J.: Princeton University Press.

Bookman, C. M. 1932. "The Cincinnati Community Chest." *Social Forces* 10 (4): 488–493.

Bourdieu, Pierre. 2014. *On the State: Lectures at the Collège de France, 1989–1992*. Cambridge, U.K.: Polity.

Boyer, Paul. 1978. *Urban Masses and Moral Order in America, 1820–1920*. Cambridge, Mass.: Harvard University Press.

Boynton, Charles Brandon. 1864. *History of the Great Western Sanitary Fair*. Cincinnati, Ohio: C.F. Vent & Co.

Bratt, James D. 2001. "From Revivalism to Anti-Revivalism to Whig Politics: The Strange Career of Calvin Colton." *Journal of Ecclesiastical History* 1: 63–82.

———. 2004. "Religious Anti-Revivalism in Antebellum America." *Journal of the Early Republic* 24 (1): 65–106.

———, ed. 2006. *Antirevivalism in Antebellum America: A Collection of Religious Voices*. New Brunswick, N.J.: Rutgers University Press.

Breen, T. H. 2004. *The Marketplace of Revolution*. New York: Oxford University Press.

———. 2010. *American Insurgents, American Patriots: The Revolution of the People*. New York: Hill and Wang.

Bremner, Robert H. (1960) 1982. *American Philanthropy*. Chicago: University of Chicago Press.

Brewer, John. 1988. *The Sinews of Power: War, Money, and the English State, 1688–1783*. New York: Alfred A. Knopf.

Bridges, Amy Beth. 1982. "Another Look at Plutocracy and Politics in Antebellum New York City." *Political Science Quarterly* 97 (1): 57–71.

———. 1984. *City in the Republic: Antebellum New York and the Origins of Machine Politics*. New York: Cambridge University Press.

Bristow, Nancy K. 1996. *Making Men Moral: Social Engineering during the Great War*. New York: New York University Press.

Brockett, Linus Pierpont. 1863. *The Philanthropic Results of The War In America, Collected from Official and Other Authentic Sources, by An American Citizen*. New York: Press of Wynkoop, Hallenbeck & Thomas.

Brockett, L. P., and Mrs. Mary C. Vaughan. 1888. *Heroines of the Rebellion; or, Woman's Work in the Civil War: A Record of Heroism, Patriotism, and Patience*. Philadelphia: Hubbard Brothers.

Brooke, John L. 1996. "Ancient Lodges and Self-Created Societies: Voluntary Association and the Public Sphere in the Early Republic." In *Launching the "Extended Republic": The Federalist Era*, edited by Ronald Hoffman and Peter J. Albert, 273–377. Charlottesville: University Press of Virginia.

———. 2009. "Cultures of Nationalism, Movements of Reform, and the Composite-Federal Policy: From Revolutionary Settlement to Antebellum Crisis." *Journal of the Early Republic* 29 (1): 1–33.

Brown, Maoz. 2018. "Cooperation, Coordination, and Control: The Emergence and Decline of Centralized Finance in American Charity." *Social Science History* 42 (Fall): 543–573.

Brown, Robert E. 1952. "Democracy in Colonial Massachusetts." *New England Quarterly* 25 (3): 291–313.

Brubaker, Rogers. 1996. *Nationalism Reframed: Nationhood and the National Question in the New Europe*. New York: Cambridge University Press.

———. 2005. "Ethnicity without Groups." In *Remaking Modernity: Politics, History, and Sociology*, edited by Julia Adams, Elisabeth S. Clemens, and Ann Shola Orloff, 470–492. Durham, N.C.: Duke University Press.

Burke, Edmund. 1993. *Reflections on the Revolution in France*. New York: Oxford University Press.

Burner, David. 1979. *Herbert Hoover: A Public Life*. New York: Alfred A. Knopf.

Calhoun, Craig. 1993. "Nationalism and Ethnicity." *Annual Review of Sociology* 19: 211–239.

———. 2007. "Nationalism and Cultures of Democracy." *Public Culture* 19 (1): 151–173.

Callahan, David. 2017. *The Givers: Wealth, Power, and Philanthropy in a New Gilded Age*. New York: Knopf.

Callen, Zachary. 2016. *Railroads and American Political Development: Infrastructure, Federalism, and State-Building*. Lawrence: University Press of Kansas.

Campbell, Bruce A. 1990. "Social Federalism: The Constitutional Position of Nonprofit Corporations in Nineteenth-Century America." *Law and History Review* 8 (2): 149–188.

Campbell, Persia. 1944. "Volunteers in Public Administration: A Case Study." *Public Administration Review* 4 (2): 108–112.

Capozzola, Christopher. 2008. *Uncle Sam Wants You: World War I and the Making of the Modern American Citizen*. New York: Oxford University Press.

Carruthers, Bruce G. 1996. *City of Capital: Politics and Markets in the English Financial Revolution*. Princeton, N.J.: Princeton University Press.

Carruthers, Bruce G., and Laura Ariovich. 2010. *Money and Credit: A Sociological Approach*. Cambridge: Polity.

Carwardine, Richard. 1972. "The Second Great Awakening in the Urban Centers: An Examination of Methodism and the 'New Measures.'" *Journal of American History* 59 (2): 327–340.

———. 1983. "Evangelicals, Whigs and the Election of William Henry Harrison." *Journal of American Studies* 17 (1): 47–75.

Cates, Jerry R. 1983. *Insuring Inequality: Administrative Leadership in Social Security, 1935–54*. Ann Arbor: University of Michigan Press.

Channing, William Ellery. (1829) 1858. "Remarks on Associations." Boston: Cosby, Nichols, and Company. Reprinted in *The Works of William E. Channing, D.D.*, 12th ed., vol. 1. New York: C. S. Francis and Company.

Charles, Jeffrey A. 1993. *Service Clubs in American Society: Rotary, Kiwanis, and Lions*. Urbana: University of Illinois Press.

Clemens, Elisabeth S. 1997. *The People's Lobby: Organizational Innovation and the Rise of Interest Group Politics in the United States, 1890–1925*. Chicago: University of Chicago Press.

———. 2005. "Logics of History? Agency, Multiplicity, and Incoherence in the Explanation of Change." In *Remaking Modernity: Politics and Processes in Historical Sociology*, edited by Julia Adams, Elisabeth S. Clemens, and Ann Shola Orloff, 493–514. Durham, N.C.: Duke University Press.

———. 2006. "Lineages of the Rube Goldberg State: Building and Blurring Public Programs, 1900–1940." In *The Art of the State: Rethinking Political Institutions*, edited by Ian Shapiro, Stephen Skowronek, and Daniel Galvin, 187–215. New York: New York University Press.

———. 2007. "Toward a Historicized Sociology: Theorizing Events, Processes, and Emergence." *Annual Review of Sociology* 33: 527–549.

———. 2009. "The Problem of the Corporation: Liberalism and the Large Organization." In *Handbook of Organizational Studies and Classical Social Theory*, edited by Paul Adler. New York: Oxford University Press.

———. 2010a. "From City Club to Nation State: Business Networks in American Political Development." *Theory and Society* 39 (1): 377–396.

———. 2010b. "In the Shadow of the New Deal: Reconfiguring the Roles of Government and Charity, 1928–1940." In *Politics and Partnerships: Voluntary Associations in America's Political Past and Present*, edited by Elisabeth Clemens and Doug Guthrie, 79–115. Chicago: University of Chicago Press.

———. 2015. "Organizing Powers in Eventful Times." *Social Science History* 30 (1): 1–24.

———. 2017a. "Dynamics of Nation-Building: Benevolence and Liberalism in American Political Development." In *Dynamics of Continuity, Patterns of Change: Between World History and Comparative Historical Sociology*, edited by Benjamin Z. Kedar, Adam Kin-Oron, and Ilana Friedrich Silber, 129–151. Jerusalem: Israel Academy of Sciences and Humanities and the Jerusalem Van Leer Institute.

———. 2017b. "Reconciling Equal Treatment with Respect for Individuality: Associations in the Symbiotic State." In *The Many Hands of the State*, edited by Kimberly Morgan and Ann Shola Orloff, 35–57. New York: Cambridge University Press.

Clemens, Elisabeth S., and James Cook. 1999. "Politics and Institutionalism: Explaining Durability and Change." *Annual Review of Sociology* 25: 441–466.

Cohen, Adam. 2009. *Nothing to Fear: FDR's Inner Circle and the Hundred Days that Created Modern America*. New York: Penguin Press.

Cohen, Lizabeth. 1990. *Making a New Deal: Industrial Workers in Chicago, 1919–1939*. Chicago: University of Chicago Press.

Coit, Margaret L. 1957. *Mr. Baruch*. Boston: Houghton Mifflin.

Colley, Linda. 1992. *Britons: Forging the Nation 1707–1837*. New Haven, Conn.: Yale University Press.

Collins, Randall. 1980. "Weber's Last Theory of Capitalism: A Systematization." *American Sociological Review* 45 (6): 925–942.

Cooper, John Milton, Jr. 2009. *Woodrow Wilson: A Biography*. New York: Vintage.

Courtis, John K. 1983. "Business Goodwill: Conceptual Clarification via Accounting, Legal and Etymological Perspectives." *Accounting Historians Journal* 10 (2): 1–38.

Cramer, Clarence H. 1961. *Newton D. Baker: A Biography*. Cleveland: World Publishing Company.

Crawford, Sue E. S., and Elinor Ostrom. 1995. "A Grammar of Institutions." *American Political Science Review* 89 (3): 582–600.

Crenson, Matthew A. 1998. *Building the Invisible Orphanage: A Prehistory of the American Welfare System*. Cambridge, Mass.: Harvard University Press.

Critchlow, Donald T., and Charles H. Parker, eds. 1998. *With Us Always: A History of Private Charity and Public Welfare*. Lanham, Md.: Rowman & Littlefield.

Cross, Robert D. 1961. "The Philanthropic Contribution of Louisa Lee Schuyler." *Social Service Review* 35 (3): 290–301.

Crozier, Michel. 1964. *The Bureaucratic Phenomenon*. Chicago: University of Chicago Press.

Cuff, Robert D. 1970. "Newton D. Baker, Frank A. Scott, and 'The American Reinforcement in the World War.'" *Military Affairs* 34 (1): 11–13.

———. 1973. *The War Industries Board: Business-Government Relations during World War I*. Baltimore, Md.: The Johns Hopkins University Press.

———. 1977. "Herbert Hoover, The Ideology of Voluntarism and War Organization during the Great War." *Journal of American History* 64 (2): 358–372.

Cutlip, Scott M. 1965. *Fund Raising in the United States: Its Role in America's Philanthropy*. New Brunswick, N.J.: Rutgers University Press.

Dahl, Robert A. 1961. *Who Governs? Democracy and Power in an American City*. New Haven, Conn.: Yale University Press.

Dalzell, Robert F., Jr. 1987. *Enterprising Elite: The Boston Associates and the World They Made*. Cambridge, Mass.: Harvard University Press.

Dauber, Michelle Landis. 2013. *The Sympathetic State: Disaster Relief and the Origins of the American Welfare State*. Chicago: University of Chicago Press.

Davies, Andrea Rees. 2011. *Saving San Francisco: Relief and Recovery after the 1906 Disaster*. Philadelphia: Temple University Press.

Davis, Allen F. 1967. *Spearheads for Reform: The Social Settlements and the Progressive Movement, 1890–1914*. New York: Oxford University Press.

Davis, Allison, Burleigh Gardner, and Mary Gardner. 1941. *Deep South: A Social Anthropological Study of Caste and Class*. Chicago: University of Chicago Press.

Davis, David Brion. 1960. "Some Themes of Counter-Subversion: An Analysis of Anti-Masonic, Anti-Catholic, and Anti-Mormon Literature." *Mississippi Valley Historical Review* 47 (2): 205–224.

De Leon, Cedric. 2015. *The Origins of the Right to Work*. Ithaca, N.Y.: Cornell University Press.

De Tocqueville, Alexis. (1856) 1955. *The Old Regime and the French Revolution*. New York: Doubleday.

———. (1839) 2004. *Democracy in America*. Washington, D.C.: Library of America.

Dewey, John. 1984. *Individualism Old and New*. Amherst, N.Y.: Prometheus Books.

DiMaggio, Paul J. 1991. "Constructing an Organizational Field as a Professional Project: U.S. Art Museums, 1920–1940." In *The New Institutionalism in Organizational Analysis*, edited by Walter W. Powell and Paul J. DiMaggio, 267–292. Chicago: University of Chicago Press.

DiMaggio, Paul J., and Walter W. Powell. 1983. "The Iron Cage Revisited: Institutional Isomorphism and Collective Rationality in Organizational Fields." *American Sociological Review* 48: 147–160.

Dionne, E. J., Jr. 2012. *Our Divided Political Heart: The Battle for the American Idea in an Age of Discontent*. New York: Bloomsbury.

Domhoff, G. William. 1974. *The Bohemian Grove and Other Retreats: A Study in Ruling-Class Cohesiveness*. New York: Harper and Row.

———. 1996. *State Autonomy or Class Dominance? Case Studies on Policy Making in America*. New York: Aldine de Gruyter.

Dorsey, Bruce. 1998. "Friends Becoming Enemies: Philadelphia Benevolence and the Neglected Era of American Quaker History." *Journal of the Early Republic* 18 (3): 395–428.

Douglas, Mary. 1966. *Purity and Danger: An Analysis of the Concepts of Pollution and Taboo*. London: Ark.

———. 1986. *How Institutions Think*. Syracuse, N.Y.: Syracuse University Press.

Douglas, Paul H. 1920a. "A System of Federal Grants-in-Aid I." *Political Science Quarterly* 35 (2): 255 271.

———. 1920b. "A System of Federal Grants-in-Aid II." *Political Science Quarterly* 35 (4): 522–544.

DuBois, W. E. B. (1903) 1994. *The Souls of Black Folk*. New York: Dover.

Duffy, John. 1968. *History of Public Health in New York City, 1625–1866*, vol. 1. New York: Russell Sage Foundation.

Dulles, Foster Rhea. 1950. *The American Red Cross*. New York: Harper and Brothers.

Eckstein, Susan. 2001. "Community as Gift-giving: Collectivist Roots of Voluntarism." *American Sociological Review* 66 (6): 829–851.

Edling, Max. 2008. *A Revolution in Favor of Government*. New York: Oxford University Press.

Edwards, Martha L. 1919. "Religious Forces in the United States, 1815–1830." *Mississippi Valley Historical Review* 5 (4): 434–449.

Eifert, Christiane. 1997. "Coming to Terms with the State: Maternalist Politics and the Development of the Welfare State in Weimar Germany." *Central European History* 30 (1): 25–47.

Einhorn, Robin L. 1991. *Property Rules: Political Economy in Chicago, 1833–1872*. Chicago: University of Chicago Press.

———. 2006. *American Taxation, American Slavery*. Chicago: University of Chicago Press.

Eisenstadt, Shmuel. 1963. *The Political Systems of Empires*. New York: Free Press of Glencoe.

———. 1964. "Institutionalization and Change." *American Sociological Review* 29 (2): 235–247.

Eisner, Marc Allen. 2000. *From Warfare State to Welfare State: World War I, Compensatory State Building, and the Limits of the Modern Order*. University Park: The Pennsylvania State University Press.

Eley, Geoff, and Ronald Grigor Suny, eds. 1996. *Becoming National: A Reader*. New York: Oxford.

Elfenbein, Jessica I. 2001. *The Making of a Modern City: Philanthropy, Civic Culture, and the Baltimore YMCA*. Gainesville: University Press of Florida.

Eliade, Mircea. 1959. *The Sacred and the Profane: The Nature of Religion*. New York: Harcourt, Brace and World.

Eliasoph, Nina. 1998. *Avoiding Politics: How Americans Produce Apathy in Everyday Life*. New York: Cambridge University Press.

———. 2011. *Making Volunteers: Civic Life after Welfare's End*. Princeton, N.J.: Princeton University Press.

Elkins, Stanley, and Eric McKitrick. 1993. *The Age of Federalism: The Early American Republic, 1788–1800*. New York: Oxford University Press.

Ellis, Mark. 1992. " 'Closing Ranks' and 'Seeking Honors': W.E.B. Du Bois in World War I." *Journal of American History* 79 (1): 96–124.

Erie, Steven P. 1988. *Rainbow's End: Irish-Americans and the Dilemmas of Urban Machine Politics, 1840–1985*. Berkeley: University of California Press.

Evans, Peter. 1995. *Embedded Autonomy: States and Industrial Transformation*. Princeton, N.J.: Princeton University Press.

Evans, Peter, and James E. Rauch. 1999. "Bureaucracy and Growth: A Cross-National Analysis of the Effects of 'Weberian' State Structures on Economic Growth." *American Sociological Review* 65 (5): 748–765.

Evans, Rhonda, and Tamara Kay. 2008. "How Environmentalists 'Greened' Trade Policy: Strategic Action and the Architecture of Field Overlap." *American Sociological Review* 73 (6): 970–991.

Faust, Drew. 1988. *The Creation of Confederate Nationalism: Ideology and Identity in the Civil War South*. Baton Rouge: Louisiana State University Press.

Finegold, Kenneth. 1995. *Experts and Politicians: Reform Challenges to Machine Politics in New York, Cleveland, and Chicago*. Princeton, N.J.: Princeton University Press.

Fischer, David Hackett. 1989. *Albion's Seed: Four British Folkways in America*. New York: Oxford University Press.

Fisher, Claude S. 2010. *Made in America: A Social History of American Culture and Character*. Chicago: University of Chicago Press.

Fisher, Edmund Crisp. 1864. *Military Discipline and Volunteer Philanthropy*. A Paper read before the Social Science Congress held in the City of New York During the month of September, 1864. London: William Ridgway, 169 Picadilly.

Fiske, Alan Page. 1992. "The Four Elementary Forms of Sociality: Framework for a Unified Theory of Social Relations." *Psychological Review* 99 (4): 689–723.

Fitzgerald, Maureen. 2006. *Habits of Compassion: Irish Catholic Nuns and the Origins of New York's Welfare System*. Urbana: University of Illinois Press.

Fitzgerald, Michael S. 1996. "Rejecting Calhoun's Expansible Army Plan: The Army Reduction Act of 1821." *War in History* 3 (2): 161–185.

Fligstein, Neil. 2001. "Social Skill and the Theory of Fields." *Sociological Theory* 19 (2): 105–125.

Fligstein, Neil, and Doug McAdam. 2012. *A Theory of Fields*. New York: Oxford University Press.

Follett, Mary Parker. 1998 [1918]. *The New State: Group Organization The Solution of Popular Government*. University Park: Pennsylvania University Press.

Fones-Wolf, Elizabeth A. 1994. *Selling Free Enterprise: The Business Assault on Labor and Liberalism, 1945–60*. Urbana: University of Illinois Press.

Formisano, Ronald P. 1974. "Deferential-Participant Politics: The Early Republic's Political Culture, 1789–1840." *American Political Science Review* 68 (2): 473–487.

———. 1999. "The 'Party Period' Revisited." *Journal of American History* 86 (1): 93–120.

Formisano, Ronald P., and Kathleen Smith Kutolowski. 1977. "Antimasonry and Masonry: The Genesis of Protest, 1826–1827." *American Quarterly* 29 (2): 139–165.

Fosdick, Raymond. 1958. *Chronicle of a Generation: An Autobiography*. New York: Harper and Brothers Publishers.

Foucault, Michel. 2010. *The Birth of Biopolitics: Lectures at the Collège de France, 1978–1979*. New York: Picador.

Fox, Bonnie R. 1969. "Unemployment Relief in Philadelphia, 1930–1932: A Study of the Depression's Impact on Voluntarism." *Pennsylvania Magazine of History of Biography* 93 (1): 86–108.

Fox, Cybelle. 2012. *Three Worlds of Relief: Race, Immigration and the American Welfare State from the Progressive Era to the New Deal*. Princeton, N.J.: Princeton University Press.

Frederickson, George M. 1965. *The Inner Civil War: Northern Intellectuals and the Crisis of the Union*. New York: Harper Torchbooks.

Friedland, Roger, and Robert Alford. 1991. "Bringing Society Back In: Symbols, Practices, and Institutional Contradictions." In *The New Institutionalism in Organizational Analysis*, edited by Walter W. Powell and Paul J. DiMaggio, 232–266. Chicago: University of Chicago Press.

Friedman, Lawrence J., 2003. "Philanthropy in America: Historicism and Its Discontents." In *Charity, Philanthropy, and Civility in American History*, edited by Lawrence J. Friedman and Mark D. McGarvie, 1–27. New York: Cambridge University Press.

Frost, Wladislava S. 1944. "Cities and Towns Mobilize for War." *American Sociological Review* 9 (1): 85–89.

Frothingham, Octavius Brooks. 1863. *The morality of the riot: Sermon of Rev. O.B. Frothingham, at Ebbitt Hall, Sunday, July 19, 1863*. New York: David G. Francis.

Frug, Gerald E. 1980. "The City as A Legal Concept." *Harvard Law Review* 93 (6): 1059–1154.

Fourcade, Marion, Brian Lande, and Evan Shofer. 2016. "Political Space and the Space of Polities: Doing Politics across Nations." *Poetics* 55: 1–18.

Fussell, Paul. 1989. *Wartime: Understanding and Behavior in the Second World War*. New York: Oxford University Press.

Gaddis, Vincent. 2005. *Herbert Hoover, Unemployment, and the Public Sphere: A Conceptual History, 1919–1933*. Lanham: University Press of America.

Gallagher, Gary W. 2011. *The Union War*. Cambridge, Mass.: Harvard University Press.

Ganz, Marshall. 2009. *Why David Sometimes Wins: Leadership, Organization, and Strategy in the California Farm Worker Movement*. New York: Oxford University Press.

Garrison, Nancy Scripture. 1999. *With Courage and Delicacy: Civil War on the Peninsula; Women and the U.S. Sanitary Commission*. Mason City, Iowa: Savas Publishing Company.

Geiger, Roger. 1985. "After the Emergence: Voluntary Support and the Building of American Research Universities." *History of Education Quarterly* 25 (3): 369–381.

Geisberg, Judith. 2009. *Army at Home: Women and the Civil War on the Northern Home Front*. Chapel Hill: University of North Carolina Press.

Gerstle, Gary. 2001. *American Crucible: Race and Nation in the Twentieth Century*. Princeton, N.J.: Princeton University Press.

Geva, Dorit. 2011. "Different and Unequal? Breadwinning, Dependency Deferments, and the Gendered Origins of the United States Selective Service System." *Armed Forces & Society* 37: 598–618.

———. 2015. "Selective Service, the Gender-Ordered Family, and the Rational Informality of the American State." *American Journal of Sociology* 121 (1): 171–204.

Gieryn, Thomas F. 1983. "Boundary-Work and the Demarcation of Science from Non-science: Strains and Interests in Professional Ideologies of Scientists." *American Sociological Review* 48 (6): 781–795.

Gilbo, Patrick F. 1981. *The American Red Cross: The First Century*. New York: Harper and Row.

Giridharadas, Anand. 2018. *Winners Take All: The Elite Charade of Changing the World*. New York: Knopf.

Godbout, Jacques T., in collaboration with Alain Caillé. 1998. *The World of the Gift*. Translated by Donald Winkler. Montreal: McGill-Queen's University Press.

Godelier, Maurice. 1999. *The Enigma of the Gift*. Translated by Nora Scott. Chicago: University of Chicago Press.

Goldberg, Chad. 2007. *Citizens and Paupers: Relief, Rights, and Race, from the Freedmen's Bureau to Workfare*. Chicago: University of Chicago Press.

Goodheart, Adam. 2011. *1861: The Civil War Awakening*. New York: Vintage Books.

Gorski, Philip S. 2003. *The Disciplinary Revolution: Calvinism and the Rise of the State in Early Modern Europe*. Chicago: University of Chicago Press.

Gould, Roger V. 1996. "Patron-Client Ties, State Centralization, and the Whiskey Rebellion." *American Journal of Sociology* 102 (2): 400–429.

Gouldner, Alvin W. 1960. "The Norm of Reciprocity: A Preliminary Statement." *American Sociological Review* 25 (2): 161–178.

Grant, Bruce. 1955. *Fight for a City: The Story of the Union League Club of Chicago and Its Times, 1880–1995*. Chicago: Rand McNally.

Greeley, Dawn. 1995. "Beyond Benevolence: Gender, Class and the Development of Scientific Charity in New York City, 1882–1935." PhD diss., SUNY-Stonybrook.

Greenfeld, Liah. 1992. *Nationalism: Five Roads to Modernity*. Cambridge, Mass.: Harvard University Press.

Griffin, Clifford S. 1959. "The Abolitionists and the Benevolent Societies, 1831–1861." *Journal of Negro History* 44 (3): 195–216.

———. 1960. "Cooperation and Conflict: The Schism in the American Home Missionary Society, 1837–1861." *Journal of the Presbyterian Historical Society* 38 (4): 213–233.

Grinspan, Jon. 2009. "'Young Men for War': The Wide Awakes and Lincoln's 1860 Presidential Campaign." *Journal of American History* 96 (2): 357–378.

Gross, Robert A. 2003. "Giving in America: From Charity to Philanthropy." In *Charity, Philanthropy, and Civility in American History*, edited by Lawrence J. Friedman and Mark D. McGarvie, 29–48. New York: Cambridge University Press.

Guglielmo, Thomas A. 2010. "'Red Cross, Double Cross': Race and America's World War II-Era Blood Donor Service." *Journal of American History* 97 (June): 63–90.

Gutmann, Amy, ed. 1998. *Freedom of Association.* Princeton, N.J.: Princeton University Press.

Hacker, Jacob S. 2002. *The Divided Welfare State: The Battle over Public and Private Social Benefits in the United States.* New York: Cambridge University Press.

Hall, Peter Dobkin. 1982. *The Organization of American Culture, 1700–1900: Private Institutions, Elites, and the Origins of American Nationality.* New York: New York University Press.

———. 2010. "Rediscovering the Bourgeoisie: Higher Education and Governing-Class Formation in the United States, 1870–1914." In *The American Bourgeoisie: Distinction and Identity in the Nineteenth Century*, edited by Sven Beckert and Julia B. Rosenbaum, 167–189. New York: Palgrave Macmillan.

Hamilton, David E. 1982. "Herbert Hoover and the Great Drought of 1930." *Journal of American History* 68 (4): 853–855.

Hammack, David C. 2003. "Failure and Resilience: Pushing the Limits in Depression and Wartime." In *Charity, Philanthropy, and Civility in American History*, edited by Lawrence J. Friedman and Mark D. McGarvie, 263–280. New York: Cambridge University Press.

Han, Hahrie. 2014. *How Organizations Develop Activists: Civic Associations and Leadership in the 21st Century.* New York: Oxford University Press.

Harris, Marc L. 1993. "Revelation and the American Republic: Timothy Dwight's Civic Participation." *Journal of the History of Ideas* 54 (3): 449–468.

———. 1995. "'Cement to the Union': The Society of the Cincinnati and the Limits of Fraternal Sociability." *Proceedings of the Massachusetts Historical Society* 107: 115–140.

Hartog, Hendrik. 1983. *Public Property and Private Power: The Corporation of the City of New York in American Law, 1730–1870.* Chapel Hill: University of North Carolina Press.

Harwood, James Glenn. 2002. "Religiously-Based Social Security Exemptions: Who Is Eligible, How Did They Develop, and Are the Exemptions Consistent with the Religion Clauses and the Religious Freedom Restoration Act (RFRA)?" *Akron Tax Journal* 17: 1.

Haselby, Sam. 2015. *The Origins of American Religious Nationalism.* New York: Oxford University Press.

Hatch, Nathan O. 1989. *The Democratization of American Christianity.* New Haven, Conn.: Yale University Press.

Haveman, Heather A. 2015. *Magazines and the Making of America: Modernization, Community, and Print Culture, 1741–1860*. Princeton, N.J.: Princeton University Press.

Haviland, Margaret Morris. 1994. "Beyond Women's Sphere: Young Quaker Women and the Veil of Charity in Philadelphia, 1790–1810." *William and Mary Quarterly* 51 (3): 419–446.

Hawley, Ellis W. 1974. "Herbert Hoover, the Commerce Secretariat, and the Vision of an 'Associative State,' 1921–1928." *Journal of American History* 61 (1): 116–140.

———. 1998. "Herbert Hoover, Associationalism, and the Great Depression Relief Crisis of 1930–33." In *With Us Always: A History of Private Charity and Public Welfare,* edited by Donald T. Critchlow and Charles H. Parker, 161–190. Lanham, Md.: Rowman & Littlefield.

Haydu, Jeffrey. 1998. "Making Use of the Past: Time Periods as Cases to Compare and as Sequences of Problem Solving." *American Journal of Sociology* 104 (2): 339–371.

———. 2008. *Citizen Employers: Business Communities and Labor in Cincinnati and San Francisco, 1870–1916*. Ithaca, New York: Cornell University Press.

Hayek, Friedrich A. 1948. *Individualism and Economic Order*. Chicago: University of Chicago Press.

Heale, M. J. 1976. "From City Fathers to Social Critics: Humanitarianism and Government in New York, 1790–1860." *Journal of American History* 63 (1): 21–41.

Healey, Kieran. 2000. "Embedded Altruism: Blood Collection Regimes and the European Union's Donor Population." *American Journal of Sociology* 105 (6): 1633–1657.

Hendrickson, Mark. 2013. *American Labor and Economic Citizenship: New Capitalism from World War I to the Great Depression*. New York: Cambridge University Press.

Herring, George C., Jr. 1964. "James Hay and the Preparedness Controversy, 1915–1916." *Journal of Southern History* 30 (4): 383–404.

Herzog, Jonathan P. 2011. *The Spiritual-Industrial Complex: America's Religious Battle against Communism in the Early Cold War*. New York: Oxford University Press.

Higham, John. 1974. "Hanging Together: Divergent Unities in American History." *Journal of American History* 61 (1): 5–28.

Hillman, Arthur. 1946. "A Federal Agency's Relation to Community Planning." *Social Forces* 25 (2): 183–189.

Hobsbawm, Eric, and Terence Ranger, eds. 1983. *The Invention of Tradition*. Cambridge: Cambridge University Press.

Hoey, Jane M. 1942. "Civilian Assistance Related to Wartime Needs." *Compass* 24 (1): 12–13.

Holt, Michael F. 1999. *The Rise and Fall of the American Whig Party: Jacksonian Politics and the Onset of the Civil War*. New York: Oxford University Press.

Hoover, Herbert. 1923. *American Individualism*. New York: Doubleday, Page & Company.

———. 1936. *American Ideals versus the New Deal: A Series of Ten Addresses upon Pressing National Problems*. New York: The Scribner Press.

Hopkins, Harry L. 1936. *Spending to Save: The Complete Story of Relief*. New York: W.W. Norton & Co.

Hopkins, June. 1999. *Harry Hopkins: Sudden Hero, Brash Reformer*. New York: St. Martin's Press.

Howe, Daniel Walker. 1979. *The Political Culture of the American Whigs*. Chicago: University of Chicago Press.

———. 2007. *What Hath God Wrought: The Transformation of America, 1815–1848*. New York: Oxford University Press.

Howe, Samuel Gridley. 1862. *Letter to Mrs. _____, and other Loyal Women, Touching the Matter of Contributions for the Army, and Other Matters Connected with the War*. Boston: Ticknor & Fields.

Huntington, Samuel P. 1968. *Political Order in Changing Societies*. New Haven, Conn.: Yale University Press.

Ikegami, Eiko. 1995. *The Taming of the Samurai: Honorific Individualism and the Making of Modern Japan*. Cambridge, Mass.: Harvard University Press.

Immergut, Ellen. 1990. "Institutions, Veto Points, and Policy Results: A Comparative Analysis of Health Care." *Journal of Public Policy* 10 (4): 391–416.

Jacoby, Sanford M. 1997. *Modern Manors: Welfare Capitalism since the New Deal*. Princeton, N.J.: Princeton University Press.

James, Erica, ed. 2019. *Governing Gifts: Faith, Charity, and the Security State*. Santa Fe, N.M.: School for Advanced Research Press.

Jeffrey, Julie Roy. 1998. *The Great Silent Army of Abolitionism: Ordinary Women in the Antislavery Movement*. Chapel Hill: University of North Carolina Press.

John, Richard R. 1990. "Taking Sabbatarianism Seriously: The Postal System, the Sabbath, and the Transformation of American Political Culture." *Journal of the Early Republic* 10 (4): 517–567.

———. 1997. "Hiland Hall's 'Report on Incendiary Publications': A Forgotten Nineteenth Century Defense of the Constitutional Guarantee of the Freedom of the Press." *American Journal of Legal History* 41 (1): 94–125.

———. 2008. "Rethinking the Early American State." *Polity* 40 (3): 332–339.

Jones, Gareth Stedman. 1971. *Outcast London: A Study in the Relationship between Classes in Victorian Society*. Oxford: Clarendon Press/Oxford University Press.

Jones, Gene Delon. 1974. "The Origin of the Alliance between the New Deal and the Chicago Machine." *Journal of the Illinois State Historical Society* 67 (4): 253–274.

———. 1990. "The Chicago Catholic Charities, the Great Depression, and Public Monies." *Illinois Historical Journal* 83 (1): 13–30.

Jones, John Price. 1954. *The American Giver: A Review of American Generosity*. New York: Inter-River Press.

Joyce, Patrick, and Chandra Mukerji. 2017. "The State of Things: State History and Theory Reconfigured." *Theory and Society* 46: 1–19.

Kaplan, Barry J. 1978. "Reformers and Charity: The Abolition of Public Outdoor Relief in New York City, 1870–1898." *Social Service Review* 52 (2): 202–214.

Karl, Barry. 1998. "Volunteers and Professionals: Many Histories, Many Meanings." In *Private Action and the Public Good*, edited by Walter W. Powell and Elisabeth S. Clemens, 245–257. New Haven, Conn.: Yale University Press.

Katz, Michael B. 1986. *In the Shadow of the Poorhouse: A Social History of Welfare in America*. New York: Basic Books.

Katznelson, Ira. 1982. *City Trenches: Urban Politics and the Patterning of Class in the United States*. Chicago: University of Chicago Press.

———. 2002. "Flexible Capacity: The Military and Early American State-Building." In *Shaped by War and Trade: International Influences on American Political Development*, edited by Ira Katznelson and Martin Shefter. Princeton, N.J.: Princeton University Press.

Kaufman, Jason. 2003. *For the Common Good? American Civic Life and the Golden Age of Fraternity*. New York: Oxford University Press.

———. 2008. "Corporate Law and the Sovereignty of States." *American Sociological Review* 73 (3): 402–425.

Keith, Jeanette. 2001. "The Politics of Southern Draft Resistance, 1917–1918: Class, Race, and Conscription in the Rural South." *Journal of American History* 87 (4): 1335–1361.

Kellogg, Katherine. 2009. "Operating Room: Relational Spaces and Micro-institutional Change in Surgery." *American Journal of Sociology* 115 (3): 657–711.

Kerber, Linda K. 1980. *Women of the Republic: Intellect and Ideology in Revolutionary America*. Chapel Hill: University of North Carolina Press.

Kestnbaum, Meyer. 2005. "Mars Revealed: The Entry of Ordinary People into War among States." In *Remaking Modernity: History, Politics and Sociology*, edited by Julia Adams, Elisabeth S. Clemens, and Ann Shola Orloff, 249–285. Durham, N.C.: Duke University Press.

Keyssar, Alexander. 2000. *The Right to Vote: The Contested History of Democracy in the United States*. New York: Basic Books.

Khan, Shamus. 2012. "The Sociology of Elites." *Annual Review of Sociology* 38: 364–365.

Kiser, Edgar, and Xiaoxi Tong. 1992. "Determinants of the Amount and Type of Corruption in State Fiscal Bureaucracies: An Analysis of Late Imperial China." *Comparative Political Studies* 25 (3): 300–331.

Kloppenberg, James T. 1987. "The Virtues of Liberalism: Christianity, Republicanism, and Ethics in Early American Political Discourse." *Journal of American History* 74 (June): 9–33.

Kolko, Gabriel. 1967. *The Triumph of Conservatism: A Reinterpretation of American History, 1900–1916*. Chicago: Quadrangle Books.

Kosar, Kevin R. 2006. *The Congressional Charter of the American National Red Cross: Overview, History, and Analysis*. U.S. Congressional Research Service 6 (March 15).

————. 2011. *The Quasi Government: Hybrid Organizations with Both Government and Private Sector Legal Characteristics*. U.S. Congressional Research Service (June 22).

Koschnik, Albrecht. 2000. "Fashioning a Federalist Self: Young Men and Voluntary Association in Early Nineteenth-Century Philadelphia." *Explorations in Early American Culture* 4: 220–257.

————. 2007. *"Let a Common Interest Bind Us Together": Associations, Partisanship, and Culture in Philadelphia, 1775–1840.* Charlottesville: University of Virginia Press.

Kroneberg, Clemens, and Andreas Wimmer. 2012. "Struggling over the Boundaries of Belonging: A Formal Model of Nation Building, Ethnic Closure, and Populism." *American Journal of Sociology* 188 (1): 176–230.

Kropotkin, Peter. (1896) 2015. *The Conquest of Bread*. Penguin Books.

Lainer-Vos, Dan. 2013. "The Practical Organization of Moral Transactions: Gift Giving, Market Exchange, Credit, and the Making of Diaspora Bonds." *Sociological Theory* 31 (2): 145–167.

Lamont, Michèle, and Virag Molnár. 2002. "The Study of Boundaries in the Social Sciences." *Annual Review of Sociology* 28: 167–195.

Lancaster, Ryon Andrew. 2005. "The Office of St. Peter: The Emergence of Bureaucracy in the English Catholic Church, 1066–1250." PhD diss., Northwestern University.

Landis, Michelle L. 1997. "Let Me Next Time Be 'Tried by Fire': Disaster Relief and the Origins of the American Welfare State, 1789–1874." *Northwestern University Law Review* 92: 967–1034.

Laves, Walter C. H. 1943. "The Face-to-Face War Information Service of the Federal Government." *American Political Science Review* 37 (6): 1027–1040.

Lawson, Melinda. 2002. *Patriot Fires: Forging a New American Nationalism in the Civil War North*. Lawrence: University of Kansas Press.

Leblebici, Hussein, G. R. Salancik, A. Copay, and T. King. 1991. "Institutional Change and the Transformation of Interorganizational Fields: An Organizational History of the U.S. Radio Broadcasting Industry." *Administrative Science Quarterly* 36 (3): 333–363.

Lee, Monica, and Daniel Silver. 2012. "Simmel's Law of the Individual and the Ethics of the Relational Self." *Theory, Culture, and Society* 29 (7–8): 124–145.

Leonard, Gerald. 1994. "The Ironies of Partyism and Anti-Partyism: Origins of Partisan Political Culture in Jacksonian Illinois." *Illinois Historical Journal* 87 (1): 21–40.

Levy, Jonathan. 2016. "Altruism and the Origins of Nonprofit Philanthropy." In *Philanthropy in Democratic Societies: History, Institutions, Values*, edited by Rob Reich, Chiara Cordelli, and Lucy Bernholz, 19–43. Palo Alto, Calif.: Stanford University Press.

Liebersohn, Harry. 2011. *The Return of the Gift: European History of a Global Idea*. New York: Cambridge University Press, 2011.

Little, John Branden. 2009. "Band of Crusaders: American Humanitarians, the Great War, and the Remaking of the World." PhD diss., University of California at Berkeley.

Lizardo, Omar, and Michael Strand. 2010. "Skills, Toolkits, Contexts and Institutions: Clarifying the Relationship between Different Approaches to Cognition in Cultural Sociology." *Poetics* 38 (2): 204–227.

Locke, John. (1689) 2004. *First Treatise of Government*, chapter 4, paragraph 42. Reprinted in *Social Justice*, edited by Mathew Clayton and Andrew Williams. Malden, Mass.: Blackwell.

Lockley, Timothy James. 2007. *Welfare and Charity in the Antebellum South*. Gainesville: University Press of Florida.

Lomazoff, Eric. 2012. "Turning (Into) 'The Great Regulating Wheel': The Conversion of the Bank of the United States, 1791–1811." *Studies in American Political Development* 26: 1–23.

Long, Katherine Teresa. 1998. *The Revival of 1857–58: Interpreting an American Religious Awakening*. New York: Oxford University Press.

Loss, Christopher P. 2012. *Between Citizens and the State: The Politics of American Higher Education in the Twentieth Century*. Princeton, N.J.: Princeton University Press.

Lounsbury, Michael, Marc Ventresca, and Paul M. Hirsch. 2003. "Social Movements, Field Frames and Industry Emergence: A Cultural-Political Perspective on U.S. Recycling." *Socio-Economic Review* 1 (1): 71–104.

Loveman, Mara. 2005. "The Modern State and the Primitive Accumulation of Symbolic Power." *American Journal of Sociology* 110 (6): 1651–1683.

Lowell, Josephine Shaw. 1884. *Public Relief and Private Charity*. New York: G. P. Putnam's Sons [reprint: New York: Arno Press, 1971].

Lowitt, Richard, and Maruine Beasley, eds. 1981. *One Third of a Nation: Lorena Hickok Reports on the Great Depression*. Chicago: University of Illinois Press.

Lukács, Georg. 1971. *History and Class Consciousness: Studies in Marxist Dialectics*. Cambridge, Mass.: The MIT Press.

Lundberg, Emma Octavia. 1932. "The New York State Temporary Emergency Relief Administration." *Social Service Review* 6 (4): 545–566.

Madden, Edward H. 1962. "Francis Wayland and the Limits of Moral Responsibility." *Proceedings of the American Philosophical Society* 106 (4): 348–359.

Maier, Pauline. 1993. "The Revolutionary Origins of the American Corporation." *William and Mary Quarterly* 50 (1): 51–84.

Malczewski, Joan. 2009. "Weak State, Stronger Schools: Northern Philanthropy and Organizational Change in the Jim Crow South." *Journal of Southern History* 75 (4): 963–1000.

Malinowski, Bronislaw. 1922. *Argonauts of the Western Pacific: An account of native enterprise and adventure in the archipelagoes of Melanesian New Guinea*. New York: E. P. Dutton.

Mann, Michael. 1984. "The Autonomous Power of the State: Its Origins, Mechanisms, and Results." *European Journal of Sociology* 25 (2): 185–213.

———. 1986. *The Sources of Social Power*. Vol. 1, *From the Beginning to A.D. 1760*. New York: Cambridge University Press.

———. 1993. *The Sources of Social Power*. Vol. 2, *The Rise of Classes and Nation-States, 1760–1914*. New York: Cambridge University Press.

Manson, John. 1906. *The Salvation Army and the Public: A Religious, Social, and Financial Study*. London: George Routledge and Sons.

Marchand, Roland. 1998. *Creating the Corporate Soul: The Rise of Public Relations and Corporate Imagery in American Big Business*. Berkeley: University of California Press.

Marshall, T. H. 1950. *Citizenship and Social Class, and Other Essays*. Cambridge: Cambridge University Press, 1950.

Martin, Frederick Townsend. 1911. *The Passing of the Idle Rich*. Garden City, N.Y.: Doubleday, Page & Co.

Martin, Isaac William. 2013. *Rich People's Movements: Grassroots Campaigns to Untax the One Percent*. New York: Cambridge University Press.

Martin, John Levi. 2009. *Social Structures*. Chicago: University of Chicago Press.

Mauss, Marcel. (1950) 2000. *The Gift: Forms and Functions of Exchange in Archaic Societies*. New York: W. W. Norton.

Maxwell, William Quentin. 1956. *Lincoln's Fifth Wheel: The Political History of the United States Sanitary Commission*. New York: Longmans, Green & Co.

May, Samuel C., and Robert E. Ward. 1942. "Coordinating Defense Activities in a Metropolitan Region." *Public Administration Review* 2 (2): 104–112.

McAdam, Doug. 1982. *Political Process and the Development of Black Insurgency, 1930–1970*. Chicago: University of Chicago Press.

McCarthy, Kathleen D. 1982. *Noblesse Oblige: Charity and Cultural Philanthropy in Chicago, 1849–1929*. Chicago: University of Chicago Press.

———. 2003. *American Creed: Philanthropy and the Rise of Civil Society, 1700–1865*. Chicago: University of Chicago Press.

McCormick, Richard P. 1966. *The Second American Party System: Party Formation in the Jacksonian Era*. Chapel Hill: University of North Carolina Press.

McDonnell, Erin Metz. 2017. "Patchwork Leviathan: How Pockets of Bureaucratic Governance Flourish within Institutional Diverse Developing States." *American Sociological Review* 82 (3): 476–510.

McGarvie, Mark D. 2003. "The *Dartmouth College* Case and the Legal Design of Civil Society." In *Charity, Philanthropy, and Civility in American History*, edited by Lawrence J. Friedman and Mark D. McGarvie, 91–105. New York: Cambridge University Press, 2003.

McKenna, George. 2007. *The Puritan Origins of American Patriotism*. New Haven, Conn.: Yale University Press.

Merton, Robert K., with the assistance of Marjorie Fiske and Alberta Curtis. 1946. *Mass Persuasion: The Social Psychology of a War Bond Drive*. New York: Harper & Brothers.

Mettler, Suzanne. 1998. *Dividing Citizens: Gender and Federalism in New Deal Public Policy*. Ithaca, N.Y.: Cornell University Press.

————. 2005. *Soldiers to Citizens: The G.I. Bill and the Making of the Greatest Generation*. New York: Oxford University Press.

Meyer, D. H. 1973. "The Saint as Hero: William Ellery Channing and the Nineteenth-Century Mind." *Winterthur Portfolio* 8: 171–185.

Minicucci, Stephen. 2001. "The 'Cement of Interest': Interest-Based Models of Nation-Building in the Early Republic." *Social Science History* 25 (2): 247–274.

Mitchell, Timothy. 1991. "The Limits of the State: Beyond Statist Approaches and Their Critics." *American Political Science Review* 85 (1): 77–96.

Mizelle, Richard M., Jr. 2014. *Backwater Blues: The Mississippi Flood of 1927 in the African American Imagination*. Minneapolis: University of Minnesota Press.

Molm, Linda, Jessica Collett, and David R. Shaefer. 2007. "Building Solidarity through Generalized Exchange: A Theory of Reciprocity." *American Journal of Sociology* 113 (1): 205–242.

Moore, Barrington, Jr. 1966. *Social Origins of Dictatorship and Democracy: Lord and Peasant in the Making of the Modern World*. Boston: Beacon.

Morgan, Kimberly J., and Andrea Louise Campbell. 2011. *The Delegated Welfare State: Medicare, Markets, and the Governance of Social Policy*. New York: Oxford University Press.

Morris, Andrew. 2004. "The Voluntary Sector's War on Poverty." *Journal of Policy History* 16 (4): 275–305.

————. 2009. *The Limits of Voluntarism: Charity and Welfare from the New Deal through the Great Society*. New York: Cambridge University Press.

————. 2015. "How the State and Labor Saved Charitable Fundraising: Community Chests, Payroll Deduction, and the Public-Private Welfare State, 1920–1950." *Studies in American Political Development* 29: 106–125.

Moss, Lemuel. 1868. *Annals of the United States Christian Commission*. Philadelphia: J. B. Lippincott & Co.

Mukerji, Chandra. 1997. *Territorial Ambitions and the Gardens of Versailles*. New York: Cambridge University Press.

Nackenoff, Carol, and Julie Novkov, eds. 2014. *Statebuilding from the Margins: Between Reconstruction and the New Deal*. Philadelphia: University of Pennsylvania Press.

Neem, Johann. 2008. *Creating a Nation of Joiners: Democracy and Civil Society in Early National Massachusetts*. Cambridge, Mass: Harvard University Press.

————. 2010. "Civil Society and American Nationalism." In *Politics and Partnerships: The Role of Voluntary Associations in America's Political Past and Present*, edited by Elisabeth S. Clemens and Doug W. Guthrie, 29–53. Chicago: University of Chicago Press.

————. 2013. "Developing Freedom: Thomas Jefferson, the State, and Human Capability." *Studies in American Political Development* 27 (April): 36–50.

Negro, Giacomo, O. Özgecan Koçak, and Greta Hsu. 2010. "Research on Categories in the Sociology of Organizations." *Research in the Sociology of Organizations* 31: 3–35.

Nord, David Paul. 2002. "Benevolent Capital: Financing Evangelical Book Publishing in Early Nineteenth-Century America." In *God and Mammon: Protestants, Money, and the Market, 1790–1860*, edited by Mark A. Noll, 147–170. New York: Oxford University Press, 2002.

Norris, David A. 1998. "'For the Benefit of Our Gallant Volunteers': North Carolina's State Medical Department and Civilian Volunteer Efforts, 1861–62." *North Carolina Historical Review* 75 (3): 297–326.

North, Douglass C., John Joseph Wallis, and Barry R. Weingast. 2009. *Violence and Social Orders: A Conceptual Framework for Interpreting Recorded Human History*. New York: Cambridge University Press.

Novak, William J. 2001: "The American Law of Association: The Legal-Political Construction of Civil Society." *Studies in American Political Development* 15: 163–188.

———. 2008. "The Myth of the 'Weak' American State." *American Historical Review* 113 (3): 752–772.

Oates, Stephen B. 1994. *A Woman of Valor: Clara Barton and the Civil War*. New York: The Free Press.

Opal, J. M. 2013. "General Jackson's Passports: Natural Rights and Sovereign Citizens in the Political Thought of Andrew Jackson, 1780s–1820s." *Studies in American Political Development* 27 (2): 69–85.

Orren, Karen, and Stephen Skowronek. 2004. *The Search for American Political Development*. New York: Cambridge University Press.

Oshinsky, David M. 2005. *Polio: An American Story*. New York: Oxford University Press.

Ott, Julia C. 2011. *When Wall Street Met Main Street: The Quest for an Investors' Democracy*. Cambridge, Mass.: Harvard University Press.

Padgett, John F. 2013. "Transposition and Refunctionality: The Birth of Partnership Systems in Renaissance Florence." In *The Emergence of Organizations and Markets*, edited by John F. Padgett and Walter W. Powell, 168–207. Princeton, N.J.: Princeton University Press.

Padgett, John F., and Christopher K. Ansell. 1993. "Robust Action and the Rise of the Medici, 1400–1434." *American Journal of Sociology* 98 (6): 1259–1319.

Padgett, John F., and Walter W. Powell. 2013. *The Emergence of Organizations and Markets*. Princeton, N.J.: Princeton University Press.

Palmer, Frederick. 1931. *Newton D. Baker: America at War*, vol. 1. New York: Dodd, Mead & Co.

Pateman, Carol. 1979. *The Problem of Political Obligation: A Critical Analysis of Liberal Theory*. New York: Wiley.

Patterson, James T. 2000. *America's Struggle against Poverty in the Twentieth Century*. Cambridge, Mass.: Harvard University Press.

Peel, Mark. 2012. *Miss Cutler and the Case of the Resurrected Horse: Social Work and the Story of Poverty in America, Australia, and Britain*. Chicago: University of Chicago Press.

Peterson, Richard H. 1993/1994. "The United States Sanitary Commission and Thomas Starr King in California, 1861–1864." *California History* 72 (4): 324–337.

Pflugrad-Jackisch, Ami. 2010. *Brothers of a Vow: Secret Fraternal Orders and the Transformation of White Male Culture in Antebellum Virginia.* Athens: University of Georgia Press.

Phillips, Kevin. 1999. *The Cousins' War: Religion, Politics, and the Triumph of Anglo-America.* New York: Basic Books.

———. 2002. *Wealth and Democracy: A Political History of the American Rich.* New York: Broadway Books.

Pierson, Paul. 2000. "Increasing Returns, Path Dependence, and the Study of Politics." *American Political Science Review* 94 (2): 251–267.

Pincus, Steve. 2009. *1688: The First Modern Revolution.* New Haven, Conn.: Yale University Press.

Polanyi, Karl. (1944) 2001. *The Great Transformation: The Political and Economic Origins of Our Time.* Boston: Beacon Press.

Polletta, Francesca. 2002. *Freedom Is An Endless Meeting.* Chicago: University of Chicago Press.

Posner, Russell M. 1964. "Thomas Starr King and the Mercy Million." *California Historical Society Quarterly* 43 (4): 291–307.

Prasad, Monica. 2012. *The Land of Too Much: American Abundance and the Paradox of Poverty* Cambridge, Mass.: Harvard University Press.

Pressman, Jeffrey L., and Aaron Wildavsky. 1984. *Implementation.* 3rd ed. Berkeley: University of California Press.

Pryor, Elizabeth Brown. 1987. *Clara Barton: Professional Angel.* Philadelphia: University of Pennsylvania Press.

Putnam, Robert D. 1995. "Bowling Alone: America's Declining Social Capital." *Journal of Democracy* 6 (1): 65–78.

———. 2000. *Bowling Alone: The Collapse and Revival of American Community.* New York: Simon & Schuster.

Quadagno, Jill S. 1994. *The Color of Welfare: How Racism Undermined the War on Poverty.* New York: Oxford University Press.

Ratcliffe, Donald J. 1973. "The Role of Voters and Issues in Party Formation: Ohio, 1824." *Journal of American History* 59 (4): 847–870.

———. 1995. "Antimasonry and Partisanship in Greater New England 1826–1836." *Journal of the Early Republic* 15 (2): 199–239.

Reich, Rob. 2016. "Repugnant to the Whole Idea of Democracy? On the Role of Foundations in Democratic Societies." *PS: Perspectives on Politics* 49 (3): 466–472.

Reich, Rob, Chiara Cordelli, and Lucy Bernholz, eds. 2016. *Philanthropy in Democratic Societies: History, Institutions, Values.* Chicago: University of Chicago Press.

Rezneck, Samuel. 1953. "Unemployment, Unrest, and Relief in the United States during the Depression of 1893–97." *Journal of Political Economy* 61 (4): 324–345.

Riley, Dylan. 2010. *The Civic Foundations of Fascism in Europe: Italy, Spain, and Romania, 1870–1945.* Baltimore: Johns Hopkins University Press.

Robbins, Kevin C. 2006. "The Nonprofit Sector in Historical Perspective: Traditions of Philanthropy in the West." In *The Nonprofit Sector: A Research*

Handbook, 2nd ed., edited by Walter W. Powell and Richard Steinberg, 13–31. New Haven, Conn.: Yale University Press.

Robertson, Nancy. 1998. "Kindness or Justice? Women's Associations and the Politics of Race and History." In *Private Action and the Public Good*, edited by Walter W. Powell and Elisabeth S. Clemens, 193–205. New Haven, Conn.: Yale University Press.

Rodgers, Daniel T. 1992. "Republicanism: The Career of a Concept." *Journal of American History* 79 (1): 11–38.

Rogers, Naomi. 2007. "Race and the Politics of Polio: Warm Springs, Tuskegee, and the March of Dimes." *American Journal of Public Health* 97 (5): 784–795.

Rogin, Michael. 1962. "Voluntarism: The Political Functions of an Antipolitical Doctrine." *Industrial and Labor Relations Review* 15 (July): 521–535.

Rokkan, Stein. 1973. "Centre Formation, Nation-Building, and Cultural Diversity: Report on a UNESCO Project." In *Building States and Nations: Models and Data Resources*, vol. I, edited by S. N. Eisenstadt and Stein Rokkan, 13–38. Beverly Hills, Calif.: Sage Publications.

Roll, David L. 2013. *The Hopkins Touch: Harry Hopkins and the Forging of the Alliance to Defeat Hitler*. New York: Oxford University Press.

Rollins, Richard M. 1976. "Words as Social Control: Noah Webster and the Creation of the *American Dictionary*." *American Quarterly* 28 (4): 415–430.

Ronsavallon, Pierre. 2007. *The Demands of Liberty: Civil Society in France since the Revolution*. Cambridge, Mass.: Harvard University Press.

Rosenblum, Nancy L. 1998. *Membership and Morals: The Personal Uses of Pluralism in America*. Princeton, N.J.: Princeton University Press.

Roy, William G. 1997. *Socializing Capital: The Rise of the Large Industrial Corporation in America*. Princeton, N.J.: Princeton University Press.

Rudbeck, Jens. 2012. "Popular Sovereignty and the Historical Origin of the Social Movement." *Theory and Society* 41: 581–601.

Russell, Fred A., R. W. Lyons, and S. M. Flickinger. 1931. "The Social and Economic Aspects of Chain Stores." *American Economic Review* 21 (1): 32.

Ruswick, Brent. 2013. *Almost Worthy: The Poor, Paupers, and the Science of Charity in America, 1877–1917*. Bloomington: Indiana University Press.

Sahlins, Peter. 1989. *Boundaries: The Making of France and Spain in the Pyrenees*. Berkeley: University of California Press.

Sanders, Elizabeth. 1999. *Roots of Reform: Farmers, Workers, and the American State, 1877–1917*. Chicago: University of Chicago Press.

Sanders, Irwin T. 1949. "The Use of Block Leaders in Effective Community Mobilization." *Sociometry* 12 (4): 265–275.

The Sanitary Commission of the United States Army, A Succinct Narrative of its Works and Purposes. New York, 1864. Published for the Benefit of the United States Sanitary Commission.

Sassen, Saskia. 2006. *Territory, Authority, Rights: From Medieval to Global Assemblages*. Princeton, N.J.: Princeton University Press.

Schneiberg, Marc. 2007. "What's on the Path? Path Dependence, Organizational

Diversity and the Problem of Institutional Change in the US Economy, 1900–1950." *Socio-Economic Review* 5: 47–80.

Schneiberg, Marc, and Elisabeth S. Clemens. 2006. "The Typical Tools for the Job: Research Strategies in Institutional Analysis." *Sociological Theory* 24 (3): 195–227.

Schneiderhan, Erik. 2015. *The Size of Others' Burdens: Barack Obama, Jane Addams, and the Politics of Helping Others*. Palo Alto, Calif.: Stanford University Press.

Schoenbachler, Matthew. 1998. "Republicanism in the Age of Democratic Revolution: The Democratic-Republican Societies of the 1790s." *Journal of the Early Republic* 18 (2): 237–261.

Schwartz, Barry. 1967. "The Social Psychology of the Gift." *American Sociological Review* 73 (1): 1–11.

———. 1991. "Social Change and Collective Memory: The Democratization of George Washington." *American Sociological Review* 56 (2): 221–236.

Schwartz, Bonnie Fox. 1973. "Social Workers and New Deal Politicians in Conflict: California's Branion-Williams Case, 1933–1934." *Pacific Historical Review* 42 (1): 53–73.

Seavoy, Ronald E. 1978. "The Public Service Origins of the American Business Corporation." *Business History Review* 52 (1): 30–60.

Seeley, John R., Buford H. Junker, R. Wallace Jones, Jr., and N. C. Jenkins, M. T. Haugh, I. Miller, with a new introduction by Carl Milofsky. (1957) 1989. *Community Chest: A Case Study in Philanthropy*. New Brunswick, N.J.: Transaction Publishers.

Sewell, William H., Jr. 1993. "A Theory of Structure: Duality, Agency, and Transformation." *American Journal of Sociology* 98 (1): 1–29.

———. 2005. *Logics of History: Social Theory and Social Transformation*. Chicago: University of Chicago Press.

Showalter, Elaine. 2016. *The Civil Wars of Julia Ward Howe: A Biography*. New York: Simon and Schuster.

Silber, Ilana. 2009. "Bourdieu's Gift to Gift Theory: An Unacknowledged Trajectory." *Sociological Theory* 27 (2): 173–190.

Sills, Paul. 1957. *The Volunteers: Means and Ends in a National Organization*. Glencoe, Ill.: The Free Press.

Simmel, Georg. 1950. *The Sociology of Georg Simmel*. Translated and edited by Kurt H. Wolff. New York: The Free Press.

Simmel, Georg, and Claire Jacobson. 1965. "The Poor." *Social Problems* 13 (2): 118–140.

Simonds, William Day. 1917. *Starr King in California*. San Francisco: Paul Elder and Company.

Simpson, Brent, Ashley Harrell, David Melamed, Nicholas Heiserman, and Daniela V. Negraia. 2018. "The Roots of Reciprocity: Gratitude and Reputation in Generalized Exchange Systems." *American Sociological Review* 83 (1): 88–110.

Sinisi, Kyle S. 2003. *Sacred Debts: State Civil War Claims and American Federalism, 1861–1880*. New York: Fordham University Press.

Sklar, Martin. 1988. *The Corporate Reconstruction of American Capitalism, 1890–1916*. New York: Cambridge University Press.

Skocpol, Theda. 2003. *Diminished Democracy: From Membership to Management in American Civic Life*. Norman: University of Oklahoma Press.

Skocpol, Theda, Ziad Munson, Andrew Karch, and Bayliss Camp. 2002. "Patriotic Partnerships: Why Great Wars Nourished American Civic Voluntarism." In *Shaped by War and Trade: International Influences on American Political Development*, edited by Ira Katznelson and Martin Shefter, 134–180. Princeton, N.J.: Princeton University Press.

Skowronek, Stephen. 1982. *Building A New American State: The Expansion of National Administrative Capacities, 1877–1920*. New York: Cambridge University Press.

Slauter, Eric. 2009. *The State as a Work of Art: The Cultural Origins of the Constitution*. Chicago: University of Chicago Press.

Smith, Anthony D. 2003. *Chosen Peoples: Sacred Sources of National Identity*. New York: Oxford University Press, 2003.

Smith, Rogers M. 1993. "Beyond Tocqueville, Myrdal, and Hartz: The Multiple Traditions in America." *American Political Science Review* 87 (3): 549–566.

———. 2003. *Stories of Peoplehood: The Politics and Morals of Political Membership*. New York: Cambridge University Press.

Smith, Steven Rathgeb, and Michael Lipsky. 1993. *Nonprofits for Hire: The Welfare State in the Age of Contracting*. Cambridge, Mass.: Harvard University Press.

Smith Rosenberg, Carroll. 1971. *Religion and the Rise of the American City: The New York City Mission Movement, 1812–1870*. Ithaca, N.Y.: Cornell University Press.

Soifer, Hillel. 2008. "State Infrastructural Power: Approaches to Conceptualization and Measurement." *Studies in Comparative International Development* 43: 231–251.

Sparrow, Bartholomew H. 1996. *From the Outside In: World War II and the American State*. Princeton, N.J.: Princeton University Press.

Sparrow, James T. 2011. *Warfare State: World War II Americans and the Age of Big Government*. New York: Oxford University Press.

Spencer, Robyn. 1994. "Contested Terrain: The Mississippi Flood of 1927 and the Struggle to Control Black Labor." *Journal of Negro History* 79 (2) (Spring): 170–181.

Spillman, Lyn, and Russell Faeges. 2005. "Nation." In *Remaking Modernity: Politics, History and Sociology*, edited by Julia Adams, Elisabeth S. Clemens, and Ann Shola Orloff, 409–437. Durham, N.C.: Duke University Press.

Stanley, Amy Dru. 1992. "Beggars Can't Be Choosers: Compulsion and Contract in Post-Bellum America." *Journal of American History* 78 (4): 1265–1293.

Stark, David. 1996. "Recombinant Property in East European Capitalism." *American Journal of Sociology* 101 (4): 993–1027.

Stead, William T. (1894) 1964. *If Christ Came to Chicago*. New York: Living Books.

Steffes, Tracy Lynn. 2012. *School, Society, and State: A New Education to Govern Modern America, 1890–1940*. Chicago: University of Chicago Press.

Steinfeld, Robert J. 1989. "Property and Suffrage in the Early American Republic." *Stanford Law Review* 41 (January): 335–372.

Stevenson, Marietta. 1942. "New Governmental Services for People in Wartime." *Social Service Review* 16 (4) (December): 595–604.

Stillé, Charles J. 1863. *How a Free People Conduct a Long War.* Loyal Publication Society, no. 13.

Stinchcombe, Arthur L. 2001. *When Formality Works: Authority and Abstraction in Law and Organizations.* Chicago: University of Chicago Press.

Suleiman, Ezra. 2003. *Dismantling Democratic States.* Princeton, N.J.: Princeton University Press.

Swidler, Ann. 1986. "Culture in Action: Symbols and Strategies." *American Sociological Review* 51 (2): 273–286.

Swift, Linton B. 1934. "Relative Responsibilities—Public and Private." *Annals of the American Academy of Political and Social Science* 176: 145–150.

Tani, Karen M. 2016. *States of Dependency: Welfare Rights and American Governance, 1935–1972.* New York: Cambridge University Press.

Tarrow, Sidney. 2015. *War, States, and Contention: A Comparative Historical Study.* Ithaca, N.Y.: Cornell University Press.

———. 2018. "Mann, War, and Cyberspace: Dualities of Infrastructural Power in America." *Theory and Society* 47 (1): 61–85.

Tennstedt, Florian. 1987. "Wohltat und Interesse. Das Winterhilfswerk des Deutschen Volkes: Die Weimarer Vorgeschicte und ihre Instrumentalisierung durch das NS-Regime." *Geschichte und Gesellschaft* 13 (2): 157–180.

Thelen, Kathleen. 2002. "How Institutions Evolve: Insights from Comparative-Historical Analysis." In *Comparative Historical Analysis in the Social Sciences,* edited by James Mahoney and Dietrich Rueschemeyer, 208–240. New York: Cambridge University Press.

Thorndike, Joseph J. 2009. " 'The Unfair Advantage of the Few': The New Deal Origins of 'Soak the Rich' Taxation." In *The New Fiscal Sociology: Taxation in Comparative and Historical Perspective,* edited by Isaac William Martin, Ajay K. Mehrota, and Monica Prasad, 29–47. New York: Cambridge University Press.

———. 2016. "The Dubious Distinction between Politics and Charity." *Tax Notes* 151 (April 4): 13.

Tilly, Charles. 1992. *Coercion, Capital, and European States, AD 990–1992.* Cambridge, Mass.: Blackwell Publishing.

———. 1995. *Popular Contention in Great Britain, 1758–1834.* Cambridge, Mass.: Harvard University Press.

———. 1999. "Epilogue: Now Where?" In *State/Culture: State-Formation after the Cultural Turn,* edited by George Steinmetz, 407–419. Ithaca, N.Y.: Cornell University Press.

Titmuss, Richard M. 1971. *The Gift Relationship: From Human Blood to Social Policy.* New York: Pantheon.

Tobin, Harold J., and Percy W. Bidwell. 1940. *Mobilizing Civilian America.* New York: Council on Foreign Relations.

Todd, Arthur J. 1932. "Some Sociological Principles Underlying the Community Chest Movement." *Social Forces* 10 (4): 476–484.

Trolander, Judith Ann. 1975. *Settlement Houses and the Great Depression*. Detroit, Mich.: Wayne State University Press.

Ullman, Claire F. 1998. *The Welfare State's Other Crisis: Explaining the New Partnership between Nonprofit Organizations and the State in France*. Bloomington: Indiana University Press.

Van Burkels, Sandra F. 1984. "'Honour, Justice and Interest': John Jay's Republican Politics and Statesmanship on the Federal Bench." *Journal of the Early Republic* 4 (3): 239–274.

Wagner, Joseph Anthony. 1952. "Thomas Starr King—Preacher of Patriotism." *Western Speech* 16 (1): 13–16.

Walker, Sydnor H. 1933. "Privately Supported Social Work." In *Recent Social Trends in the United States: Report of the President's Research Committee on Social Trends*, vol. 2, 1168–1223. New York: McGraw-Hill Book Company.

Wall, Wendy L. 2008. *Inventing the "American Way": The Politics of Consensus from the New Deal to the Civil Rights Movement*. New York: Oxford University Press.

Walters, Pamela, and Emily Bowman. 2010. "Foundations and the Making of Public Education in the United States, 1867–1950." In *American Foundations*, edited by Helmut K. Anheier and David C. Hammack, 31–50. Washington, D.C.: Brookings Institution.

Walzer, Michael. 1970. *Obligations: Essays on Disobedience, War, and Citizenship*. Cambridge: Harvard University Press.

Warner, Amos Griswold. 1908. *American Charities*. New York: T.Y. Crowell.

Warren, Robert Penn. 1946. *All the King's Men*. New York: Harcourt, Brace & World.

Watson, Frank Dekker. 1922. *The Charity Organization Movement in the United States: A Study in American Philanthropy*. New York: The Macmillan Company.

Waugh, Joan. 2001. "'Give This Man Work!' Josephine Shaw Lowell, the Charity Organization Society of the City of New York, and the Depression of 1893." *Social Science History* 25 (2): 217–246.

Wayland, Francis. 1838. *The Limitations of Human Responsibility*. Boston: Gould, Kendall and Lincoln.

Weber, Max. 1978. *Economy and Society*. Edited by Guenther Roth and Claus Wittich. Berkeley: University of California Press.

Wendte, Charles W. 1921. *Thomas Starr King: Patriot and Preacher*. Boston, Mass.: The Beacon Press.

Westbrook, Robert B. 1990. "'I Want a Girl, Just Like the Girl that Married Harry James': American Women and the Problem of Political Obligation in World War II." *American Quarterly* 42 (4): 587–614.

———. 2004. *Why We Fought: Forging American Obligations in World War II*. Washington, D.C.: Smithsonian Books.

Wilentz, Sean. 2005. *The Rise of American Democracy: Jefferson to Lincoln*. New York: W. W. Norton.

Williams, J. Kerwin, and Edward A. Williams. 1940. "New Techniques in Federal Aid." *American Political Science Review* 34 (5) (October): 947–954.

Williams, Pierce, and Frederick E. Croxton. 1930. *Corporate Contributions to Organized Community Welfare Services*. New York: National Bureau of Economic Research.

Wills, Brian Steel. 2001. *The War Hits Home: The Civil War in Southeastern Virginia*. Charlottesville: University of Virginia Press,

Wilson, Joan Hoff. 1975. *Herbert Hoover: Forgotten Progressive*. Boston: Little, Brown and Co.

Wilson, Major. 1988. "Republicanism and the Idea of Party in the Jacksonian Period." *Journal of the Early Republic* 8 (4): 419–442.

Wilson, Mark R. 2006. *The Business of Civil War: Military Mobilization and the State, 1861–1865*. Baltimore: The Johns Hopkins University Press, 2006.

———. 2016. *Destructive Creation: American Business and the Winning of World War II*. Philadelphia: University of Pennsylvania Press.

Witt, John Fabian. 2012. *Lincoln's Code: The Laws of War in American History*. New York: Free Press.

Wolch, Jennifer R. 1990. *The Shadow State: Government and Voluntary Sector in Transition*. New York: The Foundation Center.

Wood, Gordon S. 1991. *The Radicalism of the American Revolution*. New York: Vintage Books.

———. 1996. "Launching the 'Extended Republic': The Federalist Era." In *Launching the "Extended Republic": The Federalist Era*, edited by Ronald Hoffman and Peter J. Albert, 1–24. Charlottesville: University Press of Virginia.

———. 2009. *Empire of Liberty: A History of the Early American Republic, 1789–1815*. New York: Oxford University Press.

Woodruff, Nan Elizabeth. 1985. *As Rare as Rain: Federal Relief in the Great Southern Drought of 1930–31*. Urbana: University of Illinois Press.

Wright, Conrad Edick. 1992. *The Transformation of Charity in Postrevolutionary New England*. Boston: Northeastern University Press.

Wyatt-Brown, Bertram. 1970. "The Antimission Movement in the Jacksonian South: A Study in Regional Folk Culture." *Journal of Southern History* 36 (4): 501–529.

———. 1971. "Prelude to Abolitionism: Sabbatarian Politics and the Rise of the Second Party System." *Journal of American History* 58 (2): 316–341.

Young, Michael P. 2006. *Bearing Witness against Sin: The Evangelical Birth of the American Social Movement*. Chicago: University of Chicago Press.

Zagarri, Rosemarie. 1992. "Morals, Manners, and the Republican Mother." *American Quarterly* 44 (2): 192–215.

Zald, Mayer N., and Patricia Denton. 1963. "From Evangelism to General Service: The Transformation of the YMCA." *Administrative Science Quarterly* 8 (2): 214–234.

Zelizer, Viviana A. 1997. *The Social Meaning of Money: Pin Money, Paychecks, Poor Relief, and Other Currencies*. Princeton, N.J.: Princeton University Press.

Zollman, Carl. 1924. *American Law of Charities*. Milwaukee, Wis.: The Bruce
    Publishing Co.

Zorbaugh, Harvey Warren. (1929) 1976. *The Gold Coast and the Slum: A Sociologi-
    cal Study of Chicago's Near North Side*. Chicago: University of Chicago Press.

Zunz, Olivier. 2012. *Philanthropy in America: A History*. Princeton, N.J.: Prince-
    ton University Press.

Index

Abbott, Henry, 284
abolition. *See* slavery and antislavery
accountability: to donors, 98, 195, 197, 354n76; obstacles to, 22, 254; political, 23, 258, 267; for public funds, 188, 207, 254
Adams, John Quincy, 33
Adams, Julia, 301n33
Addams, Jane, 334n33
adjustment and maladjustment, 248; and role of private relief, 190–91, 201
African Americans: access to polio treatment, 17; and categorical exclusions, 13, 15, 105, 127, 132; emancipated from slavery, 267; enslaved, 15; inclusion through voluntarism and public relief, 127, 132, 186; and philanthropy, 113–14; race and relief, 107, 132, 152–53; race inscribed in philanthropy and relief, 107, 113–14, 330n104. *See also* categorical exclusions and inequalities; slavery and antislavery
agency system, 38. *See also* fundraising
Agnew, Cornelius Rea, 284
Aid to Dependent Children, 211. *See also* "categories"; social insurance
Aircraft Production Board, 122
Akin, Antoinette, 290

Alaska, 205
alcohol: and church membership, 37; policies and taxation, 197; and Red Cross in London, 221–22. *See also* Prohibition; temperance
Alinsky, Saul, 251
Almond, Gabriel A., 324n101
alms, 64, 85, 93, 259; Simmel on, 13; usage of term, 258
almshouse, 84, 88, 100
American Bible Society, 32, 36, 37, 43, 69, 82, 282, 289. *See also* Benevolent Empire
American Board for Missionaries, 37. *See also* Benevolent Empire
American Cancer Society, 243. *See also* medical voluntaries
American Colonization Society, 36. *See also* Benevolent Empire
American Education Society, 36–37. *See also* Benevolent Empire
American exceptionalism, 23, 259, 264
American Express Co., 124
American Federation of Labor, 224, 352. *See also* labor
American Friends Service Committee (AFSC), 155, 238, 239, 295, 353
American Geographical Society, 69, 283
American Heart Association, 243. *See also* medical voluntaries

American Home Missionary Society, 36, 43, 44, 310n54. *See also* Benevolent Empire

American National Red Cross. *See* American Red Cross

American political development, 9, 15, 20, 23, 25, 27–28, 46, 139, 211, 238, 259, 264–74, 299n6, 312n96, 361n27, 362n35

American Red Cross, 2, 17, 24, 72, 95, 106–9, 118–19, 154, 191–92, 198, 244, 250, 271, 295, 297; as archive, 305n100; blood-banking, 240–43, 247; charters and treaties, 105, 107–8, 113, 172, 242, 245; and civic, local, or municipal networks, 109, 111, 119, 135–36, 202; and civic inclusion, 127, 129–30, 204–6, 356n21; class divisions, 144, 171–73, 230; Colored Advisory Commission, 153; conflicts with Community Chest, 218–20, 236, 244–45, 326n25, 351n37, 355n7, 357n29, 357n32; conflicts within, 137; corporate form of, 107, 172; criticisms, resentment, rumors, and responses, 107, 130, 136–37, 154, 186, 187, 221–22, 231–33, 236, 293–94, 322n121; disaster and drought relief, 106, 109–11, 113, 118–19, 152–55, 166–72, 183, 201–3, 207–8, 246–47 (*see also* San Francisco: earthquake of 1906); as distinct from or an alternative to government and public relief, 142–43, 154, 165–67, 191–92, 200, 221, 231–32, 245–46; donors to, 97, 198, 222–23, 233–34, 235–36; endowment and finances, 108–9, 168, 113, 233, 246; as expression of citizenship and political values, 126–27, 173, 204–6; fund-raising and membership, 112, 122, 125–27, 134–38, 149, 170–71, 198, 209–10, 219–21, 229, 232–34, 244–45, 335n47, 336n70; hierarchy, organizational structure and staff,

118–19, 124, 326n24; as infrastructure, 154–55, 271–72; insignia, 125, 325n18; institutional members, 119; as insurance, 202; Junior Red Cross, 126, 130–32, 143–44, 188, 272; leadership and board, 108–9, 124, 147–58, 329n85 (*see also* Barton, Clara; Bicknell, Ernest; Boardman, Mabel T.; Davis, Norman H.; Davison, Henry P.; Gibson, Harvey D.; Grayson, Cary; Lamont, Thomas; Payne, John Barton); loans from, 111, 154, 335n62; local chapters, 109, 124, 143, 149, 220, 244–45, 340n139, 351n31, 356n29; militarization of, 136–37; mission and its limits, 106, 139, 144, 167–68, 173, 201, 214, 237; and nation-state-building, 17, 106–9, 118–19, 127, 220–21, 223–24, 234, 247–48, 352n44; opposition to public funding, 126–27, 167–72, 192, 201, 209–10, 227; and organized labor, 17, 223–24, 242–43, 259, 351n31, 352n43, 352n44, 356n24; as "people's partnership," 206, 213, 216, 223, 230, 351n36, 352n44, 356n24; political geography of, 109, 155, 165, 201, 207–8, 220, 237, 245, 326n24; politicization of, 166–75, 178, 183, 202, 340n136; public health and safety programs, 139, 144, 201; as quasi- or semi-governmental, 107, 332n1; racial conflicts, politics, and policy, 107, 152–53; reciprocity for relief, 112; relation to FDR and New Deal, 178, 186, 192, 199–200, 204–10, 219–20, 226, 229–30, 236; relation to federal government and presidency, 107–9, 111–12, 124, 126–27, 136–37, 139, 168–70, 178, 192, 207–8, 327n53, 356n21; relation to U.S. military, 108, 125, 139, 208, 219, 233; relation to USSC, 71–72, 106, 325n10; and religion or spiritual mission, 127, 222–23; and Rockefellers, 97, 222–23,

233–34, 339n122, 354n76; services for veterans and military dependents, 136, 142–44, 154, 191–92, 215, 232–33, 344n66; survey research on, 231–33, 235, 293–94 (see also *American Soldier* surveys; Gallup, George, confidential surveys for Red Cross); as undemocratic or democratic, 172, 230–31, 242, 351n36; unemployment relief, 173, 185, 340n139; and U.S. Congress, 107–8, 126–27, 168–70, 173–74, 183, 209–10; use of public relations and movies, 135–36, 143–44; WWI, 112–13, 122–32, 134, 136, 139, 157–58, 198; WWII, 209–10, 217, 219–25, 229

American Relief Administration, 151, 155

American Republican Society, 40, 310n64

American Revolution, 2, 9, 15, 16, 28, 52, 257, 258; Daughters of, 290

American Soldier surveys, 231–32

American Sunday School Union, 36, 40, 41, 47, 69, 283. *See also* Benevolent Empire

American Telephone and Telegraph, 119, 122, 165

American Temperance Society, 35, 36, 37. *See also* Benevolent Empire

American Tract Society, 32, 36, 37, 289; and conflicts over antislavery, 43–44. *See also* Benevolent Empire

Anaconda Mining Co., 124

Anderson, Benedict, 11. *See also* "imagined community"

Anderson, John A., 284

Annapolis Gazette, 78

anonymity and confidentiality, 269, 272; as protection for relief recipients, 91, 187–88

anti-communism, 235, 237, 240, 244, 359n61. *See also* communists and communism

Anti-Deficiency Act of 1905, 329n76

anti-mission movement, 41. *See also* Baptists

anti-partyism, 33, 309n36

anti-statism, 5, 21, 48, 192–93, 200, 216, 234, 237, 250–52, 259; equated with voluntarism, 251

Apocalypse, horsemen of, 216

Appalachia, 155, 221

Appleby, Joyce, 28, 306n6

architecture of governance, 6, 10, 92, 95, 104–5, 227–28, 259; business and elite power within, 95, 259; construction as metaphor, 20; and expansible state, 105, 118–25, 215, 259; as framework for collaboration, 112; as framework for voluntarism, 19, 21, 84, 94, 228, 236, 248, 259, 271; and infrastructural power, 6, 264–65; open, 6, 23, 25, 236; and political participation, 35; and trajectories of political development, 6, 10, 19. *See also* division of labor; infrastructural power

archives: as key informants, 20, 305n100; triangulation across, 339n122

Arendt, Hannah: compassion as path to totalitarianism, 14, 271; on revolution, 14, 304n72

Arkansas, 128, 129; and Congressional debates over drought relief, 167, 168, 169, 171, 172

army. *See* military

Army Corps of Engineers, 53

associational state, 5, 9, 264

associations: and architectures of governance, 19, 23–24, 29, 47, 94–95, 104, 118–25, 153, 177–79, 236–37, 254, 258, 264–65; as bulwark against despotism and limit on state-building, 5–6, 29–30, 39, 48, 107, 153, 254; categories of, 3; as coercive, 32, 39–40, 42; freedom of association, 31; and infrastructural power, 5–6, 19–20, 30, 47, 105, 237; laws governing,

associations (*cont.*)
21, 40–41, 44–47, 49, 52, 114–15, 267–69; legitimacy or illegitimacy of, 3, 18, 23, 27–29, 31–33, 40–43, 113–14; nationalization of, 21, 28–29, 236; and nation-state-building, 5–6, 19–20, 23, 46–48, 49, 51–52, 72, 107–9, 118 21, 137, 139, 152, 251–52; as political or reform organizations, 6, 18, 27–30, 33–44, 56; self-created vs. constitutional, 30–31; as threat to liberty and freedom of conscience, 3, 20, 39–44, 48, 52. *See also* Benevolent Empire; voluntary associations and organizations
Attie, Jeanie, 76

Baker, Newton, 120, 121, 154, 347n104
Balogh, Brian, 5, 9
Bancroft, George, 55
Bankers Trust Company, 124
Bank of the United States, 29, 36, 118; as model for voluntary associations, 36; as "monster bank," 40
banks and bankers, 29, 69, 77, 90, 113, 124, 129, 157, 158, 161, 165, 204, 282–84, 320n25, 329n77, 329n86, 341n15; regulation of charitable contributions, 133–34, 198
Baptists, 14, 15, 41, 45, 282, 288, 290; and criticism of moral reform associations, 41–42
Barkey, Karen, 302n36
Barnard, Chester, 222
Baron de Hirsch Fund, 117
Barton, Clara, 61, 64–65, 85, 106, 132, 260; and Red Cross, 106–9, 242, 325n10, 354n69
Baruch, Bernard, 121, 123
Bates, Robert C., 239
Beecher, Lyman, 34–35, 37, 41
beggars, begging, and beggary, 65–67, 79, 80, 84–85, 89, 91, 321n36, 331n107. *See also* poor

begging letters, 116–17
Belgium, 332n8; food relief for, 124–25, 151, 155, 216, 217, 330n89
Bellows, Henry, 60–61, 68, 73, 284, 317n71, 320n30; definition of state, 53, 61
benevolence: and categorical inequalities, 16; civic, 1, 2, 12–13, 16–18, 20–25, 50–51, 60, 64–65, 67–72, 74, 113, 136, 139–40, 144–50, 158, 166, 201, 203, 207, 213–14, 223, 232, 236–37, 240–43, 246–47, 249, 251, 253–55, 265–66, 271, 273, 305n88, 359n61, 363n57; and cosmopolitanism, 15–16; and national solidarity, 2, 15–17, 106–7, 132, 201, 232, 247–48, 356n21; and nation-state-building, 10, 12, 15–21, 64–67, 236–37, 242, 246, 249, 253, 261, 268–69, 317n71; organized, 49, 56, 141 (*see also* charity; voluntary associations and organizations); and philanthropy, 23; and political culture, 6; political uses of, 12, 15–16, 30–33, 34, 74–77, 88, 166–75, 201–2, 207, 240, 254, 265–66, 269, 309n40, 312n93, 312n99; relational geometry of, 12–13, 16–21, 28, 85–86, 97, 100, 106, 135, 140–41, 202, 259–61, 270–71; tension with self-interest and self-sufficiency, 10, 12, 25, 309n40, 315n32; as threat to democratic dignity and moral virtue, 12–13, 15–17, 18, 27, 32, 39–44, 64–65, 67, 262, 265–66, 272–73; usage of term, 258, 299n2. *See also* charity; logic of the gift; municipal benevolence; voluntary associations and organizations
Benevolent Empire, 3, 29, 32, 36–41, 49, 52, 69, 118, 188, 258, 267, 308n28; financial resources and fund-raising, 37–38; as nation-building project, 38–39; resistance and criticism, 39–41; as threat to liberty, 37, 39, 309n48

Bent, Gilbert Ray, 281
Berle, Adolf A., 198, 359n59
B. F. Goodrich Co., 149–50
Bible societies. *See* American Bible
 Society
Bicknell, Ernest: in Chicago, 96–97,
 145; and Red Cross, 118–19, 326n34;
 and San Francisco earthquake, 21,
 110–12, 326n31, 326n32
biography, 231; as carrier of legacies,
 68, 79
Black, Hugo, 169, 338n109
blacks. *See* African Americans
Bliss, Cornelius, 158
Block-Aid, 154–65, 174–75, 188, 193–95,
 200, 297, 337n90, 337n93
"block organization," 227
blood-banking, 240–42, 247, 331n110,
 356n20
Boardman, Mabel T., 108, 135, 242,
 325n20, 354n69
Board of Indian Commissioners, 69,
 283, 286
Boies, J. W., 182
Bolshevists, 172. *See also* communists
 and communism
Boltwood, Henry L., 284
bonds, 123; funding of relief, 151, 156,
 341n15; funding of war, 194, 231,
 235–37, 262. *See also* Liberty Loans,
 during WWI
Bondy, Robert E., 340n139
Boston, 52, 75, 87, 124, 286, 287–89,
 323n72, 329n86, 335n47, 345n69
Boston Committee on Donations,
 11–12, 57, 109, 258
Boston Tea Party, 11
boundaries and classification systems,
 7, 10–12, 205, 236, 269–70, 362n36,
 363n51; between political and charitable or voluntary, 143, 268–69, 273–
 74, 305n100; between public and
 private, 47, 119, 179, 211; between
 state and society, 174, 211; boundary

work, 10–12, 15, 20, 269–71, 274,
 321n36; jurisdictional claims, 194,
 200; transgression, 10
Bourdieu, Pierre, 7, 14
Bowler, S. L., 281
Boy Scouts, 143, 147, 262, 346n96
Brace, Charles Loring, 88
breadlines and soup kitchens, 80, 182,
 186–87, 321n36. *See also* mass relief
Breen, T. H., 12, 303n64, 303n67,
 311n73
Bringhurst, G. H., 281
Britain (or England), 32, 55, 57, 63,
 89, 125, 181, 306n6, 314n12; and
 American Revolution, 18, 27, 52–53,
 307n17; as case of nation-state-
 building, 301n33, 303n58, 303n62,
 313n6, 319n13; and Salvation Army
 ("Darkest England"), 23, 341n17;
 and voluntarism, 24, 35, 84, 308n29,
 309n39, 312n93, 313n6; and WWII,
 158, 214, 217–18, 221–22
Brown, John, 316n69
Brown University, 41
Buffalo, NY, 84, 319n24
bureaucracy and bureaucrats, 8, 54, 75,
 136, 142, 165; bureaucratic authority
 or hierarchy, 50, 142, 149; bureaucratic hierarchy and despotism, 55,
 71, 105; criticism and resistance,
 120, 209; Crozier on, 273–74; limits
 on growth, 6, 153; power of, 50; in
 theories of the state, 8–9, 11, 264,
 273, 302n43, 314n15 (*see also* Weber,
 Max); and voluntarism, 5, 67; and
 war mobilization, 120–22
Burghordt, Peter H., 285
Burke, Edmund, 1, 2, 6, 257
Bush, H. P., 285
business, 115, 359n59; and anti-statism,
 22, 119, 122, 216, 243–44, 246; charitable contributions and deductions,
 22, 98, 133–34, 179, 197–200, 211,
 243, 330n92, 334n35, 345n72; clubs,

business (*cont.*)
99–100; and nation-state-building, 2, 5–6, 139–40, 236–37; as organizational model, 124 (*see also* corporation: as organizational form); and war mobilization, 119, 123–24. *See also* Chambers of Commerce; Community Chests; corporation; wealth and the wealthy: and inequality

businessmen, 69–70, 144–50, 207–8; control over civic networks and voluntary associations, 69–70, 74, 125, 147–50, 156, 194–97, 226, 236, 242, 246, 250–51; and fund-raising, 92–93, 99, 156–58, 207, 223–24, 243, 249–50, 324n96, 336n70, 348n127; and government service, 121–25, 157–58, 228–29; and limitation of public relief and social services, 74–75, 77, 146, 187, 192; and municipal benevolence, 74–75, 83, 86–88, 92–93, 98–99, 144–50, 237, 333n30; and Red Cross, 124–25, 204

business methods, 99, 108; applied to charitable giving, 145–46, 194; applied to voluntary associations, 36, 108, 124–25, 147, 194–95, 197

business networks, 123, 175, 329n77. *See also* civic networks, competition among

Butler, Benjamin, 64, 316n68

Byoir, Carl, 1, 299n4

Caesarism, 33. *See also* despotism

Calhoun, Craig, 16

Calhoun, John C., 299n7, 300n20, 325n6

California, 58, 128, 132, 315n40, 331n115; model of charitable fund-raising, 57

campaign model, of fund-raising, 97, 100, 272

Capozzola, Christopher, 150, 361n31

Caraway, Hattie Wyatt, 167, 168

Caraway, Thaddeus, 171

care: of the army by the people, 58, 60, 61, 83, 94, 143, 225; of the people by the people, 54, 83, 93–94, 111, 181

Carnegie, Andrew, 113, 115

Carnegie Foundation, 117

Carruthers, Bruce, 301n33

case work, 85, 142–43, 150, 160, 184, 187, 191, 194, 218, 225–27, 248, 343n45, 344n64. *See also* social work and social workers

categorical exclusions and inequalities, 6, 13, 19–21, 83, 105, 107, 203–6, 271; between charity and politics, 198, 267–68; and citizenship, 83, 175, 179; and civic inclusion through gifts, 129–32, 160–61, 174–75, 271; and nation-state-building, 127; neutralized by relief organization, 162–64; and racial inequality, 6, 132, 175, 186–89; reinforced by local practices and relief policies, 152–53, 175, 186–89, 211, 270. *See also* boundaries and classification systems; marginal men; racial inequality and exclusion

categories: defense of distinctions, 10, 260, 171–74, 261, 362n36; of identity and membership, 3, 7, 19–21, 132; and legacies, 267–73; of the poor, 77, 80, 85, 89–90, 94, 154, 167, 186–87, 194

"categories," 209, 218, 225. *See also* social insurance: the "categories" (for the aged, dependent children, blind, and disabled)

Catholic charities, 96, 145, 190, 333n30, 346n96; and political patronage, 88

Catholic church, 8, 32, 42, 145, 313n101

Catholics, 53, 81–82, 95, 200, 230; and anti-Catholicism, 33, 43; and war mobilization, 53, 121, 230, 352n47

cement, 1, 6, 28, 257, 259; "Cement to the Union," 2, 18, 307n7

chain stores, 147, 243

Chambers of Commerce, 92, 98, 100, 112, 123, 126, 145, 147, 195, 237, 243;

charities endorsement committees, 98, 99, 195; and tax code, 362n44

Channing, William Ellery, 39, 41, 44, 310n62

charitable bequests, laws restricting purposes, 45–46, 114–16, 267–68

charitable contributions: and business, 133, 134, 197–99; compared to taxation, 148, 245–46; and division of labor with government, 21, 79, 95–96, 153, 179–80, 190–92, 204, 224, 226, 239; as expression of citizenship, 179, 231–32, 234–35, 240–41, 262, 272, 313n6 (*see also* citizen philanthropy); restrictions on, 198–99, 239, 267–69, 329n3; tax treatment of, 22, 133–35, 167, 197–99, 211, 243, 253, 255, 338n109, 345n72

charity: as alternative to public relief, 77, 83–84, 87, 89, 114–15, 169–71, 194; as antidote to militarism, 62–63; as bribery or corruption, 32, 76, 88, 181, 189–90; and categorical inequalities and exclusions, 21, 84–85, 188–89; compared to entitlements or rights, 1, 91, 175, 184–90, 210, 260, 263, 265–66; compared to loans, 111, 154, 168–71, 235, 302n41, 325n32, 335n62, 339n129, 350n23; contributions to, 92–93, 155–56 (*see also* fund-raising); coordination and centralization of, 79–80, 93, 260 (*see also* charity organization societies [COS]); as creating dependence, 77, 180–81; Elizabethan Statutes of, 45; ethic of, 302n41; etiquette of, 97, 238; exemptions from public programs, 23, 211; as form of insurance, 202; and the gift, 5–6; government control of (actual or proposed), 260–61; investigation and endorsement of, 98–99, 147–50, 195; limited capacity, 79, 173–74, 177–78, 319n5; and nation-state-building, 1–3, 10–17, 27, 49, 51–52, 258–61; politicization of, 141, 178, 202–3, 240, 321n43; and the poor, 31–32, 83–84; public funding of, 87–88, 165, 171, 178; reform, 90–91, 319n5; registration during war, 147, 349n8; relational geometry of, 10–17, 172, 175, 179; scientific, 86, 319n5; and stigma, 187; in tension with democracy, 10, 32, 100, 107, 140–41, 167–68, 173, 175, 179, 183, 272–73; as threat to civic or democratic dignity, 13–20, 50, 52, 64–65, 83–84, 136, 143, 172, 227, 231, 270, 317n72, 342n23; usage of term, 258, 299n2, 317n72. *See also* benevolence; charity organization societies (COS); dole; foundations; fund-raising; logic of the gift; philanthropists and philanthropy; poor; private agencies and relief

charity organization societies (COS), 68, 70, 74–75, 84–86, 89, 248, 295; and municipal benevolence, 86, 88, 95–96, 98, 100, 109, 110, 145, 333n30; New York City (NYCOS), 84, 89, 110, 116, 122, 124, 146, 155, 165, 177, 186, 191, 193, 195, 234, 248, 303, 336n67; and Red Cross, 119; relational geometries of, 175. *See also* New York City: Charity Organization Society (NYCOS)

Chicago, 54, 67, 69, 70, 81, 87, 99, 100, 106, 122, 145, 158, 190, 199, 251, 281, 282, 283, 284, 286, 287, 295, 321n36, 323n72, 341n15, 345n69; absence of Community Chest, 146, 155–56, 194, 199, 334n31, 334n33; Archdiocese and Catholic charities, 96, 190; Bureau of Charities, 110, 118, 145; Business Men's Relief Committee, 145; Central Relief Association, 89; Chicago Relief and Aid Society (CRAS), 81, 83–84, 89, 93, 106, 318n96, 326n26; *Defender*, 152; and

Chicago (*cont.*)
 Depression of 1893, 89, 93–94, 96–
 97, 114; Great Fire and Depression
 of 1873, 81–84, 106, 321n43, 322n44;
 Industrial Areas Foundation, 251;
 and municipal benevolence, 94,
 96–97, 145–46, 151, 335n48; *Sunday
 Times*, 82; *Tribune*, 83, 116, 117, 185;
 women's organizations, 82–83, 151.
 See also reciprocity: city-to-city
children: as beneficiaries, 21, 84, 90,
 145, 173–74, 191, 209, 211, 218, 225,
 238, 247, 248, 342n32; and categorical exclusions, 21, 84, 127; as future
 citizens, 49, 130–31, 254; participation in fund-raising, 32, 107, 127,
 130–32, 134, 331n107
China: *American Soldier* survey in
 China-Burma-India, 293–94; relief
 for, 111, 209, 216
Christian charity, 13, 107
Christian Commission. *See* United
 States Christian Commission
 (USCC)
Christianity: and civic responsibility,
 13, 16, 35, 38, 43, 55, 62, 89–90, 114–
 15, 132, 321n41, 322n59; as ideological
 framework or organizational model,
 14, 24, 35, 62, 65, 216, 307n11, 311n68
Christmas: gifts, lists, and stamps, 112,
 125–26, 189, 191, 262–63; Red Cross
 drives, 125–26, 128, 137–38
churches: and civil society or voluntarism, 194, 224, 226, 247, 253–54;
 fund-raising and organizational
 capacities, 36–37, 43–44, 126, 137,
 357n29; incorporation of, 45; and individual liberty, 37, 42–45; Mormon,
 116; as organizational model and
 source of skill, 36, 43, 46, 307n11,
 309n46, 313n101, 316n66; relation to
 government and politics, 14–15, 35,
 45–46, 311n68, 313n101; and relief,
 56, 79, 85, 89, 151, 156, 180–81, 194,

321n41. *See also* Catholics; Christianity; religion
Cincinnati, 56, 67, 115, 146–48, 208,
 224; and community chest, 147–48,
 334n46, 352n46. *See also* Society of
 the Cincinnati
cities, 35, 56, 69; as challenges and
 sites of organizational innovation,
 71, 74, 77–79, 86–89, 100, 136, 140,
 145–46, 151, 219, 334n31, 335n48; city
 or urban missions, 35, 69, 70, 79,
 89; home rule, 75, 120; local rather
 than national identity, 95, 100–101,
 110, 270; and political geography
 of voluntarism and relief, 60, 109,
 165, 167, 225, 237, 251, 309n39,
 343n36, 353n57; reciprocity among,
 81–82, 106–7, 110, 132, 326n26; and
 state-building or architectures of
 governance, 70–71, 75–76, 95–96;
 and theories of the state, 75–76;
 and urban or city missions, 35, 69,
 79, 281. *See also* Community Chests;
 municipal benevolence; United
 States Sanitary Commission (USSC):
 sanitary fairs
citizen philanthropy, 2, 22, 101, 125, 155,
 201–2, 205, 207, 224, 229, 238, 243,
 262, 272; as egalitarian form of civic
 benevolence, 17; as "infrastructure,"
 237; and national solidarity, 231–32,
 234, 239–41, 247, 249. *See also* civic
 benevolence; "divine method of patriotism"; presidential philanthropy
citizens: leading, 6, 86–87, 99, 134–35
 (*see also* elites); protective committees in San Francisco, 103
Citizens' Conference on "Community
 Responsibility for Human Welfare,"
 153
citizenship: charity and giving as models for, 35, 57, 63–64, 167, 240, 261–
 62; contradictions with benevolence
 or charity, 12–14, 17, 19, 21, 25, 32, 64–

65, 67, 74, 76–77, 80, 83, 91, 100, 103, 110–11, 140–41, 154, 168–69, 172–73, 175, 179–80, 182, 186–87, 189, 258–60, 262, 266, 270–71, 272–73; enacted through giving and voluntarism, 2–3, 5, 10, 12, 76, 130–31, 147–48, 152, 167, 174, 183, 201–2, 204–5, 207, 233–34, 235–37, 240, 266; exclusions from, 10, 13–14, 15, 17, 21, 75, 83, 84–85, 105, 127, 132, 186, 188, 314n11, 317n72 (*see also* categorical exclusions and inequalities); liberal model of, 5, 6, 12–14, 17, 19, 49–50, 52, 64–65, 80–81, 107, 175, 192, 259, 264, 266, 270–71 (*see also* dependence; self-sufficiency and self-reliance); models of, 105, 123, 129, 152, 179, 204, 258–59, 306n3, 361n31; relational geometries of, 12–14, 25, 27–29, 175, 258–60; rights of, 178, 186; social construction of, 130–31; urban citizenship and municipal benevolence, 95–101; voluntarism as model of, 152, 179, 204–5. *See also* democratic dignity

Citizens United, 269

civic benevolence, 69, 71, 166, 243; as alms-giving, 50, 64; contradictions with liberalism and democracy, 12–13, 64–65, 243, 246, 273–74; elite and business influence, 74, 86, 113–18, 133, 144–50, 158, 223, 237, 246–47, 251; erosion and dismantling of, 247–49, 254–55; and national solidarity or peoplehood, 15–17, 49–50, 60, 67, 201–3, 207, 232, 236, 242; and nation-state-building, 1–2, 17–23, 49–51, 125, 133, 139–41, 214, 240–42, 253–54, 363n57; politics of, 74–75, 110, 265–66, 271; and racial inequality, 305n88 (*see also* categorical exclusions and inequalities); as social technology, 17

civic clubs, 86–88, 99–100, 145; and elites, 70; Rotary, 99. *See also* Union League Clubs

civic dignity. *See* democratic dignity

civic discipline, 55, 62; and Christianity, 65

civic identities, 255; linked to racial identities, 132

civic inclusion, 162–64; through civic philanthropy, 204–6

civic life, relational quality of, 244, 245

civic networks, competition among, 109

civic philanthropy, 300n11, 300n12; as distinguished from citizen philanthropy, 160; institutionalization of, 133–37. *See also* citizen philanthropy

civic state, 47, 74. *See also* civic benevolence; nation-state-building

civilian: government or authority, 51, 314n18; reintegration of veterans, 142; volunteers and participants in war, 53, 62, 73, 108, 120, 123, 136–37, 141, 215, 226, 236, 316n66

Civilian Conservation Corps (CCC), 1, 186, 207–8, 228, 295, 299n1

civilians, and wartime sacrifice and service, 141, 354n71

Civilian Works Administration, 343n35

civil service reform, 74, 87

Civil War, 2, 18, 21, 24, 33, 48, 49–72, 77, 87, 105, 113, 130, 137, 138, 139, 258, 270, 313n3, 313n8, 316n66, 316n68, 332n121; and civic benevolence, 253, 258, 300n11; debt, 78; legacies of, 67–72, 76, 78–79, 82–83, 85, 93–96, 105–6, 108, 113, 120, 127, 129, 136, 139, 152, 158, 205, 214, 232, 271, 320n28; and municipal benevolence, 76, 134–35. *See also* sectionalism; slavery and antislavery; United States Christian Commission (USCC); United States Sanitary Commission (USSC)

civitism, 120. *See also* municipal benevolence

Clark, T. M., 285

Clay, Henry, 33
Cleveland, 100, 120, 220
Cleveland Foundation, 117
Coast Guard, 208
coevolution, of civic benevolence and nation-state, 23. *See also* combinatorial politics; constitutive contradictions
Coffee Day, 181–82
cognitive shift, 7; and recognition of unemployment, 164
Colorado, 128, 287
Colorado Fuel and Iron, 117
Colton, Calvin, 309n48
combinatorial politics, 51, 19, 257–75, 301n33; and American political development, 264–67; and institutional change, 7, 301n27; and nation-state-building, 7, 10, 13, 18, 23–24, 259, 264–73; and transposition of models or logics, 25; and zones of instability, 10, 260, 270, 360n13
Committee to Celebrate the President's Birthday. *See* March of Dimes
communists and communism, 161, 172, 235, 237, 301n33; as critique of Community Chests, 244. *See also* anti-communism
Community Chests, 23, 161, 209, 216, 224, 244, 261, 271–72, 355n7; business influence over, 150, 198, 216, 223, 243; conflicts with Red Cross, 218–20, 236, 244–45, 326n25, 355n7, 357n29, 357n32; conversion to war chests, 215, 218–19, 224, 261; and FDR, 192, 207–8, 216, 219–20; and fund-raising, 155–56, 165, 193, 198, 200–201, 226, 240, 243, 261, 334n46, 335n66, 347n104; as limit on expansion of government activity, 192–93, 209, 216, 218; Mobilization for Human Needs, 200–201, 207, 208–9, 218, 347n104; and municipal benevolence, 98–99, 106, 140, 145–50,

154–55; opposition to, 155, 194, 199, 254–55, 334n31; as organizational model, 146; political geography of, 165, 194, 199, 202, 219–20, 237, 245, 336n68, 345n79; and settlement houses, 198–99. *See also* municipal benevolence; United Funds
community surveys, 144
compassion, 14, 232, 271. *See also* Arendt, Hannah
Confederate States of America, 23–24, 54, 56, 68, 73, 127
Congregationalists, 36, 38, 43, 45, 284, 309n46, 309n50
Congress of Industrial Organizations (CIO), 17, 352n42; inclusion in civic voluntarism, 242–43; and Red Cross, 17, 224, 242–43, 259
conspiracy, 33, 161, 312n93
constitutive contradictions, 5, 19, 257–60, 362n35; and institutional change, 7, 15, 27–28, 260–62, 270–71, 273–75, 362n36; and nation-state-building, 27–28, 30, 71, 179, 266–67, 362n35; resolutions and relaxations of, 20, 47, 107, 179; stabilization by law, 269; voluntarism as response to, 19
contract theory, 16; and freedom of conscience, 43
contradictions, 270, 272, 360n17; between charity or voluntarism and democracy, 13–14, 20–21, 24, 40, 52, 67, 88, 100, 114, 175, 179, 259, 262, 269–72; between dependency or reciprocity and self-sufficiency, 71, 107; between liberty and slavery, 5, 27, 306n3; between military discipline and voluntarism, 55, 62–63; between national solidarity and categorical exclusions, 152–53, 188–89; between organizational models, 62; between public relief and democratic dignity, 111; between relational

logics or models, 10, 12, 19, 47, 62, 175; intrinsic to voluntarism, 18

contributions, as political speech, 269. *See also* charitable contributions; fund-raising

Cooke, Jay, 123, 316n60

coordination and centralization. *See* architecture of governance; charity organization societies (COS); division of labor; federated fund-raising

coproduction: of governance and public goods, 5, 6, 18, 104, 238, 274, 362n57; of war, 214–15, 236

corporate charters or incorporation, 14, 36, 46–47, 87, 113–14, 362n39; of American Sunday School Union, 40–41; of banks, 134; of churches, 45; of Red Cross, 105, 107–9, 112–13, 124, 169, 172, 206, 219, 229, 242, 244–45, 325n9, 327n53, 357n31; of Rockefeller Foundation, 116–18; of Society of Cincinnati, 31, 308n20

corporate philanthropy, 243

corporation: as delegation of sovereignty through corporate charters, 45, 46–47; as organizational form, 14, 28, 30, 32, 36, 43–44, 107, 124, 172, 198, 251, 253, 307n7, 307n17, 310n60, 311n68, 312n90, 312n96, 333n27, 359n59, 359n60, 362n39; Red Cross as, 172. *See also* business; business methods

corporatism, 95

corruption, 32, 77, 87–88, 95, 181, 187, 189–90, 203, 239, 265–66, 270, 273, 326n38, 328n60; Civil War rumors of, 65–67, 153

cosmopolitanism, and peoplehood, 15–16

Council of National Defense, 119, 121, 122

Council of Social Agencies (CSA), 199, 227; in Chicago, 145, 146, 199, 333n30

countermobilization, 262

crisis, 206, 265; and institutional change, 21, 23–24, 84, 90, 104, 164–65, 177–78, 249, 261, 274, 320n25; as opportunity for mobilization, 2. *See also* neo-episodic analysis

Crowder, Enoch, 120

Croxton, Fred, 335n66

Crozier, Michel, 273–74

cultural models and practices, 5, 172, 260–61, 302n51. *See also* relational geometries or logics

cultural sociology, 7, 260–61, 301n32, 360n15, 362n36

Dallas, TX, 151

Dartmouth decision, 47

Davis, Norman H., 219–22, 229–30, 348n126

Davison, Henry P., 124, 126, 158

decoupling, of giving from receiving, 86, 163, 188. *See also* disarticulation

de Forest, Robert W., 124

delegation: government contracts as, 258–59; of public authority and responsibility, 47, 84, 139, 178, 221, 236, 253, 258–59, 264, 342n17

democracy: contradictions with charity and benevolence, 13, 21, 64–65; enacted through volunteering, 234; invention of, 23–24, 28–29; and liberalism, 16; and the poor, 13–14; tension with forms of voluntarism, 258, 273. *See also* citizenship

democratic dignity, 17, 20–21, 91, 105, 107, 140–41, 189, 266; contradictions with benevolence, 20, 64–65, 67, 74, 86, 90, 98, 141, 162, 182, 187–88, 259, 270–73; etiquette of, 162–63, 186; of soldiers, 227; threatened by charity and dependence, 17, 20–21, 50, 52, 86, 98, 107. *See also* anonymity and confidentiality

Democratic-Republican societies, 29, 31, 33, 308n17

democratization, of voluntarism, 17, 243, 307n11, 356n20

Democrats and Democratic Party, 3, 22, 33, 40, 60, 76, 78, 87–88, 92, 134, 167, 169, 190, 206, 223, 236, 242, 319n18, 331n115, 338n109, 361n32; hostility to federal power, 105, 120, 122, 132; and March of Dimes, 202, 226

Demond, Charles, 57

dependence: as civic disqualification, 13, 106; created by gifts, 64–65, 85–86, 107, 136, 193, 260; created by government benefits, 142; stigma of, 135

Depression: of 1857, 77; of 1873, 77–84, 94, 95, 154, 163, 321n34; of 1893, 71, 88–95, 154, 161, 271; Great Depression, 2, 21, 113, 140–41, 147, 150, 154–75, 177–201, 239, 262, 265, 317n76; legacies of Great Depression, 210–12, 214–15

despotism, 3, 5, 62–63, 105, 200, 300n13, 311n77, 314n18; contrasted with voluntarism, 126–27, 200; military discipline as, 50, 55, 62–64

de Tocqueville, Alexis, 5, 18, 24, 28, 30, 39, 43, 107, 200, 253, 258, 300n14, 307n14, 307n15, 314n18; on solidarity, 28

Detroit, 69, 243, 283, 335n48

Devine, Edward T., 110–11, 116

dictatorship, voluntary fund-raising as form of, 246. See also despotism

direct and indirect rule, 7–9; and WWI, 120–25

disarticulation, 95, 188, 269–71; of obligations and dependence, 270–71. See also decoupling, of giving from receiving

disaster relief, 193–94, 206, 233, 271; categories of need, 80, 90, 100–111; and floods, 208; and fund-raising, 95; and nation-state-building, 19, 103–5, 119, 132, 206; and Red Cross, 106–9, 118–19, 154–55, 167, 178, 201–2, 206, 210, 220, 229, 233, 246–47; and rehabilitation, 317n76; and self-organization, 104. See also San Francisco: earthquake of 1906

Disciples of Christ, 115

disenfranchisement: of those on relief, 185; and voluntary principle, 45

District of Columbia, 53, 75–76, 116. See also Washington, D.C.

"divine method of patriotism," 49, 59–60, 67, 95, 100–101, 125, 158, 205, 253. See also citizen philanthropy; fund-raising

division of labor, 88, 95–96, 210–11; between government and voluntarism, 21, 79, 96, 153, 172, 179, 183, 190–93, 204, 208, 210–11, 217, 224–26, 228, 239, 248–49, 251–54; between national and local governments, 252; between public and private, 94, 153, 179, 190–94, 200–201, 252; between states and municipalities, 180. See also architecture of governance; responsibility

Dodge, Elizabeth, 290

dole, 93, 151, 167–68, 171; and Belgian food relief, 330n89; in England, 181; government benefits as, 167–68, 171, 173–74; as moral threat, 151, 168. See also charity; public relief and services; unemployment relief

dollar-a-year men, 122, 229

donors and donations, 46, 313n6; accountability to, 81, 97, 195, 241, 261, 329n76, 345n76; "dead hand" of donor, 116; discipline of, 85–86; as potential beneficiaries, 272; reciprocity among donors, 98, 100; recruitment of, 155, 157, 164, 193, 324n96, 336n67; relation to beneficiaries, 94, 99, 100, 135–36, 146–47, 154, 156, 161, 175, 248, 258, 271–72,

319n18; resentment of solicitation, 97, 98. *See also* charitable contributions; corporate philanthropy; fund-raising; Rockefellers

draft, 120–21, 153, 235, 270–71; and Civil War, 53; Civil War riots, 53, 60, 87, 322n59, 322n60; lotteries, 76; and WWI, 120–21, 123, 129; and WWII, 235, 293–94

Dream Act Amnesty Program, as political "gift," 266

drought and drought relief, 81, 114, 155, 167–79, 209; congressional debates, 170–73; and Great Depression, 140, 154, 167–68, 178, 262; and Red Cross, 155, 165, 167–68, 173, 183, 208–10, 229

DuBois, W. E. B., 74

Dun and Bradstreet, 195

Dwight, Timothy, 35, 309n48

Dyer, Francis Stephen, 285

Eaton, Dorman B., 320n30

Edison Electric Light, 94

education, shift from private to public responsibility, 153

Eisenhower, Mamie, 247

election: of 1824 and 1828, 33; of 1860, 33; of 1916, 138; of 1932, 179, 217; of 1936, 216; of 1940, 17, 216–17; of 2012, 266, 270, 273, 361n31

Eliasoph, Nina, 272–73, 363n51

elite networks, 361n28; conflicts and competition among, 245, 318n2, 324n100; and fund-raising, 156, 158, 175, 194, 207, 336n67

elites, 5, 62, 100; challenges to, 76, 95, 140, 207, 223; deference toward, 48; and fund-raising, 136, 214; influence over voluntarism and civic networks, 50–51, 60–61, 70, 86–88, 95, 99–100, 112–18, 148–49, 206–7, 224, 236–37; and municipal benevolence, 146; opposition to government, 146,

238, 262; political projects of, 22, 31, 33, 44, 75–77, 86–88, 99–101, 239–40, 252, 255, 264, 270–71, 301n33; and status abdication, 135

Elliot, Ezekiel Brown, 285

empowerment projects, 272–73

endowments, 45–46, 97, 111–12, 114, 324n96, 336n76; control over and termination of, 117, 168. *See also* foundations

England. *See* Britain (or England)

English Lifeboat Association, 24

equality, 146; of citizens, 10, 12–13, 16, 19, 28, 32, 48, 52, 136, 162, 259; contradictions with expectations for deference and gratitude, 16, 69; racial equality and inequality, 127, 161, 211, 305n88; and relief, 186–88. *See also* categorical exclusions and inequalities

equal rights, 105; in tension with individual situations and local practices, 142–43, 188–89

Eskimos, 205

Eslick, Edward, 174, 183

Europe, comparisons to, 28, 46, 50, 53–55, 66, 75, 78, 106, 164, 300n14, 301n33, 312n93, 320n26, 341n11. *See also* Britain (or England); France; Germany; Russia

evangelicals and evangelicalism, 24, 34, 36, 40–41, 43, 69–71, 95, 309n50

Evangelical United Front, 29

expansible state or nation-state, 5, 103–38, 213, 215, 227, 234, 236, 254, 300n20, 325n6. *See also* architecture of governance; coproduction; division of labor; infrastructural power

family: as natural association, 39; as relational model, 8, 14, 16, 360n14

family welfare and counseling, 99, 150, 154, 185, 191–92, 201, 204, 248, 340n139, 343n36, 345n79

Family Welfare Association of America, 154

Farm Bureau, 144

Farwell, John V., 69, 281

Father Basil, 96–97, 110, 145

fault lines. *See* zones of instability, or fault lines

Faust, Drew, 23–24

Federal Emergency Relief Administration (FERA), 177, 183–84, 186, 189, 199

federal government: capacities of, 22, 53, 179, 215, 314n15; exemptions from policy, 199; infrastructural power of, 227, 264; and New Deal, 1; opposition to power and expansion of, 105, 120–22, 192, 202–3, 216, 262; and Red Cross, 107–9, 112–13, 119, 152, 168, 206; responsibilities for relief and their limits, 165, 167–74, 177, 183, 194, 200, 202, 218, 228, 254, 321n34, 338n108; revenues and resources, 22, 37, 155–56, 309n50; State Department, 214; and voluntarism, 56–57, 87, 104–5, 117–19, 168, 199, 203, 217, 234, 252; and WWI indirect state-building, 120–32, 136. *See also* expansible state or nation-state; Hopkins, Harry; nation-state-building; taxation

Federalism, as source of dynamism, 306n105

Federalists, 28, 31, 40, 310n64; and Benevolent Empire, 38–39

federal-local relations, 179, 193, 250; in American Red Cross, 153; in disaster relief, 104; in March of Dimes, 202–3; not specified in Constitution, 75; programs disembedded from municipal networks, 189–90

Federal Reserve, 118

Federal Security Agency, 225, 226, 227

federal-state-local, structure of voluntary associations, 326n24

federal-state relations, 29, 75, 123, 155, 179, 193, 207–9; and antislavery, 40–41; Red Cross as mechanism for accountability, 207–8; in regulation and taxation, 134, 198; and unemployment relief, 165, 167, 208. *See also* matching grants

federated fund-raising, 100, 106, 147, 198, 200, 207, 254, 266; advantages of, 99, 146, 150, 237, 243; as alternative to taxation, 146; resistance to, 145, 244, 245; as taxation without representation, 150, 165–66, 243. *See also* fund-raising

Fenian Society, 68

Field, Marshall, 158

field theory, 10, 20, 360n14, 362n36

Fieser, James L., 139, 206, 221, 223, 352n43, 354n70; and democratic or popular character of Red Cross, 106, 230–31, 351n36

Finland and Finns, 213–14, 216, 349n2

First World War. *See* World War I

Fisher, Claude, and definition of voluntarism, 18, 44

Fisher, George Jackson, 285

Flint, MI, 246

Ford, Henry, II, 237, 246

Fosdick, Harry E., 158, 197

Fosdick, Raymond, 121

Foucault, Michel, 63, 302n40, 316n65

foundations, 71, 101, 115–16, 133, 152, 204, 211, 228; Russell Sage, 70, 117, 124, 154; as threat to democracy, 328n60. *See also* endowments; philanthropists and philanthropy; Rockefeller Foundation

France, 129, 141, 217, 303n58, 332n8; comparisons to American political development, 5, 14, 23, 27–28, 30, 273–74, 308n29, 312n87, 359n3; *fraternité* as model of order, 23, 28; French Revolution and Terror, 1, 14, 23, 27–29, 31, 44, 50, 257, 304n72,

308n28; Jacobins, 29, 44; National Workshops, 78, 84, 94–95; Paris Commune, 77; and WWI, 129–30, 132, 141, 157, 158; and WWII, 214, 217; Zouaves, 54. *See also* World War I; World War II

Franco-Prussian War, 65

fraternal orders, 14, 29, 48, 194, 224, 226, 247, 340n3; Masons and anti-Masonry, 29, 308n31, 308n34

Freedman's Inquiry Board, 65

freedom, 52, 55, 63, 237; of assembly and association, 3, 31; of choice, 48; of information, 259; of voluntary associations, 146, 190. *See also* liberty

freedom of conscience: linked to association by concept of voluntarism, 48; threatened by association, 39, 42, 150; Wayland on primacy of, 42–43

French Revolution. *See* France

friendship (*fraternité*), 118; as relational model, 23, 28, 160, 304n82, 306n4; used and strained by fund-raising, 97–98, 125, 135, 157, 160, 162, 222, 232, 249–50, 358n49

Friendship Train, 359n61

Frothingham, Octavius Brooks, 322n59, 322n60

fund-raising, 81, 104, 123, 157, 179–80, 210, 245, 250, 251; as "charitable buffoonery," 57, 214; as coercive, 37, 140, 147, 150, 165–66, 245–46, 250, 262, 267, 334n33, 334n47, 354n81, 355n7; during Civil War, 50, 57, 60; during WWI, 125–32, 198; during WWII, 214–15, 218–24, 228–34; efforts to limit, 234, 255; etiquette of, 187–88; in firms and workplaces, 92, 94, 95, 106, 149–50, 161–62, 193, 247, 250; as form of or limit on taxation, 32, 140, 191, 200, 237, 245–46, 249–50, 255; iconography of, 158–59; industry, 157, 160, 200, 324n96 (*see also* Jones, John Price); innovations, 57, 67, 81–

82, 100, 106; linking small and large gifts, 57, 93–94, 117–18, 134, 152, 272; and nation-state-building, 3, 17, 38, 50, 73–74, 127, 135, 152, 205–7, 216, 234–37, 250, 261–62, 272; relational structures of, 134–35, 161–62, 231–32; schemes and systems, 23, 92–94, 97–100, 113–14, 135, 136, 145–47, 157–66, 181–82, 193–94, 237, 245–46, 249 (*see also* campaign model, of fundraising; federated fund-raising); and solidarity, 17, 23, 50, 67, 166, 205–6, 219–21, 242–43, 254; as threat to local authority, 38, 45, 60, 254–55, 330n88; use of new technologies, 85, 156, 160–61, 218, 231, 336n70; as work relief, 160–61, 195. *See also* Block-Aid; charitable contributions; citizen philanthropy; civic philanthropy; federated fund-raising; matching grants; presidential philanthropy

Gallup, George, confidential surveys for Red Cross, 2, 232–33, 235–36, 344n51, 354n75, 354n76, 355n2

Garner, John Nance, 217

Gellner, Ernest, 305n94

gender politics: of Civil War, 70–71, 331n104; of WWI, 143. *See also* categorical exclusions and inequalities

General Federation of Women's Clubs, 95

general government, 53. *See also* federal government

generalized exchange, 57–60; blood-banking as, 240–43; as expression of citizenship, 172, 231; from general to particular, 59–60; organized projects of, 271–72; and reciprocity, 23, 58, 179, 231; and solidarity, 10, 23, 57–60, 73, 174–75, 231–32, 266, 271. *See also* "divine method of patriotism"; gifts and giving; reciprocity

General Munitions Board, 123

Germany, 23, 125, 213, 217, 239

Gibson, Harvey D., 124, 157, 329n86

Gifford, Walter S., 119, 122, 165, 173, 234, 329n77

gifts and giving: and corruption, or the appearance of, 65–67, 203, 239, 265–66, 270, 273; danger in big gifts, 113–18; gift economy, 195; "gift extraction," 139; giving as coerced, 139, 150, 160–61, 262; giving as ritual, 203; logic of the gift, 11, 57–61, 74, 202; and nation-state-building, 2–3, 10–11, 16, 22, 57–61, 81, 106, 125, 206, 209, 240–42, 253, 259, 271–73; and political or social inclusion, 129–32, 160–61, 174–75, 203–6, 249; public benefits as compared to, 77, 91, 143, 265–66, 270, 273, 361n32, 361n33; relational geometry of, 5–6, 18, 74–75, 86, 98, 106, 136, 147, 174–75, 245, 247, 249, 266, 271–72, 302n51; Simmel on the gift and gratitude, 302n51; theories of the gift, 1, 11–12, 13–14, 304n70; as threat to dignity, independence, and civic standing, 13–14, 32, 64–65, 80, 83, 107, 136, 193–94, 259–60, 261, 265–65, 270, 272. See also charitable contributions; citizen philanthropy; donors and donations; fund-raising

Gilded Age, 68, 113, 264

Godfrey, Rev. Mr., 281

Gorski, Philip, 301n33

government. See federal government; municipal benevolence; public relief and services

"government out of sight," 9, 258

Grand Army of the Republic, 72, 288

Granfield, Mr., 171

Grange, 144

Grant, Ulysses, 57, 68, 69, 289

Graphic, 78, 320n25

gratitude, 10, 13, 16, 57, 61, 68, 77, 81, 86, 132, 135–36, 147, 201, 234, 241, 259, 271, 273; Simmel on faithfulness and gratitude, 302n51. *See also* gifts and giving; reciprocity

Grayson, Cary, 124, 206, 229

Great Commissions, 55, 57, 60–62, 68, 72, 79, 94, 105–6, 137–38, 271. *See also* United States Christian Commission (USCC); United States Sanitary Commission (USSC)

Great Depression. *See* Depression

Greater New York Fund (or Organization), 19–20, 135–36, 200, 329n77, 347n102

Great Society, 22, 254

Great War. *See* World War I

Griffin, Edward, 285

Grimm, Jacob, 59

Groton School, 151, 158

"group-mindedness," 149–50

Hall, George A., 281

Hamilton, Alexander, 9, 299n7

Harriman, E. Roland, 158, 246

Harvard, 116, 284–89, 324n96, 324n194, 329n77, 336n76

Hayek, Friedrich, 24

Hebrew. *See* Jews (or Hebrews)

Heflin, Thomas, 167, 338n108, 338n109

Heilbroner, Robert, 253

Helsinki, 213. *See also* Finland and Finns

Hickok, Lorena, 186–89

higher education, 22, 70, 200, 243, 255

Hitler, Adolf, 217

Hobbes, Thomas, 13, 16, 304n70

Hollis, Henry French, 134, 331n115

Hoover, Herbert, 1, 21, 124–25, 137, 140–42, 150–52, 161, 203, 205, 207, 260; archive as informant, 305n100; on government reorganization, 359n57; and Great Depression, 113, 122, 158, 165–75, 182, 184, 262, 335n66, 341n12; as master of emergencies, 138, 154; and Mississippi

Flood of 1927, 140; and Red Cross, 166–67, 169, 209, 229; and relief for Finland and WWII, 213–14, 216–17, 350n21; and Rockefeller Foundation, 184, 239; on voluntarism and limited government, 1, 21, 151–52, 154–55, 161, 165, 167–75, 177–79, 202–4, 209, 216–17, 223, 240, 252, 265, 313n104, 329n79, 335n48; WWI and food relief, 124–25, 131, 137, 141–42, 150, 151, 329n79, 330n89

Hopkins, Harry, 156, 177–78, 323n76, 340n136, 342n30; bright line between public funding and private agencies, 177–79, 189–90, 194, 209; and Community Chests, 219–20; on division of labor between government and voluntarism, 190–91, 204; Great Depression and New Deal, 156, 166, 177–79, 183–86, 188, 190, 194, 342n32, 343n46; and Red Cross, 219–20, 221, 230–31, 351n36; and Rockefeller Foundation, 184, 239, 343n35; WWII, 219–21, 350n14

Houghton, Henry Clarke, 282

Howe, Julia Ward, 64

Howe, Samuel Gridley, 50, 64–65, 66, 316n69, 317n71, 317n72

humiliation, 32; by charity, 171–72

humility, performances of, 135

Hunt, Sandford, 282

Huntington, Samuel, 9

hybrids and hybridization, 44; of organizational form, 10, 31, 79, 253, 262, 270; state as hybrid, 238, 250, 361n31

"hydras," 40, 118, 309n48. See also Bank of the United States; Benevolent Empire

"imagined community," 12, 231, 234, 355n82. See also national solidarity; nation-state-building

immigration and immigrants, 15, 35, 38, 105, 127, 266, 322n60; and categori-

cal exclusions, 21; and eligibility for relief, 90; inclusion through voluntarism, 131, 134, 254

imperialism and anti-imperialism, 132, 216

income tax. See taxation

incorporation. See corporate charters or incorporation

Indiana, 128, 282; State Board of Charities, 95

individualism, 16, 17, 41, 48, 65, 71, 361n31; Hayek on relation to voluntarism, 24; Hoover on "group individualism," 313n104; as selfishness, 20. See also citizenship

Industrial Areas Foundation, 251

Industrial Fund, 237, 245

industrial relations and conflict, 115–16, 328n60, 343n46; Federal Commission on Industrial Relations, 117–18. See also labor

inequality. See categorical exclusions and inequalities

influenza, of 1918, 137–38

infrastructural power, 5, 51, 104, 109, 227, 260, 302n43, 361n27; and American political development, 264–65, 273; Boston Committee on Donations, 109, 258, 311n73; and mobilization for war, 120–21, 140; and nation-state-building, 104, 121–23, 138, 144, 210–11, 227–28, 237, 264, 335n60; political geography of, 237, 260; for voluntarism and benevolence, 211, 242, 251. See also architecture of governance; division of labor

infrastructures: Block-Aid as model, 157; and coordination of social life, 104; organized charity and voluntarism as, 109, 123, 138, 140–41, 157, 178, 242

inheritance tax. See taxation

institutional change, 10, 47–48, 166, 361n25, 362n36; and constitutive

institutional change (*cont.*)
contradictions, 260–67; and Great
Depression, 178–79; trajectories and
patterns of, 259–60, 273–75, 312n96,
363n56; transposition, 266–67; in
unsettled times, 261
institutional grammar, 269
institutional legacies, 23, 81, 210–12,
260. *See also* legacies
institutional theory, 301n32, 306n2,
360n14, 362n36
insurance, 136, 149, 203, 241; blood-
banking as mutual insurance, 241;
as organizational model, 202, 218.
See also social insurance
International Committee of the Red
Cross, 106, 214, 217
international relief, 142, 171, 178, 218–
19; Board of Foreign Missions, 115,
309n46; as foreign policy, 209, 217,
240, 327n53; International Committee of Relief for Wounded Soldiers,
71–72; and presidential philanthropy, 113, 209, 229, 262
Irish-Americans, 62, 68; as Union
volunteers, 53
Isham, Ralph N., 286
isolationism, 22, 113, 209, 212, 217,
220–21, 229
Italian-Americans, 131
Italy, 50, 111, 254, 332n8
iterated problem-solving, as method of
analysis, 18–20, 27, 257

Jackson, Andrew, 33, 40; Jacksonian
democracy, 6, 44, 120, 267–68
Jackson, Lewis, 79
Jackson v. Phillips, 114, 267, 269
Jacobs, Benjamin F., 69, 282
Japan, 115, 216, 355n14
Japanese-Americans, 132
Jefferson, Thomas, 32, 33, 39, 41, 44,
304n81, 310n60; Jeffersonians, 40
Jesup, Morris K., 79

Jews (or Hebrews): charitable socie-
ties, 81, 88, 145, 327n42, 333n30; and
Civil War fund-raising, 53; inter-
denominational activity, 121, 200,
230, 333n30, 352n47; Jewish Welfare
Board, 121; philanthropy, 134;
United Hebrew Charities, 89
Johns Hopkins University, 115
Johnson, Ellen Terry, 290
Johnson, Hiram, 331n115
Johnson, Lyndon Baines, 22, 254
Jones, Jimmy, and his new shoes, 188
Jones, John Price, 157, 200, 324n96,
336n76, 345n69
Jones, Rufus, 238
Judd, Orange, 286
Junior Red Cross. *See* American Red
Cross

Kennedy, John F., 254
Kentucky, 128, 205, 233
Kerlin, Isaac, 286
Kerr, Thomas, 282
Kissinger, Henry, 252
Kiwanis, 100
Knights of Columbus, 121
Knights of the Golden Circle, 56
knitting, 2, 66, 127, 129–31, 141, 205,
215, 271; as economic rehabilitation,
332n8
Korean War, 247
Kropotkin, Peter, 24

labor, 120, 321n34; and civic benevolence, 3; eligibility for relief, 12, 85,
189 (*see also* work relief); eligibility
of strikers, 186, 343n46; erosion of
independence and self-sufficiency,
77; free and unfree, 5, 65; inclusion in and exclusion from civic networks, 193, 223–24, 228–29, 236–
37, 242–43, 246; organizations and
unions, 48, 80, 223, 226; political
clubs, 92; public and private relief

and labor bureaus, 80, 93, 94, 180, 182, 189, 323n90; and Red Cross, 17, 223–24, 230–31, 242–43, 245, 351n31, 352n43, 352n44, 356n24; and right to vote, 304n84. *See also* industrial relations and conflict

labor law, exemption of private charity and religion, 199

La Guardia, Fiorello, 226

Lamont, Thomas, 232

law, and stabilization of contradictions, 269

Lawson, Melinda, 67, 324n103

legacies, 81, 123, 260; of American Revolution, 11; and categories, 267–73; of Civil War, 51, 60, 67–72, 78, 86, 106, 108, 120, 319n5, 325n20; of Great Depression and New Deal, 174, 210–12, 214, 248–49; and nation-state-building, 6, 19–21, 23, 260; of WWI, 123, 133–37, 139, 141–44, 147, 214, 328n75; of WWII, 240–48. *See also* institutional legacies

Lehman, Herbert, 183

Lévi-Strauss, Claude, 301n32

liberalism: and American political culture, 300n14; and citizenship, 12, 17, 50, 259, 260, 264, 266, 270; contradictions with benevolence and charity, 10, 13–14, 17–20, 25, 48, 64–65, 260, 262, 266, 271; market liberalism and neoliberalism, 25, 65, 274; as model of political order, 16; and multiple traditions, 12–13, 303n65; and nation-state-building, 120, 260, 273–74; problem of obligation, 16, 301n31, 304n83, 350n11, 359n59

Liberator, 50

liberty: and American political development, 3, 12–13, 16–20; as endangered by hierarchy, 55; as freedom of choice, 44–52; and obligation, 1; as protected by charity and volun-

tarism, 27–28, 35, 37, 252; religious, 14–15, 312n86 (*see also* freedom of conscience); and slavery as constitutive contradiction, 5, 362n35; as threatened by charity and voluntarism, 10, 18, 27–28, 35, 37, 39–44, 47–48, 77, 260–61; as threatened by government and standing armies, 52, 103, 115, 216, 237; voluntarism as resolution of government and liberty, 252

Liberty Loans, during WWI, 123, 127, 144, 157, 158, 160

Liberty National Bank, 157, 329n86

libraries, 113

Liggett, David, correspondence with Hopkins, 219–21

Lincoln, Abraham, 28, 51, 54, 62, 69, 220, 289

Lindsay, Samuel McCune, 134

Lions Club, 100

Livermore, Mary, 70, 290

loans, 168–73, 235, 302n41; as distinct from charity or gifts, 111, 154, 168–72, 181, 326n32, 335n62, 339n129; and foreign entanglements, 350n23; as funding for government, 2, 127, 156–57 (*see also* Liberty Loans, during WWI)

local: control challenged by national fund-raising, 38, 110–11, 206, 218, 225–26, 243; control over voluntarism, 48, 74, 98–100, 104, 110, 140, 147–48, 152–53, 163, 192–93, 195, 202–3, 209, 236–37, 242–44, 326n28; federal-local relations, 254; governance, 251–52; linked to national, 67, 110, 154, 202, 225, 245, 253; and nation-state-building, 8, 28, 38, 58, 60, 67, 104–5, 109, 112, 120–24, 138, 151, 179, 183, 203, 224–25, 228, 236–37; networks and circuits of reciprocity, 67, 98, 106, 226, 237, 265, 271, 312n99, 355n7, 357n29,

local (*cont.*)
    359n61; role in relief, 47, 114, 140, 143, 169–70, 173, 180, 183, 207, 209, 218–19, 335n48, 342n32, 343n46, 344n52, 344n54, 352n49; solidarity, identity, and prejudice, 48, 60, 67, 147–48, 152–53, 188–89, 219, 228, 243–44, 262, 307n7, 324n103. *See also* federal government; municipal benevolence; political geography
Locke, John, 13, 14, 16
lodging houses, 80, 91, 96, 185
logic of the gift, 57, 61, 65, 74, 77, 99, 150, 195, 202; and blood banking, 240–43; defined, 11; individualization of, 247; in a liberal polity, 77, 88, 260–61, 266–67; and San Francisco earthquake, 112; in wartime, 231. *See also* relational geometries or logics
Long, Huey, 299n3
Lowell, Josephine Shaw, 68, 85, 91
Loyal Leagues of the Union, 56, 86

Madison, James, 33, 310n64
Madison Square Garden, 20, 213, 223, 233
Maine, 72, 128, 281
Mandeville, Bernard, 14
Mann, Michael, 5, 7, 9, 109, 264, 301n28, 302n43, 305n94, 361n27
Manufacturers Trust Company, 157, 329n86
March of Dimes, 2, 17, 18, 22, 23, 201–3, 207, 226, 229, 240, 245–46, 265, 271, 272, 359n61; cartoon, 3–4; Committee to Celebrate the President's Birthday, 1, 22, 201–3, 265; and goal succession, 332n5; National Foundation for Infant Paralysis, 17, 202–3, 240, 305n87, 305n88; politicization of, 202–3. *See also* presidential philanthropy
marginal men, 6, 127–29, 189, 205–6, 271, 317n72
Marshall, George, 356n20, 359n61

Marshall, T. H., 349n136
Maryland, 78, 128
Massachusetts, 58, 65. *See also* Boston
mass relief, 187, 190–92, 249. *See also* breadlines and soup kitchens
matching grants, 134; from donors to recipients, 113–14; from federal to state governments, 177, 183–84, 190, 193, 208–9; "method of partial succor," 113; as model for funding within March of Dimes, 202–3
Mauss, Marcel, 1, 6, 247
Mazzini, Giuseppe, 50–52, 79, 258
McCagg, Ezra Butler, 286
McClellan, George B., 57
McCloy, John J., 239
McIntyre, Marvin, 202, 206
McKeon, Richard, 257. *See also* Rockefeller, Nelson: Special Studies Project
Means, Gardiner, 198
medical voluntaries, 243–44
mentally ill, as beneficiaries, 84–85. *See also* categorical exclusions and inequalities
Merton, Robert, 231, 354n71
Methodists, 69, 281–83, 307n11
"method of partial succor." *See* matching grants
Mexican-Americans, 188–89
Mexican-American War, 53, 61
Meyer, Mrs. Eugene, 356n24
Michigan, 90, 128, 244, 246, 283
military: as beggars or pauperized by gifts, 67, 136; and Civil War, 52–72, 79, 315n28, 316n66; as close to the people, 50, 52, 54–55, 60–62, 67, 83, 94, 125–26, 225, 232, 315n28; and disaster relief, 103–4, 110, 168, 208; discipline, 55, 61–64; and "expansible state," 325n6; funding of, 37, 316n60; and inclusion, 348n125; navy, 37, 103, 119, 130, 152, 208, 219, 329n76; as organizational model or

relational logic, 3, 50–51, 65, 135, 137, 231–32, 307n11; and political development, 52–54, 236, 300n20, 301n33; relation to Red Cross, 108, 125, 126–27, 129, 137, 144, 191, 220–21, 250; relation to voluntarism, 49, 54–56, 60, 63–67, 120–22, 217, 219, 221–22, 224–25, 230, 254, 316n66, 328n68, 328n75; resentment of civilian experts, 62; and Revolutionary War, 2; service and reciprocity, 21, 57–60, 66–67, 125–26, 139–40, 174, 231, 270–71; services for veterans and dependents, 142–43, 227, 237, 318n95; supported by gifts, 129–31; and threat of despotism, 50–51, 63–64, 314n18; veterans and Grand Army of the Republic, 72. *See also* Civil War; draft; Society of the Cincinnati; Spanish-American War; World War I; World War II

militia, 52, 56, 314n14; and Mississippi Flood of 1927, 152; National Guard, 152, 285; and San Francisco earthquake, 103–4

Mill, John Stuart, on USSC, 51–52, 79, 258, 314n10

missionary societies, 36, 38, 43, 82, 238, 281, 290, 310n54, 327n50; as organizational model, 24, 35. *See also* American Home Missionary Society

Mitchell, Timothy, 210–11

Mobilization for Human Needs. *See* Community Chests

models. *See* relational geometries or logics

modularity, 97

Monroe, James, 33

Moody, Dwight L., 68, 69, 281, 282

Moore, Clara Jessup, 290

moral framework, 240; "Moral Framework of National Purpose," 253–54

Morgan, J. Pierpont, 113, 151, 158, 160–61; J. P. Morgan and Co., 124

Mormons: and anti-Mormonism, 33; and revocation of charter, 116

Morris, Andrew, 193–94

Moss, Lemuel, 54, 282, 283

motives for giving, 10, 33, 35, 61–62, 64, 66, 86, 182, 220, 221, 223, 249, 266, 313n3, 322n60; corrupted by federal spending, 171; language of service, 99; religious, 222–23

Moton, Robert R., 153, 161

movies, 135, 143–44

multiple traditions thesis, 12–14

municipal benevolence, 70, 73–101, 189, 193, 209, 327n42; and business networks, 74–75; community as focus of identity and solidarity, 67, 146–47, 155, 221, 245–46, 254–55, 357n32; elite influence over, 76, 86–88, 245; as limit on taxation, 74–75; as model of governance, 21, 86, 95–101; and nation-state-building, 60, 110–11, 139–40, 250; networks of, 70–71, 93, 95, 109, 110, 112, 118, 124, 149, 216; responsibility for unemployed, 77–84, 88–95, 150–51, 156, 175, 180, 182 (*see also* Block-Aid); role of city government, 88, 93; and Sanitary Fairs, 67

municipal finances, impact of WWI fund-raising, 147–48

municipal politics, as model of progressive politics, 363n58

Murphy, Grayson M.-P., 124

Murphy, Starr J., 116

Napoleon, 39, 50

National Association for the Advancement of Colored People, and March of Dimes, 17

National Association of Manufacturers, 217, 350n23

National Conference of Charities and Corrections, 86

National Foundation for Infant Paralysis. *See* March of Dimes

National Guard. *See* militia

national identity. *See* peoplehood

National Investigation Bureau of War Charities, 147, 261, 339n122

nationalization of relief and fund-raising, 236–37, 240; proposed by Hoover, 154–55

national security state, 238

national solidarity, 271; generated by gifts, 25, 81, 100–101, 134–35, 166, 203, 234, 235; as threatened by competing identities and local practices, 121–23, 153, 270; and wartime voluntarism, 137–38, 236. *See also* generalized exchange

National Workshops. *See* France

nation-state-building, 2, 6, 13–15, 18, 30, 51, 61, 67, 72, 73–74, 100, 104–6, 121–22, 207–8, 219, 257–59, 270; and cities, 75–77; and disaster relief, 118–19; Federalist-Benevolent nation-building project, 38–39; indirect state-building, 120–25; models of political order, 16; nationalism and nation-building, 2–3, 10–12, 17, 19, 48, 67, 104, 107, 122, 125–32, 137, 203, 219, 234, 239; state-building, 1–3, 5–10, 12, 19, 48, 67, 75–77, 120–25, 139, 234, 235, 301n29, 301n31, 315n35, 335n60, 350n12; statism, 250; through voluntarism, 56, 71, 127–28, 207, 240, 265

navy. *See* military

Nebraska, 128; Relief and Aid Society, 81

Neem, Johann, 45

neighbors and neighborhoods, 16, 29, 85, 252, 354n75; neighborhood centers in Occupied Germany, 239; neighborhood leader system, 160–63, 227, 337n93 (*see also* Block-Aid); neighborliness, as basis for voluntarism, 103, 158, 163; and organization of WWI Selective Service, 120

neo-episodic analysis, 18–19, 270; and role of archives, 20. *See also* iterated problem-solving, as method of analysis

neoliberalism, 25, 274

networks: alignment of, 8, 111; disembedding from, 8, 189, 215, 244; elite, 158, 175, 194, 336n67, 361n28; linkages and contradictions among, 7–8, 9, 32, 118, 146, 244–45, 247, 260, 262; linking private organizations and federal government, 119–20, 123–25, 181, 237, 264, 329n77; of municipal control, 95–100, 106–9, 146–50, 209, 216, 226–27, 237, 246; and nation-state-building, 6–9, 11–12, 25, 34, 67, 70, 73, 112, 178, 211, 217, 240, 242, 258, 264–65, 271–72, 301n33, 302n43; personal, 135, 238, 249–50 (*see also* friendship [*fraternité*]); and political mobilization, 363n57, 363n58; of reform associations, 34–35; socio-spatial, 7; of urban relief, 82–83 (*see also* municipal benevolence). *See also* "divine method of patriotism"; municipal benevolence

neutrality: New York City in Civil War, 87; principle of, 217; and war relief, 125, 214, 330n89, 349n8

Nevada, 57, 128, 131

Newberry, John Strong, 287

New Deal, 153, 175, 177–201, 206, 211, 265, 323n76, 334n31, 346n88; agencies, 1; efforts to limit, 200; exceptions from policy, 23; legacies of, 240–48; opposition to, 216, 242; as state-building, 1, 215, 228, 248–49. *See also* Depression

New Hampshire, 58, 70, 128, 134, 284, 331n115

New Haven, CT, 90

new public management, 24

newspaper funds, 91–93, 323n83. *See also* unemployment relief

New York City, 53, 57, 60, 68, 75–77, 79, 87–89, 92, 94, 124, 134, 193–94, 205, 226, 227, 281–91, 319n12, 323n72, 334n31, 334n48, 345n69; absence of Community Chest, 146, 155–56, 194, 345n79; Association for Improving the Conditions of the Poor, 89, 146, 158, 173, 178, 195, 248; Bureau of Public Welfare, 178; charity and reform organizations, 80, 89; Charity Organization Society (NYCOS), 84, 89, 110, 116, 122, 124, 146, 155, 165, 173, 177, 186, 190–91, 193, 195, 234, 248, 341n10; Children's Aid Society, 73, 88, 89; Citizens Family Welfare Committee, 192; Commissioners of Charities and Corrections, 79, 82; Community Chest, 244; Community Service Society, 195, 248–50; depression of 1873, 81; Eastside Relief Committee, 91, 163; elites and civic clubs, 87, 135, 161; Emergency Employment Committee, 262–63; Emergency Unemployment Relief Committee (EURC), 173 (see also Block-Aid); Greater New York Fund, 19–20, 135, 200, 329n77, 347n102; newspaper funds, 92–93; Police Commissioner, 151, 158; private relief agencies and activities, 88–89, 146, 164, 170, 173, 178, 180–85, 195–96, 227, 343n36; Red Cross chapters, 112, 158, 205–6, 221; relief spending, 185; 6-15-99 Club, 92–94; unemployment relief, 156–65, 180–85, 193–96, 337n93 (see also Block-Aid; Prosser Committee); Union Defense Committee, 50–51
New York State, 128, 135, 198, 209, 244, 308n25, 313n101, 320n30, 341n15, 346n96, 347n96; Charities Aid Association, 70; and charter for Rockefeller Foundation, 117–18; public utilities and charitable contri-
butions, 198; Temporary Emergency Relief Administration (TERA), 156, 180, 182
New York Times, 67, 92, 117, 172; on Red Cross, 220
New York Tribune, 78, 324n101
New York Trust Company, 157, 329n86
Nobel Peace Prize, 115
nonpartisanship, 46, 161, 268, 311n64
nonprofit organizations: as contrasted with private charity, 248; as empowerment projects, 272–73, 363n51; exemptions from federal law, 199, 211; as innovators, 204; nonprofit sector, 22, 179, 195, 199, 204, 210, 249, 255; as organizational form, 22, 307n7; public funding of, 22–23, 199, 250, 254–55; and reciprocity, 249–50; state-building and contracting out, 2, 22, 250, 254, 269; and tax code, 243, 249, 268–69; usage of term, 22, 255, 258; work relief in, 195–97
North Carolina, 128, 129, 205, 304n81
Norway, 213
Novak, William, 264
nurses, 142, 242; in Civil War, 53, 61, 106, 141, 290, 291, 315n28, 315n32, 316n66; in public health, 143, 144

Obamacare, as political "gift," 266
obituaries, as data source, 69–71
obligation: culture of, 150; disarticulation of obligations and dependence, 270–71; and liberty, 1; networks of, 146; as problem for liberalism, 16, 301n31, 304n83, 350n11, 359n59. See also gratitude; reciprocity
O'Connor, Basil, 229–30, 240–47, 250, 356n20, 356n24
Office of Civilian Defense (OCD), 226–27, 295, 353n57
Office of Community War Services (OCWS), 226, 227, 295
Oglesby, Richard J., 318n96

Ohio, 37, 128, 147–49, 186, 230, 287, 289
Ohio Valley floods, 206
Olmsted, Frederick Law, 66, 76, 287
open access order, 45, 311n68. *See also* corporate charters or incorporation
open architecture. *See* architecture of governance
organizational: capacity, 74, 118, 119, 125, 137, 314n15; character of the Red Cross, 168–69; commitment, 167; conformity, 99; culture, 136; field, 268; leadership, 60; matrix, 56; mission, 194; projects, 137; resources, 36–38; technologies, 5, 85; template, 251
organizational autonomy, 146
organizational form, 76; contradictions between, 26; elaboration, hybridization, and disarticulation, 269–70; hierarchy and reciprocity, 19; and institutional change, 261–62, 266, 269–70, 273–74, 362n36; learning, 35; Lukács on, 257; nonprofit organization, 22; political parties, 28, 33; voluntary associations, 46. *See also* hybrids and hybridization; organizational innovation
organizational infrastructure, 47; of civic benevolence, 246
organizational innovation, 20, 27, 29, 204, 261, 269–70, 362n36; cities and, 76; and combinatorial politics, 10, 12, 18–20, 27, 76–77, 260–62, 266; and nation-state-building, 100; political parties as, 307n10; by private charity, 85–86, 190–91; as response to contradictions, 20, 29–30, 47–48, 77, 86, 88, 260–62, 270–74; as threat to liberty, 39
organizational landscape, 48, 52, 248–50
organizational models, 37, 69; and architecture of governance, 104; army as, 61, 307n11; charity organization

society as, 84; and combinatorial politics, 30; contradictions between, 62; corporation as, 124; as legacies, 69, 81; missionary societies as, 35; and nation-state-building, 111. *See also* relational geometries or logics; repertoire
organizational mutation, Red Cross charter as, 105, 107–9, 137, 172
organizational practice and skills, 67, 68–69, 85, 97; centralization as, 80; the pledge as, 42, 44
organizational sociology, 7, 260–61
orphanages, 35
Otis, James, 287
Ott, Julia, 123, 329n83
"over and above," 191–92, 344n62. *See also* fund-raising

Packard, Arthur W., 191, 234
Parent-Teacher Associations, 237
Paris Commune. *See* France
Park, James, Jr., 288
Parker, Edward, 288
Parker, Laura Wolcott, 290
participation: by African Americans, 338n97; alignment with military discipline, 61–64; in democratic politics and war mobilization, 95, 125, 135, 226, 238, 242, 251, 253–54, 274, 363n57; by elites, 135, 324n100; scale as relevant to large donors, 97, 345n76; in voluntary associations and fund-raising, 17, 105, 147, 193, 200, 209, 221, 223, 230, 242–43, 259, 313n104, 351n36, 352n49
partisanship and nonpartisanship, 16, 33, 38, 192, 202, 236, 240, 310n64; partisan control of charity, 88, 95; and Red Cross, 109, 141, 166–75, 202, 204, 206, 223; voluntarism as nonpartisan and not political, 46, 182, 189
patchwork quilt, 59

path dependence, 211, 341n9, 360n13

patriotic giving, and nation-state-building, 14, 133–32, 220, 259, 268–69. *See also* citizen philanthropy; civic benevolence; presidential philanthropy

patriotic solidarity, 60, 63, 76, 135, 158, 212, 221, 232. *See also* national solidarity

patronage politics, 33, 77–78, 88, 95, 189–90, 265–66, 309n40; charges against March of Dimes, 201–2

Payne, John Barton, 154, 173, 229

payroll deductions, 149, 193–94, 245, 262

Peabody, George, 113

Peace Corps, 254

Pearl Harbor, 218, 219

Pearson, Drew, 359n61

Pennsylvania, 40, 126, 173

peoplehood, 15–16, 23, 127; and national identity, 15, 105, 240, 266, 324n103; stories of, 3, 12, 132, 257

people's partnership, 206, 213, 216, 223, 230–31, 351n36, 352n44, 356n24

Perkins, Ephraim, 32

Perkins, Frances, 341n12, 342n30

Pershing, John J., 136

Phelan, James, 110, 112

Philadelphia, 40, 44, 51, 59, 69, 75, 87, 129, 283, 287, 288, 290, 311n68, 314n10, 323n72, 345n69; County Relief Board, 189

philanthropists and philanthropy, 97, 113–18, 133; civic and psychological effects, 166; foundations, 23; usage of term, 258

Pinchot, Gifford, 173

pity. *See* compassion

Plan of Union, between Congregationalists and Presbyterians, 36, 38

pledge, as threat to freedom of conscience, 42

Poland, 229

Polanyi, Karl, reciprocity as social form, 11

polio, 201, 240

political activity, as ineligible for charitable contributions. *See* taxation

political corruption. *See* corruption

political geography: of fund-raising, 219–21; of voluntarism, 41, 60, 67, 104–5, 109, 127, 237, 243, 245, 271, 326n24. *See also* sectionalism

political inclusion. *See* categorical exclusions and inequalities

political parties, 3; invention of, 28, 33, 267, 307n10, 308n31; legitimacy of, 33, 41, 309n40; relation to voluntary associations, 40, 70, 161, 309n40; "state of courts and parties," 314n15, 361n27

Pollard, Jack, 223

poor, 47, 76, 96, 131, 145–46, 318n96, 321n41, 338n108; Arendt on, 14; categories of, 77–78, 80–81, 83–85, 89–90, 194, 315n39, 321n36; and concept of charity, 91, 299n2; as dependent, 86; dignity of, 41, 91, 171–72; as exploited by voluntary fund-raising, 37, 150, 161; inclusion through giving, 3–4, 112, 270–71; paupers and pauperization, 13, 79, 136, 270, 318n90, 319n5; problem of poverty, 76–77; and right to vote, 85, 270, 304n84; the "should not have been poor," 77, 90, 154, 160, 163–64, 175, 182; Simmel on, 13, 77; tramps and vagrants, 65, 89, 93, 96, 319n5. *See also* New York City: Association for Improving the Conditions of the Poor

popular sovereignty, 5, 30–32

Post Office, 9, 139, 193; antislavery and Sabbatarians, 40–41; and Red Cross, 112, 154; rejected as site for draft registration, 120

power, 63, 312n96; cities as sites of, 74–76, 96, 113; concentrated or

power (*cont.*)
  decentralized, 203, 209, 226, 237, 242; elite, 32, 55, 74, 116–18; and the gift, 32, 67–68; networks of, 7, 9, 48, 118; obscured by open architecture of state, 20; and voluntary associations, 39, 43, 109, 138, 140, 170, 230, 252. *See also* federal government; infrastructural power; nation-state-building
Pratt, Adam Scott, 69, 282
Presbyterians, 36, 43, 45, 69, 283, 284, 286, 309n50, 311n68
presidential philanthropy, 201–10, 246; as foreign policy, 209, 211–12, 217; as model of governance, 2. *See also* citizen philanthropy; fund-raising; March of Dimes
President's Emergency Committee on Employment (PECE), 158, 165, 167, 338n106
President's Organization on Unemployment Relief (POUR), 165, 173, 338n106
President's War Relief Control Board, 262
Preston, David, 283
prisoners, 129, 205, 258–59, 271; prisoners of war, 316n66. *See also* marginal men
private agencies and relief: accountability to donors, 195, 245; claims for distinctive virtue, 174; as compared to public relief, 154, 191–94; coordination among, 89; crowding out, 200; eligibility for federal relief funds, 177, 183–84, 199; limited capacity of, 165, 177; as model for government programs, 197; relational logic of, 99; in relation to public programs, 179, 190–94, 207, 211, 215, 217, 225, 227; relief spending during Great Depression, 185; state regulation and oversight, 74; and war-time fund-raising, 218, 224. *See also* charity; unemployment relief
professional and trade associations, and wartime mobilization, 119, 122–23
professionals and professionalism: of social workers and relief work, 85, 108, 215; in tension with voluntarism, 66, 136
Prohibition, 197–99
Prosser Committee, 155, 162, 170. *See also* New York City: unemployment relief
public agencies and programs, 1, 177–78, 182–84, 188–91, 199–201; public benefits compared to charity, 143; resistance to use of, 142–43; standardization of, 142–43. *See also* federal government
public and private, 6, 9, 18, 22–24, 30, 71, 74, 79–80, 87, 94–95, 100, 113–14, 119, 153, 167, 204, 207, 211; boundary between, 47–48, 178–79, 211; delegation, 84; theorization of, 251–55, 258–59. *See also* division of labor; Rockefeller, Nelson: Special Studies Project
public employment and public works, 82–84, 151, 173, 195, 200, 218, 320n26, 322n44. *See also* work relief
public funding, 50–51, 180, 183–85, 188–93, 211, 318n96; of nonprofit organizations, 22, 254–55; and private charity, 9, 47, 74–75, 77, 87–88, 92–93, 178, 189–90, 343n36; and religious organizations, 190, 322n63; restricted to public agencies, 177–79, 183–84, 199, 225
public goods, 46, 260, 267, 269; coproduction of, 5–6, 18, 46, 90–91, 104, 274, 363n57; wealth and the private determination of, 259
public health, 152, 201, 241, 262, 288; nursing programs, 143–44; philan-

thropic support for public agencies, 114; shift from private to public responsibility, 152; United States Public Health Service, 142

public opinion, 31, 34–35, 37–38, 91, 310n62; on public relief, 208; of Red Cross, 232–33, 354n75, 354n76, 355n2

public-private partnerships and programs, 24–25, 95, 179, 225, 236, 306n102, 352n49

public relations and publicity, 1, 11, 91, 135, 160, 201–2, 215, 226–27, 236, 337n93, 348n127; and Red Cross, 143–44. *See also* newspaper funds

public relief and services, 77, 79, 88, 92, 94, 100, 140, 194, 204, 208, 211–12; arguments against, 78, 151, 155, 170–71, 173, 252, 265; arguments for, 150, 161, 165–68, 170–71, 173–74, 177, 204, 274, 334n46; categories of eligibility, 89–90, 186–87; as compared to charity, 262; and expansible state, 214–15; as government dole, 173; legitimation of, 186–87; as moral threat or corruption, 77, 151, 156, 185, 187, 192; outdoor, 88; politicization of, 189; resistance to claiming benefits, 142–43; as a right, 1, 80, 83, 91, 175, 183–90, 210, 260, 262; as threat to democratic dignity, 87; as threat to voluntarism, 170–71. *See also* poor

public subsidies. *See* public funding

Public Works Administration, 343

Puerto Rico, 233

Pyle, Ernie, 221–22

Quakers, 15, 238, 307n11

racial and ethnic solidarity, 258, 300n12

racial identity and diversity, 3, 132, 231, 300n11

racial inequality and exclusion, 15–17, 105, 120, 127, 129, 153, 161, 164, 188, 211, 331n104, 331n113; and citizenship

or peoplehood, 132, 134; and civic benevolence, 46, 116, 131, 162, 174, 200, 205, 223, 305n88; and disaster relief, 152–53; and unemployment relief and social security, 175, 186–89, 343n50. *See also* categorical exclusions and inequalities; slavery and antislavery

radio, 228; and fund-raising, 160–61, 218, 231–32

reciprocity, 302n41, 304n70; city-to-city, 81, 106, 112, 326n26; expectations of, 2, 86, 213, 326n26; extended or generalized forms of, 5, 23, 58, 60, 73, 179, 240–43; failures of, 246–47; municipal circuits of, 81–84, 249; nationalized, 240; and nation-state-building, 10, 16, 18–19, 25, 67–68, 150, 174, 183, 206, 213, 240, 244, 258, 300n12; and peoplehood, 23, 73; as relational geometry, 11, 24, 71, 98, 100, 175, 202, 244, 249, 302n51; restricted, 247; in war and disaster, 57–58, 112, 140, 231. *See also* gratitude; logic of the gift

Reconstruction Finance Corporation, 173

Red Cross. *See* American Red Cross

Reed, Senator, 169

"rehabilitation thesis," 191, 192, 200, 204

relational geometries or logics, 7–10, 302n51; among donors, 99; of charity and fund-raising, 85, 94, 98–99, 161, 224, 231–33, 244–45; charity as, 175; and combinatorial politics, 7–10, 19, 260–62, 266–70, 360n14, 360n15; competition among, 269–70; contradictions between, 47–48, 187, 224, 260–61, 266–71, 273–75, 313n7; of friendship, 23, 306n4; of the gift, 18, 266; of mentorship, 325n15; pledge as, 42; resolution of contradictions, 74, 260, 271 relational models. *See* relational geometries or logics

relational ties and networks: and nation-state-building, 7–10; transposition of, 7, 9

relief: cash vs. in-kind relief, 59, 168–69, 182, 187, 189, 208, 214; resentment of, 162, 245, 259, 270, 273. *See also* disaster relief; private agencies and relief; public relief and services; unemployment relief; work relief

religion: disestablishment of, 29, 35, 45–46, 313n104; interdenominational organizing, 36, 42, 81–82, 95, 121, 145, 200, 230; as model of political order, 14–15, 261, 300n13; motives for and practices of giving, 11, 193, 222–23; and nation-making, 11, 15–16, 34–35, 53, 63, 105, 131–32, 162, 175, 223, 271; Red Cross as spiritual organization, 222; and relief, 81–83; and republicanism, 55, 308n28; and social reform, 69; as threatened by the state, 216, 223. *See also* Baptists; Catholics; Congregationalists; evangelicals and evangelicalism; Jews (or Hebrews); Methodists; Presbyterians; Quakers; Unitarians and Universalists

repertoire, 19, 103, 135, 261, 267, 393n60

Republicanism, 55, 306n6, 308n17, 308n28; as model of political order, 16, 261; and understanding of virtue, 303n65

"Republican motherhood," 129

Republicans and Republican party, 68, 72, 87, 104, 331n115; criticism of March of Dimes, 201–2; and Great Depression, 167–71; and political geography of voluntarism, 104–5; public benefits as gifts, 266, 173, 361n32, 361n33; and Red Cross, 124, 183

responsibility: of community and civic networks, 146–48, 151–53, 174, 209,

237, 246, 303n64; of government, 67, 114–15, 136, 150–51, 192–94, 204, 209, 237, 248, 328n75; of individuals and voluntary associations, 9, 41–42, 48, 72, 74, 93, 127, 142–43, 146, 151–53, 169, 192, 200, 204, 207, 219, 225, 237, 248, 311n77, 340n139, 353n49, 357n29; shift from private to public, 153–54, 161, 188, 194, 204; shift from public to private, 46; as sign and instrumentality, 257; and solidarity, 28, 35, 235. *See also* division of labor

rights: from charity to, 210; civil and equal, 105, 143, 189, 310n62, 349n136, 359n59; effect of delegation of government authority, 22, 258–59; natural, 16; of public employees and relief recipients, 189. *See also* charity: compared to entitlements or rights; citizenship; public relief and services

Robinson, Joseph Taylor, 169; and Robinson Amendment, 168–70, 172–73, 210

Rochester, NY, 205

Rockefeller, John D., Jr., 20, 135, 136, 170, 194, 197, 200, 222, 238, 239, 339n122; on moral quality of voluntarism, 135; relation of charitable gifts and business expenses, 197

Rockefeller, John D., Sr., 113, 115, 195

Rockefeller, John D., III, 239

Rockefeller, Laurance, 249

Rockefeller, Mrs. Laurance, 358n49

Rockefeller, Nelson, 251–53, 258; Special Studies Project, 251–54, 257–58

Rockefeller Foundation, 329n77; conflicts over charter, 116–18; grants to federal government, 184, 239

Rockefellers, 97, 158, 260; and AFSC, 238–39; archives as informant, 305n100, 339n122; General Education Board, 116; gifts from, 97, 115, 125, 197, 214, 327n50, 336n67; Office of the Messrs., 98, 195; policies and principles, 135, 191, 194–95, 222–23, 305n100; as political or moral threat, 327n50, 328n60; and Red Cross, 222–23, 233–34, 354n76; Rockefeller Brothers Fund, 252; Rockefeller Center (Rockefeller City), 151, 197; support for community self-government, 251; support for public health, 114; WWII fund-raising, 214

Rogers, Will, 158

Rogin, Michael, on voluntarism as organizational ideology, 48

Romney, Mitt, 266, 273, 361n32, 361n33

Ronsavallon, Pierre, 28

Roosevelt, Eleanor, 204, 226, 230

Roosevelt, Franklin Delano (FDR), 1, 21, 236, 240, 248, 260, 261; and associational methods and voluntarism, 179, 200–210, 217, 219–23, 226, 228–31, 236, 261–62, 264–65, 329n76; and civic philanthropy, 201–10, 211–12; death of, 237, 240; differences with Hoover, 1, 113, 173–74, 216–17; as governor of New York, 156, 164, 166, 180–83, 209; and nation-state-building, 2, 21–22, 211–12, 236, 240–42; and polio, 1, 3–4, 22, 240, 299n4, 347n108; as president, 165, 177–79, 183–90, 197, 200, 201, 217, 341n12; Recession of 1938, 208, 344n54; on responsibilities of government and their limits, 1, 182–83, 209–10, 218, 228, 248–49, 343n39; and WWII, 216, 223, 229. See also March of Dimes; presidential philanthropy

Roosevelt, Theodore, 104, 108, 109–11, 120, 325n20; and foundation for industrial peace, 115–16

Rosenwald, Julius, 113–14, 145, 327n42

Rotary clubs, 99–100

Rube Goldberg state, 9, 19, 302n46

Ruml, Beardsley, 243

Russell, George Spencer, 288

Russell Sage Foundation, 70, 117, 124, 154, 291

Russia, 63, 168, 178, 213, 218, 238, 327n42. See also Soviet Union

Russian thistles, 186

Russo-Japanese War, 115

Sage, M. Olivia, 124. See also Russell Sage Foundation

Salt Lake City, UT, 187

Salvation Army, 23, 181, 221, 342n19, 342n32, 346n96, 352n47

San Francisco, 70, 287; Chronicle, 110; earthquake of 1906, 103–4, 109–13, 178, 187, 326n26, 326n28, 326n31, 326n32, 335n62; Relief and Red Cross Funds, Inc., 110, 112, 118

sanitary commission and fairs. See United States Sanitary Commission (USSC)

Schenectady, NY, 151

Schiff, Jacob, 134, 331n116

Schneiberg, Marc, 211

Schultz, Jackson S., 79

Schuyler, Louisa Lee, 66, 68, 70, 291, 318n93

Scott, Hugh L., 135

Searle, Arthur, 288

Sears, Roebuck, 113, 145

Second World War. See World War II

sectionalism, 105, 168, 220–21, 270–71; dangers of, 59–60, 67, 100. See also political geography

Seeley, John, 139

self-created societies, as political threat, 30–34

self-sufficiency and self-reliance, 13, 18, 77, 107; contradiction with charity and reciprocity, 13, 71, 74, 107, 175; degraded by charity, 32, 50, 64–65, 74, 91, 107; enabled by government bonds in old age, 329n83; as goal of relief, 106, 156, 192–93; and liberal citizenship, 5, 12–13, 17, 49,

self-sufficiency and self-reliance (*cont.*)
81, 130–31, 175, 270; of soldiers, 136;
and "those who should not be poor,"
90–91; threatened by government,
237, 343n39. *See also* citizenship;
democratic dignity
semi-governmental, 139–41, 253, 332n1
Sentinels of the Republic, 200
settlement houses, 178, 334n33; as
depoliticized by Community Chests,
198–99, 268, 334n31; as sites of work
relief, 195–97
Sewell, William, 301n32, 360n16
Sheffield, Frederick, 249
Sherman, William Tecumseh, 62
Sierra Club and Legal Defense Fund,
269
Simmel, Georg, 13–14, 77, 302n51,
303n69
6–15–99 Club, 92–93, 94, 271
Skocpol, Theda, 326n24, 330n93
Skowronek, Stephen, 9, 314n15, 361n27
slavery and antislavery, 27–28, 40, 42–
44, 50, 129–30, 132, 267; antislavery
and abolition, 42–44, 68; Anti-
Slavery Society, 40; dependence as
equivalent of slavery, 14; liberty and
slavery as constitutive contradiction,
5, 27, 362n35; work relief as form of,
153. *See also* categorical exclusions
and inequalities
Sloan, Alfred P., Jr., 243
Small, Frederick P., 124
Smith, Adam, 13
Smith, Al, 190
Smith, Elias, 14, 261
Smith, John, 188
Smith, Kate, and war bond drive, 231,
354n71
Smith, Rogers, 12–13, 300n14.
See also multiple traditions thesis;
peoplehood
Snow, Edwin M., 288
social closure, 99–100

social geometries. *See* relational geometries or logics
social insurance, 23, 265; the "categories" (for the aged, dependent
children, blind, and disabled), 209,
218, 225; exclusions and exemptions
from, 199, 201, 209, 211; as model
of relief, 94; old age, 185; proposed
federal agency, 228. *See also* Social
Security
socialism, 78, 91, 94, 171, 236, 323n90;
Socialist Party, 161; Thomas, 161–62
Social Security, 175, 185–86, 194, 199–
200, 203, 209; exclusions and exemptions from, 199, 201; Red Cross
as proposed alternative, 200
social status, 131, 271; and language of
service, 99–100; and local practices,
120, 189; and voluntarism, 51, 135,
161. *See also* elites
social technologies, 2, 12, 153, 194, 259;
cards, card files, and lists, 38, 85, 149,
156; and collective action, 2, 12, 22;
personal and mass canvass, 149, 156,
163–64, 170, 336n70; radio, 160–61,
218, 231; telephone and directory,
156–57, 336n70
social work and social workers, 85,
118, 142, 146, 156, 162, 177, 182,
189–90, 193, 214, 219, 225, 237,
272, 319n5, 333n30, 345n78; business influence over, 148, 150, 334n31;
and exceptions to federal labor law
and Social Security, 199; recruited
to government service, 150, 154,
184, 186–87, 190, 200–201, 215, 225–
26; relational geometry of social
work, 175, 189; resentment of, 110–
11, 144, 182–87
Society of Equity, 144
Society of St. Vincent de Paul, 89, 91
Society of the Cincinnati, 2, 29, 31,
33, 308n20; reforms under George
Washington, 31

sociology: cultural and organizational, 260–62, 360n15; historical, 306n2, 363n55

"soft power," 239

soldiers and sailors. *See* military

solidarity: Appleby on weakness in early Republic, 28; Arendt on incompatibility with pity, 14; as expressed through voluntarism, 126–27; performance of, 272. *See also* generalized exchange; national solidarity

Sons of the Revolution, 69, 283

Sons of Washington, 40, 310n64

South Carolina, 54, 128, 338n109

South Dakota, 128, 214

Soviet Union: famine, 168, 178; in WWII, 214. *See also* Russia

Spanish-American War, 68, 71, 108, 115, 320n28

Sprague, A. C., 149

Standard Oil, 115

Stark, Willie, 1, 260, 262, 299n3

Starr King, Thomas, 58–60, 67, 100–101, 253, 315n40. *See also* "divine method of patriotism"

state, 46, 307n14; centralized and bureaucratic, 264 (*see also* Weber, Max); definitions and limits of, 53, 183, 252–53, 301n29; embedded autonomy of, 309n18; as made by the people, 56; theories of the, 6–10, 53–54, 75, 264–65. *See also* expansible state or nation-state; nation-state-building

State Boards of Charities, 65, 74, 95, 100, 186, 288, 318n96; relation to USSC, 74

state-building. *See* nation-state-building

Stead, William T., 89, 114

Stettinius, Edward, Jr., 205

stigma, 34, 42; of relief, 86, 135, 187–88. *See also* democratic dignity; self-sufficiency and self-reliance

Stillé, Charles J., 63, 288

St. Louis, 67, 100, 333n27

Stuart, George H., 69, 283

submarines, 139

Sunday schools, 29, 32, 35–36, 38, 40–41, 47, 69, 70, 282, 283, 286

Sutton, Joseph Ford, 69, 283

Swidler, Ann, on settled and unsettled times, 261

Switzerland, 72

Syracuse University, 182, 209

Taft, Charles P., 208–9, 352n46, 352n49

Taft, William Howard, 117; and Red Cross, 108–9, 111, 124, 135

Tammany Hall, 88, 92

taxation, 8, 87, 180, 197–98, 249, 268, 316n66, 345n69; of alcohol, 197; as alternative to charitable giving, 126–27, 150, 165–66, 190, 194, 221, 260; as compared to voluntary giving, 32, 66, 93, 139–40, 146–48, 150, 161–62, 174, 191–92, 194, 205, 226, 243–46, 249–50, 262; of corporate profits, 243; as democratic practice, 114–15, 150, 165–66, 174, 179, 246, 304n84; during WWI, 133–34; exemptions, 46–47, 179; held in check by voluntary giving, 74, 87, 245–46; income tax, individual and corporate, 115, 123, 133–34, 161, 165, 167, 172, 193, 198, 235, 253, 331n115, 331n118, 338n108, 338n109, 346n88, 346n89; inheritance or estate tax, 115, 134, 161, 198, 327n47; payroll deductions, 194; political role of taxpayers, 87; and state-building, 8, 10, 74–76, 302n40; for support of established religion, 45–46; and support of voluntary associations, 22, 74, 88; tax-anticipation warrants, 341n15; tax code for 501.c organizations, 268–69; tax resistance, 31; tax

taxation (*cont.*)
subsidies to nonprofits, 22, 118, 179, 243, 268; tax treatment of contributions, 98, 133–35, 197–99, 255, 267–69, 334n35. *See also* charitable contributions
Taylor, Hannis, 115
Taylor, Lca, 199
temperance, 29, 35–38, 42–43, 65, 69–70, 267, 281, 285, 290, 309n48. *See also* American Temperance Society; Prohibition
Temporary Emergency Relief Administration (TERA). *See* New York State
Texas, 128, 188, 233
Thomas, Norman, 161–62, 164
Tilly, Charles, 75, 301n33, 310n13, 360n15
Tilson, Representative, 171, 339n127
Topographical Corps, 53
totalitarianism, 239, 249, 251–52, 258; Arendt on compassion as path to, 14; as contrasted with voluntarism, 252
Townsend, Helene De Kay, 291
transposition, 64, 66; of charity and social work methods, 187, 211; failure of Red Cross, 143–44; as mechanism of institutional change, 7, 266–67, 362n36. *See also* combinatorial politics
Truman, Harry, 242, 356n20, 356n21
trusts, 188; Red Cross as charitable trust, 107
tuberculosis, 112
Tucson, AZ, 189
turkeys, 87, 189
Tuskegee Institute, 153, 329n77; and polio research and treatment, 17
Tweed, William, 88
tyranny, 44, 63, 258, 300n14, 322n60; of a well-organized minority, 30. *See also* despotism

unemployables, 207–9, 226
unemployment, 84, 88, 100, 190–91, 346n86; and Hoover administration, 122, 140, 151, 156–57, 173, 234, 262, 335n48; industrial, 84, 140, 167–68, 320n28
unemployment insurance, 185
unemployment relief, 77–81, 83–84, 88–94, 145, 151, 227; during Great Depression, 156–70, 178, 180–86, 190, 195, 197, 200, 208, 227, 229, 322n44, 341n10; and Red Cross, 340n139; resistance to federal responsibility, 165; for white collar workers, 160–61, 182, 187–88, 195–97. *See also* Block-Aid
Union League Clubs, 69, 73, 79, 86–87, 282, 284, 325n20
Union Meeting of City Missions, 79
Unitarians and Universalists, 32, 36, 45, 53, 60, 95, 121, 253, 284
United Funds, 243–44, 357n32. *See also* Community Chests
United Health and Welfare Fund of Michigan, Inc., 244
United Mine Workers, 217
United Nations, 205
United Order of Internationals, 78
United Refugees, after San Francisco earthquake, 111
United Service Organization (USO), 218, 219, 221, 222, 225, 234, 271, 352n47, 352n49
United States Christian Commission (USCC), 50, 54, 57, 62, 64, 70, 95, 106; as alternative to state-building, 50, 54–55; biographies of volunteers, 68–71, 281–83, 320n28; compared to the U.S. Sanitary Commission, 66, 70–71, 95, 315n32; and generalized exchange, 58, 65–66, 68; as model or legacy, 68, 79, 317n89, 320n28
"United States Department of Welfare," 228

United States Food Administration, 137, 141, 329n79

United States Sanitary Commission (USSC), 50, 54, 56, 61, 63, 68, 70, 73, 91, 95, 106, 153, 315n39; biographies of volunteers, 64–65, 68, 70–71, 91, 284–91; and "charitable buffoonery," 57; compared to the U.S. Christian Commission, 66, 70–71, 95, 315n32; and generalized exchange, 58–60 (*see also* "divine method of patriotism"); inclusion through contributions, 53; as model or legacy, 70–71, 74, 79, 318n95, 320n30; and nation-state-building, 53–54, 62–63, 73–74, 100, 315n28; relation to military hierarchy and government, 62–63, 316n58; relation to Red Cross, 71–72, 325n10; relation to State Boards of Charity, 73; and voluntarism, 66; sanitary fairs, 51–52, 56, 57, 59, 67, 76, 79, 134

"unity in diversity," 95, 206

urban. *See* cities; municipal benevolence

U.S. Citizens Service Corps, 227

U.S. Congress, 15, 22, 70, 78, 85, 106, 123, 133, 211–12, 217, 227–29, 254, 327, 329n76, 350n21; bill to centralize control of war charities, 261; circumvented by private foreign aid, 113, 209, 212, 217, 229, 327n53; debates over charitable contributions and foundations, 115, 116–18, 133–34, 198; and disaster relief, 110–13; and Red Cross, 105–8, 126, 168–70, 201, 209–10, 225, 339n122; and response to Great Depression, 167–74, 178, 209, 339n124

U.S. Constitution, 15–16, 28–29, 33; amendments to, 117, 123, 197, 207–8; and cities, 75

U.S. Post Office. *See* Post Office

Vaux, Calvert, 76

veterans. *See* military

veto points, 104

Vicksburg, MS, 57

Virgin, Edward Warren, 283

Virginia, 58, 128; right to vote in, 314n11

voluntarism: as alternative to government, 24, 25, 74–75, 140, 151–52, 155–56, 166–75, 177–79, 221, 138, 249, 251–52, 328n68 (*see also* anti-statism); arguments for, 170–71, 329n79; and business, 345n72; and citizenship, 130–32, 204–5, 207, 221, 235; and Civil War, 49–72; as coercive, 66, 150, 303n61; definition and discourse of, 18, 30, 44, 46, 48, 133; and democracy or self-government, 169, 235, 249, 251–52, 267, 273–75, 351n36; division of labor with government, 79, 104–5, 141, 151–54, 166–67, 177, 179, 184, 192, 207–8, 215–16, 224; as enactment of political ideology or values, 50, 105, 126–27, 135, 170–71, 206, 232, 237, 239–40, 251–52, 258, 328n68; infrastructure or institutional framework for, 21, 44–49, 153, 157; limits of, 155–56, 165, 174, 177–78, 186; as model for governance and public policy, 24, 56, 71, 125, 127, 153, 161, 194 (*see also* public-private partnerships and programs); and nation-state-building, 3, 12, 14, 17, 19, 21–22, 49–51, 67–68, 71, 94–95, 104–6, 108, 113, 121, 123–25, 127, 133, 135, 137–38, 140–41, 144, 167, 171, 177, 179, 208, 215–17, 234–38, 242–48, 258–59, 267–73, 329n79, 363n57; paradox of, 48; and people-hood, 16; as performative, 230, 244; political geography of, 104–5, 155; and production of public goods, 49, 267–68; as relational geometry or logic, 46, 49–51, 129, 163; as response to constitutive contradictions, 19; as social technology, 2, 22, 259; and standardization/individualization,

voluntarism (*cont.*)
305n98; in tension with professionalism or corporate form, 66, 172; as
threatened by government, 169, 200,
210, 221; as threat to state authority
and military discipline, 55–56, 61;
as undemocratic, 229, 238; usage of
term, 258. *See also* benevolence
voluntary agencies. *See* private agencies and relief
voluntary associations and organizations, 2, 98, 48; as bulwark against
despotism or model for government, 3, 5, 24, 200, 254; and civic
life, 6, 28–29, 51–52; as coercive,
threatening to equality and liberty,
6, 32, 42–44, 52, 55, 262, 265, 267,
331n107; collaboration among, 145;
as conspiracy, 33; corporate and
hierarchical character of, 43, 66,
124, 136–37, 172–73, 253; illegitimate
or political threat, 31–34, 40, 52,
267–68; international activities of,
24, 105, 238 (*see also* international
relief); invention of, 28–29; mass
membership, 23, 362n37; as models
for government and policy, 153;
moral qualities of, 135, 171; and
nation-state-building, 5, 9, 19–20,
22, 47–48, 49, 54, 62, 104, 109, 121,
125, 140, 154, 177–79, 227, 258, 262,
265, 318n91; and organizing skills, 21,
52; as political parties as, 28–29, 44,
309n40; public subsidies to, 6, 87,
178; resources of, 37; as vehicle for
reform, 34–39, 68, 309n40, 309n50.
See also benevolence; charity;
voluntarism
voluntary giving. *See* charitable contributions; fund-raising; gifts and
giving
voluntary principle, 45–46
voluntary relief. *See* private agencies
and relief

volunteers, 2–3, 137, 195, 234, 241;
arguments for a volunteer force, 120;
and Civil War, 2, 49, 50, 53–56, 62–
64, 65–66, 79, 83, 105, 130, 315n32,
316n66, 318n2; compared to professionals or bureaucrats, 66, 141–42,
195, 197, 215, 272, 315n32, 316n66;
etiquette and ethics of, 135–36, 143,
224, 272–73; and government agencies, 141, 227, 235–36, 353n57; and
municipal benevolence, 84, 95, 97,
105; recruitment of, 143, 158, 160,
164, 197, 346n86; and relief, 141, 151,
160–61, 164, 172, 177, 184, 195, 197; resentment of, 64, 135, 143; usefulness
and uselessness, 130, 215, 224–25 (*see
also* knitting); and WWI, 112, 122–23,
125–26, 130, 133, 135–36, 329n76 (*see
also* dollar-a-year men); and WWII,
215, 219, 224, 226, 232, 242–43, 259.
See also military; militia

Wadsworth, Eliot, 124
Wagner, Senator, 165
Walden, Treadwell, 289
Walsh, Senator, 174
War, Department of, 109, 121, 225
Warburg, Felix, 134, 331n116
War Chests, 140, 215, 218–19, 261
War Industries Board, 121, 123, 130
war mobilization, as infrastructural,
120–21
Warner, Harry, 359n61
Warner, W. Lloyd, 324n101
War of 1812, 40, 53
War on Poverty, 22, 199
Warren, Robert Penn, 210, 299n3
War Resources Board, 229
War Revenue Acts, 133–34, 198,
327n47. *See also* taxation
War Savings Program, 123
Washington, D.C., 122, 172, 183,
318n95, 345n69. *See also* District of
Columbia

Washington, George, 15, 39; criticism
    of self-created societies, 30–32, 39;
    as quoted by Beecher, 34
Washington, William D'Hertburn, 92
Washington Benevolent Society, 32,
    40, 77, 310n64
Washington Daily News, 169
Wayland, Francis, 41–44, 48, 300n13,
    311n77
Wealth Act of 1935, 197–98, 255
wealth and the wealthy: and charity,
    93, 112, 146, 161, 193, 206, 310n56;
    and cities, 75–76, 86; incorporated
    in nation-state-building, 3, 6, 15, 25;
    and inequality, 105, 127; influence
    over private agencies and voluntary
    associations, 94, 98, 197, 206; and
    philanthropy, 98, 113–18, 327n54,
    328n60; taxation of, 74, 76, 114–15,
    133–34, 197–98, 268; as threat to de-
    mocracy, 113–15, 117–18, 259, 319n24,
    327n54, 328n60. *See also* elites;
    foundations
Weber, Max, 6, 8, 52; on the bureau-
    cratic state, 105, 264, 273, 301n26,
    301n29, 302n43
Webster, Noah, 9, 27, 29–30, 44,
    302n48, 307n14, 314n13
welfare state: development of, 21–22,
    168, 177, 210–11, 265, 341n11; and
    Great Depression, 177
Wells-Barnett, Ida B., 152–53
Western Sanitary Commission, 53, 56
West Point, 63
Wetmore, John C., 289
Whigs, 33, 44, 50, 242, 264–65,
    309n40
whiskey: jug of, 37; Rebellion, 31
White, Elon James, 361n33
white-collar workers. *See* unemploy-
    ment relief
Whitman, John S., 289
Wide Awakes, 54
Wigglesworth, Edward, 289

Wilkie, Wendell, 228
Williams, Aubrey, 186, 189
Wilson, Woodrow, 105, 123, 137, 142;
    and Red Cross, 108–9, 121, 124, 130,
    206, 229, 348n126
Winterhilfswerk, 23
woman suffrage, 70, 267–68, 309n48
women: as beneficiaries, 84, 174, 190,
    211; excluded from full citizenship,
    84, 105, 127, 317n72; relief and volun-
    tary activities, 74, 82–83, 95, 99, 123,
    127, 129–30, 136, 149, 151, 214, 226,
    230, 241, 300n11, 313n6, 330n104,
    356n24; and republican otherhood,
    129; and USSC, 70–71; as workers,
    80, 332n8
Wood, Gordon, 306n6
Woods, Arthur, 151, 158, 165
work relief, 78, 79, 82, 85, 91, 94–95,
    151, 156–57, 182, 184–85, 208, 226,
    317n76, 344n54; for the adjusted or
    "employables," 201, 210, 218; fund-
    raising as, 160–61; in nonprofit agen-
    cies, 195–97; rather than charity, 182,
    208. *See also* public employment
    and public works
work-sharing, 151
Works Progress Administration (WPA;
    later Works Project Administra-
    tion), 178, 197, 200, 204, 205, 207,
    208, 218, 228
World War I, 72, 116, 120–38, 206,
    236; aid to refugees, 141; as already
    reciprocating for relief, 174; debt
    paid by Finland, 213; food relief,
    217; legacies of, 139–44, 147, 214,
    228–29; Office of War Information,
    157
World War II, 22, 211, 213–34; and aid
    to Finland, 213; fund-raising, 213–
    14, 228–34, 261–62; government
    control of charity, 261; lendlease
    program, 205; politics of war relief,
    216–17; postwar Occupation, 239;

World War II (*cont.*)
  registration of war charities, 262;
  World voluntarism and mobilization, 209–10, 228–34; war relief as
  threat to domestic voluntarism, 218
Wormeley, Katherine Prescott, 315n28
worthy and unworthy poor, 12, 77, 80,
  82, 84–85, 90–91, 93–94, 163, 194,
  315n39, 322n44. *See also* poor

Yale University, 35, 324n104
Young Men's Christian Association
  (YMCA), 69, 87, 97, 114, 121, 135–36,
  144, 147, 281–83, 327n42, 346n96,

352n46, 352n47; in African Ameri-
  can communities, 114, 147
Young Women's Christian Association
  (YWCA), 144, 352n47

zones of instability, or fault lines, 7,
  18, 25, 259–60, 266–70, 360n13,
  362n36; and combinatorial politics,
  10, 19, 259, 266–67, 270; as overlap
  of public and private, 24–25, 251–52,
  253, 258, 259, 269
Zoological Society of London, 24
Zorbaugh, Harvey Warren, 99
Zunz, Olivier, 114